W9-DBI-723

Cultures of Darkness

Night Travels in the Histories of Transgression

BRYAN D. PALMER

Monthly Review Press
New York

Library of Congress Cataloging-in-Publication Data
Palmer, Bryan D.
    Cultures of darkness : night travels in the histories of transgression /
Bryan D. Palmer
        p. cm.
    Includes bibliographical references and index.
    ISBN 1–58367–026–2 (cloth). — ISBN 1–58367–027–0 (paper)
    1. Subculture—History.   2. Marginality, Social—History.   3. Deviant
behavior—History.   4. Night people—History.   5. Night—Social aspects.
I. Title.
HM646.P35   2000
306'.1—dc21   00–045086

ISBN 1–58367–027–0 (paper)
ISBN 1–58367–026–2 (cloth)

Monthly Review Press
122 West 27th Street
New York, NY 10001

Designed and typeset by Illuminati, Grosmont
Manufactured in Canada

10   9   8   7   6   5   4   3   2   1

For Joan

restless days & sleepless nights
looking into eyes that are not there
wanting nearness, larger changes
impossible
many questions, fewer answers
lists of worries
books of responses
assurances honestly given, at 2 AM
like coins to a beggar, freely
where and when will they be spent?
what purchase?

Contents

List of Figures

Acknowledgements

This book owes little to the greased wheels of academic production. No large grant drove it relentlessly forward. I am grateful to the Social Sciences and Humanities Research Council of Canada, which allowed me to divert to this study small sums from a grant originally secured to fund researching social relations in Upper Canada. At Queen's University, the Advisory Research Committee provided $1,600 in aid of pertinent bibliographic and illustrative work in New York City, and my department earmarked a few hundred dollars for the development of slides and other materials that I used in a large lecture course, "Dark Cultures: Histories of the Night," which was the "filthy workshop of creation" of this account.

My greatest debts are therefore to the students in that course, many of whom got a lot more (or less) than they bargained for, as they sat in lectures created in intense bouts of labor ending only the night before they were delivered. I thank them for their indulgence. I also appreciate the support and encouragement, including shared sources and knowledge, extended by a range of people, foremost among them Bill Gale, Frank Pearce, Christine Johanson, Carolyn Kay, Nicholas Rogers, Todd McCallum, Dan Malleck, James Wishart, Peter Bailey, Steven Maynard, Gerald Tulchinsky, and Joan Sangster. Steve Brier and Terry Karamanos, my concierges in New York, always make me feel at home, even when they are not there; I am thankful for their hospitality and cherish their friendship.

At Monthly Review Press I have had the good fortune to be supported by the ever laconic Christopher Phelps, a seemingly curmudgeonly acquisitions editor who can use few words to make an author feel a lot better about a long-winded manuscript. I was sorry to see him depart for greener

pastures. When Danielle McClellan replaced Christopher, I was accorded
every courtesy. Phelps secured the assessment of an anonymous reviewer
who provided an extremely helpful and admirably fair-minded critique.
An author could not have asked for a better process than I received at MR,
and I am grateful for having been treated so well.

A version of Chapter 18 was published as "Night in the Capitalist, Cold
War City: Noir and the Cultural Politics of Darkness," in *Left History* (Fall
1997), and I thank the editors for their permission to include it here.

I owe a debt to the people of the night, with whom I have long shared
some of my warmest hours. One of them, Kingston's Joe Chithalen, a
young musician barely into his thirties, died suddenly, unexpectedly, and
tragically as I was completing this book. He gave me many happy nights;
I am saddened that he himself has no more to enjoy.

Almost seven years ago I took a night ride with Joan Sangster. It was
a moment of transgression that turned into a labor of love. It was Joan
and our children, Beth, Kate, Laura, and Rob, who endured the heat of
the pressure-cooker within which this book boiled. They make it possible
for me to see the stars, even if it must often appear to them that I have
great difficulty getting out of the fog.

Introduction

We live in a curious, and potentially tragic, intellectual and political age. The times of the *fin de siècle* have, in modern historical memory, been associated with turmoil and tension which have often translated into a troubled period of transition. Revolutions have either been made in or sustained by the conditions prevailing through the last decades of both the eighteenth and nineteenth centuries. In such periods of intense destabilization, the structural moorings of society seemed to come unhinged, the prevailing ideas assailed and placed under acute challenge. These were moments when, in the words of the *Communist Manifesto*, now itself a century and a half old, "all that is solid melts into air, all that is holy is profaned."[1]

For Marx and Engels this unsettling fluidity was one feature of a relatively recently recognized socioeconomic order, capitalism. This capitalism, nurtured in the commercial empires, trading companies, and absolutist states of early modern history, as well as in the protoindustrial communities of seventeenth- and eighteenth-century Europe, traversed the globe over the course of the nineteenth and twentieth centuries. Its defining features were not so much the exchange relations, private fortunes, and corporate profits upon which its legends and lore have come to rest, but the mechanisms that sustained these material possibilities: the forced dispossessions of an "original," predatory accumulation that predate capitalist production *per se*; the coercive divisions of labor within which class formations evolved; and the fundamental extraction of surplus, designated by the wage form, that disfigured the social relations of economic life across centuries of development. These forces placed the mark of profound alienation on modern societies. Capitalism was thus unlike any social formation that preceded it, so critical to its continuity was revolutionary transformation and ongoing sociocultural change.[2]

This continuity of discontinuity has perhaps never been more apparent than in the mid-1990s. Without a doubt, the most critically important contemporary development has proven to be the implosion of the core of the actually existing socialist states, those tangible reminders that capital's reign has, historically, been challenged by the countervailing force of revolution and the workers' states that stood in opposition to capital. Many such socialist centers, including the site of the world's first successful proletarian experiment, crumbled precipitously in 1989 and, in the ensuing chaos, ushered into being a new era of instability and insecurity for many of the world's peoples. As a powerful, late-twentieth-century advanced capitalism experienced crisis in its particular, often western-based, domestic economies, moreover, the collapse of the Soviet Union and the break-up of its amalgamated buffer zones in Eastern Europe and the weakening of distant regimes dependent on its supports, from Baghdad to Havana, paved the way for a reinvigorated imperial order. Paced by the ironically decrepit industrial economy of the United States, capitalism's new reach toward global hegemony was premised on a set of powerful linked material processes. Cheapening production through the export of jobs to the low-wage economies of the Third World was complemented by opening the floodgates of "free trade" and integrating world markets and labor in a cartelization of huge regional economies, including those of Europe, North America, and the Far East. This decisively broke the back of all residual, nineteenth-century "protectionism," invading what was left of the planned economies of an increasingly bastardized or marginalized "socialism" (China and Grenada), and militarily vanquishing irksome bonapartist regimes of recalcitrance and reaction, such as Iraq. Wars ensued. Often fought over the control of territory and the highly traditional maintenance of access to resources, they also took place in the realm of thought.

The 1980s and 1990s were indeed decades of a revived ideological assault, in which the project was to capture the terrain of intellectual life for a reactionary populist purpose. Beginning with the new right's raid on the past, initiated by neo-conservatives in the 1970s and consolidated as governing policy with the electoral victories of Thatcher and Reagan, concerted attempts were made to refashion national histories. In the schools, museums, and public celebrations of commemorative events the conflictual accounts of oppression and exploitation that many 1960s-inspired writings, associated with that decade's so-called New Left, were displaced. In their stead were grand narratives of national accomplishment and individual, often entrepreneurial, attainments.[3] By the opening years of the 1990s, this ideological ground had hardened as the Soviet Union's formal disintegration and supposed repudiation of Marxism conditioned the self-confident proclamations of Francis Fukuyama that the "liberal democratic order" had now triumphed over the dark, disingenuous forces of communism, congealing the world of theory and practice in a final, millennial "end of history."[4]

No confluence of disintegrations—material and analytic—as profound as these could fail to leave their mark, including on the very left-wing, ostensibly progressive, forces that might be expected to challenge the ideological tides of a turbulent time. Indeed, parallel developments within the broad left liberal intelligensia had already prepared the way for interesting realignments of the personnel of reaction and reform. Not unlike earlier generations of disappointed advocates of change,[5] the post–New Left intellectuals, witnessing the incorporation of their own generation into the political economy of late capitalism, the ossification of Stalinist "socialism" and trade-union bureaucracies, and the seeming inability of the forces of revolution to transform the world, worked their way toward critiques of existing radical knowledges that increasingly distanced themselves from their origins in an eclectic, if Marxist-inspired, historical materialism.[6] It was not all that surprising that Fukuyama's crudely ideological and patently conservative statement elicited a range of far more sophisticated commentary, much of it emanating from a quarter of disillusioned leftists that found itself, in the early 1990s, either adrift in apostasy or enthusiast of a new polity.[7]

Whatever the complexities of this intellectual ferment and questioning of all that was once thought by some to be "solid" in the realm of dissident ideas, our current conceptual conjuncture has been much influenced by a hybrid melange of analyses that place us forever "after" past thought and experience. No prefix is more pronounced than that of "post." Postmodernism, poststructuralism, postcolonialism, postfeminism, *posthistoire*—they proclaim the angst of our current *fin de siècle*. That the immense body of writing associated with this highly differentiated collage of 'post' commentary contains insights, understandings, and perspectives of value is uncontestable. But that it also contains disturbing tendencies to reroute analytic directions in ways that politically disable our capacities to channel the destabilizations and fragmentations of the current moment in the direction of social change and transformation is also undeniable.[8]

As Ellen Wood has pointed out, in critiques both journalistic and academic, the contradiction of the 1990s is that as capitalism consolidates its
global, hegemonic, homogenizing authority, in form and content more
powerfully pervasive than ever before, fashionable analytic trends embraced
by many ostensible "post" leftists invalidate an interpretive approach that
would allow this world, and the past developments that have led toward
it, to be understood and overcome.[9] As the metanarrative of capitalism's
conquests in the 1990s broadens, rather than narrows, its purchase on the
minds, bodies, and political souls of us all deepening dangerously, those
who would challenge this process often offer theoretical ammunition that
accentuates fragmentation, difference, and particularistic parochialism. In
the name of refusing power's master narratives, "post" thought denies the
very importance of a systematic center of exploitation's and oppression's
causality and issues its clarion call for pluralism and diversity, in which
proliferating stories of class, race, and gender coexist in a discursive
ensemble of meanings. Marginalities of physical space and sociopsychic
identities, often connected only in the most playful of authorial constructions, occupy a preeminent analytic place. The best that can be done,
some seem to be saying, is to plead with liberalism to deliver some of
its promised goods.

This concrete elaboration of the experiences of dispossession, understood materially and culturally, has focused attention on previously underappreciated dimensions of the complex layering of privilege and power.
But this advance is offset by an analytic retreat. The "post" project has
spiralled inward in actual conceptual denial of ever knowing the experiential subject, let alone locating that solitary being at the powerfully
formative conjuncture of self and society where history is ultimately made
and remade. Current intellectual trends leave us with the disembodied
pieces of a puzzle, the borders and linked segments which would make
the whole intelligible either entirely absent or jumbled on the interpretive sideline. Yet this puzzle, in its rich totality, is the metanarrative that
can, in part, counter capitalism's current grand story of accomplishment,
the obscured mirror image of which is of course enslavement, the forcible
extraction of surplus value, and the endless proliferation of special oppressions associated with gender, race, and sexual identification. To make the
coerced marginalities of history a viable force of transformative alternative,
the need is to bring them together. Difference needs to be championed,
not through a reification of difference, but in the building of programs
and perspectives of possibility that fly in every way against the impulses
and structures of our current varied but connected subordinations. We

need a metanarrative of alternative and opposition, not an anarchistic refusal of all metanarrative; the capitalist process, pregnant with possibility, needs to be stood on its head.

This is, of course, a tall order, and few histories have ever achieved such a metanarrative. I am not so ambitious as to think that this book does what no other has accomplished. I am audacious enough, however, to offer a suggestion. The endless calls of the interdisciplinary "post" writing for attention to marginality and identity will never be adequately responded to by theoretical abstractions, by statements, however principled, of the need to do more than chronicle diversity. Perhaps what we need, then, is an attempt, however partial, to touch down on some chapters in the history of marginality and transgression.

Marginality is simultaneously an identity/consciousness and a structure/place. It is a construction both social and concrete, removed from power's centers in displacements physical and discursive. As such it is often related to the oppositional dualisms and polarizations within which difference is articulated in class, race, and gender terms. How such difference is perceived and lived, however, is never ultimately "set." Determinations do exist, and are historically contextualized, but they are contingent on an almost infinite complex of possibilities. This insures that the transgressive content of marginality, or how difference is negotiated within a given historical period, opens out into a range of realizations, traversing the spectrum from accommodation to resistance and settling, time and time again, within a blurring set of options along this continuum. Transgression travels, then, in many directions. In this collection of night travels, I have followed paths of transgression that, for the most part, highlight and sharpen the edge of difference in particular ways, cutting out marginality's peripheralization in acts and consciousness that slice, in varying degrees, into the conformist core of power's routinizations of daily, and nightly, life. Other voyages could have been made. But it seemed that an exploration, over time, that offered an account of some of the divergent ways in which subordination was lived as a dialectic of struggle and opposition, alternative and independence, complicity and incorporation, accommodation and escape, could enlighten our understanding of capitalism's deforming essence. To place such selected and partial narratives together, to link their development, is to begin the process whereby an historical metanarrative of transgressive travel might be mapped. Such a cartography of marginality's momentum through historical time offers the opportunity to place power and protest before a different scrutiny, to look into the night and see the day anew. This can not help but clarify understandings of social transformation in an age in which old certainties are seemingly disintegrating rapidly.

"Post" theory, for instance, is ever attentive to representation and metaphor, to image and its purposeful making, as opposed to those suspect categories—event and actuality—tarnished in the questioning of "empiricist" histories that confirm a discursive power's distorting influences. Rather than simply repudiate such preferences and perspectives I have tried to work with them, within limits, attending to image and metaphor as well as event and actuality.

This willingness to engage the fashion of our intellectual time in ways that both embrace aspects of "post" theory and challenge and interrogate its political and analytic short circuits lies behind the deliberate choices adopted in the subject matter of this book and how it is orchestrated and presented. In choosing to place transgression at the center of historical analysis, and in plotting its changing contours as a night travel through the ages, I was of course consciously seeking out the actual and metaphorical place where marginality might best be both lived as an experience and socially constructed as a representation. Although this book is not, properly speaking, a history of the night, the thread of evening's entitlements runs through its travelogues of transgression.[10] Throughout history, night's association with darkness has cast the shadowy hours of evening and early morning as an environment of transgression, a time and place where power's constraints might be shed and powerlessness's aspirations articulated. The now routine exhortation to consider class, race, and gender seemed to take on fresh possibilities if these relations of exchange and exploitation, difference and development, were presented through a related set of histories that encompassed stages of economic, political, and cultural change but stepped somewhat outside of older, directly materialist guidelines, associated with the productions of the day. In refusing as well certain compartmentalizations, of restricted chronology, confining geo-spatial limits, and reified "national" cultures, I hoped to cross the boundaries, not only of entrenched academic disciplines, but of the widening fissures that too often separate historicized totalities.

My purpose has not so much been to present the whole story, a naive utopian gesture at best. Rather, in touching down on illuminating moments of the experiences of class, race, and gender in particular historical periods of their formation, I aim to suggest ways of looking at the relations of dominance and subordination, rooted always in the social relations of production, but often lived out in dark cultures distanced from the public visibilities of the day. Setting transgression within the night as an actuality and a representation offers an opportunity to explore such cultures, which could voice dissent and alternative, as well as demoralization, defeat, and detachment, in which desire as well as danger ran their always problematized course.

Theoretically this approach also demanded a willingness to juxtapose intellectual and political traditions of analysis. In some senses I began explorations of transgression and its night travels guided by the conceptual refusals of order and the persistent embrace of alienation and transgression found throughout the work of Michel Foucault. The most sophisticated traveller in the historical night that contemporary intellectual practice has produced, Foucault was a mind temperamentally and analytically at home in human darkness.[11] In 1977, Foucault apparently remarked, "Philosophers must become journalists."[12] In a sense this is what he already was, a reporter of the metaphorical night, his by-line known for its brilliant and provocative recording of the "deviancies," estrangements, and terrifying marginalizations of times past, a story-teller who could be counted on not to fall into the traps of moral censure and judgmental dismissal. Foucault opened our eyes to the historical placement of "the other" within the field-of-force of the obscured centers of power, which pressured alienation and demanded dispossession and displacement in order to define and live its propertied authority. His "art of seeing" was an act of looking where most could not, out from oneself into realms that were not yet visible to the conformist eye, into the "absence" that was always present in the shadows, and that sometimes found a home for itself in the night.[13] Actively involved in the struggles of contingents of the oppressed whose histories were dark impositions of repression and silence, discourses of the "unsaid" and the "hidden," Foucault spoke eloquently of the rights of homosexuals, psychiatric patients, and prison inmates. But he also knew well the widening parameters of this conflict of the condemned, and linked their resistance directly to that of the traditional proletariat.[14] In his decentered agenda of power, however, Foucault remained impaled on the demobilizing stakes of isolation and particularity: gesturing toward the centrality of power, he could never quite bring himself to locate it, with the result that his politics were as much concerned with "circumventing 'frontal' nodes of class struggle" as they were in exorcizing exploitation and reconstituting a truly democratic authority.[15]

If I began with Foucault, then, I found myself turning to Marx, whose project was animated by an altogether different impulse. Necessity and desire preoccupy both Marx and Foucault, but in strikingly different ways.

Marx, too, was centrally engaged with alienation, rejecting idealist philosophy as he confronted its concept of humanity. He developed his theory of historical materialism and critique of classical political economy out of an appreciation of the meaning of estrangement. Marx struggled to demystify the exploitation and oppression that fueled capitalism's drive to world dominance, and that inverted values and seemingly naturalistic properties, making them what they were not and, in turn, reducing humanity to what it was not. Working his way through the totalizing and reciprocal relations of power in a consolidating system of coercive extraction and relentless accumulation, Marx discovered the reduction of people and their products to things, commodities in the marketplace of "liberty." If oppositional classes—bourgeoisie and proletariat—experience this alienation differently, Marx was insistent that capitalism was the first social formation literally to root its relations of power in estrangement, to constitute the self on a thoroughly alienated foundation.[16] In living its alienation as power *over* commodities, including their human variants, capital as a class also structured historical development in particular directions. Labor was forced to live its self-estrangement as annihilation and subordination, a dark process that elevated metaphors of the night and its monsters to a literary place of prominence in Marx's analytic framework. Confined to the darkness of human existence, even during the day, labor for Marx was the ultimate "other," its very being debased by an alien power.

Small wonder that one of Marx's earliest defenses of the dispossessed was an exploration of the customary right of the forest poor to gather fallen wood, a practice that crystallized debate in the Rhineland Assembly around notions of exclusionary property. Outside of civil society, the marginalized, morally maligned, and legally harassed forest gatherers were no doubt "criminals" of the night: materially propertyless they were nevertheless in Marx's view "proprietors of freedom," voices of universalist values of life and humanity in contrast to the "irrational pretensions" of those who fetishized ownership of the woods.[17] Capitalism's darkness necessitated a struggle for light; the divide of day and night could be transcended only in a revolutionary overturning of all estranged relations, central to which was class power. This constituted the core of Marx's thought from his early philosophical and political writings of the 1840s into his more structurally oriented examination of the logic of capital and a critique of conventional political economy in the 1850s and 1860s.

What Marx missed however was what Foucault, in a way, grasped. Marginality's making was not just externally imposed, but also internally, subjectively, constituted,[18] a process revealed in the awful desperation of

Edvard Munch's *The Scream* (1893). Fredric Jameson has called this quintessentially *fin de siècle* painting "a canonical expression of the great modernist thematics of alienation, anomie, solitude, social fragmentation, and isolation, a virtually programmatic emblem of what used to be called the age of anxiety." He argues, as well, that Munch's statement stands as a particular aesthetic of expression, in which a desperate cry of communication attempts an outward dramatization of inner pain, an interpretation entirely congruent with many of the portraits of transgression that follow.[19]

These dark cultures, metaphorically related to the night in the arts, a popular culture of purposeful, often derogatory, construction, and social criticism, or nurtured by night's protections, are of course situated historically: peasant dissidents and witches in the moment of feudalism's dissolution; pornographers, libertines, monsters, and Jacobin conspirators in the Age of Revolution; pirates and slaves in the ascendancy of mercantile capitalism; debased trades and dishonorable work, the sociability of the tavern and the fraternal order, the dangerous classes of the urban, industrial order, and the traumas of Third World proletarianization in the global reach of the Industrial Revolution; revolutions of the right and left, and their respective uses of the night; cultures of erotic, musical, cinematic, and poetic disaffection, many of which consolidate in capitalism's mid-twentieth-century epic of conformity's successes, Cold War America; and the ravages of race in the inner cities of late capitalism's material and cultural chaos. These are the narratives of marginality that follow, pieces of a larger, yet-to-be-collectively constructed metanarrative of transgression and its travels that is now merely an unsolved, partially constructed puzzle, in which we see moments of alternative, times of acquiescence, and blank spaces of invisibility.

Much has kept this puzzle and its pieces shielded from our view. On the one hand, night's darkness could be an imposed, self-destructive living out of alienation's ultimate negativity. On the other, freed from certain conventions of the day, its shadows shielding the oppressed from the glare and gaze of power, night could be the positive moment of alienation's transcendence, a space for the self's realization in acts of rebellious alternative. That these dualisms might, as well, merge is a possibility few historians have considered. We can see in Munch's *The Scream* both movements, both directions. To explore this past, this foreign country of the night, where estrangement walks in varied gaits and eyes different ends, we can be guided by the suggestions and insights of Foucault, but we will need Marx as our interpreter if we are to understand the language and meaning of our journey. His words, one commentator has noted, appear like bats, those archetypal creatures of the night: they are both mice and birds. And they can perhaps be appreciated in particular ways when seen emerging from the containment of their own sheltered day, crawling out of crevices to explode in flights that defy easy categorization, taking us across time and space in the night travels in transgression that follow.[20]

PART I
An Overview

1. Thomas Hart Benton, *City Activities with Subway*, from *America Today* (1930).

I

A Walk on the Dark Side

The Metaphorical Night

The night is different, its opposition to day marked by darkness and danger. But its fears are balanced by its freedoms. Night offers escape from the drudgeries of the day, the routines that define humanity in specific duties, obligations, and tasks. Nowhere is this more evident than in commentary on the metropolitan night, where a vast literature and artistic imagery convey a sense of the liberations that darkness offers an often beleaguered humanity. Consider, for instance, one of the world's capitals of the night, New York City. As early as the First World War, the artists of its Ashcan School were producing poignant night scenes of street and saloon, toil and tenements, prostitutes and pugilists—conveying in brush strokes the private worlds of the marginal and the oppressed.[1] A decade later, after literary commentary on the New York night by such architects of realist fiction as Theodore Dreiser, Georgia O'Keeffe's paintings of the skyscraper evening attempted to capture the illusive tapestry of the city's dark structures and soft lights, the heavy air of her New York—Night (1928) shadowing the explicit acts, daring desires, and unconscious mediations of a multitude of night wanderers.[2] According to that inveterate explorer of the erotic underside of the urban evening, Henrik de Leeuw, New York, "a fairly drab burg by day," was "a loud and almost garish village by night," the site of a strangely pathological craving for pleasure that was, in the eyes of the prudent and pious, "contemptuous of every ethical principle."[3]

The risqué sensuality and discarded gentility of the frenetic metropolis after dark is perhaps most strikingly presented by the radical regionalist

Thomas Hart Benton, best known for his Depression-decade murals. Benton came to New York about the same time as Dreiser, another displaced midwesterner.[4] He gravitated to socialist ideas in the 1920s; although he kept a discreet distance from the Communist Party, he befriended individuals on its cultural flank. In the early 1930s he painted the materialist panorama *America Today*. Commissioned by the New School for Social Research—an enclave of avant-garde exiles from mainstream American universities, critical theorists, and European intellectual refugees—the set of nine murals emphasized the turmoil of human diversity that encompassed a United States transformed by industrial capitalism but not reduced to any discernible homogenizing impulse save that of the people's power to leave their stamp on authority's quest to standardize. Gyrating bodies, theatrical poses, and bulging muscles congeal with technologies and work sites to produce an image of America's instruments of power, pluralized in competing representations of exploitation and the advance of "progress," counterposed to the energy of a robust, larger-than-life plebeian mass, urban and rural, animating the swirl of everyday events in the United States. Agriculture in the South and West as well as industry in the Northeast and changing West are symbolized by locomotives, cotton, coal, and steel.

Depicted as well are "city activities," especially those of the night that Benton knew firsthand. He frequented burlesque houses and prizefights and used his detailed appreciation of bodies and gestures to fuse a collage of night scenes, continuous yet heuristically paneled by sequences of simulated architectural moldings. The panel titled *City Activities with Subway* is a juxtaposition of night's varied opportunities and possibilities as well as a vision of its stubborn resiliency in the face of those who would attempt to subdue it. A caricatured soapbox revivalist lifts his hands luridly to the heavens, reaching past "God Is Love" to "Burlesque 50 Girls" and "Heat"; a convert kneels at his loins; the bared buttocks of a stripper grind perilously close to his shoulder blades. Salvation Army singers bask in the heat of a night ablaze with light cascading from the elevated train, their serenade directed to two thrashing boxers, deafened by the crowd's frenzied cries for blood and a knockout. The high culture of the symphony is directed ironically at a necking couple whose ribald flaunting of their sexuality overshadows in its groping and exposed flesh the low culture of the amusement park. On the subway itself—vehicle of the night masses— a debonair white-haired, jacket-and-tied Max Eastman, Marxist editor of the radical cultural journal *The Masses*, and known in left circles as something of a womanizer, visually undresses the famous striptease artist Peggy

Reynolds, who appears literally handcuffed before Eastman's gaze; his hand cradles a book but leans inward to a poised thigh. As a black worker rests, a bookie scans a tabloid whose "Love Nest" headline conjures up the sexual liaisons that often erupted in scandal because their rampant eroticism crossed class lines or the staid boundaries of familialist reproduction. One part of Benton's message, clearly, was that the night was a frontier of possibility—not unlike his beloved West—the taming of which was futile.[5]

Modern Manhattan's journey from dawn to dusk intensifies the experience of day/night contrasts, but this duality is far from unique and not as bound by time and place as might first be thought. Within the universalized difference of light and dark, morning and evening, there has, of course, been ample room for contradictory readings. London's most popular eighteenth-century artist, William Hogarth, for instance, presented a series of engravings, *The Four Times of the Day* (1738) that captured the contested meanings of morning, noon, evening, and night as an allegory of constant human battle. In *Morning* Hogarth centered a pious spinster and a plodding schoolboy midway between the imposing but coldly impersonal edifice of the church wall and the inviting warmth, sensual embrace, and cordial bickering and begging of Tom King's tavern. The narrow path of daily righteousness is unerring, but it inevitably threads its way past the lingering pleasures of the night. In *Noon*, the contrast of tavern and church, licentiousness and propriety, are again highlighted, a gutter separating order and chaos. *Evening* brings a seeming respite from the struggle: with day's labors done (save for the servant milking), the confinements of respectability, maturity, familial responsibility and domesticity produce a suffocating atmosphere of resigned conformity.

Shattering this climate of accommodation is *Night*, a macabre break with the order of the previous "times." Set on the anniversary of Restoration Day, 1660, when the British monarchy was reestablished after the revolutionary turmoils of 1640, the saturnalia of the dark hours is an unleashing of moral and political restraints. Fires rage out of control in the streets, symbolic of the burning Jacobite desire for a radical democratic alternative to the rule of kings. A chamber pot is emptied on the head of a leering, drunken Freemason, since 1717 the personification in England of opposition to the dogmatism and traditionalism of the Church and the class-based, monarchial hierarchies of state power. The Freemason has been relieved of his sword by his light-carrying and obviously disgruntled wife, who winds her way through the tavern-lined streets where children mock adult behaviors of indulgence and transgression. *Night* was

2. William Hogarth, Night, from The Four Times of the Day (1738).

one of Hogarth's darkest artistic commentaries. Auctioned in 1745, it was bought by a banker for approximately thirty pounds sterling. The lighter pictures—*Noon* and *Evening*—brought higher prices in the emerging art market.[6]

Nighttime—its clock is different. Night people—they stand apart. This is a matter not simply of hours and minutes—of what is "measured out with coffee spoons," in Prufrock's sad refrain—but of the tyrannies of time defied, if not displaced.[7] Nor is the issue easily reduced to occupation (what is done to live) as opposed to preoccupation (what is felt, thought, and embraced against the necessities of daytime's needs). These separations, whatever their particular rootedness in time and place, hint at larger continuities; they have the feel of déjà-vu. The night has always been the time for daylight's dispossessed—the deviant, the dissident, the different—and there is something of a bond among those who have chosen or been forced to adapt to the pleasures and dangers of the dark, a space that exists through as well as in time and place.

This book offers a speculative pastiche of commentary, exploring transgression through night travels not just in time and place but within metaphorical spaces where it is possible to see difference defined and lived, however obscured. It is not a book about dark peoples, dark thoughts, dark times, dark jobs, dark joys. It is not a book about dark demands and the imposed, darkly constraining exercise of power. It is not about the opaque agencies of resistance and opposition. It is about none of these historically situated experiences precisely because it is about all of them, how they are connected and what they look like in the mirrors of marginality, where transgression's countenance is sometimes reflected, sometimes distorted.

Otherness is much in vogue in contemporary scholarship but its depiction is usually one-sided, a discourse of powerful constructions somehow stripped of their dynamic reciprocities. In the process much is sanitized, and the terrible injuries of class, racial, and gender exploitation and oppression—most emphatically those that are generated by the victims of authority themselves—are washed and bleached clean to remain on the shelf of literary criticism, as if the deep and dark prices the subordinate have been forced to pay could be accounted for in the textuality of our times. Lost, as well, are the resources of otherness, the imaginative creations and challenges associated with the longings of the night and the license it has often provided. I want to use night travels as a metaphor for the Other, broadly and eclectically conceived, to explore the dark possibilities that have been fenced in by external limitations and brutal boundaries but have actively attempted to break such containments. These happenings (I name them, descriptively only, as cultures) with histories that reach back to antiquity and before, can of course never be captured in the totality of their complexity and historical sensitivity. But they can be gestured toward; examples can be pointed to and arguments made in ways that introduce broad themes in the diverse histories of cultural and social life.

The dark cultures of the night are thus not unified in any categorical history of sameness. Rather, they are presented here as moments excluded from histories of the day, a counterpoint within the time, space, and place governed and regulated by the logic and commerce of economic rationality and the structures of political rule. Night can be understood as lowering curtains on these domains of dominance, introducing theaters

of ambiguity and transgression that can lead toward enactments of liberation. But night has also been a locale where estrangement and marginality found themselves a home. This domicile could be one of comfort
and escape or, on occasion, a nursery of revolt. But so too could it be
darkness within darkness, a discomforting anarchy of alienation and
distress that shattered the brittle securities of daylight in fearful and terrifying dangers, in tensions and self-destructive behaviors all the more tragic
for their relative autonomy from the powers that conditioned them and
bore ultimate responsibility for their history of hurt. Transgression was
not always heroic, and it was certainly not only about resistance, although my account, undoubtedly, accentuates those sides of its histories.

Whatever its contents, the night, narrowly understood as a time or
broadly perceived as a space, has rarely been welcomed by the day. As a
challenge it has been legislated against; as a cover it has been historically
assailed by the intrusions of light, a proliferation of technologies illuminating its dark corners and opening it up to the glare, potential stare, and
threatening intervention of the custodial powers of midday.[8] By the late
twentieth century the critical theorist Jean Baudrillard would summarize
this vanquishing invasion of the night in terms of universalizing loss, the
bland homogenizing of humanity and history that lays a foundation for
succumbing to power's endless whiteness:

> Ours is rather like the situation of the man who has lost his shadow:
> either he has become transparent, and the light passes right through
> him or, alternatively, he is lit from all angles, overexposed and
> defenseless against all sources of light. We are simultaneously exposed
> on all sides to the glare of technology, images and information, without
> any way of refracting their rays; and we are doomed in consequence to
> a whitewashing of all activity—whitewashed social relations, white-
> washed bodies, whitewashed memory—in short, to a complete aseptic
> whiteness.[9]

The process is unmistakable but the prognosis too pessimistic. Against the
dominance of the day, dark cultures have existed—as depicted by Loren
Eiseley—over and through time, up to and including our present:

> In the waste fields strung with barbed wire where the thistles grow over
> hidden mine fields there exists a curious freedom. Between the guns of
> the deployed powers, between the march of patrols and policing dogs,
> there is an uncultivated strip of land from which law and man himself
> have retreated. Along this uneasy border the old life of the wild has
> come back into its own. Weeds grow and animals slip about in the
> night where no man dares to hunt them. A thin uncertain line fringes
> the edge of oppression. The freedom it contains is fit only for birds and

floating thistledown or a wandering fox. Nevertheless there must be
men who look upon it with envy.... It takes a refugee at heart, a wistful
glancer over fences, to sense this one dimensional world, but it is
there.[10]

For transgression—as either a moment of alternative or withdrawal—
to result in social transformation, however, the dialogues and detours of
its makings, often forged in the possibilities of the night, had to undergo
the difficult translation into languages that could restructure the day. This
rarely happened. One historical moment of night's victory over day, in
the metaphorical sense, was the French Revolution, stunningly depicted
in Delacroix's Liberty Leading the People at the Barricades (1830). Whereas the
gendered content of this representation has drawn deserving comment,
Liberty's emergence from the night—leading an army of darkened revolutionaries along a path lit by her luminous, bare-breasted, armed march
forward—is less noticed.[11]

More often than not, night's transgression did not produce this ominous, sometimes deadly, clash of politically uncompromising human agents
but sustained more quietly clandestine histories: times, places, spaces
where human expression was not as easily subjected to the surveillance
of high noon or blinded by the light of day. For much of humanity, the
nighttime has been the right time, a fleeting but regular period of modest
but cherished freedoms from the constraints and cares of daily life. This
is a history that often leaves no evidence, no record of a past that is, on
rare occasions, captured in its stillness by some intruding witness, such
as the photographic genius of the Harlem-born Roy DeCarava.[12]

Other histories, also obscured, can nevertheless be understood by
grappling with the night. "They lived and loved from sundown to sunup,"
wrote one historian of American slaves.[13] African Americans found a form
of freedom in the night—as runaways and as members of a collectivity—
even as they lived within a bondage that carried its legacies into the post-
emancipation period. But in that struggle to use the night lay not only
accomplishments large and small but also many dark moments of doubt,
distress, and worse—a recurring theme in the beginnings of African-
American sociology and the productions of African-American literature.[14]
This book offers an introductory version of histories of this subaltern
sort, a night stroll away from the midday historiographies of our time.

Let me close this brief introduction with an image and an interrogation.
One of Roy DeCarava's most powerfully evocative photographs is Dancers,
a depiction of two men dancing in a Harlem social club. Questioning the
depiction reveals that it lies on the cusp of spontaneity and pose: the men

are hired professionals brought in to entertain by dancing to jazz music in the style of an older generation of black vaudeville performers. DeCarava confesses to a profound ambiguity about the picture:

> These two dancers ... represent a terrible torment for me ... because they are in some ways distorted characters.... The problem comes because their figures remind me so much of the real life experience of blacks in their need to put themselves in an awkward position before the man, for the man; to demean themselves in order to survive, to get along.... And yet there is something in the figures not about that; something in the figures that is very creative, that is very real and very black in the finest sense of the word. So there is this duality.... I have to say that even though it jars some of my sensibilities and it reminds me of things I would rather not be reminded of, it is still a good picture. In fact, it is good just because of those things and in spite of those things. The picture works.[15]

Such comment casts transgression itself and its nights and days in meaningful light: to appreciate its contested meanings requires a sensitivity to complex histories of subordination and struggle, much of which will be visible only in the "still" of a momentarily imposed interpretive unity. Like DeCarava's image, dark cultures should induce an awkward torment in all of us. Behind these histories of the night lie some of the terrors and a part of the triumph of humanity.

PART II

Class and Gender in the Dissolution of the Ancien Régime

3. Pieter Bruegel, *The Peasants' Wedding* (1567).

2

Blood, Bread, and Blasphemy

Peasant Nights

The most striking demographic and class transformations of the twentieth century involve a social group—the peasantry—with a dark history. The light of late capitalism, however, has illuminated only the progressive elimination of peasants from the world order, a process of expropriation, in Marx's words, "written in the annals of mankind in letters of blood and fire."[1] But because this dispossession and this destruction have evolved, until quite recently, slowly and incrementally, the blood of these letters has been thin, the fires burning with the slow, glaring heat of embers cooling in the night.

For millennia the peasantry—those people who tilled the soil, maintained their own small tools, and retained customary or legal rights to the land through tithe payments (in kind or cash) or obligations of labor owed to their lords—were the majority of the globe's people.[2] Dependency characterized their lives: on large landowners, on the soil, and on the fickle fates of nature and climate.[3] And the continuities of peasant life—simultaneously a state, an economy, and a politics—reached across continents, cutting through centuries, blurring distinctions of time, immersing its subjects in what was, by the nineteenth century, a life cycle pattern that appeared unchanging.

Some have read into this continuity a peasant docility, a fatalistic accommodation to the powers of the nobility and the environmental governance of God, though this dualistic authority could be divided and appealed to in subversive ways at moments of crisis. Thus Johan Huizinga could introduce his study The Waning of the Middle Ages (1924) with chapters on the violence of everyday life and the pessimism and hierarchical conception of society that infused all orders of the ancien régime, declaring, "A general feeling of impending calamity hangs over all.... Is it surprising that the people could see their fate and that of the world only as an endless succession of evils? Bad government, exactions, the cupidity and violence of the great, wars and brigandage, scarcity, misery, and pestilence—to this is contemporary history nearly reduced in the eyes of the people.... The background of all life in the world seems black."[4]

When Emile Guillaumin penned his fictionalized account of a nineteenth-century peasant named Tiennon, he peppered the life story with the usual range of accidents, failed crops, diseases, illnesses, endless labors, and routine exactions that dominated mundane existence. In his mid-fifties Tiennon "began to reflect on life," finding it "cruelly stupid and dull." Particular seasons were hard, and specific times especially tough. Tiennon recalled the winter of 1879–1880 as one of distinguished distress: "There was great suffering everywhere in nature." As wandering peasant vagabonds pilfered wood for their fires, some of the poor used the cover of darkness to fell a maple on the manorial estate. The lord had no compassion. His wife, known as Mademoiselle, issued terse instructions to the groundskeeper: "You must make frequent rounds in the night, and if you happen to see any of those wretches, don't hesitate: shoot at him— you have the right to do it." Tiennon drew the obvious conclusions, suggesting that if there was a paradise, the landed nobility ought "to have some trouble in obtaining admission." But at the end of his life Tiennon had few answers as to how such a state of bondage could be broken. All he could manage was the anguished need not to be an imposition on those of his family who were continuing to work the land: "Death! Death, but not the horrible downfall of becoming a burden to the young, to the healthy, to the ordinary life of the family ... From life I have nothing to hope, but I have still something to fear. That I may escape this last calamity is my one desire."[5]

Tiennon chose this as his last request precisely because it was a means to ensure the survival not only of his family but of his class. Whatever their differences across time and space, the peasantry, as John Berger has argued, "everywhere can be defined as a class of survivors." Even eighteenth-century peasant folktales, according to Robert Darnton, took survivalist turns, as wish fulfillment remained fixed on "common objects in the everyday world." Storytelling was "a program of survival, not a fantasy of escape."[6]

The method of extracting surplus from the peasantry may change under feudal, capitalist, and socialist regimes, and new implements and technologies and crops are worked, but peasant life is nonetheless a matter of sustenance and survival. As such, it is often insular and parochial, its values highly traditional, the product of evolutions measured in centuries and generations. But the peasant's world view, eminently conservative, can also be egalitarian. Recognizing work as necessary, and scarcity and calamity as inevitable, it is grounded in an odd experience: those who produce the food are most likely to starve in times of acute want. To overcome this ultimate danger of hunger and its risks of distress and death, peasant consciousness oscillates between an almost instinctual hoarding individualism and a utopianism of mutual fraternal aid, a political economy of value premised on need and use rather than exchange and profit. When the latter impulse is aroused in a context of dire need, the peasant revolts that often erupt are a complex blend of the traditional and the modern: the spontaneity of insurrection articulates values of immediate need clothed in the rituals, superstitions, and attachments of the past. Antonio Gramsci, well placed to observe the peasantry in southern Italy, concluded that the rural poor do not understand progress: they think of themselves "as being, and still are all too much, in the hands of natural forces and of chance, and therefore retain a 'magical,' mediaeval and religious mentality."[7] In the capitalist transformation of the countryside the peasant is thus Janus-faced; with an interpretive gaze fixed on the past, the fields are plowed for a future that cannot be glimpsed.

For centuries this seemed to work, although appearances were deceiving, and the change within the world of the peasant was a potent lever of large-scale social transformation.[8] Still, the peasantry survived, its heretical stoicism summed up politely in a Russian proverb, "Don't run away from anything, but don't do anything," and rudely in an Ethiopian epigram, "When the great lord passes the wise peasant bows deeply and silently farts."[9]

Silence, in words or wind, can be maintained only so long. The peasantry, its survival allowed and nurtured by various social formations for a thousand years and more, is now a declining and displaced class, for as capitalism's global reach penetrates to the outer edges of a world economy, the distance and difference separating local modes of production and cultures from the metropolitan centers of empire are shrinking daily. Traditional rural class relations are being eroded by agribusiness and the commodification of land. Only in sub-Saharan Africa, China, and shrinking areas elsewhere in Asia have peasants remained a robust presence demographically, and even there the pressures on the landed poor are evident. Around the world the peasantry has fallen, as wage labor, proletarianization, and urbanization rise. Japan is a dramatic case in point: almost 53 percent of the country's population labored on the land in 1947; less than forty years later the figure had fallen to 9 percent. This "death of the peasantry," claims Eric Hobsbawm, "cuts us off from the world of the past."[10]

For much of the peasantry, the past was lived in the ugly night of subordination and deprivation, a repressive experience of limited possibilities that translated into narrowed horizons and caricatured constructions of what peasants were. Fixated on the land and its acquisition—literally and figuratively—the peasants were often regarded as the antithesis of civilization. Imprisoned in nature, they had no appreciation of its wonders; dependent on markets, they were the most instrumental of slaves to the dismal corners of the dark science of a primitive economics; incapable of lofty vision, they had only animalistic passions. They were reputed to be unfeeling and without ideals. "The peasant loves nothing nor nobody but for the use he can make of it," concluded one observer.[11] In La comédie humaine (1829–48), Honoré de Balzac could discern the peasantry by the smells they emitted, which were increasingly offensive not only to bourgeois sensibilities but also to urban workers, frequenters of taverns, and marginal lodgers.[12] To see, to hear, to smell, if not to touch or taste, the peasant was an unpleasant presence, an offense to the senses.

By the nineteenth century, Marx expressed the conventional pessimism regarding the peasantry's capacity to transform its material conditions:

> The great mass of the French nation is formed by simple addition of homologous magnitudes, much as potatoes in a sack form a sack of potatoes ... In so far as there is only a local interconnection among these small-holding peasants, and the identity of their interests begets no community, no national bond and no political organization among them, they do not form a class. They are consequently incapable of enforcing their class interests in their own name, whether through a parliament or through a convention. They cannot represent themselves, they must be represented.[13]

Lacking the political will to challenge, ultimately and decisively, its endless oppression and exploitation, the peasantry was a historic brake on the process of change. As Friedrich Engels argued: "The peasant has so far largely manifested himself as a factor of political power only by his apathy, which has its roots in the isolation of rustic life."[14] Marx and Engels judged the peasantry politically, and found it lacking.[15]

Others allowed their prejudices more vociferous voice. The French peasantry was routinely depicted, contemptuously so, as savage. Balzac's

The Peasants (1844), Emile Zola's *The Earth* (1887), and Jules Renard's *Our Savage Brothers* (1908) confirmed in literary constructions the popular prejudices of an age of animosity toward the poor of the countryside. As the French historians Eugen Weber and Theodore Zeldin have shown, comment on the peasantry as savage was ubiquitous.[16] Even a country priest could not summon up sufficient godly grace and charity to transcend his loathing for his parishioners—"I would love the peasants, if the peasant did not disgust me." "The peasant appears," Weber concludes, "as a dark, mysterious, hostile, and menacing figure."[17]

Something of this can be gleaned from an interestingly two-sided representation, Vincent Van Gogh's *The Potato Eaters* (1885). Gathered round a crude table, their evening meal consisting of potatoes and tea, their surroundings spartan, these peasant producers are shrouded in darkness, the light of their sociability and sustenance descending from a single bulb—the illumination of technology. The painting has been interpreted as an almost heroic depiction of the "voiceless toilers, the great majority," an artistic creation of "infinite sympathy" in which the peasant subjects are devoid of "self-pity." Van Gogh wrote to his brother while he was working on the painting:

> I have tried to emphasise that those people, eating their potatoes in the lamplight, have dug the earth with those very hands they put in the dish, and so it speaks of manual labor, and of how they have honestly earned their food. I have wanted to give the impression of a way of life quite different from that of us civilised people.

There is in this statement the same acute ambivalence that speaks to us from the painting itself. Even in his reverence for honest toil, Van Gogh could not escape the dichotomous imagery—them/us, civilization/savagery—in which the dirt of the earth and the gentility of the table come together in a profound unease. The artist cannot overcome this class knowledge of a violated taboo, however he may struggle to transcend its confining conventionality in an appreciation of productive labor. Its surroundings dark and primitive, its bodily parts and countenance gnarled, sooty, and covered, its needs and pleasures so elemental as to be measured out in the most basic of diets and shared with stoic resignation, Van Gogh's peasantry reproduces the standard evocation of landed labor's stolid physical separation from cultured life. It is "the face of misery and woe," a visage uncertain, timid, and expressionless, somber and meek, yet disturbingly threatening. Van Gogh painted the savage at the same time that he intended to offer reverence and respect.[18]

4. Vincent Van Gogh, *The Potato Eaters* (1885).

In this depiction of the peasant hearth and home, a vision of the terrible circumstances of landed labor, its darkened possibilities shadowed on the windowless walls, Van Gogh addressed not so much his own sympathies as the troubled realities of a subordinate class.[19] *The Potato Eaters*, a dark image of what a century and more of capitalist development accomplished in human terms, is not a pretty picture. It represents a class that has become what it produces, which is also what it eats: vegetation itself, a sack of potatoes. "Tell me what you eat, and I will tell you who you are."[20]

To reach past such a vision of rural life, to try to appreciate the words that might have been spoken at Van Gogh's peasant table or the ideas, thoughts and longings imagined amid the smoke and smells of this environment of toil, in which the places of work and leisure were never easily separable, one must look past the walls of this painting, through windows of time that are not a part of the structure of the artist's representation. To attempt to understand the dreams or the nightmares that punctuated the weary peasant's escape into sleep, one must grope through layers of historiographical and cultural darkness, putting together pieces of an always incomplete puzzle. In doing so, one will gain much by attending, first and foremost, to the relentless materialism of the peasant, whose days and nights were connected in the linked fortunes of man and nature, the births and deaths of people and animals, the movements of the seasons and their crops.

Peasant nights were dark, materialist extensions of the day. To know the night and its signs—the sunset and its clouds, the visibility of the stars, the moon's surroundings—was to prepare to know the prospects for the day and their effects on crops or animals. Nature had many a message for those who worked within its boundaries. Rain was on its way, the sixteenth-century Italian bailiff Giacomo Agostinetti assured the peasants, if "the herds leap, the donkeys bray, the wolves howl, the birds never cease to fly, or the cocks to crow. When flies and horseflies bite, dolphins and fish dart, frogs and toads croak, snakes, lizards and similar animals wander."[21]

The rhythms of peasant production thus often knew no clock of daylight work and nighttime rest. Emile Guillaumin complained that his days and nights were interspersed with labors, allowing him only "five or six hours of light, uneasy sleep."[22] The peasant night was broken into components associated with physiological states of being or "natural" happenings, observable and identifiable through the senses: "after sunset, at nightfall, at the hour of the first sleep, at the hour half-way through the first sleep, at cock-crow, or when the cock had crowed three times." Time was not money; days and nights had their interruptions and pauses.[23]

Governed by blood and bread, the peasant night brought forth reflections on the instabilities and precariousness of lives oscillating between abundance and scarcity. Power often seemed to conspire against the peasant; its form could be human or natural. In an effort to categorize and structure the data that presented themselves, peasant cultivators pondered the universe concretely. The aim was not an idealistic transformation of life but a modest regulation of its vicissitudes. Peasant storytellers portrayed a world "of raw and naked brutality," according to Robert Darnton: "To eat or not to eat, that was the question peasants confronted in their folklore as well as in their daily lives."[24] Blood and bread led peasants to think, and their wandering thoughts could, in the dark corners of the night, nurture an intensely materialistic, blasphemous questioning of the spiritual world as presented to them by those whose understanding of the sacred seldom confronted the ravages of hunger and want.

Blood mattered first. The particularities of peasant family forms varied considerably across time and space, with kinship networks developed in specific places and in different historical contexts. Kin densities in medieval villages ranged from the low (parts of England) to the high (France), just as the nature of the peasant household and its governance—narrow, simple, and nuclear at one extreme; extended and stem at the other—exhibited no uniformity.[25] Patterns of inheritance, the ease with which land could be alienated, the timing and implications of marriage, and other customary procedures that structured the meanings and tempo of peasant life and its generational cycles also shifted greatly from place to place, from century to century.[26]

Consider, for instance, the case of Martin Guerre, whose father and mother and unmarried uncle migrated in 1527 from the old family property in the Basque country on the border of France and Spain to the village of Artigat, located on a large plain, traversing the River Leze below the foothills of the Pyrenees. This move was a mere three-day walk. Yet in the separations of that half-week lay great differences. In the Basque village that the Guerres left, Martin's father was heir to the ancestral property, and such holdings could not be sold. So important to the villagers were these family homes that each was given a name. "They call themselves lords and ladies of such-and-such a house," snorted one disdainful critic of peasant pretensions, "even if it is only a pigpen." Their adopted village, however, knew few such traditions. Artigat was a bustling commercial center; its freedoms extended to the sale of lands and no seignior exacted manorial tribute. As the newly settled family from the Basque country had skills as tilemakers, they prospered. When their son Martin was married off, after an evening of banqueting he and his new bride were escorted back to his father's home where, at midnight, the young village revelers invaded the newlyweds' bed. They carried a heavily seasoned drink known as the *resveil*, which was said to solidify lovemaking and guarantee fertile marriages.[27] No doubt the couple drank to their future "blood." As Emmanuel Le Roy Ladurie has commented in introducing his history of Montaillou, the "basic cell" of peasant life was the family, "embodied in the permanence of the house and the daily life of a group co-resident under the same roof." These structures and processes were all designated by words that meant both "family" and "house." For the inhabitants of Montaillou, "the family of flesh and blood and the house of wood, stone or daub were one and the same thing."[28]

Not only bloodlines, but blood itself was a powerful presence in the world of the peasant, symbolizing sustenance and life. It flowed at the slaughter of an animal which, depending on its size, might be killed in the yard, the kitchen, or the public slaughterhouse. Peasant butchers were convinced that their regular inhalation of the smells of blood and entrails kept them healthy. When it could grace the table in blood puddings or "dark soups," it was proof of abundance. Blood and milk were thought to have restorative capacities for the enfeebled old, the "venerable gray-beards." Yet myth and folklore inspired fear of those who would drink blood to regain their health, as witches did in their blood covenants. "Blood is the human being's finest juice," declared a mid-fifteenth-century authority, "family remedy, household drug, ailment of life." Piero Camporesi concludes: "the taste of blood permeated yesterday's violent, cruel, immoderate society. From birth to death, the sight and smell of blood were part of the human and social pilgrimage of each and all." This "ideology of blood" knew no "lines of demarcation between the sacred and the profane."[29] Blood, then, had many powers, but one part of its profound and pervasive symbolic authority lay in its centeredness at the conjuncture of these sacred and profane dimensions: in families and kin groupings, with their associated labors and solidarities, blood found one of its most durable meanings.[30]

Pierre Rivière, a deranged peasant who killed his mother, his sister, and his brother in 1835, offered an extraordinary memoir of the violence of an intrafamily jacquerie, the bloodletting of a diseased familialism and its only possible outcome: Rivière was condemned as subhuman, the district prosecutor naming him "ignoble and shameful," "solitary, wild, and cruel," and "a savage not subject to the ordinary laws of sympathy and sociability." But beneath the accounts—journalistic, legal, medical—of the case lie layers of meaning, uncovered by Michel Foucault and his associates, in which blood's brutalities are chronicled in life as well as death. Rivière was troubled by his father's tortured relationship with his mother—who was carrying another man's child at the same time she held her husband in contempt because his property was not equivalent in value to her holdings. Pierre Rivière, who pondered religious texts as his mother taunted him, was trapped on the horns of a dilemma. To purify his blood he had to purge the bad in order to rejuvenate the good. All this was blood waiting to be spilled: a mother without love to offer her husband or her son, a woman who dominated by her control of land and lust, a father anguished and tired in the endless routine of daily alienated toil, a family devoid of otherworldly commitments, work without sociability. When night came, Pierre Rivière struck his blow against blood, the better to revive blood.[31] The problem was that such a course of action was an act of individual grace and salvation totally at odds with the codes and containments of blood relations, which offered no recourse to radical reversals. As such, this transgression required the full regulatory intervention of an emerging governing authority, one with a growing apparatus of technical and ideological expertise, capable of categorizing the state of the mind and incarcerating the "madman."

Of course, peasant evenings were not often consumed in this kind of reconstructive attack on blood. More typical were evenings of quiet sociability, their family content providing a possible antidote to the loneliness that could engulf those who embarked on journeys of independence and the formation of their own families. Fairytales were told around the firesides in peasant cottages—Red Riding Hood, Puss in Boots, Tom Thumb, Mother Goose—to break the monotony of long, cold winter evenings. These were cautionary stories of what could go wrong if routines were broken and trusts placed in hands that held no close connection to kin, warnings against transgression. Mother Goose was hardly a rhyme of frivolity; rather it was a text of "poverty, despair, and death."[32] Peasant nights were a time for human contact, then, of a sort that sealed the bond of blood in routines of instrumental talk, elemental fears, eating and sleeping. Night was, for the peasant, a rare time to observe blood, one of the few moments of respite in which there was some chance to see life's human products, whatever their many tensions and however constrained their circumstances. Claude-Henri Rocquet suggests as much in his imaginative discussion of Pieter Bruegel's peasant background: "This evening we will hold our hands to the fire and we will know we are alive for yet a while."[33] Night's work and night's pleasures, such as they were, were the productions and reproductions of blood, in which the self figured only incidentally.[34]

If this was no ideal retreat, the night was nevertheless best spent at home or close to it, in darkness broken by the illumination of a pipe or a full moon. To be out at night was to court danger, for night was often a time to settle scores, when peasants met in darkness behind a barn or in an isolated field to rendezvous for a final accounting that could end in death. Peasant homes, if deserted, were susceptible to theft, especially in seasons when darkness descended early, covering the actions of burglars. There were often strangers about, especially in forested regions, and rare was the peasant youth who was not well inculcated with fears of the night and of places known in local lore for their dangers. The night was "spirit time," a demonic darkness thought by some to harbor goblins and devils invested with supernatural capacities that always worked their powers in chaos and calamity:

> At night, the flying phantoms,
> Champing ferocious jaws,
> Do by their whistling terrify my soul.

more evident as the "natural" economy of the peasant poor oscillated between times of extreme want and scarcity and replenished periods of unhealthy abundance, a material cycle that engendered fantasies of gluttony ravaging hunger. In addition, the bread of the countryside was routinely seasoned with sesame, anise, fennel, cumin and, most notably, wild and cultivated poppyseeds. It is quite possible that, like Mexican aboriginal peoples, peasants were acquainted with "the bread of the gods," the intoxicating, hallucinogenic powers of certain small fungi and mushrooms, some of which no doubt found their way into actual breads. Thus, dreamed of in times of distress, bread was also the very stuff of dreams, as its seasonings were known to cause "the loss of reason" and generate "domestic drunkenness and a certain stupidity." Indeed, specific vegetation was cultivated for its sleep-inducing and euphoric properties: peasants knew well the poppy's erotic effects, using it to bring on arousal and sensual dreams. It was also much prized by wet-nurses, who were advised to maintain a strict diet of "boiled salad and poppyseeds," the better to lace their milk with a narcotic that would ease babies into a soft sleep and deflect the terrifying dreams and disturbing fantasies thought to puncture the potential tranquility of night. In addition to such sedative substances transmitted to infants from the breast, anointing rituals literally immersed the cradled child in hallucinogenic herbs. Doctors advised smearing infant foreheads and dousing the nostrils as well with ointments, heavily cut with poppy seeds and enhanced by a little opium. "Thus prepared and 'seasoned,'" concludes Camporesi, "the infant was entrusted to the dark arms of the night. The initiation into controlled dreaming and the artificial ease of opium-induced sleep began with swaddling clothes. From infancy to old age narcosis ruled supreme."[45]

Bread, the foundation of blood, is thus also an analytic lever through which the historian can materially pry open a part of peasant lives obscured in corners of the past and starved for evidence and empirical proofs. Rationalist intellectuals such as Galileo and Descartes constructed cosmologies paralleling but different from the peasant world view. Their systems articulated a conception of a world machine, "a mental and physical 'works' regulated by a coherent mechanical and logical apparatus, a perfectly and inexorably self-adapting system of fittings and attachments." But their personal universes were not alternatively starved by want and fed on adulterated excess, as were, in many cases, those of the peasantry. A dichotomized world of breads—"the bread of princes," "the bread of dogs"—led inexorably to a dichotomized world of thoughts, which could also translate into activities and practices of dramatic divergence.[46]

Produced and often consumed by day, bread also fed the night and its histories, leading us toward new appreciations of peasant revels and resistances.

This complex fusion of material and cultural forces in the agrarian-dominated and peasant-populated precapitalist world is perhaps nowhere more brilliantly revealed than in the paintings of Pieter Bruegel the Elder, the obscure sixteenth-century painter of the Flemish Lowlands.[47] Likely born in a peasant village—his landscape artistry reflected the natural rhythms and seasonal cycles of rural life—Bruegel was equally at home in the bustling commerce of Antwerp. He knew well the diverse cultures of the medieval political economy: town and countryside, world trade and village field, the power of empire and the dissenting heresies of iconoclastic sects—all were splashed on his canvases in explosive bold colors, intricate symbolism, and arresting images. Known to masquerade as a peasant and appear at village fairs and country weddings, claiming falsely a kin connection and bearing gifts, Bruegel was a Martin Guerre for a day, drawing his imposter's wage in acquired familiarity with the ways of the countryside, which he translated into a series of evocative scenes and powerful depictions. He observed first-hand the peasant's daily routines and intensified bouts of labor and leisure. But he lived in the heart of empire as well, where the grip of money and the blood of war affected almost every year of his life. His last decade was particularly tumultuous: denounced as a Libertine heretic and member of a clandestine sect, he was forced to flee Antwerp in 1563; settling in Brussels where "the air was loud with the rattle of Spanish musketry," the master painter looked with dismay on the war-torn ravages of civilization's descent into deathly struggles for domination, symbolized in the ugly scaffolds and gallows that dotted the coasts of a world defined increasingly by mercantilist doctrine and contending absolutist states. His paintings, marked by thoughtful contemplation and a faculty "for evaluating the moral and material components of the age," are contrasting sequels of vibrant color and shadowed darkness. As a whole, his oeuvre consists of the challenging alternatives of nature and disorder, a representation of the world that returns repeatedly to the dichotomies of day and night. His thought ordered by metaphor, Bruegel "plunged into the world of fables and proverbs," of "the obsessions of the medieval mind and the unrest of the times." The foundations of this metaphorical order were land and labor, bread and blood. Throughout it all, as Robert L. Delevoy suggests, "Man, as Bruegel perceives him in the heart of Nature, is obsessed with the basic need of earning his daily bread."[48]

Bruegel's concern with the labors of the day and his representation of them in colorful depictions of peasant work in late spring and early summer are captured nicely in The Hay Harvest and The Corn Harvest, both painted sometime in 1565. Comment on this archetypal Bruegelian representation has fixed on the seasonality of peasant work and the reciprocities binding the rural poor and the material environment, leading to a structure of dependency on and subordination to the laws of nature. Be that as it may, the sated cultivator, passed out under a tree, and his fellow villager plodding through the cut corn with another jug of refreshment conjure up a Camporesian image of the blurring of day's light and night's dreams in a substance-induced flight into fantasy.

The peasant's physiological displacement is perhaps nowhere more graphically depicted than in Bruegel's The Land of Cockaigne (1567), sometimes known as Fool's Paradise, a painting inspired by the Flemish proverb "Nothing is stupider than a lazy glutton." A soldier knight, a scholar (perhaps a religious man), and a peasant symbolize the three orders of medieval society, all of whom have overindulged themselves in an orgy of consumption. But rather than a comment on the abundance of the agrarian pre-industrial world, this representation could signify the pendulum swings of foodstuffs, basic necessities as well as delicacies, in a climate of oscillating excess and scarcity that swept the logic of rational thought and the hierarchies of station aside in cravings and needs that could not be paced or pacified. Bruegel may well have struggled to construct an image of utopian well-being, but the materiality of this universe of uncertainty resulted in unmistakable distortions and deformations. With want banished, the social orders of distinction separating peasant, knight, and noble fade as the three orders lie down together in the harmony of sleep and the full stomach.[49]

This was a far cry from what Bruegel actually saw in the dissolution of the ancien régime, however, and his art, as it moved outside the cycles of peasant production and beyond the villages and fields of the agrarian world, turned increasingly to the dark destructions of his age. "He saw the architecture of nightmares and he measured the contours of fevers. His eye pierced the belly of the earth and saw the horses of death," comments the critic Claude-Henri Rocquet. Caught in the grip of melancholy, Bruegel "knew his own fascination with black thoughts. He knew the path of darkness."[50] In The Battle between Carnival and Lent (1559), Bruegel prefaces this movement into the dark terrors of night with staged, almost census-like contrasts, dividing the painting into dualistic sides. Pitting the peasant festivals, indulgences, and displacements of want and power associated with carnival (in which raucousness and color add to the sense of frivolity) against the dire and drab presentation of the simplified, pious existence characteristic of Lent, Bruegel stands the sensuality and sociability of the peasant village alongside the austere spirituality of established religious convention.[51]

More awful were the productions of the ensuing years as Bruegel wrestled with the demons of his metaphorical mind, confronting the ravaging brutality and unfeeling acquisitiveness of the predatory commercialism of the 1560s. Peasants recede into the background, or are displaced entirely, as the countryside of rustic festivity and daily toil is overtaken by themes of an endless, all-consuming war in which evil constantly has the upper hand over good and dark predominates over light. Consumed by images of heaven's depleted forces battling a relentless hell as depicted in his morbid *The Triumph of Death* (1562), Bruegel seemed to be fighting a losing battle in the quest for his own Day of Judgment. His images are the antithesis of an abundant landscape: scorched ships of commerce sink in the quiet sea of trade, mourners gather by a chapel, wagons groan under the weight of skulls, thieves hang from the gallows, dissidents are impaled on the wheel, the dead spill out of their coffins, skeletons harvest a dying emperor's gold coin.[52] As blood flowed, bread's artistic attractions faded. Bruegel anatomized the disorder of his times.[53]

For the peasant masses the disorder was no less, but the anatomy differed. European peasants lived in a hierarchical formation in which station or place was unambiguous. "Some are devoted particularly to the service of God; others to the preservation of the state by arms; still others to the task of feeding and maintaining it by peaceful labors." So opened Charles Loyseau's *Traité des ordres et simples dignitez* (1610), feudal France's explication of the "estates" of the medieval world: the clergy, the nobility, and the *menu peuple* of town and country. Peasants were the poorest and most precarious members of the third estate, a subordinate order destined to labor in the wider interests of their superiors and the stability of society. They took their commands from the nobility and their guidance from men of God, a governance that was properly dualistic, ensuring the static, unchanging relations of servitude within which the rural poor worked and lived.[54]

It required a great deal of misery to undermine this oppressive stability. But then peasants had endured more than modernist consciousness can often imagine. Given that war, plague, and famine drew peasant blood and made bread scarce with dire regularity, and as the ordered inequalities

of society were paraded before peasant eyes in noble and clerical indulgence, it is not surprising that the taut equilibrium of the three estates
snapped in peasant revolt. "As natural to the seigneurial regime as strikes
are to large-scale capitalism," rebellious uprisings of the peasantry, Marc
Bloch long ago demonstrated, dot the landscape of nascent class formation,
from conspiracies of freemen-led serfs against landlord property in the
seventh century and Flemish plots in 821 to the Zapatista revolt of
aboriginal peasants in Chiapas, Mexico, in the 1990s.[55]

Peasant wars, from China to Cuba, from antiquity to the present, thus
blur boundary lines of distinction within the diverse history of revolt.
They encompass everything from the blind brutality of jacquerie, in which
the peasant village rises in uncontrollable anger to vent its spontaneous
rage against the hated oppressor, to burning, looting, terrorizing. In the
Beauvaisis in 1358, French peasants refused their lords' demands for new
obligatory contributions to the equipping of fortresses for war by torching
castles, quartering their owners, and sodomizing noble women.[56] Such
violent and disruptive explosions of refusal might put a brake on the
progressive erosion of peasant well-being, but they were most often short-
lived and defeatist. The peasant uprising could also take the form of a
general strike against feudal exploitation in principle, drawing unambiguous lines of opposition against dearth and waging a protracted struggle
that, whatever the final outcome, contributed to the language of "rights."
There was something of this in both the English uprising of 1381, with
its voice of "the freeborn Englishman," and the German peasant wars of
1525–1526, which Engels called "the grandest revolutionary effort of the
German people" and which started as a "worldly ban" of rural producers
against the demands of their lords.[57] Peasant rebellion could also approximate social banditry, as Hobsbawm has suggested, the wrongs to blood
precipitating acts of revenge that enclosed particular groups in an outlaw
identity where marginalization lived out its days in a marauding warfare
against the rich and a self-consciously mythologizing patronage of the
poor; the earliest example may be the legendary Robin Hood.[58] As the
twentieth century saw increasing peasant resistance to imperialism, peasant
war often took on the trappings of a revolutionary guerrilla strategy in
which the countryside, its terrain already attuned to resistance to capitalism
in so many ways, surrounded the invading commercial city. Mao Tse-
tung's assertions turned peasants into a vanguard of guerrilla revolt:
"Leadership by the poor peasants is absolutely necessary. Without the
poor peasants there would be no revolution. To deny their role is to deny
the revolution."[59] But more than seventy-five years after these words were

penned, more than fifty after the success of China's revolutionary forces, the peasant countryside is alive with agrarian capitalism. Survival, not revolution, is the peasantry's ultimate purpose; blood and bread are both its means and its end.

In this struggle for survival, peasants confronted deteriorating conditions, dearth and death within the static concept of an ordered universe that had been central to the hierarchies and hegemonies of many rural social formations from the time of the ancien régime. As a consequence, when productions on the land failed, and the state proved no more capable of providing for them, peasants questioned or mouthed the final order of God in a language of materialistic challenge. An engaging aspect of the peasant histories of transgression is thus crafted in the dark recesses of mysticism and blasphemy, which, again, blend into and blur the social, economic, and political meanings of peasant revolts, which often veered in decidedly messianic, millenarian directions. Possibly intoxicated by the delusions of hunger and the hallucinogens and narcotics of bread's debased adulterations, driven to defend their blood against the deprivations and deteriorations of voracious lords, attuned to a universe of hard material want, peasants followed an almost scripted traditionalism in which worldly wants and otherworldly desires coexisted in understandable, if often jarring, juxtapositions. As Engels suggested, "It is obvious that under such conditions, all general and overt attacks on feudalism, in the first place attacks on the Church, all revolutionary, social, and political doctrines, necessarily became theological heresies. In order to be attacked, existing social conditions had to be stripped of their aureole of sanctity. Attacks thus took the form of mysticism, as open heresy, or of armed insurrection."[60] Bloch outlined the common features, whatever the particularities of place, of the "spontaneous anarchy" of peasant rebellion: mystical fantasies; a primitive egalitarianism of the Gospel, a kind of "community of goods"; and itemized grievances that ran the gamut from the precise and far-reaching to the idiosyncratic and petty. In the rebellious Code paisant, drafted in Breton (1675), for instance, there were demands for "the abolition of tithes, to be replaced by a fixed stipend for parish priests, for limitations on hunting rights and seigneurial monopolies and for the distribution of tobacco with the blessed bread at Mass, purchased with money raised for taxation, 'for the satisfaction of the parishioners.'"[61]

In 1420, a century before the German upheavals of the 1520s, the Taborite peasant communalists of Bohemia revolted in an attempt to revive the ancient mythic ideal of total community. The path to this utopia was to be strewn with the bodies of "lords, nobles, and knights," all of whom were to be "exterminated in the forests like thieves." Private property was to be abolished, and "the merchants of the earth shall weep and mourn over her; for no man buyeth their merchandise any more." Holding land outside the common good was "a mortal sin." A sect that emerged from this milieu eventually dispensed with all biblical attachments—even the word of God being contaminated in their eyes. They contented themselves with a simple prayer—"Our Father, who art in us, illuminate us, thy will be done." Their belief that heaven and hell had no existence save for the righteous and unrighteous deeds of mankind no doubt contributed to the idea of purgatory, a doctrine born, as Jacques Le Goff has suggested, out of the social and intellectual upheavals of the Middle Ages.[62] When people of these tumultuous times who embraced dissenting, heretical convictions were burned at the stake, "they strode laughing into the flames."[63] If heresy did not fuel the fires of peasant revolt, it certainly burned in the charred remains of countless suppressed uprisings.[64]

Even though no other revolt matched in intensity or scope the German peasant wars of 1526–1527, the territories congruent to that rebellion experienced sixty-six other revolts between 1525 and 1789, and rural disturbances lasted well into the nineteenth century. Seventeenth-century France, Russia, and China saw endemic communal rural upheaval, and although it was unmistakably governed by the material world of tax, tithe, obligation, and dearth, it was not without its mysticism and religious content. France's Normandy revolt in 1639 followed years of plague and famine, exacerbated by high taxes. It took its name from its general leader, who called himself Jean Nu-Pieds (John Barefoot), and the peasants marched under a banner proclaiming, "There was a man sent from God whose name was John," carrying a likeness of Saint John the Baptist. In China, Confucian invocations of heaven's place in restoring justice, popular dissidence associated with Taoism and Buddhism, Manichaeist exaltations of the principles of light against dark, and the borrowed aspects of Christianity evident in the Taiping rebellion of the nineteenth century often figured in peasant uprisings. Russia's "Time of Troubles" ushered in a bewildering array of peasant mobilizations—most intense in the period 1604–1617 but reaching forward until 1674—at which time the divine, dynastic rule of the tsars, the debilitating consequences of famine (1601–1603), widespread social banditry, and the challenge of pretenders to the throne mixed the three orders of God, state, and production in a chaotic mix of idealism and materialism. Japanese peasants launched a series of *yonaoshi* revolts that grew in intensity from the late eighteenth century into the nineteenth; with the weakening of feudal authority, peasants embraced a violent millenarian movement of Buddhist "world renewal" aimed at reconstituting the communal village through religious rebirth and renovation. Some revolts, such as those of Cuban peasants in the late 1890s, their origins unmistakably linked to social banditry, cloaked missions of revenge in evangelistic language: "The redemptive Revolution will show the weak how the people express their protest," said one colonel in the peasant army in 1897. General Maximo Gomez was more blunt: "Blessed be the torch."[65]

It is thus difficult to underestimate the often blasphemous religious content of peasant revolt. The plots and thoughts of this diverse array of transgressions, reaching from early medieval manors into the countryside of capitalism, were often cultivated in the dark shelters of the peasant night, contextualized in want but warmed by hearth fires and the passions of challenging beliefs, many of which were ordered by reflections on established religion and its meanings in the seemingly stationary social relations of dominance and subordination. As Le Roy Ladurie has shown for Montaillou, peasant heresies were themselves often premised on the existence of dichotomous, Manichaean principles, if not deities. The Catharism of Montaillou pitted God against Satan, good against evil, light against dark. "On one side was the spiritual world, which was good, and on the other the terrestrial world, which was carnal, physical, corrupt." With powerful authorities at watch throughout peasant communities, ready to pounce with the vigor of the Inquisition on any dissident rural folk who dared question the rule of established order, heretics who saw the unity of material and spiritual deprivation (lodged in worldly inequalities such as the tithe and the sinecures and patronages of priests willing to do the bidding of kings and lords) would exercise due caution: "People who felt they were being watched used to move about at night, careful [of] what they said." Heretical friends gathered surreptitiously in barns, their clandestine comings and goings taking place after evening meals. When emboldened by the isolation of a mountain village such as Montaillou, they might conduct sermons over special dinners, for which the best wines and the largest fish would be saved, or a sheep poached. Night lowered the curtain, shielding heresy from view and, perhaps, obscuring social distinctions of status, age, and power.

The heretic families of Montaillou led lives relatively uninhibited by guilt. In the cliquish sects, carnal pleasures—again tasted most unambiguously in the night—were often unleashed, freed from the connotations of sin. Against the established Church strictures about incest, some heretics maintained a decided nonchalance; if sex was pleasurable, it was no sin;

if it was purchased from a prostitute, it constituted no violation of male and female purity; it could be consummated by any and all consenting adults, including cousins and priests. Blasphemous pronouncements drew on obscene gestures and phrases weighted down with bodily materialism. When asked how God was made, one dissident replied with laughter: "'God was made fucking and shitting' and as he said these words he clapped his hands together." Such physical demonstrativeness, a fist smacked against an open palm with its implications of erotic activity, could earn inquisitorial punishment. Wealth was not so much the object of attack as "the unhealthy fat of the undeserving rich, clerics and mendicants, who exploited the village without giving in return any spiritual aid of even those services of help and protection provided by wealthy local nobles." This fed the appetite of peasant resentment: "There are four great devils ruling over the world," said one Montaillou Cathar in the 1320s, "the lord Pope, the major devil whom I call Satan; the lord King of France is the second devil; the Bishop of Pamiers the third; and the lord Inquisitor of Carcassonne, the fourth." Montaillou's heretics survived against the Inquisition, plagues, famines, wars, and the elements, their worldly freedoms and earthy sensualities the product of a materialism born of their environment of endurance.[66]

Two centuries later another remote peasant villager, the Friuli miller Domenico Scandella, known as Menocchio, evolved a heretical cosmos that shared much with that of the Cathars of Montaillou. Skeptical about the Holy Spirit's governance of the Church, he defied the priests' monopoly over religious knowledge and threw caution to the wind in his proselytizing efforts to spread the word of rational dissidence. "Priests want us under their thumb, just to keep us quiet, while they have a good time," he told prospective but reluctant converts. Estranged from the powerful worldliness of the Church and its officialdom, which oppressed the poor, Menocchio embraced a rudimentary iconoclasm, rejecting the worship of relics and images, and urged the simplification of scripture. Articulating "an autonomous current of peasant radicalism," the heretic miller read erratically and pondered profusely, expressing the "elemental, instinctive materialism of generation after generation of peasants." He concluded that the hereafter did not exist, that future punishments and rewards were not to be, that heaven and hell were on earth itself, and that the body and the soul were one mortal unity. Good works in the here and now mattered most as man struggled with dichotomized being: "Our heart has two parts, one bright, and the other dark; in the dark one there is the evil spirit, and in the bright one the good spirit." Menocchio

enjoyed preaching "that men should live in peace," but damning men
and women to hell was another matter: "Paul says one thing, Peter says
another, so that I think it is a business, an invention of men who know
more than others." The world around him wrapped in injustice, the peasant
fear of starvation and dearth etched deeply in his conceptions of need,
Menocchio's understanding of paradise was unambiguously predictable, a
Breugelian articulation of the Land of Cockaigne: "It is like being at a
feast" without end, he thought, free from the alteration of "darkness and
light," but returning to the peasant's naturalism, he added, "I did not
know where it was." Menocchio's creationist doctrine was perhaps most
startling, however, and certainly most materialistic: "I have said that, in
my opinion, all was chaos and out of that bulk a mass was formed—just
as cheese is made out of milk—and worms appeared in it, and these were
the angels. The most holy majesty decreed that these should be God and
the angels, and among that number of angels, there was also God, he too
having been created out of that mass at the same time." As for Christ, he
was a man like any other, without divinity. On these and other subjects
Menocchio was willing to talk with traveling beggars and other acquaintances, their discussions lasting "all through the night." But thoughts such
as Menocchio's were not free to circulate. After two trials the Inquisition
silenced him at the stake. Clement VIII, himself, demanded his death. It
was something of a victory for the small voice of blasphemous transgression, educated in night readings and provoked over years of nocturnal
thought, to have elicited such divine retribution.[67]

Montaillou and Menocchio are two rationalist moments in the night of
peasant blasphemy, where heresy thrived in the evening discussions of a
sect or the dark readings of an isolated dissident.[68] But much of popular
religion in the sixteenth and seventeenth centuries, as Keith Thomas and
Christopher Hill have shown for England, circled around competing paradigms of allegiance: magic and the Church; alchemy and science; proph-
ecy and prayer; astrology and scripture. For many peasants, the night was
peopled with ghosts and fairies, its dangers evident in evil omens or
deflected by cunning men. "Terrifying apparitions, ghosts, goblins, spells,
and collective hallucinations, spread by uncontrollable rumours, disturbed
the nights," suggests Camporesi, as "un-sought-after supplements of shivers
and frights" were added to the unease of days terrorized by plague, hunger,
and war. "In a world where the sad winds of Insecurity, Fear, and Suspicion
blew," he continues, people weakly nourished on inadequate quantities of
possibly poisoned, almost certainly narcotized, bread and drawn to the
healing capacities of "preservatives," "pouches," and "amulets of arsenic"

were both physiologically and ideologically susceptible to the combined chaos of a pharmaceutically *and* spiritually induced mystical order. Cults with their origins in the preservationist instincts of bread and blood, seeking fecundity of the field and fertility of the body, were not uncommon. Peasants found their way to secret nightly enclosures, where they abandoned themselves to the forbidden games and erotic thrashings of agrarian orgies, demonic sabbaths, and lunar licentiousness. Curates, obsessed with such worshipful sensualities, loathed "the Lady of the Night," finding most repugnant the lustful gatherings of believers in the "troublesome religion" of the sacred fertility rite and the Italic serpent-goddess Melusina:

> The oration finished, they formed two groups,
> on one side the one sex, on the other side the other;
> then, having put out the lights, in leaps and flights
> they formed that most wicked embrace;
> and mothers mixed with their sons,
> brothers chanced often with sisters;
> and this custom, which began at that time,
> seems still to exist among the Bohemians.

As darkness descended, pagan sacrificial rites were enacted in caves and secluded woods where "impious sacrifices and vows are made":

> They run to the Goddess Venus (oh, wicked debauchery!),
> Having deposited the sacrifice, here they perform
>   the bacchanalia.
> They go into the cave dwelling by the friendly stillness
>   of the night.

In the late sixteenth century in the Friuli, the same Italian region that produced Menocchio, nightly battles were waged between the benandanti, or "good walkers" (peasants who fell into a trance as their souls left their bodies) and witches. At stake was the fate of the season's crops, although the "good walkers," armed only with stalks of fennel, might also perform cures or other benevolent magic.

> Sometimes they go out to one country region and sometimes to
> another, ... and they appear together jousting and playing games; ...
> the men and women who are the evil doers carry and use the sorghum
> stalks which grow in the fields, and the men and women who are
> benandanti use fennel stalks; ... when they make their great displays
> they go to the biggest farms ... and when the warlocks and witches set
> out it is to do evil, and they must be pursued by the benandanti to
> thwart them, and also to stop them from entering the houses, because
> if they do not find clear water in the pails they go into the cellars and
> spoil the wine with certain things, throwing filth in the bungholes.

To secure the "bread" of the fields and guard the symbolic "blood"—
wine—of village life the *benandanti* resorted to an implicit and materialistic
transgression, their blasphemies drawing on the thread of peasant heresy
to confront the dualistic spiritual world of good and evil, light and darkness. In their out-of-body experience, however, they crossed a threshold,
carrying the struggles of reciprocal days and nights into the territory of
the witches.[69]

3
Witches

Europe and America

Witches have had a bad press. When the nineteenth-century Marxist and labor activist Friedrich Sorge groped for words to express his indignation at the sordid graft associated with the United States railway scandals of the early 1870s, he found them in a condemnation of these figures of the night: it was nothing less than "a true witches' sabbath of corruption," Sorge charged, a mark of ignominy staining "all bourgeois enterprises."[1] When belief in the existence of witches was widespread, linked recipro- cally to religious faiths as in sixteenth- and seventeenth-century England, the witch "was an object of hatred to her neighbors."[2] Her independence and her cunning, scolding, healing, or gossiping ways elicited angers and fears that translated into denunciations of diabolical behavior.

The generic witch was a mythological construction composed of vague attributes and a culture of fear. Marked by the devil, witches could be identified by a simple mole, birthmark, or any protrusion of the epidermis. They were said to cause not only natural calamities such as death and drought, but more prosaic hurt such as the infliction of routine sickness or the loss of animals. They turned against neighbors and family, not strangers. Their supernatural powers meant that they could effect harm simply by thinking it done or by casting a spell or curse. Witches reversed the order of human society, from the backward chant to the "unnatural" act—bestiality, sodomy, incest, cannibalism. Finally, their immoral enchant- ments were worked in secret, derived from their possession by spirits and their consort with the devil, a relationship consummated in the night. Witches were particular personifications of transgression. Their lives de- stroyed by accusations, some confessed to the crimes devised for them by their neighbors, for which they were hunted down, interrogated, tortured, and even gruesomely executed by a mobilized zealotry of Christian Churches—Protestant and Catholic.

In the more secular, skeptical environment of disbelief in the late twentieth century, with satanisms an exotic marginality in modernist culture, to be called a witch still remains a gendered insult of weight, harking back to the essentializing caricatures of centuries past. With warts on their noses and evil cackling laughs, witches are generally threats to all that is good and innocent, reminiscent of Margaret Hamilton's terrorizing of Dorothy in her role as the Wicked Witch of the West in The Wizard of Oz (1939).[3] Witches thus seem a particularly potent premodern example of the modernist "female grotesque" studied by Mary Russo: in a process whereby genders and identities are constituted in subjection to evil and invested with uncanny, supernatural powers—many of which are placed in the service of acts of defilement and debasement—witches are provocative and transformative in ways that simultaneously upset and entice people. Creatures of caves and the depths of hell, they ride through the heavens on animals or broomsticks. Repulsive and highly eroticized, the witch merges oppositions: sensually linked to the spiritual world beyond, to the point of carnal relations with the devil and associations with his powers, the witch is also divorced from all that is good in godly experience.[4] Like the blood that they were said to crave on Thursday or Saturday nights, lowering themselves down chimneys to suck it from "the wee ones," witches have historically been invested with properties both sacred and profane; they embody a macabre magnetism that attracts and repels, the conjuncture of danger and desire that lies at the interface of transgression and the forbidden other.[5] With nature gendered as female, its diabolical developments were often associated with womanly manipulations, dark in their many unknowns.[6] Small wonder that witchcraft's history is one associated unmistakably with the night, with the black arts and mysteries, and with a gendered order of often highly eroticized evil.[7]

When not grotesque, the witch often stepped outside the gender boundaries of womanhood to practice protections, many of which might be gendered as male rather than female, and designated "white" in opposition to "black."[8] Thus, the witch-like benandanti of the Italian Friuli, a peasant region where German, Italian, and Slav customs met, perplexed the late sixteenth-century Church inquisitors precisely because they proudly proclaimed themselves good, not evil.[9] They confessed their nocturnal wars with devil worshipers, whom they called witches and warlocks, insisting that their spirits left their bodies at the command of either their captain, who summoned them with a drum, or an angel "all made of gold," who appeared "during the fourth hour of the night, at the first sleep." Their cult was an unmistakable unification of mysticism and materialism, its night battles fought against agents of evil in the interests of sustaining the harvest for the good of the village. Called to their goodly and godly labors by a spiritual world not to be denied, the *benandanti* embraced their white witchcraft knowing the price that might be exacted (though none was ever actually executed): "Since I have told you the truth, you will immediately have me put to death," stated one defiant "good walker" before the inquisitors. "I was born this way," said one woman, "and I am forced to be a *benandante*, and I cannot do otherwise." Obedient and pious, the "good walkers" of the Fruili served the Lord of Light, not the demons of darkness. They followed their consciences and their faiths in nightly crusades of Christian battle. But as inquisitors tried to trick them into confessions of idolatry and heresy, the *benandanti* found themselves frustrated, trapped in a contradictory dichotomy of good and evil that seemed destined to reverse their life's meaning. To enter the world of the witches was to set foot on a slippery slope. It was a downgrade that might lead to damnation, for white never could quite extricate itself from black where witchcraft was concerned.[10]

Witchcraft raises a series of vitally important universal themes in the history of human societies, themes of central importance to histories of transgression. In such histories the literal darkness of night merges with the dark side of humanity—its alienations, estrangements, insecurities, and fears—in a context that coerces an interpretive dualism, setting rationalism and irrationalism as seemingly oppositional analytic frameworks. Entering into the historical world of the witch seems to demand making a choice between the light of modernist day and the mystical dark of the enchanted night. The latter has had few unambiguous scholarly takers, although many have insisted on taking the subjective beliefs of so-called witches seriously.[11] Often this opposition managed to orchestrate itself around the rationality of the omniscient present, contrasted with the irrationality of a heterogeneous past. "For witchcraft is, if nothing else, an open window on the irrational," states one American historian.[12]

Historiographic conventional wisdom followed this course for some time. In a pioneering conceptualization of the witch craze of the sixteenth and seventeenth centuries, for instance, H. R. Trevor-Roper followed the logic of a powerful presentist intellectual liberalism to a conclusion of blinding rationality, casting something of a plague on both the houses of demonism and Inquisition. The world of the witches themselves was

irretrievably lost, abandoned as the "mental rubbish of peasant credulity,"
while the clerical hunters, pillaging the night for evidence of heresy, lost
the mind of tolerance and reason in "the intellectual regression of Reformation and Counter-Reformation, and the renewed evangelism of the
rival Churches." Ironically enough, this challenging dismissal managed to
push the beliefs, not to mention the practical activities, of the night to
the sidelines of historical inquiry, as the powerful, enlightened exorcisms
of Trevor-Roper's "day" silenced the myth of the witches' Sabbat.[13]

With Keith Thomas's remarkable synthesis of the ideas of religion,
magic, and astrology in relation to the rise and fall of witchcraft in
England, the presentation of witches as "interchangeable scapegoats sacrificed to partisan rivalry" was not so much overcome as bypassed: a highly
functionalist model of seemingly impeccable rationalist empiricism exoner-
ated the clergy from any responsibility for the witch craze just as it
suppressed a contextualized discussion of demonology and the meanings
of witchcraft outside of ecclesiastical authority's reduction of the witch to
a heretic. Thomas had little patience for the view that witches were social
rebels and nonconformists. Nor did he pay attention to the shifting material
ground of witchcraft, in which the powerful attractions of mythologies
of specific symbolic systems and their cultural transmission from generation to generation or through a particular region might be related to
alterations in the web of power in whose tangle of plebeian and patrician
relations the clerics, magistrates, merchants, and small producers of town
and country might be caught.[14]

The stimulating explorations of Carlo Ginzburg, historian of the Fruili
benandanti, challenge this rationalist blind spot in witchcraft studies most
directly. No historian of the witches' night has so relentlessly refused the
oppositional paradigm of modernist rationalism versus premodern irrationalism. Insisting that the witch is something more than the phobic
invention of the Inquisition, Ginzburg argues that the demonologies and
encounters with the dead associated with the Sabbat constitute a historical moment, lasting roughly the three centuries from the 1400s to the
1700s, in the deepest mythological structures of popular culture. In this
sense, witchcraft was less a "craze" (in Trevor-Roper's loaded language of
displacement) than a variant of a continuum that reaches across millennia
of human experience, from antiquity and the preliterate cultures of prehistory to the present. Drawing on Claude Lévi-Strauss's structuralist conception of myths as symbolic systems, where meaning is generated in
unconscious attachments in the mind, Ginzburg sets witchcraft alongside
the broader history of shamanism and the complex and constantly evolving

ensemble of folk myths. Many of these turn decisively on sets of symbolism that transcend the fixities of bodily experience by taking men and women into the spiritual world of the dead as an act of regeneration. If his own focus is decidedly Eurasian, Ginzburg's perspective draws the history of witchcraft toward parallel systems associated with African tribal rites, Caribbean and Creole voodoo, death dealers and *Oddiyan* in India, and American aboriginal spirit quests; he implicitly suppresses the powerful Eurocentric bias at the core of much of "cultural studies," even as he himself argues through articulations of such exclusions and marginalizations. From "a subterranean stratum of unitary Eurasian mythology," then, Ginzburg extracts "a stupefying dissemination of shamanistic traits" which gather together "a history of thousands of years." Unconcerned with the overt oppositional clash of antagonists, he mines the anthropological fields of human culture for "clues" to "hidden truths" that reach across the centuries, exploring aspects of transgression's continuities. "The inaccessible experience which humanity has for millennia symbolically expressed in myths, fables, rites, ecstasies," Ginzburg says in introducing his *Ecstasies: Deciphering the Witches' Sabbath* (1989), "remains one of the hidden centres of our culture, of our mode of being in the world. The attempt to know the past is also a voyage to the world of the dead."[15]

The strength of this orientation is threefold.[16] First, it takes witchcraft out of the cul-de-sac of an inordinately intellectual history associated with Reformation and Counter-Reformation thought and places it within broader social and cultural histories. Thus, Ginzburg suggests links between "moral panics" of the fourteenth century and before, when widespread fears that Jews and lepers were poisoning wells in a conspiratorial plot to crush Christendom, and phobias about Jewish agency in fomenting the Black Death, resulted in the tortured extraction of confessions of phantasmagoric iniquity—a foundation on which the Inquisition built. As the obsessions of this period, directly targeting marginal groups, worked their way beyond the original narrow concerns and victimizations, Ginzburg argues, the layered possibilities of the Sabbat's horrors were bred in the bone of Christian doctrine, where a peculiarly fertile imagination was receptive to the construction of the diabolical witch, characterized by animal metamorphoses, supernatural flight, unnatural promiscuities, and unclean tastes (for blood, among other nourishments). Originating in widely dispersed fertility cults, the ecstatic behaviors of women drawn to night goddesses and animals, and the ritual processions of men parading as animals, this construction of the Sabbat and its witch practitioners, Ginzburg suggests, can be associated with early Eurasian nomadic migrations and the process of cultural diffusion. Far from being an idio-syncratic glitch in the history of the Middle Ages, witchcraft is rooted in the cultural continuities of humankind.

Second, Ginzburg's approach—which materializes the belief system of the witches in its scrupulous, if always only suggestive, examination of contextual possibilities and causations—rationalizes the seemingly ir-rational. Thus, Ginzburg, like Camporesi, looks for physiological explana-tions of trancelike behavior, rather than simply brushing the existence of out-of-body experience aside in complacent condescension. The ingestion of hallucinogenic grains, herbs, and mushrooms, or the proverbial witch practice of rubbing oneself with ointments in preparation for the "flight" of the Sabbat, adds a materialist dimension to the interpretation of behaviors that were recounted by those such as the Fruili *benandanti*, who, whatever our own modernist skepticism, obviously believed firmly that they did indeed participate in night walks with witches.

> There take this un-baptized Brat:
> Boil it well: preserve the ffat,
> You know 'tis pretious to transfer
> Our 'noynted fflesh into the Aire,
> In Moone-light nights, or Steeple-Topps,
> Mountaines, and Pine-trees, that like pricks, or Stopps,
> seem to our height: High Towres, and Roofes of Princes,
> Like wrinckles in the Earth: whole Provinces
> Appere to our sight then, ev'n leeke
> a russet-Moale vpon some Ladies cheeke.[17]

Witches were said to concoct strange potions, spiced with exotic in-gredients such as the blood of a flitter mouse, and with this mixture they would "rubbe all parts of their bodies exceedinglie, till they looke red, and be verie hot, so as the pores may be opened, and their flesh soluble and loose. They ioine herewithall either fat, or oil in steed thereof, that the force of the ointment maie the rather pearse inwardly, and so be more effectuall." Thus did "they seeme to be carried in the aire."[18] "Most likely it was drugs rather than flying broomsticks that carried the witches off to their fantasy world," concludes William Monter's study of the Jura borderlands of France and Switzerland, adding that plants such as "bella-donna and henbane were probably the base of the unguents so often referred to in witches' confessions."[19]

Third, and finally, Ginzburg's arguments, though problematic, lead to cross-cultural comparisions that offer potential insight: his resolutely struc-turalist assimilation of folklore narratives into a metanarrative of the voyage to the dead provides connective tissues that can be used to tie European witchcraft (albeit loosely) to Greek mythology (which is replete with such imagery), New World aboriginal cultures, and the Chinese "soul-stealers" of the eighteenth century. When the Jesuits of New France challenged Amerindians about their spiritual belief system, questioning their understanding of creation and the lineage of their great Manitou, the replies were often politely evasive, but some native people did attribute their knowledge to a "dream visit to the other world." Chinese masons in the 1760s were reputed to write the names of living persons on pieces of paper and affix these to pilings in order to steal their life force, causing the persons named to fall sick and die while adding spiritual force to the blows of the masons' sledgehammers.[20]

As Perry Anderson has noted, Ginzburg's histories of witches and the night are "a gamble to admire, a pleasure to read, a provocation to think." They are not necessarily without their drawbacks. As in so much scholarship of the ostensible left in the 1980s and 1990s, a retreat has taken place. Ginzburg once wrote out of the concerns of the insurgent 1960s, which, in Italy, had considerable purchase on popular politics. The themes were identifiably ones of repression and resistance: class cultures, peasant wars, and social utopias. More recently, Ginzburg's tone and tempo have altered, placing the accent not on social transformation but on the amazing resiliency of popular beliefs and the deep structural inertias of human consciousness, slowing the attachment to change, dampening the spirit of a program of ultimate transgression. In 1972 Ginzburg's comment on a contemporary cult in Salerno, where a woman regularly welcomed the spirit of her dead nephew into her body, was soberingly materialistic at the same time that it betrayed no hint of complacency: "In wretched and disintegrating conditions, religion helps men and women to bear a little better a life in itself intolerable. It may not be much, but we have no right to despise it. But precisely because they protect believers from reality rather than prompting them to become aware of, and change it, such popular cults are in the end a mystification: to overvalue them in populist fashion is absurd and dangerous." Ginzburg's thoughts in the 1990s echo in a less challenging chamber, his words resigned to acceptance of human nature's unchanging continuities: "Growing doubts about the efficacy and outcome of revolutionary and technocratic projects oblige us to rethink the way in which political action is inserted into deep social structures, and its real ability to alter them," he warns in the Italian preface to Ecstasies. His postrationalism vanquishes the rational interrogation of superstition in the name of the subjectivity of the vanquished. It suggests much but stops the analytic project short, looking only into the night and managing, as a consequence, to see around but not through the day.[21]

Whatever the interpretive dilemmas posed by witchcraft, however, there is no denying its reach or the range of its influence. Braudel, typically sighting the geographic and the social, accentuates the primitive isolations of the uplands.[22] But witchcraft's explosive intervention into the theology and anthropology of everyday life in medieval Europe obviously drew on more than a geospatial determinism, although material contexts could, of course, help sustain impulses generating elsewhere. Among such conduits were Paleolithic fertility cults, the magnetic attractions of magic, and Christian heresies such as those of the Cathars or the Vaudois/Waldensians, the latter having earned excommunication for their refusal to subordinate their preachings to the restrictive controls of the papacy and for their supposed belief that Lucifer, the devil, had been unjustly expelled from heaven. Their position jarred with the hardening hegemony of authoritarian Christianity's one-sided appreciation of God, but coexisted easily with earlier Manichaean understandings of the world as a dualism.[23]

Popular folklore, from the time of the ancient Romans, confirmed the existence of women who could take to the skies at night in flights of amorous, murderous, or cannibalistic fantasy. One eleventh-century source asked,

> Have you believed what many women, turning back to Satan, believe and affirm to be true; as that you believe that in the silence of the quiet night, when you have settled down in bed, and your husband lies in your bosom, you are able, while still in your body, to go out through closed doors and travel through the spaces of the world, together with others who are similarly deceived; and that without visible weapons, you kill people who have been baptized and redeemed by Christ's blood, and together cook and devour their flesh; and that where the heart was, you put straw or wood or something of that sort; and that after eating these people, you bring them alive again and grant them a brief spell of life?[24]

Wicked women were said to follow the pagan goddess Diana, to ride animals "and in the silence of the dead of night cross many great lands." French tradition had it that one Mistress Abundia led cohorts of "ladies of the night," spirits in the likeness of robed girls and women, on a search for hospitable households where food and drink were easily accessible. Across Europe, such notions had considerable purchase on popular belief. In Italy, tables were set again after meals had been consumed, an offering "for the good women who enter at night."[25]

Blurring into these popular beliefs in women's nocturnal spirit world were conventional gendered wisdoms, which associated women with natural deception, inordinate vanity, and insatiable lust—a set of inferiorities, counterposed to idealized male virtues, that "harnessed [women] to the active promotion of evil in the world." Convinced of woman's "excessively gluttonous, perfectly lascivious" predilections, medieval authority, as invested in the Established Church, harbored a pathological misogyny: the most abhorrent human behavior, sexual indulgence and debauchery, was thought in women to know no bounds. Consorting with the devil, who in turn urged all to violate God's commandments, women were seemingly natural recruits to a culture of ultimate defiance in which the consecration of witchcraft was the Sabbat's copulation with the devil and his worshipers, an unrestrained orgy of intercourse, sodomy, fellatio, mutual masturbation, incest, and group sex.[26] As Lyndal Roper has suggested, when inquisitors confronted witches "both had psychic investments in the content."[27]

The almost pornographic confessions of those the devil had seduced and ravaged, introducing them to a rampant eroticism and release from all taboos, were an unconscious theater of repression, a drama that spoke of sexuality's screaming need for recognition and freedom and the reciprocal voyeuristic demands of its jailkeepers and ultimate executioners, real and symbolic.

> The devil often made her kiss ... his member, then his behind.... She saw everybody having incestuous intercourse against all the dictates of nature. She accused herself of having been deflowered by Satan and having had intercourse an infinite number of times with a relative of hers and with others who had condescended to demand her. She shrank from intercourse with the devil because, as his member was covered with scales, it caused extreme pain, besides which his seed is extremely cold, so that it never makes a woman pregnant, nor does that of the other men at the Sabbath, even though it is natural. Outside the Sabbath she never did anything wrong, but at the Sabbath she had a marvellous delight in this intercourse, apart from that with Satan which she said was horrible. She even seemed to us to take a marvellous delight in telling it and talking about it, calling everything by name more freely and boldly than we dared asked of her.

A Basque witch offered a description that no doubt provided comment on the fading attractions of her marital bed:

> When the devil has finished his Mass, he copulates with everyone, men and women, carnally, and after the fashion of Sodom.... He, with his left hand (in the sight of everyone) stretched her face downwards on

the ground, ... placed her against a tree and there had knowledge of her in the manner of the Sodomites, while her said husband ... made music. And while still in the said act, she gave a very shrill scream which everybody heard ... like a bull roaring. And when they had finished the shameful acts she went away very proud and satisfied.

C. L'Estrange Ewen's researches into the witch trials in England and Wales concluded that theologians thought the devil "directed his greatest efforts toward encouraging unchastity" because the sex act "caused the corruption of our first parents, and by its contagion, brought the inheritance of original sin upon the whole race." Accounts of incestuous unions and the ritual cannibalistic sacrifice of their offspring struck blows at patriarchal authority and broke violently the familialist boundaries within which all were confined. One authority later offered an understatement: "The most searching system of enquiry developed by Holy Church speedily unearthed other monstrious irregularities, the witches being forced to admit indulgence in every description of sexual perversion at their Sabbats."[28]

Devil worship struck a decisive blow against the connective tissues of a patriarchal religiously defined order in which the family, with its powerful male head and routinized sexuality, reflected the larger authority in civil society, materially centered in the absolutist state and spiritually concentrated in the ecclesiastical hierarchy. As Gerhild Scholz Williams concludes, the sorcerer struck blows that reached well beyond the erotic: "Witchcraft was a crime against public order. Witches embodied the essence of disorderliness, for they subverted the order of sexual and procreative practices, family structure, and the divine institution of the state."[29]

Between 1200 and 1450 the divergent strains of dualistic heresy and the peculiar vulnerabilities of women were being forced into a parody of unity in High Church doctrine. Various popes indulged the fantastic reports of their cleric informants in distant lands, many of whom labored diligently to outdo one another in cataloguing evil practices that were aimed at undermining Christendom. The devil, a shadowy figure in the self-confidence of early Christianity, came to occupy more central ground as the evil, dark other, always working his black magic against the light of God's good. Devil worship, its antihuman content assumed to run the gamut of sin, was thus associated in the subconscious of clerical authority with the unleashed passions of populations locked in the grip of evil; ritualized promiscuity, incest, infanticide, even cannibalism fed the fires of Lucifer's captives. Inquisitorial manuals, from the Directorium Inquisitorum

(1368) to the *Malleus Maleficarum* (1486), detailed the existence of a new society of the Sabbat, collections of devil worshipers who needed to be forced out of their dark night lairs into the light of pious day.[30]

The result was a phenomenon that eventually lent its name to wider, more generic, periods of repression: the witch-hunt. Between 1450 and 1700, hundreds of thousands of reputed witches were put on trial. Some histories have exaggerated the dimensions of the resulting slaughter, claiming a death toll of nine million. This is overstated dramatically, but perhaps 200,000 formally investigated witches were drowned, hanged, quartered, pressed with suffocating weights, burned at the stake. Countless others were tortured and coerced, introduced to prayer stools furnished with sharp nails, a weighted hoisting device called the strappado, and the leg irons, thumbscrews, and iron spikes that inquisitors collected in "witch-houses" which stood in the shadows of the public courts. Some escaped execution only to be punished by banishment, imprisonment, forced service on the galleys, whipping, or the public humiliation of the pillory or stocks. Most victims were women; at a rough estimate, for every male paraded before the secular and ecclesiastical courts, four females followed. An average of two women a day were executed as witches in Western Europe over the course of 250 years. The zeal and brutality of this panic-driven quest to erase the dark presence of the witch varied from region to region. The Inquisitions conducted at Venice managed to avoid mass executions of witches and Spain and Portugal saw few persecutions and prosecutions. Scotland, the principalities of southwest Germany, and the Jura borderlands of France and Switzerland had some of the most active campaigns, but their peculiarities defy any attempt to force a common pattern. On the witch craze periphery—in Sweden, for instance—hundreds were executed in the 1670s as thousands of men, women, and children were questioned or came forward with statements of denunciation.

The victims of the Inquisition's witch craze came from many different groups. Alan Macfarlane's researches into Tudor England accusations suggest that a period of demographic expansion and increasing social differentiation resulted in witch-hunts directed at the poor, thus freeing well-to-do families of their communal obligations to a growing stratum of aggressive beggars or masterless vagrants.[31] For Le Roy Ladurie, the failure of the peasantry to mount a viable social revolt, even under conditions that dictated the necessity of such a protest, led to an escapist need for a witches' Sabbat to displace the unsuccessful social Sabbath—an interpretation Marvin Harris places on its head by arguing that the witch craze was a conspiracy of the elite, a cynical device to deflect the poor peasants from their class dissatisfactions and hatred, which were then sublimated in the petty bickerings of the village.[32] Others accused or convicted of witchcraft included scolding women, sexual nonconformists, prostitutes, practitioners of herbal medicine, midwives, the insane and the marginal, and the unduly contentious and fractious.[33] In the close clashes over property and power in the villages and towns of medieval Europe lay many jealousies, even paranoias, that could lead to the naming of a witch. Keith Thomas has even suggested that those who felt guilt at passing the poor beggar-woman's outstretched hand without dropping a coin in her palm might fantasize that any subsequent poor luck was part of her curse, and, in retribution, identify the hapless woman as a witch.[34] In the end, anyone might succumb to the charge of having employed occult means (malificia) or of serving the devil (diabolism) in order to perpetuate some unexplained harmful act that had befallen a neighbor or well-known enemy. But on balance it was the poor and the marginal, the old and the accursed, who fell to the Inquisition, categories particularly open to widowed women, who were popularly thought to be on the edge of the varied temptations and transgressions—sexual and material—that the devil could offer.[35]

In 1687 Louis XIV issued an edict against sorcery, but it was relatively mild in its condemnations and signaled the passing of the luridly constructed coven of witches, which was in many ways an invented tradition, an imagined community of the nocturnal Other.[36] This is not to say that there were not witches who believed in their own powers.[37] But never again would witchcraft enjoy the notoriety of its seventeenth-century zenith, when the unbending repression of an inquisitorial panic ironically induced many to flights of oppositional fantasy, however delusional or rhetorical.[38] As power passed from the sacred to the secular, however, the diabolical moved in new directions, away from the dangers of the devil. The last witch would be burned at the stake in Switzerland in 1782.[39]

But it was a century or so earlier that witchcraft took its symbolic last stand, its meanings and substances a hybrid of Old World continuities germinating in the soil of New World conditions. The Puritans who settled the Massachusetts Bay Colony in the seventeenth century were not an easy lot to pigeonhole, their lives a heady mixture of theology and commerce, rebellion and conformity. A cosmology rooted in medieval Europe's preoccupations with doom, sin, and the desperate need to live a pious life, Puritanism was at the same time an austere repudiation of the pomp and ceremony of medieval religious excess. Governed by a search for grace, always uncertain of its attainment but ever steady in the knowledge of its vitality, the evangelical colonizers who battled and tamed the wilderness of New England walked a tightrope stretched taut between faith and fate. They looked to their scriptures and could be arrogant in their scholasticism, which armed them in battles with the high and mighty as well as with the poor and pagan. But because its beliefs were so attuned to achieving grace, Puritanism grappled with the implications of dualisitic heresy: those not in God's grip might be perilously close to Satan's ever meddlesome hands.

After more than half a century of seeming grace, New England's Puritans found themselves invaded by demons, the way to heaven was confused and obstructed, "all over fill'd with Fiery flying serpents." "Dens of Lions," "Mounts of Leopards," and "incredible Droves of Devils" stood between the elect and their God. "An Army of Devils is horribly broke in upon the place which is the center," wailed Cotton Mather, who regarded the diabolical attacks of the 1690s as "more Surprising, more snarl'd with unintelligible Circumstances than any that we have hitherto Encountered." As "the Houses of the Good People" were "fill'd with the doleful shrieks of their Children and Servants, Tormented by Invisible Hands, with Tortures altogether preternatural," Mather and the Puritan elect shuddered in fearful bewilderment. Severed spatially, economically, politically, and psychologically from their Old World origins, on the brink of moving forcefully out of the wilderness frontier that had nurtured a cultural isolation and evangelical purity for a generation and more, the New England Puritans looked toward the uncertainties of the eighteenth century and were afraid.[40] They saw the witches.

Witchcraft and Puritanism were not causally related, but neither were they entirely separable, and their histories crossed in the seventeenth century. Puritanism emerged in England at a time when the witch craze's feverish high point of anxiety was in the making. Notable witch-hunters in England were often Puritans, and the Puritan-controlled Parliament of 1645 tried many who had been accused of the crime of sorcery. But Royalists, too, feared the devil and his minions, and some thought Puritan iconoclasm, with its assault on crosses, had weakened society's capacity to ward off the evils of the black arts. The seventeenth-century civil war in England—witnessing the rise of Oliver Cromwell and the execution of a monarch before the eventual restoration of kingly rule—was perceived by some, in its Puritan excesses, to cultivate a climate of disorder peculiarly amenable to witches.

To be sure, not all American colonists were Puritan. Alongside the Mathers and others of the elect, were lesser folk, not only "profane and debauched persons," but those for whom the attainment of grace was not necessarily life's priority. Yet such ordinary settlers deployed a deliberate strategic eclecticism against the uncertainties of life: like their seventeenth-century English counterparts they mixed doses of magic with congregation-alist theology, alternating prayer and astrological cures with pious worship and spells or "conjurations"; the Bible was on occasion supplemented by horseshoes and nails, whose power to do good or ward off evil might be drawn on to good effect.[41]

The New England colonists thus brought witches and their craft with them to the New World. Puritans were ready to acknowledge their evil presence, having a considerable store of supernatural events catalogued in the wonder lore of "illustrious providences" that God visited upon them in the wilderness, ranging from dreams, visions, and omens to natural phenomena such as spectacular comets and the devastations of lightning, fires, and hailstorms.[42] As the Puritan elect tightened their grip on the colonial religious flock, the original English Puritan stress on each person's tie to God evolved into an understanding that at Massachusetts Bay the deity had entered into a new connection with the people of the colony.[43] Challenged by dissidents such as the antinomian-inclined midwife Anne Hutchinson (who refused to accept the divine authority of the Puritan elect, claiming the right to interpret grace, hold private meetings, and explain scripture to her neighbors) and proselytizing Quakers (four of whom were tried and executed for their missionary work in the 1650s), the congregational orthodox constructed a vision of a metaphorical "city upon a hill" where God's work could proceed unimpeded. Because the smallest of tremors was felt throughout this righteous congregation, "the land of Uprightness" moved decisively against any and all "Pranks of Wickedness."[44]

Witchcraft certainly qualified as wickedness. John Higginson, a senior pastor in the town of Salem, Massachusetts, where witchcraft's American presence would be most pronounced, had observed it, studied its black magic, and preached against it to two generations of parishioners. "Witch-craft," he said, "is one of the most awful and tremendous judgements of God which can be inflicted on the societies of men." From the first known witchcraft trial in Windsor, Connecticut, in 1647 to the end of the century, there were, excluding those in Salem, fifty identified trials in Massachusetts (which at the time included Plymouth colony and areas later to become Maine and New Hampshire), and forty-three in Connecti-cut; in addition some twenty-six allegations of witchcraft found their way to the courts in civil suits for slander. Factoring in the Salem outburst in

1692 brings the total number of witchcraft cases known to have been tried in New England to 234; thirty-six of the accused were executed. Over seventy years, a small outpost of empire, with a population of barely fifty thousand, managed to accuse almost one in every two hundred inhabitants of being a witch. In the words of the Reverend Samuel Parris, "If ever there were witches, men and women in covenant with the devil, here are multitudes in New England."[45]

The much-studied events in Salem in 1692–1693 overshadow all other New England witchcraft, but there is no doubt that all the accusations followed particular patterns. Accused witches were four times more likely to be female than male, and the males were often singled out because of their marriage or family relations to women who were judged to be sorcerers. Most of the accused were middle-aged and their most common denominator was that they *were* common: not often of the elite, in social background the witch was an unexceptional New Englander, although she was likely to have been involved in some sort of folk healing or "doctoring." What marked the witch was her contentiousness: a quarrelsome character, a vexatious spirit, shameful or outrageous behavior were thought to be marks of the devil.

Unlike the European witch, the New England variant was not obsessed with actual carnal relations with Satan, and the folklore and historiography of seventeenth-century American witchcraft is decidedly thin on the erotic confession, the fantasy world of incubi, and the "unnatural" sensualities of the Sabbat. Rare was the witch who even gestured toward such realms; only a few such as Hartford, Connecticut's Rebecca Greensmith, admitted to having had "familiarity with the Devil," and meeting with him and other witches.[46] The Puritans managed to confront witchcraft without peering into the orgiastic night. They did engage with possession, however, and among alleged victims of New England witchcraft were girls not yet adult but beyond childhood, adolescents overtaken by "fits" that left them writhing in shockingly distorted behavior that could only be described as "demoniac." One sixteen-year-old girl manifested the usual signs of possession in 1672: a frenzied, appallingly physical seizure in which cries of anguish or scratchings, beatings, and stranglings of her person were accompanied by "violent bodily motions, leapings, strainings, and strange agitations, scarce to be held in bounds by the strength of three or four" and also "roarings and screamings, representing a dark resemblance of hellish torments." A second category of witchcraft victim was the neighbor wronged or the villager troubled by guilt, Puritans whose luck had turned bad or who externalized inner doubts and dilemmas by projecting the evil inside themselves onto the objectified, despised Other—the witch.[47]

The evidence leads in various interpretive directions. All may have some validity. But it is difficult to avoid the conclusion that New England witchcraft was not a highly contained articulation of a collective unconscious, in which the manifold repressions of the Puritan mind were uncorked for a moment of displaced libidinal exhibitionism or the worldly satisfactions of jealous retribution. Young girls clutching at their throats, beating their breasts, and writhing in agony on the floor before their dour patriarchal elders; middle-aged women who had the arrogance to claim to cure or the effrontery to demand to be supported by the general properties of the village, put finally in their place of subordination; cantankerous trouble-makers decisively silenced—all of this took place before and through the grace of God. The witchcraft of the Puritans was an entirely "functional" undertaking, stripped bare of its richly contradictory European complexity. It was a last shot in the dark night of witchcraft's premodern history, but as such it modernized out of the picture much of the sensuality of sorcery's origins. Gone was any hint of the organic connections that constructed European witchcraft on historical foundations of fertility cults, heretical challenges to religion's power to subordinate, and the sexual power of the night. The Puritans routinized the witch; in making her so obviously one of themselves they purged the community of God of its ostensible malcontents. But they took so little as a measure of deviance and reached so far and wide in their need for conformity that in many cases they could not even secure confessions; most accused witches stood their ground of innocence with remarkable defiance. Where else would a witch bear the appellation "Goody," the shortened generic term for the Puritan "Goodwife?" Transgression's tastes had been somewhat tamed.

The 1692 Salem events are part of the popular consciousness of the nation, enshrined in early histories, published collections of documents, and Arthur Miller's 1953 play The Crucible.[48] In Salem, witchcraft's remarkable New England apogee, the diabolical arts of black magic reached a truly low denouement. What is most striking is that the Salem events turned, in their immediate origins, around the relatively rare presence of a slave woman, a domestic in the household of the Reverend Samuel Parris. Tituba had been enslaved in Barbados, and as late as 1949 she could be described as an "ageless consort" of her "loutish" husband, John, "half Carib and half Negro," a woman whose "breeding had been in a softer, more languid clime; her life at hard labor in frosty New England was none of her choosing. She found subtle ways of easing her lot, and one of these was idling with the little girls." The Parris daughter, nine-year-old Betty, and her rather wild eleven-year-old cousin Abigail, were Tituba's favorites; they were told stories of old Barbados freedoms, and, ostensibly, in times of seclusion from the Reverend and Mrs. Parris, introduced to fragments of voodoo. The melodramatic stage was set for a racially ordered interpretation of the dark designs of Tituba, one that future historians could easily fall into but that must have been full of awkward ambivalences for goodly Puritans, who simultaneously accepted the enslavement of African and West Indian peoples, adopted a liberal posture of tolerance for blacks as members of God's community, and were immersed in the color-ordered oppositions of good and evil, day and night, light and dark.[49] As Marion Starkey puts it:

> The half savage slave loved to cuddle the child in her own snuggery by the fire, stroke her fair hair and murmur to her old tales and nonsense rhymes. Never from her own mother had the child received such affection, for though godly parents loved their children as much as any heathen, they would not risk spoiling them. Basking in this warmth, Betty gave an almost hypnotic attention to the slurred southern speech and tricksy ways of Tituba. Well she knew in her Puritan heart that she was tampering with the forbidden, but she could no more resist than she could lift a hand to free herself from the spell of an evil, thrilling dream.[50]

Savage tricksters and prepubescent Puritan hearts of metaphorical gold notwithstanding, Tituba soon had an extended circle of young maidens up to nineteen years of age, drawn to her apparently exotic charms. As they graduated from fortune telling and gazing into a crystal ball to full-fledged possessions, an epidemic of "fits" broke out among the teenaged village girls and seven or eight were soon declared bewitched. Pressured by interrogators to name their tormentors, the girls identified Sarah Good, Sarah Osborne, and Tituba, a triumvirate of an outcast, a known adulteress, and the threateningly different. Marched before their accusers, the two old Puritan women denied everything and refused responsibility. The record of Sarah Osborne's testimony ends on a note of admonishment and explanation that perhaps places her "witchcraft" in understandable terms: "Why did you yield thus far to the devil as never to go to meeting? ... Alas, I have been sick, and not able to go. Her husband and others said that she had not been at meeting three years and two months." To look at "Goody" Good's leathery face was to "see" a witch; addicted to tobacco, a pipe clenched in her teeth, she begged for her sustenance, neglected her children, and had often been heard muttering threats against her neighbors. Disavowals from such a specimen would mean little to any-one: "Her answers were in a very wicked, spiteful manner, reflecting and retorting against the authority with base and abusive words," concluded the tribunal.[51]

Neither would a slave's denials have received much consideration. Asked what spirits she was familiar with, Tituba's reply was a curt, "None." Charged to answer why she hurt the children, she denied any wrong-doing. The question "Who is it then" that was causing them torment drew a sarcastic response:, "The devil, for aught I know." At this point, it seems, Tituba, in contrast to the Puritan goodwives, decided that putting on a show would do her more good than her initial dry denial; hence she drew on her Barbados knowledge to provide her judges with a riveting introduction to the invisible underworld of dark spirits and Satanic rites, naming, in the process, her Puritan accomplices. She told of the devil's enticements, of how he appeared to her in the shape of a black dog or a hog or a man from Boston, and a "hairy thing [that] goes upright like a man, it hath only two legs," and of his commands to "serve me." Tituba constructed a standard depiction of the witches' flight: traveling by night in consort with others, "I ride upon a stick or pole with Good and Osburn behind me: we ride taking hold of one another; don't know how far we go, for I saw no trees nor path, but was presently there when we were up." Finally, tiring of the performance and perhaps feeling some remorse at repeatedly naming Good and Osborne, Tituba ended with a blunt refusal to continue answering questions about who was afflicting the children in front of her: "I am blind now; I cannot see."[52]

Tituba saw better than she knew. Nineteenth-century commentators were quick to portray the "Indian" slave as "a mind at the lowest level of general intelligence" but one capable of "cunning and wariness in the highest degree." The issue was more complex, and two-sided. One part was tied to a strategy of survival in a context of intense racism. As the nineteenth-century slave Henry Bibb conceded, "The only weapon of self-defence I could use successfully, was that of self deception." For Tituba, "puttin' on ole Massa" was particularly easy. All she did was give her Puritan inquisitors what they wanted, what her accusers had already confirmed, laced with a little color from her West Indian past, where the lore of the witch and the devil's doings were rich indeed.[53] And it worked: being a slave and having confessed, Tituba, as far as any records show, was spared execution (a fate that befell, predictably, the muttering "hag," Sarah Good, and that would certainly have been the lot of Sarah Osborne—not only an adulteress but a person who, with her husband, upset the balances of property and inheritance in Puritan Salem—had she not succumbed in prison). But another part was the brutal coercions of slave status. Tituba later claimed that "her master did beat her, and otherwise abuse her, to make her confess and accuse (such as he called) her sister-witches; and that whatsoever she said by way of confessing or accusing others was the effect of such usage." Moreover, "her master refused to pay her [gaol] fees, unless she would stand to what she had said." And it appears that Tituba was eventually sold to recover the jailer's charge. All of this would certainly fit with the Reverend Parris's shame at the witchcraft epidemic emanating from his household: he considered it "a very sore rebuke and humbling providence that the Lord ordered the late horrid calamity to break out first in my family."[54]

But if Tituba was the first and most obviously marked victim of the Salem inquisition, the "possessed" girls managed to open the floodgates of accusation rather widely. For the first couple of months in 1692 they kept their tongues somewhat in check, only six people being suspected of witchcraft, but things escalated after February's and March's deliberations: twenty-two witches were accused in April, thirty-nine more in May, and after the first execution in June slowed the arrests somewhat, they picked up again at end of the summer. As the jail at Salem choked with imprisoned suspects, the hunt proceeded to other towns, and in the process the witchcraft craze descended into a dementia that engulfed the social identity of the Puritan community, consolidating tensions associated with village and religious factionalisms, property, station, and power. All the "demons" that a Puritan world confronted were conveniently reduced to one identifiable enterprise, that of witchcraft.

Having exorcised the evil among them, Puritans moved into the eighteenth-century world a more secular, materialist people, their villages more impersonal, less pious, but also less crazed. No longer would the elect be "an unquestioned authority to whom automatic obedience was due." Gone was the time when the individual of grace was the "jealous protector of [the] community from ideological contamination."[55] Factions were no longer favored; nonpartisanship was a counterweight to controversy. Tituba, sold to pay the cost of her food fees while she languished in jail, had accomplished more than she knew. The witches of Salem had seemingly done damages the devil himself could not have accomplished. All residues of the ancien régime had finally been decisively vanquished.

Over the course of three centuries, then, witchcraft in Europe and America emerged out of and was finally overtaken by forces of vast social transformation. Societies governed by intense and demanding religiosity, where belief in good and evil took an understandable detour from the day into the dark and often diabolical possibilities of the night, constructed the witch as myth and *maleficia*, an identifiable transgressive evil that required highly public interventions by inquisitorial authority. Out of this cauldron of structural change and sensual subjectivity poured the highly differentiated experiences of witches and their antagonists. But if there was much diversity in the histories of the witches, there was a commonality as well. They went to the stake or Gallows Hill by day—the price paid for difference, whatever its actuality—but they had ridden through the air to consort with the devil by night, an exhilaration that could have been imagined in ecstatic fantasy or imposed in spiritual coercion or out of all-too-worldly revenge and malice.

Science and secularism would strike hard blows at this imagined community of the witches and the superstitions that drew many to believe in it, as would money, markets, and the proletarianization of the peasantry—all forces gathering their powers over the course of the late sixteenth and seventeenth centuries.[56] But for a time, to make their particular lights shine brighter, there was a fundamental need for the darkness of the witch, her magic and diabolical alliances. As Marx once commented, "Even the pure light of science seems unable to shine but on the dark background of ignorance."[57] Largely the terrain of the poor, witchcraft expressed the often understated dissent of the dispossessed, however much its huntings and hangings were the result of elite phobias. In its often unfathomable sensuality, it struck blows at the core of repression but, for the most part, avoided articulating a politics of direct opposition. At about the same time that witchcraft fell, a movement of aristocratic and patrician challenge fused some of the same eroticized currents with a more explicit, secularized dissent, a libertinism that ran its course in a sacrilegious sexualization of politics. In pornography and obscene parody, the libertine indulged the passions of the witches' Sabbat while refusing, or refusing to take seriously, the coupling that linked the devil and God. Rather than the literal lowly netherworlds of the cave or the coven, literary (and other) undergrounds now attracted the ire of the consolidating state.[58] Once more, the night proved a hospitable climate for an order that harbored those whose "deviance" masked dissidence and alternative. With the centrality of the printed page, however, came a new historical epoch: the Age of Revolution.

PART III

Marginality and the Age of Revolution

5. William Hogarth, *Caricature of Wilkes* (1763).

4

Libertines, Licentiousness, and Liberty

The Underworld of Pornography's Political Beginnings

The irascible historian Lawrence Stone once asked mischievously, "Is it more than coincidence that witches vanish just at the time when Fanny Hill appears?" Behind the playful query lies the possible association of sexuality and its representation with particular cultural climates. The winds of change in the political economy blew across landscapes of definition and desire in gusts and breezes propelled by material forces and the challenges of varying voices of dissent. As Stone suggests, if there was a link between the demise of the sexualized witch and a genre of erotic imagining—captured in licentious eighteenth-century texts such as John Cleland's *Memoirs of Fanny Hill* (1748), a fictionalized fantasy memoir of a courtesan who managed both to enjoy her sexual adventures and to escape into a later life of privilege—then it likely developed from "different stages of rising female expectations, generated in turn by the growth of literacy and the rise of individualism that were accidental by-products of the Reformation."[1]

What Stone misses, somewhat predictably, is the gendered *and* class text of power at the base of this politics of pornography. His analytic table seems set appropriately, but the seating arrangements are backward, and one guest is missing. Acknowledging class as well as gender, one can appreciate the potency of the sexual in the politics of challenge, as well as the significance of the shift from the largely peasant concerns and constructs associated with witchcraft to the differently situated preoccupations of libertine aristocrats. Their quest for freedom posed a curiously contradictory dialectic of self and sex in which subordination was always masked but incompletely destabilized. Thus rather than pointing to a simple case of "female expectations," one might rather place the interpretive stress on male desire and voice, female negotiation within submission, and aristocratic license. As Peter Nasy's study of France on the eve of the French Revolution concludes, libertinage passed through stages of free thought and anticlericalism, finding its way to a sexual radicalism that freed some (males, aristocrats) to pursue desire by dehumanizing the erotic enslaved others (women, plebeians).[2] The meanings of Fanny Hill and other libertine writings of the eighteenth century are nevertheless more interestingly complicated than this understandable assessment, for even as early pornography confirmed certain gendered inequalities, it struck hard at the class repressions associated with the absolutist state and its servile ecclesiastical structures and authorities. Precisely because class and gendered power had been conjoined in the ancien régime, however, the complexity of early pornography meant that it could not help but confront awkwardly many of the patriarchal metaphors of power: civil rule invested with familialist connotations; sexuality subdued in the absolute demonization of lust. Eighteenth-century pornography thus turned a page in the histories of transgression.

First advertised in the London General Advertiser as "Written by a Person of Quality," Fanny Hill was "not merely a man's fantasy of the life of a harlot but—more complexly still—a very peculiar fantasy of prostitution as a quasi-domestic, bourgeois institution."[3] V. S. Pritchett and J. H. Plumb have commented on the peculiarly male fantasy of Cleland's text, and some feminist critics such as Nancy Miller and Anne Taylor see in it "a phallic pride of place," if not an undercurrent of misogyny.[4] Though relatively innocuous in its eighteenth-century context, the infamous Memoirs of a Woman of Pleasure, renamed Memoirs of Fanny Hill in 1750, would thus become a suppressed erotic text, mythologized by its underground status and a sensational and staged obscenity trial in 1963, which canonized it as a banned book for a few brief years before loosened censorship regulations in the 1970s lifted the tight net of restriction and persecution.[5]

Fanny Hill's meaning, however, was always something more than mere decontextualized, ahistorical sexual arousal. "Truth! stark, naked truth, is the word," declares Frances Hill on the first page of her memoir, which begins with the almost seditious statement (in mid-eighteenth-century terms), "I sit down to give you an undeniable proof of my considering your desires as indispensable orders."[6] This is purpose diametrically at odds with the suppression of self so prominent in the thought and practice of the ancien régime. Cleland experimented with a technique of narrative realism that masked his highly unrealistic romanticizing of prostitution, but it was the style and the unleashing of individual fulfillment through graphic depiction of sexual acts that marked *Fanny Hill* as a creative innovation, a unity of form and content that produced perhaps the first unambiguously pornographic publication in eighteenth-century England. Cleland, who as a soldier had been stationed on Bombay Island, no doubt drew on his contact with Indian culture, which confirmed his libertinism and may possibly have introduced him to eastern eroticism. There is speculation as well that Cleland was a practicing sodomite, sexually attracted exclusively to men, which, if true, might explain the undue fixation and anatomically detailed depiction of the male penis and the less focused and uncareful confused ambiguities about the female erogenous anatomy, whereby Fanny manages to place the clitoris inside the vagina. Randolph Trumbach has recently suggested that this intersection of sodomy and libertinism could well have produced Cleland's sexual radicalism, which built on deep alienations "from conventional Christian asceticism" and grew out of conscious inversions and mockeries of a range of religious and familialist practices: baptism, marriage, and holy communion. *Fanny Hill*, Trumbach implies, may have been a product of acute personal estrangement.[7]

Certainly its philosophical foundations are part of a broad culture of dissent. The novel is driven by what Leo Braudy recognized as a philosophic materialism, set firmly against the metaphysics of medieval theology with its repudiation of the body and its mystical elevation of the soul. Braudy suggests an important link between the explicit and often lyrical depictions of sexual acts in *Fanny Hill* and the "physiological and mechanical view of human nature" developed in Julien Offroy de La Mettrie's *L'Homme machine* (1747), a text that sought to liberate and humanize the self and sexuality in its insistence that the mind and the body were reciprocities conjoined in imagination and the power of the erotic. Pitted against "centuries of philosophical subordination of body to mind," Braudy argues, Cleland's novel espouses a naturalism that connects sensual physicality with the cerebral creations of the mind: the penis is, in Fanny's favored expression, "a machine"; the mechanical arts produce "erections."[8] At the core of this endeavor of reconciliation and emancipation is the appreciation of desire, the sexually charged explosion of individualism that would, in the doctrine of the "libertine virtuoso" developed by the third Earl of Shaftesbury, move through sensuality past carnality and Christianity's superstitions to a higher "philosophized" calling, elevating grace, beauty and art to a new plateau of gentlemanly breeding.[9] Such a perspective fits nicely with Cleland's domestication of brothel life and his accommodation of the gritty reality of London prostitution, with which he was certainly familiar, to a more prettified erotic elegance.[10] Lord Shaftesbury's voice seems to echo in Cleland's frontispiece statement of purpose, "If I have painted Vice in its gayest Colours, if I have deck'd it with Flowers, it has been solely in order to make the worthier, the solemner Sacrifice of it to Virtue"—although this prose could have been put forward as a pose to soften the blows of state censorship.[11]

In a later and more wide-ranging study, Braudy has also related the widening parameters of eighteenth-century aspiration—which he associates with the "sensational debaucheries" of Matthew Lewis's 1796 novel The Monk and the tales of the Marquis de Sade—to the "possibility that a fame linked with power could surmount death and compensate for the lost hope of heaven."[12] This libertine "frenzy of renown," then, propelled by a simultaneous hunger for fame and an insatiable quest for sex, placed carnality beyond the superstitious connections of devil worship and the "unnatural" by naturalizing sexuality and sexualizing the ways in which nature could be subdued by the mechanics of material constructions. As the season of the witch passed, and the superstitions of its calendar faded, between 1650 and 1750 the libertine stood poised to rearticulate, in a class language of "philosophical" clarity, the accentuated politics of Eros. This libertine culture, featured prominently in the eighteenth-century novels of Henry Fielding, W. M. Thackeray, and Pierre Choderlos de Laclos, has worked its way into the popular culture of the late twentieth century via the cinema. The explicit eroticism and freneticism of Tom Jones (1963), the detached artistry and scenic sensuality of Stanley Kubrick's Barry Lyndon (1975), and the evil, manipulative sexual politics of Dangerous Liaisons (1988) are but Hollywood's articulation of attractions and products, new in the eighteenth century, which linked the aristocratic rake and the obscene tract.

Pornography—which of course has a history reaching back to antiquity and across cultures to the rich eroticism of the East and the sixteenth-century obscene writings of the Italian Rennaissance or the England of revolution and restoration—thus came of age in its Western beginnings in the seventeenth and eighteenth centuries.[13] As a literary and graphic art, however, as well as a legal and conceptual understanding, pornography was an invention of the nineteenth century, following a semantic discovery of the ancient Greek pornographos, or writing about prostitutes. Earlier, it was more likely to be prosecuted as seditious libel or blasphemy, or relegated to the margins of aristocratic masculinity. A word unknown in English in 1755, pornography came to mean medical writing on prostitutes and public hygiene in 1857, and descriptions of prostitutes, their patrons, and obscene subjects in 1909. As early as the 1780s, however, *Harris' List of Covenant Garden Ladies*, an annual directory of call girls, was circulating in London, a compendium of offerings, prices, and lyrical descriptions of anatomical precision.[14] Closely associated with Victorian prudery, pornography's origins are thus often obscured by locating them in the repressions and cloistered sexualities of a supposedly prudish nineteenth-century population that managed to find expressive means of exposing "the secret life."[15] In France, Étienne-Gabriel Peignot's *Dictionnaire critique, littéraire et bibliographique des principaux livres condamnés au fé, supprimes ou censurés* (1806) defined pornography as obscene works associated with immorality, the suppression of which was fundamental to the protection of society and the preservation of moral order.[16] Over the next two centuries the meaning persistently narrowed, so that pornography now means the literal or visual representation of explicit sexual acts, which, in E. P. Thompson's words, is intended "to displace the imagination from any context of human actuality into an unlocated masturbatory fantasy."[17] Whether or not this constitutes obscenity, however, and is therefore open to legal suppression, has become a highly elastic issue in which so-called community standards stretch and rebound in judicial decision and reversal. There can be no doubt that in contemporary North America there are places where pornography is a public spectacle that few can escape, whereas in other sectors the access to pornographic texts, images, theater, and acts is far more self-selecting and limited. Nevertheless, as a representation, pornography now engulfs this society, proliferating at all levels of discourse to the point that its meanings—if not its sheer quantity, pervasive presence, and billions of dollars in commerce—present an almost endless set of problematic dialogues.

As a relationship to the night, pornography is at present unambiguous. One opponent, G. Steiner, has penned a critical challenge under the title "Night Words," and a segment of radical feminism that yearly takes to the streets in a campaign to eliminate all forms of male dominance and threat, partly identified as pornography's powers and debasements, marches under the banner "Take back the night."[18] Urban sex districts, strip joints, and prostitution come alive in the gaudy neon of night, where sex as simply cash-governed exchange relationship is enhanced by the obscurities of darkness, and desire is stripped of its humanity in the shadows of dimly lit street corners or the illumination of a seedy booth. A veil of estrangement prevents the process from being anything more than a fleeting encounter of lust in which power can be located in the eye of the beholder—fixed, in one party, on the receipt of currency; in the other, on the object of need. In this evening of exchange, pornography—as written word, visual image, or personal presence—is a product narrowed in time and space. Buyer and seller are agreed that "the reciprocal gaze" that makes a person both seen and seeing is denied or deflected. From the prostitute's refusal of anything but clinical "relief," or the striptease and peep show distances of stage and plastic partition, to the flattened images of videos and magazines, the pornographic moment is devoid of growth and time. As Stephen Marcus showed in his discussion of Victorian "pornotopia," "all things exist in a total, simultaneous present," the prose of which is "endlessly repetitive, formless, goalless, and cliché-ridden," a nonaesthetics that has had a remarkable continuity over the last century and a half.[19] Pornography as it is known at the end of the twentieth century, is a one-dimensional, unidirectional, eminently finite experience, never speaking directly to larger personal or social issues.[20] It is an exercise in commodification.

Contemporary pornography does of course illuminate wider matters of power, difference, and human negotiations of freedom and the forbidden. Some of this is not unrelated to transgressive impulses.[21] Pornography's historical emergence appears as a clear-cut case of obscenity's contextualization, its relationship to the world of politics and dissent being drawn in clear, broad strokes. Its beginnings, if one must generalize as to specifically Western origins, lay in "the demimonde of heretics, freethinkers and libertines who made up the underside of the Renaissance, the Scientific Revolution, the Enlightenment, and the French Revolution." In opposition to superstition and repression, writers and engravers utilized the stimulants of the erotic to challenge boundaries and restraints in acts of rationalist demystification and individualist transgression. Pornography was thus named and regulated, in its legal late-eighteenth- and nineteenth-century origins, by sets of authority, moral regulation, and governmentality which were contesting "an argument" as much as they were opposing a particular depiction or subject matter.

When Thomas Sherlock, Bishop of London, voiced his protest against what he called Cleland's "Memoirs of a Lady of Pleasure" he transposed woman and lady in an instinctual substitution of genteel construction, but his letter to the secretary of state managed to bypass any mention of the rights and wrongs of woman: "I beg of your Grace to give proper orders, to stop the progress of this vile Book, which is an open insult upon Religion and good manners, and a reproach to the Honour of the Government and Law of the Country."[22] From the other side of the prudery/prurience divide things looked quite different. Thus the French novelist and reformer Nicholas Edme Restif de la Bretonne—author of countless tracts, reflections, and novels, among them The Pornographer (1769) and The Depraved Peasant (1776)—mixed discussions of all manner of hetero-sexual transgression with (in the bibliophile Algernon Charles Swinburne's surprised judgment) chapters of "good sense, just reasoning, right feeling, and true prophetic insight." Possessed of a "fathomless capacity for fantasy," Restif constructed a personalized utopian order of political and biological renewal in which an uninhibited sexuality confirmed his own decidedly patriarchal powers. Failing to live the incest he craved, he rationalized it as a sexual politics of infinite patriarchal procreation, outlining in Les Posthumes (1802) a new world order literally fathered by an omniscient, omnipotent wizard named Multipliandre who, at age a thousand, had created an empire of inbreeding demographically cast in his own image. In a 1793 novel, one of Restif's characters writes his epitaph: "Oh, what a man! What a man! As many children as books, as many books as children."[23]

Yet Restif considered himself not only a pornographer, a title he embraced with pride, but a reformer whose literary works aimed to introduce social changes around prostitution and sexuality, changes that would enhance the stability of families and secure religious values. In his own mind, Restif linked the realities of sexual relations with the need for reform. That tradition died for a time but found something of a parodic rebirth in the 1980s' "freedom of speech crusades" of Hustler magazine's Larry Flynt.[24] The historical point is that more than two centuries ago, libertine productions were a background to a battle over ideas and social change, pitting bishops and traditionalists against dissidents and reformers. This contest took place, according to one commentator, "on the border between zones of darkness and light, the secret and the revealed, the hidden and the accessible." Now relegated to the night of ostracized consumption, whose furtive purchases challenge little and actually eco-nomically sustain much of daylight's seamier conventional debasements, pornography's beginnings were a politics of the night of dissent, a direct—if not unproblematized—opposition to the conformist day.[25]

Catalogued in Henry Spencer Ashbee's limited edition bibliographies, works of this sort might bear titles such as Restif's sixteen-volume Les Nuits de Paris (1788–1794) or the more concise anonymously published Nocturnal Revels (1779), yet another monk's tale that linked the night as a time and place for sexual transgression with pornography as a genre or a practice well suited to darkness. Nocturnal Revels described genteel London brothels in which drunkenness and disease were banished in the interests of "a domesticated fantasy" appropriate for the well-bred. Such houses of erotic repute were outlets for a new affective sexuality that paralleled the declining authorities of Church and state; in England it postdated the repressively gloomy consolidation of Puritanism after 1660, and in France it presaged the political upheavals of the French Revolution. They were built, brick by brick, out of a complex swirl of cultures, cash mediations, and commitments—religious and political—that historians have not yet untangled, but that tied together a series of social groupings whose ideas and practices, if not in any way connected to one another, did nevertheless strike blows for the widening of male sexual freedoms. Thus at the pinnacle of established power in sixteenth-century England, the restored king, Charles II, declared in defense of his own sexual libertinism that he did not think God would punish him for "a little pleasure taken out of the way."[26]

Even the revolutionary decades preceding the Restoration witnessed the proliferation of radical sectaries, many of which, such as the Muggletonians and Ranters, espoused and practiced sexual freedoms of astounding modernity. One group claimed a heaven of sexual license: "All males, not made to generate, But live in divine happy state." Others endorsed female nudism, polygamy, marriage by annually renewable contract, and quite tangible loosenings of paternal responsibilities for children—all, of course, spelling out the one-sidedness of sexual freedom. It was, in an age of ineffective birth control, a male affair, and one that might pollute the cuckolded marriage bed with problems not just of piety but of property, or leave the unmarried woman—also another man's property—despoiled. Thus the Ranter preacher and former New Model Army recruit Abiezer Coppe could pen tracts such as *A Fiery Flying Roll* (1649) and attack the monogamous family: "Give over they stinking family duties," he railed, defending an unbridled male sexual access to all women as the vehicle to grace: "External kisses have been made the fiery chariot to mount me into the bosom ... of the king of Glory.... I can kiss and hug ladies, and love my neighbour's wife as myself, without sin." Even after the religious justifications for such licentiousness had passed, it was possible that coteries of "middling" professionals might sustain local cultures of underground eroticism. In the ex-Puritan village of Norwich, for example, Lawrence Stone has uncovered a 1705–1707 outbreak of "voyeurism, group sex, wife-swapping, the trimming of pubic hair, and extensive bisexual flagellation." Such practices drew state charges of "gross and unnatural behaviour," just as earlier ranting justifications of uninhibited lust elicited fearful voices of moderation. This threat hung over the aristocracy even as its sixteenth-century context faded, and in the new seventeenth-century milieu of more moderate experimentation, with its mix of contradictory traditionalism and innovation, the polite brothel of Cleland's *Fanny Hill* was a place for libertines to cultivate their eroticism while maintaining the illusion of familial affection and the substance of protected, patriarchal, propertied marriage. In the houses of assignation where libertines gathered, Cleland's lascivious book was well thumbed and the fantasy world of the rake indulged.[27]

The openness to *Fanny Hill*'s charms had been prepared by a flood of pamphlets, in both 1649 and 1688, depicting the monarchial court as "a sink of financial corruption and sexual depravity, fit only to be destroyed by men of moral integrity." Such pornographic politics had their place in the execution and deposition of kings, and the relationship between political opposition and pornographic anticourt satire was unambiguous, as some obscene lines of verse in 1682 indicated:

> The King, Duke and State
> Are so libelled of late
> That the authors for Whigs are suspected.
> For women in scandal
> By scribblers are damned all,
> To court and to cunt disaffected.[28]

By the second quarter of the eighteenth century the politics of pornography and the linked culture of the libertine were increasingly counterposed to the Church, against which a half-century of essays, limericks, altered verse, and nocturnal scribblings were consciously set; the culmination was Richard Payne Knight's 1786 *The Discourse on the Worship of the Priapus, and its Connexion with the Mystic Theology of the Ancients*, an almost pagan attack on Christianity's repression of libidinal instincts. The libertine worshiped "the generative force," and for all its theological vacuity the phallus as symbol of homosocial desire was an enduring, if infantile, anticlerical counterweight to the prudish zeal, bigotry, and dogmatism of established religious faith, with its obvious links to state and family. As fantasy, then, licentiousness was also an articulation of liberty, the embrace of the erotic being a discourse of defiance, aimed at Church and king, rationalized by the philosophical telos of the Enlightenment. The naturalism, materialism, and mechanization of the intellectual moment was adapted to a secularized sexuality that struck blows at absolutist authorities, whose powers and properties had long been invested with "divine" idealized grace.[29]

Centers of libertine culture in England were the Dilettanti Society, founded in 1732, and a fraternity known as the Hell-Fire Club, established sometime later. Ostensibly interested in promoting knowledge of classical civilization, Dilettanti members met in robed ritual, mocking Christian convention and pricking the pompous and pious of the day. Their deism and their supposedly scholarly interest in the ruins, sculptures, and medals of antiquity were often little more than justifications for their libertine tastes and ribald attraction to phallic symbolism, which they invested with "the generative powers of God." One of the society's founders was Sir Francis Dashwood, "an amiable sensualist" and pronounced anti-Papist, who in youth gained notoriety for an alleged Good Friday invasion of the Sistine Chapel in Rome. He was reputed to have performed a ritual flagellation, horsewhipping worshipers gathered to atone for their sins and then fleeing from an outraged crowd of Catholic penitents who took exception to his discipline. Dashwood's hurried exit rang with outraged cries of, "the devil, the devil." He would later become a quintessential eighteenth-century populist—crossing the lines of old-country Tory, independent, Whig, and Jacobite—then a colonel of the Buckinghamshire battalion and chancellor of the exchequer, at the same time as he was active in establishing the raucous debauched fraternity popularly known as the Hell-Fire Club, but formally constituted as the Order of Medmenham Monks. Dashwood's principal residence was in part remodeled as a reconstructed temple to Dionysus or Bacchus, and in 1750 he renovated the converted Cistercian abbey at Medmenham, six miles from his home, placing the inscribed motto *Fay ce que voudra* (Do as you wish) over the door and a naked statue of Venus in the garden.[30]

Dressed in the habit of monks (although they were also rumored to don white suits) the inner circle of the Hell-Fire Club, limited to twelve, met at Medmenham for nights spent in mock worship of pagan deities, ludicrous pranks, lewd and profane singing, feasts of gluttonous abandon, and sexual liaisons with prostitutes and "ladies of quality," who were modestly anonymized by the wearing of masks. Blasphemy was constantly in the air—the monks fed the Eucharist to an ape—and there was an undercurrent of black magic: the caves of Medmenham Abbey may have witnessed equivalents of the witches' Sabbat. Dashwood's library contained an extensive collection not only of pornography but also of satanic and liturgical studies. As in the case of Cleland, a connection to India through the initiate Sir Henry Vansittart hints at the influence of Eastern eroticism, and the monks were aware of the *Kama Sutra*. Toasts were drunk to the goddess of love, whom the monks called Bona Dea;

obscene paintings adorned the walls; a giant phallus labeled with Latin double entendres suggestive of the the male sexual organ's supremacy over penitence, loomed large; and the penis and testicles were, in one poem possibly written at Medmenham, addressed as the "thrice blessed glorious Trinity." Dashwood, whose followers referred to themselves as Franciscans, presided over all rites, adorned in a red cap trimmed with rabbit fur, and in a uniquely revealing construction of the male erotic gaze he poured "Libations to the Goddess without eyes." Blind to those who worshiped her, this deity represented the sanctity of the grounds, which were also guarded at both ends by the Egyptian male and female gods of silence. The monks and their chosen mistresses who gathered for the carnal convivialities of Medmenham were meant to understand the cloistered privacies of the place and to speak no blemishing word of its "natural" sins, protecting, in particular, the reputations of the women involved, about whom little is known.[31] Dashwood's elaborate experiment in sustaining a libertine Sabbat was, then, a crystallization of aristocratic eroticism's link to "a recrudescence of paganism" that pushed debauchery into the "dark labyrinths" of the self.[32]

Pornography, eighteenth-century dissent, and political opposition crossed paths in the Hell-Fire Club, for one of Dashwood's recruits was the young John Wilkes, whose evolution from a gentleman of pleasure to man of the people would be inscribed in the populist slogan "Wilkes and Liberty." Born at the interface of commerce and piety, Wilkes was the consummate metropolitan figure, a Londoner who nevertheless managed, through an arranged marriage of property, to acquire a manor and the status of an improving squire. The charitable country paternalist and Anglican magistrate in his rural seat, he was also the dissolute city rake. His wife, having endowed him with aristocratic credentials and a daughter to whom he was deeply devoted, was soon displaced in divorce, and throughout the 1750s Wilkes cultivated his personal indulgences and his political stature, securing a costly seat in Parliament in 1757. His early political career was uneventful, but he had declared himself "a friend of liberty," and this was to remain his standard. Nevertheless, throughout the later years of the William Pitt regime, he functioned as a government loyalist, a small figure in the last years of court whiggery and political coalition.

By the 1760s, however, with Wilkes serving under Dashwood in the militia and consolidating connections among the libertines, the personnel and politics of the state took a turn at the accession of George III; the old stabilities of governance crumbled, opening spaces for particular politics of dissent. Wilkes was soon well on his way to becoming, in the words of a biographer, "a genuine Radical as well as an undoubted rascal." His reputation as a blasphemous incorrigible and insatiable rake was prodigious, rumors of his profligacy as a Monk of Medmenham having spread. So did awareness of his earthy political wit, which was well suited, as Nicholas Rogers and John Brewer have argued, to an age of ceremonialism. Oppositional Whigs reveled in his jaunty turns of phrase, with their always loaded charge of politicized and sexualized sarcasm. The Earl of Sandwich, a fellow monk, detested Wilkes for one of his Medmenham pranks (in which a baboon dressed as a devil landed on the dissipated peer's shoulder as he knelt in staged prayer) and laughingly wondered whether the parliamentarian would die on the gallows or of venereal disease. "That must depend, my Lord," snapped Wilkes, "upon whether I first embrace your Lordship's principles or your Lordship's mistresses." Playing on the politics of shock value, Wilkes refused to grovel in hypocritical denials of his curbless passions, with the result that he was constructed, by friend and foe alike, as even more of a rake than he likely was, his reputation for debauchery snowballing in a free fall of fact, half-truth, exaggeration, and falsehood. "Whatever was worst in his character," concludes one biographer, "was always known of him."[33]

After Wilkes's divorce, it was his friend Thomas Potter, the libertine son of an archbishop, who helped escort him into a life of sexual consumption in which "young women and whores" were preferred to "old women and wives," and evening conferences with mothers-in-law contrasted with "the Heavenly inspired passion called Lust." Potter promoted Wilkes politically, as well as pushing him in directions that would eventually contribute to his financial ruin. He encouraged Wilkes to write a number of minor sexual parodies—limerick-like verses—to be read at the male dinners that nourished gendered sociability in the libertine milieu. He may have had a hand in the 1754 production of the most notorious pornographic poem of the eighteenth century, Wilkes's Essay on Woman, which could well have figured in his young protégé's initiation into the brotherhood of Medmenham Abbey. A takeoff on Alexander Pope's Essay on Man (1751), the obscene Wilkes parody circulated informally for almost a decade before its history came to rest in the pressure cooker of oppositional politics in 1763. The poem mixed jeering anticlericalism and obsession with female sexual anatomy ("a country for men to traverse"), intercourse being the divine reason for woman's creation. Its form a typical libertine annotation of established texts, juxtaposing the routine and published comment of newspapers and literature with jarringly sexual and sacrilegious follow-ups, and accompanied by three burlesque distortions of Christian prayer, the Essay on Woman was the standard fare of ribald aristocratic parodic alteration. The verse caused no consternation, however, until Wilkes became a journalistic gadfly, a constant thorn in the side of the government of George III and First Lord of the Treasury, the Earl of Bute.

Bute had established a government paper, The Briton, to propagandize in the interests of the state. Wilkes could not resist the opportunity to put out a rival sheet, which he derisively dubbed The North Briton to draw attention to the government's undue placation of Scottish interests and over-heavy reliance on Scots staff. Relentless in its pillorying of established authority, The North Briton abused and ridiculed the government at every opportunity, making especially lurid political capital out of Bute's alleged intimacy with the king's mother. The libertine was turning the tables on aristocratic license, and Wilkes was quickly winning a place in popular politics as the impudent soul of a raucous opposition; moderate Whigs stood their distance, but the London crowd embraced the challenging barrage of ridicule and diatribe. Coeditor and former fellow of the Hell-Fire Club, the ex-clergyman Charles Churchill, author of a "very cold, long, dark, and dirty" poem titled Night (1761), played a role in constructing Wilkes as the voice of the common people:

> Wilkes—with good and honest men
> His actions speak much stronger than my pen
> And future ages shall his name adore
> When he can act and I can write no more.

Tory gentlemen and the state replied to Wilkes with demands for duels and charges of seditious libel. Parliament condemned the forty-fifth number of The North Briton as "a false, scandalous, and seditious libel," ordering it to be burnt by the Common Hangman. Yet the popular politics of Wilkesite radicalism flourished in protesting dinners, endless puns and plays on the now sacred "No. 45," crowd actions, and parade revelries. Wilkes's imprisonment, declaration as an outlaw, exile, and expulsion from Parliament (followed by repeated popular electoral victories) only solidified his reputation as defender of all the people's liberties, including the most cherished: freedom of the press.[34]

This clash of libertine license and state authority came to a head as eroticism blurred the line of distinction between the ribald and the rebellious. The true libertine populist, Wilkes maintained that "no man has the right to inquire into my private amusements if they are not prejudicial to society."[35] The calling-down of state wrath upon Wilkes occurred when he blundered into what he himself called "a juvenile performance," one justified not on principle but on "candour and indulgence." At the point that he and The North Briton were locked in relentless combat with the state, Wilkes decided to have a dozen copies of his pornographic Essay on Woman printed, possibly as some kind of tribute to the recently deceased Thomas Potter, perhaps to be distributed among his old fraternity of the Medmenham Monks. There was no intention actually to publish and commercially circulate the parody, but with Wilkes now a marked man, he was exposed to manipulation: while he was out of the country on a prolonged visit to Paris, a copy that had been left in the printer's hand was turned over to the state by an informant in the workshop. No time was wasted in bringing charges against its author before the House of Commons and the House of Lords. The poem was in fact only partially reproduced, but that portion was adorned with a phallic frontispiece and was scurrilous in its parody of Alexander Pope, whose lines,

> Who sees with equal eye, as God of all,
> A hero perish, or a sparrow fall,
> Atoms or systems into ruin hurl'd,
> And now a bubble burst, and now a world.

became,

> Who sees with equal Eye, as God of all,
> The Man just mounting, and the Virgin's fall;
> Prick, cunt, and bollocks in convulsions hurl'd,
> And now a Hymen burst, and now a· world.[36]

The typical jumble of obscenity was explicitly configured around the supremacy of the godlike phallus in ninety-four printed lines of verse available to the censorious eye of the wronged state:

> Happy spark of Heavenly fame!
> Pride and wonder of man's fame
> O Prick, how great thy Victory?
> O Pleasure, sweet thy stings.[37]

In the words of one member of the House of Lords, it was "a most scandalous, obscene, and impious libel, a gross profanation of many parts of the Holy Scriptures, and a most wicked and blasphemous attempt to ridicule and vilify the person of our most blessed Saviour."[38] It was curious indeed how authority could virtually ignore the sexual form of pornography, with its gendered content and unquestioned articulation of male power, and focus instead on the eroticized satire as an affront to God, king, and state. Even former Medmenham Monks lined up against Wilkes, including the Earl of Sandwich, whose private dissolutions and debaucheries in Wilkes's company were now conveniently forgotten in a rush to align with the king in outraged public condemnation.

Wilkes weathered it all: libertine turncoats such as Sandwich were popularly lampooned for their hypocrisy, and the printer who had turned the obscene ditty over to the authorities was castigated as an informer, blacklisted by the master printers and reduced to pathetic appeals for employment to the office of the treasury. When the sheriffs and the hangman attempted to burn No. 45 of *The North Briton*, a rampaging crowd of five hundred Londoners pelted them with debris and rescued the sheet from the flames. A city jury awarded Wilkes a thousand pounds sterling in damages at the end of 1763, and crowds gathered in the streets to cheer "Wilkes and Liberty!" But an affair of honor, resulting in a duel that left the libertine ironically wounded in the groin, tarnished the moment, as did the persistence of his enemies at the king's court, who laid further charges that he was summoned to answer. Wilkes decided to slip out of the country on Christmas Eve of 1763, finding his way to France. For years the embattled libertine remained abroad but returned to win election in Middlesex in 1768 and ride the "Wilkes and Liberty" wave, which a repressive state authority could not contain, into the 1770s.[39]

What Wilkes had managed to do was turn a politics of pleasure, originating in flamboyant hedonism, into a commerce of office, mythologized in a defensive populism and symbolized by the resounding ring of the cry "Wilkes and Liberty." The licentious libertine, whose physical appearance was one of almost mythic ugliness (a deforming squint contorted a countenance further disfigured in old age by a lack of teeth), nevertheless captured the crowd's appreciation of conspicuous finery with his dashing red waistcoats and ostentatious wardrobe. He reveled in a reputation of sexual potency and profane wit, a flair for "the common," and an ability to strike a pose in defense of popular rights. His immediate circle was aristocratic, but his appeal was to the plebeian crowd and the urban middling sort. They were captivated by his irreverence, his outrageousness, his capacity to personalize the spirit of independence and liberty in a relentlessly ribald goading of the great. The latter's defeats, humiliations, and ridiculousness the London crowd enjoyed as a politics of sensual, transgressive negation. Pornography was not an aside in this politics of repartee and risqué rebellion; as a form that lent itself readily to the rough, masculinized substance of political challenge, it was a cultural capital absolutely necessary in the struggle to displace the tentacles of ministerial interest and aristocratic clientage that penetrated the Hanoverian world. In that struggle, *private* gendered power was deployed against *public* political power, its own curbs on freedom and need to subordinate conveniently consolidated in the unquestioning security of the ribald style. Most especially this could happen in the night, as processions, gatherings, and a network of taverns and clubs offered the Wilkesite consituency an endless outlet for its expression of dissent.

Yet for all of this, Wilkesite radicalism had its limits. If the cry of "Wilkes and Liberty" was a constant challenge to the narrowly parasitical rule of the aristocratic court, for whom Wilkes represented an unthinkably coarse challenge to the boundaries of breeding and station, its highly circumscribed politics of opposition never successfully made the break into republicanism, reform, or revolution. Radicals were drawn to Wilkes and his supporters among wage workers, artisans, apprentices, and the small producers, but "Wilkes and Liberty" was a way station between "Wilkes and License" and "Wilkes and Reform." Its floating and open agenda masked traditionalism and political stasis as much as it proclaimed a politics of oppositional alternative.[40] Like the night itself, in which it was embraced most boisterously, "Wilkes and Liberty" was a possibility reaching to move beyond itself.

In later years even this effort would run its course in Wilkes's accommodations to conventional politics—whereby he would secure further elections, among them that of lord mayor of London—as well as in his personal *rapprochement* with some past adversaries, including the king. He outlived his past and came to distance himself from his old ways, even from the urban crowd that had hoisted his banner high in street procession and tavern tippling. But he did go to his 1796 grave in the old ceremonial style: at his previous direction the coffin was carried by six of the parish poor, whose services were rewarded with a guinea each and a suit of clothes. He had lived the words of his favorite quotation, Swift's "Might the whole world be placed within my span/ I would not be that thing a prudent man." The only phrase he would consider as his epitaph was judiciously restrained: "A friend of liberty."[41]

Wilkes's libertinism was never conceived overtly as a politics; his politics was not promoted, at least not frontally, as an eroticized aesthetics. More transgressive, but troublingly so, was the French libertine Donatien Alphonse François, the Marquis de Sade (1740–1814), whose history is one of pornography's articulations amid the politics of revolution. As Lynn

Hunt argues, pornography figured prominently in creating a climate of burlesque caricature, satirizing the old regime in a crescendo of sexualized representations of debauchery and lustful exploitation. It was not hard to construct the people as a feminized violated subject, objectified by king and court, the aristocratic privilege of the first estate exercising all manner of "unnatural" acts on, over, and through an innocent third estate for whom seduction, subordination, and estranged servility were meant to be conditions of life. France was a particularly glaring case of Enlightenment pornography's becoming "a vehicle of protest against the authority of Church–State."[42] As the French Revolution vanquished the old order, loosening all manner of regulatory regimes, pornography proliferated, but its political targets were no longer clearly focused in its sights—its licentiousness predominated. And as the new regime of bourgeois revolutionary power consolidated an almost puritanical conservatism over the course of the early-to-middle 1790s, this licentiousness was in turn targeted as an offense to Virtue, a hangover of the aristocratic license of the ancien régime. Libertinism, an old enemy of corrupt kings and hypocritical churchmen, was now an enemy of "the people." Sade, a committed libertine from an early age, an aristocrat raised on the doctrines of licentiousness, lived this awkward history of ambivalence.

Lawrence Stone suggests parallels between Dashwood and the libertine circle of the Hell-Fire Club, of which Wilkes was a part, and Sade—notorious examples all of "ideas carried to extremes."[43] Yet between Wilkes and Sade lies a world of difference. Wilkes's libertinage, profligacy, and politics of popular freedom were, of course, an individualized quest for pleasure as well as an assertion of rights. Metaphorically, Wilkes operated within night's recesses but never quite effected a social and political rupture with the day's light, which he simultaneously accepted and sought to extend. Unusual in his candor, creative in his adaptations, refreshing in his principles, but limited by his accentuation of the conventionalities of both libertinage and liberty, Wilkes was comfortable in his *historicized* place; he was a creation, however dissenting, of his times and as such reached into the night from the stability of accommodation to aspects of the day. One might characterize him as a *social* libertine, one who enjoyed the pleasures of masculine fraternity and the offerings of feminine sensuality, which it was his purpose to seduce and consume, to "spend"—a double entendre associated with the licentiousness of both the marketplace and the boudoir. A good-natured rake, he followed sin along well-trodden heterosexual paths (he would have found male sodomy abhorrent). If his intentions were seldom "honorable," they were neither "uncivil" nor unconcerned with particular proprieties. It would have been beneath him to besmirch "a lady" publicly, yet for the private amusement of himself and his circle he could write crudely objectifying comment on the generic "woman." In all of this he belonged to a masculine community of "refined" pleasure.

An appreciation of Sade is more demandingly difficult because, in his confrontation with evil and totalizing pornographic immersion in the moment of boundless, perversely transgressive lust, all limits were shattered and all metaphorical connection to day and its lights abandoned.[44] No matter that this moment is boringly repetitive, a quantifiable accumulation, for that is itself a feature of the ordered "pornographic imagination."[45] Sade's "tormented life," in the words of Simone de Beauvoir, was governed less by the repressive apparatus of state regulation and the constraints of material need, whatever Sade's obsessions with these forces, than it was by "the painful experience of living" without "any solidarity between other men [and women] and himself." He thus personifies the deepest of alienations, the most engrossing plummet into darkness imaginable. And he knew it. "Imperious, choleric, irascible, extreme in everything, with a dissolute imagination the like of which has never been seen, atheistic to the point of fanaticism, there you have me in a nutshell, and kill me again, or take me as I am, for I shall not change," was his defiant self-assessment.

Of all the libertines, Sade pushed licentiousness and liberty, in their individualized guises of gendered power and aristocratic license, the furthest, making "of his eroticism the meaning and expression of his whole existence." It severed him from humanity and, in its limitlessness, forced compulsions that shattered the self in a process that Foucault has referred to as "unreason transformed into delirium of the heart, madness of desire, the insane dialogue of love and death in the limitless presumption of appetite." The Sadeian night was a dark encounter with a fragmented self, unleashed from any social moorings, cut adrift from a history it needed to reconnect with. Sade lived sex, and having exhausted its carnal conventions early in his career, his work became its perversions, the wages of which were paid in currencies as inflated and debased as almost any known to humanity. This commodification of Eros, which he recognized, severed him from history and cast him into a personal hell of alienation from which there was no escape, however frenzied and compulsive his obsessions. "I have invented horrors and carried them out in cold blood," he recalled. "Since I had the resources to refuse myself nothing, however costly my projects for debauchery might be, I set out on them at once."

But resources did not buy sociability and his pornographic descent from conventional libertinage was the antithesis of the masculine club life of Wilkes; Sade fucked alone, his accomplices—whether manservants or prostitutes—were paid for their troubles. An *obsessional* libertine, Sade narrowed his circle over time to the point of focusing almost exclusively on himself—an ironic historical reification, given that he lived through a revolution that consolidated possessive individualism. As Georges Bataille suggests, "Sade's life and work are indeed connected with historical events, but in the strangest possible way. The sense of the revolution is not 'given' in his ideas: if there is any connection it is more like that between the uneven components of some unfinished figure—between a ruin and some rock, or between the night and silence."[46]

Paradoxically, but true to his boundless libertinism, Sade wanted it both ways. Choosing the night, he shattered its unspoken solitudes in an outpouring of writing that plunged the reader into licentiousness, traversed its possibilities, and pushed into the uncharted darkness of evil, which he embraced as desire. Anything but silent, he "chose cruelty rather than indifference," and his philosophical fictions detail almost every perversion imaginable, inverting the softer pornographies of the era in their refusal of anything approximating a gratified sexuality of utopian paradise. Instead, Sade presents a sexual solitude external from the world but spiraling ever downward in tragedies, damnations, and hurt. Sexuality became a matter of inflicting and tolerating pain, a tyranny of unfreedom to be not challenged but succumbed to. The true Sadeian libertine is an "exile from the world," a dominating, controlling figure whose "abominable privilege" pushes the envelope of aristocratic license past comprehension. Having made the "brutal discovery that there was no conciliation possible between his social existence and his private pleasures," Sade chose to step through the conventions of his station and assert his need to tyrannize and dominate in brothels and "little houses"; these he outfitted with sacrilegious adornments, instruments of flagellation, and other mechanical aids, thus buying the right to unleash his fantasies. For his vision of evil and the audacity to put it into practice, Sade would spend twenty-seven of his seventy-four years in prison. Among his crimes were sodomy, which the eighteenth-century state had little tolerance for; kidnappings of poor women and prostitutes, whom he beat and tortured; and affairs of truly bizarre debauchery. Sade's incarcerations by his family, his class, and his state—none of which he was truly disposed to rebel against—bridge dramatically different contexts: the ancien régime, the revolutionary reign of Robespierre's Terror, and the restored Empire under Napoleon. Sixteen volumes of writings, encompassing plays, novels, letters, and philosophical tracts, among them The Misfortunes of Virtue (1787)—later rewritten as Justine (1791) and The New Justine (1797)—and Philosophy of the Bedroom (1795), attest to his agency and voice in the creation of a system of sexual thought called sadism.[47] Yet after this prodigious production, Sade wished to be forgotten, requesting in his last will and testament to be buried without ceremony: "Once the grave has been covered up, acorns will be sown upon it, so that ... the traces of my tomb might disappear from the surface of the earth just as I flatter myself that my memory will disappear from men's memories." The epitaph that he wrote for himself (though it was not placed on his tombstone) struck a more characteristically defiant posture: "Passerby, kneel down to pray beside the unhappiest of men. He was born in the last century and died in the present one. Despotism of hideous mien made war on him in all ages; under the kings, that odious monster took hold of his entire life. Under the Terror, it persisted, and put Sade at the brink of the abyss. Under the Consulate, it returned, and Sade was still its victim." Liberty obviously mattered to the old libertine, but it meant most when it was denied to him.[48]

Although it is tempting to see Sade as little more than "an exemplary figure in psychopathology,"[49] this interpretation is clearly inadequate.[50] Sade elicits a hostile response precisely because his eroticism is charged with cruelty; it often draws blood, and even if he murdered no one in his debaucheries, he did injure. Bataille considers Sade's frenzy to be the destruction of human beings, pleasure's enjoyment peaking in the thought of death, the "one occupation in his long life which really absorbed him" being that of the tortured spilling of blood.[51]

This, understandably, turns many people off. But in fact this is not Sade's legacy, in pornography or in life. "Yes, I admit I am a libertine and in that area I have imagined everything that can be imagined," he wrote in protest in 1781. "But I have absolutely not acted out everything that I imagined, nor do I intend to. I am a libertine, but I am not a criminal or a murderer." An aristocrat of a declining feudal order whose license was extended broadly to include the pleasurable use of "inferiors," most decidedly female bodies, Sade was no friend of a narrowly constituted freedom that recognized the rights of the poor and that sought to overcome, even in a Wilkesite program of limited agendas, their oppression. Nevertheless, in his embrace of a crudely reductionist, relentlessly materialist and sexualized philosophy, Sade's private pleasures and perversions were a mirror held before the grand oppressions and exploitations of the ancien régime. His pornography thus identifies and, through images of sexuality, reflects back upon the institutions of order the inequalities and violence of a social formation in which rulership, property, religion, and family are all literally dripping in blood.[52] It was for this reason, which had little to do with Sade's actual crimes or writings, that his imprisonment in the Bastille was presented by William Blake in the symbolism of The French Revolution (1791) as a statement on the corruptions and travesties of the old feudal world:

> ...and the den nam'd Horror held a man
> Chain'd hand and foot, round his neck an iron band,
>   bound to the impregnable wall.
> In his soul was the serpent coil'd round his heart,
>   hid from the light, as in a cleft rock;
> And the man was confined for writing prophetic...[53]

Sade, as Foucault suggests, stood at the threshold of a great transformation, one that, in part, suppressed "sanguinity" and elevated "sexuality." In the confused swirl of rising and falling regimes of power, in which the symbolics of blood and the analytics of sexuality were grounded but in which slippages could indeed take place, it was understandable that a figure such as Sade, with his intransigent erotic obsession, and his own power straddling the ancient blood license of aristocrats and the libidinal pleasures of modernity, would strike sufficient blows at both feudal and bourgeois order to ensure a deep-seated personal estrangement and official hostility. Unchained from incarcerating repression by the French Revolution's initial impulse of freedom ("No Bastilles"), Sade served his time in the Parisian trenches of revolutionary citizenship—only to find that the new bourgeois order would have blood on its hands as well.[54] With the Terror he found himself back in jail, his radical atheism not welcomed by the Robespierresque Court of the Supreme Being. The overactive guillotine working its horrors outside his window took his publisher's head. There would be no cries of "Sade and Liberty."[55]

In his extremism, then, Sade does make the connection of libertinage, licentiousness, and liberty but not in ways that are obvious or prettified. Unlike Wilkes, he was incapable of becoming the libertine Lord of Misrule, mounting the hustings in defense of liberty, leading the crowd in the demand for freedom. Eroticism was more than witticism, the text of sexuality weightier than burlesque verse parodying religion and reveling in unchaste thoughts and deeds. His project was not to politicize the public but to publicize the private and promote the perverse. Yet pleasure was no less arduous a taskmaster than Parliament, and just as likely to turn on its adherents. In Sade's The 120 Days of Sodom (written 1785) the murderous denouement is a literal witches' Sabbat of blood, excrement, sexual mutilation, and torture, a perverse utopia where only the debased self rules, a devil's domain of flesh and force that banishes humanity in a timeless and repetitive reproduction of evil. With Sade the witch was indeed redundant.[56]

Libertines had done their bit to deflate sorcery's challenge and to defend liberty (for some but against others) as a limited possibility for an expanded political public. But their reach, whether in the Wilkes or Sade tradition, was cramped. Aristocratic license in the last half of the eighteenth century could be extended in various directions, but there were points beyond which it would not go. Licentiousness—as a preface to opposition or a perverse sexualized parody of the material world of domination and destruction that was consolidated in the new late-eighteenth-century regimes of power and crystallized in the fusion of state authority and capitalist interest—had discernible boundaries. Those who wanted to transcend such limitations, to orchestrate mobilizations of overt challenge and oppositional vitality, might continue to explore the politics of pornographic caricature; an underworld of ribald revolutionaries still thrived in London's tavern debating societies and among the radical pressmen who kept libertinism somewhat alive by an under-the-counter trade in obscene publications. But libertinism not only had gone subterranean in this context, it had crossed class lines; its survival was a commercial necessity for the struggling Grub Street Jacobins whose political commitments and business activities had little in common. The aristocracy, a declining class now decisively displaced, was no longer dangerous and its licentious libertinism—with an outlet in an anticlerical, blasphemous pornography—was largely a spent force. Pornography would of course still figure in the transgressive histories of the night, but as a dimension of the dangerous classes it had, by the 1790s, been replaced by other sorts of tracts and the evolving formation of new systems of thought.[57] It was on its way to "pornotopia," that state of alienated sexuality where the erotic is hived off from the rest of life. In the dark night of libidinal need the lonely masturbatory hand, incapable of reaching out in loving caress to another human being with whom it is possible to share both sensually and politically, grasps at representational straws, all of which have the same tedious form and an identical boring content.[58]

5

Conspiracies of the Night

Anglo-French Radicalism, Jacobinism, and the Age of Revolution

In 1776, as the United States was taking form by banishing British dominance, John Wilkes rose in the House of Commons to argue that "the meanest mechanic, the poorest peasant and day labourer has important rights respecting his personal liberty, that of his wife and children, his property, however inconsiderable, his wage, his earnings, the very price and value of each day's hard labour, which are in many trades regulated by the power of Parliament."[1] To be sure, Wilkes's plea for the poor's place in their own government was limited, in gendered and class ways, and he condescended that the need for reform was critically important to "this inferior but most useful set of men."[2] His was the two-sided language of the Age of Revolution, spoken on the eve of twenty years of socio-economic turmoil that would turn the political world of European class relations in new directions; and stand the realm of ideas on its head. Wilkes's words and the ideas they conveyed were a product of a three-tiered structure of social change and breakdown, out of which would emerge the modern capitalist political economy and its "freedoms," defined and bounded by the pervasive influence of the market. Each stage in this turmoil was associated with the words and deeds of discrete but inter-related revolutions whose coming together in the last quarter of the eighteenth century sounded the death knell of the ancien régime.[3]

Weakest at its furthest link, the chain of the ancien régime was broken first, but perhaps least decisively (since in British North America variants of seigneurialism remained, though confined regionally, as in the slave-holding South), in the distant colonies of the future United States. White settler societies in all parts of the Americas—Spanish, French, and British—

resented the considerable limits placed on their autonomy by imperial power. With metropolitan authority increasingly incapable of enforcing its absolute domination over its colonial subjects, its hands tied in international rivalry that usually ended in costly and cumbersome wars, its head befuddled with contradictory understandings of rights and responsibilities, the moment seemed ripe for rebellion. In America it was unleashed in 1776 as a war of independence waged in the name of property. Undue taxation on tea proved a potent symbol that rallied rich and poor alike to a standard of bourgeois revolution that managed to espouse a rhetoric of liberty and equality, while pursuing a happiness that avoided addressing the enslavement of actual people. As the colonists protested their subordination to arbitrary British rule they increasingly alluded to the pressing danger of their own slavery, but closed their eyes to the black slaves whose labor sustained the plantation economies of the South and so many other economic endeavors of the New World. Not until a second American revolution was unleashed with the Civil War of the 1860s would this blind spot begin to be addressed, and even then only partially.

More thoroughgoing was the French Revolution of 1789, a decisive, world-historic event that culminated in the vanquishing of all formal relics of feudalism and whose political reverberations were destined to register from Latin America to the Far East over the course of the nineteenth century. If the American Revolution resulted in a change of *government*, the French Revolution established a change of *society*. In France, as aristocrat and bourgeois found themselves ensnared in oppositional entanglements, dichotomous lines of allegiance were soon formed, and a compromise between feudal privilege and the market-based forms of "democratic" rule was quickly reduced to a legal and political impossibility. The Declaration of Rights, amended as the revolution progressed, established equality as the prerogative of humanity, although, of course, it offered no guarantees that all men and women would have the means to ensure that this right was implemented and used. Beyond the wall of property the bourgeoisie would and could not go. Thus, Boissy d'Anglas, an advocate of government by "proprietors," declared in a speech on the projected constitution of 1795, "Civil equality is all a man should reasonably expect. A country ruled by men of no property is in a state of nature."

By this date, radicals such as Robespierre and Saint-Just had fallen to the guillotine, and with them went the contradictory clash of the revolution's inconsistencies. "There must be neither rich nor poor," Saint-Just had written in the fourth part of his *Institutions republicaines*, confining his doubts about how to deliver such a utopia to his diary in the words,

"Must not allow the break-up of private property." On 26 February 1794, Saint-Just spoke more than he knew when he exhorted the revolutionaries to stand firm: "Do they talk about mercy in the courts of the European monarchs? No! Do not let yourselves be softened," he thundered "Those only who aid in freeing it have any rights in this our Fatherland." He closed with what could be the gravestone epitaph of Jacobinism: "Those who make revolutions by half, are only busied in digging a grave."

Six months later the evening meetings of the Jacobin Club were a scene of sober realization at the magnitude of the defeat. "You have heard my dying testament," Robespierre reported one night, "I saw today that the league of the wicked is so strong that I may not escape it. I fall without regret." Among those sacrificed with him was Saint-Just. In the struggle to create civil equality, however, new visions were released from the virtual Pandora's Box of contested meanings and popular aspirations pushed to limits previously unimaginable. This is why the French Revolution (no mere representational illusion, as some historians have proclaimed) managed to attain a mythic stature in the popular consciousness of revolt, the liberation of the Bastille remaining a symbol of emancipatory insurrection for generations and the "Marseillaise" a lyric battle cry of freedom to this day. But the directing social and intellectual forces of the revolutionary bourgeoisie nevertheless managed to straddle the fence of a proclaimed juridical liberty and equality while balancing a commitment to fraternity on the pillars of property.[4]

The limitations of the political revolutions of the late eighteenth century were thus not unrelated to the revolution in property that was developing at precisely the time that feudalism was on its last tired, embattled legs. The fundamental determinative context within which governmental authority was displaced, state power consolidated, and society transformed was the Industrial Revolution. Though slower and less visible than the mobilizations of 1776 and 1789—lacking proclamations and unruly champions in the streets and constituted assemblies, and definitely not reducible to a fixed point in time—it is pivotal to the Age of Revolution. Its coming was recognized late; probably not until the 1820s did French and English socialists actually identify, perhaps invent, the historical process of industrial revolution, though no doubt the origins of this vast transformation in productive life lay buried deep in a complex past. But economic growth and the detailed division of labor—spurred to new heights of achievement by ideas, science, technological innovation, expansive markets associated with demographically exploding populations, the resources of conquered colonies, new sources of labor (slave and coerced, as well as free), the profits of commerce, and the rapacious monopolization of landed property associated with clearances, enclosures, and the ending of common right traditions—marched through a long gestation of proto-industrialization. Gathering speed into the 1760s, this economic transformation of accelerating capitalist accumulation restructured the meaning of everyday life, establishing the factory system and its impersonal regimes of discipline and labor control as models not only for the making of goods but for the running of society. States, schools, social life, churches and the punitive institutions of regulation, from the asylum and the prison to the temperance society, all felt the weight of the Industrial Revolution's hand pressing on their place in the new order of commodity production.

Strongest in Britain, where the cotton and textile industry was the new king of an accumulative order, the Industrial Revolution restructured life in all of Europe and left its mark, in deformed ways, on such outposts of empire as India or the Caribbean. There, astronomical profits were made in a triangular trade that linked Africa as a source of slaves, plantations growing and harvesting cotton (and more addictive products, such as sugar, tobacco, and, later, coffee), huge Lancashire mills, and new markets for cheap textiles in the populous peripheries of consolidating imperialism. The pattern repeated itself in countless variations, but by the late eighteenth century money ruled as it never had before. Whatever the public program of the Age of Revolution, private power was ensconced in a new layer of entrepreneurs whose "only law was to buy in the cheapest markets and sell without restriction in the dearest," Hobsbawm explains. Since few barriers could block this revolutionary procession, marching to the tune of profit, by the end of that century, "the gods and kings of the past were powerless before the businessmen and steam-engines of the present."[5]

Few moments of history belonged so decisively to a rising ruling class. Nevertheless, ideas of dissent germinated, formed in direct opposition to the crude, often vile, rants of Edmund Burke and others, who saw in events such as the French Revolution the threatened collapse of the civilizing influence of men of property and standing. Burke despised ordinary people, and as the ideologue of reaction he penned defenses of property that reached memorable lows in their assaults on what he indiscreetly referred to as "the swinish multitude." His Reflections on the French Revolution (1790) drew an irate outbreak of hostile pamphleteering that parodied his language of contemptuous dismissal in titles of ironic derision: Hog's Wash, Pig's Meat, and Politics for the People: A Salmagundy for Swine. "Whilst ye are gorging yourselves at troughs filled with the daintiest wash; we, with out numerous train of *porkers*, are employed, from the rising to the setting sun, to obtain the means of subsistence, by picking up a few acorns," declared the typically overdone tongue-in-cheek *Address to the Hon. Edmund Burke from the Swinish Multitude* in 1793. Less jocular responses included Mary Wollstonecraft's impassioned *A Vindication of the Rights of Men* (1790), which preceded her historic articulation of feminism's project, *A Vindication of the Rights of Women* (1792). "Your tears are reserved, very naturally considering your character," she railed at Burke, "for the declamation of the theatre, or for the downfall of queens, whose rank throws a graceful veil over vices that degrade humanity; but the distress of many industrious mothers, whose *helpmates* have been torn from them, and the hungry cry of the helpless babes, were vulgar sorrows that could not move your commiseration, though they might extort an alms."

Thomas Paine's *Rights of Man* (1791–1792) emerged out of this intellectual moment of anti-Burkean tirade, consolidating what E. P. Thompson calls "a new rhetoric of radical egalitarianism ... which penetrated the sub-political attitudes of the urban working people." Emboldened by the American and French Revolutions, Paine's uncommon common sense expressed the aspirations of the disenfranchised and subordinated masses of the first industrial nation. "I have an aversion to monarchy, as being too debasing to the dignity of man," he proclaimed with straightforward bluntness—and his words fueled the fires of republicanism that burned in thousands of radical booksellers' back rooms, debating societies, and dissenting chapels. Paine historicized the skeptical interrogation of the institutions of aristocratic privilege, asking as early as 1776, in *Common Sense*, hard questions about the "divine" origins of kingly rule: "A French bastard landing with an armed banditti and establishing himself King of England, against the consent of the natives, is, in plain terms, a very paltry, rascally original. It certainly hath no divinity in it.... The plain truth is that the antiquity of English monarchy will not bear looking into."

This irreverent plain speaking earned Paine high regard among a growing constituency of transatlantic dissidents. Some, under pressures of expedience, dissociated themselves from his more extreme postures, but few found tolerable his victimization by the state, which in 1793 declared *Rights of Man* a seditious libel, banned the book and drove its author into exile. Paine's popularity soared with the emergence of a working-class opposition, and in many circles he was a figure of almost untouchable repute for generations, the foremost advocate of a radical republicanism embraced enthusiastically by the producers and proletarians driven to protest capitalism's political oppressions and economic exploitations. In the Chartist agitations of the 1830s, Paine was often discussed at meetings. "One night somebody spoke of Tom Paine. Up jumped the chairman. 'I will not sit in the chair,' he cried in great wrath, 'and hear that great man reviled. Bear in mind he was not a prizefighter. There is no such person as Tom Paine. Mister Thomas Paine, if you please.'" At the interface of the American, French, and Industrial Revolutions, a language of class opposition was taking shape.[6]

It took the form of "Jacobinism."[7] The Jacobins were a section of the French Revolution; the Jacobin Clubs established in 1790 and 1791 overlapped with societies that declared themselves "Friends of the Constitution." As the revolution proceeded, the clubs came more and more to reflect the politicized disputes of the revolutionary process, and the Jacobins were associated with intransigence, academic debate, "national" centralized policies, and "left" positions. Believers in republican forms of government, universal manhood suffrage, separation of Church and state, the abolition of all hereditary distinctions and social privileges, private ownership of property, the alleviation of dire poverty, the independence of the individual and the nation-state, and the virtues of an austere work ethic, Jacobins were the theoreticians of bourgeois order, architects of a systematic dismantling of the curbs on freedom associated with the old regime. A Jacobin constitution, drafted in 1793, was marked by its democratic procedures and concern with the needs of the poor; Jacobins abolished slavery in the French colonies in 1794; and Jacobins spearheaded a national system of public education and a centralizing code of law, both of which were meant to safeguard equality as a universal, abstract right. Incapable of being reduced to a simplified class essence, Jacobinism nevertheless forged a political dictatorship of "the lower and middle sections of the bourgeoisie" and cultivated the support of the popular masses through a commitment to democracy and an economics of liberty in the productive realm. Jacobins personified the program and principles of the bourgeoisie, as well as its contradictions: abstractly, their position led deeper and deeper into the tangled underbrush of a forest of popular aspiration; concretely, they constructed the institutions and ideological authority of class-based governance. This politics thus has two histories: the one as architect of bourgeois order and the orthodoxies of rule; the other as a symbol of radical commitment centered in a party premised on political ideas and an unbending resolve. Recently this tradition has been obsessively assimilated to the Leninist notion of the necessity of a revolutionary vanguard. The new historiographical revisionism of François

Furet's "galaxy," a constellation of academic and journalistic repudiation of the French Revolution, persistently likens Jacobinism to a centerpiece in the history of a simplified and always totalitarian Bolshevism.[8]

Little of this complexity registered in the 1790s. When reformers in England challenged the state with demands for a more inclusive political process, they ventured into the confused swirl of Jacobinism, although they themselves might have preferred the titular identification "Friend of Liberty." And when, in 1792, they expressed their solidarity with the course of the French Revolution and began to champion the rights of Irish Catholics or endorse the demands of Scottish radicals, their gestures toward the right of self-determination drew sharp antagonism from established political authority. Then came an onslaught of caricature and repression, evident in the loyalist Association for the Preservation of Liberty and Property against Republicans and Levellers, founded late in 1792, and the publication of the *Anti-Jacobin*.[9] An 1881 English text explained the pejorative use of the term "Jacobin":

> Its application to the early reformers arose from the terror it inspired during the first flush of the French Revolution, when the minds of the easy-going classes were disturbed at the popular demands for Liberty and Equality. They did not stop to inquire what sort of "equality" was wanted: or to discover that it was *equality before the law* for rich and poor alike which was meant. There has never been any such enduring terror as that in modern history. "What they did not understand, they dreaded and abhorred." So it came to pass that the people and the cause which they did not understand were dreaded as monstrous and dangerous; the cry of "Jacobins and Levellers" was freely raised; and a prejudice was encouraged which has not entirely been dissipated to this day.[10]

But there was another way of looking at this dark moment of repression. "The struggle carried on by the Jacobins in England was the beginning of the class war in this country," wrote Robert Birley in 1924.[11]

This class war had its origins in decades of exploitation and oppression, often lived during the day. But to ponder it and to organize it required the "leisures" of the night. At least this was how one Thomas Hardy, founder and first secretary-treasurer of the London Corresponding Society (LCS), put the matter in 1799 when he offered an account of the organization's beginnings. Throughout November and December 1791, Hardy, a shoemaker who would rise to the status of small master by 1795, spent his evenings "reading some political tracts which I had formerly perused with much pleasure during the American War." Short though they were (averaging two to eleven pages), these tracts convinced Hardy that "a *radical reform in parliament* was quite necessary." He talked with an intimate friend about forming a society to include "all classes and descriptions of men" committed to universal suffrage, and then met this man and two more for supper a few evenings later, reading them passages on reform. They all agreed to meet with such others as could be attracted to their cause the following Monday night at an Exeter Street tavern off the Strand. There, sheltered by a landlord whom Hardy knew to be "a friend of freedom," nine men gathered for bread, cheese, and porter, following their dinner with the usual pipes. Then, "well-meaning, sober, and industrious," they commenced a discussion of the dire circumstances of the people and the ignorance and prejudice of the bulk of the nation, which they considered the greatest obstacle to redressing the many defects and abuses of government. Two more evening gatherings increased their numbers to twenty-five, and for five nights running they debated whether or not tradesmen and mechanics had the right to seek parliamentary reform. They concluded that they did. Hardy soon communicated with a similar society in Sheffield which had an impressive membership of two thousand, signing his name to a short address accompanied by a series of resolutions. Later he showed the manifesto to an American friend, who responded, "Hardy, the Government will hang you." It did not, but not for want of trying.[12]

Over the course of the next two years the London Corresponding Society grew phenomenally, drawing on the common practice of unmarried mechanics and workingmen to gather after the day's labors at a public house or tavern for a light meal and modest drink. Divisions were soon established throughout the metropolitan center of London, convening all nights of the week, communicating with one another and similar societies across the country through their central committee. "That the numbers of our members be unlimited" was thus the first of the leading rules of the society, where a belief in the inadequacy of political representation, a commitment to universal male suffrage, and endorsement of all justifiable means of reforming Parliament were the foundations of popular involvement. All business was conducted without remuneration, and all members paid the same modest dues. Within six months Hardy claimed the allegiance of two thousand Londoners; probably between five to ten thousand eventually came to involve themselves in one way or another with the cause of reform.

Among them, as the advance guard of English Jacobinism, were Tom Paine, for whom the society organized a defense fund after the indictment against *Rights of Man*; Maurice Margarot, son of a wine importer known to have entertained patriot gatherings during the era of "Wilkes and Liberty" and himself a classically educated reformer who traveled among the leaders of the 1789 uprising in France; the scrupulously respectable (at least in later life) voice of artisan republicanism, Francis Place, who thought the LCS "the very best school for good teaching" and a cause of considerable moral improvement "among the People"; and a nonmember, John Horne Tooke (who once confessed that although he would not use violence in the reform cause, he would sit still and say a prayer for those who did), a committed advocate of parliamentary reform to whom Hardy and others turned for advice, a patrician figure who enjoyed his stature among his "inferiors" but was capable of opportunistic proclamations of distance from them when it suited his personal interests.

Hardy was the organizational center of this expanding reform constituency, linking an older London radicalism, the transatlantic ideas of Paine, and the expanding popular ranks of reform-minded mechanics and tradesmen. The uninhibited Hardy coauthored an impudent September 1792 address, delivered to France, praising the accomplishments of the National Convention. With the English state poised to declare war on revolutionary France—a position that unleashed a bellicose patriotism spurred on by cries of "Church and King"—these internationalist words of fraternity were dangerous indeed. Hardy's nights of thought were bringing him and many like-minded but lesser-known men to the brink of what the state, unaccustomed to political gatherings of unenfranchised tradesmen, considered treason. There was a certain gentility and postured accommodation in those disaffected oppositional Whigs and literary circles drawn to the cry "No Bastille" that was simply not allowed into the considerations of the tavern-gathering tradesmen, artisans, and small masters who dominated the Corresponding Societies, let alone the wage earners from the docks and larger workshops drawn to radicalism after 1794.

Little of this patrician propriety could be construed to cloak the personage of the London Corresponding Society's principal speaker, theoretician, and agitator, John Thelwall. Hardy "dressed plainly, talked frankly, never at any time assuming airs or making pretensions." He was the stable center of the LCS tradition, the selfless organizational laborer working through the night for the cause of reform, conscientious in recording the minutiae of meetings and guarding scrupulously the records and dues of members. Thelwall, in contrast, was the Jacobinical performer, a national leader and rousing orator who, if occasionally given to flights of self-dramatization, appeared as the people's champion. His tours drew thousands to the radical cause; his twice-weekly lectures were a wildly appealing political theater of extreme rhetoric and symbolic gesture. Something of Thelwall's politics and panache are summed up in his manner of taking refreshment. At the night gatherings of the LCS he was conspicuous among the radicals whose business was conducted amid tables of bread and beer, loud with jokes about sans-culottes and "the Swinish Multitude." Cutting the frothy head from a pot of porter, he was known to exclaim, "This is the Way I would serve Kings."[13]

Thelwall had been born to a pretentious but struggling commercial family in which the premature death of the father constrained the well-being of his wife and children and left John at the mercy of a violent and dissipated brother. The experience instilled in him a hatred of corporal punishment and perhaps drew him in later life to the figure of John Howard and the need for reform in penal institutions. Educated in his youth to the private world of study and poetry, Thelwall adapted poorly to the economics of family need. While apprenticed to a tailor, he was in a perpetual state of distraction, stealing time to study and reading even as he walked home at night, the pages illuminated by a candle he carried in his pocket. He found it more to his liking when articled to a lawyer but soon grew disconsolate and miserable with the knowledge that the law generally bore down mercilessly on its victims. On at least one occasion, he gave his last shilling to a poor client. "Lawyers," he later charged, had "spread more devastation through the moral world than the Goths and Vandals, who overthrew the Roman Empire." By the late 1780s, having found little he could live with in any aspect of the business world, he turned to painting and literary endeavors, but they paid poorly. He soon took on the trappings of a moderate reformer, denouncing slavery, deploring the fate of seduced women, and adopting "the simple principles of materialism" to challenge orthodox religious assumptions about the soul. With the French Revolution, and above all with Burke's outrageous assaults on the popular classes, Thelwall received the push he needed, propelling him into the ranks of radicalism. Repression would be the midwife of his rebirth as a Jacobin.

After the Society for Free Debate, which Thelwall helped to manage, was suppressed in the anti-Jacobin repression of late 1792, his politics grew more intransigent. He next joined the Society of the Friends of the People, founded by Major John Cartwright (who had also established the Society for Constitutional Information in 1780), but when it was crushed by government opposition Thelwall was precipitated into the more lower-class ranks of the much larger London Corresponding Society. Known by this time as something of a firebrand, he could not at first rent a room for open political discussion anywhere in London. Soon, however, he was the LCS's most frequent and undoubtedly most talented speaker. By 1793, he was paying the price for this notoriety: Thelwall, Hardy, and others were tracked by state spies who worked their way into society meetings and even got themselves elected to influential committees. In addition, government-hired thugs and magistrate-induced loyalists hounded LCS meetings, heckled speakers, and tore up handbills. Each radical word, whether spoken or printed, was scrutinized for sedition, and Thelwall brushed close to imprisonment on a number of occasions. In this climate of repression, from 1794 to 1796, his series of lectures in a small Soho room not only articulated the tenets of popular, Jacobinical radicalism but moved it beyond the narrowly constitutional issues of parliamentary reform into the expanding causes of economic grievance and their social resolution. Thelwall, more than any other eighteenth-century Jacobin and certainly more than the better-known Paine, had the vision to link the political oppression of state power and aristocratic privilege to the exploitive power of capital, asserting, moreover, that the social force of a waged working class created by the latter would inevitably address the former. As Gregory Claeys has recently argued, Thelwall "herald[ed] the interest in economic conditions that was to define nineteenth-century radicalism by contrast with the more predominantly constitutionalist concerns of the past."

Soon the night lectures were drawing a thousand and more, and a larger hall on the Strand was secured. Still having to turn away hundreds at the door, Thelwall and the LCS pioneered several huge outdoor meetings, some with as many as five "tribunes" or stages, from which speakers addressed throngs of fifty thousand and more. The message was no longer merely that of the people's need for representation, a reformist constitutionalism. Thelwall, like other LCS leaders, was increasingly drawn to the more revolutionary content of the French Revolution, espousing not so much the platform of 1789 as that of 1792. He declared himself "a Republican and a true Sans-Culotte," defended Robespierre, and cast his lot with the "men of the Mountain (Jacobins)." America, twenty years past its revolutionary zeal, he now found possessed of "too great a veneration for property, too much religion, and too much law." "I adopt the term Jacobinism without hesitation," Thelwall declared, first because "it is fixed upon us, as a stigma, by our enemies" but also, because although he had no taste for the guillotine, Jacobin ideas were "the most consonant with my ideas of reason, and the nature of man, of any that I have met with." Jacobinism in the 1790s meant an enlarging commitment to reform independent of what Thelwall christened the "authorities and principles of the Gothic customary." In their sharp break with libertine privilege and the popular politics of the eighteenth-century hustings, Thelwell and the LCS charted new democratic paths. Their doctrine of "members unlimited" led them from mobilizations originating in demands for political rights to an appreciation of the fusion of the political and the economic.

Thelwall and the leading English Jacobins were thus groping toward resolutions of the dilemmas posed not just by formal, legalistic equalities but by the social inequality of the Industrial Revolution, the exploitation of class power that was increasingly evident in the world's first advanced capitalist economy. London, whose radical constitutionalist heritage had been proclaimed in the electoral streets of Westminster for generations, was taking a back seat to the provinces. Jacobin ideas, bred in the city, were "driven into weaving villages, the shops of the Nottingham framework-knitters and the Yorkshire croppers, [and] the Lancashire cotton-mills." Jacobian commitments to equality reverberated in working-class knowledge of hard days of labor, exacerbated by rising prices and narrowing possibilities. As Thelwall wrote in The Rights of Nature (1796), the workplaces of the Industrial Revolution were now nurseries of radicalism, the experience of proletarianization cross-fertilized with Jacobinical notions of equality in the long evening of reason's reflection.[14]

With ideas like these germinating in the night of Jacobin radical thought, espoused in public meetings that drew thousands out into the after-work hours of an oppositional culture, the powers of the day struck blows in defense of privilege and property. With a sense of humor biting in its sarcasm, Thelwall was known to lecture on "the moral tendency of spies and informers," well aware that provocateurs and government agents were among his audience. On occasion those sent to disrupt his talks were dissuaded from their harangues, perhaps even convinced to think through their mercenary loyalism. One duo, dispatched to sing "God Save the King," were converted to silence by Thelwall's effective blend of bitter vehemence, historical analogy, reasoned argument, and coarse wit. "I am afraid," reported another spy, "they left the room with different sentiments to what they entered it with."[15] When the London Corresponding Society convened a huge assemblage at Chalk Farm Tavern in mid-April 1794 to consider the widening boundaries of reform agitation, spies and informers did their best to provoke disturbances, the military was marshaled in case of revolt, and the landlord was ordered by several attending magistrates to refuse refreshments to any reformers in attendance. Yet Hardy recalled that the reform masses conducted themselves with order and dignity, refusing to succumb to the "insulting language of some of the

the most barbaric of "Church and King mobs," whose penchant for beatings, "rough music," and attacks on halls seemed to occasion no concern from the guardians of order, either magistrates or soldiers, the latter being prominent in many loyalist vendettas. Hardy's paper, *The Tribune*, was suppressed in April 1796; innkeepers passed declarations or posted signs banning Jacobians from their premises. Thelwall faced relentless harassment; he was attacked, threatened with kidnapping, impressment or forced transportation to Siberia, pursued, jostled, and persistently prevented from speaking. He genuinely and justifiably feared for his life. There were times when he defended himself with a pistol, his back pressed to the wall as a corps of thugs advanced with some menacing object in mind. The savage climate of the times is perhaps best captured in Charles James Fox's claim that "Church and King" mobs were known to parade effigies of reformers through the streets, their straw likenesses containing the heart of an animal. Pierced by a pike at an opportune moment, the heart would bleed through the straw, conveying a message of mutilation and death. The effigy would then be burned, and to climax the loyalist display, the heart would be eaten by members of the mob.[20]

In this climate of coercive repression, as Thelwall and other leading Jacobin figures were pushed into corners of retirement, popular Jacobinism with its constituency of artisans and mechanics was waning. A contingent of Romantic poets and literati such as William Wordsworth, S. T. Coleridge, Robert Southey, and William Godwin, who had, for a few years, nourished Thelwall's radical thoughts in a Jacobin society of revolutionary aesthetics, would make a most precipitous rush from radicalism in these troubled times of repression. They differed in their politics of attraction to revolution, of course, and exited from the Hall of the People in various ways, Coleridge being the most offensive in his apostasy. In the disenchantment of this milieu Thelwall and other Jacobins, whether stalwart supporters who flocked to lectures and flogged the press or agitators of the first rank, felt the sting of generalized abandonment and disillusionment.[21]

It was the end, seemingly, of Jacobin transgression. The dream gave way to the disgruntled prose satire of *Nightmare Abbey* (1818), Thomas Love Peacock's portrait of a generation's slide into "obscurantist accommodation." Peacock prefaced his "comedy of humours" with the insightful verse of Samuel Butler, whose poetics of defeat had a particular resonance with the trials, literal and figurative, of the embattled Jacobins:

> There's a dark lantern of the spirit,
> Which none see by but those who bear it,
> That makes them in the dark see visions

> And hag themselves with apparitions,
> Find racks for their own minds, and vaunt
> Of their own misery and want.

In Peacock's character, Mr. Flosky, drawn from Coleridge, the denouement of Jacobin disillusionment emerges:

> He dreamed with his eyes open, and saw ghosts dancing round him at noontide. He had been in his youth an enthusiast for liberty, and had hailed the dawn of the French Revolution as the promise of a day that was to banish war and slavery, and every form of vice and misery, from the face of the earth. Because all this was not done, and from this deduction, according to his system of logic, he drew a conclusion that worse than nothing was done, that the overthrow of the feudal fortresses of tyranny and superstition was the greatest calamity that had ever befallen mankind, and that their only hope now was to rake the rubbish together, and rebuild it without any of those loop-holes by which the light had originally crept in. To qualify himself for a co-adjutor in this laudable task, he plunged into the central opacity of Kantian metaphysics, and lay *perdu* several years in transcendental darkness, till the common daylight of common sense became intolerable to his eyes.... The good old times were always on his lips: meaning the days when polemic theology was in its prime, and rival prelates beat the drum ecclesiastic with Herculean vigour, till the one wound up his series of syllogisms with the very orthodox conclusion of roasting the other.

To lose an intelligentsia such as this—"The catastrophe is excellent," Southey said to Peacock in 1819—was an undoubted setback for Jacobinism, but there were more tangible, organizational losses as well. "Members unlimited" went, in part, the way of other ideals.[22] Among the most significant casualties were the societies themselves. As of July 12, 1799, the London Corresponding Society was prohibited from meeting on pain of fines, imprisonment, or transportation. Its every move reported on by spies, its last days were inconsequential. Discussions turned on clandestine meeting procedures, connections with such bodies as the United Irishmen, and fears of state repression. A conspiracy of state power conditioned a conspiratorial atmosphere among those Jacobins who did survive the 1790s, and the driving force of the earlier LCS—a mass movement of disaffected ranks—sank in seas of repression, resurfacing only rarely and carefully.[23]

Things were not helped by events in France, where Bonaparte had succeeded in replacing revolutionary republicanism with an aggressive imperialism ruling with as much authoritarian power as the absolutist kingdoms of the ancien régime. Thelwall wrote to Hardy in 1805 that the "tyrant Bonaparte" had destroyed, "perhaps for ever, all my glorious speculations of the improvability of man, & blasted the best hopes of Europe." Still, Thelwall qualified his disappointments with a useful "perhaps." He wrote poems that never conceded to counterrevolution, and, very much unlike Coleridge or Wordsworth, he never allowed his lapse from active Jacobinism to plumb the depths of overt rejection of his past or to embrace a comfortable complacency. He remembered the rights of man, and he harbored knowledge and resentment of the wrongs done to him and other reformers by a powerful state and its ideological and material hirelings. Never would Thelwall forget the tirades of the *Anti-Jacobin*:

> *Thelwall's* my man for State Alarm:
> I love the Rebels of *Chalk Farm*;
> Rogues that no Statutes can subdue,
> Who'd bring the French, and head them too.

There was honor in this revolutionary history. "The Storm is past," he wrote to a friend, "but I do not forget the Mast I clung to in the hour of wreck." He knew that as a political figure he was "*defunct*." Principles, however, he still cherished: "Have I *shifted sides*, like a common prize-fighter?" he asked in rhetorical amazement. Like many others he bided his quiet time, taking some small solace in the modest victories that might be secured in the name of a less tumultuous reform. When the Nottingham electors overturned a sitting conservative member in 1802 a victory procession brought out the old symbolism of radical Jacobinism: "The Goddess of Reason attended by four & twenty Virgins dress'd or rather half dress'd in white in the French fashion followed by the Tree of Liberty and the tri-colou'd Flag; a Band of Music playing the Tune "Millions be free" and the multitude singing the chorus."

This was too much, however, for the state that had so resolutely vanquished Jacobinism: on appeal to the House of Commons the election was overthrown. It was, Thelwall and other radicals knew, a "bad world" for politics. They went to ground, remembered better times, and hoped for some kind of future.[24]

Radicals elsewhere, however, were less benign and not given to such patience. The Jacobin night had not so much succumbed totally to the dawn of power's repressive day as it had been driven underground and here politics was indeed a conspiracy of the night. Forced into darkness by state repression, the Jacobism of the late 1790s withdrew into the shadows of political culture and the last of the decade's revolutionaries, their democratic, public agitation outlawed, nurtured the radicalism of the clandestine cell and the politics not of mass education and mobilization but of armed uprising and the terror of the deed. It was a distortion of authority's own making, but it posed a considerable challenge.

An outbreak of naval mutinies in April and May 1797 blockaded the Thames and threatened to push the government to end hostilities with France. Bred of economic and political motivation, the mutinies constituted a classic case of incipient proletarian rebellion, leavened by the intervention of democratic, Jacobinical ideas (thanks to the influence of members of the London Corresponding Society on the politics of the seamen) but constrained by popular loyalism. This two-sided process was personified by LCS member Richard Parker, who became the reluctant "admiral" of a "floating republic" of mutinous ships. He went to his execution "a Martyr in the cause of humanity," much disappointed in those rough sailors he had tried to touch with the ideas of The Rights of Man. The attempt to extend the mutinies into a general strike for revolutionary peace failed badly, and Jacobinism was driven further underground.

One mutinous sailor, John Pollard, who led the takeover of a ship at Portsmouth, managed to avoid punishment in spite of striking an officer twice and continued his "seditious and disorderly conduct." Eventually flogged but not prosecuted to the full extent of naval law, which would undoubtedly have led to the gallows, he was turned ashore, sent "as a sick person to the Royal Hospital." He pushed the radical posture too far, however, in 1800 when he was arrested and prosecuted for his tavern toast, "Success to the French," and his rebuke to a loyalist jeer: "Damn & Bugger Government ... for not making peace yet." There is no knowing how many similar toasts were hoisted by the defeated naval mutineers, but among the fifteen thousand Irish sailors and marines the residue of a revolutionary impulse remained.[25]

In Ireland, unmistakable echoes of Jacobinism could be heard in the rise and fall of the insurrectionary United Irishmen, in which staunch republicans such as Wolfe Tone cultivated the belief that a mass uprising of Irish rebels would be aided by the French. By the time the Irish rebellion was launched, however, the hour of possibility had passed; despite efforts by France to aid the 1798 revolt, a bloodbath ensued, a "fratricidal massacre" of the United Irishmen's leaders being one of radicalism's "worst nightmares."[26] Nevertheless, the links between this revolutionary, Jacobin-leaning Irish nationalism and an insurrectionary underground were evident in the dispersed international community of Irish immigrants and exiles. Their reach extended to America where, in the company of English Jacobins, their politics aligned with the rising

Jeffersonian movement, mellowing considerably in the less rigidly hierarchical political economy of the New World. But even here, perhaps,
lies a buried history of nighttime rendezvous and clandestine correspondence. In the loyalist enclave of Upper Canada and neighboring
Francophone Lower Canada there were hints of revolutionary agitations
in the years 1804–1807. Rumors spread of an uprising, thought to be
financed by cattle sales in American markets. The money was to be spent
procuring arms for a ship, said to be outfitted in France, which was to
sail to Lower Canada manned by United Irishmen. One plot's leader was
said to be "as great a Jacobine as any of that Character either in England
or in this country." Another disgruntled yeoman claimed that "he would
wade up to his knees in blood for the cause"; he was for blowing up
His Majesty's garrisons, and boasted that "nothing was then in wanting
for that purpose but the match." It was in England, however, that the
ultra-left of the London Corresponding Society and the thwarted revolutionaries of the United Irishmen merged in the formation of the United
Englishmen, spawning an opaque culture of conspiratorial intrigue and
clandestine revolutionary commitment.[27]

The post-1798 counterrevolutionary panic and the increasingly, and
justifiably, clandestine countenance of Jacobinism collapsed the movement
for liberty further inward, especially in the most pronounced working-
class sectors of the movement. There were abundant indications that a
penchant for wage increases, an end to war, trade-union-like combinations,
and the politics of liberty thrived in manufacturing hamlets, milltowns,
and industrial neighborhoods. In Jacobin Sheffield and its Yorkshire environs, Nottingham, Lancashire, and elsewhere the immediate post-1800
years saw an underground of night agitations, announced by handbills
that appeared mysteriously under doors or were posted on market stalls.
"Shake the earth to its center," declared one revolutionary pronouncement.
It called for an end to high prices, oppressive taxation, and the horrors
of war; it demanded education, support for the aged and distressed, and
the reform of government. The Leeds Mercury complained of frequent midnight meetings of sedition-minded reformers, lurking in their nocturnal
holes "like a lawless banditti." Such dark gatherings were said to be
generalized throughout the West Riding in the winter of 1801–1802. Their
tracks covered well by darkness and deliberate care, the radicals and their
leaders proved an illusive foe to the state. All that could be ascertained
was that a committee known as the Black Lamp, meeting on Friday nights
with some two hundred in attendance, had hatched a plan to force their
demands for the abolition of taxes and enjoyment of democratic political

rights. "On one night the rise was to take place in every quarter," reported the mayor of Leeds. Eventually, two radicals were arrested and sentenced to seven years' transportation. Their trial revealed that they had recruited a thousand "friends of liberty" in the town of Sheffield alone. Members of the underground association, bound together in oaths of secrecy, had manufactured pikes and buried caches of arms in readiness for the uprising. "Directors & Conductors" officered the rebels and drilled them nightly. "Thousands carry about with them a Secret Conviction & Indulge a Hope that Matters are growing Ripe," worried a local official.[28]

The London center of this revolutionary underground was a constellation of taverns frequented by laborers, soldiers, and Irish immigrants. One pub in particular, Furnival's Inn in Fetter Lane, contained a cellar which, as early as 1798, was "the very general resort of the most radical Jacobinical politics in London." Drowning their words of conspiracy and dissent in the atmosphere of a raucous "free and easy singing and debating society," United Irish expatriates, LCS radicals, and other convinced oppositionists met in efforts to link London and the country core of disaffection and organization with Ireland and France. Out of such nightly gatherings would crystallize the United Englishmen (or Britons); in their midst rose to prominence Colonel E. M. Despard, "a mild gentlemanlike man," "singularly good-hearted." This disaffected military figure, who had earned the respect of Lord Nelson, was an Irish officer without wealth or family influence. Having been overlooked for promotion in the spoils of army patronage, banished to the colonies, and recalled to half-pay inactivity in 1790, he served in the ranks of London's Jacobin societies and, with the Irish uprising of 1798, was drawn to increasingly more insurrectionary politics; much of his later life in England was spent in His Majesty's jails. Despard was supported by a devoted common-law wife, Catherine, an African-American woman, possibly once a slave, with whom he had formed a loving union during his colonial outpostings in Jamaica, Honduras, or the Yucatan. Catherine's revolutionary ardor must have pulled Despard through many a dark moment, and it would continue as the Jacobin officer faced his truest test of leadership.

Despard's authority and stature in the radical underground grew throughout 1798–1799, and he was eventually arrested and imprisoned on the basis of allegations that he was organizing a secret military force to strike for freedom and a piece of the state pie. Released in 1800, he continued to work for the cause of treason and revolution in the broad Jacobin underground, now composed of various united brotherhoods and clandestine societies. Whether as its architect (as claimed by the state and his prosecution) or advocate, Despard did aim to forge a revolutionary army that would launch a coup d'état. Proposing to seize the Tower of London and the Bank, the conspiracy planned next to secure the army barracks, break down the walls of prisons, and take the king prisoner. When the mail coaches were stopped, the whole country would know that London had commenced the revolution and would fall into step. The government, knowing of all this through informers since September 1802, in November arrested Despard and forty others, some of them guards-men. Catherine organized the prisoners' wives and made it her business to worry worthies such as the home secretary, Lord Pelham; the sheriff of London thought her an irksome nuisance. In February 1803 Despard and six accomplices were found guilty and condemned to execution.

It was the sorry suppression of the dark desire of a long, hard night of unrelieved repression. In the Despard conspiracy Jacobinism sank in a rough sea of unreality, driven to extremist exasperation by a climate of coercion and cold, implacable power. The colonel had traveled far from the days of "Members unlimited," and of Thelwall's capacity to stand before a known spy, insult him, and suggest he tell his masters the import of a meeting of thousands. In 1802, when Despard was arrested, the Jacobin underground had come to believe that "a revolution was not to be effected by extensive associations ... but by a small party of desperate men, who, having struck one great blow, such as the assassination of the King, and filled the city with consternation, would find thousands to support them." It didn't end this way.

"Behold the head of a traitor," declared the London executioner of Edward Marcus Despard to the London crowd. There had been difficulty in finding someone to erect the scaffold; rumours had circulated that public riots would break out with the execution; and the cabinet decided that it would be prudent not to display the heads of the traitors but to bury them with the corpses. Catherine, penniless with her husband's death, saw to it that the gentle colonel was buried. "Shall Despard's headless corpse walk into every tap-room, to make proselytes an hundred fold?" asked one source. Despard died a martyr to liberty's cause; his execution platform speech to the radical throng, who believed him an innocent victim of a state frame-up, was a final "inflammatory" call to treason, "persevering in infidelity." Interrupted twice by the crowd's cheers, Despard and his comrades went to their death proud and defiant, silent as to any other co-conspirators or other plans. They were condemned, in their own accounts, as friends "to the poor and the oppressed." In the anguished eyes of state power, however, they were monsters, damned as the danger that lurked in the night society of Revolution and Terror. Another monster, whose history in the popular culture of the transgressive night would prove more durable and widespread, could also trace its lineage to the Jacobinism of the 1790s.[29]

6

Monsters of the Night

Historicizing Fantasy

Revolution in France, Jacobinical challenges to the English state, the rights of men *and* women, and the threat of proletarian uprising blurred in the counterrevolutionary panic of the 1790s. To many, this was monstrosity itself, a tragic reversal of the stable order of things that seemed to give birth to an unnatural "chaos of levity and ferocity," a "monstrous tragi-comic scene" of staged oppositions: attraction/repulsion, laughter/tears, affection/scorn, joy/horror. Edmund Burke's *Reflections on the Revolution in France* (1790) railed against the "arbitrary and total destruction" of 1789, condemning the French "monster of a constitution" as an inversion of the body politic, governed by "the shallowest understanding, the rudest hand." "Rage and phrenzy will pull down more in half an hour, than prudence, deliberation, and foresight can build up in a hundred years," concluded Burke.[1]

Belief in monsters predates the Age of Revolution, the hideous creatures of destruction being both myth and metaphor, living entities and repre-sentation of the world turned upside down.[2] Conceptions of monsters grew out of many sociocultural and political processes, including peasant superstition and attraction to the practices of the supernatural as well as ruling-class fears of social unrest and rebellious rumblings among the masses.[3] "What the classical period confined," writes Foucault, "was not only an abstract unreason which mingled madmen and libertines, invalids, and criminals, but also an enormous reservoir of the fantastic, a dormant world of monsters supposedly engulfed in the darkness which had once spewed them forth."[4]

Yet with the Enlightenment's values of rationality and reason the monster ironically attained more secure footing in popular culture, its presence cultivated in a literary genre, the Gothic novel, which harks back to medieval mysticism and magical creations, among them the creatures of the night. Following the publication of Horace Walpole's The Castle of Otranto (1765) a proliferation of texts fantasized, accepted, and explained the eerie and supernatural phenomena of the medieval tale.[5] The Gothic tradition perhaps reached its apogee in an early-nineteenth-century triad: Mary Shelley's Frankenstein (1818), John Polidori's The Vampyre (1819), and Charles Robert Maturin's Melmoth the Wanderer (1820).[6] As Foucault has suggested, there was both continuity and change in this rebirth of the monster. On the one hand, "the fortresses of confinement functioned as a great, long silent memory; they maintained in the shadows an iconographic power that men might have thought was exorcised; created by the new classical order, they preserved, against it and against time, forbidden figures that could thus be transmitted intact from the sixteenth to the nineteenth centuries." On the other, "the images liberated at the end of the eighteenth century were not identical at all points with those the seventeenth century had tried to eliminate," for "something had happened, in the darkness, which detached them from that secret world where the Renaissance, after the Middle Ages, had found them," resulting in a new maze of human contradictions and consequences.[7]

It was in the disappointed and disillusioned aftermath of the French Revolution that the literary construction of the modern monster emerged. The representation was rooted in the very medieval mysticism and magic, with its nocturnal fantasies and potent blood symbolism, which had been decisively vanquished by the revolutionary transformations of the Age of Revolution/Reason.[8] But now it was invested with new contents: "the complicity of desire and murder, of cruelty and the longing to suffer, of sovereignty and slavery, of insult and humiliation."[9] The monster thrived in theatrical productions and popular consciousness.[10] This was because a troubled, if enlightened, cultural elite had need of a suitable metaphor to mask the ugliness of bourgeois society's monstrous creations with even uglier caricatures, as extreme and as grotesque as the mind could imagine.[11] As Gilles Deleuze and Félix Guattari argue, "It is not the slumber of reason that engenders monsters, but vigilant and insomniac rationality."[12] Monsters offer boundaries to bourgeois order at the same time as they threaten to overflow them.[13] "The literature of terror is born precisely out of the terror of a split society, and out of the desire to heal it," concludes Franco Moretti.[14] And such a split and its terrors yet again reproduce the oppositions of day and night, the fear of the monster being the quintessential terror of the dark and its unknowns, of places and spaces where shadowed peoples and experiences nurture powerful challenges that no printed text can quite subdue. However often the monster may be sacrificed on the altar of literary convention, it remains a fearful earthly and earthy presence, the metaphorical power of terror residing less in the imagery of horror than in the horrible realities of human social relations. Haunting humanity, the monster—the desires it awakens and the nightmares it induces— "disappears into the darkness."[15]

As R. E. Foust has argued, this process is less a product of theology than of the psychology of modern men and women. "The monster," he suggests, "mediates between the daylight society of the self-created Ego and the boggy night country of the inchoate and imperfectly repressed Id, which it imaginatively represents.... [It stares] at us loathing and longing from some dark geography lying in a past we attempt repeatedly to forget." Drawing on Freud's essay "The Uncanny," Foust suggests that the creation of the monster is a doubling of the self, an "uncanny harbinger of death" whose grotesque extremism actually provides a representation of the secretly, unconsciously familiar. "[The] uncanny," in Freud's view, "is in reality nothing new or alien, but something which is familiar and old-established in the mind and which has become alienated from it." Its "eternal malevolence, its more-than-human pitifulness, its universal doom" all become, in Foust's Freudian reading of the antagonistic fantasies of the monstrous image, "a chapter in the spiritual autobiography of the human race." It "reconstitutes within us the dark and potent portion of our nature."[16]

Obscured in this homogeneously naturalized reading of fantasy are the historical origins of the Gothic genre, which offer explanations and contextualizations of meaning vital to any appreciation of the monster as a social and, hence, changing construction. Women vampires, for instance, from the time of J. Sheridan Le Fanu's 1872 novel *Carmilla*, articulate transgressive sexualities that subvert rather than confirm order, for Carmilla, in Nina Auerbach's words, is "one of the few self-accepting homosexuals in Victorian or any other literature"—a factor, no doubt, in the utilization of the vampire theme in modern lesbian literature.[17] One writer has suggested that contemporary lesbian vampire film has the capacity "to overturn mainstream gender authority, carrying within it the "potentiality for a feminist revision of meaning [because] in turning to each other, women triumph over and destroy men themselves."[18] Indeed, the entire vampire oeuvre can be read as a homoerotic gender inversion related to and paralleling the construction of the modern identity of homosexuality, which—whatever its accommodations—is never easily reduced to a conformist reproduction of the familialist, gendered, and erotic conventions of bourgeois society.[19] To read the monster historically, then, may suggest a complicated genesis of the Gothic tradition: emerging at the revolution/counterrevolution interface as an erotic fiction that at its root engaged with sexual taboos, it articulated ambivalences that struggled with the awkward challenges and contestations of order in its varied guises.[20] "Never wholly reactionary nor wholly liberatory," the Gothic monster "represents the disruption of categories, the destruction of boundaries, and the presence of impurities," Judith Halberstam has recently argued. The appeal of the monstrous, she concludes, lies not in some instinctual conservatism, as has recently been suggested by pop horror writer Stephen King, but in the "need to recognize and celebrate our own monstrosities."[21]

Thus Bram Stoker's fantastic creation in Dracula (1897), at the high water mark of bourgeois Europe's consolidation, draws on age-old mythologies of the vampire and other night creatures such as werewolves to construct an admittedly sexualized and unambiguously transgressive metaphor of violation, one that can be seen as the monstrosity of capital's accumulative essence, the extraction of surplus value.[22] But it does this by way of an intensely materializing metaphor. The body is placed at the very center of its meaning, introducing into the relations of class the "perversions" of orthodox sexology, which understands the vampire in terms of necrophilia, sadism, and fetishism.[23] What blood is to physiology, value and its production are to political economy. In creating the monster of alienated labor—by which the bulk of humanity is reduced to toiling to produce the dead labor that is capital with its endless, ruthless craving for surplus—capitalism, like the ascetic count in his suspension as the undead, is driven by its accumulative need; it is never satiated, but must always return to seek increased profit, expanded domains, and newer and fresher victims. The productions of the day, rationalized by a century and more of the dismal science composed of the writings of Adam Smith and his intellectual offspring, have their macabre reflection in the horrors of the night. The desire for power and capitalist expansion finds its metaphorical fall in the curse of Dracula, who must consume all rivals, not in the realm of ideas or things but as substance and sustenance of a particular bodily sort. The (un)freedom of the class society that proclaimed its historic advance in the right to acquire succumbs, finally, to the overpowering, frenzied need to subjugate all competitors and reduce the entirety of humanity to a final extractive resource. Dracula is transferred from Transylvania—that othered land beyond the forests, midway between East and West, North and South—to the commercial center of nineteenth-century empire: London.[24] There he will, among the city's "teeming millions, satiate his lust for blood, and create a new and ever widening circle of semi-demons to batten on the helpless, a new order of things." Simply, if ironically, this new order reverses the trajectory of the capitalism/imperialism relation, much as the monster inverts the social relations of the human landscape. That Dracula is ultimately killed by a mysterious American, who is able to mask his own vampire needs in a façade of youthful vitality, is an allegory of competing national capitalisms all too truthful in its representation of global competition and the scramble for world markets at the turn of the century. At precisely the time of the Stoker novel's appearance, the United States was surpassing Britain as the world's preeminent capitalist nation. And as American capital subordinated the globe in the twentieth century, no crucifixes, garlic buds, holy waters, sanctified wafers, or magic flowers would impede its lustful consumption. The wooden stake that might be driven through the all-powerful heart of capital would be that of an organized proletarian opposition. But the revolutionary challenge, mounted most powerfully in 1917, struck first at the metaphorical vampire's most vulnerable refuge, where development betrayed the weakest links in the chain of capitalism's uneven global expansion, a Transylvania of possessive individualism: tsarist Russia.[25]

Decades before Stoker published his *Dracula*, Marx and Engels utilized similar imagery in their depiction of a new ruling class, repeatedly employing the analogy of capital as a vampire-like parasite that "lives only by sucking living labor, and lives the more, the more labour it sucks," dragging "with it into the grave the corpses of its slaves." In *The Condition of the Working Class in England* (1845), Engels drew on this conceptualization when he discussed the much-vaunted philanthropy of the rising capitalist class, dismissing the paltry impact of charity with sarcastic bite: "As though you rendered the proletarians a service in first sucking out their very life blood and then practising your self-complacent, Pharisaic philanthropy upon them, placing yourselves before the world as mighty benefactors of humanity when you give back to the plundered victims the hundredth part of what belongs to them!" Driven to consume excessively, Marx's vampire-like bourgeoisie was identified at the same time that James Malcolm Rymer's *Varney the Vampire* (1845–1847) alarmed the middle classes by reflecting the lack of effective curbs on predatory behavior and the instinct of acquisition that threatened the destruction of all class constraint.

In the *Grundrisse*, Marx repeatedly likened capital to a vampirish body dependent on the soul of living labor, drawing on Gothic imagery to darken his presentation of capitalism's class and moral meanings. In the opposition of the British bourgeoisie and its advocates to the passage of legislation limiting the work day to ten hours, Marx saw proof that industry, "vampire-like, could but live by sucking blood, and children's blood, too" (alluding to the ravages of child labor). Extended working hours, Marx claimed in *Capital*, only "slightly quench[ed] the vampire thirst for the living blood of labour," an endless need that was satisfied, partially but appropriately, by the introduction of the night shift. Dripping with blood, capitalism was a systematic draining of labor, and the vampire bourgeoisie could not let go "while there remains a single drop of blood to be exploited."[26]

Stoker's *Dracula*, and the vampire subgenre of Gothic writing, struggled with this radicalized imagery but attended to its meanings far differently than did Marx and Engels. Like much of the evolving twentieth-century horror genre, the vampire literature attempts to condition a readership always frightened of the monster the better to consolidate ideological convention and to secure repression. As Moretti comments, *Dracula*, a product of capitalism's unambiguous late Victorian triumph, "mirrors and promotes the desire for a capitalism that manages to be 'organic.'" In its dialectical relations, the text reconciles the harsh oppositions of everyday existence by dehistoricizing them. In the process, time is suspended and individual reflection discounted as fear, its powerful suppressants working their capacity to numb. Anything but escapist, such a literature reproduces the social order. Fear overtakes reason; suspense conditions the insecurity that is the fundamental bulwark against oppositional politics. Dracula's message is that of capitalism's continuities, the monster boasting, "My revenge is just begun! I spread it over centuries, and time is on my side."[27]

Historicizing Frankenstein's monster, conceived a century earlier and a product of a more ambivalent moment in the crystallization of bourgeois power, produces a more complicated fantasy of night monsters and their meanings. The literary construction of Frankenstein is a layering of monstrosities. Its author, Mary Wollstonecraft (Godwin) Shelley, was the offspring of parents representing Jacobinical radicalism and a scandalous feminism which refused bourgeois conventions of family and sexuality. Her father, William Godwin, was notorious as a radical of the 1790s, although his resolve was shaken by the actual prospects of revolutionary activism and the lives of those around him who followed principles with practice. Godwin's path first crossed that of Mary Wollstonecraft in 1791, and eventually they forged an intense, tempestuous, and loving union, consummated in the post-1796 days of Jacobin disillusionment.

Mary Wollstonecraft symbolized the nightmarish implosion of gendered conventionalities that arose from the 1790s ferment over equality.[28] She quickly assumed a place of prominence as a "writing woman" and an advocate of women's rights; her publication in 1792 of A Vindication of the Rights of Woman refused to excuse "the tyranny of man" that thwarted the acquisition of female virtue. But her fame as a public defender of women's rights was not matched by success in private life. Twice rejected by men she loved, one having fathered a daughter with her, Wollstonecraft attempted suicide and was, when she met Godwin for the second time, in the process of healing the hurt inflicted on her by a lover of particular insensitivity. Within a matter of months after their meeting in 1796, Wollstonecraft and Godwin had struck up an intimate relationship. Neither was a proponent of marriage, but with the discovery in December 1796 that Mary was pregnant, the two staunch opponents of marriage softened their antipathies. They were joined in wedlock in March 1797.[29]

Their daughter Mary was born at the end of August 1797; Godwin recorded in his diary that she had come, almost predictably, "at night." Wollstonecraft developed puerperal fever and, in considerable pain, died ten days later.[30] Godwin was shattered. Probably motivated by a deep sense of loss he commenced a memoir of Wollstonecraft's life, a defense of her decision to pursue love and liberty against the grain of conventional gender relations. Published at the beginning of 1798, Godwin's Memoirs of the Author of a Vindication of the Rights of Woman appeared at the height of the anti-Jacobinical backlash. This climate of reaction no doubt affected the reception of the grieving radical's defense of his recently departed wife, but the scurrilousness of the reviews was directed more at Mary Wollstonecraft herself, now marked more publicly than ever before as the example of woman's scandalous capacity for immorality. Godwin was attacked in predictable loyalist reviews and ostracized by the respectable literary establishment, but it was Mary Wollstonecraft who was vilified for generations as the womanly evil lurking behind the guise of equality. Typical were these anonymous lines of verse appearing in the Anti-Jacobin Review (1801):

> Then saw I mounted on a braying ass
> William and Mary, sooth, a couple jolly:
> Who married, note ye how it came to pass
> Although each held that marriage was but folly—
> And she of curses would discharge a volley

> If the ass stumbled, leaping pales or ditches—
> Her husband, sans-culottes, was melancholy,
> For Mary, verily, would wear the breeches—
> God help poor silly men from such usurping b———s.

Godwin suffered this abuse with dignity, replying to critics, when attack merited response, with admirable restraint.[31]

Wollstonecraft and Godwin's daughter followed in her mother's footsteps, charting a course of troubled and ambiguous independence early in her life. The younger Mary, tragically, was a child whose desperation drove her to be a woman before she had a chance to be a child. She traveled in literary circles that she regarded as "the elect." Dependent on her father for sole support (material, social, and intellectual), revering his judgment, the daughter left motherless at her birth understandably developed both an idolization of her radical mother—whose status as an icon was promoted by Godwin and a small circle of literary radicals—and a close, perhaps at times unhealthy, attachment to her father, who could be overly cerebral and somewhat coldly demanding in his need for both intellectual and filial devotion. Mary's first book, *Frankenstein, or the Modern Prometheus* (1818) was "respectfully inscribed," not to a dear father, but to "William Godwin, author of *Political Justice, Caleb Williams* & Etc." When in *Mathilda* (1819), she presented a story of a father's incestuous desire for his daughter, however, Godwin called the novella "disgusting and detestable" and refused to return the copy Mary had sent him, undoubtedly sabotaging its publication. Her early writing therefore exhibits a dualism, straddling conventionality and rebellion. As Katherine C. Hill-Miller has suggested, Mary Shelley examined "the ambivalence, horror, and loss characteristic of the female condition, and she located their sources in the individual paternal rejection that became emblematic of the culture's general rejection of the female. She expressed the daughter's affection, guilt, and hostility toward individual and cultural fathers who give too little and expect too much, and expressed her sense that daughterhood, which is a version of and doorway to motherhood, is a deadly proposition." But although she could write this experience, implying the need to transcend it, Mary Shelley herself was trapped in this dualism, unable either to shake its confinements or to accommodate comfortably to them.

Raised as a literary "son," she was expected to assume the familial legacy of writer/reformer, but with adolescent emergence into womanhood her father distanced himself from her, and Mary, having absorbed the expectations of accomplishment upon which she was nursed from infancy, moved decisively but painfully away from him and into the realm of a woman of letters. Once she had secured her place in this world, a kind of "monstrous daughterhood" was overcome, but her father's return into her life laid new demands on her adult, maternal character, for she was expected to provide her ageing patriarchal parent with material support and psychological consolation.

This troubled relationship was marked by a single, sexual, decisive rupture when Mary fell quickly in love with one of her father's admirers, the radical poet Percy Bysshe Shelley. Already married, this young aristocrat at twenty-two was five years Mary's senior, and when they eloped in the summer of 1814, it was an act of rebellion that even the Godwin circle found difficult to accept, for Shelley had abandoned his pregnant wife. Over the next half-decade Mary would suffer the loss of three children, all of whom died before they reached the age of four, and another pregnancy ended in a near-fatal miscarriage; only one son survived to adulthood. Percy, who developed a series of flirtations and sexual liaisons with other women—among them Mary's stepsister Claire Clairmont— died prematurely in 1822, the victim of a drowning accident. Mary, who may well have entered into liaisons of her own when Shelley was alive, later married Thomas Jefferson Hogg, but she was sustained chiefly by a circle of woman friends and her commitment to publish the surviving writings of Percy, her first love and affectionate literary tutor. Like her mother she was a woman whose defiance of convention led her inexorably in the direction of convention's unfortunate and unforgiving tragedies.[32] It may well be that in constructing Victor Frankenstein, the creator of the monster, she drew on the imagined if unconscious conception she harbored of Percy Bysshe Shelley, providing a prophetic statement in which her own future meshed with that of her fiction.[33]

Mary Shelley's *Frankenstein* is a novel of the night, its monster a creature of darkness whose making is a product of the crazed compulsions of science's cloistered evening labors. Victor Frankenstein recalls his discovery of the secret of creation, the product of days and nights of toil, through which finally broke "a light so brilliant and wondrous" that, ironically, it drove him to "midnight labors," as he "dabbled among the unhallowed damps of the grave, or tortured the living animal to animate the lifeless clay." Collecting bones and body parts from graves and charnel houses, his profane fingers probing the decayed matter of the dead, Frankenstein pursues his brilliant researches to the lowliest of locales, even the slaughter-house furnishing some of his materials. In pursuit of the mystery of creation, the scientist is thrust into a darkness from which it is impossible to emerge: "Every night I was oppressed by a slow fever, and I became nervous to a most painful degree.... I grew alarmed at the wreck that I perceived that I had become." And then, "on a dreary night of November" Frankenstein "beheld the accomplishment of [his] toils."

> Did I request thee, Maker, from my clay
> To mould Me man? Did I solicit thee
> From darkness to promote me?—

Startled from the darkness of a disturbed sleep by the ugliness of his creation, he escapes "the demoniacal corpse to which [he] had so miserably given life" and "passe[s] the night wretchedly." When the scientist falls ill, the monster takes his leave, and then, through the monster's killing of Frankenstein's brother, creature and creator are reunited, a process of troubled resentments, rejections, and reconciliations always shrouded in darkness. The plot, as well as the monster's socialization, is advanced through recourse to the night: "It was completely dark when I arrived in the environs of Geneva"; "the scene was enveloped in an impenetrable darkness"; "I passed a night of unmingled wretchedness"; "if there was any moon, or the night was star-lit, I went into the woods, and collected my own food and fuel for the cottage"; "When night came, I quitted my retreat, and wandered in the wood; and now, no longer restrained by the fear of discovery, I gave vent to my anguish in fearful howlings"; "I generally rested during the day, and travelled only when I was secured by night from the view of man"; "He was borne away by the waves, and lost in darkness and distance."[34]

The cover of darkness is thus for Shelley a context in which desire and necessity meet, providing a space for the irreconcilable clashes of modern society, which eclipses justice and equality at the very point that it calls them into being. At the height of their romantic union the Shelleys saw their creative powers as conjoined, the strength and stability of Mary balancing the mercurial brilliance and imaginative creativity of Percy, a Romantic voice frustrated by the worldly materialism that forced them into an itinerant life forever threatened by financial insolvency. "My mind without yours is dead & cold as the dark midnight river when the moon is down," wrote Percy.[35] In the darkness Mary would construct a ghost story that illuminated the night recesses of society's blind spots, where the oppressions of gender and race and the exploitations of class found their metaphorical residence in what would become the classic Gothic tale of monstrosity.

Frankenstein, like the Gothic genre of which it is a cornerstone, is obviously, if ironically, gendered. The creator and the created are masculine prototypes, to be sure—the one of tortured mind and morality; the other of grotesque bodily matter, a "creature." It is a terrifying tale, but in a twisting difference that separates it from many other scripts of the supernatural constructed to induce horror, there is no heroine, no female victim who can draw out the woman's capacity to retreat into unfathomable fear, engaging—in both text and readership—the chivalrous intervention of male rescue. One critic has even suggested the appropriateness of subtitling the text *Men without Women*.[36]

Nevertheless, though superficially a male text, *Frankenstein* is an obviously womaned book and one guided by a sense of the monstrosity of women's lives. As a woman whose mother died of the complications of her birth, herself a woman who had by her early twenties seen her children die and one pregnancy terminate in near fatality, Mary Shelley—as countless critics have shown—constructed her account with a decided eye to how her "hideous progeny" exposed the tense anxieties, brutal terror, and deadly consequences of birthing.[37] The idealization of motherhood, often a male construction and likely one that permeated the Romantic milieu in which Mary Shelley was immersed, is criticized from a distance in *Frankenstein*: the author genders the monster's birth as male creation, distancing it from the womanly virtue of maternalism.[38] The gender inversion allows an earthy assessment of birth's material ugliness, which takes place in "the filthy workshop of creation," a phrase of almost misogynist connotations.[39] Victor Frankenstein, beholding his creation, responds in a language that mocks motherly adoration, juxtaposing wonderment and disgust, constructing the "child" in whom the scientist father/mother has invested two years of labor as a being of beautiful revulsion:

> How can I describe my emotions at this catastrophe, or how delineate the wretch whom with such infinite pains and care I had endeavoured to form? His limbs were in proportion, and I had selected his features as beautiful. Beautiful!—Great God! His yellow skin scarcely covered the work of muscles and arteries beneath; his hair was of a lustrous black, and flowing; his teeth of pearly whiteness; but these luxuriances only formed a more horrid contrast with his watery eyes, that seemed almost of the same colour as the dun white sockets in which they were set, his shriveled complexion and straight black lips.[40]

When the creature reaches out to touch his creator, his countenance wrinkled in the raw imperfection of the newly born, Victor Frankenstein flees in fear, and much of the novel then addresses the shame and guilt of this traumatic rejection and its awful social consequences.[41]

Anne K. Mellor has suggested that "*Frankenstein* is a book about what happens when a man tries to have a baby without a woman." That may well be an insight of particular strength into Mary Shelley's ambivalent politics of femininity, in which the aggressive self of the womanly writer was forever entangled in the subordinations of daughter, lover, and mother.[42] But more suggestive, perhaps, is the possibility that Frankenstein is about the fear and loathing of birth that many articulate Age of Reason women must have suppressed as their protestations of the need for equality were smiled on benevolently by the William Godwins of Romanticism, the ultimate challenge of the hideous progeny being beyond their male grasp. To have creation become the provenance of men, Shelley may have understood, would allow its fearful meanings and disturbing consequences, even perhaps its "filthiness," to be addressed for the first time. Perhaps Frankenstein is the daughter's conclusion to the mother's A Vindication of the Rights of Woman, posed in the masculinization of experience that alone could give voice to the biological discontents that no abstract treatise on equality might address.[43]

In other ways as well, Frankenstein addressed the gendered construction and confinement of an early-nineteenth-century context. Johanna M. Smith and Mary Poovey have commented at length on the tyrannical dichotomization of masculine public avocation (in the sciences and arts) and the privatized femininity of domestic propriety. It is a process that grows outward in the monstrous confinements of family that encase the Frankensteins of the novel and the Godwin–Shelley circle, pushing Mary herself out of youthful radicalism toward a myriad of gendered adult accommodations.[44] In its treatment of technology, the novel presents a forceful analytic repudiation of the objectification of nature as the gendered feminine and science as the gendered masculine, a project of "patriarchal encoding of the female as passive and possessable, the willing receptacle of male desire."[45] The monster emerges as the product of Victor's male ambition. He—who was ironically born of a mother who "had much desired to have a daughter"—is driven by a "fervent longing to penetrate the secrets" of creation and succeeds only by the light of the moon in pursuing "nature to her hiding-places."[46] But the positive potential of science as a liberator of humanity, possibly even an emancipatory force in lessening women's biologically overdetermined oppression, can not be easily dismissed. The creature's creation thus reveals science as a complex amalgam of repressed, sublimated sexuality (the penetration of the "fortifications and impediments that seemed to keep human beings from entering the citadel of nature"); male usurpation of women's command over nurture, broadened to a gendered nature of secret recesses; and perhaps an enlightened force in lessening the physical travails of humanity—birthing foremost among them.[47]

The trauma of birthing and its social ramifications are also the silent presence at *Frankenstein*'s end. The monstrosity of the text's inverted relations, with science's promise and perversions all too apparent, is nowhere more evident than in Victor Frankenstein's anguished horror of responsibility, when he weights his personal relief against the ominous outcome of his freedom from the monster. Asked to create a female with whom the monster can live in "the interchange of those sympathies necessary for [his] being," the scientist at first reluctantly agrees, hoping to secure release from the nightmare of his creation, who has consented to a voluntary and benevolent exile beyond the reach of ("civilized") humanity if his wish is granted. Victor secures the placidity of the monster with the promise to furnish him with a companion, dismissing him with the Conradesque words "depart, depart and leave me in darkness."[48] But he finds himself incapable of honoring his commitment, fearing the global consequences of such an act. In creating a man, his science of discovery was a singular accomplishment, whatever its abominations. But if he were to create a woman, the outcome would be too terrifying to countenance.

At this point Victor Frankenstein faces frontally the true, gendered power of creation, over which males have historically had only limited knowledge:

> Even if they were to leave Europe, and inhabit the deserts of the new world, yet one of the first results of those sympathies for which the daemon thirsted would be children, and a race of devils would be propagated upon the earth, who might make the very existence of the species of man a condition precarious and full of terror. Had I a right, for my own benefit, to inflict this curse upon everlasting generations? I had before been moved by the sophisms of the being I had created; I had been struck senseless by his fiendish threats; but now, for the first time, the wickedness of my promise burst upon me; I shuddered to think that future ages might curse me as their pest, whose selfishness had not hesitated to buy its own peace at the price, perhaps, of the existence of the whole human race.

He could not enter into this night of transgression. And the monster's revenge, suitably, is not to kill Victor in immediate wrath but to promise the scientist the same truncated fate that he has been forced to accept. "I will be with you on your wedding night" is the unambiguous and terrifying final threat to Victor's identity, patriarchal and masculine, and the monster does eventually strangle Frankenstein's beloved Elizabeth. This gendered reading parallels another monstrosity, for it is Victor Frankenstein's final fear of creating a race of monsters that imperils monster and creator, forcing their reciprocal, fugitive journeys of vengeance and death.[49]

Race may seem to be a distant fear in the hierarchy of Shelley's monsters, but *Frankenstein* has proved a transgressive text in societies committed to race purity: it was banned as indecent and objectionable in apartheid South Africa in 1955, and Nationalists there were chastised in 1972 for creating a "political Frankenstein which is pointing the way to a non-white political revival." (Also prohibited by the apartheid state was the high camp, gender-bending, *Frankenstein*-inspired 1970s film, *The Rocky Horror Picture Show*, starring Tim Curry as the extraterrestrial, transsexual, erotically motivated Frank N. Furter and featuring such soundtrack productions as "Over at the Frankenstein Palace," "Touch-A, Touch-A, Touch Me," "Sweet Transvestite," and "I Can Make You a Man.")[50]

Scorned and condemned to an intolerable isolation because of his physical difference, the monster is obviously not of the white race that peoples the European text. The point at which Mary Shelley produced the novel was one in which racialized categories of difference were being forged in the crucible of empire formation and the radical cause of the abolition of slavery. H. L. Malchow has recently suggested that Shelley would have been aware of "the wider, enfolding, external environment of shifting values, attitudes and observations" that consolidated in popular racial thought and that likely combined comfortably with the "black theodicy" of Miltonesque allegories of Satanic otherness, upon which *Frankenstein* obviously drew.[51] Gayatri Chakravorty Spivak notes that the proliferating inversions at the core of Shelley's construction of monstrosity include the reversal and dispacement of traditional gender roles: male power, usually deployed in constituting the subject of subordination within imperialism's economic and military agendas, is forced to adapt to the idiom of constraining sexual reproduction, which is not the conventional colonial masculinist practice. *Frankenstein* thus combines the language of racism and the "hysteria of masculinism," ever worried about patriarchial lineage and progeny, in a preemptive genocidal strike against the horror of racialized malignant procreations.[52]

Shelley's monster, as Malchow suggests, is also othered in racial ways: his size alone would have been reminiscent for literati such as Shelley of the almost superhuman strengths and features mythologized as characteristic of African blacks. With "dull yellow eyes," "black lips," "lustrous black hair," and skin the color and texture of "a mummy" (that is, a parched brown or "black"), the monster was presented as hideous in ways not unlike those commonly adopted in the social construction of racial physiognomy. In his pathetic wretchedness, moreover, the monster resembled the debased and enslaved Africans whom many radicals believed capable of the worst atrocities and the most wanton sexual indulgences, specifically because oppression and ostracism had denied them the civilizing grace of education and enlightenment. The monster was a savage much as the savages of other races were monstrous: they were creations of their superiors. And nothing physiologically presented this contrast more clearly than Victor Frankenstein's creature. With his animalistic bulk, low-browed countenance, and dull demeanor, he is a dark inversion of Frankenstein's angelic Elizabeth, an Aryan beauty classically adorned with golden hair and cloudless crystal blue eyes, "a being heaven sent, and bearing a celestial stamp in all her features." Gender and race constructions and phobias blurred into the Frankenstein monster's "savage" revenge on his creator's Teutonic beauty, an "unmanly" assault that may have brought to mind sexualized images of black males ravaging white womanhood. It is possible that Shelley actually anticipated rather than reflected such sexualized racism, her novel being written before the Victorian hardening of such lurid associations.

But as Malchow and Chris Baldick have suggested, such images were transferred to various racialized others throughout the Victorian period, the caricatured Irish Frankenstein becoming a popular motif in the mass marketing of ethnic prejudice over the course of the middle to late nineteenth century. Thomas Carlyle racialized the monster Irish in passages of literary diatribe that solidified conservative phobias of French Revolution–inspired democracy and bitterly xenophobic attack. The Irish, often dubbed the sans-Potato, were portrayed as a material and political retributive scourge on mid-nineteenth-century English society. Carlyle's Irish are Frankensteinized as "Huge Democracy, walking the streets everywhere in its Sack Coat." Popular magazines such as Punch routinely reacted to Irish nationalist mobilizations—Daniel O'Connell's Repeal Movement of the 1840s or Charles Stewart Parnell's campaigns of the 1880s—by printing woodcuts of the threatening monster of Irish rebellion stirred by aspirations of political independence and Home Rule.[53] An almost generic racialized savagery was evident in Thomas Edison's first cinematic depiction of Frankenstein's monster in a 1910 silent film. The monster was a horror to behold, then, because in his savage extremes he threatened the worst of the nightmarish imaginings of the political status quo, the dangers of an uninhibited masculinity, and the unknown terror of racialized otherness. His hideousness worked upon the minds of genteel reformers and a wider populace precisely because it also intersected with the crass construction

6. Irish
Frankenstein,
Punch (1882).

of the proletariat—to the bourgeois age, the most common and dangerous monstrosity.

Victor Frankenstein's creation is a monster who strives for sociability
but is denied the basic warmth and companionship of humanity; he is
a living being who, ironically, seems to need human contact far more
than does his creator, a crazed and aloof man driven by the compulsion
that ultimately destroys him.[54] The monster values labor and knows its
worth, sympathizing with the poor cottagers from whom he learns the
art of language and something of the meaning of existence. But as he
comes to know them from the distance of his undetected observations,
he realizes that he is a creature divorced from the collective experience
of both individual and class formation. Deprived of a past, family, childhood, and the capacity to work, he is estranged not only from his nonexistent peers, but also from his self, which he can know only in the
most rudimentary way. He lives in darkness, both literally and figuratively:

7. Reform Bill
Frankenstein,
Punch (1867).

given the instantaneous nature of his creation, his knowledge of himself
is confined to the immediacy of his short time on earth, a life spent in
hiding and retreat, in which only the night affords him the opportunity
of acquiring the basic necessities of survival. He is propertyless and
powerless, marked by his impoverished nature, which identifies him to
all he has contact with as the truly alien being that he is. Even when he
engages in selfless acts of good will, he is repudiated and reviled. Frankenstein's monster is thus the proletarian at his most debased, an isolated and
endangered self, an individual ostracized, stripped of collectivity and
humanity, reduced to the solitary estrangements of acute marginalization:

> I learned that the possessions most esteemed by your fellow-creatures
> were high and unsullied descent united with riches. A man might be
> respected with only one of these advantages; but, without either, he was

considered, except in very rare circumstances, as a vagabond and a slave, doomed to waste his powers for the profits of the chosen few! And what was I? Of my creation and my creator I was absolutely ignorant; but I knew that I possessed no money, no friends, no kind of property.... When I looked around, I saw and heard of none like me. Was I then a monster, a blot upon the earth, from which all men fled, and whom all men disowned?[55]

Writing in the aftermath of disillusionment with the French Revolution's decline into conservatism, and on the heels of the abdications and defeats of the radical English Jacobins, Shelley is not just depicting the monstrous proletariat. She is elaborating on its defeat and alienation, its inevitable collapse inward as the promise and potential of collective class consciousness faded in the post-1800 years.

Shelley's monster is thus not only hideous; it is repressed and, in the process, pressured into tragic acts of self-destruction. Such a perspective is exactly what we might expect from a Jacobin in retreat, once committed to the cause of reform but chastened by its increasingly gritty working-class substance. Thus, in September 1817, between the completion of *Frankenstein* and its publication, Mary Shelley wrote to Percy Bysshe Shelley of her fears of William Cobbett's agitations among the poor, which she thought designed to foster blood conflict: "He appears to be making out a list for proscription—I actually shudder to read it—a revolution in this country would [not?] be bloodless if that man has any power in it. He encourages in the multitude the worst possible human revenge."[56] And when the monster speaks, its words are fearful indeed: to Victor Frankenstein's defiant "Never will I create another like yourself, equal in deformity and wickedness," the creature replies in anger: "Remember that I have power, I can make you so wretched that the light of day will be hateful to you. You are my creator, but I am your master." The modern Prometheus, with an unyielding will, noble suffering, and concern for mankind, has been perverted by proletarianization, an alienating experience of hurt and deprivation that leaves only the embittered anguish of venom and retribution: "I had feelings of affection, and they were requited with detestation and scorn.... Your hours will pass in dread and misery, and soon the bolt will fall which must ravish for you your happiness forever. Are you to be happy, while I grovel in the intensity of my wretchedness? ... I am fearless, and therefore powerful ... you shall repent of the injuries you inflict."[57] What the bourgeoisie creates, ultimately, is also what can destroy it, as Marx pointed out: "Not only has the bourgeoisie forged the weapons that bring death to itself; it has also called into existence the men who are to wield those weapons—the modern working class—the proletarians.... What the bourgeoisie therefore produces, above all, are its own gravediggers."[58]

This is the "spectre haunting Europe," the proletarian insurrection of revenge that Marx and Engels introduced in the opening pages of The Communist Manifesto (1848), a Gothic fantasy of contrived fear bred of the irreconcilable oppositions of bourgeois and proletariat. As Franco Moretti observes, like the proletariat the monster has no name. Lacking a history, created overnight by an Other, he lacks individuality. He is the product of an assemblage of parts, not unlike a working class drawn together from the dispossessions and destructions of enclosures, forced migrations, and impoverishments associated with the breakup and agonizingly long death march of the feudal body. The result is a physical articulation of the deforming difference that designated capital and labor as unequal in an age that proclaimed equality to be the right of all human beings. Yet the more this rational, enlightened, civilizing order, with its advances in technology and science, took the productive process in its grip, the more misshapen the worker, as Marx noted in Capital. The process lies at the center of Frankenstein: what Victor Frankenstein conceives is beautiful and life-enhancing, a mystery solved in the interests of humanity; what he creates is ugliness, an evil of prodigious and threatening hideousness. The novel, like bourgeois order, is a progression of negations: whatever "man" is, the monster is not—but their fates are intertwined.[59] And the monster will be remembered not as Other but as Frankenstein; historically, he overshadows his creator, appropriating his name in popular culture and memory.

The truly insightful centerpiece of Mary Shelley's Frankensteinian under-standing of the making of bourgeois society was thus the distorting reciprocity in capitalism's class relations, her book's allegorical elaboration of the double-edged character of the modern Prometheus being especially pertinent in the early to middle nineteenth century.[60] What Marx's dialectical inversions underscored was the two-sided meaning of capitalist creation: the monstrosity was not simply the making of a debased sector of humanity, condemned to alienated labor, but the refraction of that process back into the creationist process, resulting in the duplication of the monster: "The capitalist produces labor as alien; labor produces the product as alien. The capitalist produces the worker, and the worker the capitalist." As the literary critic Martin Tropp has noted: "Linked in life and death, Frankenstein and Monster are separate entities and one being. The power of technology gives Frankenstein's dream self a concrete reality and a separate existence, allowing it to act out its maker's fantasies with terrible results." In 1856 Marx would pose this Frankensteinian dilemma with disturbing acuteness:

> In our times everything seems pregnant with its contrary. Machinery, gifted with the wonderful power of shortening and fructifying human labor, we behold starving and overworking it. The new-fangled sources of wealth, by some strange weird spell, are turned into sources of want. The victories of art seem bought by the loss of character. At the same pace that mankind masters nature, man seems to become enslaved to other men or to his own infamy.... All our invention and progress seem to result in endowing material forces with intellectual life, and in stultifying human life into a material force.

Seventy-five years later, as radical working-class communists met in places such as New York City, they would hear speeches on the "Frankenstein" of capitalist production.[61]

The answer provided by Marx and subsequent revolutionaries to the dead end of capitalism's Frankenstein-like social relations was revolution. It was precisely what Mary Shelley—who, when she wrote Frankenstein, was a member of an increasingly disillusioned circle of the Jacobin intelligentsia and, later in her life, an advocate of bourgeois proprieties—could not countenance. Her novel ends with a prophetic journey, symbolic of capitalism's highest stage: imperialism. As Victor and his creature find Europe too constrained for their expanding antagonism, the quest for a resolution of their monstrous relationship takes them to the outer limits of the earth's surface. "The need of a constantly expanding market for its products chases the bourgeoisie over the whole surface of the globe," declared Marx and Engels in The Communist Manifesto.[62] In the novel the private war of Victor and his creation ends in the mutual destruction of the isolating maker, whose compulsions lead him to his death, and the isolated monster, whose reluctant fall into the darkness of revenge weighs heavily on his soul as he flees the murder of his creator, setting off into the cold night of an Arctic exile that will supposedly end in suicide. In her monster of the night, Shelley anticipated the transgressive trajectory of a radical repudiation of self-destruction and immobilization, but this was a light too blindingly revolutionary for her to accept. She remained trapped in the darkness of her social station, which, however reform-minded, could never really shake its fears of the gravedigging working class that threatened to turn day into night and night into day, burying the conventionalities of power. The modern Prometheus of Frankenstein thus ends in monstrosity's continuities, lived out in the dark recesses of estranged labors and the displaced subordinations of racially riven empire.

PART IV

Exchange Relations, Empire's Underside, and Early Capitalism

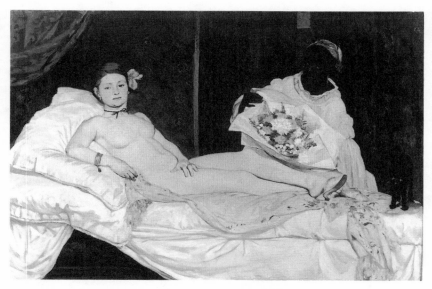

8. Edouard Manet, *Olympia* (1863), Musée d'Orsay, Paris.

7

Productions of the Night

Dark and Dangerous Labors

Lofty ideals animated the thought of the Age of Revolution. But property remained a fortress of power, and in the place of kings stood capital. Money was the symbol of its governing authority; accumulation, the material law and logic of its being. As the bourgeois revolutions of the late eighteenth century consolidated particular forces and as the increasing impersonality of productive relations locked workers—men, women, or children—into the status of proletarians, the heights of abstraction associated with the *philosophes* and their discourses of liberty, equality, and fraternity faded into the seemingly more mundane contests over what limits would be placed on the exploitation of labor. The ubiquitous struggle exposed the essential division of capital and labor, their antagonisms as fundamental as the foundational separations of day and night.

Marx reserved some of his more impassioned vitriol for his analysis of the working day, a subject, he thought, that exposed the rapacious inhumanity of capitalism. Facing "nibbling and cribbling at their meal times," nineteenth-century laborers were the victim of capital's relentless "petty pilferings of minutes," a process of theft that lengthened the working day with meaningful consequences for employers. "If you allow me to work only ten minutes in the day over-time," one master explained, "you put one thousand a year in my pocket." His conclusion was an exacting metaphorical accounting of bourgeois vision, powerfully terse in conveying the ledger-like measure of capital's scrutiny of the productive process and its human relations: "Moments are the elements of profit." Especially appalling were the fifteen hour days reported by children, no older than nine, who from the age of seven had been at their work six days a week, from 6:00 A.M. until 9:00 P.M. Nothing incensed Marx more than this "coining of children's blood into capital."[1]

To the question "What is the working day?" Marx replied that it is little more than an act of theft, an appropriation undertaken by a crazed capital, with deleterious consequences for the worker. With labor thus commodified and alienated, reduced to a mere mechanism of production, capital's ultimate power was reflected in its suppression of nature—its obliteration of the difference of day and night, and its subordination of all time to the dictates of production and profit: "Even the ideas of day and night, of rustic simplicity in the old statutes, became so confused that an English judge, as late as 1860, needed a quite Talmudic sagacity to explain 'judicially' what was day and what was night. Capital celebrated its orgies." And so it was that "in place of the pompous catalogue of the 'inalienable rights of man' comes the modest Magna Carta of a legally limited working day," one that Marx insisted should "make clear 'when the time which the worker sells is ended, and when his own begins.'"

The history of nineteenth-century class relations is littered with factory acts supposedly protecting workers and limiting the hours of labor, as well as working-class mobilizations to secure the shorter working day— a testimony to the epic confrontations over the boundaries that would define the space and time of productive activities. Few such legislative enactments had the teeth required to bite into capital's feeding frenzy on labor, and if working-class struggle over the length of the working day was able to secure some minor concessions from employers, the battle would have to be fought and refought throughout the nineteenth and twentieth centuries. Some workers therefore took it upon themselves to establish the night as their own time, a space for productions that they defined as opposed to those of an exploitive process that appropriated their output for the benefit of others. Transgression had its transparently material aspects.

A contingent of mid-nineteenth-century French workers, many of whom aligned themselves with various oppositional, utopian socialist movements, sought to claim their nights in reconstitution of their identities. Their days of exploitation and precarious lives of want, need, and insecurity were pushed to the backs and corners of their nights of production and creativity, evening labors spent in the writing of poems and prose that attached these workers not to the material self-interest of workers' struggle but to the literary and philosophical aspirations of their class Other, the bourgeoisie.[2] This, of course, was one measure of marginalization, a class denial of worldly travails that sought its particular solace in the spaces of the night.

But early capitalism's darkest work was not usually of this sort. Rather, it was associated with the dishonorable trades, labor unmistakably defined by squalor, suffering, and sweat rather than by skill and security. By the early nineteenth century many trades had been darkened by the shadows of sweated labor and subcontracting systems which, if they did not overtake the production of goods in a specific economic sector, restructured the wages and conditions of all workers.[3] Often associated with the exchange relations of an ossified mercantile capitalism, sweating and subcontracting were systems of production that bypassed the factory system and direct employment by creating a layer of middlemen who supplied producing capitalists with goods and services drawn from a reserve army of labor that was hungry for whatever piece of the wage pie it could secure. Without the costs of overhead associated with sanitary and safe facilities, unencumbered by union regulations or restricted hours of labor, these innovations were the underside of capitalist social relations. Often hidden from direct and obvious view, they distanced workers from one another and from their employers, passing the price of exploitation down the line of working-class "power." They encouraged the self-exploitation of families and children, thereby absolving large capital from responsibilities that social protest had demanded and state legislation was supposed to enforce. Sweating and subcontracting thus fed the coffers of the capitalist enterprise, swelling its accumulative appetite, but they did so not in the open day of acquisition but in the nocturnal recesses of a process of production cloaked in night's darknesses and ambiguities.

This coming together of debasement, evening toil, and the sweated exchange of the subcontracting system affected diverse sectors of early capitalism's labor force, from woodworkers and building tradesmen to the gendered divisions of the needle trades. The classic locale of capitalist night work, however, was the bakery, a workplace that foreshadowed the rise of sweating in many industrial sectors. Bakers had a long history of honorable accomplishment, cultivated in early artisanal expressions of their guild origins and indispensable role in providing society with the staff of life. When American bakers marched in support of the ratification of the newly independent nation's Constitution in 1788, they displayed proudly a huge "Federal Loaf" and proposed the motto "May our country never want bread." In early nineteenth-century parades of civic and developmental celebration, bakers linked their centrality in community well-being to their origins in medieval times. But centuries of heritage would unwind as the baker's image, both self-constructed and popularly generated, darkened under the impact of night work.[4]

Eighteenth- and nineteenth-century urban tastes and the problem of perishability dictated that bread be fresh, hot, and available for morning purchase. Bakers thus came to symbolize the limitless exploitation of capitalist production, their working day stretched to fifteen and sixteen hours, six or seven days a week. Some in the trade worked 365 days a year. Always tired, the baker was occasionally feted by his appreciative customer, one thankful French admirer commenting in 1788, "He burns the midnight oil for me, let us salute him." But more often than not the working baker was out of daylight sight and thus forgotten by minds that little appreciated the labors of the night. The baking environment was one of unhealthy extremes, alternating between searing heat and chilly dampness, and the basement "caves" of production were dirty, low-ceilinged, and poorly ventilated. Throughout the night the groans of bakers and apprentices could be heard in the side streets adjacent to the dungeonlike workshops, "a painful and savage cry" that George Sand likened to that of "the last scene of murder." In fact, baking was known to produce broken bodies: the baking boys who stood in the doorways of the shops, covered in flour, were sallow and haggard, reminding passers-by of scarecrows.

The endless night toil was what the bakers protested in union efforts and labor politics. "The night, a time of rest, is for us a time of torture," complained the journeymen bakers of Paris as early as 1715 in an attempt to draw attention to their general "misery." For centuries, bakers would protest that night work was "against the laws of nature," and they repeatedly claimed that the inversion of night and day associated with the trade perverted life and reduced it to an animalistic level. Tired of living like "bats," the prisoners of a "nocturnal slavery" sought to escape the incarcerating segregation of night work, which they judged made them a class apart from society, a "vulgar and brutal" group despised and despoiled by the deprivations of an unnatural rhythm of production:

> 'Tis six at night,—see! who goes there
> With faltering steps and looks of care,
> His eyes half closed and visage wan—
> An object of pity to gaze upon?
> Who is he, and what can his calling be,
> He looks so haggard and pale to see!
> 'Tis the Baker, who toils both night and day
> In heat and steam, for his humble pay.
> ... United be, and spare no pains,—
> The white slave yet shall break his chains.

Laboring "in silence and in darkness, trapped in the stifling heat of the bakeroom, enveloped in smoke and flour dust, at a time of night when all of Nature is at rest," bakers were a craft driven underground, into the depths of dark and dangerous obscurities. Night work had taken them from proud productive citizenship to a lost world of "white" slavery whose dark leitmotifs were articulated in terms of "purgatory," "hell," "captivity," "torture," "prison," and "forced labor."[5]

If trades once honorable and honored could be brought to such debasement by night labor it is not surprising that those less ensconced in a former identity of privilege suffered equally. Servants, whose presence in particular homes signaled the affable affluence associated with cherished middle- and upper-class status, might snatch moments of the day for rest, away from the watchful eye of mistress or master. But their nights were long, and six hours of sleep was a rarity for the servant, four a more normal—and inadequate—respite. Brought into the homes of the bourgeoisie, made responsible for its dirt and its dinner, its children and its character, servants were the dark class difference of the emerging capitalist order, an exploited group that imported the contradictions of dependency into the very bedrooms of intimate domesticity. As such, they were uniquely situated in the awkward relations of property and propriety, a layer of the laboring classes that was at once capable of being bathed in pious affection or criminalized as deviant, undependable, or worse. Not surprisingly, female servants—second only to prostitutes, whose ranks they often found themselves reduced to—were the most likely women to end up in jail, charged with drunkenness or theft, the true prodigal daughters of the familialist order.[6] Servant work was isolating, its freedoms few, its days long, and its nights occupied.[7]

It was not, moreover, without its truly dark and bizarre narratives, for the cauldron of conventionality associated with domesticity and service could bubble over into transgressions that inverted, distorted, and recast the class and gender conformity of Victorian social relations. This was most emphatically the case in the strange world constructed by Arthur Munby—a Victorian civil servant, photographer, barrister, poet, and obsessional night traveler—and a maid-of-all-work, the amazingly versatile Hannah Cullwick, who became his secret wife. Together, Munby and Cullwick, who have become something of an analytic cause célèbre for cultural studies, elaborated an intensifying fantasy world of domestic deception and unusual fetishes in the night of the power/subordination reciprocity that was pivotal to familial service in general, with its endless reproduction of a domesticity riven by class and gender.[8]

Munby, raised by another maidservant named Hannah, was an obscure Victorian gentleman occupying the fringes of Christian-socialist and workers' education circles. His paid post with the Ecclesiastical Commission proved something of a bore and a burden to him, but its leisurely employment and assured income gave him the freedom to indulge his true interest: the fetishization of women's rough labors. Never having worked with anything heavier than a pen, Munby was fixated on the muscular femininity, reddened hands, broad shoulders, and sooty physicality of the street women of London and the provinces. He photographed, sketched, and collected representations of hundreds of such women, among them colliery girls, farm servants, flower sellers, scrubwomen, laundresses, prostitutes, and others who seemed to reverse conventional gender physiology, from circus performers and girl acrobats to the eight-foot, one-inch "Gentle Giantess" of Nova Scotia, whom he met at the Egyptian Hall in 1869.

Obsessed by his voyeuristic need to encounter women capable of overshadowing men with their strength and brawn, Munby was but the dark neurosis of a generalized bourgeois fascination with commingled sexuality and labor, subordination and dirt, which surfaces elsewhere in less outrageously fetishistic quarters and undoubtedly reflected an unconscious ambivalence. Sheltered from both physicality and strenuous labor by their class station yet educated to regard the service of work as man's proper calling and raised by women of the working classes, Victorian gentlemen were curiously confined. Bred to occupations that were abstracted from exertion, accustomed to divorce the bodily sensuality of both labor and sexuality from the refinements of the home and the ethics of genteel work, and dependent on the washings, cradlings, and feedings of their working-class servants, these men of the rising middle class nurtured longings and attractions that spoke to the *domestication* of their lives, with its attendant class and gender ramifications. Thus, the French painter Edgar Degas, writing to a friend during a visit to New Orleans, expressed his incredulity at the beauty of everything around him—but confessed that he would "exchange it all for one Paris laundry girl with bare arms."[9]

Munby's bare-armed girl was Hannah Cullwick, whom he met in 1854 and with whom he carried out a clandestine relationship that involved a wide array of ritualized and fetishistic behaviors, including cross-dressing, role playing (slave/master and infantile regression), bondage, discipline, and hand, foot, boot, and dirt worship. When Cullwick accompanied Munby on continental trips, she dressed as a lady of substantial means, an act of class transvestism, but she also at times donned masculine attire and cropped her hair to pass as a man, wore chains as symbols of her domination, and blackened herself with soot. For his part, Munby willingly nestled in Hannah's ample lap, cradled in her huge arms, and nursed like an infant. The relationship was one of mutual agreements and negotiations (or at least as reciprocal as any male/female relations), and although they married secretly in 1873, Hannah chose to remain, in her words, Massa's "slave." It was a station she preferred to that of "wife" and one which she regarded as the equal of that of any "vulgar man." She absolutely refused to enter society as a proper Victorian mistress, and continued to live and labor as a rough maidservant, stealing her nights to be with Munby. Perhaps her Massa had trained her all too well. Some critics suggest that Munby's years of disciplined teaching, in which he apprenticed Hannah to the lowest and most servile of work, where subservience was fetishized as her freedom and degradation as the badge of love, bore their ultimate perversion in a permanent incarceration in drudgery. Others, however, stress Hannah's active involvement in her own making as a woman liberated by a fetishistic manipulation of "the slavish obedience to conventions of power"; such commentators see a sadomasochistic theater governed by an "economy of conversion." This reading of the Munby–Cullwick relation highlights the inversion of hegemonic roles of authority and subservience.

It was at night, hidden from the public scrutiny of conventionality, that much of this transgressive sociosexuality unfolded and that Hannah's independence was lived. During the day she scrubbed and cleaned the homes and shoes of the master class, whose aversions to her dirt, her powerful stride, her bulging biceps, and her rough demeanor shielded her from the necessity of ladylike behavior. Her labors done, however, Hannah "[went] out alone to public houses at night, walk[ed] through crowds of drunken men without fear, wander[ed] at night across fields and waste ground, and all without molestation or harassment." Munby, the Massa, no doubt appreciated the extent to which his slave was free in ways that he was not. After their marriage, Hannah insisted that she be paid wages for her domestic labors; she had no desire to be a mother; she kept her own lowly quarters and preferred cleaning to the easy chair, soft music, and vacuous pleasures of the bourgeois parlour. Her slave bracelet, which she chose freely, was to her preferable to the marriage license and the wedding band.[10]

The spaces for servility, subordination, and sex created by Arthur Munby and Hannah Cullwick were a secret enclave in a Foucauldian underworld, a place purchased by certain forms of power associated with gender and class where, in darkness, two individuals might reorder power to their mutual satisfaction. The sadomasochistic fetishism of this enterprising risk worked, apparently, for Hannah and Munby, playing, as Foucault might suggest, the practices of power backward in rituals of reversal that codified desire.[11] But the limits of their night world were always profoundly obvious. Their eroticized games of postured class and gender place worked precisely because they mirrored exactly the daily routine of bourgeois society without shattering its material fragilities: Hannah would scrub the doorsteps of Munby's home while he sauntered down the street, jauntily swinging his cane; Munby would check into a boarding house where Hannah worked in order to be waited on by her. This was all the functionalist reproduction of order and subordination; the transgressive embrace of gentleman and maidservant (which itself cloned many an unspoken seduction), the posed photographs, the cross-dressing excursions, the stroking of boots, and blackening and washing of bodies were concealed and covered in darkness both real and metaphorical. And yet it had all begun with a voyeurism that was far more generalized. Munby and Hannah simply extended the limits of class and gender relationships, acting out the logic of desire that drew so many of the consolidating bourgeois order to the squalor that it spawned. That Hannah made a place for herself in all of this was possibly unique; that she found nothing to be gained by accepting an elevated station was an expression of tragedies and triumphs shared with many others of her lowly rank.

Other undergrounds, less individualistic and idiosyncratic, were more visible to the ever needful bourgeois voyeuristic eye. It was as though the revolutionary settlement with the ancien régime demanded a visual ordering and opening of these underworlds. Foucault has suggested that the latter half of the eighteenth century was haunted by "the fear of darkened spaces, of the pall of gloom which prevents the full visibility of things, men and truths.... The new political and moral order could not be established until these places were eradicated.... A form of power whose main instance is that of opinion will refuse to tolerate areas of darkness."[12] In an effort to see through this darkness and its underworlds, the nineteenth-century bourgeois order probed intrusively into the labors of the night, offering a statistical dissection of the amazing array of the underemployed on the margins of the newly established factory system. In those for whom sporadic employment had become a way of life— street sellers, cadgers, paupers, beggars, buskers, ballad-vendors, letter-writers, costermongers, dung gatherers, ragpickers, and the young who pitched pennies against warehouse walls, hocked newspapers on corners, or polished shoes—the emerging accountants of class propriety, from Henry Mayhew and Charles Booth to other minor functionaries of moral regulation and state data gathering, discovered a dark, deliciously suited resource to expose to the light of censorious "science."[13] Journalists and novelists sensationalized the underside of Victorian life in lurid depictions of the dark recesses of society.[14]

The actual underground labors associated with sewers, subways, and mines came to occupy a place of prominence for such a gaze; the realities and representations of the labyrinth of tunnels and cavernous environments beneath the affluence of polite society ran through the fiction and form of class relations. As Rosalind Williams has indicated, the engineered underground spawned an imagined space of darkness and danger in which all manner of degeneration, defiance, and deviance were thought to lurk.[15] In works such as Victor Hugo's Les Misérables (1862) and Eugène Sue's Les Mystères de Paris (1842–1843),[16] sewers were associated with the criminalization of class experience that Louis Chevalier has explored in his controversial but brilliantly imaginative Laboring Classes and Dangerous Classes in Paris during the First Half of the Nineteenth Century.[17] "Underground man" emerged out of this fictive reality. "A creature of the city," wrote Irving Howe, "he has no fixed place among the social classes; he lives in holes and crevices, burrowing beneath the visible structure of society.... Even while tormenting himself with reflections upon his own insignificance, the underground man hates still more—hates more than his own hateful self—the world above ground."[18]

It was as though the invisibility and filth of the underground, a foundation on which the visibility of civilization rested precariously, produced a human equivalent of opposition, as well as a new frontier that had to be tamed, controlled, and opened to the light of intrusive sight. Thus the "industrialization of light" that Wolfgang Shivelbusch has explored as an incessant and merciless illumination of the city street was a precondition of extended state surveillance and control, paralleled by attempts to see through the tunnels of society's excrement and refuse.[19] The sewer was, in Hugo's words, "the conscience of the city," a place where all "things converge and confront one another." As a resting place for what bourgeois order discarded and denied, sewers were ghastly places of shadowed truth, in a darkened atmosphere of social pathology that was often seen to nurture the subversions of alienated peoples and ideas.[20] Exposure of this dark and dangerous underground was a class imperative, and by 1867 the Parisian sewer administration was offering guided tours of the

9. Underground Men (no date).

subterranean system, appropriately sanitized: visitors descended into the urban depths by way of an elegant iron stairway, and rode in style to sluices, where they boarded a plush gondola, lowered themselves into cushioned seats, and made their observations by the illumination of large lamps. Towed against the slow current of the underground stream of refuse by sewermen wearing white canvas overalls and shirts, the tourists of this underworld were treated to an otherworldly journey in which the dark debris and dirty work of the bourgeois order were repositioned and revisioned in the glare of a staged spectacle.[21] The sewer as a night fusion of criminalization and proletarianization had been reduced, through the commodified and ordered gaze of bourgeois intrusion, to the merely picturesque.[22]

The Parisian sewers and the night labors of prostitutes, who would also be the subject of a particular set of bourgeois visions, came together in the writings of Alexandre-Jean-Baptiste Parent-Duchâtelet, a public health expert whose voluminous investigations of dirt and disease brought him face to face with the dark social necessities served, in his view, by the underworlds of filth associated with both streetwalkers and sluices. Parent-Duchâtelet saw his entry into the sewers, where he walked among the most abject and disgusting discards of society, as an apprenticeship leading logically to his work in urban brothels. The social orifice of the sewer

was not unlike the bodily orifice of the prostitute: both served a social
need, and both demanded the regulatory attentions of the state to spare
society the scourge of infection, disease, and calamity.

The quantitative dimensions of potential catastrophe were truly astronomical. London boasted its share of prostitutes by the 1860s: one claim
of 3,300 known brothels and 8,600 prostitutes understates the trade significantly; an earlier authority put the number of women working the
streets and houses of ill repute at 24,000; other accounts, which no
doubt included persons who supplemented their wages in factories,
sweatshops, and outwork with casual and poorly paid prostitution, estimated 80,000 to 100,000. Paris, however, was the unrivaled metropolitan
center of nineteenth-century prostitution. With only half the population
of London, it supposedly contained 34,000 prostitutes, but in addition to
its official brothels and clandestine houses, the rougher, more independent,
and less regulated street trade swelled the numbers of working "girls" to
the hundreds of thousands. In the last three decades of the century 155,000
Parisian women registered with the state authorities as prostitutes, and an
amazing 725,000 were arrested on suspicion of "professional" activity.[23]
"Prostitutes are just as inevitable in an urban district as are sewers, dumps,
and refuse heaps," declared Parent-Duchâtelet, adding, "The authorities
should take the same approach to each."[24] In some ways they did. The
prostitute was subject to a dualistic depiction. Vulgarized as a conduit of
filth, disease, revolt, and corruption in some quarters, she was also
sanitized in practice and in portrait, medically and economically regulated
by the state, and inserted into the representational structure of nineteenth-
century society through venues of voyeurism, the aim of which was to
enlighten the dark dramas of sexuality's commodification.[25]

Here, too, the complex meanings of night and day connected in the
spatial and material intersections of a bourgeois order that privileged one
class over another and relegated segments of the poor to the most acute
oppression. Chevalier suggests that Parisian prostitution's plebeian "walk,"
a stationary display visible to this day along the twilight-shrouded alleyways, seedy courtyards, and narrow crib corridors of Rue Saint-Denis,
had its origins "in the demographic and occupational characteristics of
work at Les Halles," a district of central Paris:

> The workers are mainly men and young men at that, but this labor
> force is also unstable, vagrant and occupationally, socially and morally
> underprivileged, finding jobs here that it could not find elsewhere,
> crowding in from all the working-class districts of the city. Most of the
> work is biologically abnormal because it has to be done mainly at night,

because all the implications of work and all the impressions of night combine in a state of mental and bodily confusion, and because it leaves the whole vast daytime free, for rest maybe, but far more probably for pleasure once again, providing an unrewarding but necessary clientele for the prostitutes who find their best customers among the workers of Les Halles.[26]

But like the sewers of Paris, or its Degas-drawn washerwomen, the prostitutes of the street were seldom exposed to the light of accurate public portraiture. Rather, they were depicted according to the politics of the moment: as dangerous revolutionaries leading uprisings of the people in 1830 and 1848, Delacroix's prostitute in Liberty on the Barricades (1831) blurring into the depiction of "La Louve," the rehabilitated whore of Eugène Sue's Les Mystères de Paris. There was in fact little in the way of a union of prostitution and revolt in the first half of the nineteenth century; nevertheless in bourgeois fantasy the construction of danger was imaginatively creative, its nightmarish excesses a bountiful melange of "dangerous bodies in circulation, ... violated bodies in search of change, ... marginals whose interests could be championed, ... women whose desires could be profitably represented." Deplored as yet another "monstrosity" bred of the Age of Revolution, the prostitute was the bodily expression of a freedom that threatened the repressed order of civil society. "The excess of liberty engenders licentiousness," declared the Parisian chief of police during the Revolution of 1848.[27] The republicanization of prostitutional imagery—a picturesque "Liberty" who retained little of the whore's flouting of gender proprieties or class tensions—allowed proper citizens to visit the underworld of the body's dark labors, comfortable in their visual complacency. It was a process not unlike that unfolding in the tours of Parisian sewers, where bright lights kept the rats at bay and white uniforms bleached the dirtiest of work in a ghostly cleanliness.[28]

Something of this was at work as well in the artistic representations of prostitution in post-1848 France. The divergence between the medicalized sociology of prostitution as disease and infection (an affliction of animalistic carnality associated with decay and decomposition) and the imagery of the kindhearted whore or the elegant pose of the bordello (associated with the writings of Balzac, Hugo, Sue, and Gustave Flaubert, and the paintings of a wide circle of minor Parisian artists) stands as evidence of a conflictual consciousness of oppositions: attraction/repulsion, humanity/venality, innocence/degradation. It was the practice of prostitution that unleashed fears in bourgeois society, social traumas that public hygienists such as Parent-Duchâtelet and the dreaded Saltpêtrière asylum attempted to alleviate. A sore on the body politic, prostitution was judged responsible for the plague of syphilis that by the 1880s was corrupting the very physicality of Paris, infecting upward of eighty-five thousand people. But the idea of prostitution had a magnetic pull on the voyeuristic imagination in a social order of fundamental repression; its dark transgressions, in which boundaries of class place and gendered propriety were shed in naked material exchange, lured the likes of Flaubert, Degas, and Edouard Manet, who in varying degrees sought to make the ugly beautiful and the beautiful ugly.[29]

Prostitution's imagery, like its actuality, often represented the oppositions of day and night. In the elite mansions of prostitution's upper echelons, ceiling paintings such as Paul Baudry's *Day Hunting Night* (1864) employed an exaggerated obviousness to scaffold the complexities of the predatory hunt and the supine seduction, casting the relation in the gendered constructions of power and metaphor: an armed, erect, masculine day pursuing and threateningly sighting a reclining, welcoming female night.[30]

More unsettling was Edouard Manet's *Olympia* (1865), a scandalous modernist representation of the prostitute that dissolved the easy clarities of shame and modesty, power and subordination, gender and class in juxtapositions of difference that flew directly and starkly in the face of the polite conventions of impressionism. The immodesty of the reclining nude is offset by the oddly masculine hand that covers the genitals. A body unencumbered by clothing is adorned with the delicate bondage of an elegant choker and the entirely decorative slipper. Unchaste sensuality is supported by chaste materiality, the dark context enlightened by the bright grayness of linen, the colors of class one of contrasting white leisure and black, laboring servitude. Nature's beauty and innocence, an offering of flowers, are disconcertingly displaced by its evils, the shadowed presence of a black cat symbolizing sinisterness, as if plucked out of a witches' sabbath.

Although hailed as "the founding monument of modern art," *Olympia* shocked Parisian audiences in 1865. One contemporary critic described the painting as "armed insurrection in the camp of the bourgeoisie: it is a glass of iced water which each visitor gets full in the face when he sees the BEAUTIFUL *courtisane* in full bloom." The bloom, upon careful consideration, was quick to fade into a "vicious strangeness": Olympia (a favored adoptive name among Parisian prostitutes) came to be seen as a prematurely aged, fatigued, corrupted expression of sourness, "a woman of the night ... from the mysteries of Paris and the nightmares of Edgar Poe." Most commentators likened the reclining pose to that of a decomposing corpse laid out on the counter of the morgue. Others deduced Olympia's illness: "Insomnia and colic have disturbed her serenity; her colour indicates as much." Reference was made to the "hideous Negress," a servant who unfortunately had "nothing about her that *recalls the amorous night.*" All this was social construction, overdetermined by the ideology of the moment, more than an exploration of technique and representation: *Olympia* elicited the anxieties surrounding prostitution precisely because it declined to portray the prostitute in the conventional imagery of depravity and disease.

In refusing the representations of station, service, and sex that would have clarified Olympia's social place for viewers, Manet presented ambiguities and open-ended possibility. The unclothed Olympia's *class* location in the hierarchy of prostitution was unknowable; that she receives flowers, rather than bathing paraphernalia or a gentleman's calling card, leaves her sexuality's meanings and purposes uncertain. As T. J. Clark has suggested, *Olympia* scandalized because it refused to scandalize. It destabilized and problematized the dark labors of the prostitute, presenting a woman of the night in the leisured ambiguities of the day, evoking ambivalence and indeterminate reaction. Whatever the "station" of the prostitute, this was a dangerous denial of the night work that classified her as an imaginary, representational Other, the symbolic embodiment of urban vice.[31] Few were the zealous reformers who did not want the prostitute constructed in the brutalizing idiom of dark decay. Perhaps *Olympia* generated such controversy and loathing because it played into the fears of late-nineteenth-century social purity activists who wanted to depict the prostitute in the oppositional hues of black and white, with their connotations of night and day, disease and health—a representation Manet's painting refused.[32]

The prostitute's night harbored dangers that might well feed on and into the realm of representation, but they also affected prostitutes materially: beyond the social construction of "the curse of Babylon" lay an environment in which coercion and violence were all too common. As indicated by the intrusive state campaigns in England around the Contagious Diseases Acts of the 1860s, the regulation of the women of the night was not merely a matter of imagery.[33] However much "white slavery" panics were the fantastic creations of moral purity advocates, designed as powerful inducement to cleanse urban vice with repressive restrictions, some prostitutes did find themselves orchestrated by powerful rings of internationally connected merchants of vice. Charles van Onselen has suggested that a virtual triangular trade in "fallen women" linked New York City, European ports, and South Africa.[34] Caught between the state and their controlling madams and pimps, prostitutes cultivated numerous discontents. But their ultimate fears were of a range of true occupational hazards that had unmistakable gendered boundaries: "It is men, only men, from the first to the last, that we have to do with! To please a man I did wrong at first, then I was flung about from man to man. Men police lay hands on us. By men we are examined, handled, doctored, and messed on with. In the hospital it is a man who makes prayers and reads the Bible for us. We are up before magistrates who are men, and we never get out of the hands of men." Such a prostitute's lament, directed to a feminist ally, found an echo in the impassioned words of the French socialist-feminist activist Flora Tristan, author of The Workers' Union (1843). She deplored the "infamy" and "revolting degradation" of "the most hideous of the afflictions produced by the unequal distribution of the world's goods." In her view, the confining despotism of paternal power ensured that some women would prefer infamy over oppression. It was a "choice" that the prostitutes themselves should be absolved of any responsibility, and Tristan declared unequivocally that the dangers and deprivations society imposed on women who opted for the dark labors of the night meant that there could be "no moral law" expected from those who earned their wages in the ever threatening sale of their bodies.[35]

Prostitutes could generally be divided among the finely dressed and elegantly presented inmates of the expensive maisons and brothels, catering to aristocratic tastes and commanding a price that put them well out of the reach of the rough and uncouth; streetwalkers of some independence; and the downtrodden "squatters" who serviced the lowliest of clients for gin money and the cost of a night's lodgings. For the last group, the perils of the street could be deadly, with gruesome consequences. It was in London's notorious Whitechapel district that Jack the Ripper killed and mutilated five poor women in 1888. His crimes plunged these congested alleyways and side streets—an eerily transgressive environs of dirty, sweated work, public licentiousness, and subterranean cultures charged with the excitement of dangerous liaisons—into an "autumn of terror" that exposed the extremities of danger faced by all prostitutes but that bore down with particular violence on the "fourpenny knee tremblers" who solicited clients in slum rookeries and thoroughfares such as Dorset "Do as You Please" Street. At almost the same time, a peripatetic serial killer, Dr. Thomas Neill Cream, was poisoning his female victims. His deadly web of victimization connected abortion, prostitution, and drugs, crossed the Canadian–United States border with abandon, and reached into the music halls and commercialized vice of London.

The grisly mutilations performed by Jack the Ripper, in which sexual and reproductive organs were literally carved out of the female body, articulated a misogynist violence indiscriminate in its generalized assault, but hitting hardest and most directly at those women dependent on the dark labors of the night. Not only prostitutes, but also servants, seamstresses, scavengers, and barmaids necessarily found themselves, in time and place, endangered. Never apprehended, the Ripper terrorized women, particularly the poor of Whitechapel, but he mobilized men: the social reformers who managed to turn the tragedy and terror of 1888 against the very victims of its violence. Constructing an image of deplorable depravity, the voices of vigilance campaigned to close down the "nurseries of crime" that sustained street prostitution (and so much else) in Whitechapel: the common lodging houses which, whatever their flaws, offered some protections from the dangers of the night. "The stories which they have to tell," reported the British Medical Journal of the resulting dislocations, "are of saddening uniformity: uncontrollable brutality; women turned into the streets ... and shivering on the stones at night fleeing from the execrations and the violence of drunken men ... tragedies and horrors of public obscenity treated by the police as the ordinary incidents of dark alleys, unlighted courts, and low neighborhoods." In the night of terror that was Jack the Ripper's Whitechapel in 1888 the police could see only dark, the social purity campaigns only light. Lost from sight were the prostitutes themselves, their night labors shrouded in distasteful condescension, sensationalized in bodies that mattered only as objects of mutilation and murder.[36]

Across the Atlantic the sensationalization of death was associated more with casual sexual commodification. In the summer of 1841 a beautiful and "well-bred" tobacco girl and boarding-house keeper, Mary Rogers, disappeared; shortly thereafter, her body was discovered floating in the shallows of the Hudson River. Rogers, who had arrived in New York as part of a vast rural influx in the 1830s and 1840s, quickly found a niche in the risqué sexual openness of tobacco shops, sporting culture, and "houses of assignation" that provided a space for the easy virtue and commercialized sex associated with lives and livelihoods unconfined by family and the traditional home. Perhaps not herself a prostitute, Rogers was young, unmarried, and sexually available. That trilogy of attributes, in conjunction with defiance of conventionality and willingness to take a number of lovers, linked her to the dark labors of the sex trade and, certainly, the kinds of class and gender transgressions that inevitably brought her into danger. The list of men she associated with—a cork cutter, a clerk, a sailor, a shopkeeper and rising real estate magnate, a naval officer, and a politician's son—was a veritable catalogue of those frequenting the city of Eros, a newly constructed urban space that seemed to flout the long-established rules ordering class and gender behavior. Mary's death, an unsolved mystery that captured much attention in the popular culture, was variously attributed to a rowdy gang, a lover's rage, suicide, a botched abortion. Whatever the cause, it lay embedded in the dangers and desires of New York's liberating licentiousness, where bodies were exchanged in new and emancipatory ways, purchased not only with the materiality of buying power but also with the ubiquitousness of danger. For Mary Rogers, that danger ended in her death, an event mythologized in the penny press and immortalized in Edgar Allan Poe's archetypal detective story "The Mystery of Marie Roget" (1842–1843).[37]

If Mary Rogers lived on in fiction, her life course was reproduced in fact for generations in countless locales where the urban working girl rubbed shoulders (and sometimes more) with the prostitute. The "girl problem" of large cities persisted into the late nineteenth and early twentieth centuries, a text of countless pages often recording sexuality's darker moments in which the pleasures and perils of urban life seemed inseparable. It was not just that such young women confronted a culture of confinement and limitation, a "boy problem" unacknowledged in the sociology and political economy of the times, although that was a part of their difficulty. But class deprivations, accentuated by the special oppressions of gender, worked themselves out against the backdrop of danger that ultimately ended Mary Rogers's life and that left its mark on all young working-class women, especially those who sought the last resort of abortion. Locale might produce its peculiarities (port cities were notoriously likely to steer women toward prostitution because the pull of the seafaring market was enhanced by the push of minimal industrial or sweatshop employment) but throughout urban North America most nineteenth-century women struggled with a basic problem of survival. "I know no other means of getting a livelihood without sleeping with men," declared a prostitute arrested in Halifax, Nova Scotia in 1862.[38]

In New York City, the stronghold of metropolitan republicanism, the impoverishing wages of female labor, the dullingly routine rigors of domestic service, and the irregularity of much of the available work, combined with the lure of the promenade and the offerings of a seemingly insatiable male sexual appetite to produce an explosively public prostitution. Modest treats, lodgings, and the ultimate leveler, cash, were all deployed to procure girls' and women's bodies. Professionals and amateurs abounded, for the vice trade embraced the elegant mistress, the hardened whore, and the seemingly innocent but eminently streetwise, working girl whose "walking outs" on the Bowery could easily end with casual sex in a "house of assignation," the basement of a half-finished building, or a dark spot obscured from view by a churchyard wall. The coins and fineries, dinners and theater dates that made up the exchange medium of such liaisons eased the intimidations of male sexual exploitation and conquest. Often regarded as a gendered prerogative of workingmen and bourgeois night travelers alike, such relations produced a slippery accommodation to eroticism that became, in limited ways, more reciprocal than it might have been had women not bartered their bodies for small, tangible materialities or simply succumbed to the power—physical and cultural—of men. A republic of virtue thus spawned a subterranean vice that spilled out of the streets and alleys, bars and bagnios, into the notorious clip joints and Canal Street cigar stores.

This dark culture of bargained desire blurred the boundaries of Eros and exploitation. Between 1818 and 1855, when Dr. William Sanger was commissioned by New York to research this "enormous vice," his estimate of the number of women involved in the illicit commerce of prostitution rose from ten thousand to eighty thousand. This may have been an exaggeration, but Sanger had no doubt that the problem was proliferating, its variety and extensiveness presenting a disconcerting threat to civil society. It was not only the professional woman of the brothel who presented herself for sale; in New York's materialistic marketplace the sale of sex seemed to be everywhere. Working-class prostitutes plied their trade in tenement apartments adjacent to those of the laboring poor, and in the most destitute neighborhoods a family might even rent out a room or a corner space to a downtrodden streetwalker. Dance halls featured naked performers; pornographic paintings enticed customers into concert halls and eating establishments that catered to particularly lustful clienteles such as sailors; the customers of girls who sold phallic-like ears of hot corn on the street might also make a less wholesome purchase. Tastes that turned to more exotic and perverse realms were catered to as well, the most troubling result being the growth of child prostitution. Moreover, the containments of class were made more fragile by an increasingly urbane culture of money and fetish which placed a fashionable premium on commodified erotic encounters between bourgeois men and working-class women. The hierarchies of prostitution remained, its classifications of elegance and debauchery as evident in New York as they were in London or Paris. But the "fallen woman" was now more visible, more varied; she more casually combined her dark trade with the poorly paid labors of the day at which she might well still toil. Prostitution, complained Sanger, "no longer confines itself to secrecy and darkness, but boldly strikes through our most thronged and elegant thoroughfares, and there, in the broad light of the sun, it jostles the pure, the virtuous, and the good."[39] Things were apparently not all that different in Toronto, a supposedly placid outpost of British culture and reserve. Promoted as Toronto the Good, the city had its dark underside. "Houses of ill fame in Toronto?" asked the irrepressible, muck-raking journalist C. S. Clark in 1898, "Certainly not. The whole city is an immense house of ill fame."[40]

With prostitution established in this generalized manner, most North American urban locales supported thriving centers of the commercialization of sex, common in their offerings but diverse in their ways of doing night's business. In St. Paul, Minnesota, the trade was monopolized throughout the latter half of the nineteenth century by forty madames whose houses had a life span of eight to ten years each. Chicago, the industrial metropolis of the Midwest, was said to have more than five hundred brothels by the 1860s, at their pinnacle the aristocratic Everleigh Club. Foreign-born German and Irish women and teenage girls who established the sex trade in New Orleans built a foundation for the infamous Storyville, the early-twentieth-century red-light capital of the deep South. Hard pressed to find work outside the poorly paid and excessively confining rigors of domestic service (where an African-American and Creole reserve army of labor ensured that the oppressions of the servant plumbed new depths) these women were an accumulative resource of considerable magnitude. In 1911 it was estimated that in the close quarters of Storyville "well over ten million dollars a year, probably closer to fifteen million, found its way into the stockings of the prostitutes, the cassocks of the clergymen who owned the whorehouse property, the pockets of the politicians, and the swelling accounts of the landlords." San Francisco's elegant "parlor houses" were the toast of the West Coast trade, but its Asian "cribs" off Chinatown's alleys (two-thirds of the 3,500 Chinese women in California in the 1870s listed their occupation as prostitute) were closets of incarceration: impoverished immigrants signed themselves into years of sexual slavery to pay off the debt of their passage from China.[41] To observe the doings of this range of tenderloins and promenades, red-light districts and notorious "houses," whether hard or glamorous, was to come to the same conclusion as Walt Whitman, who wrote of the streets adjacent to New York's East River in 1857: "The great doings, in these quarters, are at night."[42]

In this bustling traffic in bodies it was impossible not to see the class and gender content of sexuality's commodification. How race figured in the transgressive trade is more problematic, a complex layering of special oppressions and subordinations intersecting the already intricate amalgamations of difference. Yet the dark labors of the prostitute's night, contextualized in time and place, was racialized as well. The origins of American pornography perhaps lay at the intersection of intense anti-Catholic nativism—with its lurid anti-papist tales of erotic priest–nun encounters and the despoliation of innocent womanhood—and the rough cosmopolitan sensuality of the street. *The Awful Disclosures of Maria Monk, as Exhibited in a Narrative of Her Suffering during a Residence of Five Years at the Hotel Dieu Nunnery at Montreal* (1836), a sensationalized tale of Catholic debauchery, culminating in Monk's pregnancy, was made and marketed to appeal to the anti-immigrant nativism of North American society as well as its emerging prurient interests.[43] Halifax's prostitutes, according to Judith Fingard, did not discriminate against one another on the basis of race. The garrison port obviously provided a market in which African-Canadian women could sell themselves: overrepresented in the commercialized sex of the street, blacks were barely 3 percent of Halifax's population but accounted for 40 percent of all prosecutions of prostitutes.[44]

Aboriginal, black, and Mexican prostitution on various North American frontiers no doubt added the inferiorities of racial otherness to the subordinations all too obvious in prostitution, but the presence of racialized sexuality may also have fed the destabilizing powers of nights in which boundaries normally erected with rigidity were transgressed or circumvented, however fleetingly or problematically.[45] New York's Five Points district, for instance, early achieved a reputation for interracial debauchery, a "spot where black and white promiscuously mingle, and nightly celebrate disgusting orgies." A destitute, spatially disordered neighborhood of the pre–Civil War poor, Five Points was "the social melting pot of New York's underground economy," a congenial and enterprising environment of profitable vice and criminality. Two of every three blocks housed prostitutes and brothels, and after nightfall the saloons, theaters, dance halls, and cheap lodging houses were awash with "members of the whoreocracy in most slatternly *deshabille.*" Much of the sex was public, and not a little was interracial. A watchman arrested a white man and a black woman for fornicating in an unimproved lot one hot summer evening in 1838, a not uncommon occurrence that might draw "a great mob" to cheer on the carnal display. One preacher on a police-escorted nocturnal tour was repulsed by the "motley multitude of men and women, yellow and white, black and dingy, old and young, ... a set of male and female Bacchanals dancing to the tambourines and fiddle; giggling and laughing ... and making "night hideous" with their lascivious orgies." Black saloonkeepers and madams might cater to a purely black clientele, but haunts such as the Diving Bell, Swimming Bath, Cow Bay, and Squeeze Gut Alley were notorious for white–black sexual intercourse, characterized as "amalgamation" by its opponents. Miscegenational eroticism elicited racist condemnation, but the hardened segregation of black and white prostitutes characteristic of the post–Civil War years was quite subdued, if it existed at all, in early-nineteenth-century Five Points.[46]

The presence of blacks in North American prostitution thus balanced the meaning and historical context of a racially ordered tension around emancipation and subordination. In Europe the same process could well have been at work, but the representational fixations and fetishes of a voyeuristic layer of bourgeois authors and artists rewrote the prostitute body racially. Manet's *Olympia*, a high statement of modern art, poses the racial poles of service: the prostitute, who services the reproductive continuities of the familialist order by making sex available to those without families as well as those trapped in sanitized, asexual domesticity—thereby securing the future of productive labors—is in turn serviced by the black domestic. Just as capitalism thrives on the dark labors of marginality, the margins of capitalism—its colonial conquests—are themselves provisional forces imported into the realm of reproduction. Modernity's moment is the coexistence in labor of class power and need, gendered eroticism, and racial subordination, all presented as subjectivity.

In the twentieth century, cubism and abstractionism had their founding representation statement in yet another image of prostitution, Pablo Picasso's *Les Demoiselles d'Avignon* (1907). Charles Bernheimer has suggested that this unity of the modernist subject, a recurring fixation on the prostitute reaching from Manet to Picasso, can hardly be accidental: "From the mid-nineteenth century to the beginning of the twentieth," he argues, "modernism obsessionally and anxiously displays its innovative desire by fragmenting and disfiguring the female sexual body, epitomized in male fantasy by the prostitute." Missing from this insightful gendered reading, however, are the class and race associations, which are also of historical significance. Painted a brief decade before the publication of Lenin's *Imperialism, the Highest Stage of Capitalism* (1917), Picasso's *Demoiselles* constructs the prostitute body colonially, the brothel women being displaced in the angularity of African masks. The primordial fetish of "tribal" culture is transformed into the coin of timeless commercial exchange, covering the

10. Pablo Picasso, *Les Demoiselles d'Avignon* (1907).

face-to-face contact of client and courtesan, empire and exploited outpost. As Leo Steinberg has argued, moreover, in eliminating two male
bodies from the scene—one a sailor, a working-class figure unmistakably
linked to both the trade in sex and the global movement of goods—and
in presenting the brothel figures as "almost entirely freed from humanity,
... [as] naked problems, white signs on a black board," Picasso shattered
the form of impressionistic modernism with its presentation of the subject. He offered in its stead the fragmented displacement of subjectivity
that imperialism imposes, a process that often also marginalizes, obscures,
and disturbs the clarities of class (hence the erasure of the sailor). In the

words of Fredric Jameson, "a significant structural segment of the economic system as a whole is now located elsewhere, beyond the metropolis, outside of the daily life and existential experience of the home country, in colonies over the water whose own life experience and life world— very different from that of the imperial power—remain unknown and unimaginable for the subjects of imperial power."[47] *Olympia* and *Demoiselles* are thus the representational forms expressive of the configurations of class, gender, and race at two connected but differentiated points in capitalism's history. Their meeting place was along the axis of empire, where the dark labors of an accumulative night would once again present an imagery and a materiality of the social relations of class, race, and gender, within which production and reproduction, dark and light, happened.[48]

8

Dark Continents

Empire and Race

Just as the prostitute and the dark labors of the nineteenth-century metropolis contributed to the emergence of the social survey and the sociology of urban pathology, so too did Henry Mayhew and the Booths (both Charles and William), who charted the course of this initial wave of inquiry, draw on the sighting and mapping techniques of the "imperial eye." The immensely popular Salvation Army publication *In Darkest England and the Way Out* (1890) by General William Booth—which sold over 200,000 copies in one year—drew explicitly on colonizing attempts to penetrate the "dark continents," whose history was then being constructed and codified by imperialism's relentless intrusions and explorations. It appeared at the same time as H. M. Stanley's two-volume *In Darkest Africa; or The Quest, Rescue, and Retreat of Emin, Governor of Equatoria* (1890). Victorian imperialism—encompassing scientific classification, evolving cartographic precision, literary representations, the piety of serving underdeveloped peoples, and the economics of exploitation, accumulation, and unequal exchange—naturalized a global order of dominance balanced on the knowledge and moral worth associated with lightness and darkness, oppositional states that reproduced and then refocused the city's bifurcation into slum and society just as it divided civilization from nature's wastelands. Darkness could be lifted by the rescue work of those committed to the cause of whitening, cleansing improvement; the face of degeneration could be turned to a countenance of civilized contentment.[1]

This was the view from on high, a Kiplingesque conception of imperialism as service. Over time, that nineteenth-century imperial ethic, always more promotional than practical, rotted in its own contradictions;

even Rudyard Kipling wrote a book called *The Light That Failed* (1890). By the early twentieth century the sons of the aspiring colonialist bureaucratic middle classes, on whom the sun of empire set in the last bright light of an administrative career, had lapsed into apathy or worse, a process of debasement explained by George Orwell.

Orwell joined the Imperial India Police and, like his father before him, served in the Far East as "part of the actual machinery of despotism." He wrote *Burmese Days* (1934) after a 1920s' struggle in which the lure of empire tugged incessantly but unsuccessfully at his realization that the imperial dream was a nightmare, less governed by the burden of benevolence than by the crass materialism of capitalist accumulation.[2] "All over India there are Englishmen who secretly loathe the system of which they are a part," he would write in 1937 in the Left Book Club–commissioned *The Road to Wigan Pier*.[3] Kipling's nineteenth-century order found it difficult to withstand blunt statements such as Orwell's 1927 rationale for ending his stint as a colonialist gendarme: "I could not go on any longer serving an imperialism which I had come to regard as very largely a racket."[4] His brief career as an arm of imperial power may seem idiosyncratic and fleeting, but it captures the complex layering in imperialism's global reach, which commenced with the economics of exploitation and proceeded through the intricate interrelationships of class, race, and gender.

First, as Orwell emphasized, and as an extensive early-twentieth-century set of writings established conclusively, the British Empire was a preeminently economic creation. Orwell's most important job in the imperial police was overseeing two hundred men whose occupation it was to guard the industrial area of Syriam, Burma's oil-refining capital, where the huge processing and storage tanks housed the life blood of the subcontinent's political economy.[5] J. A. Hobson's *Imperialism: A Study* (1902), Rudolf Hilferding's *Finance Capital: A Study of the Latest Phase in Capitalist Development* (1910), Rosa Luxemburg's *The Accumulation of Capital* (1913), Nicolai Bukharin's *Imperialism and World Economy* (1917), and V. I. Lenin's *Imperialism: The Highest Stage of Capitalism* (1917) all accentuated the astonishing late-nineteenth-century acceleration in capital outflow to the less developed colonial world from the advanced capitalist economies of England, France, Germany, and elsewhere. As the banks and their international networks of exchange swelled into a bloated infrastructure of expanding capitalist power they dragged, in the words of one 1930 commentator, "the political and military power of their governments behind them."[6] Armies, like industries, grew into octopus-like organisms, wrapping their tentacles around the world in an increasingly bellicose posture and practice of conquest that the revolutionary left had no difficulty in associating with the drift to war that culminated in the catastrophic implosion of 1914–1918.[7] This process of material exploitation and crusading imperial might reached across centuries and through various stages of colonialism and imperialism.[8] If its meanings vary, its general importance is clear: the dark continents were exposed to the light of capitalism's bright benevolence precisely because it was very much a paying proposition.[9] Orwell acknowledged in 1938 that seeing "imperialism at work in Burma" had been something of a schooling in "the real nature of capitalist society."[10]

Second, Orwell's Burmese days were an acute reminder that within the economics of imperial exploitation lay an archive of the relations of class, race, and gender. Although each colonial encounter could produce particularistic orderings of this ensemble of ideas and practices, the general genealogy of this trilogy of power sprang from the universality of domination and its hierarchies. Orwell's recollection of his time as an officer of colonial rule shows how pride and prejudice, nurtured in the metropolitan center and founded on the structured meanings of class and sex, were translated to a colonial context where they assumed different demeanors, and how they became infused with the content of race:

> In an "outpost of Empire" like Burma the class-question appeared at first sight to have been shelved. There was no obvious class-friction here, because the all-important thing was not whether you had been to the right schools but whether your skin was technically white.... except for the common soldiers and a few nondescripts [whites] lived lives appropriate to "gentlemen" ... and officially they were regarded as being all of the same class. They were "white men," in contradistinction to the other and inferior class, the "natives." But one did not feel towards the "natives" as one felt towards the "lower classes" at home.... One looked down on them as "natives," but one was quite ready to be physically intimate with them; and this, I noticed, was the case even with white men who had the most vicious colour prejudice.... I felt towards a Burman almost as I felt towards a woman. Like most other races, the Burmese have a distinctive smell—I cannot describe it: it is a smell that makes one's teeth tingle—but this smell never disgusted me.... I found the English "lower classes" so much more repellant than Burmese "natives." ... they were "common people" and I did not care to be too close to them. In the hot mornings when the company marched down the road, myself in the rear with one of the junior subalterns, the steam of those hundred sweating bodies in front made my stomach turn.... All I knew was that it was lower-class sweat that I was smelling, and the thought of it made me sick.

Orwell thus brings into one rambling passage the gendered content of servile intimacy, the color of prejudice, homoeroticism, and the aesthetics

11. The Empire as Brothel from *The Cremorne* (1882).

of economic class, all blurred together in a colonial encounter of material
and cultural explosiveness, infused with the sexualities and sensibilities of
domination/subordination. In his writing one sees the colonial contest as
a matter of economic exploitation, through which run threads of class,
race, and gender. At their base, these were all relations of power which
were preserved, ultimately, by violence.[11]

This colonial conjuncture is illuminated in the erotic frontispiece of a
Victorian pornographic publication, *The Cremorne*, which appeared in 1882
but was dated 1851. This historical inaccuracy was perhaps plotted to
confuse the censors but may also have articulated a subconscious sense of
the freedoms of a lost era of imperial licentiousness.[12] The scene is one
of plantation power, the voyeuristic gaze of the master enjoying simultaneously the staged, unbridled lasciviousness of black women and the
public sexual performance of a young male. Certainly a subordinate—
possibly an example of Foucault's symbolic "class body" with its complex
appeal to the unique configurations of race, gender, and class afforded by
empire's distorting materialism—the performing male fuses homoeroticism
and concubinage, which could coexist easily if packaged in deeply structured commitments to whiteness and unimpeded access to bodies of
color.[13] The entire representation draws on emerging nineteenth-century

European notions of black women as possessed of a particular primitive sexual appetite (thought to be biologically overdetermined in enlarged genitalia that dictated an insatiable erotic need) and on the extensive colonial practice of institutionalizing sexual regimes of concubinal subordination, the better to acclimatize the shock troops of empire to their tropical outposts, whether in Malaysia, Indochina, or French- and British-ruled Africa.[14]

Some have seen in this constructed hypersexuality of the Other a mere reflection of repressed desire.[15] According to V. G. Kiernan, one attraction of Orientalism was its nocturnal mysteries and pleasures, from the magic of the *Arabian Nights* to evenings of indulgence textualized in sex manuals and medicalized in concocted aphrodisiacs. Male fantasy seemed constructed by Asiatic abundance: the sumptuous bodies of belly dancers; the potential for domination, possession, and endless delight associated with the women of the imagined baths, slave markets, and harems. Certain early feminists and priggish ruling-class patriarchs in the West often found such imagery upsetting, its potential for lasciviousness running simultaneously and contradictorily in the directions of both freedom and restraint. Lord Palmerston once told a pasha that "nothing would go right in Turkey … until polygamy was abolished."[16] The issue, however, was never simply that the denied sexuality of the European was finding its revengeful genital outlet in empire, as Ronald Hyam has suggested, but rather that the relations of class, race, and gender in imperial outposts reconstituted one another, and this reconfiguration ordered and reordered power in both metropole and colonial hinterland.[17]

What is critically important about the sexualization of empire, exhibited in crude pornographic or artistic scenes of the Orient, is that a male fantasy of power was capable of eliding tensions of class through a carnalization of rule, knitting together an always unraveling center of authority and domination in the gendered and racialized metaphors of European supremacy and native subordination.[18] On the one hand, just as imperialism has often been interpreted as providing crumbs from the colonial table to placate the domestic working class of the advanced capitalist nations by bribing its union leaders and a privileged layer of labor aristocrats,[19] so too did the sexual opportunities of empire afford a measure of concession and placation for the class "refuse" of imperial power. Outposted to the colonies, this class structure was dressed in eroticized power over peoples of color, allowing a displaced stratum (both explicitly proletarian and marginally petty bourgeois) the pleasures of patriarchal authority with very little of its familial responsibilities. On the other hand, this sensual class pact with the devil of accommodation was sealed in the dualism of global power: the actions of rich and poor individuals mirrored the practices of larger civil bodies, with nations assuming the gendered relations of conventional sexual relations. As Edward W. Said and Anne Stoler suggest, the penetrations, silencings, and possessions of Oriental women by European men stand for the "pattern of relative strength between East and West," an iconography of rule in which "sexual assymetries are tropes to depict other centers of power."[20]

The early modern association of gendered and racial subordination with imperial, economic designs has cast a dark shadow, fusing the mythologies of sexuality and the perversions of racism in an "amalgamation" of deeply ironic significance, given the pains taken by the architects of empire to separate the mechanics of interracial sex and the purities of "blood."[21] Racism and empire met in the encouragement of the social relations of the brothel and their denial of the inevitable miscegenatious offspring. Mixed-blood children of the imperial connection were often refused their legal, property, and social rights as members of the dominant class, a destabilizing demographics that had its impact in cultural and religious formations of often defiant demonism.[22] Defined by a European whiteness that refused any suggestion of race mixing, a censoriously hypocritical elite maintained its superiority in the powerful fiction of carnal restraint and cultivated concubinage which it doled out to the common and inferior whites, whose sexual lives of indulgence marked them as incapable of exercising the responsibilities of colonial rule and self-governance. In the empire's shifting relations of class, race, and gender, power found a vehicle eminently suited to its ongoing reproduction.[23] Yet a more protracted view sees that power unable to extend itself infinitely.[24] The marginalized "damned," literally bred of licentiousness, took their revenge by fostering a state of disorder—visible in its vagrancy, idleness, and irreverent noncompliance—that might erupt in overt rebellion.[25]

Empires, of course, are of longstanding antiquity; they come and, however long they might last, inevitably go. The collapse of the Roman Empire over the course of the fifth, sixth, and seventh centuries seemed to Edward Gibbon "the greatest, perhaps, and most awful scene in the history of mankind," a tragic instance of a "stupendous fabric [yielding] to the pressure of its own weight." Historians have thus traditionally interpreted the fall of classical civilization as an almost naturalized inevitability, Peter Brown's The World of Late Antiquity (1971) declaring "altogether, the prosperity of the Mediterranean world seems to have drained to the top."

Yet as the great Marxist account of G. E. M. de Ste. Croix argues, the drawn-out demise of Rome's imperialism was neither as innocent nor as passively automatic as such metaphors imply. It was not just that an unwieldy economic order succumbed to its own pressures but that those pressures, exploitive in their origins and hardening over time, exacted tremendous costs. The increasing burden of maintaining an imperial army and a bureaucratic apparatus that could effectively knit together a disparate geocultural collectivity of vast regional reach—contemporary Britain, Gaul, Spain, and north Africa in the fifth century; all of modern Italy and the Balkans in the sixth; Syria, Mesopotamia, and Egypt in the last stages of Rome's seventh-century dominance—fell largely on the peasantry, with urban producers and city slaves suffering secondarily. As a Christian Church began to take its share of the surplus, and the leisured class of absentee landowners grew both in absolute size and in its expectations of a life of conspicuous consumption, merciless exploitation intensified. An economic process of squeezing more and more out of direct producers was paralleled by the cultural decline of citizenship rights and a climate of violence increasingly marked by torture, imprisonment, and execution. As the dark shadow of class difference, dependence, and destruction loomed over an empire confronting hordes of barbarian invaders, its lower classes saw little reason to offer their hard taskmasters much in the way of support, military or moral. As Ste. Croix concludes, "Those who have been chastised with scorpions may hope for something better if they think they will be chastised only with whips." Rome's fall, then, had little to do with a mechanical process of yielding to inevitability or the gravitational pull of a naturalized system of drainage. Ste. Croix prefers the metaphor of the vampire bat: in antiquity's dark night of imperial degeneration, exploitation sucked the lifeblood out of the Roman Empire; it fell to its weakened state exhausted by a ruling class's insatiable demands.[26]

A ruling-class craving ever larger accumulations is a fundamental feature of world history. From at least the time of the thirteenth-century travels of the Venetian merchants Niccolo and Maffeo Polo, and Niccolo's son Marco, the world and its history began to be reconstituted as travel and trade. If the first "dark" continent was the Orientalized East with its demonic hordes of Islamic barbarians and seemingly uninhibited sexual license—evident in cuckoldry, adultery, prostitution, and the potentate's harem—its lush offerings of sensual surplus brightened an often mis-understood geographic landscape. As late as the fifteenth century, how-ever, the European world was still bounded by the land masses bordering the Mediterranean, and ignorance and accident governed the first phases of the misnamed explorations of Columbus and others. In search of the fictive wealth of Marco Polo's East, these adventurers went looking for lands such as the fabulous isle of Zipango (Japan), where it was reported there was "gold in the greatest abundance, its sources being inexhaustible." Marco had in fact constructed a mythology of Eastern wealth from stories circulating throughout the Orient. Nevertheless, his exotic concoction of tales galvanized Spain's Catholic rulers to mobilize expeditions of crusading warriors and transoceanic brigands whose intended conquests would unite religious, territorial, and material purpose. Columbus declared that God had "reserved for the Spanish monarchs, not only all the treasures of the New World, but a still greater treasure of inestimable value, in the infinite number of souls destined to be brought over into the bosom of the Christian Church." Columbus hoped to sight more than converts, however. He was on the lookout for the wealthy islands of the Indian East, where, along with giant red pearls and mountains of gold and silver, the rich preservative flavorings of pepper, ginger, cloves, nutmeg, and cinnamon spiced the material inducements of such dangerous voyages. Instead, he "discovered" the "unknown" continents of the Americas; his sails driven by the winds of acquisition and accumulation, his sense of his whereabouts in 1492 was geographically skewed but socially and economically momentous.[27]

Then began America's Dark Ages. "I was attentive, and took trouble to ascertain if there was gold," wrote Columbus in his diary the day after his landing in the Bahamas. Gold was in fact in relatively short supply in the West Indies; hence the Spanish monarchy's appetite for it propelled Iberian imperialism toward Mexico and Peru. The Caribbean economy, transformed by the European presence, became monoculturally fixed on sugar cane, making labor recruitment of paramount importance. The fierce resistance of the native people known as Island Caribs allowed Columbus and others to construct them as savage cannibals, which, under the Spanish legal and moral code, justified their enslavement.[28] A humanitarian Catholic bishop estimated in 1552 that fifteen million natives had died in their resistance to forced labor. This figure is generally regarded as wildly exaggerated, but whatever the precise numbers, chaotic disruption and brutalizing violence unquestionably brought about immense demographic devastation and widespread physiological and spiritual malaise. Among the losses were the obliteration of Amerindian cultures and civilizations that ranged from nomadic hunting groups and settled farming communities to the dazzling Aztec societies, with their elaborate, urban-based dominions ruled by emperors resplendent in their dress and rhetoric.[29]

The most recent reliable (though conservative) estimates of the native population of the New World in 1492 put forward a figure of approximately fifty-four million. The comparable number for 1650 is less than six million, a calamitous loss of 90 percent of two continents' peoples over a century and a half. This racially structured, materially ordered holocaust was a proclamation of empire's ultimatism: its willingness to ravage peoples and places transformed not only the mind of an epoch but its ecosystems and population structures as well.[30] In their quest for the bright metals, shining of wealth, Europeans lowered a night of despair and destruction over the native peoples of the Western Hemisphere. George Abbot's highly popular and confidently immodest account of empire-building, *A Briefe Description of the Whole World* (1599), summarized Eurocentric assessments of the Amerindians: if their virtues lay in hospitality, affability, and candidness, these positive traits were balanced precariously by a set of Satanic vices, most of which had their origins in sexual perversion—incest, sodomy, adultery—and the monstrous savagery of cannibalism. Such a litany of "beast-like" behaviors could be used to justify any act of cruelty, even the collective extermination of entire tribes and aboriginal cultures.[31]

Inhabitants of the New World thus lay beyond and outside the legal codification of natural rights that was crystallizing in Europe; they became the first outlaws of nascent empire. This dissonance between the theory of natural right, international law, and the rapaciousness of imperial power was somewhat uncritically reproduced in the writings of Daniel Defoe, a literary advocate of colonialism, and lay at the heart of Jonathan Swift's satirical genius in *Gulliver's Travels* (1726). As Warren Montag, guided by a Swiftian sense of irony, has usefully put it, "No greater misfortune could befall the inhabitants of Africa and the Americas than to be declared by the Europeans to live in a pre-social state of nature: the lands that they inhabited were sure to be taken, as armies and navies arrived to assist their voluntary subjection to a legal state whose institutions would ensure their transition to a civilized condition."[32]

The violence of European conquest and political order was, according to a recent account by Richard C. Trexler, intricately related to the gendered violence of the invading institutions of colonialism, for which the warrior natives of the Americas were sexually othered as sodomites. Trexler contends that extremely punitive restrictions on male same-sex erotic acts, as well as a range of sexual behaviors associated with churchmen, women, and soldiers, prepared the conquering armies of Spanish imperial might for carnal relationships that linked power, property, and the varied practices of sex. As they confronted Amerindian berdaches—males who dressed as women and adopted women's domestic and sexual roles in military, diplo-matic, and religious circles—hostile associations hardened. Almost from the moment of native-white contact, then, the Spanish invaders linked power with sexual dominance. Columbus's doctor wrote in 1494 that the Caribs were fierce savages who captured young boys from the surrounding islands, castrated them, used them sexually until they grew to adulthood, and then killed and ate them. Sexual defamation and ritual mutilation were commonly practiced by native warriors: the warlike Tumucua of old Florida never left a battlefield without symbolically sodomizing the dead enemy, piercing the anus with an arrow. In Peruvian Andean temples, the conquering Spanish concluded "the devil made the Indians of these regions believe that it was an offering pleasing to their gods for them to have Indians as temple assistants so the chieftans could have carnal knowledge of them, thus committing the heinous sin of sodomy." To the imperial eye, set contentedly within the constructed patriarchal body of emerging European civil society, masculine and feminine were power's polar oppo-sitions. Empire's invasions, conquests, and subsequent dominations were of course about material acquisition and accumulation, but the path to the new world of riches followed the gendered logic of established old-world practices.[33]

Women, as Anne McClintock has suggested, were thus boundary markers and threshold figures in the process of conquest, a means by which colonizing males oriented themselves and rationalized their use and extension of power. Doing so could take the form of a chivalrous defense of white womanhood, which stood threatened by rebellious uprisings of peoples of color and enslaved or subordinated Africans, a nightmare fantasy of gendered apprehension that could flare in the imagin-ation. In the aftermath of the Indian Mutiny of 1857 an outpouring of literary productions symbolized the revolt in the rape of British women by Indian men. Simmering below the surface of race relations for gen-erations in the American slave South, this reification of white womanhood's precariousness could erupt in controversy, as with the publication of William Styron's The Confessions of Nat Turner (1967). The book outraged African Americans with its allusions to the Southampton slave insurrection of 1831 and its leader's supposed masturbatory longings. At the actual historical point of empire's conquests, however, indigenous peoples confronted male warriors. This clash provided the context in which gendered humiliations and feminizations rationalized a process of othering that opened out into justification of brutalizing subordinations. In its dangerous marginality, femininity had to be banished from some theaters of sociability, sexuality, and spirituality, first segregated in order to be reintegrated in an act of social placement and containment. Male violence, given free reign, took some of its cues from the gender ambivalences of native culture and custom, perceived by Europeans as simultaneously passively and hospitably receptive *and* savagely sexual, unnaturally transgressive, even cannibalistic.[34]

This sad chapter in the history of imperial plunder can be closed with the conquest of the Incas of the Peruvian Andes, already weakened by the first forays of Spanish invasion, which brought disease if not military subordination. The first blows of destruction rained down on the young Inca civilization—little more than 150 years old—in the second quarter of the sixteenth century. The Incan network of provinces—knit together by an impressive synthesis of economy and culture that included roads, suspension bridges, towns, temples, fortresses, irrigation canals, and warehouses of provisions used to sustain the poor, the handicapped, and the widowed—was a hierarchical order headed by the Supreme Inca, humanity's representative to the gods, the highest deity being the sun. Among the smallpox epidemic's thousands of victims was the ruling monarch, and in the wars of succession that followed Incan society was diverted from the due attention required to be paid to the invading Spaniards. The victor in the contest for the Inca throne, Atahualpa underestimated the conquistadors, judging them to be "bearded thieves" and "lazy robbers." Overconfident, buoyed by the sheer numbers of his own army and the seemingly ragged crew of the invaders, Atahualpa refused to be cowed by the crosses and Bibles the Spaniards offered as symbolic of their power, mocked the notion that a distant lord known as the Pope could possibly "give away countries which [did] not belong to him," and proceeded unarmed into a massacre that left between five and ten thousand of his retinue dead. Puzzled by the European lust for precious metals, which to the Incas were aesthetic and iconic substances—without monetary value but representative of the gendered basis of the universe: gold was the sweat of the sun, symbolizing man; silver, representing woman, was the moon's tears—the emperor sought to buy his freedom by pillaging the temples and palaces of tons of gold and silver, which was melted down into ingots and presented to the conquering Spaniards. But Atahualpa found these imperialists to be without honor: instead of being freed, he was tried for treason and executed. There could be no compromise with imperial power. The Incas themselves recognized the eclipse of their civilization's day and the imposition of a night of terror and death:

Hail fell,
Lightning struck,
The sun sank,
Night came.[35]

For other conquered victims of empire the night's terror would be more protracted.

Empire's New World colonies and their growing economies demanded, above all else, a labor force. Nowhere in history has the enslavement of native peoples been an unambiguous success. Among Amerindian populations it was a decided disaster. Spain acknowledged necessity as a virtue by 1540, banning the enslavement of aboriginal populations; the English and the Portuguese found in the African slave trade a more effective and bountiful source of labor. The Dark Continent was born in the night of empire's material need.

Diverse human streams fed the appetite of the new plantation economies. Various nonslave but coerced labor migrations pushed indentured servants and others out of the Old World's declining opportunities and pulled them in the direction of the demanding productions of the new.[36] But chattels were attractive to power in ways that citizens, however circumscribed, never could be. Economic inducements made slaves cheap and servants dear, and in a hardening racist atmosphere white Europeans, however lowly their class status and material dependency, could never quite be othered like blacks brought from Africa. These circumstances ensured that the slave trade became the major disfiguring chain of labor recruitment linking the globe's increasingly connected continents.[37] The fortunes of capitalism and slavery were inextricably meshed, the progress, enlightenment, and lofty ideals of the Age of Revolution shadowed by the dark triangular trade in sugar, tobacco, and cotton from the New World, textiles manufactured in the rising factory system of England, and black bodies herded into the slave ships and plantation compounds of empire's most sordid transactions.[38]

The first architects of this systematic barter in human flesh were the Portuguese, whose mid-fifteenth-century trading posts along Africa's sub-Saharan west coast initiated the importation of black slaves into the Iberian peninsula and the cluster of Portuguese-controlled islands extending south from the Madeiras to Cape Verde. But the small numbers involved in this exchange, approximately a thousand a year, were a mere drop in the bucket of an exploding trade that grew annually from 1502 to 1860, consolidating on the bedrock of New World plantations and drawing in all the advanced trading nations—the Dutch, the French, the British. Over the course of these three and a half centuries almost ten million Africans were forcibly transported to the Americas. Sugar production—in the British West Indies, the French Antilles, Brazil, and the Louisiana Territory—absorbed 60 to 70 percent of all slaves who survived the Atlantic passage to labor in European colonies. These New World slaves accounted for a mere 1 percent of the world's population between 1600 and 1800, yet they produced the goods that dominated the channels of world trade. Increasingly, as well, the sugar plantations of Cuba and the British West Indies followed a division-of-labor trajectory that foreshadowed later economies of scale in the mass production factories of advanced, mono-poly capitalism. Economic specialization led to monoculture as sugar pushed other crops to the sidelines and then toward virtual extinction; slave labor eliminated indentured servants and waged workers; large plantations overtook smaller ones; gang labor chipped away at other forms of production until it reigned supreme; new technologies of transportation (railroads) and refinement (steam engines for grinding the cane and powering huge rollers) complemented the labors of the fieldhands. One Louisiana plantation housed a brick processing plant longer than a city block, serviced by cars on iron rails and the most advanced industrial equipment of its day. Colonial exports in this massive economy soared upward of 17.5 million pounds sterling by the 1770s, dependent on half a million tons of shipping and more than a hundred thousand seamen and dock workers.[39]

Slavery sustained empire; it also made it more precarious. The stakes were high, and enslaved workers were a gamble that wagered immense economic return against a set of fears, tensions, conflicts, and pressured accommodations both psychic and material. The slave was a dark imperial-ism's even darker underside. When scrutinized, slavery exposed imperial-ism's contradictions, costs, and vulnerabilities. In this climate of often unspoken contest much could go wrong.[40] Slavery was one of history's great ironies, as well as perhaps its supremely exploitive tragedy: the articulation of unfreedom, it expanded globally and consolidated its peculiar accumulative regime in an age that proclaimed freedom a fundamental and universal right. At odds with so much associated with the emerging capitalism of the Industrial Revolution, its contribution to the economic origins of the two leading empires of the modern world—Great Britain and the United States—is, however one assesses significance, of unques-tioned importance. Now regarded as a thing of the past, at least in the Western economies of advanced capitalism, slavery has left legacies that distort and demean the social relations of the modern world. Slavery was the dawn of imperialism's brightest waking day, as well as the nightmare of its longest, darkest sleep. The ugly accelerations and polarizing prejudices of nineteenth-century racist thought and the heroic struggles of enslaved Africans to strike blows for their own freedom were mutually reinforcing processes that emerged directly out of empire's destabilizing distortions.

It was perhaps an understandable paradox that as slavery filled imperialism's coffers in the late eighteenth and early nineteenth centuries, abolitionist and antislavery tracts, lectures, and societies proliferated. Their image of Africa was two-sided: patronizingly romanticizing a land of noble, innocent, and simple savages, reformers constructed a conception of a continent despoiled by rapacious European slave traders. It was a liberally well-meaning but derogatory representation that prettified, flattened, and caricatured reality. Still, between 1780 and 1840 the writing on Africa did not, for the most part, present the continent "darkly." As Philip D. Curtin, Douglas A. Lorimer, and Patrick Brantlinger have argued, the image of the Dark Continent was a later nineteenth-century construction. It was molded in a historical moment that saw pseudoscientific racism crystallize in anthropology's beginnings, the economic and social decline of the British West Indies, and the chaos of the American Civil War (1861–1865) in which the issue of slavery drove a violent divide down the middle of U.S. society and threatened the material interests of Great Britain and other trading nations. Ironically, as the slave trade was suppressed within the British Empire in 1807 and slavery abolished entirely in 1833, a discourse arose not of racial harmony and coexistence but of racist antagonism. From the 1860s to the publication of Stanley's In Darkest Africa in 1890, a plethora of publications presented an increasingly deprecatory view of blacks and their continent. Many of the writers were missionaries, their evangelical disdain for the savagery of Africa presented in the usual composite of piety, prudery, and profane contempt.[41] Under titles such as Daybreak in the Dark Continent, Dawn in the Dark Continent; or, Africa and Its Missions, and Savage Africa, black/white oppositions found expression in metaphors of lightness and darkness, the light unmistakably equated with civilization and human advance. "Loving darkness rather than light," suggested one missionary's autobiography, "the natives ... resent all that makes for progress."[42]

As Anne McClintock has suggested with interpretive brilliance, this racism adapted itself to and was extended by the emerging market in small consumer goods as imperialism cultivated a commodity spectacle of racialized domesticity. One company mass-marketed its soap through advertising campaigns that displayed the cleansing authority of a product that could scrub the blackness of skin color into the racialized whiteness of civilization and progress. A stove polish highlighted another side of this racialized cult of color's oppositional hues: the staying power of blackness could be deployed to useful purpose in the shining of certain surfaces. Imperial themes, accentuated by images of civilization and savagery, white and black, conquest and subordination, insinuated themselves throughout the growing marketplace of consumer goods in the late nineteenth century, reinforcing in the low culture of the shop and the advertisement stereotypes of racism that had already found an articulation in science, religion, and the power of the state.[43]

Mirroring these products and their racially scaffolded iconographic presentations was the black-corking of the stereotypical minstrel show, in which racist caricature was physically and culturally presented to transatlantic audiences in the middle to late nineteenth century. Henry Mayhew discovered fifty such "Ethiopian serenaders" plying their trade in the streets of mid-century London. One reported that they got the best-paying response from working people: "The evenings are the best times.... The City is good, I fancy, but they won't let us work it; it's only the lower parts, Whitechapel and Smithfield ways, that we have a chance in. Business and nigger-songs don't go well together."[44] The first postage stamp of British Central Africa, the mail being a symbol of imperial invasion, bore the motto "Light in Darkness" on a shield flanked by natives holding a spade and a pickax—implements, as Brantlinger suggests, for building the future white civilization on the Dark Continent.[45] Children's literature constructed similar understandings, as did drill and dance.[46]

Wherever one looked in late Victorian Britain, it seemed, a Foucauldian-like discourse of racialism gave new meanings to things. Through active human agents of imperial ideology, "this violence ... [done] to things, or, at all events, a practice ... impose[d] upon them" constructed racialized identities of opposition that fed into the structures of exploitation and oppression.[47] From inherited racial prejudice, the legacy in part of a slavery long renounced, a hierarchically coded imagery of skin colors and cultures worked its way around the world, continuing the violence of slavery in the white settler dominions that had rooted their social formations in the suppression and subordination of aboriginal Others.[48] One of the founding fathers of Australia's literary canon, Marcus Clarke, proclaimed with certainty in 1868 that "'Aborigines' are a mistake." His program for white development, prompted by an outbreak of violence between settlers and Maoris in New Zealand, differed from those adopted elsewhere only in its forthrightness:

I regard the occupation of New Zealand by the British as a gross swindle from beginning to end.... but having got the land, established ourselves there, and built churches and public houses, and so on, we would be fools not to use our best endeavours to keep [it]. To do this in peace, the Maoris must be exterminated. ... To make treaties and talk bunkum is perfectly useless; they must be stamped out and utterly annihilated. If England will send out a sensible man with a genius for slaughter, New Zealand should be grateful. Free fire and sword for six months, and a "smoking-out" or two would speedily put matters to rights.[49]

Thus the imperial dream remained a nightmare for some. Its darkness was most evident at precisely those moments of repression associated with attempts to mobilize resistance. Slavery, for all the sophisticated attempts to conjure away its evils, was indeed a horror. If the lash did not rule, it was at the least a last resort. Given the slave masters' known willingness to exploit their women slaves sexually and, in some regions, to encourage high levels of fertility among slave women, thereby increasing their assets in a reproductive process that might see offspring sold to plantation states in need of a labor force, is it any wonder that rebellious antagonism was bred in the bone of one of history's most acutely oppressed social groupings?[50] Whatever methods the slaves had at their disposal to subvert the systematic mechanisms by which their bodies, and their labors, were produced and reproduced as the property of white masters (and these were many, creative, and varied), and however differentiated the specific locales of slave political economies that reached from Brazil and Cuba into the West Indies and the American South, the threat of slave rebellion and revolt simmered persistently beneath the surface of the class, race, and familial relations of a social order rooted in an inequality as intense as any the modern world has known.[51]

Slave revolts ran the gamut from the abortive uprising of the militant few to massive contests that galvanized entire societies. "Whatever else may be said of the revolts," notes Eugene D. Genovese, "they everywhere formed part of the political opposition to European capitalism's blood conquest of the world and attendant subjugation of the colored peoples." Within this hemispheric clash of those oppressed by their class and race place against those whose privilege and color marked them for lives of leisure and largesse, a turning point was the great black revolution of the 1790s in Saint Domingue, led by Toussaint L'Ouverture and studied by C. L. R. James. This event of world-historic proportions established itself as an important chapter in the long battle for human liberation and enshrined itself in literature. The Haitian Jacobins linked their resistance to slavery to the bourgeois-democratic ideals of the Age of Revolution; in doing so they shifted the terrain of slave revolt from an attempt to win freedom from slavery to a wider struggle to overthrow slavery as a social system. A South Carolina publicist grasped this intuitively in the aftermath of one rebellion, commenting, "We regard our negroes as the 'Jacobins' of the country, against whom we should always be on our guard, and who, although we fear no permanent affects from any insurrectionary movements on their part, should be watched with an eye of steady and unremitting observation." Although this may seem a slaveholding voice of uncommon moderation, the same writer picked up the pace of diatribe: "They are the *Anarchists* and the *Domestic Enemy*: the *common enemy of civilized society, and the barbarians who would if they could, become the destroyers of our race*."[52]

Throughout the non-U.S. New World plantation economies—British Guiana, Jamaica, Saint Domingue, Brazil, and much of the Caribbean— black slaves outnumbered whites, sometimes constituting 80 to 90 percent of the population. Revolts occurred in these outposts of empire with explosive regularity: in the Brazilian Bahia, 1807–1835; British Guiana, 1731–1823; Jamaica, from 1669 to the great "Christmas Rising" of 1831, in which twenty thousand participants waged a virtual general strike which, despite its defeat, prefigured modern Jamaican nationalism and doomed the slaveholding minority. These uprisings took place against a backdrop of ruling-class crisis and disintegration—an ideological ferment in which the banner of freedom (whether for class, race, or nation) was invariably unfurled—and the economic, military, and political chaos born of European imperial rivalries. The preponderant numbers of slaves, then, and the ongoing crisis of a seigneurial order insecurely placed at the intersection of diverse and tightening capitalist rivalries, made such protests revolutionary events, campaigns in what was in effect a protracted guerrilla war.

Within the U.S. South the situation was markedly different. There slaves only rarely outnumbered whites; the free black population tended to disperse north or integrate into a buoyant capitalism's marginal opportunities; and America's revolutionary national contest with empire was settled decisively, and relatively quickly, in the late eighteenth century. To be sure, slavery disfigured and divided the republic, creating factions within the ruling class, but nowhere within the governing elite was fractiousness, destabilization, or commitment to abolition sufficient to draw battle lines favorable to the slaves. Even during the point of Civil War, which took on the appearance of a last-ditch stand of slaveholders against northern capitalists, issues other than slave freedom were very much in the forefront. Slave revolts in the English-speaking colonies and the United States could be quite bloody, but they had even less chance of success than those elsewhere and were more likely to be politically confined. That outbreaks in New York City (1712), Stono, South Carolina (1739), and Louisiana (1795 and 1811) took place at all was a testimony to the resilience and determination of slave rebels. Nevertheless, slave conspiracies and revolts in nineteenth-century America—Gabriel Prosser's Richmond, Virginia, plot of 1800; Denmark Vesey's Charleston, South Carolina, revolt in 1822; and the Southampton County, Virginia, uprising of Nat Turner in 1831—kept southern slaveholders and their northern allies on the knife edge of a class and race paranoia that was unleashed with terrifying brutality in the aftermath of each rebellion.

When some two to five hundred poorly armed slaves marched in revolt on New Orleans in 1811, they were quickly suppressed by federal troops aided by a free Negro militia. Thereupon, vengeful whites began an indiscriminate slaughter, killing sixty-six of the rebels and subsequently executing sixteen leaders. Decapitating their victims' bodies, the whites placed heads on spikes and lined the road from New Orleans to the plantation where the uprising had commenced. At times even the hint of a black revolt could draw the irrational terror of retribution. A rumored uprising in New York in 1741, which never in fact took place, resulted in the arrest of 150 slaves and twenty-five whites. Five of the latter—an innkeeper and his wife, a soldier, a priest, and "a woman of unsavory reputation"—were executed. Of the slaves arrested, thirteen were burned alive, eighteen were hanged (some in chains), seventy were banished, and seven went mysteriously missing, never to be found. Civilization and its saviors had their dark side.[53]

Resistance to the slave order, something of a given, was understandably organized and launched, at least at the height of actual rebellion, in the relative freedoms and clandestine collectivity of the night. Most of the large American slave revolts of the early nineteenth century are thought to have originated in all-night prayer meetings. It was not for nothing that slaveholders often imposed an evening curfew beyond which all blacks—free and slave—were expected to be housebound. Frederick Law Olmstead commented on the Charleston ban on night activity: "I found that more than half the inhabitants of this town were subject to arrest, imprisonment, and barbarous punishment, if found in the streets without a passport after the 'evening gunfire.'" The equivalent of apartheid's pass laws, such regulatory zeal addressed ruling-class fear that the night gave the slaves license to create pieces of freedom. Virginia sheriffs routinely broke up nocturnal meetings of slaves and expressed their consternation that religious dissidents in the white community were "determined to encorige our Negroes to Wrong & the other day they sent to the Captain of the Patteroles that on Friday night they wood have a meeting & if they came there & offered to tuch a Negroe that they wood protect the Negroes & if they said a word wood beat them." It was common to announce that revolt would be struck at the hour of midnight. Gabriel's conspiracy in Virginia in 1800 was orchestrated through a series of slave encounters, some of which—barbecues, afternoon drinking sessions under a bridge, market gatherings, or outdoor preachings—did happen during the day. But it was at night that recruitment was most likely, darkness providing a cover for conversations that tested the convictions of potential slave recruits. It must have been the same elsewhere, night being a time propitious for freedom, an interlude between the endlessly repetitious routines of the slave's daily labors, a moment that could be used to run away or plot rebellion.[54]

The slave's night therefore differed dramatically from empire's nineteenth-century night. On the one side, nights of resistance and rebellion spawned quests for freedom; on the other, nights of nostalgia and escalating fear led to terrifying campaigns of repression and containment. Hope stood counterposed to the high walls of coercion that incarcerated a rising proportion of the world's peoples in confines of class, race, and gender that global power found profitable and purifying. Empire produced order, as well as satisfying the accumulative addictions of Europe's ruling class. Slave revolt was often "the ultimate manifestation of class war under the most unfavorable conditions," but it managed to knit together the vision of an alternative order, one of transatlantic transgression and challenge.[55]

The central event was the Saint Domingue revolution, which Genovese sees as indicating the development of a "revolutionary ideology that emerged in the 1790s ... fed from both sides of the Atlantic." Leaders of American slave revolts consciously looked to Haiti for inspiration, and one rebel leader in the 1811 Louisiana uprising was a free "mulatto" from Saint Domingue. White and black mariners battled the press gang in American ports such as Boston in the decades leading up to the Revolutionary War, and when the first battle of that struggle broke out, the black seaman Crispus Attucks was in the crowd, standing at the head of "a motley rabble of saucy boys, negroes and mulattoes, Irish teagues and outlandish jack tarrs." Among the French troops stationed in Savannah in 1779 to bolster the revolution and aid the Americans against the British

were 545 blacks, one of whom was Henri Christophe; he would serve
fifteen years later as one of Toussaint L'Ouverture's corps of chief officers,
all free blacks. As late as the 1860s, echoes of the French Revolutions—
European *and* Haitian—could be heard in the deep South, evident in the
New Orleans creole call for black and colored unity in response to the
Emancipation Proclamation:

> Brothers! The hour strikes for us; a new sun, similar to that of 1789,
> should surely appear on our horizon. May the cry which resounded
> through France at the seizure of the Bastille resonate today in our
> ears.... Let us all be imbued with those noble sentiments which charac-
> terize all civilized people.... In sweet accord with our brothers, let us
> fill the air with these joyous cries: "vive la liberté! vive l'union! vive la
> justice pour tous les hommes."

Slaveholders found little to like in the celebrations of Haitian independence
staged by free black workers in St. Louis, Missouri in 1859.[56]

But traffic in the ideas of the Age of Revolution and the practice of
rebellion were not simply inserts in the politics of the "peculiar institution," a rough-edged reminder of the American republic's racial limitations. Conversations and travels were more wide ranging than this. The
African-born former slave Olaudah Equiano, for instance, led a life of
extraordinary adventure: he witnessed a slave ship's captain's brutal and
deadly flogging of an English sailor; he saw a Highlander scalp an Indian
at the battle of Louisburg; and his wanderings in the Americas and England
put him in contact with abolitionists, Wilkesite libertarians, and Jamaican
rebel slaves. Along with Ottobah Cugoano, he was a leading figure in the
black community of 1780s London. There he promoted the emancipation
of slaves and worked on behalf of the black poor who, after a taste of
empire's slavery and racism, wanted to relocate to Sierra Leone. He may
well have touched down in the Corresponding Society milieu of 1790s
Jacobinism; some say he met Thomas Hardy. He certainly read Milton,
and he imagined himself and his community possessed of the rights of
freeborn Englishmen. An African, a slave, a rebel—Peter Linebaugh calls
Equiano "the boomerang of the triangle trade," an agent of change who
kept returning to those who attempted to relegate him to imperialism's
oppression. And there were others of his kind.[57] They rubbed shoulders,
metaphorically at least, with all marginalized peoples in the Age of Empire,
including those self-constructed maroon communities of runaway slaves
and their seafaring buccaneer equivalents, the pirates.

9

In the Shadow of Empire

Pirates and Maroons

Empires, like the capitalism within which they grow and whose historical consolidation they paralleled, are often regarded by scholars as structures of controlling governance, drawing loosely on the panopticism of the Foucauldian mechanisms of power or the totalizing institutionalism evident in Stanley Elkins's thesis on slavery in the United States. "The practice of placing individuals under 'observation' is a natural extension of a justice imbued with disciplinary methods and examination procedures," noted Foucault, who was then prompted to ask: "Is it surprising that prisons resemble factories, schools, barracks, hospitals, which all resemble prisons?" The prison, that "darkest region in the apparatus of justice," was the most wide-ranging metaphor of power, its meanings circulating throughout various socioeconomic realms in which the regulation and rationalization of inequality—among individuals as well as global domains—were inscribed.[1] As early as 1609, Robert Johnson's Nova Britannia articulated the regulation and discipline that wedded empire to class formation, a cycle that was simultaneously one of punishment and accumulation attendant on the rhythms of imperialism's core states and peripheral conquests: "Two people are especially required herein, people to make the plantation, and money.... For the first, we need not doubt, our land abounding with swarms of idle persons, which having no means of labor to relieve their misery, do likewise swarm in lewd and naughty practices, so that if we seek not some ways for their foreign employment, we must provide shortly more prisons and corrections for their bad condition."[2]

Within this disciplinary circularity, empire and its political economies of plantation, slavery, racism, and ever-widening imperial domain mapped, counted, and recorded an archive of hierarchical authority, relations of subordination, and economics of predation, extraction, and decidedly unequal exchange. From within this seemingly all-encompassing circle it was difficult to see through power to other possibilities. But there were creole pioneers who, in the words of Benedict Anderson, forged the "imagined communities" of New World nations in the Americas out of the acute fears of slave revolution and the material fissures in the panoptic walls of the Spanish-American Empire's edifice of repression and containment. Through print, pride, and the stigmas of Old World prejudice this colonial stratum produced the imagined communities of New World nationalism: within a brief period in the nineteenth century the Spanish-American Empire, an institution of three centuries' duration, exploded into eighteen autonomous nation-states.[3]

The total, panoptic institution, then, was never quite as imposingly "carceral" as Foucault's positionings suggest. In the shadows of empire stood remarkably resilient and resourceful "nations" of marginality, imagined communities of destabilized geographic and cultural-economic place that, when scrutinized, illuminate disciplinary power by locating the circulatory flow—from nation to colony and back again—of punishment's processes and personnel. Indeed, Foucault himself suggests as much in his typically cryptic and subjectivist comment on "the completion of the carceral system." He locates this endnote in the dying words of a child inmate of the Mettray. An aptly dubbed "colony" of juvenile detention, Mettray was little more than a prison for youth (many of them not even convicted of crimes but stigmatized by allegations of wrongdoing). "What a pity I left the colony so soon," was the young offender's last sentence.[4] There were those who exhibited no such resignation, men and women for whom neither the blow nor the cell were acceptable. Among these were empire's exiles, runaways from the institutions of the ship and slavery—the former, imperialism's material conduit; the latter, a foundation of its commerce. Within the darkly obscured histories of the pirates and maroons, under the banner of King Death or the flag of flight, lie experiences of those who refused empire's many incarcerations.[5]

Piracy is as old as humanity's limited mastery of the sea. Like the empires that consolidated their power and political governance in part on conquests and adventures secured by sailing ships of war and trade, the pirates flourished—and flouted the laws and peace of such society as existed—at times of instability and turmoil.[6] They soon acquired a socially constructed character as "harsh-voiced and sullen-faced [men who] loved the groans and violence of war." In the ancient Mediterranean world, pirates were robbers and early slavers, plundering the unwary ships of the coastal waters and raiding sea towns for merchandise—the most valuable of which were robust young men and comely females who could be reduced to chattels. The Greeks thought piracy a reasonable vocation, enshrining it in myth and legend and placing it at the center of their written histories, while Roman rulers routinely bargained with pirate bands and sealed pseudo-political/military alliances with them.[7]

As the Roman Empire faltered, piracy flourished. In the political vacuum created by Rome's inability to retain its Mediterranean hegemony, the Dark Ages made a space for marauding bands of seafaring robbers. Among them were the much-feared Vikings from the north and west and, to the east, the pirate fleets of the various straits that connected India, the Middle East, and the trade in religious pilgrimage and commercial exchange. As late as the 1580s, the Venetian authorities, whose frustrations occasionally exploded in deadly repressions—blockades, indiscriminate coastal burnings, and public hangings—found the Mediterranean pirates "practically immune from any pursuer." It would be easier, declared one anguished senator, "to stop the birds flying through the air with one's hands than to stop" sea robbers with the large galleys of conventional sea war. Farther east, in the uncharted waters off the Malay Archipelago and the South China coast, ancient communities of boatmen and fishermen practiced sporadic acts of piracy. With the invasion of European ships and the commerce of late eighteenth- and nineteenth-century empire, these pirate fleets burgeoned into fierce battalions of seafaring power, a force to reckon with in the contests over sovereignty in the Orient.[8]

The early history of piracy, as Robert C. Ritchie has indicated, was one of simultaneous accommodation with and resistance to empire and its logics of domination and subordination. There was space in this seaborne expression of crude acquisitive individualism for officially sanctioned piracy: absolutist states literally hired out the seas to robber barons who, for the license of state sanction, functioned as both profiteers and protectors of empire's always dubious boundaries. This venture in global subcontracting produced entrées of world-historic significance into the transoceanic political economy of the early modern period, among the most noteworthy being Sir Francis "Sea Hawk" Drake's circumnavigation of 1577–1579. That two-year pirate voyage piled the spoils of plunder high in the court of Queen Elizabeth, who rewarded Drake with the status of a revered patriot.[9] But whole regions, such as the Mediterranean, may have been ceded to pirates by embattled empires such as those of the Spanish and the Turks, whose overhead costs weighed heavily on their everyday undertakings. Established ruling orders saw much advantage in shifting the exacting costs of empire's defense to the backs of privateers, whose willingness to combat rival colonizing powers was whetted by an appetite for potential booty.[10] When states did not bankroll this process, merchants might; sixteenth-century capital, often organized in imperial monopolies such as the English and Dutch East Indies Companies, provided sanctuary for pirates for more than a century, the rapaciousness of sea robbers supplementing the transactions of commerce.[11]

If sponsored piracy was seafaring plunder's dawn, its night was represented by those who broke from all official sanction, refusing to be either mercenaries of empire's seas or contractors of coastal looting. These freebooters sometimes established themselves in ports such as the famous pirate stronghold of Port Royal, Jamaica (eventually destroyed by an earthquake) or the New Orleans of Jean and Pierre Lafitte. But they could just as easily forgo all ties to conventional settlement, wandering the seas for years at a time, building self-contained floating societies sustained by the accumulations of relentless predation. As Ritchie suggests, these were marginal men (and the rare woman) of the Age of Empire, whose lives knew few conventional restraints and whose sense of "nation" and "community" was an imagined refusal of the restrictive agendas of property and power. Many such marauders had so thoroughly disengaged themselves from their cultures of birth that they crossed over into whatever non-European societies offered them the continuities of freedom they had come to appreciate.[12]

Wherever most pirates had come from, it was not a place of privilege. Likely to be in their twenties, many were former naval or merchant seamen who became pirates when their own ships were captured; in the words of Marcus Rediker, they were already "grimly familiar with the rigors of life at sea and with a single-sex community of work." Virtually all seemed to be without ties of family and marriage, or to have abandoned them; indeed, pirate vessels, to avoid having to deal with later desertions, often resolved "to take no Married Man." Drawn from the lowest social classes, they were easily castigated by authority as "desperate Rogues." If their orgins were the colonial populations of the West Indies, pirates had social backgrounds decidedly lacking in prestige. Island populations were a melting pot of pauper immigrants, deportees, exiled prisoners, highwaymen, and dissenters, a hodgepodge of the miscreant and the marginal described in 1685 by one commentator as "convict gaol-birds or riotous persons, rotten before they are sent forth, and at best idle and only fit for the mines," and by another as "a company of sodomists." These were hardly letters of reference to polite society.[13]

The true pirate was one, simply, who robbed on the high seas or from coastal towns, without consideration as to the prey's nationality. Having been driven out of desperate Old World circumstances or absconded from the imperial sea or the mercantile trading ships of empire's commerce, the pirate settled into nights of planning and raiding, followed by further nights of festive entertainment. Night was often his time of work, darkness his most trusted ally. "They resolved to execute their Plot at ten a-Clock the Night following," reads a typical account. One buccaneer commenced his life as a pirate by breaking his indenture, stealing a skiff from the Tortuga harbor one dark night and, at great risk from the winds and currents, making his way to the island of Saint Domingue. "We came very near the vessel before the people saw us, by reason of the darkness of the night," explains Alexander Esquemeling, recounting the seizure of a Spanish barque in August 1679. Sir Henry Morgan's 1668 subduing of the entrepôt of Portobello, a Costa Rican way station for galleons en route from the conquered lands of the Spanish New World to the treasuries of the imperial capital, was an archetypal pirate raid on a fortified town. His plans a well-kept secret, Morgan eventually told his captains and their crews that "he intended ... to plunder Porto Bello, and that he would peform it by night, being resolved to put the whole city to the sack, not the least corner escaping his diligence." Their night's labors done, Morgan's pirates spent the next fifteen days in looting, eating, and drinking, "committing in these things all manner of debauchery and excess." The spoils of the raid, divided up in Morgan's common place of rendezvous in Jamaica, amounted to 250,000 pieces of eight, as well as tons of merchandise, including linens and silks, all of which was dissipated with the usual "huge prodigality." The pirate night was a lucrative one, and the transgressions of the high seas could pay windfall dividends.[14]

By the seventeenth century the Golden Age of the nocturnal buccaneer had attracted sufficient attention and romanticization to enshrine piracy in the literary canon of succeeding generations. Blackbeard (Edward Teach), Captain (William) Kidd, and the indefatigable Welsh "gentleman" pirate Sir Henry Morgan, the knighted Lieutenant Governor of Jamaica, provided the historical foundations for an outpouring of fictional accounts and best-selling, sensationalized "eye-witness" treatments. Alexander O. Esquemelin/John Esquemeling's Netherlands-published The Buccaneers of America (1678) is among the latter. So is A General History of the Robberies and Murders of the Most Notorious Pyrates (1724), published under the name of one Captain Charles Johnson, but, since 1932, usually attributed to Daniel Defoe; that identification, however, was undermined subsequently by P. N.

Furbank and W. O. Owens, whose researches reestablish the enigmatic Captain Johnson as the creator of this immensely influential text.[15] Defoe did, however, pen the 1720 fictional The Life, Adventures, and Pyracies of the Famous Captain Singleton and the historical The King of Pirates, being an Account of Famous Enterprises of Captain Avery, with the Lives of Other Pirates and Robbers (1724). The theme would also be exploited by Sir Walter Scott in The Pirate (1821); in J. H. Ingraham's memorialization of the famous Louisiana-based Jean Lafitte, The Pirate of the Gulf (1837); and in the 1879 theatrical presentation of W. S. Gilbert and Arthur Sullivan's The Pirates of Penzance. Near the end of the nineteenth century, Robert Louis Stevenson's Treasure Island—first serialized in the children's magazine Young Folks in 1881–1882—brought the romance of the pirate into thousands of Victorian homes, as did J. M. Barrie's Peter Pan, performed in 1904 and published in 1911.[16]

Few of these histories, travelogues, and romantic fictions contained the insights and Swiftian ironies of Gulliver's Travels (1726):

> But I had another reason which made me less forward to enlarge his majesty's dominions by my discoveries. To say the truth, I had conceived a few scruples with relation to the distributive justice of princes upon those occasions. For instance, a crew of pirates are driven by a storm they know not whither, at length a boy discovers land from the top-mast, they go on shore to rob and plunder, they see an harmless people, are entertained with kindness, they give the country a new name, they take formal possession of it for the king, they set up a rotten plank or stone for a memorial, they murder two or three dozen of the natives, bring away a couple more by force for a sample, return home and get a pardon. Here commences a new dominion acquired with a title by divine right. Ships are sent with the first opportunity, the natives driven out or destroyed, their princes tortured to discover their gold, a free license given to all acts of inhumanity and lust, the earth reeking with the blood of its inhabitants: and this execrable crew of butchers employed in so pious an expedition, is a modern colony sent to convert and civilize an idolatrous and barbarous people.[17]

Colonies and pirates, in Swift's presentation, were part of the same water-borne process of conquest and accumulation. "Fortune is to be found on the sea, where one must go to collect it," philosophized one Caribbean buccaneer.[18]

Indeed, the term "buccaneer" derives from a method whereby Spanish colonizers cured the meat of wild cattle in Hispaniola (Saint Domingue/ Haiti), drying and smoking the long strips of flesh over a grating of green wooden sticks after the fashion of the Carib Indians.[19] Native peoples called the place of this cooking a boucan and the dried meat viande boucannée; and the European hunters themselves were known as buccaneers. As these

Spanish colonists combined their trade in flesh and hides with that of piracy, the name of buccaneer stuck, gradually merged into the nomenclature of West Indian piracy, where French corsairs plundered the seas along with English freebooters.[20]

Esquemeling, the Dutch physician, who lived among these buccaneers from 1668 to 1674, recalled that they ate scarcely anything but meat on their voyages of robbery and destruction, provisioning their ships by nocturnal raids on hog yards, where they secured the requisite supply of pork at the point of pistols and swords. Pirates then met in council on board their ship and laid out their voyage's constitution, or *chasse-partie*, a document signed by all on board. It set down the details of special compensation for captain, carpenter, and surgeon, plus extra payments to be made to each pirate who suffered a specific physical injury or loss (a right arm was valued at six hundred pieces of eight or six slaves). Beyond this, all shared in the booty, it being "severely prohibited to every one to usurp anything in particular to themselves ... all they take is equally divided." Likewise, if the plunder was poor, all equally, suffered. "No prey, no pay" was the supreme law of the pirate seas. The buccaneers exhibited little accumulative instinct, their lives of stealth and seizure contributing to a cavalier consumption of the spoils of their predatory labors. Their voyage done, the pirates squandered their perilously acquired wealth indiscriminately in nights of debauchery, indulgence, and camaraderie. Esquemeling noted that they were "civil and charitable to each other ... if any wants what another has, with great liberality they give it one to another": "O! Many a brave carouse I've known,/ as many a seaman may,/ A melting of the dollars with/the boys at Negril Bay."[21]

The buccaneer's life was thus one of wildly oscillating materiality: brief periods of excess, fed by a predatory expropriation, gave way to stints of scarcity during which preparations for the next voyage were made in haste. The evolving society of buccaneers adopted survival strategies that reflected the conditions of this life. Largely without wives and children, the West Indian pirates commonly associated in pairs and developed a system of inheritance known as *matelotage*. B. R. Burg accentuates the sexual and subordinate dimensions of this practice, suggesting that *matelotes* were most often youthful companions or servants of pederastically inclined pirates, *matelotage* being a codified system of protection and debt not unlike that which has developed in modern prison populations. As such, it could descend into abusive exploitation, but over generations of buccaneer experience it emerged as an institution of brotherhood among the pirates, sufficiently flexible to encompass the sexual and the material.

The gendered inequalities of a conventional land-based, property-defined familialism were stretched in new directions to accommodate the realities of the pirate's unconventional occupation and lifestyle. Homoeroticism might well figure prominently in these relations, but so could ties of long-standing sociability, admiration, and companionship or short-term material self-interest. According to a buccaneer known as Louis-Adhemar-Timothee Le Golif—whose memoirs present a raucous account of his wedding night, his *matelot* Pulverin, and his wife's subsequent fatal infidelities—*matelotage* was an intense form of male, brotherly bonding in which all was shared, including future wives:

> It is known that each of us in America has in the normal way a Brother of the Coast, or *matelot*, with whom he has to share everything, including the favors of madame, if one of them happens to marry.... I told [my wife to be] that in our case it would not be required hereafter to ask who was her husband, since my brother Pulverin allowed me, of his own free will, the title of spouse, not feeling disposed to receive the sacrament of marriage. This speech left the girl a little surprised. No one had warned her of it when she had embarked. But having taken a good look at Pulverin, who was younger than myself, lowering her pretty eyes, the fair one agreed that it would be ungracious to come to a country and not conform to all its usages and customs, and that, strange as this law was, she felt she would be, in this as in everything else, too docile a spouse not to submit.

As the two buccaneers shared the young woman in a discreet domesticity that managed to last three months, outfitting Madame Le Golif's household with a largesse that made the residence the favored supper lodging and watering hole of the local pirate community, all seemed well. When Le Golif and Pulverin debarked for a most profitable raid on the city of Saint Iago de Los Caballeros, however, Madame availed herself of the amours of a local island libertine and loafer. After Pulverin avenged his wronged master by killing the two in their bed, he was forced to flee, leaving Le Golif to mourn the loss of his loyal brother, a masculine companion of extraordinary talents. The loss of his wife occasioned less anguish.

Matelotage was thus an innovative pirate creation, one of many bred of the sailors' superstitious belief that once having passed the "Tropic," the seafarers had "drowned all their former obligations." Family surnames were discarded and, with them, complex histories, not only of lineage but of societal formations and cultural codes. A common saying among West Indian pirates was that one knew a man only when he was married, an indication that the last name of patrimony was irrelevant to the buccaneers, who had the rare freedom to construct identities and dismantle them according to which ship of fortune they joined. Outsider law had no meaning to these sea robbers; the only rules that applied to them were those they devised themselves. "Though Out-Laws, we keep laws among ourselves," explained Purser the Pirate "else we could have no certain government."

Seamen whose ships were pillaged might join the pirate crews precisely because the seeming self-autonomy of the buccaneer stood in stark contrast to the oppressive tyranny of the merchant ship. In 1723 off the coast of Barbados an armed sloop carrying thirty to forty pirates overtook the Princes Galley, a slave-trading vessel; they tortured its captain, seized its cargo of slaves, gold, guns, and ship's stores, and forced two of its skilled mates—an apprentice surgeon and carpenter—to join the buccaneer ranks. Two of its seamen, however, abandoned their waged employment willingly, witnesses later testifying that one of them voluntarily signed "a paper which the said pirates called their Articles of Regulation." Thus, beneath "the banner of King Death"—the Jolly Roger—pirates forged a new social order that took shape, in the words of one sea raider, through "the choice in themselves" exercised by these masterless men:

> Here was the Form of Justice kept up, which is as much as can be said
> of several other Courts, that have more lawful Commissions for what
> they do. Here was no feeing of Council, and bribing of Witnesses was a
> custom not known among them; no packing of Juries, no torturing and
> wresting the Sense of the Law, for bye Ends and Purposes, no puzzling
> or perplexing the Cause with unintelligible canting Terms, and useless
> Distinctions; nor was their Sessions burthened with numberless Officers,
> the Ministers of Rapine and Extortion.

In Virginia in 1720 one of six condemned pirates called for a bottle of wine on the gallows and defiantly drank "Damnation to the Governour and Confustion to the Colony," and his five fellow buccaneers pledged the same. When George I extended general pardons to all pirates in 1717–1718 in an attempt to rid the seas of this unruly menace, some took up his offer, but most seemed indifferent or "used the King's proclamation with great contempt, and tore it unto pieces." One pirate crew toasted the edict with the saucy salute "Curse the King and All the Higher Powers." In short, the pirate "nation" abhorred conventional power and its myriad forms of rule and governance, whether centered in law, in family, or in state.[22]

The rough democracy of the pirates was evident also in the relations of captains and crews. As Le Golif's memoir indicates, captains were made by their crew's regard for their strategic daring and leadership abilities, which included prowess in battle and the capacity to work their way out of difficult, often deadly, situations—as well, no doubt, as a certain uncompromising brutality that might save pirate lives at the expense of their enemies.[23] Although obeyed faithfully, the captain was no ruling-class authority; pirate leadership was earned, then willingly deferred to in specific circumstances. Captains governed precisely because buccaneers recognized the need for a decision-maker, particularly in the heat of chasing, or being chased. Prisoners were the property of the captain and decisions regarding their treatment understood to be his sole domain. Captains also had the recognized right to execute any pirate who challenged or refused orders during the commission of a raid. At all other times, however, captains were removable at the will of the crew "and had scarcely more prerogative than the ordinary pirates." Those with "gentleman-like" pretensions incurred the wrath of their men, many of whom had sufficient first-hand experience with the cruelties and brutalities of naval law and its mercantile enforcers to demand an immediate end to any hint of despotism or distinctions based on a sense of class superiority. The galling favoritism of other maritime occupations was quashed in a series of democratic checks and balances that elevated quartermasters and councils of the whole ship's workforce to the status of adjudicating bodies in the event of any disquiet. Merchant or naval captains who were captured by pirates might find themselves the victims of the oceanic crowd's rough justice, for many a sea raider remembered the floggings and tortures of his previous maritime servitude. Having escaped those inequalities and terrors, such pirates no doubt supplemented the spoils of material plunder with the sweet taste of revenge. Upon his apprehension in 1726 the buccaneer Philip Lyne confessed that his tenure as a pirate had allowed him the opportunity of considerable blood retribution: he claimed to have killed thirty-seven masters of vessels in his years under the banner of King Death.

The pirate ship, then, was a floating republic whose relatively egalitarian order seemed to the seamen of empire to be something of a kingdom of justice, materially rooted in the comradely distribution of seafaring life's largess as well as its tribulations. In *The Navy Royal; or, A Sea-Cook Turned Projector* (1709), Barnaby Slush commented on its attraction for early eighteenth-century maritime laborers:

> *Pyrates* and *Buccaneers*, are Princes to [Seamen], for there, as none are exempt from the General Toil and Danger; so if the Chief have a Supream Share beyond his Comrades, 'tis because he's always the

Leading Man in e'ry daring Enterprize; and yet as bold as he is in all other Attempts, he does not offer to infringe the common laws of Equity; but every Associate has his due Quota.... thus these *Hostes Humani Generis* as great robbers as they are to all besides, are precisely just among themselves; without which they could no more Subsist than a Structure without a Foundation.

Out of the shadows of empire's many and terrorizingly enforced inequalities sailed, in the words of Marcus Rediker, a "collectivist ethos of life" premised on looting the ill-gotten gains of imperialism's varied thefts. To many of the laboring poor, the "refusal to grant privilege or exemption from danger," as well as the "just allocation of shares," democratically determined, placed pirate theft beyond the moral compromise of colonialism's acquisitive individualism.[24] It was no doubt this unique historical experience that led the mysterious and exotic Marie Le Compte, a.k.a. Miss Le Compte, Proletaire—a Boston anarchist and Social Revolutionist, associate editor of the *Labor Standard* and a socialist orator especially drawn to tramps and outlaws—to hold forth in Stratford, England, in 1881 on "The Rebels of the Sea," a paean to pirates.[25]

Pirates, then, as part of a tradition of social banditry usually associated with peasant protest against poverty and oppression, rode the winds and sails of empire to extend to the high seas the cause of primitive justice and a contradictorily conservative egalitarianism, governed by the highly gendered rough masculinity of the maritime trades.[26] They were of course more than the merely "riotous, quarrelous, teacherous, blasphemous and villainous" lot they were routinely caricatured as in the seventeenth century.[27] Buccaneers formed something of a premodern collectivity, dispersed geographically but tied together through the camaraderie of their like labors, governed loosely by their own institutions and leadership hierarchies, which included ethical codes and taboos, laws, command structures of admirals, lesser officials, and captains, as well as symbolic representations of their community, most notably the pirate flag. In all of this, of course, the "revolutionary traditionalism" of the social bandit surfaced in a constructed community which, for the most part, mirrored the established structures of the ancien régimes the pirates had in fact repudiated.

National animosities—materially rooted in piracy's complicated historical origins as licensed (often furtively) by imperial authority and outlawed by that same metropolitan power—could be evident among them, particularly in the almost endless periods of declared war among rival colonial empires. The antagonism between Spanish and English pirates is legendary. Nevertheless, piracy was a community of sorts, one well known to its foes and recognized by itself. When the black or red flags of the floating "states" of the boundaryless buccaneers—emblazoned with the skull and crossbones, an hourglass, spears, cutlasses, or a bleeding heart: insignias of death, violence, and limited time—appeared on the horizon, potential victims fled in fear, while comrades in the art of sea raiding fired welcoming volleys of sociability. These floating principalities might strike separately or, in times of acute aggravation, battle among themselves, but they seemed to march together in their irreverent, often deadly, blood feud with the standards of private property and state power. The pirate nation thus consisted of a loose confederacy, encompassing as many as thirty to forty vessels and a thousand men among English pirates in the seventeenth century, a body that grew to almost 2,500 by 1718; in all, perhaps 5,500 seafarers may have gone "upon the account" at the high-water mark of Anglo-American buccaneering. In the French West Indies in 1684 approximately twenty corsairs were manned by almost two thousand pirates. Floating factories of pillaging accumulation and dissi-pating debauchery, pirate ships might sustain workforce crews of up to three hundred.

Their "production" was prodigious: in the opening decades of the seventeenth century French and English merchants sustained losses in the tens of thousands of pounds sterling. Peter Easton, a northern pirate captain in command of nine ships, terrorized the Grand Banks of Newfoundand in the summer of 1612, inflicting losses of 20,000 pounds sterling; Trinidad, plundered in 1673, yielded a booty of 100,000 pieces of eight; a decade later the sacking of Vera Cruz, the richest city of the New World, brought buccaneers some $6 million dollars. The notorious Captain Kidd, whose vast treasure is still reputed to await its modern finder, was rumored to have had 400,000 pounds sterling on board one of his ships before he went to the gallows in 1701. For a time, plunder was more profitable than production, though that state of economic parasitism could not last forever. If colonialism was one component of early capitalism's accumu-lation, piracy—when not bankrolled by established mercantile and state powers—was yet another measure of the retribution the dispossessed of the countryside and the city attempted to mete out to their rulers.[28]

Christopher Hill has speculated that the pirate community could well have harbored an intellectually subterranean but continuous seaborne attachment to the radical ideas of the seventeenth century, articulated in the doctrines of the Ranters, Diggers, and Levellers.[29] Making its way through religious dissent and obscure clandestine bodies such as the Robin

Hood Society (a tavern order of the mid-eighteenth century) to new refuges in Jamaica and Madagascar, such utopian commitments could have found a home in the pirate's imagined community of rough, white, masculine egalitarianism, built in the shadows of empire. When eight pirates were tried in Boston in 1718, a merchant captain whose ship had been captured by the accused buccaneers testified that they "pretended to be Robin Hoods Men."[30]

A rare rebel pirate presented in Johnson's *History* was the fictional Captain Mission, a religious dissident who synthesized and symbolized the utopian possibilities that pirate democracy seemed to promise, especially in the buccaneer outpost of Madagascar. Mission refused to bend the knee to theological orthodoxy, insisting that Established Church doctrine was "no more than a curb upon the minds of the weaker, which the wider sort yielded to in appearance only." Aligned with a "lewd diest priest," he exhibited a pronounced skepticism that pointed to the contradictory character of the scriptures and promoted the view that God had granted man reason so that he could better pursue his "present and future happiness." All curbs on the liberty to do so were unnatural constraints, and Mission justified waging piratical war on the ships of the sea as a means of breaking down the barriers erected by despotic governments that oppressed all humanity. Mission regarded his crew, then, not as pirates, but as "men who were resolved to assert that liberty which God and Nature gave them and own no subjection to any farther than was for the common good of all." On Madagascar, a long-standing African refuge of temporary pirate settlement, Mission and his extraordinary band supposedly founded a democratically governed utopian outpost in which slavery was abolished, property made available for all, and money held in a common treasury. Mission called the settlement *Libertalia* and gave his people a universal nationality named "*Liberi* ... desiring in that might be drown'd the distinguish'd Names of *French, English, Dutch, Africans, Etc.*" Commandeering two sloops named *Liberty* and *Childhood*, Mission mercilessly attacked the commerce of monopolistic trading companies and vessels transporting cargoes of enslaved Africans; "knocked off their Chains, and of Slaves made them free Men, and Sharers in his Fortunes." The residents of his community were said to have "enjoy'd all the Necessaries of Life; were free and independent of the World," regarding it as "Madness again to subject themselves to any Government, which, however mild, still exerted some Power." Even in fictional life, however, *Libertalia*'s longevity was limited: its inhabitants were suddenly subjected to an unprovoked attack, and "all their propos'd Happiness was vanquished; ... in the

Dead of Night, the Natives came down upon them in two great Bodies, and made a great Slaughter, without distinction of Age or Sex." Founded on the spoils of night raids, Libertalia succumbed to similar violence.[31]

Captain Mission's utopian settlement, with its obliteration of the color line of race that ran so prominently through the histories of both empire and piracy and its egalitarian displacement of class power, went a considerable distance toward erasing traditional oppressions. But what of the placement of women in the pirate world? There is no doubt that the buccaneer's life was gendered as masculine in ways that reflected to the point of caricature the powers of patriarchal dominance. As Burg suggests and the memoir of Le Golif constantly attests, the relentlessly rough and uninhibited predatory character of pirate sexuality placed women— whether slaves, prostitutes, or free agents of desire—in positions of subordination. This may, as Burg argues, have had a homoerotic dimension; there were no doubt pirate sodomites whose sexual pleasures favored males, and especially young boys, over women. But pirate sexuality was also unashamedly lustful; in port, women were prizes—fought over, seduced, raped, and purchased (often with the buccaneer's characteristic material abandon). This was most emphatically a male nation, although the odd woman could find a place in it—either on the proverbial pedestal of beauty deified (as in Morgan's kidnapping of a white Christian woman of elite status in Panama, and his failure to seduce or coerce her into a sexual liaison); in an almost mythic reputation of sexual skill (most pronounced among certain prostitutes); or, as in the rare cases of Mary Read and Anne Bonny, by cross-dressing and joining the fighting ranks of pirates directly.[32]

The pirate's taste for women, one senses, was not unlike his taste for all that could be acquired to satiate an appetite: acquisitions were meant to be spent rather than savored. The notorious Blackbeard, after wedding his fourteenth wife, a girl of sixteen, followed his usual custom of bedding his bride and then asking five or six of his crew to do the same while he watched. In Libertalia and other utopian settlements in Madagascar, polygamy was ostensibly the common familial form and one area where the powerful and humane authority of Captain Mission appeared to have little weight. When his pirate crews seized a hundred Muslim girls and their families on the way to Mecca, Mission was determined to set the prisoners free but could not dissuade the buccaneers from keeping the young women, whom they wanted for wives. Amid the wailings of the separation, Mission pleaded with the Liberi men, but his exhortations fell on deaf ears.

There were undoubtedly limitations to the democratic experiment of the pirates, but these must be balanced off against its possibilities. In an age of rigidly gendered constraints in the sexual and familial realm, pirates pioneered new freedoms: for example divorce by mutual consent seems to have been recognized. Certainly a woman like Anne Bonny demonstrated little of the subservient spouse: she changed husbands by means of a properly written and witnessed document, acted on her physical attractions to new members of the crew despite marriage to the captain, and bluntly addressed her husband on the day of his execution with the cold dimissal that "she was sorry to see him there, but if he had fought like a man, he need not have been hanged like a dog." Like her comrade Mary Read, she herself escaped the gallows by "pleading her belly": that is, informing the court of her pregnancy. Read was no less outspoken and certainly not one to succumb to domineering males. She found her shipmates preferable to those Old World authorities "who are now cheating widows and orphans and oppressing their poor neighbours."[33]

Bonny and Read, who may well have shared a transgressive lesbian relationship, as well as the irreverent social world of piracy, situated the ideas and practices of seaborne resistance within the widening circles of eighteenth-century dislocation and dispossession. Against property and power they offered a defiant set of repudiations, lived out in a politics of dissenting deviance that embraced conspiracies against the Crown as well as cross-dressing, the occasional forcible freeing of slaves chained in ships, and the torching of empire's buildings of commerce and profitable exchange.[34]

It was not ideas such as these, ultimately, that brought piracy to the end of its days and nights on the seas, but they must have helped to stoke the fires of intense antagonism already burning wherever the buccaneers threatened the capital moving over empire's commerical waterways. By 1720 the imperial outposts of the New World had lived in terror of pirate atrocities long enough. The pleadings of authorities, which peaked around 1717–1718, were remarkaby similiar. "I think the pirates daily increase, taking and plundering most ships and vessels that are bound to this island," reported the harried commander in chief of Jamaica in 1717. From the governors of South Carolina and old Massachusetts came similar tales of woe; without aid, they knew their "trade must stop." The timing of the supposed pirate settlements in Madagascar was perhaps not accidental: between 1690 and 1710 the buccaneers sensed that their dominance of the seas was coming to an end, and they looked to far-off lands of exotic potential to find shelter from a new storm of repression. By 1723 the number of pirates active in the Atlantic and the Caribbean had dropped to around a thousand, and in 1726 the dwindling buccaneer ranks were barely two hundred, with only half a dozen pirate raids reported annually.

A judicious deployment of legislation aimed at making the trials and punishments of pirates more effective, pardons designed to entice the buccaneers away from the lucrative trade of sea robbery (although this ploy had little effect outside of the Bahamas), the licensing of private ships that were no more than oceanic bounty hunters, an outpouring of religious and other propaganda (New England's Cotton Mather issued pious anti-pirate sermons, including the luridly titled 1726 *Vial Poured Out upon the Sea*), and the stepping up of increasingly public trials and executions of captured buccaneers (though the youngest might be granted reprieves) all took their toll. Some pirates went to their final punishment besieged at the scaffold by clergy and by print-minded hucksters who craved a few lines of verse to sell. Others refused to confess to their crimes and accepted no interference from religious figures. William Fly, facing the hangman in Boston in 1726, showed a total lack of penitence: carrying a small bouquet of flowers in his hand, he walked to the scaffold with a sprightly step, called to the crowd, and admonished the executioner for not knowing his trade; as his last act among the living, he showed the hangman how to work the ropes in the most effectual manner.

Many, however, exhibited a mixture of defensive obstinacy and final contrition. Cotton Mather ministered to the last needs of eight condemned pirates in Boston in 1717. One twenty-four-year-old expatriate New Yorker, who had taken up with the buccaneers of the West Indian island of St. Thomas, was willing to confess to some of his sins, including undutifulness to his parents and profanation of the Sabbath. But when Mather insisted that he acknowledge the wickedness of murdering his brethren of the deep, the young man replied bluntly, "We were forced men." Mather did not appreciate the explanation. One wonders if he grasped the precious sarcasm of a Jamaican pirate:

> You see yourself then a most miserable sinner?
>> Oh! Most miserable!
> You have had a heart wonderfully hardened.
>> Ay, and it grows harder. I don't know what is the matter with me. I can't but wonder at my self!
> There is no help to be had, anywhere, but in the admirable Saviour, whom I am now to point you to.
>> Oh! God be merciful to me a sinner!
> A sinner. Alas, what cause to say so! But I pray, What more special sins, lie now as a more heavy burden on you?

> Special sins! Why, I have been guilty of all the sins in the world!
> I know not where to begin. I may begin with gaming! No, whoring,
> that led on to gaming; and gaming led on to drinking; and drinking to
> lying, and swearing and cursing; and all that is bad; and so to thieving;
> and to this!

Macabre rituals sometimes accompanied pirate hangings. Those in England were not atypical. At Execution Dock on a bend of the Thames (now overlooked by the pub called the Captain Kidd), amid a jumble of wharves, timberyards, and ships' masts, gallows were erected on the shoreline at low tide. After a hanging the bodies were submerged by the swirling waters of incoming tides, and not until three high tides had washed them were they cut loose and hauled away. The most notorious pirates were then tarred—to preserve the cadavers from the elements, carrion-feeding birds, and decomposition—and hung in chains or suspended from a gibbet, their remains strategically placed on long-term display for the seafaring community to behold. When capital punishment took place "within the flood marks," all knew that the executed man had committed crimes on "territory" governed by the Lord High Admiral. Four to six hundred Anglo-American pirates were executed in the decade 1716–1726, and "truck, barter, [or] exchange" with buccaneers was also punishable by death. Empire's property, the high seas, was not to be a common treasury for all.[35]

Pirates had their own customary practices of punishment among themselves which, in spite of the lore of "walking the plank" (almost never practiced), more likely involved summary execution and torture. But the most common response of buccaneer crews to violations of their code, or to the presence of merely inconvenient prisoners whom they did not wish to kill, was marooning: putting them ashore on a desolate or deserted island. Such a fate could lead to a slow and agonizing death but might afford the possibilities of survival evidenced in Defoe's tale of the shipwrecked Robinson Crusoe. The naming of this practice perhaps links to marginalized communities of outcasts made up of runaway slaves, who established "maroon" societies in the most isolated and rugged territory surrounding the plantations of the New World. In this perhaps original sense the term derived from the Spanish cimarrón (wild, unruly); it referred to domestic cattle pastured in the hills of Hispaniola which were often captured, first by Indian slaves who had escaped their captors and, later (after the mass importation of African slaves), by "bush negro" runaways. Another linguistic connection is made to the wild hogs hunted in the Spanish colonies by the people who came to be known as maroons. By the seventeenth and eighteenth centuries these slave exiles had created "wild" African-American societies of notable fierceness, which the pirates could see as sharing much with themselves. They may well have considered the term applied to these isolated, often mountain-based groups, in which a warlike defensiveness dominated an outlaw culture, as somehow appropriate to the banishment they imposed on backsliders and bodies seized in acts of plunder. Both as a structure built from slave resistance and as a practice of pirate punishment, then, maroons as people and marooning as a process emerged at approximately the same time and found their common histories linked in islands of rough inaccessibility.

Pirates as a whole were hardly staunch abolitionists—Captain Mission and Libertalia notwithstanding—but neither were they blind to material self-interest. Although they often traded in the black slaves of Africa and the West Indies, they also forged alliances with runaway slave rebels, whom they knew to be fierce opponents of slaveholding regimes in the New World. Early in the history of empire's rivalries, the pirate lord Sir Francis Drake recruited maroons to aid in his Panama adventure. Runaway slaves might be helped by pirates, who knew that a price could be exacted from them for their freedom. Some blacks escaping the plantations were even known to sign on with pirate crews; at least one Cuban maroon rose to the rank of buccaneer captain. The New Orleans–based pirate Jean Lafitte cultivated a relationship with the maroon palenques (barricaded settlements) of Cuba as late as the early 1820s. Pirates and maroons, then, shared a history in the dark shadows of empire.[36]

Maroon societies, born of the irrepressible need for freedom, might form anywhere that mountains, swamps, forests, or other inaccessible terrain afforded rebel chattels the chance to fortify themselves against recapture. Cuba revealed a common pattern. As early as 1503 the governor complained that black slaves were fleeing to the woods of the island, where they taught the native Indians innumerable bad habits and instilled a sense of insubordination. They built fortified villages, barricaded by tree trunks, in the Oriente and Pinar del Rio Mountains or the Zapata Swamp, outposts in which maroon warriors fashioned machetes, wooden arrows, and iron spears.[37] Usually small, precarious enclaves of freedom fighters, numbering only in the tens or hundreds but jealously protective of their hard-won liberty, might forge loose alliances with aboriginal peoples, pirates, or others of their kind. More often than not, however, they were locked in a parochialism they could trust to be true to their interests and clandestine existence. Societies originating in nights of flight and rebellion extended from Brazil and Peru, through the islands of the West Indies, to the Florida and Georgia swampland of the 1837 Seminole War, and into the slaveholding states of the American South. Some were powerful enough to force European powers into treaties that legitimated their freedom in return for pledges of allegiance to colonial authority and law. But the maroon experience was one of considerable diversity. In the seventeenth century the great quilombo African state of Palmares, Brazil, boasted a population of hundreds, well cultivated lands, cereal production, irrigation systems, village concentrations, and an established political hierarchy headed by a monarch and his officials. More fragile were the settlement aspirations of runaway Africans in Virginia and the Carolinas, where the Dismal Swamp region and other uncolonized frontiers provided some limited chance to raise small livestock, plant crops, and construct huts, as well as geographic protection from the expeditions of white reprisal which periodically set out to destroy whatever stable structures of community life the fugitive slaves had managed to sustain.[38]

The largest maroon community in continental North America was that of the Florida Seminoles, where the always ambiguous relations of slave blacks and Native Americans came together in a complex fusion. The Seminoles, a branch of the Creek Indians, owned slaves, but allowed them a far greater degree of integration into their society than did white owners. Black slaves acted as translators, bridging the gulf between white colonizers and the native people. High rates of slave–aboriginal intermarriage, as well as the Spanish practice of encouraging slaves from the bordering states of Alabama, South Carolina, and Georgia to flee their Protestant masters, resulted in a mixed-blood community in which mestizo, slave, and Indian were almost indistinguishable. After the War of 1812 left British guns and a cannon-defended fort abandoned, the Seminole maroons occupied the structure, took up arms, cultivated the surrounding land, and waged their own guerrilla struggle against the American planters. Between 1817 and 1843 they fought repeated battles, suffered losses and the recapture of five hundred slaves, but also succeeded in creating constant havoc for the southern planter class, serving as a magnet that drew runaways from across the southeast. Fierce warriors, the black newcomers earned a rough equality with their native allies, to the point that General Thomas Jessup declared, "This, you may be assured, is a Negro, not an Indian, war." Pirates of the plantation economy, the Seminole maroons were judged by their opponents "a most cruel and malignant enemy. For them to surrender would be servitude to the whites; but to retain an open warfare, secured to them plunder, liberty, and importance." Their wars finally subsided when an American general forged peace with a promise to transport the black rebels to the free soil states of the southwest. Similar wars elsewhere had similiar ends.[39]

In Jamaica the powerful maroon communities of the eighteenth century had their origins in the Spanish masters' abandonment of their plantations in the face of British conquest. Some fifteen hundred former slaves found themselves emancipated freedom fighters in a guerrilla war that pitted Spanish and black against an invading army of British. The blacks formed bands, struck for the hills, and cultivated communities but were unable to knit themselves together into a coherent unit. The problem was exacerbated when one of the most powerful maroon leaders aligned with the British in return for acknowledgement of his village's rights to freedom and property. Groups of dissident maroons retreated into uninhabited sectors of the island where, for generations, they kept largely to themselves. As the British imported more and more African slaves, revolts erupted with regularity, and runaways escaped the confines of the plantations in large numbers to form new communities that eventually began to connect with the older settlements of more domesticated maroons. By the 1730s these amalgamations of complexly layered African ethnicities had constructed fighting battalions that struck terror into the heart of white colonial power, drawing on a history of eighty years of intermittent warfare. Governing authority deplored the endless desertions and raids as a "height of insolence" that left "frontiers ... no longer in any sort of security." As maroon rebels seized plantations, the island divided into warring isolations, and slaves left their owners in droves; the slaveowning caste grew more and more restive, its hegemony eroded even among those slaves who remained at their work. British authorities thought that incorporating powerful wings of the maroons into their structure of governance and repression would prove more successful than fighting on so many unprotected fronts and therefore signed treaties with some maroons. These agreements solidified the rights of maroon citizenship, but also called on them to suppress rebels who refused to accept the terms of peace and to function as slave catchers in the case of future runaways.

The resulting accommodation divided maroon communities and left a bitter residue of factionalism and feud that eroded the strength of the former slave rebels, pushing them into a series of tumults and disorders. When a final war broke out in 1794–1795, precipitated by the British use of slaves to whip two maroon culprits, some of the once proudly defiant settlements of former slaves were reduced to fighting the world's greatest imperial power without support from the plantation blacks or from the rest of their scattered communities. A few hundred maroons battled, then, against long odds: with armed slaves hunting them down, other free black battalions arrayed against them, and vicious dogs imported from Cuba to track them through the hills, the rebels eventually had to bend the knee to British and planter authority. They found themselves cruelly served by their military betters: promised that they could remain on their land, 556 maroons were marched aboard transport ships a year later and "resettled" in the inhospitable climate of Nova Scotia. "I have saved the island," declared the complacent official who engineered the deceit, a subterfuge compounded by the subsequent unceremonious shipment of the Jamaican bush rebels from Nova Scotia to Sierra Leone.[40]

The remaining Jamaican maroons struggle to maintain their culture in a world of increasingly pressured assimilations and incorporations. Their music and dance, cooking and dress, unique technologies originating in their adaptation to the mountainous terrain, and customary celebrations— as well as a distinctive pride and appreciation of their historic accomplishment of freedom—are forceful reminders of the resilience of communities forged in resistance and rebellion. Unlike the pirate nation, which rose and fell on the volatile seas of plunder, maroons sustained their presence— through years of history in which dark defeats often threatened to overcome them—largely because they never relinquished the vitality of their autonomy. Novels such as Vic Reid's *New Day* (1948), *The Jamaicans* (1978), and *Nanny Town* (1983) are premised on this sense of independence and selfhood. One fictional figure thus angrily rebukes the youth, who appear overly envious of the finery of coastal towns: "Old cast-off clothes from a Red-Ants slave owner! That is what they wear! Our pigskin and lace-bark shirts we got by our hands! Not ashamed of mud on our feet either, boy. Mud on the feet is a sign that we broke away! Mud on the feet and burr in the hair—signs of freedom, boy!" This reverence for a rebellious past of flight is central to the making of the maroon community, which has constructed a powerfully positive mythology of its breakaway beginnings. Another fictional character declares, "We, all of us who call ourselves Maroons, form a chain. A chain of freedom all along this great backbone of mountains. If any link in that chain is weakened, all of us will become weakened. Somewhere, we will break."[41]

In this language of historical continuity lies a great difference that separates maroons from pirates. Aside from the truly inspirational imagined communitarian longings of Libertalia, pirate consciousness and identity was developed in the warfare of the moment, in the spoils of battle seized and squandered with wild abandon. Maroon wildness and guerrilla warfare, however, were not about the moment and certainly not about a carousing consumption; rather they were essential to sustaining freedom and surviving, through and over time. One result was an entirely changed set of gender relations, and in the history of maroon societies it is not accidental that women occupy different, and centrally recognized, ground.

Both pirates and male maroons were known to have shared women, but for the Jamaican maroons the practice was carefully monitored through specific understood codes of conduct. And although the Madagascar buccaneers experimented briefly with polygamy, the runaway blacks of the Jamaican hills institutionalized systems of multiple (most often two, occasionally three) wives for their leading warriors—a not surprising development, given the necessities of ensuring the reproduction of a social order often ravaged by war's human losses. European commentators tended to equate these familial, gender, and sexual norms with barbarous brutality to women and children, whom they condescendingly portrayed as being savagely handled and prostituted by authoritarian warrior patriarchs. Filtering through the admittedly dense underbrush of accumulated conventional wisdom, however, is a possible different view of gender relations among these breakaway mountain communities.[42]

What is striking is how potent remains the myth of the original maroon chieftainess/warrior, called Nanny, after whom rebel towns have been named. The representational production and reproduction of a rebel woman has two-sided implications. The "Grandy Nanny" of maroon folklore is now ensconced in legend and literature, but, as Kamau Brathwaite has shown with great insight, the "Nanny" has been constructed as an icon, an image rather than a living historical presence. In reports of Nanny's supernatural capacities, mythologized by nineteenth- and twentieth-century commentators and symbolized by repeated tales of her capacity to catch bullets in her buttocks and fart them back at her European antagonists, lies a process of reducing centuries of resistance to the inexplicable miraculousness of a singular woman. Depicted as an "unsexed woman who [led] ... a freebooter's life," Nanny was "ten times more ferocious and blood-thirsty than any man among the Maroons." Yet "nannies" were actual historical actors; they were fighters and healers, prophets and producers (of generations as well as general sustenance), not otherworldly warriors of supernatural stature but struggling people of the maroon world. They were women who battled on a daily, routine basis (medicinal and religious, for instance) as much as in episodic events. In accompanying men into battle they may have fought as young warriors or, as old ohemmaa ("past the menopause"), led maroon soldiers as Keepers of the

Tribe. Women's roles, in short, were many and varied, not at all adequately contained in the mythology of the "witch" Nanny. Contemporary maroon poetry attempts to recapture this diversity for women of the breakaway culture, incorporating the mythic battle prowess of Nanny but pluralizing her identity and multiplying her roles, from the rebel wars of the seventeenth and eighteenth centuries to the contemporary quest for education and equality.

Lorna Goodison's "Nanny," published in her poetry collection *I Am Becoming My Mother* (1986), recounts the historical creation of the woman rebel: an African reared to be childless ("My womb was sealed/ with molten wax"), but schooled in the spirit and sense of her people ("From then my whole body would quicken/ at the birth of everyone of my people's children"), and trained "in the rhythms of the forest.../ I could sense and sift/ ...death's odour/ in the wind's shift." With her eyes rendering "light from the dark," she was sold to the slave traders, physically barren but socially a powerful force for reproducing resistance:

> all my weapons within me.
> I was sent, tell that to history.
> When your sorrow obscures the skies
> other women like me will rise.

With the ascent of such women, maroon societies—unlike the world of the pirate—secured a historical continuity, most evident today in the maroons of Jamaica.[43]

Few episodes in the history of New World maroons would prove as complex and convoluted as that of the Jamaican survivors, and none would retrace the transatlantic currents of the triangular trade. But in virtually all Atlantic colonies the very existence of an alternative culture and social formation—emerging out of flight and rebellion and carved out of wilderness isolations in ways that threatened planter security and property— could only lead in the direction of conflict. In Palmares, Brazil's stronghold of maroonage, it took a seventeenth-century onslaught of expeditions by two of the strongest imperial powers of the day—Portugal and the Netherlands—to crush the great quilombos, which may have supported a population in excess of ten thousand. The Bantu-speaking maroon leaders fought valiantly, but white colonizers had their eyes on the rich Palmarinos lands, and in 1695 a ravaging coalition of "ruffians, hastily recruited northerners, and a larger army of Indians" put an end to the singularly successful reconstruction of African civilization in the New World.

Maroons figured prominently, if ambivalently, in the Haitian–Saint Domingue revolt of 1791. And in the Dutch sugar kingdom of Surinam, a "Blood Spilling Colony" where some fifty thousand slaves, many of them recently arrived Africans, were brutally exploited by three thousand European whites, maroonage produced "a theatre of perpetual war." There the rain forests bordering the plantations proved an inviting route of escape for blacks who served the most profligate and philistine plantocracy in the Americas: nude house slaves waited on masters' tables, fanned their sleeping owners day and night, and bathed their children in imported wines, while fieldhands produced revenues far exceeding those of other colonies. Cruelties excessive even in the exaggerated annals of slavery's many horrors were often associated in the European mind with Surinam; Voltaire used this planter economy to satirize the evils of enslavement in *Candide* (1759). The bands of maroons who rebelled with flight and resettlement were not large—from a few hundred, conservatively estimated, to a few thousand—but they managed to wage a series of preemptive strikes against the plantation economy, risking death and mutilation if captured. They palisaded their settlement bases deep in swamplands fordable only by secret paths submerged in shallow water; in mountainous or forested terrain their protections included pits bottomed with sharpened stakes. Maroon success, as Michael Craton notes, "depended on convincing the colonial regimes that they could not win in battle while disguising the fact that no maroon community could live permanently in a state of war." It was an uphill fight but one that was waged constantly, striking directly at the slave-based sinews of empire.[44]

For centuries, for generations, the maroons waged this relentless battle. A community forged in freedom's nocturnal flights, the rebels solidified their culture in the darkness of guerrilla warfare, where the rough inaccessibility of their precariously occupied lands and the shadowing protections of the setting sun gave them an advantage over the conventional military powers of imperial enemies. But as the plantation economies and slave societies of eighteenth- and nineteenth-century empire gave way to more hegemonic cultures of rule and absorption, the maroons faced potent new imperial forces:

> come down the hill at sunrise w/ eyes that read the dark
> m16s that are not
> crutches
> though we might hold them o so casual against our sides
> ......
> & yet today the hawks on their warm rising roundabouts
> look like dark sorrows. for the Portuguese
> have beaten us at last at their own game
> surrounded us. camped hard all year against us. caius

> revved rockets up into the very kidneys of our cooking pots
> beguiled the younger female fauns w/ foolish fans & beauty
> contestants. have taught them how to shave midden hair & brave
> ly bear a bene buonorott' bikini sheer & mare & tender
> lion & how I gonna bring you in an early morning breakfast plate a
> fruit
>   ......
> tourists led inwards by the sweeper at the marketgate
> rush in & shoot us with their latest nikkon liekas & many of our men
> are lured away to work at chipping ice in sin[45]

New empires wore new clothes, even if the age-old fashionable goal of accumulation seemed unchanging. Over the last century, their tight fit on the peoples of the colonial world, however willingly they were sported, have proved yet another powerful mechanism of restraint upon transgression, a dark containment showered in the blinding light of commodities, consumptions, and cultures of contentment.[46] This process of incorporation would be fought, negotiated, and constituted anew, again and again[47]—and not only in the shadows of empire.

PART V

The Transforming Power of Capital

12. Paul Cézanne, *The Card Players* (1890–1892).

10

Sociabilities of the Night

Fraternalism and the Tavern

Capitalism, empire, slavery, and the forms of resistance that they spawned restructured the social relations of the world between 1600 and 1900. As marginal communities of outlaws challenged the dominant configurations of power—on the high seas, within plantation economies, and in the peasant and proletarian networks of laboring peoples at the centers of Europe's great transformation—others adapted to the threats and insecurities of the new age. Much of this difficult adjustment had to do with mechanisms of dispossession that severed relations to land and craft skills, or with the creation of new human "natures" acclimatized to the rigors of time discipline, or with economies governed by the wage rather than oriented to the task. The politics of class formation, the rise of the trade union, and the upheavals of overt rebellion developed in this context, as did the disorder of criminality's acquisitive individualism.

Histories of transgression and acclimatization blur in the differential responses to immiserization and its many threats. Two locales where male streams of nineteenth-century humanity flowed with some regularity, their intentions embedded in overlapping cultural negotiations with the material and social pressures of insecurity, were the fraternal order and the tavern. Sites of night's sociability, the lodge and the saloon offered divergent routes away from the isolations and constricting individualism of nineteenth-century society. They were cultures of collectivism that could, alternatively, ensure respectability's continuity, or barter it for the gratifications of the immediate moment.

There is a tendency to see in the process of class formation a one-sidedness of workers' lives, an overriding dominance of the class struggle, conceived mechanically as relentless *physical* confrontation over the wage packet, the hours of work, or the politics of disenfranchisement. There was, to be sure, plenty of this in the first stages of adjustment to the Industrial Revolution. But class struggle was also about carving out a niche in the cultural corners of nineteenth-century society, creating spaces for mundane securities and devising strategies of survival—for many workers, the first necessary step toward launching a more combative program of social transformation. As E. P. Thompson has argued, this too was a battle, striking hard at the confinements of class place that denied working people a voice in so many aspects of society. In constructing fraternal societies to shield themselves from the ignominy of a pauper's burial, or to protect their families from the ravages of unemployment, sickness, or injury, workers who dressed themselves in the rhetoric of respectability and gravitated to the idea of mutual aid struggled no less than those who waged their war at the point of production. "The discipline essential for the safe-keeping of funds, the orderly conduct of meetings and the determination of disputed cases," concludes Thompson, "involved an effort of self-rule as great as the new disciplines of work."[1] But in that disciplined self-rule lay many a contradictory impulse.

The fraternal orders that dotted the organizational landscape of nineteenth-century society had their origins in an age-old human pro-clivity to join voluntary associations that would provide aid to their members in times of financial need. Organized to offset the danger to families should the male breadwinner or female wage earner suffer un-employment, injury, or death, mutual benefit societies have historically offered families a material buffer zone, insulating them from the debilitat-ing impact of various personal tragedies. Over time and across national and cultural contexts, from the benevolent bodies of the ancient world through the guilds of medieval and renaissance Europe and the *compagnon-nages* of the early modern period to the sworn brotherhoods and sisterhoods of industrializing China and Latin America, mutualism and the fraternal order have been a ubiquitous presence wherever society has attained a level of economic diversification sufficient to provide not only for the accumulation of wealth but for the debilitations of its scarcity. As a recent collection of essays suggests, the comparative history of mutual benefit societies is rich indeed, with a reach as broad and as wide as that of almost any other cultural form.[2]

The names of these fraternal orders often constructed a purposeful sense of antiquity (Ancient and Honourable Fraternity of Free and Accepted Masons,[3] Ancient Order of United Workmen, Loyal Order of

Ancient Shepherds, Ancient Order of Foresters) or harked back to an epoch of chivalrous service (Knights of Pythias, Knights of Columbus) or adopted a titular independence (Independent Order of Oddfellows). Many mutual aid societies were formed as *national* bodies (Sons of England, St. George's Society, and a host of immigrant orders). In the particular case of Ireland, such institutions might shade the cause of patriotic affiliation into that of cultural–religious identity (Ancient Order of Hibernians, Emerald Beneficial Association, the Loyal Orange Association).[4] Ironically, these stabilizing intentions were either entirely mythical (the fraternal order as a mutual benefit society was a product of the post-Enlightenment modern period,[5] most decidedly a late-eighteenth- and nineteenth-century institutional phenomenon with a carryover into the twentieth century) or an exaggerated articulation of nation at the very moment that both people of the British Isles and eastern and southern Europeans were finding their way to all corners of the globe.[6] The Oddfellows explained their particular attraction to tradesmen, who they felt were "daily becoming more migratory in their habits, and who are also emigrating in great numbers from [our] shores to our colonies and distant lands."[7] As Margaret C. Jacob suggests, with pointed reference to the admittedly particularistic history of Freemasonry, for all its national trappings fraternalism was an "international phenomenon" that built a "polity within sociability" and cultivated a specific vision and discourse, drawing on quasi-religious symbolism to develop an "imitation and initiation of forms of governance."[8]

This governance was a hybrid of democratic commitment and acknowledgement of hierarchy. In its Enlightenment origins, for instance, Freemasonry was led by progressive aristocrats who were used to challenging political despotism and calling for a meritocracy, even as they separated themselves from "the common people" beneath them in "talents" and "worth." They established thirty-three degrees, or measurements of an individual's station, and few fraternal lodges managed to avoid some kind of tiered structure. To climb the mutual benefit society ladder, moreover, meant a cash outlay: each of the five degrees of the Oddfellows cost one dollar, and there were other possible expenses associated with the purchase of pins, regalia, and other paraphernalia. And yet there is no mistaking the rhetorical core of democratic purpose in many fraternal society manuals and guidebooks. "A single individual, if he labor with a will, may accomplish much in the field of fraternity," proclaimed the *Correct Guide to All Matters Relating to Odd-Fellowship*, "but a host, united in a solid phalanx in the service of Benevolence, may revolutionize the world." The democratic impulse was evident in one lodge's statement of intent: "to abolish all considerations of wealth or poverty in our fraternity, ... to make all feel ... they are not only brethren, but equals." The motto of the Ancient Order of United Workmen was blunt, betraying no hint of caste or class privilege and superiority: "The one needs the assistance of the other."[9] This duality present in early fraternalism has prompted historians such as John Gillis to state that Freemasonry was "both fraternal and patriarchal. Its organization was hierarchical and at the same time fundamentally egalitarian." Jacob provides a similar interpretation: "The lodges mirrored the old order just as they were creating a form of civil society that would ultimately replace it."[10]

What was it like to spend an evening in one of the tens of thousands of friendly society halls or rented lodge rooms that figured so prominently in the nighttime sociability of the Victorian era's culture of masculine respectability? We know too little about these nocturnal happenings, but the experience of nineteenth-century Freemasonry suggests patterns that were likely reproduced in other orders. Lodges often employed dramatic lighting techniques and elaborate costuming to accentuate the passage from the dark, uninitiated isolation of nonmembership to the light of brotherhood and inclusion. Theatrical accouterments—robes, sashes, and other lavish alterations of dress—lent the proceedings a purposively staged atmosphere, furthered by the particularly ornate artistic images that hung in lodge rooms. Initiation rituals situated blindfolded newcomers in a space of vulnerability and chaos, from which each prospective candidate would be rescued by ritual incorporation into the collectivity and con-firmed identity of fraternal brotherhood. Many orders constructed rites of passage along lines of symbolic death (associated with the dependent status of childhood or youth) and the resurrection of manhood. They embedded this movement in the relationships of age and labor. In the Masons, for instance, the three basic degrees symbolized the stages of life and their interaction with the skills of the universal craft: Entered Apprentice was youth; Fellow Craft, middle age; and Master Mason, old age. The symbols of the trade of masonry—square, plumb, twenty-four-inch gauge—further solidified the connection of station and toil. Ritual incantations, which drew on understandings of natural developments such as the seasons and on human constructions with their geometric designs, all led—albeit through convoluted and often unknowable routes repre-sentative of life's uncertainties—to the highest station of "hieroglyphic bright, which none but Craftsmen ever saw, as the emblem of divine truth." Movement from one stage to another was a journey, the proceedings often taking place over a checkered black-and-white carpet indicative of humanity's alternating passage through periods of good and evil. Each candidate would, at various times, pause on this carpet to receive guidance through lectures, dramatic presentations, or readings from the Bible. An 1890s Masonic publication called this lodge activity "the greatest of all plays, containing the highest sentiments, the most beautiful allegories, historical representations [with] dramatic force and settings."

The Independent Order of Foresters often displayed on their walls a set of paintings in pre-Raphaelite style to illustrate their mottoes: "Moral Courage, Physical Fitness, and Stability of Character" and "Liberty, Concord, and Benevolence." These images, contrasting the virtues of light and the dangers of the dark, showed mounted horsemen symbolic of courage and fitness, draped in white and glowing in armor, overtaking figures with their heads bowed in fear and despair, preceded by a scythe-carrying, heavily shrouded, blackened representation of death. Some societies opened with prayer, and many drew on religious motifs, secularizing obedience to God in the mainstays of virtuous, temperate, prudent, just behavior. Masons described the new initiate as standing "on the threshold of this new Masonic life, in darkness, helplessness, and ignorance. Having been wandering amid the errors and covered over with the pollutions of the outer and profane world, he comes inquiringly to our doors, seeking new birth, and asking a withdrawal of the veil which conceals divine truth from uninitiated sight."

Fraternalism, then, was a night quest for light, a search in the leisured hours of the evening for sociable station, an attempt to transcend the compromises and threatening chaos of the day. The stability offered, however, was sealed in secrecy's protections, each Masonic degree candidate having to swear an oath of allegiance, the breaking of which had—symbolically, at least—violent repercussions. Practices and promises such as these provided entry for fraternal society candidates into a culture of night collectivity, separate from households and the outside world of labors and tensions. They admitted men into a brotherhood marked by dress (the lambskin apron worn at masonic meetings) and insignia (the small square and compass Masons might wear on their street clothes) that were badges of respectability, signifying a place in the limited democratic order of the lodge. If the waged work of the day provided the capacity to purchase the sustenance of life, the night labors of the fraternal orders were put to higher purposes, cultivating an ostensibly spiritual purity. It was as though fraternalism's night, "free and accepted," could transcend the confines of the day.[11]

Critical here is the intriguingly complex meaning of fraternalism, associated with its explosive importance at a particular historical juncture in the maturing years of the first Industrial Revolution. One interpretation is fundamentally material and economic, the other decidedly cultural and ideological. Fraternalism proliferated at precisely the moment that a working class was being forged out of the dislocations of capitalism's *original*, or primitive, accumulations, through which the ties that had bound the *menu peuple* of the seventeenth- and eighteenth-century feudal and commercial regimes were shattered. The resulting historical process, which took generations to complete, left a layer of society entirely dependent on the wage, a precarious economic relation premised on the impersonality of market relations. Gone were the flimsy protections of a nebulous "moral economy" to which the poor could turn in moments of want and crisis. Not yet born was the welfare state. The last half of the nineteenth century was thus a vacuum in the history of informal and formal social provisioning, a time in which class relations had been reconstituted in ways that obliterated the social responsibility of the rich for the poor but which predated the acknowledgement of the place of the state in ensuring minimal standards of living. Mutual benefit societies emerged and grew in this context precisely because they represented a historical moment in the *primitive accumulation* of the welfare state, a way in which the poor could shoulder the first, and truly immense, costs of their own forms of crude social insurance, providing for their *reproduction* as a labor force.[12]

One Oddfellow acknowledged as much in 1870, suggesting that friendly societies had been the means of "vast saving to the revenue of England, in poor rates and otherwise ... pauperism has decreased ... as Friendly Societies have increased." He did not stop, however, at the significance of the purely economic role of fraternalism; rather, he noted that "better still [was] the vast regeneration in the habits, and mental tone of the working classes [that the mutual benefit societies] are slowly, but surely, effecting, teaching them to prize and attain the virtues of self-help, and manly independence."[13] In this cultural and ideological work lay a parallel process of primitive accumulation in which the material securities of reproduction were accompanied by the dualism at the heart of fraternalism's potent attractions. On the one hand, the brotherhood of the various orders was a self-constructed creation, a vibrant and energetic milieu of self-definition and bonding which took on collectivist as opposed to individualist trappings and which was associated closely with the values of egalitarianism and democratic leveling of the separate strata of the emerging class order. On the other hand, fraternalism's assimilation of many underlying social distinctions also reproduced the wider hierarchies evident in the society as a whole. Segments of the working class, which was as a whole expected to sustain its own precarious security through voluntary fraternalism and the collectivity of mutual aid—a process reinforced by a powerful rhetorical and representational attachment to equality—were also drawn into the fragmenting ideological cauldron of the friendly society lodge. An attachment to nation and empire was often reinforced in mythologies of an imagined community's heroic, warlike beginnings, where racial distinctiveness and superiority were promoted and where gendered difference was deepened.

In short, fraternalism was born at an interface of economic collectivity—seemingly egalitarian and rooted in class needs, a material making of the recognition of workers' distinct and increasingly insecure place in the social order of international capitalism—and social isolation and "possessive individualism," in which nations, "races," and genders were kept ideologically distant from one another the better to sustain various levels of power's multifaceted practice. Fraternalism cultivated collectivity; it also fractured broad solidarities. The friendly society was an arena in part made by and for workers as an expression of their material interests; it was also a place where the experience of class was submerged in divisions that were routinely accentuated.

Workers whose wage allowed them the illusion of security and respectability valued these cultural commodities (as did many who could do little more than aspire to such a level of material well-being). Their days of labor sustained families in which wives might not have to suffer the degradation of factory employment and in which there was some hope that the children, through education, training, or the acquisition of sufficient "culture" to separate themselves from their origins, might escape to the middle classes. A portion of these same workers' nights were spent in friendly society halls trying to achieve the same ends. Whatever the likelihood that this familialist respectability would continue or future upward mobility be secured, the fraternal order, with its promise of mutual benefit aid in the event of the loss of a job or a life, was a hedged bet in the larger gamble of working-class life.[14] Although fraternalism was therefore not a uniquely and uniformly working-class phenomenon, it did draw hundreds of thousands of workers to its ranks on both sides of the Atlantic and throughout the industrializing economies of the Third World. Millions of dollars flowed from working-class pockets to fraternal treasuries, some finding its way back to those in need.[15]

Diverse settings produced remarkably similar outcomes in which the beginnings of trade unionism were often linked to the necessities of mutual aid. In England and Wales, small independent lodges had reached a total membership of over 900,000 by 1815.[16] But the affiliated orders multiplied more remarkably in the period of working-class agitation associated with Chartism and the Anti–Poor Law campaigns (1834–1842). The Oddfellows grew by leaps and bounds over a single decade, expanding the number of lodges from 560 to 3,500 and increasing their membership sevenfold, to 221,000. One 1839 account commented on the stimulus of the Poor Laws "in the formation of such societies" and suggested that the swelling ranks of fraternalism were related to "the opening of unions throughout the kingdom." In the same decade, across the Atlantic, carpenters and joiners in the Upper Canadian colonial center of York (now Toronto) formed their first trade union out of the fraternal impulse, their 1833 declaration highlighting mutual aid intentions as well as a willingness to confront employers. A century later, in the port of Dar es Salaam, the African Labour Union of casually employed dockworkers reproduced this mutual-aid/trade-union parentage, declaring (not unlike comparable workers in Quebec in the 1850s) that "their union is for the purpose of helping one another when sick and for burial purposes."[17]

These purposes were carried out in the nightly meetings of lodges and orders whose jealously guarded rituals often marked the accommodationist friendly society as a transgressively dark milieu of exotic mysticism and proselytizing potential: "We hold the hand of fellowship to all./ Could but the world our secret actions see,/ Mankind one mighty brotherhood would be."[18] The abduction and disappearance of William Morgan, an American Mason who threatened to publish Freemasonry's secrets in Batavia, New York, and who did eventually produce the revelations of *Illustrations of Free Masonry* (1826), contributed to this transgressive aura surrounding fraternal practices. Morgan's exploitation of the commercial potential inherent in exposing Freemasonry's secrets resulted in a series of night raids and other threatening activities that culminated in his imprisonment for debt, supposed seizure after being coaxed from jail by a bail-paying Mason, and subsequent kidnapping. In the aftermath of rumors that Morgan had been spirited away by vengeful Masons, speculation as to what had become of the renegade lodge brother spiraled out of control: he was now living in Canada among the Indians; he had departed for foreign lands; he had been murdered for breaking his Masonic oath and his body disposed of so that it would never be found. Over the course of the next five years some twenty grand jury investigations were held and dozens of Masons indicted; eighteen trials took place; proceedings developed as far as the Supreme Court; many judges, law officials, and prominent public figures were suspected of covering up the Morgan abduction and subverting of justice; Masonic supporters defended themselves from what they equated with "popish plots" and Salem witch trials; and anti-Masonry figured forcefully in the later politics of the United States. In the process, Masonry was constructed as a conspiratorial intrigue determined to subvert the young republic and to insinuate its members into all positions of governing and economic authority in the land, thus establishing a Freemasons' monarchy. In *Masonry Proved to Be a Work of Darkness* (1830), Lebbeus Armstrong asked provocatively: "If the government of France was revolutionized in three days, might not the government of these United States have been changed to Monarchy in one day by the Mystic Power of Masonic Stratagem? Nothing could have prevented such a revolution, but the interposition of that Divine Providence which has broken asunder the strongly fortified enchantments of Freemasonry, and exposed its works of darkness to the world."[19] With the Morgan affair, fraternalism's nightly sociability had come to seem a nightmare of political irrationality and social paranoia.

This climate of escalating fear found its way to the working classes, who were also often judged to be conspiratorial practitioners of the art of nocturnal gathering and dangerous collectivity. Early trade unions drew on the secret rituals and oaths of fraternalism:

> Strangers, the design of all our Lodges is love and unity,
> With self-protection founded on the laws of equality,
> And when you have our mystic rights gone through,
> Our secrets will be disclosed to you.[20]

Montreal tailors in the 1830s were said to be bound together by such sworn bonds, reinforced by threats that those who refused to support the trade in its collective confrontation with employers would have their thumbs cut off. By the end of the nineteenth century there was no mistaking the extent to which workers had been drawn to the friendly society. When asked in the 1880s, "What kind of membership constitutes these societies?" one working-class reformer replied bluntly, "Working classes—nine-tenths of them."[21] The Oddfellows described their order as, "most adapted to working men," and various North American community studies have uncovered the important place of fraternalism in the consolidation of a working-class presence.[22] Historian of the American working class David Montgomery was led to conclude that the later nineteenth century witnessed an institutional and social shift of considerable importance to laboring people. "During these decades workers created a wide variety of institutions, all of them infused with a spirit of mutuality. Through their fraternal orders, cooperatives, reform clubs, political parties, and trade unions, American workers shaped a collectivist counter-culture in the midst of the growing factory system."[23] On occasion this kind of analytic reading of the clandestine culture of nineteenth-century working-class sociability and solidarity drew the fear and ire of authority. The English plebeian community of Macclesfield was described in 1812 as "a nest of illicit association ... full of sick and burial societies which are the germ of revolution."[24] Yet there were others at century's end who saw such associations as "merely poultices on the cancer" of an unjust social system. "If there were no benevolent societies there would be a revolution among the workingmen of the country," thundered one North American radical in 1891.[25]

Nights of fraternalism did not lead in the direction of revolution. In fact, mutual benefit societies often fostered a masculinist attachment to empire, promoting a brotherhood of bellicose patriotism that accentuated "love of country" in various ways. The Ancient Order of United Workmen gave this nationalist creed a loyalist twist: "Any member guilty of any crime, indictable offence, treason or participation in any riot, revolt, or rebellion against his country or its people, shall be expelled from the Order, and can never again be received into membership." Few associations pushed this chauvinism as far as did the turn-of-the-century Orange Order in Canada, which officially advocated "close supervision of all new settlers and the encouragement of suitable white immigration from the British Isles, the United States, and Northern Europe."[26]

As the Orange Order's allusion to race suggests, fraternal orders in their nineteenth-century North American forms often restricted admission to "whites only," forcing Asians and African Americans in the New World to charter their own separate lodges or distinct brotherhoods.[27] Women fared similarly, for although some friendly societies had women's affiliates, most barred females from their halls.[28] The Masons stipulated early that "no atheist, eunuch or woman can be admitted." This statement of exclusion was never rigidly enforced, however, despite a ritual provision for the lifting of a prospective candidate's waistcoat to ascertain anatomical correctness. More significant was the pervasive gendered meaning of the mutual benefit society as a brotherhood of protectors, ever vigilant in its efforts to sustain familialist values, for which dependent wives were to be dutifully thankful: "Remember how it cheers the wife/ When sickness lays her husband low——/ To feel that brothers guard her life/ And strive to avert the dreadful blow." Fraternalism's brotherhood, then, was an associational construction that fed directly into larger processes of the formation of gender identities, reproducing societal polarities: masculine/ feminine, public/private, domestic/political-economic.[29] In time, moreover, fraternalism's powerful early sense of collectivity and egalitarianism faded as the mutual benefit society became little more than a marginal insurance broker, activated less and less by its former idealisms and more and more by the actuarial business acumen of paid officials and organizers who saw recruits in terms of premiums.[30] By the second quarter of the twentieth century the mutual benefit society survived as a forum of sociability largely among the immigrant cultures of North America, where population groups locked out of the "white" mainstream took solace in ethnic collectivity.[31]

The dark side of fraternalism's egalitarianism was therefore a protectionism which, instead of widening the sociabilities of the night into solidarities of all oppressed groups, actually reconstructed and replicated the patterns of exclusion and difference evident in the larger social world. National chauvinism, racial prejudice, and gender exclusiveness were all deepened and dispersed throughout the industrializing world within which fraternalism's often contradictory messages were propagated. This was done in the name of a wide-ranging respectability, whereby the sociability of the night served as a defense mechanism against those crises and accidents that could undermine the earning power of the day.

Not all of those who suffered through the intensifying atmosphere of insecurity opted for the society of the fraternal lodge, however. Some turned to the tavern, where drink and conviviality could be had throughout the nineteenth century without the monthly dues and ritual encounters of the friendly society.

It is difficult to grasp just how central drink was to the laboring poor of the late eighteenth and early nineteenth centuries. Featured in workplace customs, it punctuated their endless toil, quenched thirst that adulterated milk and polluted water could not satiate, and "purified" other products. Intoxicants were thought to energize workers in the strenuous trades, as well as enhance festivities and certain rites of passage: apprenticeship, courting, marriage, and independence from parents were all occasions for drinking. The ways in which spirits and liquors were taken (by the refined glass or from a rough jar or scoop) and purchased (by the dram or pail or in the larger cask) marked class place, as did income, food, clothing, and occupation. At moments of high social tension, alcohol was often a stimulus to acts of riot or rebellion. But it could also prove a depressing sedative, acclimatizing the poor to lives of incredible oppression. Thomas Carlyle regarded gin as "the black throat into which wretchedness of every sort, consummating itself by calling on delirium to help it, whirls down, ... liquid Madness sold at ten-pence the quartern." The sheer quantities of drink consumed annually were staggering, especially by subsequent standards: between 1831 and 1931 United Kingdom per capita imbibing of hard liquor fell from 1.11 proof gallons to 0.22 and beer consumption from 21.6 gallons to 13.3. The number of licenced establishments per head of population fell by two-thirds.[32]

Prohibition rendered meaningless such comparisons for the United States in this same century-long period, but there is no mistaking the social significance of liquor and beer, as well as of the establishments that dispensed them, in the middle to late nineteenth century. Well over 250,000 licensed liquor dealers and illicit "blind pigs" existed in the United States by the middle of the 1890s. In cities such as Chicago, saloons were as numerous as groceries, meat markets, and dry goods stores taken together. In many urban, immigrant, working-class districts there was at least one tavern on any given block, one saloon for every fifty adult males in the neighborhood. Boston had the dubious distinction that more than half its population frequented a bar or tavern over the course of a typical twenty-four-hour period. And even though consumption of distilled spirits declined from midcentury to the First World War years, the corresponding figures for beer rose dramatically: adult per capita consumption climbed from just under three gallons annually in 1850 to almost thirty gallons in the years 1911–1915.[33]

There is therefore no common international pattern to drink's social history, although in general there were ever widening networks of censorious ideology and institutional monitoring. At the base of alcohol's increasing regulation and governance lay a vital social imperative: the new capitalist industrial order demanded a rigid separation of work and life, insisting on workplace sobriety and the regimentation of daytime's productions. Drinking, once a part of the perpetual motion of life's varied and related cycles, now had to be confined to leisure time, most especially the nonwaged night. Although this change curbed the consumption of beer and spirits, it also concentrated their accessibility in the evening hours. The result was a growing saloon culture, associated with vice and public drunkenness, which both pioneered new forms of popular entertainment and stimulated the nineteenth-century growth of temperance and prohibition crusades. Individual business enterprises came and went with the business cycle and the shifting tastes and appetites of the consuming public: in the years 1897–1901 one-third of Chicago's saloons folded or sold out, and in some wards taverns might open or close at the rate of one a month.[34] But the whiskey and beer sellers were always a presence, their draw especially strong in the evening hours. Nights of nineteenth-century leisure often meant nights of drink.

Taverns, of course, have a history as old and continuous as that of the benevolent society. Innkeepers in the revolutionary colonies of the 1770s and in the more staid loyalist outposts of British North America in the 1830s were known to cherish their "independence," their establishments being nurseries of oppositional sentiment, incubators of discontent and rebellion.[35] In Paris, café society shaped working-class politics, cultivating a popular sociability that influenced the birth of modern republicanism, socialism, bohemianism, anarchism, and syndicalism.[36] And if the numbers of licenced taverns in London declined over the course of the nineteenth century, the significance of drink did not. Temperance, as Brian Harrison has shown in great detail, no doubt had its impact, but the plebeian attachment to liquor and beer was hardly lessened. The expansive working-class club milieu defined a part of its separation from patrician tavernkeepers and slumming aristocrats in its possession of a bar to which patrons flocked, especially on Friday and Saturday nights. Music hall culture lampooned the "cold water" cause; working-class ballads extolled the "manly" art of hoisting a pint. Even as gin palaces declined, the generalized venues for leisure activity, and their close relationship with the consumption of alcohol, expanded.[37]

Nowhere was this more apparent than in the pages of the penny comic weeklies such as *Ally Sloper's Half Holiday* (1884–1923), which celebrated the picaresque adventures of its hero in large front-page cartoons. Sloper, a philandering toff, frequented seaside resorts, the racetrack, public exhibitions, and the music hall, but it was his discolored and bulbous nose that signified for readers his jocular attraction to drink and the world of the tavern. A caricature of the gendered pursuit of pleasure, Sloper was a petit-bourgeois hedonist, uninhibited by the insecurities and material boundaries of working-class life. But that may well have been a large part of his attraction to an essentially plebeian audience, for whom his preservation of "the spirit of licence and the carnivalesque" leaped off the page in vitality, social energy, and cultural defiance. Ally Sloper magnified the choice so many laboring males harbored as an ideal but had to pursue through connivance and subterfuge. As Peter Bailey remarks, "Sloper's own unabashed enthusiasm for strong drink may represent one of the irreducibly plebeian features of his behaviour and a corrective to undue delusions of refinement, but it may also reflect the persistent drinking that took place in the commercial world, particularly in the City."[38]

There was no *typical* tavern, where nights of homogenously gendered sociability might be spent; rather, like prostitution, the institution had many faces. Fine hotels catered to those of aristocratic pedigree or pretension; other houses attracted moderate artisans or city swells and dandies. Then there were "the Great Houses of the Vulgar People" and hundreds of "low rum holes" spread throughout the metropolitan centers of Europe and North America, a tavern underworld haunted by "the undeserving poor."[39] Yet end-of-the-century surveys of the more plebeian and working-class habits generally indicated that more was at stake in the attractions of the tavern than simple access to intoxicants.

The working-class saloon in the United States—according to an 1899 investigation headed by the statistician Carroll D. Wright which probed the "economic aspects of the liquor question"—was a "workingman's club, in which many of his leisure hours are spent, and in which he finds more of the things that approximate luxury than in his home, almost more than he finds in any other public place in the ward." Canvassing the taverns of distinct districts of New York, Boston, Pittsburgh, Chicago, and San Francisco, the investigators found a dense network of social functions. In Chicago they kept a detailed list of saloon services offered in the 157 taverns of a cosmopolitan sector of the city that was dominated by un-skilled labor and housed approximately fifty people of more than two dozen "nationalities." Drinking was actually quite moderate, but thirty-five saloons contained tables and chairs used for card games and con-versation, ninety-two provided free lunches, seventy kept newspapers for their patrons' regular use, fifty-eight had billiard tables, three contained a piano or organ, two had well-equipped gymnasiums, and one a complementary handball court. "At bottom," Wright and his colleagues concluded, "it must be a craving for fellowship underlying the unrest of the workingman's idle hours that draws him to the saloon. There he finds what the average family life cannot supply and what no other institution offers." San Francisco's drinking culture bridged class divisions; the city's "sporting population" set a "wide-open" tone to night life that saw widespread gambling throughout the hotels and saloons, and tavernkeepers were well known as cordial brokers of the small loan that might get a habitué out of a tight spot. Grocery stores were routinely also drinking establishments in late-nineteenth-century San Francisco; women and children frequented them in the day to fetch pails of beer to their laboring husbands, while "at night the men drop in as [they would to] an ordinary saloon." In many locales there was "nothing even suggesting any mid-night or Sunday closing regulations." Well into the twentieth century the saloon was "a rendezvous for those who want companionship and for those who want special meetings or conferences, but have no convenient place elsewhere," a situation quite common in left-leaning working-class circles. In turn-of-the-century Buffalo most of the city's trade unions (sixty-three of sixty-nine) conducted their regular meetings in halls provided by saloonkeepers, and as social critics became aware of the declining fortune of the neighborhood tavern, they noted that it had for decades nurtured the "ideas underlying the labor movement."[40]

Teamsters, bakers, shipbuilders, and brewery workers routinely punctu-ated their workdays with a trip to the tavern. Itinerant or unemployed laborers used the saloon as a mailing address, a bank where they could deposit or borrow small sums, a social center of recreation and convivality that could double as boarding house, a restaurant (the free lunch represent-ing undeniable value at the price of a five-cent beer), or even an employ-ment bureau—a place where waged work could be advertised and secured. Walter A. Wyckoff, who wandered the United States as an itinerant laborer in the 1890s, gathering research for his two-volume study *The Workers* (1898–1899), claimed that the saloon was "perfectly adapted" to the social needs of workingmen and that no other social institution apart from the family exercised comparable "influence upon the lives of workingmen in America." Wyckoff's comment grew out of a patrician paternalism; he was seeking to impress upon late-nineteenth-century reformers the need to offer alternatives to the saloon, which he regarded as responsible for the wreckage of many individual lives. His account of American casual laborers contains references to the tavern's dubious two-sided character, evident in this complexly layered description of a Chicago tavern:

> We enter a large room brilliantly lighted [where] ... a coal fire burns
> furiously. In the corner near us are three men, slouching, listless, weary
> specimens of their kind, who are playing "Comrades" with a gusto
> curiously out of keeping with their looks of bored fatigue. One has a
> harp, another a violin, and the third drums ceaselessly upon a piano of
> harsh, metallic tone. There are a dozen round tables in the room, and at
> these are seated small groups of men and women drinking beer. ...
> They are simply commonplace... . Suddenly you note that the social
> atmosphere is one of strangest, complete camaraderie. The conversation
> is the blasphemous, obscenest gossip of degraded men ... unrelieved by
> anger or by mirth, and varying only with the indifferent interchange of
> men's and women's voices. The naturalness and untrammelled social ease
> have blinded you for a time to what you really see, and then the black

reality reveals itself in human degradation below which there is no depth—as though lost, sexless souls were already met upon a common plane of deepest knowledge of all evil. And yet in very truth they are living fellow men and women, in whom have centered the strength of natural love and hope.[41]

The saloon, for Wyckoff, presented an image that should be passed on to the reformers of the age, a representation of darkness through which he could not quite stop the light of humanity from shining. Jack London saw the tavern's boisterous male bonding less piously, writing in *John Barleycorn* (1913), "Men talked with great voices, laughed great laughs, and there was an atmosphere of greatness ... Terrible they might be, but then that only meant they were terribly wonderful." The brass rail of the tavern, to one Prohibition-era commentator, had been "a symbol of masculinity emancipate."[42]

As such commentary suggests, tavern life was fundamentally masculine, a school of gendered posturing that educated many an adolescent boy hanging around its loud entranceway or peering into its recesses in search of an errant father or a view of the forbidden adventures of adult male sociability. Married men might frequent the tavern to escape what they perceived as the confinements of domesticity and the family; "young stags" and older bachelors, because of its masculine allure, in which the warmth of fellowship and the pluck of independence attained heights of illusory ease. In Hutchins Hapgood's 1913 comment on the legendary McSorley's Saloon, his language and analytic framework betrayed and privileged the gendered world view of the tavern: "No woman ever passed or passes the threshold of McSorley's saloon. The dignified workingmen who sit quietly for hours over one or two mugs of ale, look as if they never thought of a woman. They are maturely reflecting in purely male ways and solemnly discoursing, untroubled by skirts or domesticity."[43] Bought cheaply, this kind of male freedom challenged few of the truly debilitating material ties that bound the lives of the "lowly" in knots of oppression and chains of exploitation. But its purchase seemed, in the spaces of the night, substantial enough, especially when lubricated with the rounds of the "treating" table, in which male friends stood each other the proverbial symbolic glass. The absence of women—save for the prostitute and, in some English pubs and American establishments, the barmaid—distanced the saloon from the complexities of familial hetero-sexuality with its attendant obligations, responsibilities, and direct appro-priation of the "family wage" portion of the weekly pay envelope. For these it substituted the one-dimensional parasexuality of simple sexual purchase or the alienated gaze and constructed, if unrealizable, fantasy. In the male night of the saloon lay, perhaps, the displacement of desires and needs sacrificed on the altar of masculine bonds of affection and long since bartered for shadows of their once sought-after substance.[44] In this often difficult negotiation lay the possibility of psychic scarring that could constrain lives in tangible ways, just as it could on occasion fuel the viciousness of domestic violence and find its troubled end product in the squandering of scarce resources, desertion of families, and abusive behavior both verbal and physical, including wife and child beating.[45] The tavern night was, like many evening pastimes, the site of both desire and danger, possibility and problem.

In Victorian Montreal, a port city that housed some twelve hundred licensed drinking establishments, a waterfront tavern called Joe Beef's Canteen provides a glimpse of the particular night life of a specific clientele of canalmen, longshoremen, sailors, and former soldiers—the "unkempt, unshaven, fierce-looking specimens of humanity" that frequented the dark corners of nineteenth-century grog shops and saloons.[46] Joe Beef's was founded by Charles McKiernan, an Irish Protestant ex-soldier of republican attachments, a man with one foot in the New World of the exile and the migrant, another in old country attachments to Home Rule freedom. Patronized by day laborers, his canteen was furnished with rough tables and chairs, had a sawdust-covered floor, was adorned with skeletons and bottles of preserving fluid containing mementos of interest, and housed a fantastic menagerie of monkeys, parrots, wildcats, and even bears, which McKiernan named and regularly jostled with. Beer was sold for five cents, and some of the bears were known to consume twenty pints daily, a "cruelty" the authorities of moral regulation harped on with some consistency. Animal insobriety as well as client rowdiness made Joe Beef's Canteen an object of attack by crusading reformers, zealous newspaper editors, and temperance advocates. As part of a criminal subculture that thrived on the margins of working-class life, particularly in proximity to the comings and goings—material and human—of an international port, the tavern was a well-known rendezvous for the "sun fish and wharf rats" of the harbor and also much frequented by youth gangs. In his *Autobiography of a Super Tramp* (1908), W. H. Davies claimed that "not a tramp throughout the length and breadth of the North American continent ... had not heard of [Joe Beef's Canteen] and a goodly number at one time or another patronized the establishment."

McKiernan's tavern attracted casual laborers, the unemployed, and transients for three reasons. First, it offered them sustenance along with drink:

huge piles of bread, cheese, and beef were there for the taking by those who paid for brew. Dollar bills and notes of credit could be deposited with McKiernan, tucked into an engraving above the beer taps and drawn upon by regular customers who found themselves out of work or behind bars. The tavern also functioned as an informal hiring hall (McKiernan was known to lend out shovels and picks to the unskilled) and as a cheap boarding house: for ten cents, "guests" were provided with a blanket, access to a tub and barber, and "medical" advice and "cures," as well as a bed. As many as two hundred men could be crowded into the sleeping quarters on any given night. Newspaper boys aged twelve to fourteen made up three-quarters of McKiernan's boarders; for twenty cents a day they received both food and lodging.

Second, Joe Beef's provided an escape from the cares and troubles of the world in an atmosphere of reckless abandon and hilarity. Any given evening might see McKiernan engaged in a game of billiards with one of his bears, or setting the dogs upon the same animal. If a Salvation Army preacher or an official of the Society for the Prevention of Cruelty to Animals combatively entered the establishment, the raucousness might even escalate. Musicians were commonly employed, despite legal prohibitions against their performing in low taverns of Joe Beef's type, and McKiernan was prone to provide his own performance art, haranguing the crowd in rhyming couplets, firing out ammunition drawn from local newspapers and Irish journals published in New York in an endless stream of debate and critical commentary.

The third attraction of Joe Beef's Canteen was its unmistakable role as defender of the poor, an institution with a direct message of the equality of men and the worth of the supposedly worthless. McKiernan promoted Joe Beef's Canteen through newspaper advertisements as a house in which social outcasts could find a niche uncrowded by the condescension and deference that "Beaver Hall Bogus Aristocrats" practiced and demanded:

> Citizens, we eat and drink in moderation;
> Our head, our toes, and our nose are our own,
> All we want is to be left alone!
> We eat and drink what we like,
> and let alone what we dislike.

He lent this rhetorical flourish substance by offering food and lodging free of charge to the destitute and—although supported mainly by the white Protestant English speakers—by refusing to cater to the prejudices of the age:

JOE BEEF OF MONTREAL
Who will feed a Poorman, if [he] is hungry
Cure him if he is sick—He does not give a damn
Whether he is an Indian, a Nigger, a Cripple, a
Billy or a Mick—He never let a poorman die on
The floor and never went back on the Poor.

Adept at bridging contradiction, McKiernan could challenge the arbitrary and class-bound nature of the law at the same time that he provided information to local police; vilify the British Empire while ruling his own "den of robbers and wild beasts" with "infernal majesty in loyal style"; or satirize the crass commercialism of the age and the tyranny of the "lousy dollar" yet proclaim that "all Joe Beef wants is the Coin." "Son of the people," Joe Beef cared not for "Pope, Priest, Parson, or King William of the boyne." Thoroughly materialist, he provided the transient poor with what they needed to survive—beer, beef, a bed, and pride—and denigrated the empty promises and salvations offered by "Churches, Chapels, Ranters, Preachers, Beechers and [other] stuff [of which] Montreal has already got enough."

Although a notorious partisan of the Conservative cause, which would enlist his ranks in the time-honored practice of electioneering by riot, McKiernan could also turn his activities toward the unfolding class struggles of his time. The most explicit demonstration came in the midst of an 1877–1878 strike of laborers on the Lachine Canal, when over a thousand French and Irish workers on the sluice enlargement project dropped pick and shovel to resist a wage cut and protest other indignities. Joe Beef's provided the strikers with wagon-delivered daily rations—three hundred loaves of bread, thirty-six gallons of tea, and a like quantity of soup—and housed three hundred out-of-work canallers. As the private charities closed their doors to the striking workmen and their families, Montreal's working class was given a stark lesson in the essential difference between the undependable charity of the upper class—with all its attendant strings tying the "gift" of benevolence to appropriate behaviors—and the mutual assistance generated in the name of their own ranks.[47]

McKiernan complemented the bread and soup donated to the strikers with an elementary lesson in political economy:

My friends, I have come here tonight to address you on "the Almighty Dollar." The very door bells of Montreal seem to ring with "the Almighty Dollar." The wooden-headed bobbies nail you, and you have to sleep on the hard floor provided by the City Fathers, and the next morning the fat Recorder tells you: "Give me the Almighty Dollar, or down you go for eight days." The big-bugs all have their eyes on the

"Almighty Dollar," from the Bishop down, and if you die in the hospital, they want the almighty dollar to shave you and keep you from the students. No one can blame you for demanding the "Almighty Dollar" a day. The man who promises 90 cents a day and pays only 80 cents is no man at all. The labourer has his rights.... . Now I won't ask you to cheer for prince, bishop, or any one, but for the canal labourers.

The loud cheering that followed this speech prompted one contractor to overstate McKiernan's role in the dispute: "All of the trouble which we have had on the canal this winter has been caused mostly by men that have never worked a day on the canal," he claimed, adding that the conflict was "started in a low Brothel kept by one Joe Beef who seems to be at the head of it all." In the end, though, Joe Beef's role was not insignificant, and in popularizing the grievances of the men and helping them to carry out their work stoppage, he did contribute to the canal laborers' eventual victory.

McKiernan's strike support was but a part of a more wide-ranging commitment to the "liberty tree" with which he had adorned his wife's grave in 1871. His libertarian stand often vented itself in satirical rage, directed especially at evangelical pietists and temperance advocates; he was known to set his bears on those foolish or naive enough to enter his rooms for the purpose of proselytizing. By the late 1870s, however, the forces of moral regulation and social order were on the ascent, and Joe Beef's Canteen began to face competition from the Young Men's Christian Association rooms recently established in the waterfront area. When a regular customer died of overconsumption of drink in 1879, the public attack on McKiernan was stepped up, and the next years saw the erosion of Joe Beef's reputation as a patron of the poor. As workers gravitated toward more explicit forms of class action, centered in their economic programs and potential challenges of the rising Knights of Labor or the growing trade-union movement, tavern life at Joe Beef's became less and less associated with the class position it had taken in the 1870s. Its convivial atmosphere, for years a jocular chaos of good-natured hilarity, was replaced by somber, dull, and vacant silence, expressive less of the old combativity than of a growing resignation.

Charles McKiernan must have found this changed context of the 1880s difficult to adjust to, and his displacement from the center of the rough waterfront world no doubt proved a hard and bitter pill to swallow. "Always the poor man's friend," when he died on January 15, 1889, McKiernan's body was accompanied to its grave by representatives of fifty Montreal labor societies. Not everyone mourned his passing, however; one virtuous bourgeois editor scoffed that Joe Beef's "talented proprietor," had operated "a resort of the most degraded of men" and actively worked "for the brutalization of youth." An advocate of Christian philanthropy, this editor revealed the limitations of a reformism that could not comprehend the laboring poor any more than it could appease them. Joe Beef's, the product of an age of transition in which class perspectives were coalescing, had attempted to provide for the unemployed, the casual laborer, the tramp—persons outside of respectability; they had only the mutual aid they themselves could muster, with the help of an odd enigma such as Charles McKiernan. Though perhaps atypical, Joe Beef's Canteen thus bridged the gulf separating rough and respectable. It provided the warmth of the tavern, the protection of the mutual benefit society, and the fraternity of an egalitarian order, all the while refusing concession to the hypocrisies of the consolidating bourgeois ethos and its class prejudice.

Let me close this chapter with a textual reading of an artistic expression of high modernism, with its transforming of traditional images and ability to invest in them a "disinterested contemplation" that lent to aesthetic experience a new spirit of interpretive possibility. Paul Cézanne is generally recognized as a painter whose use of color and line intentionally blurred distinctions between appearance and its artistic construction, affording new potential for analytic expression. Among his major serial works, The Card Players, painted sometime in the 1890s, can be usefully read as a comment on the broad meaning of fin-de-siècle plebeian sociabilities of the night.[48] Its actual locale is impossible to ascertain. Probably neither a friendly society hall nor a tavern, the aesthetically constructed setting is nevertheless one of potential insight into those two spatial contexts of plebeian and working-class nights of leisure and recreation.[49]

What is conveyed in The Card Players? First, the general scene is one of somber shadows, receding planes, stark backgrounds, murky colors. Billowing material, in its folds and capacity to encompass, shields or obscures humanity, pushing the players almost to the edge of the canvas or dwarfing them in the flowing darkness of coats and the covering tilt of hats. Second, the placement of players and onlookers is one of aligned poses, constructed angularity, and repetitious, almost clashing, arrangements of knees, hands, shoulders. Third, the studied separation of the human figures, from the downcast eyes of the child and blank standoffish curiosity of the pipe-smoking onlooker (said to be Cézanne himself) to the introspection of the three seated participants in the game, contributes to a "hauntingly self-reflective composition."[50] Fourth, the gendered stereotypes and sameness of the players, all male, is so deceivingly obvious as to go almost unnoticed. All told, the image is anything but an expression

13. Paul Cézanne, *Still Life with Skull* (1895–1900).

of sociability; it exudes a poised stoicism and distanced detachment that seem the very antithesis of good-humored collectivity.

It would be an immense inferential leap to suggest that Cézanne was directly commenting on fraternalism or the tavern with this painting, but it is perhaps not impossible that he was reflecting on the general demise of night's sociability at the end of the nineteenth century. So many institutions, once the site of vitalities and energies associated with evenings of collective sociability, had faded into resigned shadows of their past prominence and pale reflections of previously invigorating cultures of vibrant human interaction. Certainly fraternalism, by the end of the century, had adapted to the morbid actuarialism of the insurance company, its metaphorical nights of ritual and symbolism passing (and unsuccessfully at that) into the dull days of the balanced ledger book. Something of this same process overtook much of tavern life, which succeeded as a social institution for a time but largely failed as a small business, thus compromising its continuity as a cultural presence.[51] Way stations in the cultural making of class difference, fraternalism and the tavern had, by the end of the nineteenth century, served their time in the service of class formation; both increasingly found themselves a cultural reservoir turned to by marginalized social groups for whom the process of assimilation in North America's mainstream was thwarted by ethnocentrism, nativism, and racism. Other institutions and mobilizing collectivities now galvanized and represented—both in speaking for labor and in symbolizing its meanings to others—the growing and increasingly vocal ranks of the working class as a collective whole. Nights of fraternity and tavern sociability remained, but they often took on the appearance of deadening, enervating weights on the table of plebeian actuality, which could hardly be limited to the gendered confinements of masculinity's moments of retreat and retrenchment. Was Cézanne saying as much when, at the same time that he was experimenting with The Card Players, he also painted his obviously related, deeply dark, and richly symbolic Still Life with Skull (1895–1900)? Fraternalism and the tavern thus stand as stark reminders of how complicatingly difficult it would prove to sustain transgressive impulses in the face of the deadening shadows of accommodation.

I I

Nights of the Bomb Throwers

The Dangerous Classes Become Dangerous

In the spring of 1886, North American workers huddled on street corners, exchanged knowing looks as their eyes met across the aisles of foundries, factories, breweries, and mills, shrugged matter-of-factly as they headed down the mine shaft, or gathered outside cooperative groceries after shopping for the week's foodstuffs. They talked of the forthcoming visit of a well-known labor lecturer, an upcoming strike, the much sought-after eight-hour day, the article or serialized novella published in the last issue of their trade or reform journal. Or they might pass the word of the next meeting of the Knights of Labor:

> To-night we meet within the mystic halls
> Of these our brothers, whose emblazoned shields
> Glow forth in golden splendor on our walls,
> Greeting with joy the sword our Order wields,
> ...
> But while we dream of the chivalry of yore
> And wish for knighthood to redress all wrong,
> We know our time has braver deeds in store.[1]

The "braver deeds" that the Knights of Labor looked forward to did not go unnoticed in 1886, even across the Atlantic, among the often condescending elite of continental Marxism.

A distinguished German socialist Wilhelm Liebknecht, Karl Marx's daughter Eleanor, and her lover, Edward Aveling, visited the United States that year. They found the progress of the class struggle to be surprisingly advanced. At the forefront of what would come to be known as the Great Upheaval were the Knights of Labor, "the first spontaneous expression by the American working people of their consciousness of themselves as a class."[2] For the "Old General" of international socialism, Friedrich Engels, 1886 and the Knights of Labor occupied a similiar point of significance. As "the raw material out of which the future of the American working-class movement, and along with it, the future of American society at large, has to be shaped," the Knights were a powerful if at times contradictory phenomenon: "an immense association spread over an immense extent of country, ... held together ... by the instinctive feeling that the very fact of their clubbing together for their common aspiration makes them a great power in the country; a truly American paradox clothing the most modern tendencies in the most medieval mummeries."[3] Engels regarded the explosive U.S. class mobilizations of 1886 as "one of the greatest events of the year."[4]

Behind this shocking transition were days of exploitation and oppression, to be sure, but they were supplemented by nights of sociability that, in locales such as Chicago, nurtured an oppositional culture of ribald, lampooning revolutionism, paralleling the Knights of Labor but distinct from it. As the mundane but materially attractive features of fraternalism and the tavern were incorporated into a network of mutual benefit clubs, athletic and drinking associations, gymnasiums and singing societies, schools, unions, and target-shooting militias, the transgressive possibilities of class were highlighted. Woven together by the anarcho-communist politics of proletarian insurrection and conscious antagonism to bourgeois society, the working-class night evolved into a merciless challenge that erupted across the spring of 1886 in poems of derision, parades of protest, and, ultimately, class battles that ended in repression and state hangings in the aftermath of the Haymarket bombing. Night, a nursery of class consciousness in 1886, proved a nightmare to those who feared the implications of proletarian power. As the dangerous classes became truly dangerous, bourgeois authority unleashed its dark "psychic revenge" in campaigns of terror.[5]

The "dangerous classes" were a social construction of fear and loathing, made in the realm of ideas, perceptions, and intuitions. As class society hardened during the Industrial Revolution the spatial separations—evident in the consolidation of different neighborhoods and experiences—of social and cultural life widened in the capitalist economies of Europe and America. In the first half of the nineteenth century the dangerous classes were a blurred category, associated not only with the threatening demands of laboring people for better wages and conditions or some semblance of political equality but also with crime, chaos, and the conflagration of epidemics and death, all of which were of course embedded in destitution and immiseration. Indeed, there seemed to be a layered development of the irrationalities of categorization as the dangerous classes were made in the push to police and incarcerate all offenders against social stability; to sever the ill from the supposedly healthy in penitentiary-like isolations, whether officially monitored quarantine or more informal social ostracism; to crush dissidence by invoking the repressive apparatus of the state in times of conflict (strikes, riots, rebellions, revolts); and generally to outlaw all who refused to adapt or succumb to authority's powers and proscriptions. As the American labor reformer George McNeill wrote in editorial protest at the time of the 1870s business crash and the Great Railway Strikes of 1877, "When [the worker] is at work, he belongs to the lower orders, and is continually under surveillance; when out of work he is an outlaw, a tramp,—he is a man without rights of manhood,—the pariah of society, homeless, in the deep signifiance of the term."[6] Eugène Buret's *De la misère des classes laborieuses en Angleterre et en France* (1840) made much the same point: "The lower classes are gradually expelled from the usage and laws of civilized life.... They are outside society, outside the law, outlaws."[7]

This criminalization of the poor was, as Louis Chevalier has suggested, perhaps the central social fact of developing class relations in Paris in the first half of the nineteenth century. It was lent a certain authority by the othered meaning of the night. "We are back in the palmy days of the Middle Ages, when the streets were dark and deserted," wrote Vicomte Charles de Launay in 1843. "For the past month the sole topic of conversation has been the nightly assaults, hold-ups, daring robberies." What disturbed this commentator was that crime, knowing no distinctions between wealth and material precariousness, attacked all indiscriminately, as if the night lowered a suffocating darkness over both perpetrator and victim alike: "What is so terrifying about these nocturnal assaults is the assailants' noble impartiality. They attack rich and poor alike.... Paris is much perturbed by these sinister occurrences." Night was easily associated with particular crimes, from the theft practiced by prostitutes who picked the pockets of their often inebriated clients to the act of ultimate violence, murder, or its self-inflicted counterpart, suicide. Police reports routinely referred to "the attacks by night," stipulating which was the most terrifying. Jules Janin's *Un hiver à Paris* (1845) was perhaps the most melodramatic in its construction of the dangerous classes as creatures both of the night and apart from the genteel society of the day:

Paris at night is fearsome. This is the hour when the tribe of the underworld sets forth. Darkness reigns, but little by little the gloom lifts in the flickering lantern of the ragpicker going off, basket on back, to seek his fortune amid those foul rags that have no name in any language. At that hour, too, bespattered carts draw up to the door of sleeping houses to carry off every kind of filth. At the corner of the gloomiest streets through the blood-red curtains the pothouse lamp shines out with funereal gleam. Along the walks slink marauding robbers, ever and anon uttering the cry of some night bird; women come and go seeking the cellar where they are to spend the night; for this abominable population spends its nights in the cellars. So the terror is vast, horrible, formidable. Those steps you hear thudding on the muddy paving are the gray patrol starting out on its voracious prowl.... In the hideous lairs which Paris hides away behind its palaces and museums ... there lurks a swarming and oozing population that beggars comparison. There are crusts and wretched remnants all around. They speak a language spawned in the jails; all their converse is of larceny, murder, prisons, and scaffolds. A vile bohemian world, frightful world, a purulent wart on the face of this great city.

This was danger and darkness at their metaphorical deepest.[8]

The dangerous classes, exiled from the soul and center of the body politic, were then reduced to the status of sores on that physique. In fact, their health did suffer from the darkness in which they lived, the congested neighborhoods so shadowed even in daylight that they assumed the foreboding character of the night. Claude Lachaise's *Topographie medicale de Paris* (1822) offered an early commentary:

The inevitable result of the congestion of the houses and their excessive height is that the sun shines for a short time only in some of the streets, hardly at all in others and never in most of them, and that the people living on the ground floor are still in the dark when the sun is far up the horizon.... persons who are compelled by their occupation to live in low-lying and dark places, such as porters, certain workmen, even persons who, though well enough off, live on the ground floor in dark, narrow streets, fall prey to the so-called intermittent fevers, scrofula, scurvy, dropsies, arthritis and rheumatism and the like, and to a multitude of other illnesses similar to the wilting of plants. This perpetual dusk, and the damp that accompanies it, are the main causes in Paris of the scrofulous complaints, the rickets, scab and white swellings which are so common.

One newcomer linked the vast gulf separating rich and poor in mid-nineteenth-century Paris to the darkening of night itself, the loss of a country evening's clarities being connected to the "black" atmosphere of the city's impersonality and suffering.[9]

In this dark congealment of biology and bigotry, of culture, climate, and class, the poor were seen as a naturalized, homogenized organism—a beast. Even as sympathetic an observer as Flora Tristan, a proponent of women's unionism, confided in her diary that she found workers a "brutal, ignorant, vain people, so disagreeable to rub shoulders with, so repulsive when seen close up." Engels regarded the Irish in England's industrial cities as dirty, bestial drunkards, more attached to their pigs than to even minimal standards of civilization, contemptuous of genuine human enjoyments, their simple savagery confirmed in a cheery, carefree temperament that only reduced them to lives of exploitive filth and poverty. The Irish fared little better in the New World, where they were customarily categorized as racially inferior—simian, lazy, wild, low-browed, groveling savages; they were regarded as a race apart, a dark people closer to African-American slaves than to the freeborn communities of "white" people among whom they settled. Many immigrant workers in North America continued to be associated with physical brutishness. As late as 1893 the Boston-based reformer B. O. Flower referred to a "night of poverty and despair" that engulfed a "commonwealth of victims" in a "democracy of darkness," a subterranean vault of incarcerating wretchedness. In Flower's rhetorical constructions, the men, women, and children of this Dantean inferno "wallow[ed] in animality." This underworld of crime commingling with poverty, bestial passions, and sensual gratifications threatened civilized order with the likelihood of "a bloody cataclysm." Authors, caricaturists, and commentators reduced this view to its barest physicality, depicting striking workers in "racial" ways. Adding an ideological hostility, they presented an image of the working-class activist as a Frankensteinian monster, lunatic in its raving ugliness, possessed of a socialist savagery that showed to good effect as a dark representation of revolution.[10]

Homogenizing representations of the laboring and dangerous classes were ideological constructions, but they did address the process of universalizing proletarianization, albeit in ways that served only to distort the experience of class formation. The nineteenth century saw the making of a global, and highly international, working class. In Europe alone the numbers of proletarians doubled, rising to some two hundred million. Driven by demographic and structural growth, working populations expanded six- and sevenfold in a hundred-year period. If much of this explosive class expansion was associated with the phenomenal rise of the city—Berlin, Paris, London, New York, and Melbourne grew dramatically in the last half of the century, as did the new settler economies of Australia and North America—and the subordination of the countryside, it was also inseparable from the active human agency of those who were proletarianized.[11]

In Britain, home of the first Industrial Revolution, the early working class fought simultaneously for economic rights in the workplace and for the extension of political democracy, summed up in the demand for universal male suffrage. These activities culminated in the Chartist agitation of the 1830s and 1840s, a richly complex mobilization of hundreds of thousands of workers who established their own newspapers, fostered an articulate reform leadership, and cultivated a class identity of shared interests. One result of this process was a culture of robust defiance in which working-class men, women, and children stood together against employers who attempted to contain their rebelliousness with threats of dismissal from their jobs and other punitive measures. The night figured prominently in this resistance: twenty thousand factory workers marched menacingly on one town in a torchlit procession; other nocturnal meetings were punctuated with volleys of pistol shots. One mill, owned by a particularly despised pair of "tyrants," burned to the ground one evening under what the magistrates termed "highly suspicious" circumstances, while the about-to-be-unemployed workers cheered the conflagration and refused to help put out the fire. Events such as the South Wales Newport Rising of 1839, in which thousands of miners and iron workers marched against "the reign of terror" unleashed on the Chartists, was preceded by the creation of an underground organization, sustained by nights of secret meetings and the gathering of arms. Timed to coincide with the annual night raucousness of Guy Fawkes celebrations, the Newport Rising ended in bloody defeat when troops fired on the assembled crowd, leaving twenty-two dead.[12]

Meanwhile, U.S. workers had won access to the ballot box and formed a series of workingmen's parties by the 1830s. Skilled French workers in the artisanal trades led the way in the formation of unions and utopian movements, taking to the barricades in 1830 and 1848. In 1871 they helped to launch a struggle for state power in a short-lived insurrectionary experiment, the Paris Commune. Following midnight marches down the Champs-Elysées, early morning debates on the barricades, and bonfires at the Arc de Triomphe, the Commune would fall to the fire of reaction, initiating "tragic nights" of repression in the words of one of the first unambiguously positive histories of the Commune, Lissagaray's *Histoire de la Commune de 1871* (1876). "There were nights that were louder, riven by more awful lightnings, of a more awful grandeur, when the flames and the cannonade enveloped all Paris; but none left a more funereal impress upon the imagination."[13] As capitalism penetrated underdeveloped areas such as China, India, southern Africa, and Latin America, the working classes that developed faced special oppressions and intensified exploitation.

Everywhere the strike came to be the symbolic statement of working-class resistance. Organized by shadowy figures who "emerged suddenly from out of the night for one brief moment," these protests and the workers' activists who led them are too often marginalized and obscured by historical accounts that present "their barely glimpsed faces" as "a mere blur."[14] Exploring the nights of labor that sustained working-class agitation and conflict may help place them more prominently on the pages of history.

It is appropriate to begin such a discussion with an account of the Noble and Holy Order of the Knights of Labor, a body begun as a secret society in Philadelphia in 1869. Workers who had previously experimented with class organization had often faced strong opposition, and many were victimized and blacklisted, hounded from one workplace to another, driven from their jobs and their homes. In this context, secrecy made profound sense. Founded by skilled workers who drew explicitly on Masonic rituals, it spread slowly over the course of the 1870s and by the 1880s had established itself in most of the major urban and industrial regions of the United States and Canada. It also developed a weak presence in England, Ireland, Australia, and New Zealand, and the odd continental Europe locale, where the base was Belgium. Believing that craft unions restricted to a particular trade were a narrow and outmoded means of protecting broad working-class interests, the Knights organized all workers in particular geographic sectors after first gathering them together in local assemblies. These could be composed of employees in a specific workshop, members of a trade group, heterogeneous collectivities of laborers from a particular place, or any combination of men, women, blacks, whites, and members of other ethnic groups willing to band together in the cause of labor's solidarity. The local assemblies then sent representatives to District Assemblies, which in turn chose delegates to annual continent-wide General Assemblies, at which the body's leadership was elected. As such, the Noble and Holy Order was an organizational innovation that departed dramatically from the sectional interest-group form of the established unions of skilled labor that dominated the labor movement in nineteenth-century Canada and the United States.

This mobilizing breadth adapted well to all manner of working-class settings, from the one-industry resource towns of the mining belts to the diversified manufacturing cities, huge factories, and milltowns of the industrial heartland, to the small "island" communities and transportation links dotting the landscape of the political economy. The Knights, unlike the craft unions, welcomed unskilled workers, racial and ethnic minorities (with the exception of Asian laborers, for whom they generally reserved a racist antagonism), and, eventually, women (after being excluded in the pre-1881 years of secrecy, female workers fought their way into the organization and were thereafter a presence of considerable importance). If the Knights' commitment to marginalized groups (which, after all, could be absolutely central to particular work settings or a majority of all workers in a given locale) was not complete, in the 1880s this inclusiveness was a tremendous advance over previous practice, which had limited working-class organization to a narrow base of privilege, materially rooted in white skins, male powers, and the secure and relatively well-paying occupations.

Moreover, this new reach across class divisions was paralleled in the range of purposes embraced by the Knights. Not just a defensive protector of job interests, the Order was, to be sure, a union, founded in the materiality of the workplace, but it was also a political reform society, an educational body, and a lodge in which fraternalism, working-class religiosity, and sociability all commingled. The Knights of Labor established their own newspapers, political parties, and courts, in which they tried transgressors on all manner of charges, from traditional acts of disloyalty such as strikebreaking to other breaches of proper knightly conduct such as sexual seduction, failure to pay off debts, revealing the secrets of the Knights' ritual, and violations of domestic norms (poor treatment of stepchildren, wife beating). Strikes were organized and improved conditions fought for, of course. But additionally Sunday labor sermons were preached in Knights of Labor halls, tracts of political economy read and discussed, and poems and prose written in ways that reproduced the values of the movement. Picnics and parades, public concerts, dances, and balls, as well as smaller soirees took place under the Order's banner, providing a network of sociability that gathered together entire communities in a labor-centered collectivity. More than any other nineteenth-century body, the Knights of Labor struggled to make workers' organizations a *movement culture*, a striving for justice and equality that, whatever its shortcomings, attempted to go beyond narrow self-interest.[15]

Hundreds of thousands of laboring people were drawn to the symbolic universe of class resistance in night gatherings held in Knights of Labor halls or rented rooms. The Order's ritual, the secret work known as the *Adelphon Kruptos* (AK), stipulated a set of opening services, an allegorical evening journey that had to be traveled before business of any sort could be conducted. "A Globe being placed on the outside of the Outer Veil; a copy of the Sacred Scriptures closed; and a box or basket containing blank cards on a triangular Alter, red in color, in the center of the vestibule; a Lance on the outside of the Inner Veil, or entrance to the Sanctuary, over the wicket; that the initiated may know that an Assembly of the [Knights of Labor is] in session." Secrecy, certainly (the Globe was placed *outside* the sanctuary), and perhaps even combativeness (the Lance signified defense) were enshrined in this opening ritual, as was the solemnity of membership (blank initiation cards resting on an inspiring red altar) and a closing of the book on sectarian differences (the Bible being shut). The Master Workman's podium was marked by a column three feet high, the shaft of which resembled a bundle of sticks. As one leading Knight explained, the tightly bound rods indicated strength: "One attempt to break a bundle of sticks is sufficient to prevent a second effort in that direction [for] ... 'in union there is strength.'" An entire world of symbolism thus rooted the membership in the movement, and specific symbols reinforced traditions of collectivity in an age of individualistic pieties.[16]

The pull of this imagery and representational world was powerful. Members made their way, alone or in small groups, through the darkness of the night, their every step taken with resolve and meaningful awareness of how much was at stake in the clash of class cultures that pitted workers and their organizations against capital and its supporters. The centrality of class pride and the significance of solidarity and collectivity reverberated throughout the AK, echoing in Knights of Labor halls across the length and breadth of the United States and Canada and drawing workers out of their days of toil and, through the muted working-class collectivity of the fraternal order, into a movement culture where class needs were finally addressed frontally.

The parades, dinners, festivals, and dances that were organized by Knights deepened commitments to this cause, as did the solemn attendance of members at funerals, when the Order appeared "in a body" at a special memorial assembly, having appointed a historian, a "knight of the unbroken vow," a poet, and a eulogist.[17] From these and other mobilizations emerged a contingent of labor intellectuals known as "brainworkers," who touted the Knights at huge rallies, edited newspapers, researched and wrote articles, and traveled throughout their districts, "spreading the light."[18] To read the working-class newspaper of this era is to appreciate the unwaged evening toil that went into the production of thousands of lines of verse and serialized stories and novels, a stylized reflection of the solidarity and sentimentality that blurred into the "Great Upheaval" of popular culture associated with the Knights of Labor. In just one of the Order's newspapers, the *Journal of United Labor,* 530 poems appeared in the fourteen-year stretch from 1880 to 1893. Members, moreover, were a mass market for a range of publications that marked the first foray of "cheap fiction" into the ranks of the working class, where the "mechanic accents" of a labor readership renegotiated the meanings of romaticized stories of working-class struggle with and ultimate accommodation to bourgeois America.[19] No previous labor organization in North American history had made such inroads into the nights of the working class. Daily concerns and leisure activities stepped off the workplace floor and onto the platform of public sociability, so long dominated by the masculinist tone of the fraternal order or the tavern.

The trouble with the Knights of Labor night was that it promised a new day. When dawn broke in the middle to late 1880s with the explosive campaigns of de facto independent labor parties, almost two hundred working-class tickets were mounted electorally in the United States and Canada, encompassing thirty-four of the thirty-eight states and three of the core industrial provinces. Surging strike waves spread along railway lines, reached into mining communities, and rocked milltowns and factory cities alike, bringing robber barons such as Jay Gould to their knees. Capital sensed that more was going on in the Order's nightly assemblies than strange oaths and secret handclasps.

The year 1886 struck fear into the heart of capitalist America. With the Knights of Labor behind him, the labor reformer Henry George narrowly lost the New York City mayoralty campaign, and labor candidates across the United States were elected as assemblymen, judges, and other civic officials. More than three times as many strikes were fought out in 1886 in the United States as in any previous year between 1881 and 1884. Led by the Knights of Labor in Chicago, New York, and Milwaukee, nearly 340,000 North American workers waged a battle for the eight-hour day. Thousands of small conflicts erupted, but it was the mass strike that proved most terrifying to authority. "One go, all go" was the revealing cry of a Polish worker in Detroit. What had been a slogan on a coopers' banner in 1880, "Each for himself is the bosses plea/ Union for all will make you free," seemed less rhetorical in the tense climate of 1886 as Toronto's workers overturned streetcars. Chicago's immigrant-staffed packing-houses exploded in conflict, and transport laborers—from New York City's freight handlers to the laboring crews of the southwestern railway lines—walked off their jobs. "All I knew then of the principles

of the Knights of Labor," remembered union pioneer Abraham Bisno, was
that the motto was "One for All, and All for One." A year later the *Boston
Labor Leader* was drawing the worrisome conclusion that the strength of the
Knights of Labor lay "in the fact that the whole life of the community is
drawn into it, that people of all kinds are together, ... and that all get
directly the sense of each others needs." Such strength could have
disturbing consequences. Out of the night had come obvious class
challenges to the established powers of the day.[20]

From the small backwater of Alvinston, Ontario, a semiliterate man
wrote to Knights of Labor figurehead Terence V. Powderly, his frame of
reference defined by organized workers' new offensive, the rising tide of
antilabor sentiment, and the class battle on Jay Gould's southwestern
railroad system. Having seen the efforts being made to "shield the
labouring man/ from the ... tironizin cruelty of monopolies and Rich
Men," Howard Rickard requested information about the procedure for
"organising the Nigts of Labour" in his area. He advised the General
Master Workman that the Order should proceed "cautiously and with all
due respect to a well organize bodie of opponents," but he wanted to see
the wrongs to workers righted so that "beter days [could] be brought
around." He understood that this was "no small task." As for the fight on
Gould's railways, he knew where he stood: "To look after and in speaking
of the strikes of the Labouring of those railroads now unsetled as yet I
regret that their should been any necesity to resort to fier arms as that
nearly always results bad. But it is necessary sometimes to fight for your
rights."[21] In Chicago there were those who had long before taken such
words to heart.

The Knights of Labor made up a highly heterogeneous political body.
Within its generalized politics of working-class advocacy its radicalism
was eclectic rather than focused, and each District Assembly harbored a
range of positions: those who favored independent labor politics might
rub shoulders with those more conciliatory to established parties. Reform,
not revolution, dominated the political agenda of the Order's leadership.
But wherever immigrant radicals, especially Germans, congregated in
sufficient numbers to cultivate revolutionary cells, the red and black flags
of the European International Working People's Association might lie
unfurled, ready to be flown on the barricades should the occasion arise.

The politics of Social Revolution—the ultra-left of the workers' movement in the 1880s—revolved around what might best be called anarcho-
communism, a Marxism not yet indelibly stamped with hard opposition
to the often rhetorical "terror of the deed" associated with British and

Continental anarchism. By 1886 this revolutionary current was established in Great Britain. William Morris and the Socialist League found them-selves embroiled in a two-year-long contest with committed anarchists, most of whom were aligned with recently arrived European exiles such as the fiery propagandist and author of the terrorist manual *Revolutionary War Science* (1885), Johann Most, or the famous Russian anarchist Prince Kropotkin, whose paper, *Freedom*, was often sold by socialists hawking their own *Commonweal*. Anarchism proved attractive to some revolutionary socialists in the 1880s largely because it refused any and all compromises with reformist politics.[22] The politics of anarchism were crystallizing in the Social Revolutionary movement, where socialism was increasingly pushed away from Marx and Engels's historical materialism and toward a distinctively conflagrationist anti-statism; parliamentary reform was wildly denounced as counterproductive and the leading cadre propagandized for a direct, and decisively final, confrontation with capitalist power. Johann Most and a group of Continental militants organized the International Social Revolutionary Congress in London in July 1881, but it was soon apparent that the epicenter of anarchist politics had shifted westward to the burgeoning industrial cities of the American Midwest. Chicago would be the hub of this dramatic political development.[23]

By the early 1880s Chicago was the most radical city in the United States. Its workers' movement was a contentious coalition of socialists, anarchists, and trade unionists, organized in locals of the Socialist Labor Party, the Workingmen's Party of Illinois, the International Working People's Association, and a competing if overlapping network of trade-union "centrals."[24] The Central Labor Union attracted anarchistically inclined Social Revolutionaries and the radical Bohemians and Germans; the Knights of Labor drew on Irish and Anglo-American workers; and the Trades and Labor Assembly united the foreign- and native-born socialists who favored political action. All found a place in the Eight Hour League, from which would be launched a continent-wide struggle to reduce the daily hours of labor. Much could be made of the ideological, ethnic, occupational, and programatic rifts that separated the various tendencies. But if these divisions were tangible and at times quite debilitating, they never man-aged to override entirely the generalized atmosphere of radicalism that touched all sectors of the Chicago workers' movement, lending it a revo-lutionary fervor unrivaled in any other metropolitan center.[25]

As early as 1879 a Chicago anniversary celebration of the Paris Commune filled the huge Exposition Building on the lakefront with a crowd esti-mated to range between twenty and forty thousand. A hostile reporter explained to readers of the *Tribune* how such a huge throng had been assembled:

> Skim the purlieus of the Fifth Ward, drain the Bohemian socialist slums of the Sixth and Seventh Wards, scour the Scandinavian dives of the Tenth and Fourteenth Wards, cull the choicest thieves from Halsted, Desplaines, Pacific Avenue and Clark Street, pick out from Fourth Avenue, Jackson Street, Clark Street, State Street and the other noted haunts the worst specimens of female depravity, scatter in all the red-headed, cross-eyed and frowsy servant girls in the three divisons of the city and bunch all these together and you have a pretty good idea of the crowd that made up last night's gathering.[26]

This was a particularly virulent construction of the dangerous classes, Americanized in its nativist venom, misogynized in its disgust at the presence of women among the ultra-revolutionaries of Chicago's socialist community. Under the headline "Grand Carousal of the Communists," the press harangued the socialists as "prostitutes," "steaming mobocrats," "prowling wantons," "lowbrowed villains," and the "offscouring of the slums." In the boarding houses of the ethnic ghettos, respectable society saw the huddled masses of revolutionism breeding their pernicious doctrines of chaos and destruction. That women could carry their heads high in this degrading darkness bewildered authority. Captain Michael Schaack, who investigated the anarchist milieu in the aftermath of the 1886 Haymarket bombing, was shocked that a "Red Sisterhood" was prominent in the parades and demonstrations of the Social Revolutionaries; carrying banners and babies, these women could only be judged "crazy ... creatures in petticoats ... the most hideous looking females that could possibly be found." By the 1880s, the dangerous classes, criminalized from the outset, were being demonized by respectable society.[27]

The Chicago revolutionaries reveled in returning the favor. They seized with remarkable zeal every opportunity to strike blows for the cause of social transformation, and no issues so effectively mocked bourgeois standards as women's equality and an armed working class. One Fourth of July parade, for instance, was headed by "a brigade of Socialist Amazons, in bright costumes, splashed with vermilion bonnets, arm bands, sashes, scarves." The Workingwomen's Union float, decked out in pink and white fabrics and ribbons, was adorned with a banner that read: "WHEN WOMAN IS ADMITTED INTO THE COUNCIL OF NATIONS WAR WILL COME TO AN END, FOR WOMAN, MORE THAN MAN, KNOWS THE VALUE OF HUMAN LIFE." Reinforcing this theme with ironic intention was a *tableau vivant* comprising a group of men around a leather cannon and a gun carriage piled high with cannonballs. Satirizing the established newspapers, which had publicized rumors of a forthcoming communist uprising, the staged burlesque was also aimed at a proposed military law that would prohibit unlicensed displays of arms. In mock uniforms of blue blouses, red scarves, and deliberately outlandish, oversized, conical red hats, the marching militia sported huge wooden replicas of revolvers and elongated painted daggers, taunting the class enemy with the slogan "WHO'S AFRAID? FOR WE'RE NOT AFRAID." Laughter rippled through the watching throngs as authority was lampooned and the exclusiveness of the elite eroded with wild witticisms. But such ribald displays were not just empty jest: the Bohemian Sharpshooters, the Irish Labor Guards, and other defense corps often formed up in military procession, shouldered their guns, and marched to the tune of the "Marseillaise." Social Revolutionaries lambasted their opponents with endless hyperbole. One leaflet called workers to a huge protest, promising that after the ceremonies and sermons a charivari-like "serenade" would be offered to "the priests and officers of King Mammon." Already the movement had a sense of its past: "All the French and German Communists wanted during the dark days of '48 and '71," proclaimed one revolutionary orator, "was to establish a self-governing Republic, wherein the working classes—the masses—would partake of the civilization which their industry and skill had created." The endnote of the speech was unambiguously blunt: "We mean to place Labor in power."[28]

Chicago, then, more than any other locale, exemplified the extremist construction of the dangerous and laboring classes and drew bourgeois antagonism to the politics of revolution. As economic conditions worsened in the mid-1880s, the impoverished and often out-of-work revolutionaries were thrown into a downwardly spiraling climate of material distress, exacerbated in Chicago by a local police force with a well-deserved reputation for ruthless repression. The notorious Captain "Black Jack" Bonfield was known even in polite circles as a sadistic brute; his suppression of a street railway strike in 1885 was but a prelude to his violent and uncontrolled actions in the 1886 events on Haymarket Square. Strike after strike pitted destitute workers against powerful bosses, who drew on the resources of the state (the local constabulary, the militia, and federal troops), scabs, private Pinkerton detectives, and employer organization blacklists and lockouts to drive organized labor into retreat.

Many in the local workers' movement looked back in terror on the violent events of 1877, when socialist workers—men, women, and children—had taken to the streets and the factories in a July rampage that unleashed the combined forces of a weak police force, the militia and cavalry, and a merchant-led "veteran's corps" and "citizens' patrol"—euphemisms for vigilantism—on behalf of the city's elite. That confrontation had left thirty workingmen dead and two hundred wounded. And in 1884, one of Chicago's leading revolutionaries, August Spies, lost his nephew to a police bullet; he was fatally shot in the evening street, while trying to protect a drunken friend from arrest by an Irish cop. None of this was forgotten as May 1, 1886 drew close. The potential of socialist political action seemed more and more remote, the appeal of ultra-revolutionary rhetoric had become increasingly potent and attractive in its immediacy. The Socialist Labor Party had faded to a hundred members by 1886, but the Social Revolutionaries in the predominantly German Chicago branches of the International Working People's Association, buoyed by a successful 1883 convention in Pittsburgh that drew Most to America, expanded their numbers to almost three thousand. This ultra-left was particularly strong among the long-standing German and Bohemian radicals led by Spies and a new contingent of English-speaking revolutionaries headed by Albert and Lucy Parsons.[29] The anarcho-communist movement in Chicago was blessed with talented leaders, dedicated ranks, and the most active left-wing press in the country. The dangerous classes were becoming truly dangerous. *Alarm* was more than the title of an anarchist journal.[30]

As class relations further polarized in the tense climate of 1886, with hundreds of thousands of North American workers scheduled to strike for the eight-hour day on May 1, the Social Revolutionaries continued to prod and push the working class in the direction of armed self-defence. Johann Most's cult of dynamite had become deeply rooted in certain quarters by 1885:

> Dynamite today, dynamite tonight,
> Most tells us how, he shows where,
> He says all in *Freiheit*
> And his good little book on warfare.

Originally contemptuous of the reformist essence of the demand for the eight-hour day, the revolutionaries reassessed their position as masses of North American workers flocked to the banner of the shorter workday. Anarcho-communist journals exploded with the rage of class vengeance; hundreds of thousands of leaflets, books, and pamphlets were sold, among the most popular being Lucy Parsons's *To Tramps, the Unemployed, the Disinherited and Miserable*. Indeed, Albert and Lucy Parsons were central figures in the

Social Revolutionary community, editing the *Alarm*, marching in processions, speaking from a plethora of podiums. They merged into the eight-hour agitation with surprising ease.

Both the southern-born, fastidious, and articulate Parsons and his beautiful, vivacious part Native American, part African-American wife reached well past the issue of the hours of labor, being uncompromising advocates of a violent overthrow of the entire existing order. The *Tribune* reported Lucy as saying that "every dirty, lousy tramp [should] arm himself with a revolver or knife, and lay in wait on the steps of the palaces of the rich and stab or shoot the owners as they come out. Let us kill them without mercy, and let it be a war of extermination and without pity. Let us devastate the avenues where the wealthy live as Sheridan devastated the beautiful valley of Shenandoah." Perhaps the newspaper exaggerated this exhortation for political purposes, but it was unlikely that Lucy Parsons was misquoted in the *Labor Enquirer*, where she wrote that dynamite could be put to good use in defeating armies and toppling governments. "If some tyrants must be put out of the way," she concluded, "it should be looked upon as a blessing, inasmuch as the more oppressors dead, and the fewer alive, the freer will be the world." Albert was no less vitriolic. At a night rally to protest the opening of the new building of the Chicago Board of Trade, he assailed "the vampires and parasites" who fed on the flesh of the poor, drawing the cheers and interjections of a crowd ready for ruling-class blood. In the soaring oratory for which he was justly famous, Parsons declared that each stone of the new financial edifice had been "carved out of the flesh and blood of labor, and cemented by the sweat and tears of the women and children of toil." To end this state of oppression "every man must lay by a part of his wages, buy a Colt's navy revolver [*Cheers and 'That's what we want!'*], a Winchester rifle [*'And ten pounds of dynamite—we will make it ourselves!'*], and learn how to make and use dynamite. [*Cheers and cries of 'Vive la Commune.'*]"[31] The mainstream press was aghast, the *Chicago Tribune* exclaiming: "They parade at night with their black and red flags in the very shadow of the buildings which have furnished them full employment and menace the lives of their owners and threaten the destruction of the buildings with dynamite which they were paid to construct!"[32]

In the spring of 1886, as the working-class insurrection appeared to be unfolding, Parsons, Spies, Adolph Fischer, George Engel, Michael Schwab, Samuel Fielden, Oscar Neebe, and Louis Lingg—all of whom would soon be indicted—were among the revolutionaries who threw themselves into the massive mobilization. The First of May 1886 saw forty thousand Chicago workers out on strike, their Saturday one of jubiliant festivity: eighty thousand marched in what was one of the earliest May Days, the procession led by Albert and Lucy Parsons and their two children. As the city assumed a pre-conflagration quiet, "a Sabbath-like appearance," Spies and his comrades exhorted the rising proletariat to fulfill its historic destiny. "Bravely forward! The conflict has begun.... Cowards to the rear! ... The die is cast.... NOW OR NEVER," proclaimed the leaflets and the anarchist press. "Brand the curs," replied the bourgeois press. Police, Pinkertons, and deputized civilians lined the rooftops along the procession route, their hands clutching loaded rifles. In the city armories the militia stood poised to intervene, its Gatling guns primed for battle. Parsons and Spies were particularly singled out by the Chicago Mail: "Mark them for today. Keep them in view. Hold them personally responsible for any trouble that occurs. Make an example of them if trouble does occur." Parsons himself left Chicago almost immediately after leading the parade, traveling to Cincinnati to address the strikers there.[33] Nothing untoward happened, and the momentous beginning of the battle for the eight-hour day was capped with an immensely successful evening ball held under the auspices of the Trades and Labor Assembly.[34]

On Monday, May 3, the walkouts and protests continued in a climate that seemed anything but volatile. In the afternoon, however, things took a turn for the worse. Cyrus H. McCormick's agricultural implements factory had a bitter history of labor–capital conflict exacerbated by police and Pinkerton violence. For almost a decade the company's workers had been embroiled in skirmishes, strikes, lockouts, attacks on scabs, resistance to technologies that would displace employees, and picket-line brutalities that had earned the plant the name Fort McCormick. Weeks before the May Day events, the plant had been the scene of a typical clash. With workers engaged in union activities discharged, negotiations between management and labor stalled, the company locked all its employees out of the factory, hiring scabs in their stead. Protest meetings followed, many of which were addressed by leading anarchists, including Parsons, Spies, and Schwab. On May 3, Spies was addressing a gathering of several thousand striking lumber workers just down the street from McCormick's. As he concluded a quite moderate speech, the end-of-workday bell rang at the reaper works, and hundreds of workers swarmed toward the plant to support the locked-out employees and heckle the scabs. August Spies hurried to the scene, now inflamed by the arrival of patrol wagons of policemen. The picketers and their supporters escalated the battle from a harangue of the blacklegs to physical intimidation, driving the strikebreakers back into the plant. Stones rained down on the building, breaking windows, and the police were greeted with the same treatment. They responded by firing revolvers into the crowd and beating unarmed workmen, wounding many and killing two.

As the crowd fled, Spies attempted to draw the remnants of the lumber workers' assembly to the support of the McCormick's workers, but his pleas fell largely on deaf ears. He rushed to the offices of the *Arbeiter-Zeitung*, quickly drafted a fiery leaflet headed "Revenge! Workingmen to Arms!!!" and calling for "uncompromising annihilation" of "the beasts in human form who call themselves rulers." A horseman galloped through the city, dropping off Spies's inflammatory statement, written in German and English, at points where workers were known to gather. One of the distribution points was Greif's Saloon, where an evening meeting of German anarchists was in progress. Later depicted as "the Monday night conspiracy," this was a meeting of the most revolutionary segments of the armed militias of the International Working People's Association. Two of the later Haymarket martyrs, Engel and Fisher, were in attendance, and discussion had turned on the strategic direction to be taken should police and protesters clash over the issue of the eight-hour day. Apparently the anarchist circle determined that the signal for armed sections of their ranks to meet at Grief's in response to police violence and provocation would be the publication of the letter "Y" in the correspondence column of the *Arbeiter-Zeitung*.

These and other clandestine plans in place, the anarchists turned their attention to the day's events at McCormick's and to Spies's call for retaliation. After much debate it was decided to hold a protest rally at 7:30 the following night at the spacious Haymarket Square, which could accommodate twenty thousand people. Fischer immediately drafted a circular announcing the meeting and, apparently on his own initiative, added the concluding advice, "Workingmen Arm Yourselves and Appear in Full Force!" Spies struck off that line before handing the leaflet to the printer, but some of Fischer's original handbills had already circulated. Moreover, with highly charged accounts of the McCormick massacre appearing in the anarchist press the next day, the original calm of the eight-hour protest was decisively shattered. Chicago's working-class districts were soon seething with demands for retribution, allusions to arms and dynamite, and exhortations for all who were "manly" to rise to the occasion.[35] Police and protesters battled on street corners, and a crowd destroyed a drugstore from which police had relayed messages to their headquarters. A coded message appeared in the *Arbeiter-Zeitung* summoning the armed groups of the International to assemble and begin the work of "downright revolution." Conspiracies were no doubt afloat, but who had orchestrated them and how they were to unfold remain, to this day, something of a mystery. Whatever the case, the night of May 4, 1886, was shaping up to be a momentous one.[36]

As evening approached, tension mounted. Concentrations of police officers were stationed strategically about the city; plainclothes detectives were dispatched to mingle with the Haymarket crowd. Yet the night began anticlimactically. August Spies meandered into the meeting forty-five minutes after its announced time. Barely three thousand had come, and some were starting to drift away because of the late beginning. Albert Parsons, expected to speak first (English addresses conventionally preceded German ones), was still nowhere to be seen; he and Lucy were involved in a meeting of the American group of the International which had been called to organize the city's sewing girls. There had in fact been a mixup in establishing speakers for the meeting: Parsons did not even know he was expected at the Haymarket. Spies reconvened the remaining listeners, mounted a truck wagon, and spoke to the crowd in English. The mayor himself was in the crowd, but Spies's speech, aside from a few inflammatory declamations, was peaceful and law-abiding, and the city's leading civic official thought there was no need to intervene.

By 9:00 P.M., Parsons and other leading anarchists, summoned to the Haymarket, had adjourned their meeting with the sewing girls and walked the half-mile to the protest rally. Albert Parsons mounted the wagon as Spies, no doubt exhausted, stepped down. He gave the usual impassioned plea for socialism, deflecting cries for individual vengeance with reasoned arguments to attack not the personalities of oppression and exploitation but the causes. He did declare that Americans who loved liberty should "arm themselves," but his tone was judged "moderate." Even the mayor conceded that the gathering was calm and orderly and violated no laws; there was the usual bitter denunciation of capital, but neither Spies nor Parsons had made any suggestion "for the immediate use of force or violence toward any person that night." Convinced that there was no cause for concern and certainly none for suppressing the meeting, the mayor made his way home.

Parsons stepped down around 10:00 P.M. to join his wife, his two young children (four and six years of age), and a female anarchist, Lizzie Holmes. As the final speaker, Samuel Fielden, took the makeshift podium, and rain threatened, the crowd began to thin further; the women and children left, Parsons and his family among them. Fielden spoke for only a few minutes, but attacked the law as something to be throttled, killed, stabbed, wounded, and impeded in its progress of degrading the working class, reducing it to "mere things and animals." This was the language the police were waiting for. A phalanx of officers spilled out of a nearby station and marched menacingly on the now quite small crowd. Pushing their way to the wagon, the officers stood poised to attack as their captain demanded that Fielden and the rest of the assembly disperse. The revolutionaries were actually shocked; the meeting, now well over two hours old and all but finished, hardly seemed to merit this intrusive show of police power. "But we are peaceable," was all the numbed Fielden could mutter. After another police order to disperse, he complied. "All right, we will go," he said, stepping down from the wagon.

And then it happened. A sputtering object sailed over the heads of the police and dropped in their midst. Seconds later an explosion ripped through the Haymarket; windows shattered; officers fell. Round one, brief as it was, went to the bomb. The second round would belong to an infuriated mob of police who fired into the crowd and pursued the fleeing protesters. With the bell in the nearby police station tolling the riot alarm, five minutes of "wild carnage" ensued. Many were shot, including Fielden. Spies was saved by his brother, who grasped a police officer's gun as it was aimed at the German anarchist leader's back, taking the bullet in the groin. "Fire and kill all you can," shouted one lieutenant; the dark night literally exploded with bullets. "Goaded to madness, the police were in a condition of mind which permitted of no resistance," commented the *Chicago Tribune*. "They were blinded by passion and unable to distinguish between the peaceable citizen and the Nihilist assassin." Indeed, the officers shot one another, many of the seven dead and sixty wounded among them sustaining injuries that could not have been inflicted by anything other than the guns of the law. At least four workers were killed, but the count of civilian casualties has remained unknown, for those shot, trampled, or beaten largely made their way to drugstores, alleys, and homes, where their wounds were quietly dressed and hidden from those who might use them as indictable evidence in the subsequent repression. The bombthrower, despite much speculation as to his (it was not likely to have been a woman) identity, also remains unknown. Whether agent provocateur, individual, or conspirator, it is unlikely that he will ever be found out. The dark night of repression covered his tracks.[37]

What followed has been designated the first American "Red Scare." The immediate climate was one of inflamed venom, as the actual Haymarket events were distorted to confirm headlines proclaiming, "Now It

Is Blood." The *New York Times* reported that three explosive devices had initially been thrown and that a crazed mob "with a frantic desire for blood," poured "volley after volley into the midst of the officers." Across North America and Europe the anarchists were assailed as murderers. "Hang them first and try them afterward," seemed the commonplace response. Revolutionaries were vilified in the mainstream press: the only good anarchist was a dead one; too many rebels went unhanged. The *Cleveland Leader* offered a particularly lurid construction of the Social Revolutionary as vicious beast: "The anarchist wolf—unwisely permitted to take up its abode and propagate its bloodthirsty species in this country— has fastened its hideous, poisonous fangs in the body corporate of the American people." A law journal in Albany, New York, deplored the depraved indifference to respectable society of "a few long-haired, wild-eyed, bad-smelling, atheistic, reckless foreign wretches, ... who, driven half crazy with years of oppression and mad with envy of the rich, think to level society and its distinctions with a few bombs.... This state of things almost justifies the resort to the vigilance committee and lynch law." In short, American depiction of the diabolical face of the dangerous classes was not unlike that of the racialized criminalization of anarchists developing in pseudoscientific circles in Italy. There rebel terrorists were typed as a subhuman species as they waged a relentless war against European authority, figuring in the assassination plots that rocked France, Spain, Austria, and Italy from 1878 to 1900.[38] Popular dime novels of the period such as *The New York Detective Library* depicted the hairy, disheveled anarchist against a backdrop of "the red flag of Chicago anarchism," and a floor strewn with bombs, revolvers, and daggers. *Frank Leslie's Illustrated Newspaper* told stories of "the Rogues Gallery" that was being compiled in the aftermath of May 4: anarchists, socialists, and other workingmen were photographed by police so that their physiognomic traits (skull shape and facial features) could be compared and a eugenically developed understanding of innate criminality established.[39] Captain Schaack's *Anarchy and Anarchists: A History of the Red Terror and the Social Revolution in America and Europe* (1889) saw the dangerous classes as an underground brotherhood of destruction.[40]

Oscar Ameringer, a recently arrived immigrant in Cincinnati, later recalled with understatement the demoralization in the ranks of eight-hour activists: "The bad news from Chicago fell like an exceedingly cold blanket on us strikers. To our erstwhile friends and sympathizers the news was the clarion for speedy evaporation. Some of our weaker fellow Knights broke ranks. The army of the social revolution was visibly melting away.

The police grew more numerous and ill-mannered. And so did the tempers of our diminishing irreconcilables."[41]

The Haymarket bomb would be heard around the world, but the dark aftermath of that night lowered most decisively on Chicago's rebellious working class. Picketing workers were threatened, physically attacked, and forced back to their workplaces. The headquarters of anarchist and socialist groups were raided, their meeting places invaded, leaders and literature seized, and presses shut down. More than two hundred men and women were arrested in their homes, workplaces, or neighborhoods. Suppressing anarchy became a business, its entrepreneurial zeal exemplified by the notorious Captain Schaack, who, according to one contemporary,

> saw more anarchists than vast hell could hold. Bombs, dynamite, daggers, and pistols seemed ever before him; in the end, there was no society, however innocent or even laudable, among the foreign-born population that was not to his mind engaged in deviltry. The labor unions, he knew were composed solely of anarchists; the Turner societies met to plan treason, stratagems, and spoils; the literary guilds contrived murder; the Sunday schools taught destruction. Every man that spoke broken English and went out o'nights was a fearsome creature whose secret purpose was to blow up the Board of Trade or loot Marshall Field's store.

With spies infiltrating anarchist, socialist, and labor groups (even the Imperial German Police sent agents) the hopes of that early May Day, celebrated with such festive promise and honored by so many workers prepared to sacrifice their wages for a cause, came crashing down. Cautious, reformist labor leaders, especially those in the Knights of Labor and the craft unions of the Trades and Labor Assembly, issued proclamations of denunciation as the revolutionary milieu was driven underground. To be sure, defense committees and other organizations kept the idea of revolution alive, but the severe and unrelenting repression of radicalism, all too evident in the trial of the eight defendants charged with murder as a result of the Haymarket bombing, struck tangible blows against all workers.

The trial was a legal travesty, the verdict a foregone conclusion. Parsons, Spies, Schwab, Fielden, Fischer, Lingg, and Engel were found guilty and sentenced to death; Oscar Neebe, also convicted, had his penalty fixed at fifteen years in the penitentiary. Parsons, Spies, Fischer, and Engel would be executed on November 11, 1887; Ling would cheat the hangman by taking his own life; Engel, Fielden, and Neebe would eventually be pardoned by a progressive Illinois governor, John Peter Altgeld.[42] This act of clemency earned Altgeld the enmity of many staunch conservatives, and when reactionary Republicans scored electoral victories that fall, the *Tribune* envisioned the governor cast "into outermost political darkness ... with his mob of Socialists, Anarchists, single-taxers, and office-holding louts at his heels."[43]

The condemned men and their comrades knew that their fate had been sealed by the very injustice they had dedicated their lives to opposing. Lingg's final address to the court was unequivocal:

> It is not murder ... of which you have convicted me ... the con-
> demnation is—that I am an Anarchist! ... Anarchy means no domination
> or authority of one man over another, yet you call that "disorder." A
> system which advocates no such "order" as shall require the services of
> rogues and thieves to defend it you call "disorder." ... The universal
> misery, the ravages of the capitalist hyena have brought us together in
> our agitation, not as persons, but as workers in the same cause. Such is
> the "conspiracy" of which you have convicted me.... I do not recognize
> your law, jumbled together as it is by the nobodies of by-gone
> centuries, and I do not recognize the decision of the court.... I tell you
> frankly and openly, I am for force. I have already told Captain Schaack,
> "If they use cannons against us, we shall use dynamite against them". .
> I am the enemy of the "order" of today, and I repeat that, with all my
> powers, so long as breath remains in me, I shall combat it ... let me
> assure you that I die happy on the gallows, so confident am I that the
> hundreds of thousands to whom I have spoken will remember my
> words; and when you shall have hanged us, then, mark my words, they
> will do the bomb throwing! I despise your order, your laws, your force-
> propped authority. Hang me for it!

An advocate of dynamite, Lingg had comrades who supported him. One smuggled bombs into his cell at Springfield, Illinois. Even after their discovery and the tightening of security, Lingg managed to secure an explosive, embedded within a cigar, with which he would kill himself the day before he was due on the scaffold. There was a certain morbid poetic justice in this man's refusal to allow bourgeois justice to lead him to the gallows, and Lingg may well have savored his last moments alone, knowing well that it would give his jailers fearful pause to know that he could defy their incarceration and their capital punishment with his own hand. If even the jails cannot be secured from anarchist terror, Lingg was proclaiming with his own blood to authority, how can you expect to keep your social "order" intact? He died knowing that he was part of a revolutionary community. "I shall be as proud of you after your death as I have been during your life," his mother wrote to her only son just days before his suicide. "Whatever happens—even the worst—show no weakness before those wretches," wrote his aunt. Dead at the young age of twenty-two, Lingg made bourgeois society wince. "All over the world people must be asking themselves, What cause is this really, for which men die so gladly, so inexorably?" wrote William Dean Howells.[44]

As Parsons, Spies, Engel, and Fischer walked to the gallows on November 11, 1887, they symbolized the retribution that bourgeois order would demand when the dangerous classes actually became dangerous. They stood condemned of no actual crime save that of confirming the worst nightmares of property and propriety. The lower orders were constructed as savages by their "social betters"; savages they had now become. The Reverend Dr. Robert Collyer, ensconced in a New York pulpit, endorsed the hangings as an effective blow against the "plague" of anarchism and an act of education meant to lift "the worker to a higher stage of life." The Reverend C. C. Bonney, sermonizing in the Union Park New Jerusalem Church barely two weeks after the bombing, deplored anarchy as religious infidelity and chastised ruling authority for having allowed "the dangerous classes of the great cities to hold the balance of political power," thus bringing on social order and the urban environment an inevitable catastrophe. Lizzie Holmes, a comrade of the executed martyrs, would write in 1902 that the crime of Haymarket was not murder, and the weapon of Haymarket was not the bomb. Rather, the crime and the weapon were the same: the powerful idea of resistance, which "civilization" could reduce to its own antithesis only by constructing anarchy as irrational, "a wickedly secret, dark and bloody band intent only on violence and murder." Parsons spent his last minutes reciting Marc Cook's poem "A Farewell": "Poor creatures!/ Afraid of the darkness,/ Who groan at the anguish to come./ How silent I go to my home!/ Cease your sorrowful bell—/ I am well!" Spies—who had particularly outraged bourgeois propriety by courting Nina Van Zandt, the twenty-four-year-old daughter of a businessman, throughout the trial and marrying her by proxy in January 1887—proclaimed from under the hangman's hood, "The time will come when our silence will be more powerful than the voices you strangle today." Fischer and Engel simply shouted, "Hurrah for anarchy!" Minutes later the four comrades were dead.[45]

The next day, in the Bad Lands of Dakota, the executed anarchists were hanged in effigy by Theodore Roosevelt and a band of cowboys. There could never be enough repression for some; the dangerous classes demanded an ever vigilant coercive apparatus. Haymarket lived, however, in the memory of the workers' movement, a moment of potential that could not, ironically, be killed, however many times the scenario of bourgeois

14. The Haymarket Riot, from *Harper's Weekly* (1886).

order would be enacted. In Latin America, in Europe, and across the length and breadth of North America, the Haymarket events and the names of the martyrs remained a ubiquitous presence in the consciousness of a class opposition.[46] Wherever the dangerous classes threatened to become dangerous, the dark history of one of bourgeois order's uglier episodes soon came to mind, echoing Albert Parsons's last words to his children: "Your Father is a self-offered Sacrifice upon the Altar of Liberty and Happiness." Late one night in 1929 the revolutionary communist James P. Cannon, expelled for "Trotskyism" from the United States Communist Party he had helped to found, commemorated Parsons in verse:

> They say he was defeated, he went down
> To everlasting failure and disgrace,
> On that gray morning when they woke the town
> To see him hanging in the market place;
> No more will he rebel, long has he lain
> In sombre silence in the graveyard gloom;
> His words and deeds and dreams were all in vain,
> The dust of forty years is on his tomb.
> And yet his footsteps on the gallow's stair
> Resound like drumbeats, quickening the feet
> Of men who hear and even now prepare
> The march of stern avengers in the street;
> And blazoned on their banners overhead
> Is the accusing silence of the dead.[47]

12

Working for the Devil

Dark Dimensions of Exploitation

To travel from the centers of capitalist accumulation, with their exploitation of factory production workers, to the margins of proletarianization is to enter another world of inequality, subordination, and sociocultural imbalance. In the heartland of industrialized extraction of surplus value, class battles were dressed in the modernist rhetoric of "class against class." More distant economies produced a wide range of tensions and overt clashes: some followed the logic of unambiguous labor–capital conflict, but others trod paths of violence, complex negotiation, and accommodations bound by forces well outside the Eurocentric rationalities of market society. Exploitation in the increasingly important "underdeveloped" worlds of Africa and Asia, Central and Latin America, and the Caribbean was doubly dark. As a process of brutal coercion and relentless repression, it secured profitability for colonial capital at levels that massively outstripped those of the industrial-capitalist nation-states of Europe and the white settler societies of the United States, Canada, and Australia. When peasants and independent producers in such settings were proletarianized, moreover, they negotiated their acclimatization to a new order of inequitable wealth and power—mediated always by the many meanings of money (as wage, symbol, defining essence, category, and commodity)—in the shadows of aged and traditional cultures of ritualized engagements and occult power.[1]

Sorcery and magic, present at the birth of capitalism's first faint stirrings in early modern Europe, reappeared as a zone of engagement. The process of proletarianization in the so-called Third World was masked in dark and often diabolical attempts to trade the waged and marketed materiality of capitalist relations for the seemingly intangible powers and integrities of individual souls. As early as 1605 a black slave in a New Spain textile workshop confessed that he had appealed to satanic forces to deliver him from the oppressions of toil. "Is there not a devil somewhere," he wailed, "who might help me out of these labors in exchange for my soul?"[2] If capitalism eroded, even destroyed, devils and witches in its core states, anthropologists have suggested that on its margins they were reborn, proliferating in the cauldron of inequality that money and its meanings everywhere brought to a newly intense boil.

When German and British colonization of the south and west sectors of Cameroon, for instance, introduced large-scale banana cultivation, the plantation boom of the post–First World War era threatened a traditional people, the Bakweri, with extinction. This traditionalist and fundamentally egalitarian African tribe had evolved mechanisms to avoid proprietarial attachments and break the progress of an instinct of accumulation. In potlatch-like ceremonies that redistributed the symbols and material substance of wealth—dwarf cattle, pigs, and goats—they had weakened the need for jealousy-driven liemba, a system of witchcraft aimed at righting an aggrieved party's sense of material wrong. It was but a short step for the Bakweri to interpret the new wealth-generating possibilities of the banana-boom plantations in light of such sorcery; hence they avoided wage labor and modern houses, thus acquiring a reputation among Europeans for laziness and apathy. Colonial capital then encouraged the in-migration of other African groups, who soon flooded the Bakweri areas of Cameroon and weakened old ways with their entrepreneurial zeal: traditional lands were sold or rented to these strangers, who also provided clients for prostitutes and possibilities for concubinage seized upon by Bakweri women. Belief was widespread that the newly arrived and wage-labor-rich African plantation workers were nyongo witches, sorcerers who, unlike past variants, did not eat their victims but drew them to the Bakweri lands and reduced them to zombies forced to work on the "invisible plantations" of white colonial capital. (This process of belief paralleled the gendered appropriations happening as well in the sexual realm, for would not Bakweri women who sold themselves to outsider men take on the symbolic and psychological status of the undead?) These nyongo men lived in houses with tin roofs, and to preserve their opulent lifestyles they constantly had to recruit more zombie labor. But to spend a night in a modern house was to risk being trapped forever in the servitude of the plantation economy. The concubines and prostitutes who lived there, having abandoned their indigenous culture, must also have fallen under the spell of a particular incarceration.

As a powerful brake on labor recruitment, this Bakweri perception of sorcery and its fusion of the discontents of labor and culture was a curb on the accumulation process. It was broken decisively only in the 1950s when, encouraged by a contingent of Bakweri intellectuals, the group entered into the banana trade by organizing a cooperative venture. The immense wealth generated in the project encouraged the village council to seek the aid of a powerful shaman from a neighboring region. Lured with considerable cash, the shaman—buttressed by a crowd of wild dancers in long robes and masked in a fearsome crocodile skin—exorcised the *nyongo* witches and paved the way for full-scale Bakweri entry into the banana business. For almost a decade prosperity and economic boom prevailed, until the Bakweri farmers lost their privileged market position because of unification with the formerly French Cameroon and the new state's association with the European Economic Community. Thus sorcery originally provided a form of resistance to proletarianization among the Bakweri, erecting a barrier to labor recruitment and blocking access to the relatively lucrative wage and the ultimate profits of enterprise. After more than half a century this resistance was reversed for a brief period as "sorcery was transformed, almost overnight, from a barrier to a stimulus for accumulation." But in the end the witches seemed to have the last word, the local economy of the banana falling prey to distant devils. In other Cameroon cultures similar processes were at work.[3]

This kind of negotiation with the transformative impact of the colonizing conquest of capital appears as a regular feature of proletarianization in the underdeveloped world. Well into the 1980s various Third World societies sustained powerful beliefs about devil pacts and possession: known to have experienced such phenomena in the twentieth century are Bolivia, Colombia, Ecuador, Peru, Chile, Argentina, Panama, Puerto Rico, Cuba, Trinidad, Mexico, Guatemala, Honduras, El Salvador, Nicaragua, Costa Rica, Spain, Greece, and some African and Indo-Asian societies.[4] As Clifford Geertz suggests in a study of Java, "The spirit world is the social world symbolically transformed," an analytic sensibility congruent with Fredric Jameson's suggestive interpretation of "magical narratives," which often evolve out of social formations in which individual psychological subjectivity is inhibited, displaced by the power of a mystified but collectively concrete social realm.[5] Whatever its variations and particularities, devil lore, reaching from Malaysia to Central America, is unmistakably related to the social relations of capitalist production: when propertyless laborers confront new technologies and regimes of accumulation, they must make not only a material but a spiritual accounting, a process of adaptation that is often disconcerting and disruptive. Female factory hands in Malay transnational electronics corporations complain of spirit possession, believing that devils dominate workplaces that are unclean in both the physiological (dirty) and spiritual (haunted) senses, the environment of remunerative labor being one of debased "pollution."[6]

As anthropological analysis suggests, such devil lore is often a repudiation of the distorting powers of capital, which have reshaped the natural benchmarks of life, from family and landscape to day and night; they fracture time and subordinate it to the clocked paycheck, commodifying fundamental structures and relations of life—both geological and human—that have been pried loose from their traditional moorings and increasingly subjected to the rule of property and profit.[7] Whatever the modernist skepticism concerning human–devil relations, the imagery of devil-associated machines of capitalist predation, engines of extraction and accumulation, has a certain representational validity with respect to the history of modern empire.[8] Conquered and partially proletarianized, shaped in conformist contortions which offer them only a caricature of development's commodified civilities, peoples of the Third World necessarily seek to understand how they have been taken over. They seem to have bartered their lives with a devil whose demands on their natures and their bodies apparently know no limits. In an attempt to negotiate this barter in the interests of life, some colonial subjects choose the devil that they perceive as a gamble with some chance of return, a reinvented tradition at least partially of their own making, rather than the more distanced and less accommodating devil of unmediated exploitation. (Others, in contrast, explain power and its hoarding in terms of devil alliances with which they will not compromise.) In the process they have often bargained, of course, for more than they knew, opening their lives to a nightmare that oscillates between illusive, emancipatory hope and deadening debasement, between jealousy and fear. Frantz Fanon commented, "Believe me, the zombies are more terrifying than the settlers; and in consequence the problem is no longer that of keeping oneself right with the colonial world ... but of considering three times before urinating, spitting, or going out into the night." He longed for an end to "centuries of unreality" plagued by "the most outlandish phantoms," a time when the "native" may finally stand in a pose of armed resistance against the colonial foe and heap scorn upon the spirits of the ancestral world, "the horses with two heads, the djinns who rush into your body when you yawn."[9]

But as the vampire mythologies elaborated by Luise White indicate, the terrifying fear instilled in colonial peoples subject to new and alienating work with its sacrifices, estrangements, and coercions has been deep and debilitating, its multiple meanings quite telling in their complex staying power. Strange vehicles and labors have been linked with the dangers of blood loss, an extractive process easily associated with work and the circulatory system of money—an innovation in the first half of the twentieth century in African society, and one that drained the body and reduced its physicality to the symbolic exchange of currency. (In Mexico, similarly, folk gossip associated engineers with murder, their motivations supposedly linked to the need for body oil for automobiles.) [10] For Africans, understanding their relations with Europeans was facilitated by a mythology of the making of the undead, an image with powerful resonances in their varied lives of exploitation. Stories of children lured into vehicles, fattened on special foods, drained of their blood by thirsty Europeans, and left to return to their homes in emaciated condition, might well receive a sympathetic hearing in regions ravaged by famine. War-torn Kenya could easily see the medical department patrol as a vehicle of the vampires, equipped to siphon the blood of strangers and deposit their wizened remains in the gutter—especially if bodies did end up decomposing on the roadsides, as some undoubtedly did. Priests, shopkeepers, and labor recruiters all had their vampire-like qualities, as did white mine supervisors in the 1940s.[11] A materialist sensibility grasped intuitively that dead labor was what capital thrived on, and nowhere was this death more visible than in the terror of colonial capitalism.[12] The imagery of vampires and devils could easily merge in associations with exploitation and subordination.[13]

Contemporary gold miners in the Brazilian Amazon work their way through the displacements and sufferings of the transient quest for riches with a range of similar spiritual beliefs. Violence unrelated to the search for gold supposedly draws the appearance of the precious metal, which is often provided by a female Enchanted Being with whom the *garimpeiro*, or miner, meets secretly at night. Gold is humanized, an agent to be conceptualized properly: "Gold, it asks a lot of us. You can't go about thinking of riches—a car, a nice house, these sorts of things, when you set out after gold. Because if you set your mind on them, it gets mad and disappears, see? No, you have to think about that gold and nothing else. Because gold is like fire, it moves about, and then, vanishes like smoke." Sexualized and gendered as feminine, gold selects those males whom she will favor, but it is then the responsibility of the miner to take possession of her, satisfying her lustful needs: "Man, you have to grab gold in the moment. Because if you go soft, *she* straightaway goes running to another, see." And like riches secured in all devil pacts, such gold as comes to the *garimpeiros* in this way can never be hoarded, accumulated, or invested; it must be spent quickly and recklessly so that more will be given; "because it is gold itself that never stays with anyone. It gets tired [of the man] and goes away, leaving the miner feeling betrayed. Always, always. So then, it's better to spend the last penny in order to strike it rich again." Money procured in pacts with the netherworld of the spirits is fundamentally resistant to being saved; it exists to be *used*.[14]

In some regions of Colombia, Nicaragua, and northern Costa Rica the power of landowners grown rich off traditional and modern enterprise, especially agribusiness, was said to be sealed in a pact with the devil. Marc Edelman details the case of a powerful local landowner in Filadelfia, Costa Rica. Francisco Dubillo Incer, a transient Nicaraguan, arrived shortly after the turn of the century as a peon looking for work. He managed to rise to prominence in the livestock market through his shrewd bargaining, indefatigable accumulations, and business intelligence. Because of his initial poverty and meteoric rise to wealth and power, Don Chico, as he came to be known, was widely thought to have made a pact with the devil: he "signed a pact, a document, with the devil, because of the fact that from night to morning, well, in the night he didn't have anything and in the morning he did.... peons tell that at night first there would be a strong wind and then he would get up to go and converse with the devil." Envy and esteem fueled these narratives of a devil alliance that secured land, money, and women.

It was that last "commodity" that eventually dissipated the immense fortune of Don Chico, for as a profligate paternalist who may have fathered as many as one hundred offspring, his legacy was spread thin. A man who rose rapidly, he was a figure who accumulated relentlessly and whose appetite for acquisition—cattle and land, wives and daughters—was always appeased by his ready recourse to money, which he sported on his belt or spilled out of huge saddlebags. Don Chico was the personification of unexplainable power interpretable only as a result of the black arts, satanic magic. His conquest of the social order took place not only in the commodified marketplace of the day but in the sexualized hours of night, within which he seduced and secured the women of the community. This final statement of his totalizing, materialized ownership linked him decisively with the devil.[15] Catherine LeGrand has uncovered a remarkably similar instance of devil lore in the banana-producing enclave of Santa Marta on the Caribbean coast of Colombia. Other instances include the widespread Haitian and Dominican belief that those who accumulate unexplained wealth have negotiated with demons, and the Honduran conviction that the economic success of newly arrived Arab immigrants must be due to negotiations with the devil.[16]

The most developed appreciation of devil pacts is associated with the studies of Michael Taussig and June Nash. Bolivian tin miners and their relationships with the Tio (Uncle)—the devil said to hold the power of life and death as well as ownership of the resource in the deep extractive caverns of the country's critically important mines—were first studied extensively by Nash, whose work provides a foundation for Taussig's exploration of demons and commodity fetishism. Taussig presents a highly contentious but endlessly stimulating account of how groups of semi-proletarianized Latin Americans work for the devil.[17] His analysis of devil pacts in the Cauca Valley of Colombia posits a dichotomous divide distinguishing peasant household economies structured around production for use, and a growing plantation sector of capitalist agribusiness, where profit is premised on the impersonalities of hired workers. Caught in the vise-like grip of an inexorable and relentless transition to agrarian capitalism, the partially proletarianized peasantry acclimatizes to the commodifications at the essential core of its being as a waged sugarcane-cutting workforce by solemnizing pacts with the devil in order to increase output and amass wealth. The riches accumulated in this negotiation, however, cannot be spent on livestock or land but only on commodities of a transitory, consumable sort, for all wealth accumulated through demons is touched ultimately with death, not life, and will inevitably exact its cost in premature death, pain, and suffering. At bottom, then, "the neophyte proletarians and their surrounding peasant kinsmen understand the world of market relations as intimately associated with the spirit world of evil. Despite all the possibilities of increasing their cash incomes, they still seem to view this new mode of production as productive of barrenness and death as well. To them, therefore, this new socio-economic system is neither natural nor good. Instead, it is both unnatural and evil, as the symbolism of the devil so strikingly illustrates." Peasant proprietors, mindful of the long-term interests of their own small plots, do not make pacts with the devil to increase their own subsistence productions. Nor do women, whose lives are associated with households and the reproduction of generations of cultivators, consort with demons. The devil is a dark presence, a negotiated acknowledgement of both resistance and accommodation. As peasants sacrifice their lives to the wage, they see no reason not to carry the barter through to its logical conclusion, risking all for the accumulated gratifications of the moment and, in the process, ceding the productive capacities of the soil and its cane, now alienated as the property of capital, to the ultimate evil of the demonic world.[18]

Taussig historicizes this process by situating it within the general struggle over the land in which large capitalist interests eventually took advantage of a series of developments to consolidate their commercialized holdings, enclosing more and more of the small proprietors' lots, fencing huge plantations, and restructuring the landscape.[19] Colombian history is rife with periodic explosions of social protest and banditry, oscillating moments of resistance and repression, the most famous recent outbreak of which was the frighteningly bloody civil war of 1948–1958 known as la violencia. The end result has been an alienation of humanity and nature both brutally violent and devastatingly unambiguous, a barren, death-like social psychosis that has overtaken an entire social formation. As a percentage of the Colombian population, the peasantry was halved between 1951 and 1973, an impersonal statistic behind which lie the horrific human consequences of disruptive, despair-riddled dispossession. At stake is nothing less than a way of life, increasingly lost to a generation whose choices sometimes seem limited to outlawry or subordination. The latter, given the bloodshed of the violencia, is an option chosen by many of the young, but it spells the death not just of bodies but of spirits. One peasant proprietor commented: "My sons and daughters are uninterested. They are only concerned with getting by daily and grabbing the money in the afternoon; to go to work in the dawn and return at nightfall. They live day-by-day. But agriculture is an art; they don't understand that. For this art the first thing is constancy and land."[20]

Generations acclimatized to these kinds of accommodations and estrangements are already the undead, their pact with the devil of capitalism's alienations metaphorically sealed. It is but a short distance to actual belief in negotiations with demons. Linking crop and capitalists, the devil pact is an ultimately ironic form of resistance, directed not so much at overthrowing the large landholders and their commercialization of everyday life as at bypassing their regulatory regime, in which the wage is payment for a supposedly fair day's labor. In refusing that individualized logic of reciprocity, in which money is the measure of a moral ethic of the capitalist spirit, peasants who make pacts with the dark force of evil transgress unspoken rules in order to turn the spoken contract of the wage against itself, violating the foundation of the socioeconomic order. "The magic in the devil contract is directed not at the plantation owners," Taussig concludes, "but at the socio-historical system of which they are part." He adds intriguingly that although the devil-dealers "have lost a class enemy susceptible to magical influence [for all peasants recognize that colonial plantation owners do not believe in the world of demonic power], ... they stand to win a new world in their realization of that enemy's disbelief."[21] The ultimate birth of the proletariat is thus a still birth; a form of working-class rebellion arises out of the refusal of sectors of the Colombian peasantry to be unambiguously proletarianized, its "hidden transcript" being the countercontract with the devil, nullifying the wage bargain central to capitalism's being.[22]

Nowhere in Latin America is this devil and his cold touch of death more evident than in the tin mines of Bolivia, the second largest producer of tin in the world. By the 1960s the country's twenty-eight thousand miners nurtured a highly policitized, revolutionary tradition of militancy that earned them a place of unquestioned prominence in national trade-union circles as well as in the working-class politics of Latin America. Yet surrounding this archetypal modernist drama of class mobilization and labor–capital conflict in the workplace is a highly traditional folkloric legend of the spirit world.[23] Monsters and ogres are widely believed to live in the hills surrounding the mining encampments, and the people are thought to have been enticed from their virtuous peasant tilling of the soil by the devil, or Tio, of the mines. This powerful spirit lured with the riches of his caves; once ensnared in the ill-gained wealth of the mines, the people faced the onslaught of four ravages—a monstrous snake, a lizard, a toad, and an army of ants descending to devour them—but all these hideous attacks were beaten back by the powerful Tio. As owner of all of the mines' wealth, this devil is sometimes seen at night, guiding teams of llamas laden with tin, iron, zinc, bauxite, lead, copper, magnesium, gold, and silver into the earth, where the riches are deposited for the miners to find.[24]

To appease the Tio, who is easily offended, the miners erect images of the devil in the main shafts on each level of the mine and adorn the coca-chewing niches of their underground workplace with smaller icons. With bodies made of metal and their hands, face, and legs constructed of clay, the devil images can be as large as a man; bright pieces of glass or metal are stuck on them, and eyes are often fashioned out of light bulbs from the miners' helmets. Clothing provides additional creative touches, sometimes seeming to mock the rapaciousness of "gringo" capital: the devil is often outfitted with flamboyant cape, huge boots, and outlandishly incongruous cowboy hat. The mouth is always open, ready to receive what is given or to take what it needs, with teeth sharpened like nails; hands are stretched out to receive. The Tio is sexualized in his representation as a cock or a bull, or by a huge erection. The theme is unmistakable: Tio is a particular kind of power, greedy, insatiable, and ever demanding; he gets, in great quantities, what everyone wants. Not unlike the mines themselves, which are unforgiving of error and persistent in their hold over the workers, or the wage that both provides and enslaves, Tio gives but never does so without receiving his due.[25] After three young miners died in an accident in 1970, their comrades sacrificed a llama to the demon. "We eat the mines and the mines eat us," explained one Bolivian worker. "For that reason, we have to give these rituals to the spirit of the hills so that he will continue to reveal the veins of metal to us and so that we can live."

Indeed, twice weekly miners traditionally perform after-work ceremonial ch'alla, in which liquor, coca, cigarettes, and other items are first offered to the Tio and then shared among themselves. Banners, streamers, and representational figures are presented to the Tio, sacrificial burnings are made, and the miners drink, ask the devil for his protection, and talk among themselves about their labor and its exactions. At other times individual miners sacrifice an animal, save its blood, and sprinkle it around the mine or on their tools to ensure good favor from the devil, whom they further appease by burning the bones of the animal or burying them in red or white wool in a segment of the mine where they will remain undisturbed.

Such rituals have a long history but in their recent past have been increasingly suppressed by state authority in the nationalized mines, just as new technologies and workplace rationalizations have changed the team complexion of mining work by reducing work units from groups of fifteen to isolated duos. Old miners bemoan the passing of working-class collectivity and solidarity, an ethos of mutuality that has withered with the ch'alla's enforced disuse: "And so it was in the ch'alla," recalls one mining militant fondly, "we used to talk of our problems and what to do to change things." Another states more decisively the need to keep to the old practices of negotiating with the devil, seeing in such ritualized activity the foundations of proletarian power:

> The tradition inside the mine must be continued because there is no
> communication more intimate, more sincere, more beautiful than the
> moment of the ch'alla, the moment when the workers chew coca
> together and it is offered to the Tio. There they give voice to their social
> problems, they give voice to their work problems, they give voice to all
> the problems they have, and there is born a new generation so revolu-
> tionary that the workers begin thinking of making structural change.

This is their university. The experience they have in the *ch'alla* is the best experience they have in the mine.

Keeping the Tio alive becomes a transgressive process of resistance—challenging the post-1974 militarized and bureaucratized control of the mines—linked to the many sacrifices now embedded in the historical memory of the mining community. Miners remember the massacres of the past, such as the violent suppression of unions in the 1920s, when workers were killed by government troops. "It is our history," one said, in explaining why on the anniversary date of 1923 killings they light fires in the streets, "We must remember that night and carry on." One worker noted on another occasion, "The Tio is the real owner here. The administrators just sit in their offices and don't help us in our work." When managers skimp on the odd public ceremony meant to appease the devil, the miners nod knowingly; a divide separates those who work for the devil and those who do not. As Taussig suggests, the miners have created an art around Tio, an iconography of blended oppositions in which nature and ownership contend, the fetishized authority of the magic world of landscape and spirituality standing in inverse relation to the reified power of commodities and the profitability of things. The miners can make "the petrified world speak and live, but the shadow of death and sterility constantly threatens to consume this flicker of life." Nash notes that miners and their wives regard the earnings of their labors as the devil's wages, and as such they always quickly dissipated. Saving money has historically proved impossible. "The Tio is still hungry," say the miners with knowledge of what it means to be exploited, "and so are we."[26]

The entire month of August, traditionally among peasants a time of preparing the land for planting in September, is for the miners a period given over to placating Tio. Sacrifices and ritualized offerings are made to the Supay, or spirit devil of the hills. If such traditions have been allowed to lapse under the modernist governance of the mine by nonbelieving superintendents, any accidents or bad luck—especially if they involve death or failure to strike a productive vein of ore—will be understood by the miners as acts of revenge by the devil owner of the mine. Such a belief system simultaneously deflects a consciousness of revolutionary class antagonism, holds a managerial stratum responsible for unfortunate developments, and cultivates a strand of oppositional denial of the power of capital. One miner, who participated in sacrificing a pair of llamas, and who draped the female llama's fetus over his shoulders as he delivered gifts to Tio, explained the significance of death in the mines and of the negotiations that had to be made with the powerful devil spirit:

This is the luck of the working class. It is our thing because of our faith in the Tio Lucas. He is the owner of the mine. We walk with him. He takes care of us and we arrive with him. He is still owner of the mine. Before, we worked with greater strength and without accidents. It is the fault of the security engineers that we had this accident. They are in collusion with the administration. We make claims without any effect.

Working for the devil is thus something of a rehearsal for revolution, a ritualized negotiation of exploitation in which the ultimate power of capital is bypassed in a refusal whose final meaning will be realized when the devil is no longer given his due, when all deities are displaced in a decisive reversal of power.[27] But belief in the power of the satanic connection is difficult to overcome: the Mexican revolutionary Pancho Villa, nicknamed El Demonio, was reputed to have garnered his military acumen and physical prowess through a pact with the devil, consecrated in a cave with gold walls.[28]

The importance of the devil pact surfaces at various times. Public placation of the mine devil Tio is often part of communal carnival celebrations. During the official Bolivian carnival week, for instance, the entire mining community, including all trade unions and fraternal societies, is immersed in the pageantry, which includes collective ch'allas, masked dancers, dramatic reenactments of pre-Conquest mythologies, and persistent allusion to the class conflicts and political struggles of the miners. Devil masks and dances figure prominently in the carnivalesque fusing of revelry and revolt. The diablada, or devil dance, is driven by "epochal music" that one anthropologist regards as "a stimulus to a movement of insurgency." The wild dress of carnival, similarly, is a rich and beautiful negation of "a system of impoverishment." As June Nash concludes, carnival in the Bolivian tin-mining encampments blends good and evil, historicizing struggles that have embedded both resistance and accommodation in the social relations of the mines. This history, one of dark negotiations with evil, cannot escape the ways in which working for the devil is a necessarily contradictory and ambivalent experience. Carnival serves to remind those impaled on the horns of this demon's dilemma that resistance is necessary, and that in forging revolt they can shed some of the everyday drabness in the struggle for a better life.[29]

This commingling of carnival, devil lore, and the inversion of power is a generalized theme in the social relations of the developing world. Nineteenth-century Caribbean carnival was often associated with moments of slave and class revolt. In the sugar-producing center of Martinique the night celebrations of February 1831 witnessed an outpouring of songs and dances that whites regarded as threatening, insulting, or seditious.[30] As Trinidadian blacks appropriated carnival in the aftermath of emancipation, their celebrations grew more raucous, less respectable, and increasingly menacing. Marauding bands of stick-wielding men, masked as bats, jam-jabs (devils), pirates, and "Indians" paraded the streets, often in whiteface. Sometimes they carried flaming torches known as canboulay, a linguistic creolization of the French cannes brulées (burnt canes) and an articulation of the former slaves' resentment at having been commandeered, usually by violent means, to fight the arson fires of slave sabotage and cut the burning cane fields before the crop was totally destroyed.[31]

During carnival in locales such as Port of Spain, dominated by an underworld of prostitutes and their "sweetmen," gamblers, stick fighters, dock and warehouse workers, and the marginally employed wretched residents of slums and barrack yards, the traditional street rowdiness often escalates and threatens to get out of hand. Calypso bands and neighborhood gangs blur in celebrating lives of ribald irreverence, especially those of the notorious chantuelles, whose rough songs were the vocal expression of a culture of disregard, dominated by commitments to drinking, fighting, and singing. White chantuel Cedric LeBlanc sang of two such figures, both of whom had died by the late nineteenth century: "Bodicea first, then Piti' Belle,/ The devil waiting for them in Hell."

Riot punctuated Trinidadian carnival throughout the last decades of the nineteenth century, a time of rising class conflict that escalated into a generalized labor unrest in 1882–1884. As class and gender proprieties were lampooned mercilessly in transvestism, obscene parodies of phallic power, and lewd presentations of defecation and menstruation—all accompanied by the din and clamor of African drums and innovative instruments constructed out of whatever came to hand—an aesthetic chaos and street macho-bravado created a climate of intimidating polarization.[32] Vile songs were directed at the island's leading ladies, and costumed revelers mocked figures of the governing elite and the socially prominent. When police banned African drumming—as a prelude to seizing the Shango drums used by the Orisha, a voodoo-like faith that fused features of Catholicism and the African Yoruba religion—crowds fought back, bombarding the constables and taking over a town before they were dispersed and some of their ranks thrown in jail. With steel bands naming themselves "the Red Army," authority moved to suppress the more riotous aspects of carnival in the early 1880s, and arrests and street confrontations were yearly features of the attempt to tame and tailor the carnivalesque. Trinidadian carnival was thus born bemoaning:

Class legislation is the order of the land,
We are ruled with the iron hand.
Britain boasts of democracy,
Brotherly love and fraternity,
But British colonists have been ruled
In perpetual misery—*sans humanité*.[33]

Small wonder that one contemporary Brazilian participant in carnival declares, "The facet of Carnival that I like the best is to be playing, understand? not working. This is Carnival for me. The pleasure of knowing today I don't have a *patrão* [boss].... *I even give him the elbow and so on while I'm dancing*.... You don't feel like his employee."[34]

The carnality of carnival could give way to a challenging politics of opposition, then, but it could also spiral downwardly inward, in the resigned fatalism of the contemporary Brazilian *carnaval* song: "Happiness is fleeting. Sadness is forever. And playfulness comes to an end on *quarta-feira* [Ash Wednesday]." Daniel Touro Linger suggests that carnival liberates dangerous passions "in tenuously controlled outbursts of song, dance, and play ... going to the brink ... [and] challeng[ing] people to undertake what it would seem to define as the supremely human task—the willful donning of the mask of hope and solidarity in defiance of their own desperate plight and quarrelsome nature." It does so successfully only by holding certain lines, delivering the final, unstated, message that "the danger at the heart of both person and collectivity can still be held in check."[35] The freedoms of night's transgressions are often somewhat fleeting.[36]

Interpreting the carnivalesque has become something of an academic industry, and one with many sectoral tendencies. It is enough here to lay stress upon its inversions and the space it creates, expects, and demands, which has historically opened out into the possibility of transgression and resistance. The devil, as a figure of original recalcitrance, is regularly linked to such historical processes. Early European Christian carnival drew out just such practices of subversion, which were quickly met with authority's arsenal of repression. Laypersons were forbidden to go about in "the devil's skin" in some locales, and edicts against this and other threatening and insulting behavior—perceived to be directed against spiritual and secular leaders of impeccable social standing—proliferated in the fifteenth and early sixteenth centuries.[37] Emmanuel Le Roy Ladurie provides an account of the dualities of urban/rural France, with its commoner-versus-noble political economy of grievance and repression, mounting debt and food-sector excise strikes, taxes and folk festival protest, and parades of armed artisanal workers on a rung-by-rung construction of the February Mardi Gras, which erupted in a bloody people's uprising in the city of Romans in 1579–1580.[38] Three hundred years later James Ensor's *Christ's Entry into Brussels in 1889* presented a carnivalesque canvas of Mardi Gras revelers, many masked or posed in the guises of modernism's deceptiveness, death, and artificiality. With the teeming conformity and scandalous procession surrounding Christ on a donkey, eyed by such on-lookers as the Marquis de Sade, Ensor conveyed the terrifying chaos of contemporary life's authoritarianism (with the routinized mask of mili-tary sameness) and hedonism. As a depiction of carnival's seemingly spontaneous celebration of "the social," a realm of infinitely shocking potential transgression, Ensor's bold colors and thick, crusted paint were in fact a planned statement that so shocked nineteenth-century audiences and critics that the painting was not exhibited until 1929.[39]

As William Rowe and Vivian Schelling conclude, carnival "temporarily inverts the social order, [but] this inversion is also relativized. All negations are themselves open to negation; thus ambiguity permeates the language and symbolism of carnival. Moreover this ambiguity is manifested in the fact that it brings together through the use of mask and disguise the most disparate elements: devils as gods, men dressed as women, humans as animals."[40] Carnival, like the devil pact, is thus an expression of both inversion *and* fluidity, a moment of dislocation in which those experiencing social transformation seek out ways of symbolically turning a world already upside down, upside down again.[41] This is best done, as all accounts of carnival implicitly acknowledge, at night. Amid cries of "Anything goes, it's carnival," pandemonium reigns from dusk until dawn.[42]

In New Orleans, blacks who parade during Mardi Gras present them-selves as Indians, the elaborate costume of their chief protected by a devil-like wild man who clears the way, while others rhyme a language without script: "Wild Tchoupitoula, uptown ruler, blood shiff ahoona, won't kneel, won't bow, don't know how."[43] By the twentieth century, the New Orleans Mardi Gras Indians had taken on intensified meanings for neighborhoods of the city's black population, whose organization in bands led by hierarchies of chiefs produced an atmosphere of intense competition. Outfitting themselves outrageously and dancing and drum-ming through the streets, these rivals might clash in violent battles known as "humbugs." Drawing on Caribbean and Latin American carnivalesque adaptations of Indian costuming, as well as the commercialized Wild West shows of U.S. popular culture, they were a historical voice of ethno-cultural fluidity. The Creole Wild West Tribe, ostensibly descended from the founder of the first masked Indian grouping, conveyed some sense of this in saying of the 1920s and 1930s, "French and Indian, in them days, was all mixed up. Black folks registered as white. Things were all crossed up."[44] In a segregationist South, this was the devil's work.

An entire iconography of the devil—not unlike that dotting the landscape of the Bolivian mines—links festivity, celebration, work, and life, fusing discontents and desires. The devil masks of carnival reappear in artisanal and literary productions, creative moments of mediation in which the transformed cultures of colonialism negotiate the meaning of exploitation through recourse to a complex, intuitively understood symbolism. Migratory workers who seek jobs in the cities of Mexico, for instance, might find their journey to work, with its many unknowns, eased by the ceramic devil depictions of the artesanos of Ocumicho, Michoacán. Since the 1960s they have been molding devil figures associated with features of the modern city unknown in small villages: police, motorcylces, airplanes. One such ceramic depicts a busload of happy devils headed for the urban congestions where waged work is available; another presents a schoolroom of devils learning to read. One artisan was asked why the devils in his ceramic figures were jostling to see themselves in a mirror. "The mirror is appearance," he replied. "You look at yourself and you're there. You take away the mirror and you are not there any more."[45]

This is the strength and weakness of the Third World negotiations with the devil. As a means of self-making, in which the script of proletarianization is rewritten and thus subverted, the devil pact is a mechanism of displacement, an imagery of defiance *and* debasement, a mirror of illumination and distortion which clarifies *and* clouds the social relations of production. The mirror can be studied at length, revealing the materialism and death at the core of wage labor, or it can be withdrawn, leaving no record of the negotiations of labor and its imagined taskmasters. For capital, this can be a maddeningly illusive contractual two-step in which the impersonalities of the wage are draped in an exchange as fantastic as it is unfathomable.

This is the way much of the class struggle of the "developing" world must look to the modernized consciousness of those who, in the material moment of the twentieth century, actually do own the mines and the mills, the factories and the fields, capitalism's reservoirs of profit and production. To be told, in word and deed, that a spirit has supplanted their essential proprietary rights over the things and relationships of land, machines, and working people does violence to the foundations of capital's many conquests.[46] How could a Dominican coffee farmer who employed Haitian labor, for instance, exercise his rightful capitalist dominance when he knew that these workers possessed "seemingly unlimited [voodoo] powers"? "Dark, secret, and opaque," in the eyes of their employers, the Haitians were a repository of threatening spiritual authority: they had protective spirits capable of transmogrifying into animal beings and overseeing the health of livestock and crops as well as humans; their sexual powers were legion, and their women, if they died virgins, could return to haunt men and seduce them at night; certain Haitians, often associated with moneylending, were said to trade in the undead (the zombie transactions taking place at midnight), and a special Haitian region, Arcahaie, was the sacred home of these corpses that could come to life.

At its base, this seemingly continuous repertoire of sorcery was rooted in money. As Lauren Derby concludes, "In the predominantly non-commoditized border economy, Haitians came to represent the impinging market and Dominican fears of a value cut loose from the social relations that produced it. This links Dominican fears of money and the threat of Haitian voodoo: both were exterior to Dominicans and lay outside their control." Haitians presented a seemingly unstoppable threat. Since their rituals were rumored to involve a ceremonial mixing and drinking of gold coins and the blood of sacrificial animals, and since Haitian money "ran" inland to the major Dominican interior city of Santiago, an imagery linking blood and money was constructed: "The value which Haitians embodied was obscene because it represented pure exchange; antithetical to the natural economy of the border, Haitians were linked to usury, their money appeared to grow on trees." The final chapter in this mythology was tragically predictable: in 1937 the Dominican dictator Rafael M. Trujillo dispatched machete-wielding soldiers to cleanse this blood-money impurity in a massacre of thousands of Haitians, many of them women who were subjected to gruesome, womb-directed ritualized gougings.[47]

Proletarianization and its extractive essence, exploitation, take on new meaning in such contexts. Capital faces challenging obstacles in its quest to recruit labor and subject it to the economic law of the market when money has powers other than, and sometimes decidedly inferior to, those attributed to it by the rule of commodities. Among the cargo cults of New Guinea, prophetic religious figures promise an end to the world of oppression and want and the liberation of the people's needs in a new power's provision of endless goods and an eternity of bliss. This assurance precipitates a popular abandonment of fields, killing of livestock, gluttonous indulgence, and discarding of money—the very antithesis of capitalist acquisitive individualism. In the "boycotts by bewitchment" and the odd "strike by witchcraft" on the mine compounds of Southern Rhodesia (now Zimbabwe), the dark engagements with exploitation that have become routine fixtures of culture and social life in capitalism's widening circles of global reach presented repetitious evidence that class is made in ways as complex and contradictory as they are defiant of any simple formula.[48]

As Jacques Chevalier suggests in a study of the shamanism of the Peruvian rainforest, where wage labor has made tentative inroads on social life, capitalist forms of domination and traditional, occult means of engaging with such disruptive interventions have clashed repeatedly in modern history. Both sides of this contestation are pulled in new directions; class formation becomes "the site of a constant rebellion led by the forces of a totally alien domain ... which recognizes neither the distinct existence of "this material world" nor the disembodied supremacy of other–worldly saints." On the one hand, capital's day of conquest is darkened by the material and mental clouds of traditionalist sorcery, magic, and dialogues with the devil; on the other, the rebellious content of the spiritual cosmos of "blue nights lit by stars" loses some of its clarity and capacity "in the nocturnal silence" of ritualized practices that, in the words of one functionalist anthropologist, "vanish in the reality of day."[49]

The pact with the devil—so common in various forms wherever capital and wage labor confront those legions of putative proletarians who refuse to bow down unequivocally to the myriad demands and hard extractions of exploitation—seems ironically poised on the cusp of a double negativity. Refusals of subordination are often articulated in a bastardized contractualism, an illegitimate fusion of the material and the mental, the dark and the light, the day and the night, which somehow serves to guide coerced workers of the developing world along a path neither of labor nor of capital, neither of life nor of death. Like Marx, they seem convinced that their immediate prospects are doomed, and they insist on choosing a path that negotiates a different direction, awaiting times more welcoming in their long-term prospects than the present, in which all roads of work lead to sorcery and evil: "When a great social revolution shall have mastered the results of the bourgeois epoch, the market of the world and the modern powers of production, and subjected them to the common control of the most advanced peoples, then only will human progress cease to resemble that hideous pagan idol, who would not drink the nectar but from the skulls of the slain."[50] Yet as those many Third World peoples working for various devils know all too well, "a long time will be needed before misfortune and good fortune cease to be the work of dead gods who do not wish to die and have never stopped feeding off the flesh and the thoughts of living men—off their and our relations."[51]

PART VI
Eroticism and Revolutions
The Pleasures and Dangers of Difference

15. Bertall, *Les Pétroleuses* from *The Communists of Paris* (1871).

13
Nights of Leather and Lace

Transgressive Sexualities

The devils that figured so forcefully in the experience of proletarianization in the developing world were sexualized beings; their needs included those of the erotic realm, and among their gifts were the wages of sin and the flesh as well as those of paid labor. So-called deviancy was never all that far removed from their presence. "See how the Devils laugh, whom we have serv'd," bemoans a seventeenth-century "Lament of the Sodomites."[1] In Haiti, lesbians were thought to have a particularly potent relation to the evil retributions of sorcery, being able to cause such natural disasters as epidemics, earthquakes, and droughts.[2] Carnival, with its licensed transvestism, inversion of dominant relations and authorities, masked festivity, and ribald tolerance was a natural venue for homoeroticism. In Bolivia, June Nash notes, "Only men can dance the role of the *chinas*, or seductresses who are the consorts of the devil, since the obscene gestures required would make the role too much for a woman to overcome after Carnival.... The role often attracts men with homosexual tendencies ... who can find in the Carnival an acceptable outlet."[3]

Among black miners in southern Africa, isolated in both terms of their underground work and their compound living arrangements, the institution of the "mine marriage" solidified formal rules, sexual practices, domestic responsibilities, and a patriarchal set of oscillating relations of coercion and affection linking older workers and their boy "mine wives." While such liaisons were generally accepted as necessary by all parties, those boys who refused the advances of their older suitors would find themselves eventually subjected to the final pressure, that of witchcraft.[4] Small wonder that those who rebelled against the seamless web of power's endless entanglements broke the chains of righteous conduct's codes, not only in the particular links of the body politic and the organism of the economy but in the sexual practice of "unnatural vice." The introductory volume of Michel Foucault's *The History of Sexuality* (1978) opens with an appreciation of sexuality's significance in this kind of historically situated order, which coincided with the rise of the bourgeoisie, but his innovative interpretive contribution was to refuse to see the history of sexuality as a one-dimensional exercise in modernist repression: "We must therefore abandon the hypothesis that modern industrial societies ushered in an age of increased sexual repression." Instead, as Leo Bersani has suggested, Foucault's purpose was to point out that "power in our societies functions primarily not by repressing spontaneous sexual drives but by producing multiple sexualities, and that through the classification, distribution, and moral rating of those sexualities, the individuals practicing them can be approved, treated, marginalized, sequestered, disciplined, or normalized."[5]

One of these multiplicities has been same-sex activity, sexual acts that in their historical concreteness defy essentializing and conventional categorizations; they offer up not some timeless "vice" but motions of transgression, differing in their meanings, associated with widely separated times and places. For Foucault, homosexuality must be seen as historic opportunity that reaches out for sexual potentiality, rather than some intrinsic quality of act or agency; it is a position of marginality, a standpoint from which to survey standardizations and glimpse and devise possibilities otherwise obscured and obstructed. Foucault's grasp of homosexual meaning fractures commonsensical understandings of the homosexual as Other, as only a third gender, as purely oppositional inversion: the man–woman, body–mind reversal.[6] In the night—as both metaphor and time—of homosexuality's making, then, it is the manifold possibilities of historicized eroticisms that demand attention. If their ultimate subordination to the mainstream powers of the day seems all too evident to a modernist view of the constructed category the homosexual, the long historical night in which this marginalization was, in part, made is infinitely more complicated and complicating.[7]

Precapitalist social formations, for instance, gave rise to an amazing array of same-sex, homoerotic practices. Few of these conform to modern understandings of homosexuality, whatever the problematic dimensions of post-Victorian thought on the stereotypical third sex. From the crossdressing and sexualized berdaches of Amerindian peoples—with their military, religious, and domestic connotations—to the male cult prostitution of the archaic civilizations of the Mediterranean, the diverse cultures and political economies of the separate worlds of the distant past spawned institutions and erotic encounters that crossed established lines of hetero-sexuality and familialist procreation. Harems in the Near East and India were but one of many possible nurseries of lesbianism, the exclusion of men and the pressing companionship of women encouraging emotional and sexual relations among the cloistered co-wives.[8] The Turkish baths supposedly provided inspiration for the sapphic proclivities favored by ladies at court during the French Renaissance.[9] European travelers to six-teenth-century China deplored the widespread practice of sodomy, which they declared "a vice very common in the meaner sort, and nothing strange among the best."[10] Ancient Greece produced the lyrical, almost mythical, woman-centered physicality of Sappho, an invitation in its own time and in ours to see past what John J. Winkler has designated the phallocentric vision of sexuality, of which the end product can only be the objectification of women and the denial of their eroticized subjectivity.[11]

The Greeks also constructed, indeed institutionalized, a pederastic aesthetic through which the powers of an elite—the familialist continuity of noble pedigree, the militarized foundations of class rule and the preser-vation of empire, and the democratic civilization and culture enjoyed by the privileged—were conserved in a sexual life cycle that bonded adoles-cent boys with adult males and encouraged youthful male prostitution. Indeed, a range of writings suggest that the phallocentric culture of the Greeks fused erotic pleasure, pedagogy, and the martial and moral arts in an aesthetic of the self which, in dramatic contrast to that of later periods of history, decisively eschewed an ethic of repression.[12] When Philip of Macedon, father of Alexander the Great, defeated the Athenians and Thebans on the battlefield of Chaeronea in 338 B.C., the valiant warriors who resisted him had been led by Pelopidas's "Sacred Band," a military unit composed of paired lovers, none of whom wished to survive with-out his partner.[13] John Boswell presents copious evidence of marriage-like same-sex unions that developed in this and later periods.[14]

The Use of Pleasure (1985), the second volume of Foucault's History of Sexuality, addresses this moment in sexuality's history, concluding: "The moral reflection of the Greeks on sexual behavior did not seek to justify interdictions, but to stylize a freedom—that freedom which the "free" man exercised in his activity. This produced a state of affairs that might well seem paradoxical at first glance: the Greeks practiced, accepted, and valued relations between men and boys; and yet their philosophers dealt with the subject by conceiving and elaborating an ethics of abstention."[15] What was not contained in this new ethics of interdiction was outside of it, othered as alien and foreign and thus scorned by power and labeled in discourses of cultivated authority as deviant, pathological, perverse. Homosexuality was being made on the one hand, unmade on the other.

One part of its making and unmaking was the mythological, dualistic construction of Sodom, a dark city of renowned perversions and treacheries, marked in the Talmud as a site of great deceits and frauds, and in Genesis 19 of the Bible as a locale of Foucault's "utterly confused category": sodomy.[16] God eventually took his vengeance on a city so consumed by outrageous transgression that the very heavens cried out for retribution: fire and brimstone rained down on Sodom, and "the smoke of the country went up as the smoke of a furnace." Wickedness drew upon itself a decisive act of destruction that sealed the fate of the Sodomites in their final transgression, anal intercourse being a sterile sexual act, pleasurable but barren, "as though the proclivities of the Sodomites answered biologically to their utter indifference to the moral prerequisites for survival."[17]

Sodom remained associated with death and destruction for centuries, consolidating in the latter half of the twelfth century a virulent and repressive Christian assault on same-sex practices as "unnatural." Part of a constricting climate of intolerance, directed as well against Jews, lepers, witches, and other "deviants," this emerging sexual fanaticism with its arsenal of indictment, punishment, and ideological terror was unambiguous in its condemnation of sexual minorities. In the nascent kingdom of Jerusalem, Europeans attempting to establish a Western feudal order within Muslim society supplemented their crusades with legislation that specified death by burning for all sodomites; by the sixteenth century both the Ottoman Empire and the Arabic principalities of North Africa and the Near East were considered to be racial and sexual domains of degeneration, environs of "the brutal sodomite." The opinion expressed in Genoa around 1300, that sodomy was "so filthy and grave that anyone who commits it deserves death by fire," was apparently widely held. Coercive codes in France, Spain, and Italy in the years after 1250 often stipulated that executions for homosexual acts were to be preceded by torture, dismemberment, or castration.[18] As part of the "unnatural, the alien, and the demonic," sodomy was linked with sorcery and heresy as an unforgivable crime that no ruler could pardon.[19]

But for all this, its attractions were apparently many to those in search of pleasure. A primer of accumulated objections to sodomy was gathered in the thirteenth century, verses of denunciation that name Chartres, Sens, Orleans, and Paris as latter-day Sodoms sustaining what John Boswell describes as "a flourishing and well-developed gay subculture of prostitution and highly specialized erotic interests."[20] But Sodom lived, as idea and act, through an age of sexual repression and terror, finding polite expression in the Shakespearean canon and elsewhere.[21] In Renaissance and Enlightenment Europe the pursuit of sodomy by a beleaguered minority of erotic outlaws, as well as by court figures and patronage-sponsored scholars, established new boundaries of male–male relations. Violently dichotomous images—the universal admiration for masculine friendship and the equally generalized repugnance for the sordid, heretical sodomite— were parallel, as Alan Bray has suggested, in uncanny ways.[22]

This incongruous pairing resurfaced, far from European Christianity's hegemonic shadow, in the Caribbean outposts of the pirates, seventeenth-century Port Royal being described by B. R. Burg as "the Sodom of the Universe."[23] In colonial Brazil, subject to Portuguese law that condemned sodomites to death, those with a taste for same-sex anal intercourse included the aristocratic governor of the plantation economy from 1602 to 1607 and some Catholic priests; their promiscuity drew the ire of the bishop of Rio de Janeiro, scandalized by the confession of one that he had enjoyed carnal relations with forty individuals. New France's first convicted sodomite was condemned to death in 1648 but cheated the hangman by agreeing to become the colony's official executioner.[24]

Transgressive sexualities in this precapitalist context extended beyond sodomy into other realms.[25] Early modern female same-sex pleasure seldom reveals either an unambiguous lesbian consciousness or explicit erotic acts of woman–woman love, but as Lillian Faderman, Valerie Traub, and others have suggested, the period was not without indications of female same-sex desire.[26] Much of the evidence filters through the pages of literary "sapphic platonics" or the spiritual sensualities of the con-vent.[27] The emergence of the hermaphrodite in this period also blurred gender distinctions in confusions concerning the body which invariably produced sexual transgressions. Complicated further by the beginnings of transvestism, which reached beyond the Renaissance stage, this blurring of the received categories of conventional sexuality was seized upon, if Antonio Beccadelli's ribald Italian text Hermaphroditus (1425) is any in-dication, in the "active and varied night-life" of a developing subculture of Eros that was often perceived as debauchery.[28]

Milton's Paradise Lost (1667) personified this generalized lewdness in the person of Belial ("than whom a spirit more lewd fell not from heaven"), a seventeenth-century characterization composed of one part urban vice, one part sodomy, and one part dark desire, seared and sealed in the secrets of the night:

> In Courts and Palaces he also Reigns
> And in luxurious Cities, where the noise
> Of riot ascends above thir loftiest Tow'rs,
> And injury and outrage: And when the Night
> Darkens the Streets, then wander forth the Sons
> Of Belial, flown with insolence and wine.
> Witness the Streets of Sodom, and that night
> In Gibeah, when the hospitable door
> Expos'd a Matron to avoid worse rape.

In George Lesly's *Divine Dialogues: Fire and Brimstone, or, the Destruction of Sodom* (1684) this dark culture of promiscuous indulgence was marked as a dangerous threat.[29] But John Wilmot, Earl of Rochester, proclaimed sexual transgression's defiance in the prohibited play *Sodom* (1684), the monarch Bolloxinian declaring his sexual preference:

> Come my soft flesh of Sodom's dear delight,
> To honour'd lust thou art betray'd to-night.
> Lust with thy beauty cannot brook delay,
> Between thy pretty haunches I will play.

The play ends with lines of intransigence: "Let heav'n descend and set the world on fire,/ We to some darker cavern will retire."[30]

Were those who pursued Sodom homosexuals? The question orders two schools of thought that divide the historiography. On the one hand is the dominant interpretive paradigm, influenced by a Foucauldian understanding of the significance of discourses of social construction and attentive to the fluid nature of erotic desire and the need not to categorize identity through a rigid correlation of sexuality and the sexual act. From such a perspective, before the medical and psychoanalytic "invention" of heterosexuality *and* homosexuality in the late nineteenth century, premodern sexual transgression transcended any particular essentializing homosexual orientation. This view lays stress not on homosexuality but on a plurality of desires, practices, and, in some cases, obscure cultural enclaves of possibility, needs, acts, and places which—however much they broke with conventionality or reconstructed the boundaries of erotic life—lacked the conscious self-articulation of *a* or *the* homosexual role before the late nineteenth or the early twentieth century.[31] Though pointing to the importance of the ways in which sexualities are socially constructed in oppositional categories related to power's rigid need to designate "deviant" and "normal," the Foucauldian "new inventionists" (as they have been dubbed by one historian of Renaissance masculinity) have perhaps overstated the linguistic side of homosexuality's making. They rely, perceptively but rather one-sidedly, on discourses of pathologization and their appropriation and reversal at a certain point in history by a community of sexual outlaws who finally took the decisive step of seizing their own oppression and proclaiming it a way of life.

On the other hand, some historians of gay life (whose work tilts toward the masculine, since evidence on pre-1800 lesbian activity is decidedly thin) have rejected the seeming abstractionism of the social constructionist view, claiming for homosexuality a more prominent place in the historical past of erotic behavior. Acknowledging that the pederasts of antiquity and the sodomites of the Renaissance may well present endless variations of sexual consciousness and identity—many of which blur the distinctions of modern categorization—they have staked out interpretive ground that claims a more decisive divide in the history of sexuality. They suggest that the active agency of sexual preference and choice has been inscribed more clearly on the admittedly murky record of past societies.[32]

What is perhaps most striking about the polarizations of this interpretive contest is the extent to which they have been dehistoricized. Whether marginalized as an acceptable but limited functional activity (Greek pederasty) or relegated to the confinements of the dark and the night (Puritanical heresy), homosexual acts and desires, thoughts and practices, choices and constraints have always been shadowed in the rhetorics and reasons of day's determinations. In this sense the constructionist/essentialist duality dissolves in the practice of possibility, which offered historically concrete but ever changing if always contained options within which variations of sexual transgression could be acted out. "Men make their own history," Marx wrote, "but they do not make it just as they please; they do not make it under circumstances chosen by themselves, but under circumstances directly encountered, given and transmitted from the past." Homosexuals make their histories the same way, in that awkward, historicized friction of agency and necessity, parts of which are "theirs" and parts of which are not.[33]

As an aristocratic culture of libertinism consolidated in the seventeenth and eighteenth centuries, pushing the possibilities of licentiousness, it opened doors for lesbianism, even if such woman–woman eroticism was often regarded as but foreplay for the dominant phallocentric heterosexuality of this milieu.[34] By the 1770s and 1780s, some authorities contend, tribadism, or lesbian simulation of heterosexual intercourse, had become fashionable among actresses (whose routine transvestism schooled them in particular possibilities of deception and seduction) and women of the court. Women who moved in such circles of sexual transgression crossed paths with their male counterparts, frequenting cafés known to attract those with venturesome sexual tastes, although much of their erotic lives were lived out in the exclusive company of women. Lesbian clubs were said to exist, one in England reputedly devoted to flagellation.[35]

In cosmopolitan centers such as Paris, London, and Amsterdam, sodomitical subcultures thrived. Their meeting places in the open air and in designated houses, on known cruising boulevards and in parks, clubs, and taverns; their argot of mimicry, signs, and names; their effeminate, exaggeratedly aristocratic dress; their networks of sexual markets, friends, and contacts—all constituted a veritable underground of places, prose, and practices and certainly suggest a consciousness of particular sexual identity, if not of outright homosexuality.[36] One historian of seventeenth-century Lisbon notes that "there were inns openly patronized by sodomites, balls where transvestites danced and played instruments, much street prostitution, and men who served as go-betweens for male sexual encounters.... All classes participated."[37] This promiscuous and pluralistic transgressive grouping of sexualities blurred distinctions between men and women; in fact, its erotic nocturnal underworld of transvestisms, inversions, crossovers, reversals, and refusals has prompted one historian of London's sapphists to suggest the need to transcend the boundaries of gender categorization and proclaim this period a moment in the making of modern sexual culture which moves it "from three sexes to four genders."[38]

London's Molly-Houses—immortalized in Ned Ward's infamous tract The Secret History of Clubs; Particularly the Kit-Cat, Beef-Stake, Vertuosos, Quacks, Knights of the Golden Fleece, Florists, Beaux, Etc., with Their Original; and The Characters of the Most Noted Members Thereof (1709)—were symbolic centers of the emerging subculture of heretical sexuality, appropriated space where male effeminacy, the exaggerated aping of a woman's speech ("they try to speak, walk, chatter, shriek and scold as women do") cross-dressing, and casual sex predominated. Jonathan Wild—the notorious thief trainer and taker, police informant, receiver and returner of stolen goods, urban crime boss and prop of metropolitan authority—described the assemblage at one such establishment as "He-Whores ... rigged in Gowns, Petticoats, Head clothes, fine lac'd Shoes, Furbelow Scarves, and Masks ... tickling and feeling each other as if they were a mixture of wanton Males and Females." Such a carnivalesque display of deviance makes unmistakable the nurturing nature of the transgressively erotic evenings that drew the "sodomitical Mollies" to what were widely known as "Festival Nights."[39] The anonymous author of Satan's Harvest Home (1794) found this subculture of debauched sexuality a degeneration that left any participant "unfit to serve his King, his Country, or his Family, this man of Clouts dwindles into nothing, and leaves a Race as effeminate as himself; who, unable to please the Women, chuse rather to run into unnatural Vices one with another, than attempt what they are sensible they cannot perform." Such condemnation fused economic class ("nothing" being a reference to material worth), gender ("unable to please the Women"), and "Race" in layered repudiation of the "Unmanly, Unnatural Usage" that was easily identified as "the first inlet to the detestable Sin of Sodomy."[40]

For all Foucault's insights, his suggestions about the making of homosexuality in the psychological, psychiatric, and medical categorizations of the later nineteenth century (where he locates homosexuality's "birth," like a biological "delivery" at the point of Carl von Westphal's 1869 article on "contrary sexual sensations") have led others to simplify historical process.[41] Just as the entire prehistory of homosexuality, most emphatically its rich eighteenth-century urbane effervescence in subcultures of same-sex eroticism, complicates Foucault's focus on discourse and identity, so too does the nineteenth- and twentieth-century experience of men and women who broke the boundaries of sexual conformity.[42]

Romantic, aestheticized friendship, quite common in the same-sex histories of both men and women, continued into the nineteenth century. In the United States it was associated with the poet Walt Whitman, just as, no doubt, the hidden histories of darker embattled "perversions" continued to insist on small spaces for their continuities.[43] The subdued Whitmanesque homoeroticism of this period, however, could produce nights of loneliness and longing:

> Who was not proud of his songs, but of the measureless ocean of
> Love within him—and freely poured it forth,
> Who often walked lonesome walks, thinking of his dear friends, his
> lovers,
> Who pensive, away from one he loved, often lay sleepless and
> dissatisfied at night,
> Who knew too well the sick, sick dread lest the one he loved might
> secretly be indifferent to him.[44]

Still, the nineteenth century also afforded a more abundant diversity of oppportunity and sexual transgressions, despite ideological pressures that worked to coerce conformity to the increasingly public enforcement and endorsement of a compulsory heterosexuality. These possibilities and practices extended beyond the pathologization of homosexuality in the emerging scientistic medical discourses and, perhaps, contributed to the "expert" attention that came to be riveted on the so-called third sex.[45] No matter how much the naming of homosexuality led to its containment, regulation, and governance via the state, however, these developments also produced a dialectics of seeing in which the observed and monitored pathological subject was capable of appropriating his or her oppression. A consciousness of sexuality and self that was defiantly and even oppositionally transgressive resulted. An outlaw band of same-sex practitioners of "unnatural vice" emerged for whom the medical text was not known or influential. Neither the state nor its guardians of virtue could have figured as overwhelmingly decisive agents in the making of this sexual identity. Like the working class, then, homosexuality was a "historical phenomenon, unifying a number of disparate and seemingly unconnected events, both in the raw material of experience and in consciousness." As E. P. Thompson suggests, this was not just a structure, or even simply a category, so much as something that in fact *happened* "in human relationships ... an active process, which owes as much to agency as to conditioning." Named or unnamed, sexual transgression was historically an "it" (what Oscar Wilde would call "the Love that dare not speak its name") that "was present at its own making."[46]

To look at the history of same-sex relations in the nineteenth century and into the twentieth is to glimpse, with homosexuality's more public emergence, both an aesthetic and a practice. A textual, often artistic, sensibility—an enlightening idealization of masculine desire—wrote and sculpted itself across the standards of beauty in ways that legitimated homoerotism by equating it with classicalism.[47] Something of this was at work, as well, in freethinking and socialist milieus where the new life of personal gender relations was being worked through by advocates of feminism, by masculine desire, and by broadening, eroticized conceptions of fellowship associated with the thought and practice of Edward Carpenter, the young Havelock Ellis, and others.[48]

The politely accepted separations between aesthetics and practice faded quickly, however, as desire crossed a *class* divide. A mass bourgeois propriety that could appreciate a homoeroticism sublimated in classical allusions and the refinements of texts, in *objets d'art*, and antiquity's allurements, could hardly be persuaded to countenance such "ugliness" as messenger boys prostituting themselves to gentlemen. When the Cleveland Street Scandal of 1889–1890 exposed this sordid underside of homoeroticism, threatening to reach into the royal family and implicate the heir apparent, Prince Albert Victor, in male–male sexual activities, a moral panic was in the making; the enlightened day of cultural aesthetics was pushed aside, and the dark night of homoerotic practice was increasingly subjected to a criminalization that generally spared the rich and famous but universally outlawed the working street poor associated with male same-sex desire.

The exception to this class divergence was the unfortunate Oscar Wilde, whose novel The Picture of Dorian Gray (1890–1891) seems on its face to embody much of the classical aestheticism of homoeroticism's established Victorian presence. Largely devoid of overt eroticism, Dorian lives not in a sodomitical subculture but in a homosocial environment. Yet Wilde's notorious dandyism and his indifference to social station, shored up by his feigned elitism and aristocratic pretensions, angered the high moralists who presumed to speak for bourgeois order through the repressions of law and the courts, which, between 1885 and 1895, demonized homosexuality. Wilde's book was the wrong voice of aestheticism in the 1890s precisely because Wilde himself had been in the wrong places. "Mr Wilde has brains, and art, and style," wrote one former friend turned virulent critic, "but if he can write for none but outlawed noblemen and perverted telegraph-boys, the sooner he takes to tailoring (or some other decent trade) the better for his own reputation and the public morals." At his 1895 trials much was made of Wilde's alleged consorting with "men who were not his equals," but "illiterate boys," and of his pose as a "sodomite." Eventually he was convicted of "committing acts of gross indecency with another male person." His jail sentence, served under quite harsh and vindictive conditions, silenced his aesthetics: Wilde would produce next to nothing of literary worth in its aftermath. Before his death in 1900, he lived out most of his last days in exile in France, often masking his identity with a pseudonym. Wilde had bridged the day/night divide of Victorian homoeroticism, threatening to bring artistic sensibilities and acts of anal pleasure closer together; he found his days of literary endeavor forcibly restrained as the dark night of victimization descended upon him.[49]

Not surprisingly, those sexual transgressors who lived their homoeroticism generally did so in their own subcultures, which they kept deliberately dark in an effort to obscure the regulatory gaze of the moral police. Small wonder that the Russian maverick Christian philosopher Vasilii V. Rozanov discussed his ambivalent thoughts on "the third sex" in a book titled People of the Moonlight (1911).[50] In England this night culture of the homoerotic reached from the White Swan Public House, Vere Street, Clare Market, London—where the Sodomitical Club assembled on Sunday evenings in the opening decade of the nineteenth century—to the "twilight world" of the "professional Maryannes" who frequented transvestite parties and the well-known pick-up spots around Piccadilly Circus in the time of Oscar Wilde. Occasionally rouged and dressed as women, these male prostitutes were more likely to consider themselves "trade" than to identify self-consciously with the sodomitical culture, but they serviced that milieu. "He wore me like a badge," recounted one young prostitute of his relationship with a gregarious figure from the gay intelligentsia.[51]

All the world was not London, of course, but beyond the European metropolitan centers the histories of sexual transgressors could be found in the long-obscured case files, transcripts of "unnatural vice" trials, and other corners of a past kept deliberately dark but subject to police surveillance. A homosexual self-identity might come, for instance, via the "discoveries" available through the holes of lavatory walls or in the lanes and shadowed parks of an urban subculture of nocturnal sex. It could be negotiated in the class- and age-ordered power of the man–boy erotic act, bartered in the darkened seats of vaudeville theaters, burlesque houses, or all-night lunchrooms and cafeterias that had become known landmarks in turn-of-the-century city "cruising."[52] Work sites restricted to males—the navy, the prison, the logging camp, the rough frontier—all functioned as nurseries of the "abominable sin," to which migratory workers, soldiers, and seamen seemed especially attracted.[53] Corners of empire might harbor "deviant" sexualities; Sir Francis Burton's elasticized "Sotadic Zone," stretching the Mediterranean world eastward into Indochina and south through Morocco and Egypt, was illuminated in the pages of The Book of the Thousand Nights and a Night (1886) as a place of pederasty, understood as a virtual "racial institution."[54]

To turn to the major metropolitan center of homosexual culture in the 1890–1940 period, New York City, is to open a window overlooking the urban night and its sexual transgressions. One German homosexual noted that he was "always immediately recognized as a member of the confraternity" in the United States, and the 1879 publication, Sodom in Union Square, supposedly penned by a former police captain, offered revelations of the "doings" in one notorious urban locale. At an 1880s homosexual nightspot called Armory Hall the waitresses were supplemented by "a number of simpering males," whose effeminate style and unambiguously flirtatious banter signaled to the patrons the availability of what a reporter labeled "moral depravity." The owner also hired powdered, rouged, crossdressing "inverts" to entertain his clientele; they sang, danced, and often joined the better-paying customers in curtained booths, where a sexual "circus" could be had for a price. "This type of pervert was then something new," added the journalistic voyeur, who signed himself "Paul Prowler."[55]

By the 1890s the novelty had worn thin: gay sex could be found in a proliferating set of institutions. In 1892 a detective, Charles W. Gardener, took the crusading reformer Dr. Charles H. Parkhurst on a nocturnal ramble through the city's vice dens and wrote an exposé published as *The Doctor and the Devil; or, The Midnight Adventures of Dr. Parkhurst* (1894). Among the most shocking revelations, and one from which the good doctor fled in horrified haste, was the scene at Scotch Ann's West Third Street Golden Rule Pleasure Club, a homosexual brothel staffed with youths whose faces were painted and eyebrows blackened; the boys talked in the supposedly universalized high falsetto voice of the "fairy" and addressed each other by women's names. At about the same time the city boasted an annual black trans-vestite ball, eventually suppressed by the police (a similar "orgie of lascivious debauchery" was staged yearly in Washington, D.C.). Specific bars were known to draw upward of fifty "degenerates" on any given night, and one in particular, called Paresis (a medical term for insanity) Hall, was known to the City Vigilance League as the favored haunt of a hermaphrodite. In the Bowery district of the Lower East Side a conglom-eration of clubs, nestled into the red-light district of that immigrant, working-class quarter, catered to the fairies and their clients. The Slide on Bleecker Street was well known for "the unspeakable nature of the orgies practiced there." The Sharon Hotel, affectionately known as "Cock Suckers Hall," offered a menu of public sex acts for the price of a drink.[56]

Police repression was a constant; the nightly festivities were routinely broken up by bar closings and arrests. Gay New York, however, refused to die; it was busy being born. Havelock Ellis's 1915 edition of *Sexual Inversion* described the subculture as large and organized, recognizable through its language, customs, and meeting places. It came out at night in certain streets where "every fifth man [was] an invert," and in dance hall "clubs" attached to saloons, where evening gatherings of "inverts of the most pronounced type, i.e., the completely feminine in voice and manners," filled the small rooms with patrons drawn to a same-sex eroti-cization of the tavern's usual offerings: drinking, singing, dancing, and gossip.[57]

Between 1890 and 1940 this New York gay subculture flourished, as George Chauncey has recently shown in a rich book that details its changing and complex character. Composed of distinct but overlapping milieux, this world was simultaneously heterogeneous and homogeneous. On the one hand, discrete neighborhoods with their own spatial con-figurations sustained particular class and ethnic or race groupings of homo-sexuals, who were also differentiated by their cultural and sexual choices and preferences and adoption of specific roles and public personae. On the other hand, these varied networks nurtured a sense of commonality in the face of repression, in alienation from dominant sexual norms, and in the cultivation of events such as the massive transvestite balls of the 1920s, which for one evening of spectacle and invigorating "queerness" drew thousands of New York homosexuals from various walks of "the life" into a space of relative sameness. "Once men discovered the gay world," Chauncey concludes, "they knew they were not alone."[58]

So extensive were the networks of bathhouses, cafeterias, bars, saloons, speakeasies, street promenades, park pickups, public lavatory connections, apartment parties, drag balls, codes, signs, aesthetics, and sensibilities in this urban gay world that it was possible for gay Americans in the early twentieth century to high-camp their presentation of the homosexual self, mimicking female rights of passage in "society" circles. The transvestite galas, held at such illustrious New York venues as Madison Square Garden, the Astor Hotel, and the Savoy and Rockland Palace, were likened to debutantes' "coming-out" balls. These declarations of sexual identity, like many lesser forms, solidified the gay subculture not as one of closeted degeneracy but as a world of difference that could, at appropriate moments of the night, be put on spectactular or sexualized display. A doctor interviewing working-class homosexuals in New York's city jail in the 1920s bemoaned their resistance to his offers to release them from their pathology. "Proud to be degenerates," he lamented, they did "not want nor care to be cured."

This kind of consciousness was a creation not of days of exposure but of nights of discovery: homosexual identity was made in the dark. Writing under a series of pseudonyms that have left his life disguised, one New Yorker of this period wrote his recollections of life in the underworld of androgynism, where he discovered a social center for his marginalized sexuality. He saw a culture that was assailed and brutalized but one that refused to succumb. In the same-sex pairings, witty conversations, and cultured subtleties of the Bowery sex dives, this advocate of Victorian homosexuality saw degeneracy and depravity from another vantage point. Since "the 'classy,' hypocritical, and bigoted Overworld" considered him a "monster and outcast," he "was driven to a career in the democratic, frank, and liberal-minded Underworld" and seized his freedom in the night travels of what was then known as a bisexual world: "While my male soul was a leader in scholarship at the university uptown, my female soul, one evening a week, flaunted itself as a French baby-doll in the shadowy haunts of night life downtown."[59]

Over the course of the first half of the twentieth century, this night of the fairy gave rise to a layered complexity of plural identities and heterosexual–homosexual interaction. Dark streets under railroad trestles, wee-hours speakeasies around Times Square, midnight encounters off Union Square, evenings at the baths, nocturnal park promenades, shadowy burlesque houses or movie theaters, and the public comfort stations and subway washrooms known as "tearooms" were among the locales supplementing the saloons, clubs, and festive drag balls of gay New York. For gay men who lacked private quarters—because they were of the working poor or leading the double life of a clandestine sexual identity masked in conventional appearance—"public" sex almost invariably took place under the cover of night. Sodomy trial depositions might later tell the dark tale.

As the ironic closures of the Prohibition era (1920–1933) sustained new cultural openness in the jazz clubs and speakeasies of Times Square, gay life and night life became more, not less, flamboyant. The pansies, as homosexuals came to be designated in the 1920s, were on parade. *Broadway Brevities* for 1924, a year-long series of articles, described New York's gay world and its institutions under the title "Nights in Fairyland." Ten years later *Vanity Fair's* 1931 "intimate guide to New York after dark" singled out "the pansies" as a Broadway tourist attraction. Less crassly theatrical were the scandalously eroticized buffet flats and speakeasies of Jazz Age Harlem, where celebrities and gays in quest of "rough trade" rubbed shoulders and crossed the race divide in a climate of cultural sensuality and sexual transgression. Clubs such as Harry Hansberry's Clam House, fictionalized in Blair Niles's gay novel *Strange Brother* (1931), cultivated a city-wide and even national reputation for their entertainment, clientele, and unmistakably gay atmosphere.[60]

Gay New York in the first half of the twentieth century thus fundamentally revises the conventional wisdom that homosexuality was so isolated and closeted in the pre–Second World War period as to be virtually invisible. A product of the night, it was apparent to those who lived in the dark and those willing to walk into the night's many offerings. Even the men who led double lives did not experience the monolithically self-policed repression that the term "closet" has come to convey. Although at work and within their families many pre-1940 gays adopted the stylized masculinity of the mainstream, they were able, as well, to elaborate a shifting set of characters in the night spaces of one of the world's premier cities of sexual possibility.[61]

Ironically enough, gay New York's very visibility and the homosexual night's diversity, engaging spontaneity, and institutional richness in the first third of the twentieth century may well have contributed to the increasingly repressive climate that followed.[62] By the 1930s and 1940s the "pansy parade" had, in the eyes of some, gone on too long; its flaunted culture of same-sex desire enraged other sectors of American society. Drag balls were canceled or forced out of highly visible arenas and posh midtown hotels. Further, political dissidence and sexual transgression seemed to be linked in repression's chain reactions: the New Star Casino, a venue often patronized by communists and drag queens, who both rented the premises for their galas, came under police scrutiny in 1931, and sweeps of gay clubs invariably resulted in arrests of figures active in the ultra-left.[63] During and immediately after the Second World War the gay world's gender ambiguities and hedonistic subculture came under increased attack. Pansy clubs closed; gay-bashing violence escalated in the streets; female impersonation (whether vaudeville art or lifestyle choice) was literally outlawed; arrests on various degeneracy and dress laws increased; and stage, screen, and (later) television saturated popular culture with contrasting images of the straight male and the pathologized homosexual.[64] The closet closed in on many gay men, given the coercions of a quite terrifying extremist enforcement of "consensus" in an anticommunist, familialist Cold War America. Elements of the black literary gay community escaped the constricting nooses of both racism and homophobia by opting for exile.[65] Gay New York, the most vital and vibrant of transgressive sexual communities in the opening decades of the twentieth century, by 1950 was struggling to survive.

It did so—again with the helpful protections of the night. But darkness, as always, was very much a two-way street.[66] In the 1950s and early 1960s, gay males necessarily lived and loved within the boundaries of a culture that demanded they be hidden. The night was, in many ways, the place to hide, but, given repression's upper hand and the dominance of the day, only with particular demands and deformations. A British account of male homosexuality from the 1940s to the 1970s draws on W. H. Auden's lines from "Lullaby": "Nights of Insult let you pass/ Watched by every human love."[67] As Drucilla Cornell argues in her study of sexual difference, "what is done in the dark" is seldom done without costs. Insisting that "we must always remember the dark side that will be with us as long as we are mortal human beings," Cornell quotes Gananath Obeyesekere: "What is hidden is dung and death. And like dung and death, pain and human suffering are also confined to a sanitized environment. There are, however, the few who will be attracted to such forms of experience and thought, in spite of the physical and social environment in which they live, because they have searched, as Freud did, the dark recesses of their own lives and from there have had a vision of the dark side of life in general."[68] Gay men were among those few, and their embattled struggles, personal and political, sustained them through difficult decades marked by both self-doubt and self-realization. The ambivalence of a consciousness of being homosexual and the need to address that in political ways scratched itself into the intimate and public lives of those whose love, for the most part, dared not speak its name.[69]

Still, in cosmopolitan centers such as New York and San Francisco, as well as in resort enclaves such as Fire Island (off the south shore of Long Island), the gay world hung on tenaciously. These years left a legacy for the generation that would build the gay liberation movement in the decade spanning the New York Stonewall riots of June–July 1969 and the White Night rebellion in San Francisco's Castro community in 1979. In New York, homosexuals responded to police raid and reprisal with rebellious opposition. In San Francisco, gays and lesbians vented their rage after former city supervisor Dan White was convicted of manslaughter (the lightest possible verdict) for the murder of gay-sympathetic Mayor George Moscone and homosexual activist-elected official Harvey "the Mayor of Castro Street" Milk.[70]

For a brief historical moment the articulate demand for rights co-incided with a subculture of ever intensifying libidinal pleasures that yet again shattered constraints on desire and restructured the meanings and possibilities of pleasure. The gay milieu of the 1970s and early 1980s was an explosively pluralistic network of discrete but interconnected institutions and yearnings, sexual practices and political agendas, many of which came together in pioneer publications such as The Body Politic (1971–1985), the Toronto-based centerpiece of North American gay politics, journalism, and sociocultural dialogue. Its pages bristled with defiance and difference, articles ranging from the etiquette of fist-fucking, the politics of man–boy love, and the age of consent to histories of gays and lesbians, book and theater reviews, and accounts of the lives of single gay fathers. In the baths and the bars, the bookstores and the gay-owned bakeries, on Saturday nights among political activist friends or out on the increasingly adventure-some town, the boundaries were being overtaken.[71]

Most shocking to the mainstream heterosexual culture was the sado-masochistic (S/M) scene, which had astounding appeal in San Francisco's South of Market district, the westside docks of Manhattan, Griffith Park in Los Angeles, and lesser-known enclaves that mushroomed wherever homosexual energies charted the new paths of previously unanticipated desires and dangers. The gay life had always been, fundamentally, a risk. Now sectors of it entered a Georges Bataille-like universe of Eros in which breaking taboos in ways that unified pleasure and danger, good and evil, brought transgression to its ultimate zone of sexual engagement. In the warehouse catacombs along San Francisco's Folsom Street, one witness recalled his reaction to the almost surreal, shadowy merger of pleasure and pain in an S/M club where "they were doing something that couldn't be realized by the daylight world." A new and expanding gay world was being born, again. And, like its predecessors, it came out at night.[72]

Its difference from the past was that it *also* marched into the day, demanding visibility and space, organizing Gay Pride Days and protest rallies, petitioning, meeting, cajoling, talking, electing, writing, leafleting, and working for the cause of homosexual rights. None of this was easy; the repressive forces of state power came down hard on the symbols of an almost ancient gay degeneracy. Sodomy statutes and bath raids reasserted the capacity of police and law to move decisively against the gay life when it threatened to offend the public sense of propriety. Isolated sex killings unleashed a vicious assault on male homosexuals, who were demonized as threatening, violent pedophiles. "Fag bashing" was virtually licensed, a blood sport for those needing proof of their masculinity. As gay pride organizers drew 200,000 marchers to San Francisco's festive parades in the late 1970s, and 100,000 people descended on Washington in a 1979 national protest, an antigay backlash erupted, orchestrated by the religious fundamentalist right of Jerry Falwell and Anita Bryant. Gays were now visible as never before, but they were also under attack.[73]

When gay men, in one of the most tragically destructive and horrifying accidents of health history, began to be diagnosed with what would later be scientifically identified as the Human Immunodeficiency Virus (HIV) and the deadly Acquired Immune Deficiency Syndrome (AIDS), homosexuals found their "wasted bodies" scrutinized, as Leo Bersani has shown, with a newly devastating intensity and repugnance in the 1980s. "The normal fear of homosexuality has been promoted to a compelling terror as a secret fantasy becomes a public spectacle," Bersani notes with evident sadness, explaining that this morbid attraction is presented as nothing less than "men dying from ... the suicidal ecstasy of taking their sex like a woman."[74] The night's sexual abandon was to blame, stated Professor Opendra Narayan of the Johns Hopkins Medical School with obvious distaste: "These people have sex twenty to thirty times a night.... A man comes along and goes from anus to anus and in a single night will act as a mosquito transferring infected cells on his penis. When this is practiced for a year, with a man having three thousand sexual intercourses, one can readily understand this massive epidemic that is currently upon us."[75]

AIDS snuffed out so much of gay life that one activist called the physical devastation a holocaust; within a few years he alone could count five hundred acquaintances among the hundreds of thousands, projected to be millions, who had succumbed. Gay enclaves of urban America suffered in ways that statistics only hinted at: by 1993 San Francisco had 280 cases of AIDS per 100,000 people, and the comparable New York figure was 155; in Youngstown, Ohio, the number was 5.[76] The staggering loss of life was exacerbated by the homophobic ravings of a coalition of "family-value" advocates, religious fundamentalists, and New Right reactionaries who pushed mainstream politics in widening circles of conservatism. Little was forthcoming at first from the liberal, often silent, center; the political and economic structures of power took a rather jaundiced view of a viral death count that seemed weighted toward a population of "abnormals." Not until AIDS began to touch the bodies of heterosexual America— decimating the arts milieu, taking icons of conventional sexual attractiveness such as Rock Hudson, and threatening blood banks, babies, and the sexually active young of both sexes[77]—did the market mentality of the pharmaceutical companies and the opportunism of the state kick-start a long-overdue but still grossly inadequate response. Meanwhile, much had been lost, and the anti-queer backlash had so swept through mainstream sexual circles that it was next to impossible to dislodge hatred of homosexuality from the issue of AIDS as a catastrophe that demanded immediate attention. Talk spread of quarantining or firing from their jobs those who tested HIV-positive, of sterilizing AIDS carriers to curb their prodigious sexual appetites, and of recriminalizing homosexuality (the last option pleasing over 50 percent of News of the World readers). Lurid denunciatons of the "orgiastic behavior of multiple-partnered" homosexual males overtook the discourse of transgressive sexuality, burying the possibility of deviant desire in an avalanche of hate. The AIDS crisis did not so much spawn an attack on disease as precipitate an assault on desire.[78]

The deluge was difficult to sidestep; even those who refused it outright were deflected from aspects of the transgressive content of their homosexuality, moved obviously but also subtly out of the deep night of their own erotic making and into sober early evenings of respectability.[79] Some gays regarded once-vibrant neighborhoods such as San Francisco's Castro district as a war zone, the scarred landscape of a sexual battlefield now littered with human loss. "So exhausted with death, with the care of the dying, with fear of dying" were the gay warriors of the 1970s that by the late 1980s many of them "had gone numb." To be sure, others fought back, and AIDS activists have rekindled the fires of gay rights in angry, demanding voices.[80] Desire under the shadow of death has pushed sexuality in new, creative, and "safe" (but often promiscuous) directions; artists and cultural critics and commentators have forced the dignity and worth of gays back into the domain of social and political life, insisting on transgressive sexuality's right to be lived, seen, and—even at the point of its physical demise—remembered. In the interrupted night of gay male sexuality of the turn of the twenty-first century, transgression has been forced again to take a leap in the dark.

Lesbian sexuality and its evolving transgressions paralleled but did not follow directly or derivatively the more visible and flamboyant subculture of male same-sex eroticism. Throughout the nineteenth and twentieth centuries women were sometimes situated in the same spaces of sexual and gender ambiguity as many marginal men, their romantic platonism and long-term, monogamous "Boston" marriages reaching—whether tentatively or more decisively—into nights of erotic potential. But these were almost exclusively the terrain of women in a particular social station, the "new women" professionals of the relatively effete eastern seaboard, a culture corresponding to that of the "independent woman" in the British Isles.[81]

Women's historical same-sex activity is both less known and likely less well developed than men's because the conformist constrictions of gender roles tightened more repressively around women's possibilities. One measure of this was that for women, cross-dressing was not so much the exaggeration of a sexual persona—poised publicly (in the saloon or the street) in the obvious pursuit of relatively immediate gratifications, offering to be taken sexually—as it was a life's labor, a totalizing movement across the line of gender difference that might or might not involve same-sex eroticism. When the jazz musician Billy Tipton died in 1989 and was discovered for the first time to have been a woman, one of his adopted sons attested to how all-encompassing some women's cross-dressing could be: "He'll always be Dad to me." Tipton's former wife explained another side of constructed gender identity: "He gave up everything. There were certain rules and regulations in those days if you were going to be a jazz musician." Possibly motivated by lesbian attractions, as in the case of New York's late-nineteenth-century Democratic Party political boss and bon vivant Murray Hall (who passed as a man for twenty-five years, was twice married, and was "sweet on women"), female transvestism was early linked to womanly sexual perversion. By the Victorian era women's cross-dressing had assumed a secrecy that differentiated it from its more partial, more flaunting public male counterpart: from the closet of male attire, women in masculine drag proclaimed not simply their sexual availability, but their gender ambiguity and, in some instances, their desire for the rights of manhood. One transvestite from the 1850s left her husband, wore men's clothing in order to find work and earn men's wages, adopted the posture of a preacher, and set up a household complete with loving wife. In Missouri a laborer who became secretary of the International Brotherhood of Boilermakers, and who could drink, swear, and court the girls with the best of his working-class confreres, was a successful passing woman.

When women's same-sex desire was discovered in this dress, it was almost always forcibly suppressed, as was the transvestism itself, except if it was of the most instrumental sort. San Francisco's most infamous nineteenth-century female cross-dresser was a French immigrant, Jeanne Bonnet. Her run-ins with the police were ostensibly about her male wardrobe, but their derisive descriptions of her as a "man-hater" who sported "short cropped hair, an unwomanly voice, and a masculine face" signaled a more explicitly erotic crime of sexual transgression. Bonnet met her end because of it: frequenting brothels as a male patron, she fell in love with a prostitute, enticed her away from the life, and was then murdered by her newly liberated companion's pimp. Transvestite passers of this sort so flagrantly violated a range of social norms that they routinely skirted the law in ways other than their clothes. Prison—in which early-twentieth-century reformers often located "women in love" who violated not only sexual but racial taboos, consolidating black–white couples—provided one unfortunate venue for female homosexuality. Although lesbian exoticism and evil lurked in the voyeuristic poetry of Baudelaire and in the seduction-driven pornographic imagination, then, it had not managed by the 1890s to construct a quasi-public subcultural presence for itself.[82]

At precisely this moment, as "new woman" feminism and romantic friendship blossomed in the Boston marriage, and the first sustained hints of the presence of woman–woman eroticism surfaced among the poor and laboring classes, lesbianism was named by early sexologists. The German psychiatrist Carl von Westphal, who first coined the term "congenital invert," drew his language and perspective of homosexuality from the case study of a young woman attracted sexually to other women. His disciples Richard Krafft-Ebing and Havelock Ellis continued his work, presenting a view of lesbian pathology that was even more damning and

Others, too, remembered lines and nets of various kinds. Leslie Feinberg, a butch patron of the tough, working-class lesbian bars of the 1960s, was a factory-working prefeminist who passed as a man in order to survive into the early 1970s. In her 1993 novel, Stone Butch Blues, she offers a quasi-fictional account of the terrors and triumphs of gender and sexual transgression and closes her acknowledgements with words of recollection: "There were times, surrounded by bashers, when I thought I would not live long enough to explain my own life. There were moments when I feared I would not be allowed to live long enough to finish writing this book. But I have. History take note: I did not stand alone!"[88]

What is made collectively in the dark has a certain historical longevity, evident in the 1980s subculture of New York City's transvestite balls, which has been captured cinematically in Jennie Livingston's powerfully evocative, stimulatingly emancipatory, and depressingly tragic Paris Is Burning (1990). To come out of the night that has nurtured it for centuries, however, transgressive sexuality needs a day willing to welcome it, a society open to any and all erotic possibilities, a morning sunrise that will not expose, harrass, ridicule, terrorize, and eventually kill those whom the light's glare spotlights as deviant.[89] This, the repressive culture of dominance has never been willing to countenance. John Rechy's powerful novel of transgressive Eros, City of Night (1963), opens with acknowledgement of the night's centrality, its undeniable possibilities, and its familiar alienating isolations:

> Later I would think of America as one vast City of Night stretching gaudily from Times Square to Hollywood Boulevard—jukebox-winking, rock-n-roll moaning: America at night fusing its dark cities into the unmistakable shape of loneliness. Remember Pershing Square and the apathetic palm trees. Central Park and the frantic shadows. Movie theaters in the angry morning hours. And wounded Chicago streets.... Horror movie courtyards in the French Quarter—tawdry Mardi Gras floats with clowns tossing out glass beads, passing dumbly like life itself.... One-night sex and cigarette smoke and rooms squashed in.... And I would remember lives lived out darkly in that vast City of Night, from all-night movies to Beverly Hills mansions.[90]

But the nurturing darkness also suffocates; it is a night of long birth and slow death. Sexuality, like all sites of oppression, requires nothing less than a revolution to free it from its many fetters. Just as Marx saw that "labor cannot emancipate itself in the white skin where it is branded in black skin,"[91] conventional sexuality will never be truly free until class, race, and gender break the barriers standing between humanity and its freedoms, liberating transgressive sexuality from its dark exile. Then and only then will men, women, and all the Others marked as different exercise their choice and their compulsion without constraint and in ways welcomed by their erotic comrades.

14
Festivals of Revolution
Light Out of Dark

The modern world was born in revolution. The continuity of revolution marks the calendar of "progress" for some and symbolizes the barbaric for others. No other event so captivates the attention of literary and artistic publics, focusing the politics of past and present on the important episodic nature of historical process and change. Revolution is often presented, in the contrasting metaphors of darkness and light, as a movement from the long night of oppression and exploitation into a new day of dawning possibility—even though the repressive onslaught of authority's vengeance is usually present as well.[1] When five revolutionary free-speech fighters, members of the Industrial Workers of the World, were killed in the booming lumber town of Everett, Washington in 1916, their martyrdom was commemorated by a Wobbly bard: "Out of the dark they came; out of the night/ Of poverty and injury and woe—/ With flaming hope, their vision thrilled to light/—Song on their lips, and every heart aglow."[2] In the cauldron of transforming modernism and capitalist ascendancy, the American Louise Bryant captured the revolutionary's sense of fearful anticipation in lines of verse that appeared in the *Voice of Labor* as her comrade and lover, John Reed, sat behind bars with hundreds of other communists, socialists, unionists, and "criminal syndicalists" during the Red Scare of the First World War epoch: "Into every sun-filled morning,/ Into every star-filled night,/ Till the blossoms wither blackly/ And your blood is cold with fright."[3]

Jan Valtin's 1941 revelations of Stalinist espionage—played out against the backdrop of early-twentieth-century revolutionary Europe: a seafarer's global adventures and the degeneration of the Communist International

in the interwar period—is a constant alignment of the contrasts of night
and day. Drawing on William Ernest Henley's

> Out of the Night that covers me,
>   Black as the Pit from pole to pole,
> I thank whatever gods may be
>   For my unconquerable soul,

Valtin titled his text *Out of the Night* and divided his account into three
books: "They Called It Dawn" outlines his role as a sailor courier for the
Comintern, a "red vagabondage" that carried him from Hamburg to
Leningrad, from Shanghai to San Quentin; "The Dance of Darkness"
chronicles the powerful constraint of Stalinist authority in international
revolutionary circles and the failure of the workers' movement to block
Hitler's rise to power; "The Night of the Long Knives" explores Valtin's
final, dark despair over Stalinism's betrayals and fascism's viciousness.[4]

Three decades later, during the cataclysmic "feverish *journées*" of May
1968, a revolutionary new left, undaunted by fascism, but still deeply
despairing of the constraining role of Soviet Communist Party politics,
launched nights of transgressive rebellion in which all order was reviled.
These French events, paralleled by similar happenings across Europe, Great
Britain, Japan, the United States, and Canada, were ostensibly precipitated
by the anti–Vietnam War protests of students at the University of Paris's
Nanterre campus and the harsh response meted out by the state. But as
indicated by the slogans of the moment—"When examined, answer with
questions!" and "Professors, you are past it and so is your culture!"—the
politics of the time was a heady concoction of countercultural antagonism to all authority. Led into a celebration of spontaneity by agitational
figures such as Daniel Cohn-Bendit, student protesters demanded amnesty
for their Nanterre comrades and then used the night to seize the streets
of Paris's Latin Quarter, erecting barricades made of pushed cars and
torn-up paving stones, fighting police, and taking over the institutional
center of higher learning in France, the Sorbonne. Evening marches, thirty
thousand strong, shut down the boulevards of Europe's cultural capital,
the youthful chant of "*hop, hop, hop*" ringing in the cosmopolitan ear of
metropolitan life. The intense desire for root-and-branch change, however, was matched by the savage brutality of official reaction: on one
bloody Monday night of pitched battle the scorecard of hostilities read
422 arrests and 345 injured *gendarmes*; the smell of tear gas hung in the
air; grenades exploded against the defensive street fortifications of the
students, now aided by supporters from the congested urban neighborhoods of Paris. From midnight to six in the morning during the second

week of May, the Parisian night was a war zone. Jean-Jacques Lebel described the carnage of the night of May 10 in the pages of the anarchist journal *Black Dwarf*:

> 1 A.M.: Literally thousands help build barricades ... women, workers, bystanders, people in pyjamas, human chains to carry rocks, wood, iron....
>
> 2 A.M.: It is now obvious that the police are preparing a powerful attack ... the general mood was defense, not offensive; we just wanted to hold the place like an entrenched sit-down strike.... [The police] tactics are simple: at one hundred yards distance they launch gas grenades by rifle which blind, suffocate, and knock us out.... Also explosive grenades.... we are forced back. Our barricade burns. At this point all I can remember is that I faint from lack of air.
>
> 6 A.M.: Still fighting outside.... The police are searching house by house, room by room. Anybody with black hands and gas spots on clothes ... or wounds is beaten and arrested.... people in cars and taxis volunteer to take us out of police zone. Everywhere we see enormous buses full of our people, tired, beaten, bloody prisoners.

A leading French intellectual, the Gaullist Raymond Aron, acknowledged that the discovery of "such a fund of violence and indignation in the masses" was "both staggering and bitter" for the ruling regime.

Within a few days of the infamous May 10 "Night of the Long Batons" France appeared headed toward a decisive rupture. The students, dressed in red and black, hoisted high the banner of revolution and plastered the columns of their educational institutions with inflammatory posters and the visages of Marx, Mao, and Che Guevara; from the Chinese they borrowed the tradition of the wall newspaper, a public exchange of views and information that gathered thousands of people around daily "hangings" of news and views. The aspiring revolutionaries, however, cast their collective manifesto of social transformation in the language of a festive surrealism, declaring, "Everything is possible"; "The imagination takes power"; "Take your desires for realities"; "It is forbidden to forbid." To Raymond Aron it was all "psycho-drama, ... a verbal delirium." But with demonstrations now drawing 200,000 and protest sweeping out of Paris into cities like Lyon—where a policeman was killed in a riotous confrontation on May 24—intellectual dismissals were of little consequence.

As the French workers' movement downed tools, proclaiming a general strike and seizing workplaces in nighttime occupations, the revolt took on material significance. Spreading from a base in the car and aviation factories of western France near Nantes, the trade-union rebellion escalated quickly: coal mines closed, national railways ground to a halt, red flags flew over the shipyards, teachers and civil servants declined to report for duty. Within a week two million workers were on strike; by May 22 the number of French men and women refusing to do their jobs had soared to nine million. Strikers' wives formed proletarian family associations that established distribution networks for food supplies, pricing them according to the costs of production and issuing coupons to those in need. Capitalist dealers were forced to close. A central strike committee, composed of farmers, workers, and students, installed itself in the Nantes town hall, displacing the mayor and prefect, proclaiming a People's Republic. Many workers followed their unions' urging to demand better wages, reduced hours, and improved conditions, but some strikers remained truer to the students' refusals. One plant, occupied for ten days, staunchly resisted union pressure to draw up a list of demands. The workers' silence spoke loudly about the reasons behind their revolt: they wanted not this or that piecemeal change but a resoundingly complete reversal of all past relations. Work had to become play. Small wonder that plant meetings, adjourned by the traditional singing of the "Internationale," often turned into film festivals or volleyball tournaments.

In Paris the nights of late May 1968 looked like a celebration of revolt. Latin Quarter cafés overflowed, their atmosphere one of politicized anticipation. Students wearing armbands directed traffic; the boxes were passed to collect coins for medical aid; action committees sprang up in every quarter. But the climate was one of questioning, rather than directing: "What is going to happen?" were the words most commonly heard. In the end, what Norman Mailer called (in the context of similar events in the United States) "the armies of the night" knew not where to march or who to look to for answers. Consequently, the final crowd, celebrating not rebellion but reaction, marched to the tune of General de Gaulle's orderly drummer: a forest of *tricolores* and nationalist salutes, backed by the armed stick of the state and riding the carrot of placation and concession, overflowed into the Paris streets of May 30, and the evening was swamped in the well-dressed respectability of affluent urbanity. Up the Champs-Elysées tramped the cordons of complacency in what Stephen Spender called "the triumphant bacchanal of the Social World of Conspicuous Consumption." Amid chants of "France back to work!" "*La police avec nous!*" "Clean out the Sorbonne!" and "We are the majority!" the promise of May 1968 imploded in disappointment and disillusionment. Workers found their way back to jobs that remained bleak and boring, and students were allowed the summer to ponder their month of revolt before returning to classrooms little different from those they had stormed out of weeks before. On June 1 the mood was less festive, the ugliness of the hour captured in the notorious chant of repression: "Cohn-Bendit to Dachau!" The student reply, "We are all German Jews!" was an honorable rejoinder but one chillingly cognizant of defeat.[5]

One part of the history of revolutions is thus the ambivalence of the festival, a ritualized consecration of accomplishment: it supposedly celebrates "progress" in parade and pious pronouncement, but it has the tendency to turn into its opposite. Such festivals were a traditional component of the popular culture of the ancien régime. Trade processions, school celebrations, palace and academic parades, and religious feast days had so inundated pre-revolution Paris that, in addition to the Sundays of respite and revel, thirty-two festive holidays tended to reproduce the gluttony and indulgence of the "Land of Cockaigne." Those days of carnivalesque excess worried *philosophes* and encyclopedists such as Montesquieu and Diderot, preoccupied as they were with calculations of lost national revenues and fears of "dark little places" in which festered consciousness of social stratification. Festive crowds troubled authority on the eve of the French Revolution, presenting transgressive "occasions of confusion, indecency, the improper mingling of the sexes, the blurring of social roles, the reign of night and wine ... all too likely to harbor elements ready, at any moment, to erupt into violence—a constant threat to religion, to the state, or to morality."[6]

As the French Revolution attempted to restructure much of life, from the calendar of days and nights to the thoughts and allegiances of men and women, the festival became a battleground. In the first years, contending understandings of the place of festival clashed. Peasants in the provinces insisted on utilizing hastily decorated and quickly trimmed maypoles and liberty trees to establish their emancipation from rents, which they mistakenly believed the revolution had abolished. Around the *mai sauvage* (wild maypole) they danced in almost anarchistic abandon, burning church pews, striking noblemen, and proclaiming a new reign of equality. This people's festival, which often grew out of nights of resentment and misunderstanding, was gradually tamed by the authorities of the revolution, however, who implemented a more rational, scientistic, and utopian celebration of the planted, cultivated Liberty Tree. Transgression accommodated to revolution's agenda: such festivals became an expression of man's link with nature (a national reforestation campaign), cultivation of the revolutionary essence (responsibility, harmony, the disappearance of private interests, the significance of communal life and its symbolic centeredness in a strong, visible, growing tree, recognized publicly), and a planned community. Words of conscious commitment, not acts of retribution and demands for rights, were now the festival's foundation. The planting of official liberty trees required a ceremonial officialdom and a text of righteous service, a laborious construction.

With the festival straitjacketed by officialdom, it was the regulation of celebration, as much as its content, that left its imprint on a changing history of revolutionary activity. Daniel Guerin contrasts the early popular festivals, marked by the spontaneous eruption of revolutionary fervor, with the managed bureaucratism of the official revolutionary state's calendar of anniversaries.[7] James Leith, in his exquisitely illustrated account of monuments, squares, and public buildings in revolutionary France, outlines a similar process.[8]

Consider, for instance, the foundational Federation festival of the French Revolution, the anniversary celebration of July 14, 1789, when the people stormed the Bastille and signaled the end of the old regime. Four days later Charles Villette expressed a desire to see this unprecedented revolutionary act commemorated with a huge civic meal that would gather, symbolically and practically, the whole of France around "the great national table." A year later, the revolution not yet irreconcilably divided against itself, the people did spontaneously launch a series of improvised celebrations. From the streets of Paris to the turbulent armed march of peasants in the countryside, they united in fear and joy at the prospect of preserving their newfound liberty from various poorly understood threats. Decidedly military, these early Federation festivals in the countryside and provincial towns featured processions, open-air meetings and speeches, the blessing of the tricolor, and the taking of oaths, capped by night bonfires, fireworks, and dancing. At Angers, "each of the municipal officers insisted on taking the arm of one of those women who are called women of the people." But the provincial Federation festivals were soon disciplined by the revolutionary authorities in Paris, who feared the popular autonomy that threatened to break out into anti-aristocratic disorder.

In Paris the 1790 Festival of Federation commenced as a singular display of popular revolutionary zeal, pushed past its official limits by the collective enthusiasm of the people, who insisted on bypassing the moral order of the austere revolutionary leadership. Anticipating an influx of liberty-loving provincials, they blanketed the city with broadsides, printed guidebooks offering "salubrious and patriotic plans of the brothels of Paris" and "a price-list of the filles de joie of the Palais-Royal," prepared lodgings for the incoming fédérés, and did what they could to secure adequate supplies of food and sufficient seating at the major public celebrations. Women and young ladies were particularly encouraged to participate, and, when this push for a "female federation" was rebuffed by the Constitution Committee, an event involving five hundred women was organized for a week immediately following the official festival. The city, in short, was being opened up, emancipated, for the revolution and its advocates. The possibility of post revolution transgression was being kept alive. Construction on the Champ de Mars exemplified the new order: in the face of administrative incompetence the people gathered with wheelbarrows, picks, and shovels and literally transformed the site into a sacred place of civic festivity—leveling the soil, making terraces, building a triumphal arch. At nightfall those who had worked with their hands to beautify the Champ de Mars left the scene arm in arm, carrying garlands of Liberty Tree branches, led by a fife-and-drum band. The butchers came under a banner decorated with a knife. One guild proposed showing up at the Champ de Mars behind a hearse crawling with toads, rats, and vipers, to represent "the ruin of the clergy and the aristocracy."

In mid-July a long military procession, a mass, and an oath ceremony were the austere centerpieces of the officially sanctioned festival, but a phalanx of smaller entertainments provided the assembled throng with carnivalesque sights and sounds that included greased-pole hoistings of the tricolor, jousts on the Seine, and parades around the Bastille. Present largely as gate-crashers at the official events, the people managed to break out of their designated role as witnesses. Although peripheralized in circles of oath-taking, the people were sometimes able to demand that they, too, be administered the new sacraments of citizenship, which were supposed to be restricted to the inner circles of soldiers and notables. Jean Paul Marat stood in awe of the masses' remarkable good humor, knowing that the revolution had yet been but "a sorrowful dream for the people!" "Why this unbridled joy?" he asked. "Why these evidences of foolish liveliness?" For Kropotin, writing in 1909, the answer was simple: in 1790 the revolution was still moving, and that was enough; there was nothing to suggest the "dark and savage character" that would be revealed within a year, when the Champ de Mars would be the site of repression and the shooting down of the people. On that first anniversary of the taking of the Bastille, "everywhere the people's hearts were filled with life." One banquet participant proposed that, "a number of poor people, equal to the number of guests, be given a supper in the evening." The festival, a public spectacle of revolution having turned darkness into light, now found itself looking to the night to find a place for those on its margins.[9]

The working-class revolution that established the Soviet state in 1917 also had its festivals, drawing on tsarist practice to orchestrate huge mass spectacles that commemorated past moments of glory. In the first such festive celebration the municipal theater department of Voronezh gathered together foot soldiers of the Red Army, stunt men from a touring circus, and local yachtsmen to perform a two-hour, five-scene presentation of Peter the Great's conquest of the Turks by means of a naval expedition outfitted at the Voronezh wharves. With the sloping banks of the river forming a natural amphitheater and an island representing the Turkish fortress, the audience of four thousand was separated from the performance by a distance that made spoken dialogue impossible but accentuated fireworks, onshore megaphone commentary, and a ninety-piece brass band. At the conclusion of the event, spectators were ferried to the island for a carnival that lasted well into the morning hours.

The cultural politics of Alexander Kerensky's transitional Provisional Government, which came to power in February 1917, was highly attuned to the tradition of the French Revolution's festivals, and there were proposals for a "grandiose carnival-spectacle" of Bastille Day–like celebrations, the construction of a prop city of Paris, and other ambitious doings. At the level of the street this fervor took on a particular bohemian tone. One American radical likened the Nevsky cafés after midnight to Fifth Avenue, an exotic festival of pluralities: "The cafés had nothing to serve but weak tea and sandwiches, but they were always full.... Men and women wear what they please. At one table would be sitting a soldier with his fur hat pulled over his ears, across from him a Red Guard in rag-tags, next a Cossack in a gold and black uniform, earrings in his ears, silver chains around his neck."[10]

After the October Revolution this traditional attachment to cultural celebration presented problems for the Bolsheviks, whose energies and material resources were expended in the herculean and endlessly frustrating task of building war communism. Having long participated in illegal May Day celebrations and at ease with the socialist conception of the mass character of theatrical display, after 1917 they nevertheless faced the difficult task of building a revolutionary festive culture true to the class and national purposes of a proletarian state suspended within a peasant economy and assailed by a worldwide capitalist opposition. Lacking a revolutionary iconography, incarcerated in the neoclassicism of the Romanov streetscape, the Bolsheviks adapted the first Soviet May Day, in 1918, to a highly traditional presentation of freedom. Petrograd's celebration was a curious hybrid of old forms and new ideas and practices. On a Romanesque float stood a goddess, outfitted in a tunic of purest white, her upraised hand holding a torch illuminating the slogan "Having proudly made it through centuries of oppression, we celebrate the worldwide May Day holiday." Labor was allegorically depicted in the guise of another classical, tunic-clad female figure, and workers were presented as embracing revolution by leaping astride a winged horse, the classical Pegasus. The heroes were wreathed in laurels, surrounded by angels blowing trumpets and Grecian arches and columns. It was a stylized celebration of revolution dressed in the glaring incongruities of antiquated autocratic representations.

As the Bolsheviks battled insurmountable odds, tightening material circumstances, and considerable ideological disarray, the revolutionary working-class festival hardened into a propaganda arm of governing authority. By 1920 the mass festival was conceived as a fusion of cultural dialectics in which the spontaneity of the masses, with their deep organic need for ritualized festive articulation, fused "naturally" with the collective creations of state-directed authorities and professionals. The Bolshevik cultural apparatus merged festival and theater in the drama of the revolution's myth. One production proposed for 1920, opening with the Promethean worker bound to the black deity of capitalism, would have shown the dark forces of a constraining night overcome by the progressive emancipatory rays of Red Army light; audience and actors were then expected to come together in song. Out of this kind of scripted *spectacle* came a stylized presentation of dynamic development, an aesthetics evident in the consciously spiraling modernist monument to the Third International, with its symbolic reifications of technology and technique, created by the Moscow artist Vladimir Tatlin in 1919.[11] The mass dramas of 1920—*The Mystery of Liberated Labor*, *Third International*, and *From the Power of Darkness*—were exercises in separation, the militia cordoning off stage and audience, notable government officials and foreign visitors separated from the mass of spectators.

Where the people did participate, they were needed, as ever, for actual toil. May Day's symbolism grew increasingly pragmatic as Bolshevik festivity underlined the pressing needs of the revolution's "new beginnings." If 1917 had swept away tsarist autocracy and capitalist exploitation, much dirt nevertheless remained to be cleared as the revolution built from the ground up. One poet proclaimed "Labor's Holiday" as anything but restful. May Days turned into work fairs: groundbreaking for new buildings, factories, and cities; apartment buildings constructed over the course of a holiday fête. The work might be taken up with enthusiasm, but it could suffer as the holiday culture faded in the year of labor's more mundane days. One May Day, sixty thousand trees and bushes were planted on the Field of Mars, but the pressured work festival had not allowed time for their careful cultivation and afterward nobody came to tend them. By midsummer the foliage had wilted, and all the shrubbery died. Nevertheless, the mass spectacle managed to center the Bolshevik Revolution, to proclaim its world historic destiny, and to solidify the legitimacy of the workers' state. A 1920 evening dramatization of *The Storming of the Winter Palace* was, in spite of poor weather, witnessed by 100,000. The 8,000-member cast far exceeded the actual army of opposition in 1917. At midnight the spectacle ended, the revolution accomplished, its victory crowned by red banners, flashing lights, a cannon salute, and fireworks. Born in the night, revolution's new age was sealed in the mass spectacles of dramatic authorization that presented a mythology and a legitimacy for the consolidating workers' state.

Once the trials of war communism had been weathered, the festival as spectacle was already considered to have served its purpose. "We reject the strict centralization of celebrations that was once necessary to demonstate to the West the power of the Soviet Republic," declared the Moscow May Day Commission in 1923. But that freeing of local initiative would be rechanneled in even more narrowly conceived purpose with the ascent of Stalin in the middle-to-late 1920s. In 1927 the tenth anniversary of the Russian Revolution was highly bureaucratized: the masses were kept rigidly separated from the major spectacles in various urban centers, and the message unmistakably urged production for the socialist program of collectivized industrialization. As Stalin stood with his leadership atop the Lenin Mausoleum, Moscow's Red Square, to which public access was restricted, was opened up to an invited regiment of mounted Georgian Cossacks. When a Trotskyist contingent of protesters tried to make themselves heard their slogans and shouts were drowned out by the saber-rattling Cossacks' ritual charge. The revolutionary festival, like the revolutionary state, had degenerated into a mere expression of power, a public statement of whose voice—and whose voice alone—would prevail.[12] A culture of mobilization and potential was hardening into the cultist reification of the leaders and the led, accentuating not the reciprocities of revolution's makings but its stylized differences.[13] As cultural historians have come to appreciate, the underside of the programmatic and theoretical "pluralism" of the New Economic Policy (1921–1928) was a curiously ambivalent prelude to Stalinism's later political and economic closures, an almost gothic corruption that disfigured sexuality, fantasy, the longings of utopianism, and the primitive myths of everyday life.[14]

In the long interval separating the French and Russian Revolutions, insurgent workers had struggled to sustain moments of revolutionary challenge and opposition that often drew on festival traditions. To write the history of nineteenth-century Paris is to be drawn into this melange of the insurrectionary carnivalesque, in which the night and the underground (again, as place, darkened space, and metaphor of transgression and resistance) figure forcefully.[15] The Paris Commune—created amid the collapse of imperial rule, a threatened Prussian invasion and defeat of France, and an immense popular uprising calling for the deposition of the emperor and the establishment of a workers' government—was one such mobilization.[16] Described in one 1896 text as a groundswell of early September 1870 protest, the beginnings of the Commune can be located in the midnight crowds forming in the streets, fearful of invasion by German armies, their cries for change ringing into the next day as the boulevards thronged with animated people singing the once-outlawed "Marseillaise." Months later, in February 1871, the established government was reduced to a state of impotence, and the people's power was displayed in awesome gatherings at the Place de la Bastille, where increasingly insurrectionary crowds honored the revolutionary tradition. Flags inscribed "The Republic or Death" flew boldly in public squares, and at night the troops fraternized with the people. On March 18, 1871, the streets of Paris were, according to conservative comment, a threatening carnival of insurrection. The crowd appeared on the verge of revolt:

> The streets and heights of Montmartre continued to be crowded with the excited populace.... Drunken with blood and wine, passionate with hate, delirious with their achievements, mad with the moment's yield, and knowing neither past nor future, these biped brutes, in pandemoniacal array, shrieking and shouting, men, women, and children confusedly joined together, many half-nude, and all entirely possessed with an uncontrollable hellish frenzy.

A central committee controlling 200,000 citizen soldiers "had no difficulty in now considering itself the master of Paris." Throughout the late night and early morning of March 18–19 this central committee of federates released political prisoners and constituted the workers' republic. During these same dark hours the established ministers of Paris fled the city and, not unlike an earlier monarchial authority, headed to Versailles.[17]

Paris was now a festival of the oppressed. As early as the first week of April one newspaper was remarking that the city had become "truly picturesque ... a permanent concert, a sort of perpetual fair: a new fair!" Churches were taken over in the evenings by clubs that discussed and debated, among all manner of ideas, the need to abolish the prudery of a class-based restraint of sexuality rationalized by such coercive concepts as "modesty, decency, and public morality." A threateningly festive atmosphere of licentiousness seemed to some to be overtaking Paris. A letter to the Central Committee of the National Guard declared:

> There is no such thing as public decency, shame, vice or prostitution. Nature is not concerned with such stupidities. She has her needs, her demands, and she must be satisfied as is thought best, in her way, when and where one wishes, taking any opportunity, as one pleases, completely by chance, after waiting a long time or at the first meeting, with whoever one wants to, as we do, we other proletarians, among ourselves. Only today what we need are your girls, O idle rich, your women. What is needed is that they return for the benefit of the proletarians, and of everyone in the great communal family.... I am too old to do anything but simply watch the show of this great and magnificent priapic festival that will be the inauguration of the true community. Besides, even if the result will not be as grandiose as I hope, the proletariat is owed this festival.

The streets were alive with drama; the walls shouted the slogans and politics of change; the newspapers bristled with caricature; the air was thick with the imagery of revolutionary promise.[18]

As the gendered boundaries of politics were stretched to breaking point with the forceful presence of the unruly women of Paris in the streets of turmoil, age-old conceptions of masculine and feminine place and their dichotomized associations with nature and civilization, private life and public pursuits were both challenged and reinforced. To the many enemies of the Commune, the breakdown of order associated with the events of 1871 unleashed the furies not only of class but of gender. In the bloody repression that followed, the *communarde* was replaced in reactionary caricatures by the vindictive torch-bearing *pétroleuse*, a misogynist representation of woman's inherent viciousness, uncaged by revolution, its incendiary rage finally directed at Parisian property in the *semaine sanglante* of May 22–28, 1871. But in the weeks leading up to that debacle, before the communards lost the struggle for the assemblies, the streets, and the imagery conveying the meaning of their battles, women of the people were a part of the festival of revolt. Singing and dancing and laughing in their collective emancipation, they stood on the barricades, unarmed, bodies posed defiantly against the soldiers of the state—an indication of how far femininity had traveled from its historical confinements.[19]

The laughter and *joie de vivre* of the masses had become a weapon of class struggle, "ringing out joyfully ... like a shaft of lightning in a terrible storm." For one advocate of the revolutionary festival, "no better reply could be made to our stubborn enemies'" ceaseless cannonade than the refrain that a thousand voices intone every night in the twenty music-halls of Paris: "The peoples of the world are brothers to us,/ Our enemies are the Versaillais." Louis Barron, like many others, flocked to Paris in 1871 to join the social revolution: "In these solemn ceremonies, these festivities, these battles joyously fought," he concluded, "are born the great and sublime movements that cause people to break out of their habits and set their sights on a new ideal." Convinced that these public festivities were the very cement of viable revolution, Barron praised their spontaneity as an exalted experience, likening it to awaking from a dream whose memory "remains ... a brief moment of ectasy, an illusion of fraternity." Anthems bellowed from evening concert halls, posters proclaiming the people's worth at night performances at the Tuileries, the red flag flying in the clear wind of dusk, the ritualized pulling down of Napoleanic icons, the public burning of guillotines, the democratization of theater and other sectors of the arts—all such events confirmed the Commune as a festival of revolutionary creation and imagination. As cannon shots punctuated "this amazing show of merriment and sentimentality," how, Barron asked, "could one imagine that such a varied, entertaining play could ever have a tragic end?"[20]

But revolution is never just a festival; it always faces the concerted power, and often the terror, of counterrevolution. The Commune's accomplishments for actual reform were modest: it struck a strong and decisive blow for women's involvement in public life; it advanced the social significance of industrial education and day nurseries, materially undercutting the privileges of class and the subordinations of gender; and it pioneered important labor reforms, including the abolition of the notorious night work in the bakeries. A proclamation was issued, a commemorative coin struck. But the power of the Commune, proclaimed in part in its festivity, was the possibility of workers' self-rule; the Communards lived, however briefly, their own self-emancipation.[21]

This Paris of liberation would be sacked, European capital putting aside its national squabbles to connive in the restoration of traditional class rule. The Commune's reign was short, and its repression bloody. It succumbed to military defeat in the blood-soaked weeks of late May and early June 1871 as the Versailles forces invaded and ravaged the short-lived workers' republic. Paris became a graveyard, the mass carnage deposited in hastily dug trenches, cavalierly covered with earth that barely managed to conceal the bodies of those summarily executed; it was even rumored that the wounded living were indiscriminately buried with the dead.[22] A festival of revolution ended in class slaughter, with more than twenty-five thousand Communards dead and almost thirty-six thousand arrested. One contemporary commented, "Oh, yes, Paris is quiet now, as quiet as a battlefield the day after victory, as quiet as the dead of night."[23] As the dark curtain of repression lowered, festivities ceased; the restoration of Parisian order was marked by barefoot corpses left lying against the executioners' wall and the return of those women of the evening, the prostitutes whom the Commune had so zealously attempted to reform and reintegrate into society. "This evening, for the first time," reported one contemporary on June 6, 1871, "one begins to have difficulty carving a path amidst the sauntering of the men and the prostitution of the women."[24]

The Commune quickly assumed a place of martyred privilege in international working-class thought. English radicals such as William Morris and Walter Crane revered its memory, as did the anarcho-communist movement in the United States. Socialist Belfort Bax regarded the dearly paid-for fraternity of the Communards as "the only true religion for human beings."[25] Commemorative meetings would figure prominently in the history of the ultra-left, and in Chicago they set part of the stage upon which the Haymarket events of 1886 would unfold.[26] In the repression that followed that event, other martyrs were sacrificed on the altar of capital's and the state's combined hostilities to working-class revolution in general and the demand for the shorter working day in particular. Out of this cauldron of class struggle, repression, and internationalism would emerge the celebratory May Day, a festive seizure of working-class initiative that encompassed demands for shorter hours, improvements in conditions and wages, and socialist agitation and organization.

Building on the traditional spring calendar of class confrontation, in which strikes in many trades were endemic, May Day also constructed powerful myths of solidarity and working-class fraternity, within which class relations were moved in both festive and revolutionary directions. Nineteenth-century utopian socialists had charted paths in this direction, but their attachment to a ceremonial fête of international humanity never quite attained the reach of the revolutionary promise of May Day, first articulated in 1888–1889 by the combined forces of European and American workers, some associated with the Second International. "The Proletariat is about to do something unique in the annals of the world!" declared these originators of May Day, and their followers often took the day of respite from wage labor with an insurrectionary bravado: "On the First of May, either we'll get the eight-hour day or the knives will be out," declared one resolute French worker. Others thought that food would be theirs for the asking and that bosses and landlords would finally be held accountable. Gangs led by women "furies" were rumored to be terrorizing country notables, some of whom were "in some apprehension of the damage which might be caused to their property by demonstrators, especially when the latter are returning at nightfall to their respective localities." "Shall we have a journée?" asked the French radical paper, L'Eclair, in playful anticipation of the first May Day in mid-April 1890. In Russia, May Day strikes and demonstrations, especially among the factory workers of St. Petersburg, "became a political school for millions of toilers," as the New York Times pointed out in 1944. Days of protest, marches, speeches, and demonstrations were typically followed by evenings of celebratory sociability. France's La Défense des Travailleurs printed a classic account of May Day as, in Michelle Perrot's words, "a true workers' festival" and the "perfect expression of a counter-society." A morning of socialist education was followed by an afternoon of picnicking, a joyously sensual coming together of food and drink, song and laughter, which many thought "was like being in the Land of Make-Believe." A night of ballads, socialist song, and comedy followed, a politics of solidarity and an expression of workers' power that seemed "an extraordinary mixture of high mass and village fête."[27] Yet when John Sommerfield penned his English novel May Day in 1936, its austere popular frontism managed to convey something of how festivity had been stripped from the workers' holiday and night reduced to a depressed adjunct of the demonstrative day, something always "trickling away in a thousand little incidents."[28]

A different approach to the festive surfaced in the creative coming together of striking workers, revolutionaries in the Industrial Workers of the World, and Greenwich Village intellectuals at the time of the famous Paterson, New Jersey, silk industry work stoppage.[29] The February 1913 strike, dragging on for months, united skilled weavers and unskilled dyers' helpers. Cultivating the emergence of a rank-and-file female leadership, the protest also drew on the revolutionary agitational skills of Wobblies such as Big Bill Haywood, Elizabeth Gurley Flynn, and Carlo Tresca. The strikers held firm throughout April and May, huge gatherings of twenty-five thousand and more meeting in nearby Haledon (Paterson being the preserve of the silk magnates and their police protectors). As May weather blossomed, the Haledon Sunday afternoon rallies became massive displays of working-class solidarity and festivity, the hopes and aspirations of diverse ethnicities and distinct occupations, all suffering want and privation together but all standing fast against oppression and tyranny. Greenwich Village radicals from the salon society of New York's avant-garde traveled to Haledon to witness the workers' revolt. The singing and cheering struck a chord among the visitors, who experienced the "stage spectacles" of working-class protest as a unique "creative energy." To become convinced of the justice of the workers' cause, one New Yorker declared, "the spectacle before me was enough." Another remembered, "Haledon was always like a picnic, and it was a joy to go there." That men, women, and children could face "hungry days and supperless nights" for months and remain united in a sea of solidarity that every Sunday "brightened with sharp colors several areas of the grassy slopes" of Haledon was a powerful statement that New York intellectuals assimilated and translated, through revolutionary figures of immense romantic stature such as Haywood, into their own world.[30]

By mid-May 1913 it appeared that the strikers, for all their impressive accomplishments, were about to be beaten into submission if supportive funds could not be raised to continue the struggle. Haywood, Harvard-educated revolutionary John Reed, and the salon figure Mabel Dodge Luhan—whose weekly "evenings" provided a forum where working-class revolutionaries and intellectual rebels could meet—hatched the idea of a pageant. "Why don't you bring the strike to New York?" responded Mrs. Luhan to Haywood's complaint that the metropolitan center was losing sight of the struggle and not providing sufficient material support. "There's an idea!" exclaimed Haywood with enthusiasm, followed by Reed's exclamation, "We'll make a Pageant of the strike! The first in the world."[31] The strikers would enact the drama of their struggle before a New York audience, who could then be counted on to offer monetary support.

With a cast of approximately twelve hundred strikers, a script directed by John Reed, a plot that encompassed the clash of heroic labor and villainous capital and that detailed the funeral of a strike supporter killed by a detective's stray bullet, as well as an inspirational May Day parade, the Paterson pageant was a gala festival of representational class struggle. Preceded by band-led marches—one headed by Reed and another by the fiery Carlo Tresca—the strikers, dressed in work clothes, carrying something red, singing the "Marseillaise" and "the Internationale," descended on Madison Square Garden early in the evening of June 7, 1913. Before an overflow crowd of fifteen thousand, the Paterson workers introduced themselves, their plight, and their history. "No such spectacle, presenting in dramatic form the class war raging in society, has ever been staged in America," claimed the pageant committee. Radical journalist and future communist Rose Pastor Stokes, like many New York rebels, devoted herself to this new festivity, an art form that actively participated in the class struggle: "Hail the new pageantry! Hail the red pageant—the pageant with red blood in its veins." Riveting acts drew the assembled together in narratives of violence and power, the final episodes of the performance leading toward revolution and May Day's emancipatory message. Leaving the stage, the workers wove through the audience, shouting "Strike! Strike!" Spectators and actors blurred into one: "The people on stage had long ago forgotten the audience," explained one reporter. "The audience had long ago forgotten itself. It had become part of the scene." The class struggle had been translated into a spectacle that galvanized not only the immediate audience but a portion of America. One night of drama conveyed months of desperation. "No spectacle enacted in New York has ever made such an impresson," proclaimed the *International Socialist Review*.[32] The pageant recharted the relations of festivity, spectacle, and revolutionary class struggle, if only for a few weeks of exhilaratingly creative innovation. It drew upon the deepest well of laboring life, the lived experience of struggle, and in so doing it broke the barriers separating rank-and-file workers, revolutionary leaders, and avant-garde intellectuals.

But the festivity of working-class struggle, moving dramatically in the direction of revolution, appeared to some in darker dress. "Under the direction of a destructive organization," declared a *New York Times* editorial diatribe, "a series of pictures in action were shown with the design of stimulating mad passion against law and order and promulgating a gospel of discontent." Moreover, it proved, unfortunately, a financial failure, and when the strike was ultimately defeated, even some revolutionaries came to regard the pageant as having been a diversion from the more traditional tasks of class struggle. But in the euphoric festivity of its actual staging, the revolutionary power of labor had perhaps never seemed more tangible and immediate:

> 'Tis the final conflict,
> Let each stand in his place,
> The Industrial Union
> Shall be the human race.[33]

In "Red" cities of the European revolutionary working class, such as Vienna, festivals of proletarian insurgency marched to a similar purpose, albeit one constrained by different forces. As a mass culture of radio, film, and spectator sport, plus Catholic passion and mystery plays performed on high religious holidays, threatened to inculcate resignation and resistance to socialist ideas in the workers, revolutionary leaders organized mass festivals of explicit oppositional alternative. In Vienna one of the most successful, aimed at aestheticizing worker politics and deflecting crude insurrectionism, was the spectacle presented at the July 1931 Worker Olympics. The playing field of the newly built stadium came alive as four thousand singers, actors, musicans, speakers, gymnasts, and socialist youth assembled against a backdrop of props and stage effects. A spectacle of laboring humanity—its historic struggles from the Middle Ages to the coming of industrial capitalism—was presented, and the golden calf of acquisitive individualism was overthrown by thousands of youth, their collective power clothed in purest white, marshaled under the red flags of proletarian internationalism. Yet despite repeated performances, a total audience of 260,000, and unadulterated praise in party publications, the 1931 festival may well have been a "mass theatre of illusions" that merely masked the political reversals of the Vienna socialists and the declining fortunes of municipal socialism. Tightly orchestrated and choreographed with exquisite detail, the festivals of Red Vienna were as much a displacement of revolutionary enthusiasm and energy, a containment of this exuberance within party channels and conventional socialist thought, as they were an unleashing of spectacle's festive power.[34]

This two-sidedness of the festival in the balance sheet of revolutionary possibility was nowhere more evident than in Spain's seething cauldron of political tension. Right and left clashed repeatedly, their confusing contentions pitting language and nationality, anarchism, communism, republicanism, monarchism, and fascism against various aligned and fracturing alliances of combined affiliations. In Barcelona, where by the 1920s and 1930s dictators such as Miguel Primo de Rivera and Francisco Franco were tightening the constraints on popular initiatives, civic festivals had a long history of embodying political volatility and violence. May Day was celebrated in the Spanish city in 1890 both as a festival and as a general strike, with mass marches of twenty-five thousand and strikes involving almost as many workers. Catalan separatists and anarchists complicated the political scene, expressing their politics of opposition in acts of terrorism, which were often staged, for maximum impact, in conjunction with public marches and ritualized celebrations. Bombings, assassinations, and the ensuing police reprisal cultivated an atmosphere of acute class and political tension. Civic festivals such as the Corpus Christi procession, a traditional proclamation of summer's relaxations, were often the scene of conflicting politics. By 1930 all civic festivals in Barcelona had been banned in an effort to stifle the apparently irrepressible relation between festival, spectacle, and forms of resistance that threatened order.[35]

16. Pablo Picasso, *Guernica* (1937).

Even Pablo Picasso's art, unmistakably associated with both Barcelona as a cultural center (bullfights, flamenco dancers, cafés, brothels, music halls, carnival, and masked balls) and the left as an international presence, became a symbol capable of galvanizing intense political polarizations.[36] His *Guernica* (1937), commissioned by the Spanish government for its pavillion at the Paris World's Fair, was inspired by the political crisis of the middle-to-late 1930s. The painting's animalistic ugliness was an articulation of life's festivity plunged into a nightmarish authoritarianism of anguish, pain, and dark despair. This was the politics that Picasso saw being lived in 1936–1937, with fascism aggressively in pursuit of a multitude of destructions:

> The Spanish struggle is the fight of reaction against the people, against freedom. My whole life as an artist has been nothing more than a continuous struggle against reaction and the death of art. How could anybody think for a moment that I would be in agreement with reaction and death? ... In the panel on which I am working, which I shall call *Guernica*, and in all of my recent works of art, I clearly express my abhorrence of the military caste which has sunk Spain in an ocean of pain and death.

Described by critics as "a cry of outrage and horror amplified by the spirit of genius" and as a rectangle of black and white announcing "all that we love is going to die," *Guernica* was an explosive artistic statement of the turning tide of political civilization.[37] As Stephen Spender commented in the *New Statesman*, moreover, the mural's dulling collage of "non-color" (black, white, and gray) captured visually "a waking night-mare of second-hand experience." In this sense, it paralleled the horrifying prospective plunge into the fascist counterrevolution's abyss, which could be grasped by most of the world's people only in newspaper, wireless, or newsreel partialities—an alienated vision of documentary footage that, in Picasso's elongated canvas of catastrophic clutter, appeared to stretch endlessly on and on.[38]

This dark dialogue of despair seemed confirmed by Spain's incomparably chaotic circularity of revolution and counterrevolution. In the 1936 elections the Barcelona Popular Front of communists and other leftists secured a victory that would soon be challenged by a contingent of army generals, led by Franco and supported by Catholic landowners and fascists. In April 1937 the Nazis, in a bloodthirsty maneuver of no strategic military significance, bombed Guernica, the symbolic center of the Basque nation, killing sixteen hundred and wounding eight hundred. Two weeks later Barcelona erupted in the "May days" of class conflict that pitted the city's small but influential Communist Party against the militias of left-wing insurgents who demanded the immediate goal of working-class revolution. One million Parisians marched in protest of the Nazi bombing and their government's neutrality, but the capitalist nations of the world kept a discreet distance from the unfolding atrocities. The Soviet Union contributed to the failure to build unity by self-interestedly channeling its military and medical aid in ways that exacerbated tensions among the various left-wing factions, pitting Stalinists and workers' militias against each other with a violence and vehemence that sealed the fate of working-class insurgency. Barcelona's mayor canceled the traditional May Day parade, the festival's historic meaning in affirming popular support for republican and socialist causes now a potential site not of solidarity but of bloodshed.[39] With the festival of revolution divided against itself and the specter of Nazism sweeping Europe, the dark night of counterrevolution appeared to be eclipsing the bright light of revolutionary promise.

15
Decade of Darkness
The Fascist Night

National Socialism—the pairing of these words is one of those contradictions that meet in the dark night of political economy, where a catastrophic collapse of the material foundations of civil society pressures a politics of counterrevolution from below, in which much is borrowed from the program of revolution so that any actual revolutionary transformation may be decisively stopped in its progressive tracks. The great Soviet film director Sergei Eisenstein once chastised Joseph Goebbels in an "open letter," declaring the rhetorical and propagandistic term "National Socialism" a self-canceling "mongrel of lies" incompatible with truth and realism.[1]

Adolf Hitler despised the masses as stupid, easily (mis)led, and weakly "feminine." But fascism—as the reactionary mobilizations associated loosely with Hitler's Germany, Mussolini's Italy, and lesser known (but powerfully successful) movements such as the Hungarian Arrow Cross and the Romanian Iron Guard came to be known in the 1920s and, more especially, the 1930s—gloried in the manipulation and orchestration of "mass" power, which it maintained symbolically in festivals of the *Volk*, from morning school exercises and flag raisings to the Nuremberg rallies and propagandistic cinema such as *Triumph of the Will* (1935).[2] In 1941, there were almost daily Nazi school celebrations, conceived as "festive hours" that would serve as "confessions of faith," and throughout the year there were special flag or colors rituals, entrance and graduation festivals, historical memorials, and eight major national holidays (honoring the *Reich*, the *Volk*, the *Führer*, Labor, Farmers, National Heroes, the German Mother, and the pre-Christmas Festival of Light).[3] As Leon Trotsky noted in 1933, "If the road to hell is paved with good intentions, then the avenues of the Third Reich are paved with symbols."[4] None was more effective than the swastika, its black articulation of the Aryan race emblazoned on the red "socialism" and white nationalism of the Reich flag.

What Hitler's National Socialism promised was not a revolution that would overturn class power and its consequent inequalities but a "breakthrough" into tradition, a reformation of the past in a present that craved order, hope, and a decisive *national* leadership.[5] That this could be dressed in borrowings from the revolutionary left—evident in the name National Socialist Workers Party, its modified red flag, and its appropriation of May Day as the official holiday of labor—was an obvious part of its success. For many who lusted for change, its dynamism, its action-oriented youthful leaders, and its grandiose view of a reconstructed world marked it as a unique conjuncture of what had been valued in the past and what might be radically new in the future. As a *putsch* carried out in the name of community, fascism festered in years of street violence before the crisis of the old regime catapulted it to power.[6] Once lodged in the institutions of precarious bourgeois authority, fascism distinguished itself from other reactionary political agendas by refusing to curb its appetite for domination dressed in excess.[7]

But even conservative critics were disconcerted by the course being charted in the 1930s. Considering traditional dissidents little more than "mourners at a funeral," Hermann Rauschning, once an official in Hitler's party, came to deplore the Nazi coup. "The skies are tempestuous, with heavy clouds, some of them sharply outlined storm clouds," he declared in 1941. "Patches of sunlight and shade pursue one another.... I am sitting for a while in the sun. The world holds its breath: the beast from the abyss is lurking, waiting to pounce."[8] Those Freikorps officers who led a volunteer contingent of German soldiers serving the cause of domestic repression in the aftermath of the First World War, paving the way for Hitler's ascent to power and constructing a protofascist cult of virulent racism, aggressive anticommunism, and the soldier state's presentation of hypermasculinity, battled similar fears in the warrior-generated fantasies of the 1920s. In Thor Goote's 1932 novel *We Shoulder Life*, a nurse—love object and mothering sibling in the collective unconscious of these soldiers—expresses her distaste at the proximity to these early Nazis that she is required to experience, declaring: "There was so much fear lodged in my gullet that I was embarrassed in front of everyone. And at night, a bald-headed vulture with claws sat on my bed. Night after night."[9] This imagery of darkness, of "a long night of barbarism," hung over the representation of fascism in the 1930s, a symbolism not unrelated to the fear that day's end would bring the Gestapo to the door.[10] Indeed, there is no better entrée into the methods and politics of Nazism than three specific nights of orchestrated fascist repression: the nights of the Reichstag fire (1933), the Long Knives (1934), and Broken Glass (1938) illuminate Hitler's tactical orientation and strategic ends, exposing them in hindsight as a systematic deployment of the power of state terrorism and its reduction to an agenda of exterminism.

This dark and diabolical deformation, in which so many would pay with their lives and whose debasements would distort the first half of the twentieth century, had its origins in the failed working-class revolutions of an earlier epoch. Their defeat registered in the crushing of the German uprising of 1918–1919, the vanquishing of the workers'and soldiers'councils that had the temerity to seize political and military power, and the Freikorps murder of the Communist leaders Karl Liebknecht and Rosa Luxemburg. Following the Allied capitalist powers' rapacious subordination of a defeated Germany to a position of abject economic crisis and demoralization, the Weimar Republic was a fertile breeding ground of ultra-nationalist resentment and irrationality. Its economy was suspended in a seemingly perpetual state of externally imposed chaos; its politics appeared poised persistently at the edge of a defensiveness always threatening to embrace extremist solutions; and its culture gravitated at times toward obsessions with sexual violence that Maria Tatar has outlined in her study of the aestheticization of Lustmord, or sexual murder.[11] When the world capitalist economy crashed in the depression of 1929–1930, fascism's totalitarianism, racial sense of order, and crusading promise to obliterate the enemies of the "national community"—whether Gypsies or Jews, communists or homosexuals, tramps or trade unionists or social democrats, the mentally deficient or the physically disabled—provided the powerful antidote to Germany's long-standing material and sociocultural sicknesses, whether eugenic, sexual, racial, or ideological.[12] Hitler rode this wave of structural malaise until his newly proclaimed power could plunge the plethora of real and perceived economic dislocations, political disorders, and sociocultural degenerations into a pogrom. This potent politics of reaction reclaimed, materially and spiritually, the fatherland for the chosen people, an act of rejuvenation implicitly sustained by a deeply historical German ideology that joined utopianism, romanticism, and a sense of race destiny.[13] By the time the blinding light of this promised day of the Volk's realization had dimmed sufficiently to allow a refocused vision of the new Reich's measures and means, authoritarianism and its state-directed terror were firmly in control of a nation that had been a centerpiece not only of European culture and civilization but of working-class radicalism and sexual and artistic freedom. A dark night colonized a country and demanded that the country colonize the world.

Germany would not, at a superficial glance, have seemed an ideal climate for this repression. It boasted an ostensibly militant working class, unrivaled in its institutions and political organizations. Yet, as Trotsky noted in March 1933, "The most powerful proletariat of Europe, measured by its place in production, its social weight, and the strength of its organizations, has manifested no resistance since Hitler's coming to power and his first violent attacks against the workers' organizations."[14] Trotsky thought this fundamental *class* power of strategic importance, and, indeed, it was of pivotal significance on three levels.[15]

First, as Hitler and the Nazis reached for power at the end of January 1933, they utilized their uncompromising, decisive seizure of the apparatus of the state to mold together wavering segments of the despairing petty bourgeoisie and elements of large capital with the promise that fascism alone had the resolve to vanquish the threatening presence of organized labor and working-class radicalism[16]—associated most publicly with the communists but also linked to the discredited politics of reformist social democracy.[17]

Second, as Nazism justified itself and its terrorist tactics on the basis of the pressing need to crush a potential communist insurrection, it pioneered the extra-parliamentary suspension of civil society and constitutionalist procedure which would come to be the hallmark of Hitler's violently authoritarian regime.[18] As an act of staged violence the February 27, 1933, burning of the Reichstag—occurring on the eve of an election that would in all likelihood have left Nazis, Social Democrats, Communists, and others sharing political power—signaled the suspension of bourgeois democracy: scapegoated as the evil enemy of national institutions, the Communist Party was presented as the arsonist and, in the immediate aftermath of the fire, outlawed. Hitler stood amid the scorched ruins of the once white-columned, neoclassical German parliament building and proclaimed, "This is a sign of Providence from above. Now nobody will dare stand in our way when we crush the Communist menace with an iron fist."[19] Its leaders subject to Brownshirt beatings and arrest (ten thousand on the night of the conflagration and in the immediate days following), the communist movement, unprepared for such a cunningly manipulative campaign, was thrown into debilitating disarray. The radical constituency rebounded in the March 5, 1933, election, where the

Communist Party made a reasonably good electoral showing, given the climate of irrational reaction, winning more than 12 percent of the recorded vote—almost five million ballots for what was in effect a banned body. No matter: the next day Communist Party activity of almost any sort was declared illegal, and when the newly elected Reichstag convened some two weeks later, the places of the eighty-one Communist members were empty. No voice of protest was heard in the parliamentary hall.[20]

Third, the reign of terror successfully waged against the Communists was a warning to all sectors of German politics and society that any group could be subjected to the vengeance of the fascists. The suppression of labor and its left voices was thus a pivotal moment in the consolidation of Nazi power: it forged a class alliance in opposition to a perceived communist insurrectionary threat; in the process it initiated a pattern of political terror that would be repeated in future repressions; and it sent a message to all potential detractors that the Nazis would brook no challenge to their new order.

The night of the Reichstag fire, in which the Nazis exploited fears of communist revolution to initiate a campaign designed to extinguish the challenge of labor and the left, was followed by similar orchestrations and manipulations of prejudice and powerful phobias. Again, the targets were often associated with established centers of strengths judged impure and impolitic.[21] For instance, Germany had become a stronghold of the homosexual emancipation movement; it boasted an Institute for Sexual Science headed by the gay Jewish physician and liberal crusader Magnus Hirschfeld, whose prolific writings totaled nearly two hundred books, articles, and pamphlets. Hirschfeld's indefatigable proselytizing had a dual impact: it publicized the need to reform punitive sex legislation (paragraph 175 of the German Criminal Code, instituted in 1871, called for jail sentences for all males indulging in "criminally indecent activity" with other males), but ironically it also stigmatized the "third sex" as a marginal, medicalized minority. In alignment with the growing women's emancipation movement, Hirshfeld established his institute in 1919. He amassed a unique library of twenty thousand volumes and an invaluable collection of artifacts and visual material, as well as dispensing doctor's counseling on sexual matters, venereal disease, and abortion. In 1921 he also convened the First Congress for Sexual Reform, which gathered experts from all over the world to discuss genetics, sexology, and law and to establish an international organization dedicated to sex reform. Impaled on the pathological construction of homosexuality that was the foundation of the sexology discourse, Hirschfeld nevertheless managed to garner enough support in left-wing circles to threaten the striking down of paragraph 175 in parliamentary committee. But the stock market crash of 1929 pushed the bill to the sidelines, where it would soon be lost in the swirl of political and economic crises.

Weathering various storms, the early German gay and lesbian movement nevertheless thrived. Organized lesbian costume balls, luxurious lesbian bars and nightclubs, and lesbian theater and magazines all flourished. Berlin's sexually transgressive bars were world famous, the city an urban night of sexual fantasy, a culture of erotic bargaining. As early as the First World War years, Berlin boasted forty or more openly homosexual gathering places—from elegant clubs to ordinary pubs—all staffed by openly gay men and supplemented by private baths and "queer" walkways. A scene that came to be designated as "Boyopolis" was alive with homosexual possibilities as a segment of the city's unemployed youth displayed their masculine beauty in tough, out-of-the-way working-class bars, bartering their bodies with a clientele drawn to an atmosphere of sexual openness. No city in Europe was better known for harboring, even flaunting, cultures of cross-dressing, fetishism, and sadomasochism. Notorious Christmas transvestite balls were but the most visible of what the English writer Christopher Isherwood called a wide-ranging "masquerade of perversions," one that he explored with a group of friends and youthfully exciting male prostitutes in evenings he regarded as a perpetual "Journey to the End of the Night."[22]

Hitler's early second-in-command and faithful sponsor throughout the 1920s, military founder and leader of the Brownshirt SA (Sturmabteilung) Ernst Roehm, was openly homosexual. Elements of the antifascist left were not immune to the homophobia of the epoch, associating Roehm's penchant for violence and terror with the "perverse" accommodations Nazism made to "unnatural" male bonding.[23] Roehm and Hitler were trusted friends, survivors of the conspiratorial 1923 Beer Hall Putsch, in which Hitler made his first bid for power. Throughout the middle to late 1920s, Roehm's sexual and political indiscretions forced him into exile in Bolivia. But when the Brownshirts, indispensable to Hitler's capacity to parade Nazi street muscle, were threatened with a factional mutiny in 1929, the Führer called on his old ally to piece things back together. Returning to Germany, Roehm mopped up the oppositionists and expanded the SA, recruiting thousands of new young members. Pivotal in the anti-communist street violence of early 1933, his Brownshirts also launched the beginnings of a terroristic assault on homosexuality: bars were raided, apartments sacked, literature and organizations banned. On May 6, 1933, Hirschfeld's institute was attacked, the library seized, the furniture smashed. Days later the books and photographs, a precious visual archive of homosexuality, were ritualistically burned in a public ceremony. The Institute of Sexual Science was declared an "international center of the white-slave trade" and "an unparalleled breeding ground of dirt and filth." Roehm's SA skyrocketed from 300,000 members in January 1933 to thirty million a year later. Communists and homosexuals made convenient targets.

Roehm misjudged his usefulness, however, or at least misperceived the importance of timing and context. His Brownshirt street thugs paved the way to power for Hitler, and they consolidated the new order in its transitional days of anticommunist terror. But once the Nazis were ensconced in the bastions of bourgeois legislative authority, the unruly, irksomely undisciplined bullying of the Brownshirts became a liability. Soon Roehm's power base, ambitions to take over the German army, and open homosexuality were subjects of jealousy and consternation among other Nazi figureheads such as the Führer's bodyguard leader, Heinrich Himmler of the SS (Schutzstaffel).[24]

The Night of the Long Knives, a bloodbath that began on June 28 and continued to July 3, 1934, was made of power relations such as these. Hitler arrived in Munich to meet Roehm on the evening of June 28. Bolstered by a contingent of SS storm troopers, he barged into SA headquarters, hurled epithets of "homosexual pigs" at the Brownshirt regulars, arrrested a number of leaders, and proceeded to round up Roehm and his immediate entourage. A similar fate befell stunned SA lieutenants in Berlin and elsewhere, as well as other Nazis who, for whatever reasons, Hitler desired to purge. They were beaten, tortured, executed summarily; the body count reached three hundred in a few days. Two weeks later, Hitler stood defiant and unrepentant before the Reichstag. "If anyone reproaches me and asks why I did not resort to the regular courts of justice, then all I can say is this: in this hour I was responsible for the fate of the German people. I became the supreme judge of the German nation.... Everyone must know for all future time that if he raises his hand to strike the state, then certain death is his lot!"

A year later, on the anniversary date of the Night of the Long Knives, harsh new laws prohibiting homosexual relations among men were implemented. The crime of "contragenics" was stretched from sodomy to body rubbing to lewd glances.[25] Between fifty and sixty-three thousand males were convicted of such homosexual offenses between 1933 and 1944, and every gay German knew that the concentration camp might be his final destination, where he would wear the mark of the pink triangle. Reviled by their Nazi jailers, more isolated and fragmented than the antifascist, Jewish, or foreign inmates, homosexuals in Dachau and Buchenwald were treated in ways that accentuated their special oppression.[26] They were subject to hormone injections, glandular implants, and various lurid experiments; forced to visit camp brothels; required to sleep with their hands outside the blankets in order to ensure that they did not masturbate. Sadistic beating of their genital areas was routine, as was assignment to work details that spelled a sure, slow death, including labor in underground tunnel factories where the dripping humidity, lack of sanitary facilities, and poor ventilation proved an incubator for diseases such as tuberculosis. Eugen Kogon's *Theory and Practice of Hell* (1968) outlined the plight of homosexual prisoners, caught between the homophobia of other inmates and the terroristic regime of the camps. Between five and fifteen thousand homosexuals died under these conditions; others considered themselves fortunate to be castrated and "released" to work in the essential war industries.[27] Himmler made it known that he regarded them as "weeds" to be pulled out, thrown on a heap, and burned. In the name of blood purity the SS leader advocated humiliating all suspected homosexuals publicly, moving expeditiously to court proceedings, and, finally, sending all convicted "sexual inverts" to concentration camps where they would be shot "attempting to escape." The Final Solution had a trial run in the violence orchestrated against homosexuals.[28]

As tragically debilitating as were the acts of repression and politico-cultural genocide associated with Nazi attacks on communists, the workers' movement, and sexual transgression, they pale in quantitative comparison with the murder of approximately six million Jews—the holocaust that has understandably cast the darkest shadow over the long night of fascist atrocity.[29] It had been evident since the 1920s that anti-Semitism and commitment to racial purification infused Hitler's politics of an ordered *Volk*.[30] But few saw the virulently racialized eugenics of his vague generalizations leading in the direction of the Final Solution. Hitler regarded himself as a revolutionary prophet declaring everlasting war on racial "defectives." Nevertheless, as late as his takeover of the chancellorship in January 1933, despite his obvious attraction to demographic "cleansing and regeneration," attacks on the Jews had been extralegal instances of Brownshirt thuggery, and the organized persecution was kept within politically expedient boundaries. Terror in the streets was unleashed in 1933, of course, and many Jews knew firsthand the nights of census-taking that the early Nazi state used to monitor and record "illegals."[31] But it was the systematic discrimination of the Nuremberg Laws against the Jewish people that spelled out the real course of "Aryanization."[32]

The Night of Broken Glass (*Kristallnacht*), November 9–10, 1938, brought Hitler's genocidal intentions to a head. When a Nazi diplomat was murdered in Paris by a young Jew, Goebbels made it clear in an address to party leaders in Munich that anti-Semitic riots would not meet with discouragement from the state authorities. A national pogrom resulted, as Nazi storm troopers and SS regulars—out of uniform but armed with hammers, axes, crowbars, and incendiary bombs—descended at 3:00 A.M. on Jewish stores, homes, and synagogues; they smashed windows, looted icons, artifacts, and goods, and gutted buildings. Thousands were brutalized, possibly as many as a hundred killed, and twenty thousand Jewish males were herded into concentration camps. The streets were littered with broken glass. To add insult to injury the Nazi state passed a decree stipulating that "all damage to Jewish businesses or dwellings ... through the indignation of the people over the agitation of the international Jews against National Socialist Germany must be repaired at once by the Jewish occupant." Further legislation imposed a collective fine of one billion marks on German Jews; other laws eliminated Jews from the economic life of the Reich, strictly limited Jewish social and property rights, and codified the boundaries of citizenship within mixed marriages.[33]

Having been marked as Other for more than a decade, Jews in the Third Reich were by the end of 1938 classified as expendable. The first result was state-enforced emigration, but the threat of war moved Hitler to more radical ground, and as early as 1939 he promised "the annihilation of the Jewish race in Europe!" By 1941 the Nazi leadership was speaking of the Final Solution. Deadly SS squads organized mass killings; six special extermination camps were constructed in conquered Poland and outfitted with gas chambers (some built to hold two thousand people at a time), the most infamous being that established at Birkenau alongside the huge labor camp of Auschwitz. At the Wannsee Conference of January 1942 the Final Solution was officially established as state policy. Just over a year later, in April and May 1943, the Warsaw ghetto was burned to the ground, and tens of thousands of Polish Jews were shot in the streets and alleys, asphixiated in the sewers, or burned in the buildings. Europe, in the words of one Nazi report, had been "combed through from west to east." Possibly as much as 68 percent of European Jewry went into the dark decade of fascism never to come out of it.[34]

Resistance to this ugly night of brutality and genocide would seem to have been, in historical hindsight, a necessary act, the only means of embracing and espousing a humanity worth preserving in the face of such deep darkness.[35] And many did resist: sectors of the military, workers, communists, socialists, liberals, students, professionals, and intellectuals all contributed to the ranks of those who opposed, often at the cost of their lives, the fascist regime. Numerous traditional avenues of protest, especially in working-class circles, had been closed down, but union militants and radical activists continued to struggle against the Third Reich even as the swastika lowered over the unions, political parties of the left found themselves literally outlawed, and underground freedom fighters worried constantly that their families would feel the tightening noose of Gestapo terror.[36] In the face of totalizing containment, workers committed sabotage, Communists published clandestine papers, unionists held to staunch principles as their institutions were dismantled and leaders deposed. In the working-class slums rebelliousness inscribed itself in the alleyways of "foul-smelling dead-end streets" and under dark arches where night scrawlers inscribed crusted walls with slogans of resilient ferocity: "Death to Hitler!" and "Long Live the Revolution." An idea could not be killed. Daniel Guerin concludes an account of his travels in "the other Germany" with the assurance that nights in Nazi Berlin still rang with the refrain of the "Internationale": "This evening, as every evening, deep in countless households, lips take up the chorus and sing with low voices: 'Tis the final conflict.'" One memoir of 1930s resistance was appropriately entitled *Out of the Night* (1967).[37]

The student authors and distributors of the White Rose leaflets, which circulated in Munich and Hamburg and were found by the Gestapo in Vienna in late 1942 to early 1943, used the cover of darkness to draft anti-Hitler statements and, eventually, conduct a clandestine graffiti campaign proclaiming the Führer a mass murderer and urging the German intelligentsia to stand up for "freedom." Their nights of illicit meetings and nocturnal travels to post offices, train stations, and distant towns were efforts aimed at widening the emerging fissures in National Socialism's hegemonic hold over the German people. Convinced that German intellectuals had "fled to their cellars ... struggling in the dark ... gradually to choke to death," the youthful members of White Rose preferred "an end in terror" to "terror without end." Urging the people to sabotage the Nazi regime and adopt a strategy of passive resistance, they pleaded against blind patriotism: "The military victory over Bolshevism dare not become the primary concern of the Germans. The defeat of the Nazis must *unconditionally* be the first order of business." As revolutionary defeatists, the White Rose authors ended their first leaflet with a passage from Goethe's *The Awakening of Epimenides*, act 2, scene 4, where Hope declares:

> Now I find my good men
> Are gathered in the night,
> To wait in silence, not to sleep.
> And the glorious word of liberty
> They whisper and murmur,
> Till in unaccustomed strangeness,
> On the steps of our temple
> Once again in delight they cry:
> Freedom! Freedom!

But six of the White Rose leaders were eventually arrested and executed, and a number of supporters sentenced to prison terms of six months to ten years. Their effort to "shatter the German night" ended, like so many acts of resistance, in incarceration and death.[38]

The passive revolution that the White Rose proclaimed the only possible option for a Germany dominated by the fascist night had in fact been germinating in diverse realms of Weimar and Nazi popular culture.[39] In evenings of revelry and retreat lay subcultures of irreverence and indulgence that cultivated transgressive identities complexly related to the politics of race purity and reaction. Within the cabarets, youth gangs, and swing enthusiasts of the 1920s and 1930s, for instance, Nazism was negotiated in ways that defied easy assimilation of its politics.

Berlin cabaret reached back to the turn of the century, a spectacle delicately balanced on the edge of conservatism and critique, where a metropolitan wit of sex and politics involved censors and performers in constant clashes over the constraints within which comments on and expressions of blasphemy, obscenity, and political satire could be staged.[40] Complicated by the Berlin Dadaists, who pushed the limits of the cabaret culture's capacity to mock political convention, the immediate post–First World War years and early 1920s saw an outpouring of radical aesthetics culminating in the First International Dada Exhibition of June 1920. Often sympathetic to rebel politics, some Dadaists were drawn to the German Communist Party, but the staid proletarian revolutionaries of the KPD had little time for the laughter and high camp of absurdist spectacle. Lampooning institutions of bourgeois politics and economics, as well as eroticizing satirical slams at the personalities of power, Dada conditioned a new climate of permissive frivolity and savage humor.

In the 1920s period of hyperinflation, popular taste drifted toward revues, presentations often enhanced by "Americanized" musical idioms, in which a ribald display of female nudity played on the audience's lasciviousness. Black jazz musicians and dance troupes and performers such as Josephine Baker parodied European culture but were hailed as embodiments of primitivist modernity, a German "expressionism" attuned to urban sensualities. American chorus lines of dancing girls also gained popularity, presenting a racial contrast of Fordist assembly-line precision and a militarization of the erotic. Cabaret thus fused diverse and often contradictory cultural forms, sustaining a spectacle whose paradoxes and parallels eroticized the Weimar Republic's classic ambivalences. As the political climate's ugliness intensified with fascism's increasingly threatening street presence and rising political visibility from 1930 to 1933, however, cabaret fractured into factions of silence and satire with respect to the future Führer and his vitriol or, in Red Reviews and agitprop theater, adopted an aggressive stand of overt political opposition.[41] But in the aftermath of the Reichstag fire most cabaret entertainers—overwhelmingly Jewish, liberal, or leftist—fled the country. By the later 1930s the world of the politicized cabaret had been snuffed out by National Socialism's silencing of critical commentary and virtual ban on "degenerate" art forms and musical genres.[42] This was a process that forced artists such as the communist satirist George Grosz and the dissident painter Max Beckman to opt for exile (1933–1937) rather than face the suffocating climate of Nazi repression.[43] Any cabarets that failed to meet the acid test of compliance and conformity were simply shut down by the Gestapo.[44]

Illustrative of the cabaret milieu and its meanings is the fictional chanteuse and dancer Sally Bowles, created by Christopher Isherwood in a 1939 short story that originally appeared in his collection Goodbye to Berlin. Bowles, as Linda Mizejewski has stunningly suggested, became the twentieth century's icon of "divine decadence," a character rewritten across the third quarter of the century but always in ways that refocus Nazism's horrible dominations through the lens of eroticism. An obvious interplay between Hitler's rise and the wildness of Weimar Berlin's nights of debauchery and decadence has proved a fascinating attraction for stage and screen audiences from the 1950s to the 1970s; indeed, it exercised this lure much earlier, with Marlene Dietrich's film The Blue Angel (1930) and Margarete von Falkensee's novel of erotic escapades in the 1920s, The Pleasure Garden (1931).[45]

In Bowles one finds a point of convergence for the shedding of sexual inhibition, the unmistakable appeal of a pervasive masquerade of erotic indulgence, the pleasures of voyeurism, and the powerfully raw horror of a public political authority marching in disciplined depravity across and through the supposed privacies of intimate life. As Bob Fosse's 1972 musical film *Cabaret* (starring Liza Minnelli and Joel Gray) made abundantly clear, Sally Bowles is the sexual body that scripts the politics of fascist darkness, however glitteringly sanitized Hollywood's imagined cabaret. In its cinematic drive to wildness lay complex negotiations of the meaning of Nazism, bringing into view the interrelated challenges and accommodations to the horrors of political life which the cabaret mirrored. A milieu of entertainment and eroticism, cabaret was a passive reservoir of sexuality, spectacle, and consumption which found itself displaced: fascism's culturalist final solution had no place for the divine decadence that had possibly eased its movement into power but ultimately threatened its hold over minds, bodies, and the state. Isherwood's model for Sally Bowles, the former cabaret dancer Jean Ross, was a politically active aspiring writer and mother who, like so many other left entertainers, had fled Berlin before the Nazis moved decisively to destroy the culture of the cabaret. When reporters sought her out, they were singularly interested in sex, but Ross wanted to pursue different matters. "They say they want to know about Berlin in the Thirties," she exclaimed in exasperation, "but they don't want to know about the unemployment or the poverty or the Nazis marching through the streets—all they want to know is how many men I went to bed with. Really, darling, how on earth can anyone be interested in that?"[46]

This two-sided passive revolution animated sectors of German youth as well. Gangs of fourteen- to eighteen-year-olds, neglected teenagers who had been lumpenproletarianized at an early age, proliferated on the outskirts of Berlin. Their subcultures of criminality were marked by a romanticization of marginality evident in the names they appropriated: Blood of the Indians, Forest Pirates, Red Apaches, Gypsy Love. Governed by a hierarchy of affiliation, often initiated into the ranks through practices of sexual exhibitionism and rough hazing, distinct in their dress, adorning their bodies with earrings and tattoos, these gangs stood outside all forms of order. Sexually promiscuous, they often embraced homosexuality, sadomasochisic ceremonies at night gatherings in secluded woods, and male prostitution; their politics and economics were those of a predatory underworld of fences and pimps, tavernkeepers, hustlers, and thieves. Six hundred such gangs were estimated to have existed in Berlin alone in 1931, and the total German membership was said to approach fourteen thousand. Daniel Guerin describes one such gang, which he encountered outside Berlin in 1932:

They were very much "toughs." They had the depraved and troubled
faces of hoodlums and the most bizarre coverings on their heads: black
or gray Chaplinesque bowlers, old women's hats with brims turned up
in "Amazon" fashion adorned with ostrich plumes and medals, proletarian navigator caps decorated with enormous edelweiss above the visor,
handkerchiefs or scarves in screaming colors tied any which way around
the neck, bare chests bursting out of open skin vests with broad stripes,
arms scored with fantastic or lewd tattoos, ears hung with pendants or
enormous rings, leather shorts surmounted by immense triangular
belts—also leather—both daubed with all the colors of the rainbow,
esoteric numbers, human profiles, and inscriptions such as *Wild-frei* (wild
and free) or *Rauber* (bandits). Around their wrists they wore enormous
leather bracelets. In short, they were a bizarre mixture of virility and
effeminacy.

Leaders of these "masquerade Indians" often called themselves Winnetou,
supposedly the surname of the last of the Apaches. Rebels against all
order save that which could be orchestrated to display their contemptuous
hatred of the society that left them to their culture of primitivism, the
Winnetous and their followers were a volatile, unpredictable collectivity,
capable of almost any response to fascism's consolidation. More than one
found his way into the SA or the SS, but there were also Communist
efforts to organize these ragged gangs.[47]

Some later youth cultures, however, moved overtly in the direction of
resistance. By the end of the 1930s a less alienated, more respectable and
stable contingent of traditional working-class gangs had come into being.
Known as the Edelweiss Pirates, they obviously borrowed much from the
wild, homeless, criminal youth of the previous decade, but given the
labor shortages of the immediate pre–Second World War years they had
access to jobs and an endless supply of casual work, plus sustained connections to families, neighborhoods and former school friends. Thus they
exercised a territoriality based on homes, incomes, leisure sites, and
workplaces. Hiking, cycling, or hitchhiking for miles over the course of
a weekend, these clubs made the rounds of the countryside. Their nights
spent in bars, their days in odd jobs or avoiding work, lounging along
a canal or on the fairgrounds, these proliferating associations of wandering youth creatively resisted the bureaucratized routinization of life in
wartime Germany: "Master, give us cards,/ Master, give us pay./ We've
had enough of slaving,/ Women are better any day." The Pirates, like their
criminal predecessors (long since rounded up and sent to the front) took
names such as Navajos and Traveling Dudes. They defied bans on movement, bypassed police controls and ration books, prided themselves on
their freedoms (physical, sexual, and political), and sustained nights of

ribald singing in which official Nazi songs and sanctioned popular hits were adapted and reworked to espouse a stand of opposition. Glorying in Nazi-bashing, the Edelweiss Pirates seldom passed up an opportunity to beat up on the Hitler Youth, signalling a refusal to be subordinated. The Dusseldorf Pirates explained their slogan, "Eternal War on the Hitler Youth," by noting that every order given by the Nazi regime was premised on a threat.

The politics of the Pirates embraced the passive revolution of sensuality and pleasurable companionship but added a clarion call for freedom and physical resistance:

> Hitler's power may lay us low,
> And keep us locked in chains,
> But we will smash the chains one day,
> We'll be free again.
> We've got the knives and we'll get them out.
> We want freedom don't we boys?
> We're the fighting Navajos.

Hitler's authority was regarded as the absolute enemy, against which a guerrilla warfare was to be waged:

> Polar Bear, listen, we're talking to you,
> Our land isn't free, we're telling you true.
> Get out your cudgels and come into town
> And smash in the skulls of the bosses in brown.

A youth resistance that drew on class resentments and the politics of freedoms that the established Communist, socialist, and trade-union mobilizations could barely fathom (although one group of youth gangs in Leipzig with approximately fifteen hundred in its ranks did borrow from the radical tradition), the Edelweiss Pirates had, by the early 1940s, come to the attention of the Gestapo. It regarded them as agents of sabotage and demoralization. "The youths mentioned display an extraordinary degree of cynicism and impertinence in their behaviour towards their older work colleagues and superiors," noted a 1941 report on fifteen Pirate youths who were said to have been absent from work for a total of fourteen hundred hours between January and July, reducing the Reich's galvanized zinc production by 400,000 kilograms. Nazi officials worried that cliques among German youth threatened a "political, moral, and criminal subversion" of the young.

A series of raids crushed Pirate groups in Dusseldorf, Duisburg, Essen, and Wuppertal in December 1942, and a little over a year later the chief public prosecutor for Cologne claimed to have used "special procedures" to deal with a thousand or more such individuals. But the state needed proletarian youth in order to produce, so there could be no "final solution" for the young of the working class. Thus they continued to proclaim their independence in the formation of clubs that adopted militant-sounding names such as Halle's Proletarian Troops or, more commonly, designations of the culturally rebellious: Dresden's Mobs, Hamburg's Death's Head Gang, and Munich's Crews or Crowds. Late in 1944, with the Third Reich in ruins, members of the Edelweiss Pirates joined alien workers, escaped prisoners of war, and German antifascists in the debris of bombed Cologne, stunning Nazi officials with surprise attacks on military supply sites and mounting impressive strategic assaults on units of the Gestapo, Wehrmacht, and police. Twelve of these young rebels were promptly and publicly hanged in the working-class district they had fought to liberate.[48]

Among the more well-to-do youth of the upper middle class the swing movement served a similar, although less explicitly oppositional, function. In large urban centers such as Hamburg, the craze swept energetic youth into a carefree culture of dance hall abandon. "Swing" was a social dance based on the American Lindy Hop of the 1920s, emphasizing loose gyration and frenetic jiving; at its hottest it juiced up the watered-down jazz of the officially sanctioned clubs to a radically eroticized articulation of sensual casualness that translated into an implicit critique of National Socialist order. The swing youth wore their hair longish (male) and loose (female), and cultivated a casual demeanor that bordered on an embrace of decadence and sleaziness. They had the money, clothes, status, and brazen sense of self to frequent nightclubs, where they repeatedly violated Nazi injunctions against the "hot" jazz of Benny Goodman and other banned Jewish and African-American musicians, defaced signs prohibiting swing, pushed bands to test the limits of artistic censorship, and exuded a cultural rebelliousness that always spoke loudest in a voice of sexual nonconformity. In their defiant flouting of convention, appropriation of foreign (especially British and American) styles, tastes, and argot, friendships with Jews, and refusal to shut their ears to the Nazi-designated racially impure "nigger-like cacophony from the USA," swing youth were a thorn in the side of a culturally coercive state.

A February 1940 report on a swing festival in Hamburg codified the Nazi regime's discontent:

> The dancers were an appalling sight. None of the couples danced
> normally; there was only swing of the worst sort. Sometimes two boys
> danced with one girl; sometimes several couples formed a circle, linking

arms and jumping, slapping hands, even rubbing the backs of their heads together; and then, bent double, with the top half of the body hanging loosely down, long hair flopping into the face, they dragged themselves round practically on their knees. When the band played a rhumba, the dancers went into wild ecstasy. They all leaped around and joined in the chorus in broken English. The band played wilder and wilder items; none of the players was sitting down any longer, they all "jitterbugged" on the stage like wild creatures. Several boys could be observed dancing together, always with two cigarettes in the mouth, one in each corner.

By 1942, Himmler was advocating that swing ringleaders be incarcerated in concentration camps for two to three years, and fascism's thin skin was breaking out in violent antagonism to the Anglophile tendencies and mocking postures of those who regarded the Nazi state as "all lies, all rubbish." Practitioners of "cool," swing aficionados challenged with their bodies the rigidities, disciplines, and paramilitary regimen of everyday life under the Third Reich. Surrendering to rhythm and spontaneous movement, swing youth twirled and sleazed their way into the small hours, ears cocked to the aphrodisiac of jazz. The affected culture of the boys and girls of swing was a deliberately provocative challenge to the attempt to subordinate all aspects of life under the swastika to the state's pronounced understanding of order.

When leaders of swing in Hamburg resisted the demand that all teenagers join the Hitler Youth, repression followed quickly. Swing took its stand against Nazism's idealized constructions of gender identity—males were, in Hitler's words, to be "hard as Krupp steel, tough as leather, swift as greyhounds"—and paid for it in beatings, arrests, jailings, assignments to work gangs and concentration camps, spy reports, denunciations, ugly allegations of sexual deviance, and public humiliation. In cities such as Hamburg the dark night of fascist coercion was challenged by the light night of the "sleazy life." Sweeps of swing nights, when halls could be rented on the Rothenbaumschaussee, or premises secured at the dance casino Alsterpavillion (maliciously dubbed the "Jewish Aquarium" by the Nazis) netted the Gestapo hundreds of fingerprinted detainees: 408 in one such raid, 391 of whom were under the age of twenty-one. Most were released except for those ringleaders the authorities earmarked for special consideration, such as the nineteen-year-old "half-Jew" who carried the monicker Wolf.

The swings were hardly resistance fighters, but their defiant culturalism carried a sting nonetheless. "We were going to tell these dumb bastards that we were different, that was all," recalled swing leader Hans-Joachim

"Tommie" Scheel. As one member of a Kiel club, the Plutocrats, wrote to a friend who had left the city to travel: "Be a proper spokesman, ... won't you? ... make sure you're really casual, singing or whistling English hits all the time, absolutely smashed and always surrounded by really amazing women." The message moved with an internationalist tempo. In 1942, Parisian youth were arrested in the Metro by German soldiers and carted off to labor camps for the crime of dressing in "flash, impertinent, provocative suits and dresses, and wearing a badge with the words "*une France* swing dans *une Europe* zazoue." If not a revolutionary program, such words were at least a transgressive *style* subliminally resistant to fascism's every cherished value.[49] The music to which the swings snapped their fingers and jived in trance-like fixation on the intoxicating beat was the product of yet another oppressive racial order, one that predated fascism by more than a century and was destined to survive it by many generations.

PART VII
Making Cultures in the Heart of Capitalist Commodification

17. Ellen Simon, *Savoy Ballroom* (1937).

16

Blues, Jazz, and Jookin'

Nights of Soul and Swing

The Marxist historian Eric Hobsbawm discovered jazz at the age of sixteen. Hitler had just assumed power in Germany, and the Hobsbawm family, having fought a losing struggle against the economic slump in the Berlin movie business, returned to England. There, in a sparsely furnished depression-decade attic, the young Eric and a cousin hand-turned the gramophone as it cranked out classics such as the Fletcher Henderson band's "Sugar Foot Stomp" or "House of David Blues" and the Louis Armstrong–Earl Hines productions, "St. James Infirmary," "Knockin' a Jug," and "West End Blues." Twentieth-century adolescence seemed somehow quintessentially captured in the boys' hyperenthusiasm, consumption of junk food, and penchant for evening sociability. "We preferred to have these sessions at night," Hobsbawm recalls. "When the days were too long, we drew the curtains." When Duke Ellington came to London, his band booked into the ballroom of the Streatham Astoria for a midnight to early morning "breakfast dance" (Duke's recording of the same name was famous), the boys overreached their financial wherewithal to buy tickets. They nursed the single glass of beer they could afford and sat enthralled, "the image of the band burning itself on our brains forever." The money gone, the cousins ventured out into the dawn and walked the four miles to their suburban apartments. "I was hooked for good," confesses Hobsbawm.[1]

The history of jazz and of its folk predecessor, the blues, is a history of various fusions and cross-fertilizations, a creolization of culture and musical genres that begins with African enslavement, enforced transportation to the Americas, and the oppressive routines of work and life associated with particular regions such as those of the southern United States. Blues and, eventually, jazz had their beginnings in this slave society, where the rhythmic percussion and call-and-response shouting traditions of West Africa and the Americanized fieldhand slave came together, not in a racial sense, but in the conditions of life associated with southern plantations, work gangs, and, later, the beginnings of urbanized leisure.[2] Encouraged by some masters, the slaves who worked the rice, tobacco, and cotton plantations—or harvested grain, shucked corn, slaughtered animals, and otherwise provided for their own sustenance—punctuated and paced their work with song, as would the black prisoners on the chain gangs of the twentieth century.[3] Their rhythmic adaptation of "shouts" and "hollers" to their daily tasks and to the collective needs of slave people was a process of negotiating class exploitations at their most coercive and brutal, as well as acculturating persistent but increasingly distant African idioms to New World conditions and contexts, in which power and domination had bluntly racial content. The work song could be both "strident lament" and satirical improvisation, a voice of often transgressive inflections. Linked to a paced output, the quick-time singing overseers and masters saw only as a means of stepping up the tempo of production was extended by the singers into other areas, "puttin' on ole massa":

> Massa in the great house, counting out his money,
> Oh, shuck that corn and throw it in the barn.
> Mistis in the parlor, eating bread and honey,
> Oh, shuck that corn and throw it in the barn.

Songs also spelled out areas of private life to those denied such spaces, often designating the night as a peculiar preserve of some small measure of freedom,[4] which often unfolded in the gendered construction of sexuality:

> Saturday night and Sunday too
> Young gals on my mind.
> Monday morning 'way 'fore day,
> Old master's got me gwine.
> Peggy does you love me now?

For a people stripped and lashed of individuality, the slave song provided the possibility of self-expression in a social order that allowed African Americans so little voice.[5]

The peculiarities of the Deep South, the Mississippi Delta and its slave capital, New Orleans, proved a particularly fertile breeding ground for the cultural hybrid of African, European, and American forms. There the drumbeat of West African culture and its Caribbean counterparts could still be heard in Congo Square as late as the 1880s, and the dominance of French culture produced more space for the survival and expression of African forms in the looser religious context and more celebratory calendar of festivities. Complex religious and spiritual traditions intruded.[6] All of this produced a layered transplantation: distinctly American, drawing on English-language songs and on traditions and genres largely European, but with an unmistakable echo of a distant African past. Premised on a history of oppression and exploitation, uniquely American jazz and blues often managed to allude to the night's place of significance.[7] By the late nineteenth century two developments of paramount importance had emerged out of this context of creolization and transplantation.[8]

First, with the adaptation of spiritual and gospel themes, this music moved beyond the Delta and New Orleans. In the aftermath of slavery it figured forcefully in the self-definition of African Americans. As James Cone writes about growing up in Bearden, Arkansas, blacks worked long hours through the week in mills and factories and fields, and by Saturday night they were tired and weary but fundamentally in need of a process by which they could come to grips with themselves and the oppression they lived:

> They needed to express their moods and feelings, their joys and sorrows. They needed to refresh their spirits in the sound and rhythm of black humanity. And they did, sometimes peaceably and sometimes violently, often doing to each other what they wished they could do to white people.... In Bearden, the spirituals and the blues were a way of life, an artistic affirmation of the meaningfulness of black existence. No black person could escape the reality they expressed. B. B. King, Johnny Lee Hooker, and Mahalia Jackson created essential structures that defined my blackness. I affirmed the reality of the spirituals and blues as authentic expressions of my humanity, responding to them in the rhythms of dance. I therefore write about the spirituals and the blues because I AM THE BLUES and my LIFE IS A SPIRITUAL. Without them I cannot be.[9]

Second, the explosive economic dynamism, evident by the 1890s in the American conquest of longer-established but now declining nineteenth-century empires, situated the United States as the premier capitalist nation in the world, creating an expanding commercial marketplace of popular culture that translated into particular class possibilities for the emerging idiom of African-American folk music. Barely a generation removed from slavery, locked out of many occupations and economic and social possi-bilities by the deeply rooted segregationist practices that were everywhere in the republic of mass citizenship a legacy of slavery, African Americans moved quickly into mass entertainment and music: they became dancers, singers, musicians, comics, and actors. Often they eased their way into the performing arts via the racist stereotypes of the minstrel troupe which, by the 1850s, had become a staple of popular culture and in which there was increasing space for African-American performers by the 1880s and 1890s. That this "profession" of entertainment was a mere cut above that of the prostitute was reflected in the close connections that developed between black musicians and the brothel world of the urban tenderloins and vice districts. But in its evolving structures of simultaneous marginality *and* centrality to popular culture, the exceptional melange that was co-alescing as African-American music approached the twentieth century uninhibited by the cultural standards of the upper classes. Unique among nation-states, America spawned a distinctive modernist musical idiom that fused experiences of oppression (*race*) and exploitation (*class*) in which the initiative of the masses was relatively uncorrupted by elite sensibilities and strictures.[10] "Well the blues ain't nothin'/ But a workingman feelin' bad./ Well, its one of the worst old feelin's/ that any poor man's had."[11] As Iain Lang suggested decades ago, in the particular historical context of late-nineteenth-century America "only people insulated by class and poverty from cultural orthodoxy and convention could have created a new, independent, and dynamic musical language." In the freedoms af-forded by its academic illiteracy, this creative hybrid managed to reach beyond the sameness and social conventionality of a sort of European musical Esperanto, in which an assumption of the grammar of excellence and standards of beauty had ossified over the course of centuries.[12]

The blues evolved as songs of personal experience during African Americans' adjustment to their emancipation from slavery. Freedom contained many challenges and diffculties, some related to racism's con-tinuities, but others simply associated with lives now more open to choice and its consequences. These tensions often played out in the realm of gender relations: masculine–feminine difference, broken relationships, love's ups and downs, and sexuality's balance sheet of gain and loss.[13] Early folk blues were simple and repetitive, albeit often with irregular chord sequences, and easily standardized as the genre developed. Although the earliest use of "blues" in an African-American song title was identified by a folklorist in 1898, it did not appear on sheet music until the im-mediate pre–First World War years, when "Memphis Blues" and "Dallas Blues" were published. Commonplace use of the term in the United States was a nineteenth-century, apparently largely rural, phenomenon. (In English popular usage since the 1500s it had described a troubled or anxious state of mind, and the 1600s colloquialism "the blue devils" meant evil spirits that caused despair.)[14] Capturing the low spirits of disappointment and frustration, associated with routines of loss—in which love, work, and violence figured centrally as sites of complaint, and sex and mobility as illusory roads to freedom and fulfillment—the blues grew out of the post-Emancipation and Reconstruction (1863–1877) climate of intense African-American expectation that was destined to sour in the New South's racial retrenchment of Jim Crow laws, the squalid economics of sharecropping, and the embittered revenge of the rising Ku Klux Klan and the lynch mob.

Former slaves tasted the first exhilarating breath of freedom in this period, only to find themselves the losers in a "counterrevolution of property." A black preacher urged his peers in Florida to use freedom to redefine social relationships in ways that reached past the age-old racial subordinations of power and its association with place: "You mus' move clar away from de ole places what you knows, ter de new places what you don't know, whey you kin raise up yore head douten no fear o' Marse Dis un Marse Tudder."[15] If there was, in fact, no such place to go, some black males (who could shed familial relations more easily than women) did embrace the life of the "travellin' man," with its mythology of hard-living masculine independence; the immediate gratifications of drink and women were counterposed to the immobilizing stabilities of jobs and homes.

Small wonder that this period of male African-American mobility was also the age of the railroad, which would figure centrally in the blues tradition—less as a metaphor of capitalist industrialization, alienating technology, and mechanization, than as a symbolic engine of the personal capacity to escape oppression: "Gonna catch a train fifteen coaches long,/ When you look for me, I'll be gone."[16] That this process was gendered was unmistakable: "When a woman blue, she hang her little head and cry,/ When a man get blue, he grab that train and ride."[17] Associated with a late-nineteenth-century tradition of wandering singers such as "Ragtime Texas" Henry Thomas, father figure of the East Texas blues, the railroad song was also easily adaptable to ribald sexualization. The "Easy Rider Blues" of Thomas's Texas successor, Blind Lemon Jefferson, used the metaphor of the train to plead erotic desire and mount the bluesman's usual claim to prowess:

> Now tell me where my easy rider gone
> Tell me where my easy rider gone
> *I need one of these* women always in the wrong ...
> The train I ride don't burn no coal at all

> Train I ride don't burn no coal at all
> The coal I'm burning: everybody says its cannonball.[18]

In the late-nineteenth-century context of African-American freedom thwarted, blacks attempted to lose their discontents and constraints in these fused meanings of mobility and sexuality. There was no escape into private, individualized solutions to the collective experience of racial oppression and the related poverty and material want of a class-ordered society: "I dreamed last night, thought the whole world round was mine,/ I woke up this mornin' didn't have one lousy dime."[19] For all the reverence invested in the canonization of the travelin' bluesman, however, and the life of independence painted in colorful strokes of liberation's wanton indulgences, the songs themselves often reveal another side of freedom's road: "I'm awful lonesome, all alone and blue/ Ain't got no body to tell my troubles to," or, "Money's all gone, I'm so far from home,/ I just sit here and cry and moan."[20]

Blues, then, was not so much a language of overt rebellious challenge as a necessary precursor to an oppositional stand, an articulation of grievance and a negotiation of unfairness that had crystallized into a powerful presence in the black plebeian and working-class community by the opening decades of the twentieth century.[21] Born of freedom, it was nurtured in freedom's denials. As the legendary bluesman Lightnin' Hopkins noted, blues came "out of the fields," and its origins in work songs are undeniable.[22] But it moved easily with the migrations of black Americans into urban settings and articulated universal, rather than particularistic, themes of class, race, and gender identities. By 1900 there was a black urban audience for blues in cities such as Washington, New Orleans, New York, Philadelphia, St. Louis, Chicago, Baltimore, Memphis, and Atlanta, where tens of thousands of African Americans had settled.[23] If the punctuated rhythms of blues had their origins in the plantation's profit needs, by the later nineteenth century its form and content were the antithesis of output's sense of rural toil's order. Personalized, but always striking a chord in the collective consciousness of African Americans, blues was a cautionary tale, a road map whereby the dispossessed could ease their way through the difficulties of their transformed but still highly constrained lives. "My blues is built on human beings," noted the New Orleans Storyville blues guitarist Lonnie Johnson, on "their heartaches and the shifts they go through.... It's understanding others, ... that's what makes a good blues singer."[24]

Those who made this intuitive grasp of oppression the foundation of their personal exploration of freedom embraced travel and recreation, a life of pleasures that signaled a deep alienation from the conventional ethics and values of either work or sexuality. Their music was an artistic statement—sensual and secular—that appeared both blasphemous and antithetical to the material culture of genteel acquisition which drove capitalism's message of subordination deep into the minds and bodies of its most oppressed and exploited victims: "White folks on the sofa/ Nigger on the grass/ White man is talking low/ Nigger is getting ass."[25]

The first fifty years of the twentieth century would see the blues ensconced in African-American communities.[26] It was an art form that intersected a particular sociology of class and race formation as black migrations to the North and West culminated in the making of the ghetto and its layered subcultures, in which blues figured forcefully.[27] As a treatment of Malcolm X's background, "The Nightmare Night," stresses, these years of black movement and urban settlement were never separable from the ugly darkness and intimidating violence of racist America.[28] This structural context of oppression was also embedded in the exploitive political economy of the emerging African-American mass market, where "race" records and nightclubs generated profits for some blacks, but where the large money almost always went to powerful white corporations and promoters or the criminal underworld.[29]

Memphis's Beale Street was a case in point, and a corrective to seeing the blues world through the filter of the Harlem or Southside Chicago club. The Memphis red-light district was a powerful attraction, drawing the marginalized ethnicities of the not yet blended American melting pot to an array of material and cultural possibilities: Jews owned the pawnshops and grocery stores; Greeks established the restaurants; Italians ran the saloons and grocery stores as well as the enticing numbers racket; and African Americans were both customers and performers in the Beale Street bars. Marijuana and cocaine, dispensed legally from drug stores as late as 1906, were readily available. Moonshine liquor, despite Prohibition, was a mainstay of the speakeasies and "blind tigers" that catered to crowds looking for prostitutes, gaming tables, drink, and the lively blues of black musicians. The hedonistic subculture of Beale Street epitomized the tough outsider status of the blues and its unmistakable if ambivalent integration into the criminalized milieu of fast money and endless rounds of dissipation.

Sunnyland Slim recalls Beale Street as a procession of "rough joints": the Panama, the Harlem Night Club, the Goshorn Quarters, the Hole in the Wall. "I used to make all them joints and there was no closin' at that time," he remembers, recounting a nightly round of bar hops that would net him, in the prosperity of the 1940s, twenty-five to thirty dollars. No other locale produced lyrics as aggressively antagonistic to authority, defiantly violent and self-destructive, and brazenly masculine as Memphis. That this was not purely and simply gender subordination and male power was evident in Bessie Smith's angry gutteral rasp in "Beale Street Mama": "Don't *mess around* with me." The classic female blues number, "Tain't Nobody's Business," was popularized by Bessie Smith and Billie Holiday, but its folk chorus origin was a Beale Street anthem before it appeared on the national "race" records:

> It ain't nobody's business, honey,
> How I spend my money,
> It ain't nobody's business but mine,
> It ain't nobody's business, honey,
> Where in the world I get my money,
> It ain't nobody's business but my own.

Living poor and being powerless, as Bill Barlow notes, were the hallmarks of Memphis blues, but those drawn to Beale Street lived on marginality's many-sided sociabilities and sensualities. They knew about addictions and assaults firsthand, the "killing you by degrees" that haunted the decisions made in the Memphis night, yet they returned time and time again to the many indulgences of life in the blues. A black disc jockey who had worked the minstrel circuit and ended up in Memphis as a dancer and mimic impressed B. B. King with his wit and wisdom. "If a white man could be black on Beale Street for just one Saturday night," he was fond of saying, "he'd never want to be white again."[30]

By the early 1920s a series of small, often locally oriented black-owned record companies had pioneered the release of music by blues artists nurtured in such settings as Beale Street, especially the salable women singers who had loyal homegrown followings. But these efforts were faltering by mid-decade, for the small companies lacked the capacity to advertise and distribute nationally; most produced only a handful of recordings and failed to survive more than a few years. The ground they had arduously cultivated was quickly eaten up by the three large, predatory white-owned record companies. Okeh Records, the smallest of these, had broken the race barrier by releasing Mamie Smith's rendition of the vaudeville blues performer Perry "Mule" Bradford's "Crazy Blues" in 1920, selling a phenomenal one million presses in its first year. In what would prove a sadly repetitive process of bilking black artists of their rightful royalties and fees, Okeh paid Bradford less than half the $40,000 to which he was legally entitled, pressuring him to waive his financial rights.

Bradford replied: "Please be advised that the only thing Bradford waives is the American Flag."

The real flag waiving in race recording, however, was being done by the two larger companies, Columbia and Paramount. At Columbia the incomparable Bessie Smith recorded 160 titles between 1923 and 1933, thirty-eight of them copyrighted in her own name. She may have sold as many as six to ten million records, some of her smash hits topping out at 800,000 in the first seven months. Yet she never received a penny in royalties, being paid a total of less than $30,000 in fees and guarantees over the decade of her prodigious production. In the later 1920s, race records were selling five to ten million blues discs a year. By 1928, more than five hundred titles had been released, and leading mainstream labels were devoting one-fifth of their catalogues to blues recordings. The Great Depression crushed this emerging market, but blues records resurfaced as a commercially viable genre after the Second World War. Two émigré Polish Jews, Phil and Leonard Chess, one-time allies of Al Capone and operators of a string of Southside Chicago bars and clubs, launched Aristocrat Records (renamed Chess in 1950) and signed the leading bluesmen of the late 1940s. They rode a wave of increasingly urban and electrified blues into the 1950s, recording the city's talented roster of performers, from Muddy Waters and Howlin' Wolf to Sonny Boy Williamson II, Chuck Berry, Bo Didley, Sunnyland Slim, Junior Wells, James Cotton, and Otis Spann. With the emergence of rock-and-roll in the 1950s and the "British invasion" of the 1960s, blues music was appropriated by whites, whose fame and fortune of course phenomenally outstripped those black artists from whom they "borrowed." Elvis Presley swiveled "Hound Dog" to the pinnacle of rock-and-roll stardom; its creator, Willa Mae "Big Mamma" Thornton, had recorded the song on the Duke label, a Houston-based blues and gospel outfit notorious for ill-treating its artists.[31]

Beyond the sociologies and political economies of blues lie its aesthetics. The black migrations and urban class formations of the post–First World War years produced a cultural context in which blues was inseparable from the night, with respect not only to where and when it was performed but also to its dark content and unmistakable affiliations. Sterling A. Brown's poetic tribute to Ma Rainey acknowledged the centrality of a troubled darkness: "It rained fo' days an' the skies was dark as night/ Trouble take place in the lowlands at night." The blues artist Leroy Carr recorded, in a single two-day session, "Midnight Hour Blues," "How Long Has That Evening Train Been Gone?" "Lonesome Nights," and "Moonlight Blues," and a number of other titles, most of which made the unmistakable connection between blues and "the wee midnight hours, long 'fore the break of day,/ When the blues creep up on you and carry your mind away." The legendary Robert Johnson—whose fatalism was expressed in acknowledgement that dark forces (including the devil he supposedly had a pact with) were pushing him to a supernatural cross-roads—lived and died his music: he was murdered at the young age of twenty-seven. As a music of darkness, the blues was seldom far removed from the night's duality, expressed in Charley Patton's deliberately two-sided "Moon Going Down': "Oh yea, evil walkin' at midnight/ When I heard the local blow/ I was evil at night when I/ Heard the local blow/ I got to see my rider/ When she's getting on board."[32]

As centrally important as work was to the evolution of rural blues, then, in the genre's traveling fluidity and ultimate urbanization the pleasures and problems of the night came to override the routine tasks of the day. It was almost as though the emerging black working class of mid-twentieth-century America found a voice to articulate its *estrangement* from labor: a focus on eroticism, sexual need (male and female), and a raucous refusal of conventional order chipped subversively away at the work ethic and its obligatory subordinations of the self.[33] The suffocating racism of America, bred in the bone of generations of black workers, may well have overridden the often unsubtle extractions of the capitalist system, and black music was perhaps overdetermined by this oppressive weight of prejudice.[34] As Huddie "Leadbelly" Ledbetter indicated in the power-fully evocative "Bourgeois Blues," however, class power was not separable from racial exclusions:

> Me and my wife run all over town,
> Everywhere we'd go the people would turn us down ...
> Lawd, in the bourgeois town, ooh the bourgeois town,
> I got the bourgeois blues, gonna spread the news aroun' ...
> Me and Marthy we was standin' upstairs,
> I heard a white man say, "I don't want no niggers up there." ...
> Tell all the colored folks t'listen to me,
> Don't try to buy no home in Washington, D.C.

To be sure, bluesmen did address class grievance: "Ninety men were laid off at a railroad shop,/ Ninety men were laid off, Lord, at a railroad shop,/ And the strike in Chicago, Lordy Lord, it just won't stop." L. C. Williams's "Strike Blues," sounded, however, not the call for class struggle but the worried refrain of what protest could cost African Americans: "No more 'joying, no more 'joying, baby, no more fun for me./ Well, you know, my strike is on, and its trying to get the best of me." The concern of traditional rural blues with the weight of work's oppressions, articulated in early African-American ballads such as "John Henry," found detours in the alienated refusals of the interwar period and the depression decade's laments about lack of employment. Mississippi John Hurt's "Spike Driver Blues" struck a new note of separation, distancing the blues from the entanglements of exploited labor: "This is the hammer/ that killed/ John Henry;/ But it won't kill me;/ But it won't kill me;/ Ain't gonna kill me."[35]

All of this drove the blues inevitably in the direction of the night, a fertile ground in which to plant other worry and anxiety:

> Black Jack Frost laid out at midnight, nightmares right 'til
> the break of day,
> Black Jack Frost laid out at midnight, nightmares right 'til
> the break of day,
> What's the use of lovin' some woman, some man done stole
> your girl away?[36]

But the night was equally receptive to the rollicking good times that were the trademark of fun-loving blues pranksters. Charley Patton, a mercurial rambler known for his womanizing, eight marriages, taste for drink, flamboyant dress, and the inspirational dreams out of which he composed much of his social commentary blues, also wrote songs espousing indulgence and excess: "I love to fuss and fight,/ I love to fuss and fight,/ Lord, and get sloppy drunk off a bottle of bond/ And walk the streets all night."[37] In the "street-wise, self-confident, jive-talking blues rebel" Peetie Whitestraw, a St. Louis blues guitarist and pianist who aligned himself consciously with the dark forces of the devil (and who appeared in the pages of Ralph Ellison's Invisible Man in 1952), the blues found a spokesman for a program of raw vitality in which work was most often a secondary consideration.[38]

Indeed, among most bluesmen the legacies of post-Emancipation freedom lived in the almost mythic elevation of independence into an ironically understated marginalization of the structured responsibilities of the day (work and family) and a pressured reification of the possibilities of the night (sex and style, both of which could extend into realms of substance abuse, violence, and the travelin' loner's alienation).[39] Those blues figures, and there were many, who died tragically and achieved a certain immortal status—Whitestraw, Robert Johnson, Blind Lemon Jefferson—exuded a hypermasculinity that sexualized gendered freedom as footloose independence and gendered sexuality as a predatory process of male mobility. Work, in this sense the alienation of being, was tied directly to freedom's fundamental constraints, which included not only the repressive institutions of the police and the church but the family itself: "I got a job in a steel mill,/ Trucking steel like a slave,/ Five long years every Friday/ I went straight home with all my pay." With the language of work blurring into a language of sexual conquest, blues artists mechanized the sexual as they offered an erotic escape from the mechanical:

> Well, I'm gonna race your motor, baby,
> I'm gonna heist your hood.
> Spark plugs getting old, generator ain't putting out good.
> But, oooh, yeah, let me overhaul your little machine.

Robert Johnson's "Terraplane Blues" continued this motorized metaphor:

> I'm going h'ist your hood, mama,
> I'm bound to check your oil....
> I'm gonna get deep down in this connection,
> Whoo-well keep on tangling with the wires
> And when I mash down on your little starter,
> then your spark plug would give me fire.[40]

In this blues tradition, sexual passion was, like the wage, something to be spent, not saved and certainly not savored in relationships of confining familialism. Mercy Dee's "After the Fight" codified the capacity to equate waged labor and the work of family life: "I know I'll always love a woman, and I'm gonna always try and treat 'em right./ But 'fore one of 'em marries me off to a job it'll be a long, long time after the fight."[41]

This trajectory could have devolved into mere misogyny had it not been for the powerful presence of a contingent of blueswomen whose strength of self-presentation ensured that the music carried a message of potential gender equality. These black divas of the blues scene, whose popularity and presence in the rising race-record market of the 1920s far outstripped that of the men, explored the same themes as bluesmen and with the same intensity. They lived female versions of the cherished independence that had its work and sexual connotations. If anything, the blueswomen of the 1920s were raunchier, more raucous, and certainly richer than their largely rural male counterparts, who seldom made it in the New York scene that a woman such as Bessie Smith could, for a time, actually conquer. Hard-drinking, uncompromisingly in control, sexual predators at ease in the conquest of their hired musicians or slipping into the transgressive world of bisexuality, many of the women of the early blues lived by Ma Rainey's dictum: "Take me to the basement.... Let's get dirty and have some fun." Rainey, fond of young men and young women, was defiantly unrepentant, even in the face of arrests at intimate "women only" parties: "I went out last night with a crowd of my friends,/ It must a been womens 'cause I don't like no mens." Among the most notable of these female performers, rural born but eventually urban based, were Bessie Smith, Rainey, Victoria Spivey, Mamie Smith, Alberta Hunter, Ethel Waters, and Ida Cox. Innovators whose instruments were their voices, such women introduced blues to mainstream white audiences, paved the way for African-American entrance into the commercial music business, and stood at the very center of the blended potpourri of performance— minstrelsy, vaudeville, burlesque—that came together in the tours organized by the Theatre Owners Booking Association (TOBA, known among blues artists as Tough on Black Asses), which presented "classic blues" to discerning black audiences throughout the United States.[42]

"Classic" in their concerns, the blueswomen reiterated the common themes of all blues, their fundamental materiality moving easily into the universal oppositions of work/life. Ma Rainey's "Misery Blues" declared bluntly, "Work is the thing that's breaking my heart,/ So I've got those mean ol' misery blues."[43] Blues women could be as anarchically reckless as their male counterparts. Merline Johnson's "Reckless Life Blues" gave wild drinking, gambling, and violence a female drive. Julia Moodie's "Mad Mama's Blues" took this pent-up rage and extended it to a night of urban conflagration: "Give me gun powder, give me dynamite,/ Yes, I'm gonna wreck this city,/ Gonna blow it up tonight."[44] Small wonder that New Left anarchist revolutionaries in the 1960s reached back to Moodie's lyrics as confirmation of their politics, reprinting such lines in the English and American journals *Heatwave* and *Resurgence*. But the most potent legacy of the women blues singers of the 1920s was the message of sexual liberation, which was presented with a libidinal gusto previously unmatched in the history of popular culture.[45]

Few bluesmen equalled the crude explicitness of these "down and dirty" women, whose records were marketed on the basis of their brazen raunchiness, often directed at male inadequacy: "Here's my baby all out of breath,/ Been workin' all night and ain't done nothing yet,/ What's wrong with that thing—that ting-a-ling,/ I've been pressing your button and your bell won't ring." The womanizing central to the travelin' man drew female blues singers such as Clara Smith into blunt rejoinder: "I wear my skirt up to my knees,/ And whip that jelly with whom I please." Lil Johnson's "Hottest Gal in Town" articulated the frank desire that burned sensuality into the soul of audiences captivated by the public exhibition of erotic need:

> He's the kind of man I want around,
> Handsome and tall and a teasing brown,
> He's got to wake me every morning 'bout half past three,
> Kick up my furnace and turn on my heat,
> Churn my milk, cream my wheat,
> Brown my biscuits, and chop my meat.
> He's long and tall, and that ain't all,
> He's got to be just like a cannonball.
> That's why I want him around
> 'Cause I'm the hottest gal in town.

Playfully dressing sexuality in metaphors of cooking, women posed erotic pleasures in a feminine imagery easily grasped by the black sisters they were addressing, moving past the representations of mechanization favored by their male counterparts:

> Men, they call me oven
>   say that I'm red hot
> They say I got something
>   the other gals ain't got...
> I can strut my pudding
>   spread my grease with ease
> 'Cause I know my onions
>   that's why I always please.

It was the irrepressible Bessie Smith, in songs such as "Kitchen Man" and "Empty Bed Blues," who pushed such associations to their limits:

> His jelly roll is so nice and hot
> Never fails to hit the spot...
> His frankfurters are oh so sweet
> How I love his sausage meat
> I'm wild about my kitchen man.

Undisputed "Empress of the Blues" in the 1920s, Smith, who got her start singing in Tennessee gin mills, was initially rejected by record companies as "too rough"—"Check all your razors and your guns,/ We're gonna be wrestlin' when the wagon comes.../ Gimme a reefer and a gang of gin,/ Slay me 'cause I'm in my sin"—but later profited enormously from her refusal to take a back seat to any bluesman in her open assault on prudery: "He boiled my cabbage and he made it awful hot./ Then he put in the bacon and overflowed the pot."[46]

More than any other blueswoman, Bessie Smith captured the two-sided meaning of the blues. Reveling in the nightlife of the urban underworld, at home in the dark cultures of marginality that afforded her bisexuality, alcoholism, and notorious rages a space unavailable to her in the U.S.

mainstream—and certainly closed to the poor African-American men and women whom Smith considered her audience—Bessie oscillated between excessive generosity and violent abuse. She was notorious in the black community for her outrageously inflammatory behavior, good and bad. Courageous in the face of male violence and Ku Klux Klan attack, she stood her ground with scurrilous invective and the strength of an inner rage bred of years of racist ostracism and oppression. She had no time for the effete liberals who courted her as the erotic underside of the Harlem Renaissance, but neither was she terribly considerate of those in her own entourage who might, for whatever reason, draw her ire. Self-conflicted and deeply troubled, Smith was a woman who, in the words of one admirer, performed like "a woman cutting her heart open with a knife." Neither did she lower the blade against those who wronged her in particular or women and African Americans in general. "Get your pistol, I've got mine,/ I've been mistreated and I don't mind dyin'," warned Bessie in "Sinful Blues." No other woman blues wailer, save perhaps her mentor and long-time supporter Ma Rainey, was so unambiguously in touch with the poverty and injustice associated with being poor and black in white America.

Two songs summarize Smith's life. One of her last depression-decade recordings at Columbia, a somewhat embittered "Nobody Knows You When You're Down and Out," reflected the unfortunate doldrums into which her career had sunk. The song would prove doubly tragic when the Empress of the Blues died following a car accident in the late 1930s (in part, it was said, because doctors hastened to attend to injured whites before they helped the dying singer). But if Smith had a signature piece, it was probably the unrepentantly defiant "Tain't Nobody's Business If I Do": "If I go to church on Sunday,/ Then just shimmy down on Monday,/ Tain't nobody's business if I do do do do." Known in every speakeasy from Chattanooga to Chicago to Cincinnati, a shameless frequenter of the "buffet flats" that catered to sexually transgressive black railroad crews and traveling musicians, Smith lived her life outside conventional rules.[47] She managed to mythologize her presence in the African-American world of the interwar period; her exclamatory "I never heard of such shit!" often led into some tirade that would within days be the talk of whatever town she was passing through. The Harlem of the 1920s had a phrase for behaviors whose voluble volatility, sheer brazenness, and uncultured defiance resonated with African Americans all too acclimatized to resignation and silent resentment: "I never heard such Bessie Smith!"[48]

Bessie Smith of course proved an inspiration to later generations of musicians, most especially rock diva Janis Joplin. Other white rock musicians who assimilated the blues drew particularly on the plethora of talent that had traveled the twentieth-century underground railway connecting the rich traditions of Delta blues to the northern ghetto to the undisputed capital of post–Second World War American blues culture—Chicago. Muddy Waters, Howlin' Wolf, Lightnin' Hopkins, Sunnyland Slim, Willie Dixon, Junior Wells, Buddy Guy, and many others were a transitional generation that linked the sorrowful lyrics, pulsating rhythms, and mythical aura of the legendary masters to the increasingly electrified and driving beat of the northern city.[49] In this heady concoction of past and present, the blues roots of rock would bring Robert Johnson and his peers to life in the robust crossroads of the 1960s.[50] Through the long blues night that reached from the "classic" creations of the 1920s to the adaptations of the 1960s walked the ghost of tradition: "That unseen eye reminds me of a midnight dream/ It reminds me of someone, someone I have never seen."[51]

The "Unseen Eye" of Sonny Boy Williamson II looks back to turn-of-the-century New Orleans, that cradle of creolization where slave song, Caribbean voodoo, African idioms, and French instrumentation came together in a unique musical creation. By the 1880s New Orleans boasted a distinct population of *gens de couleur*, freed slaves who had assimilated with French settlers and their descendants. Their dialect was French, their evolving social life increasingly indebted to the Mediterranean and Catholic tradition of carnival, with its profusion of fraternal (burying) societies, public festivities, and parades. The French influence was felt in New Orleans not only in language and words but in sound, the woodwinds and marching bands early making their mark on the Crescent City, where they adapted well to a culture seemingly always on parade and display. Moreover, it was one that gave a high priority to the pleasures of life (sex and sociability, food and drink, and the sensuality of sound).

As a cultural and economic hub of the Deep South, moreover, New Orleans was a magnet for many musical forms, from the funeral dirge to the concert ensemble. The most important venues were undoubtedly the sporting houses, saloons, nightclubs, brothels, bistros, barrelhouses, and dance halls of America's premier city of vice. "Jelly Roll" Morton, disowned by his parents for playing the New Orleans houses of ill repute, was one of the many piano players who could bring in as much as fifteen to eighteen dollars a night, an unheard-of amount that outpaced the earnings of horn players (whose job security was also minimal) by as much as nine to one. The atmosphere of carnal sensuality eased together varying strands of rural migrant blues, honky-tonk piano (popularized by the St. Louis partnership of Scott Joplin's ragtime and a rare white who was willing to publish the music, John Stillwell Stark), and small, wind-instrument bands that adapted to the sexualized "slow drag" dancing of the New Orleans night. Few if any of the thousands of musicians who worked this turn-of-the century milieu read music or the written word; they played by ear, their technique displayed in good-natured but highly competitive "carving contests" of improvisation.[52]

The music born of this moment, originally designated "jass," was defined by its rough proletarian and plebeian edge, its raucous and unmistakably sexual energy, and its essential urban character. "If I wanted to make a living I had to be rowdy like the other group," remembered the high-caste Creole violinist Paul Dominguez in disgust. "I had to jazz it or rag it or any other damn thing." The man Dominguez blamed for this degeneracy was Charles "Buddy" Bolden, a tough black barber who had emerged out of the blues and funeral-march ranks to play the roustabout's morgue, Tin Type Hall, using his cornet to scream his way into cakewalking hip-swinging improvisation, his trumpet blaring in the streets to announce a dance or assembly in the park. By 1897 his band was filling the dance halls and streets of New Orleans; a decade later he was gone, either to an insane asylum or to the minstrel circuit of the north. But in the interval, Bolden had pushed blues in new directions. After hearing him play in Plaquemine, Louisiana, in 1906, thirteen-year-old Clarence "Frog-man" Williams hotfooted it to New Orleans: "I had never heard anything like that before in my whole life," said the boy in awe. Bolden's inspired rough form found a fertile spawning ground in the newly created thirty-eight-block red-light district called Storyville (named after the alderman whose panicked ordinance restricted sex-for-sale to a designated area); there jazz came alive, a music of the night that, in parts of New Orleans at least, helped push the hours of sunlight into the shadows: "I could sit right here and think a thousand miles away,/ Got the blues so bad I cannot remember the day."[53]

Storyville was shut down in 1917; born of panic, it was closed in the same spirit of impulsive fear, the United States Navy running scared of its potential devastations.[54] With the nascent jazz community of New Orleans now left homeless, the musicians scattered to search out work throughout the United States, following the same northern and western migratory routes as their rural blues cousins. More than blues, however, jazz had attracted white enthusiasts. A group of white kids who stood open-mouthed as they drank in the new music at one Storyville cabaret, the 101 Ranch, would later form the Original Dixieland Jazz Band and introduce white New Yorkers to jazz at the Reisenweber Café on Columbus Circle.[55]

Jazz moved with the black migrants. St. Louis drew musicians from the Mississippi Valley, Kansas City from the Oklahoma–Texas hinterland. Northern industrial cities such as Chicago and Detroit and eastern seaboard metropolises such as New York attracted budding jazzmen from throughout the United States. The music soon developed enclaves of white support, a body of white practitioners (many of whom were Jewish), and a diluted style known as Tin Pan Alley which infused a smoothed jazz into the nightclubs of the 1920s. A domesticated variant soon evolved as the dominant idiom of popular music and dance, bringing Sophie Tucker, for example, to prominence. The Lindy Hop, the Black Bottom, the Charleston, and the Big Apple carried a taste of Harlem dance halls and obscure "jook" joints into white cabarets, creating something of a moral furor. Exemplars of virtue such as the Ladie's Home Journal were calling for an end to the madness in 1921: "Unspeakable jazz must go!" Nevertheless, Bud Freeman, a white musician, recalls the totalizing captivation of the music and dance of that time: "We did not live as other people did. Music was twenty-four hours a day.... bodies seemed glued together, as though they were trying to move through each other." The cornet-blowing Bix Beiderbecke remains a staple in the mythology of America's all too rare avant-garde, a soul lost in the pursuit of his sound's purity. Relinquishing wealth, station, philistine comforts, and acquisitions, as well the security of his bourgeois upbringing, Beiderbecke lived the fast indulgence of the jazz life until it overtook him.[56]

The center of jazz shifted from Chicago in the early 1920s to New York's Harlem later in the decade, and blacks often played in the increasingly larger white bands that packed ballrooms such as Roseland. To be sure, some of the white jazzmen lived as proverbial "outsiders," and even in the most sedate clubs the atmosphere was seldom untouched by the persona of a music that cut loose in leisure's darkest hours. Clubs came alive with "night people" on the weekends—"gamblers, bootleggers, madams and their entourages." "You may not make much money," one black musician told midwesterner Hoagy Carmichael, "but you won't get hostile with yourself."

Tension did exist in the jazz world, however, and it was never far removed from differences that turned on race.[57] The unmistakable divide that separated the "hot jazz" of a young Louis Armstrong and lesser known black musicians from the emerging "swing" of Benny Goodman, Artie

Shaw, and others was impossible to miss. The former found its nurturing ground not in the public night of the metropolitan clubs but in the house-rent parties of Chicago's Southside and New York's Harlem. Speakeasy jams gave musicians the freedom to wail. In Kansas City's gangster-controlled tenderloin district, for instance, jazz remained a significant presence late into the 1930s, connected to its blues sibling. But as the "Jazz Age" wound down in the late 1920s and swing's unanticipated popularity reconfigured the class and race components of audiences and musicians, authentic jazz was exiled to the margins, a casualty of spawning too many fashionable and accommodating reflections of itself.[58]

If the hottest of the swing bandleaders, Benny Goodman, lived the jazzman's life of the night (he once declared, "There are more towns in America that I have only seen after dark than I care to think about"), he still stood light years, and lucrative earnings, apart from the old New Orleans traditionalists such as Kid Ory, Jelly Roll Morton, and King Oliver.[59] George Dixon, who played with the Sammy Stewart band, was not alone in remembering lynchings, Jim Crow ordinances, even white southern paternalists marching on stage to reclaim their runaway workers. Aesthetically too the rift between white and black was quite acute: African-American jazzmen provided much of the raw imagination and innovative improvisation that had been critical to the genre since its birth in New Orleans at the turn of the century; whites, however, were taking the biggest public bows and certainly drawing the best paychecks, turning jazz, via swing, into a crooning commercialism. "Give me Sinatra's money," mocked the black jazz singer Billy Eckstine, "and I will give him my voice."[60]

But the transition in jazz idiom and its popular diffusion were not without their benefits. For one thing, as swing captured American popular culture in the post-1935 years, the black founders managed a modest revival and exported their original jazz to an increasingly receptive Europe.[61] For another, at the intersections of a modulated jazz and blues the great Billie Holiday found a niche. Continuing in the tradition of Bessie Smith, dazzling audiences in the late 1930s, she recorded the stunningly poignant "Strange Fruit," its gruesome imagery and jarring juxtapositions purposively constructed to haunt a self-selecting white audience that could be expected to cringe at the horror of the lynch mob:

> Black bodies swinging in the southern breeze
> Strange fruit hanging from the poplar trees
> Pastoral scene of the gallant south
> The bulging eyes and the twisted mouth
> Scent of magnolia, sweet and fresh
> Then the sudden smell of burning flesh[62]

In other songs, her tempo slowed from that of her predecessor blues-women, Holiday explored the longings of love she herself would persistently be denied:

> The night is cold
> And I'm so all alone
> I'd give my soul just to call you my own
> Got a moon above me
> But no one to love me
> Lover man where can you be

The finest of jazz singers to come out of the 1930s and 1940s, Billie Holiday's life would end in tragedy, like that of so many performers of her generation. But she had done with her voice and its dissonant notes what a new generation of jazz innovators, pioneers of bebop, would do with their horns: chill the blood so that the soul could warm.[63]

The success of "Strange Fruit" was indicative of a shift in the climate of race relations in America. Entertainers such as Paul Robeson, whatever their field and however much they were still victimized by racist oppression, were increasingly acknowledged as legitimate artists. Black workers were fighting their way into both jobs and unions as the hungry 1930s gave way to the labor shortages and productive needs of the Second World War era, and the postwar prosperity gradually and partially eased African Americans into the occupational mainstream. Although the "progressive" milieu was not without its differences on the "black question," left organizations did wage serious battles against the structures and practices of racist segregation and exclusion. As the United States armed forces confronted desegregation, the beginnings of a working-class-led black civil rights movement flared in A. Philip Randolph's challenging pressures on the White House to shift the unequal terms of material trade within a racialized American order. All of this set the stage for a volatile progressive cultural context, leavened by race rebellion, in which black workers fought the stigma of racism and oppression in a politics not only of reform demands and rare adherence to a revolutionary program but of *style*. Even the zoot suit could be a brash statement of independence from the conformist black petit bourgeois and the demands for quiet, servile subordination that emanated from every corner of white power and authority. Ralph Ellison wondered at the mysteries of this moment, asking in the 1943 *Negro Digest* whether "the zoot suit conceals profound political meaning."[64]

More pointedly, Duke Ellington's fusion of swing jazz and blues in the musical revue Jump for Joy (1941) captured the particular quest for social significance, sensitivity to race, and break from past stereotypes that typified a period of Popular Front politics and musical explorations. Premising his musical commentary on the thought of Langston Hughes, Ellington contended that "the Negro is the creative voice of America.... we fought America's wars, provided her labor, gave her music, kept alive her flickering conscience, prodded her on toward the yet unachieved goal, democracy." Claiming that "a statement of social protest ... should be made without saying it, and this calls for a real craftsman," he explained to one radical journalist, "Hear that chord. That's us. Dissonance is our way of life in America. We are something apart, yet an integral part."[65] Dissonance and even discord would soon reach new heights of meaning, for the revolution in black consciousness was, not surprisingly, paralleled by a revolution in black musical aesthetics. Jazz improvisers of the early 1940s were taking the orthodox music of African Americans in wildly innovative directions.[66]

Around 1940 a group of young black musicians, many of them having served an apprenticeship in the swing bands of the preceding decade (where they were sometimes the most outrageous of cutups and non-conformists), began to improvise and implement a new sound. It would ultimately turn on innovations that refused to bow to mainstream popularizations and that broke decisively from the conventional rhythms and tempos of the now well-heeled bandleaders. Among the first to give signs of what was to come were Charlie Christian—barely twenty years old at the time he screeched his way into Benny Goodman's quartet with an almost unheard-of jazz instrument, the amplified guitar—and John Birks "Dizzy" Gillespie, a rowdy trumpet player who, two years Christian's senior, had managed by 1941 to get himself kicked out of both Teddy Hill's and Cab Calloway's bands. Christian used his guitar to produce wryly discordant notes, chording irregularly and frequently resorting to the higher end of the scale, breaking from the rhythmic and harmonic conventions of traditional jazz. He was an innovator whose potential impact on the jazz world was cut short by his death in 1942, the result of a long-standing battle with tuberculosis complicated by an inability to tone down his extended nights of drink and sex. Gillespie had more instinctual resistance in him, and in 1940 when he began dropping in on a free-swinging house band at Minton's Playhouse, a seedy New York club on 118th Street, the results were an incubator for jazz change. Minton's brought together Thelonious Monk on piano, Kenny Clarke on drums, bass man Nick Fenton, and trumpeter Joe Guy.[67] Gillespie and countless others waited their turns to sit in, and the band soon recruited a midwestern import, a relatively unknown alto saxophone player named Charlie "Bird" Parker, who was gaining a reputation on the after-hours scene.

The "wrong" notes of Charlie Christian now dominated Minton's, the harmonies of the music slipping and sliding just off the normal production, groups of chords substituting for related ones. But the more glaring changes were rhythmic; Gillespie, Parker, and the others altered the sound of jazz by changing its momentum. The medium tempo of swing was no longer discernible in the alternating speed of a music coming to be known as bebop: ballad-like numbers dropped to the pace of slow blues; other compositions raced to "machine gun tempos." In the breakdown, jazz actually moved, ironically, closer to its blues and African-American roots. As Sidney Finkelstein notes, the most discordant of the bop innovators, Charlie Parker, was "almost wholly a blues performer," and his background was deeply in the Kansas City jazz–blues mix of the Count Basie–influenced Buster Smith and Jay McShann bands. Parker's magic, according to Whitney Balliett, lay in "the stomach-punching combinations that ... could, at lightning speed or in the languor of a slow blues, manipulate these contradictory bits and pieces." Within a few short years jazz had been transformed: from a marginal music played by a few outcasts in 1941, bebop was a decided presence in the jazz world by 1945.[68]

For a decade, bebop revolutionized jazz; its dynamic was an "unceasing and uncanny projection of surprises," an erasure of the boundary lines within which most jazzmen voluntarily agreed to swing. The movement was one of rebellion, a searing repudiation that stood in cacophonous rejection not only of the successful white bandleaders and crooners who had Tin-Pan-Alleyed jazz into the commercial mainstream but also of those "colored" jazzmen who had gone along with the show. Screaming its urgency in a cascade of discordant notes, bebop was an art of protest, a separation from what was often perceived to be sycophancy, an angry wail against authority's violent repressions. The bebop drummer Roy Porter, who played with the likes of Charlie Parker and Dexter Gordon, was typical in his hatred of racism. He grew up in the coal-mining communities of Colorado and recalled white workers' taunting farewells as his family was forced to flee another racially hostile community, the song "Bye Bye Blackbird" ringing in their ears. "To this day," he declared years later, "I can't stand that tune and never play it even as a request with my bands." Once established in the jazz scene, Porter found racist cops the worst harassers. Langston Hughes has a fictional character explain bebop as coming from the repression of the police, whose billy clubs "bop, bop, bebopped" on black heads: "That's where Be-Bop came from, beaten right out of some Negro's head into them horns and saxophones and piano keys that plays it." Gillespie could refer to Louis Armstrong as a "plantation character," and many in the bebop milieu had no time for what they considered "Uncle Tom" music, no patience with a jazz form catering to a dance beat. They considered their cause a struggle to eliminate all inhibition on the free-flowing melodic ideas that were nothing less than artistic self-expression. Frustrated orchestra sidemen, the bebop innovators railed against big-band instrumentation and claimed the free expressionism of the small combination. Cultural revolutionaries who found the scorn of the paying public a bitter pill to swallow, the inner circle of 1940s bebop created a subculture of distanced superiority. Their style of "hip," in its indifference to material acquisition, proclaimed a higher authority than possessive individualism and struggled to break free of the subordinations of race. The music historian Martin Williams, a white southerner, once commented that what struck him in seeing Charlie Parker's combo was "the *attitude* coming off the bandstand—self-confident, aggressive, it was something I'd never seen from black musicians before." "The bebop era was the first time that the black ego was expressed in America with self-assurance," declares A. B. Spellman in his 1970 book *Black Music*.[69]

Few moments in the history of blues and jazz have been more of the night than the bebop of the immediate post–Second World War period. A singular jazz novel, John Clellon Holmes's *The Horn* (1958), captures this fact brilliantly; its unfolding drama, like the lives of those it chronicles, is entirely an event of the night.[70] It is surely no accident that bebop's trademark composition was "Round Midnight," a 1944 creation of Thelonious Monk, first recorded by Cootie Williams and later adapted by Gillespie, Monk, Miles Davis, and countless others.[71] The creativity of the 1940s jazz breakthroughs was undeniably associated with the jam sessions and clusters of bars and clubs to which musicians flocked in most major North American metropolitan centers, milieus that came alive around midnight. "We just used to walk the streets at night and go from one place to another," recalled Art Farmer. Tommy Turrentine remembered a Harlem club, Small's Paradise, in the mid-1940s: "You would hear so much good music each night that, when you went to lay down, your head would be swimming." Art Pepper described a similiar Central Avenue scene in Los Angeles in the 1940s, hub of a West Coast jazz explosion. Montreal's Café St. Michel, which nurtured a young Sonny Rollins, came alive with bebop on Saturday night in the mid-1940s, the musicians putting in a grueling twelve-hour shift that stretched from nine in the evening to nine the next Sunday morning. "Nobody cared about sleeping in those days," said Wilk Wilkinson, whose recording "Wilk's Bop" was the first bebop disc produced in Canada.[72] Jazzmen and their critics understood themselves to be people and creatures of the night.[73] Jazz "turned the midnights loud and long."[74] But these nights were not without a downside, in which depression and despair were deepened by repression and racist attack.[75] The revolutionary intensity of bebop, the velocity of its sounds representing a musical form that paralleled its accelerated rise to artistic prominence, was lived in nights of frenzied creativity fed by often disordered days. The hip cats of bop did everything out of tempo, living lives racing on the edge or slowed to a junkie's nod; their pace was deliberately out of step.[76]

Like Bessie Smith before him, Charlie Parker oscillated between charm and generosity on the one hand, and on the other a dark, bullying arrogance that spiraled out of control in alcoholism, drug abuse, and a shameless willingness to live off anybody who made the necessities of life available. By 1948 even the bebop musicians who admired Bird most, such as Miles Davis and the drummer Max Roach, had tired of his abuse and quit Parker's band. His life a chaotic shambles, marriages and relationships with women in a constant state of dissolution, Parker fought off bouts of acute depression that necessitated institutionalization. He suffered the death of a young daughter, let his health descend into a nightmare of physical and mental disorder, grew increasingly dependent on drugs and alcohol, and eventually died in Greenwich Village, virtually homeless, in 1955 at age thirty-four. His insides wracked by stomach ulcers, his overweight body sustained largely by stimulants, Bird looked, according to the medical examiner, like a man in his mid-fifties. The night of bop had taken its tragic toll. Parker, who angered and alienated almost everyone with whom he came in contact, had lived only in the night of his art. The human emotions and affections he could not articulate in words or relationships or deeds of decency seemed to spill out of his horn, and for a few hours, 'round midnight, he became human. The tragedy was that his legacy to jazz, his generous contribution to art, could not save the creative, improvising genius from his own self-destructiveness. "Music is your own experience, your thoughts, your wisdom," Parker once said. "If you don't live it, it won't come out of your horn." Bird's horn was his only means of living his humanity, of articulating his experience of racial oppression and artistic improvisation. Jazz took all of what he had to give.[77]

Billie Holiday, whose relationship with bop solidified in her 1940s alliance with trumpeter Joe Guy, followed a similar downward spiral of drugs and alcohol, which led to a series of 1940s and 1950s arrests and jail sentences, to dysfunctional relationships, and to a career that finally faltered badly and left her largely alone until the booze so eroded her health that she died in 1959. The men in her life had treated Billie atrociously, turning her on to drugs, turning her in to the police to save their own addicted skins, and living off her money and the perks of her fame. If even the greatest of jazz singers could be objectified in this way, what were other women in the bebop milieu to face?[78]

As indicated by countless oral recollections, many of them from the mouths of the boppers themselves, the dark side of the jazz revolution of the 1940s was a debilitating ugliness in which art and individualism congealed in an extreme self-centeredness. "I don't let anyone get close to me. Even ... my wife," Parker is reputed to have said. His second wife, whose time with him would be short, noted, "When I met him, all he had was a horn and a habit. He gave me the habit."[79] From the cultivated darkness of the white bopper Art Pepper to the apprenticeship of bass player Charlie Mingus—served not only in the company of Parker, Gillespie, and Davis but with pimps, hoodlums, junkies, and hookers—the jazz memoir of this period is a narrative of lives that began in deprivation and moved into the art of the music in ways that accentuated the dissolute side of genius and obsession. Addiction, prison, suicide, misogyny, and theft lace through the stories of modern jazz's revolutionary beginnings.[80] "I had a beginning so humble that there was no way to go but up" was a typical jazzman's self-conception of his origins.[81] But beboppers soon found that nights of the presentation of hip, with its relentless quest to realize freedom and its recognition of unfreedom, invariably ran headlong into the powerful coercions of the state. This was true especially for black musicians but also for those whites who immersed themselves in the jazz life.

Most black beboppers experienced vicious racism firsthand, often through run-ins with urban police, who could be particularly vindictive if white women were involved with the musicians. Since the 1920s, jazz had been associated with "wildness," a wanton disregard of convention that was judged responsible for corrupting honest womanhood. That it was traceable to "the negro influence," in some minds, made the emerging connections all the more pernicious. Drugs gave the cops all the ammunition they needed. One admittedly loose estimate suggests that 50 to 75 percent of all bop musicians experimented with drugs, while as many as one-third of their number were seriously addicted. Parker's mystique, and the aura of drug use and addiction that he carried with him, influenced many a young musician. "Pony" Poindexter, whose life admittedly ran on the racier side of chronic substance abuse and misogynist treatment of women, took his leave from New Orleans after a police beating occasioned by his challenging segregated seating in the Catholic church. Like others in the jazz milieu, Poindexter eventually ended up in jail, victim of an old cop ploy to charge black jazzmen with contributing to the delinquency of minors or with statutory rape if they were found to have been present at parties where drugs and sex had been an integral part of the late night scene. Having had his fill, Poindexter eventually preferred exile in Paris.

By the early 1950s jazzmen were routinely being arrested on drug charges, many of which seemed to be obvious setups. The net of moral repression and panic was dragged over the already flagging bebop community with particular rigor. From the 1930s on, New York's musicians had been subjected to fingerprinting and licensing (infringements with which many "national" entertainers such as Frank Sinatra refused to comply). In the center of world jazz, New York and its 52nd Street clubs rigidly enforced cabaret laws that prohibited musicians with a criminal record work cards. A drug bust spelled the end of a jazzman's career. Most offensive was the victimization of Thelonious Monk in 1951 and the subsequent lifting of his cabaret card. The bebopper regained his club status in 1957 only with the help of some well-heeled, influential friends. Art Pepper took a harder fall, doing time in the Los Angeles County Jail, the U.S. Public Health Service Hospital in Fort Worth, and the notorious San Quentin, spending a good part of his life behind bars.[82] Jazz musicians who found their way north into the seemingly more hospitable climate of Montreal's openness discovered that the pinch of moral panic extended even across the 49th parallel. By the early 1950s the Royal Canadian Mounted Police were routinely rousting the dressing room of the Café St. Michel and harassing and arresting beboppers in their hotel rooms or en route to performances.[83]

The more bebop raced to improvise and topple tradition, the more it inevitably confronted the limitations of artistic innovation.[84] Its almost overnight popularity had placed pressures on the genre to adapt to mass audiences, but musicians steeled in their sense of themselves as revolutionaries challenging all convention could only sustain so much transformation and creative energy, especially when it was supposed to happen night after night. As bebop was attacked, intellectually and practically, in reviews and bookings, in police repression and actual jailings, its coherence came unhinged; Parker was but the personalization of this social, artistic process. In the long night of bop, its spiritual quest for the musical art's purity contaminated by tensions and substitutions, talented jazzmen crossed swords and retreated into their own personal darknesses, or were forced into them by crusading racist agents of the state.

Miles Davis, born of bop, led the music of hip revolt out of its impasse toward new avenues of the avant-garde, roadways of jazz fusion which after 1955 would reconfigure African-American musical idioms and elaborate stylistic improvisation that reached through hard bop, free jazz, and the pulsating vitality of John Coltrane's innovations.[85] Bebop had ushered in an epoch of permanent revolution that was capable of shattering conventionality *and* reviving traditions in ways that refocused attention on the original Dixieland of New Orleans (where jazz sustained itself with relations to life and death, families and funerals) or of channeling African-American expression in creative innovations, as with the rise of a second— Ornette Coleman-influenced—school of Chicago jazz.[86] It also stimulated an infectious internationalism that played off an emerging youth rebellion in national cultures as diverse as those of the United Kingdom and the Soviet Union.[87]

But it was with the birth of Miles Davis's original 1950s "cool," a direct offspring of bebop, that jazz nights took on new meaning. For "cool" was a word which, more than any other, would be adopted by the largely white working-class and lower-middle-class youth who, throughout the late 1940s and 1950s, gravitated to the new jazz. Lacking the musical idioms of African Americans, however, many used words and the road rather than music to proclaim their estrangement from the suffocating cultural conformity of the postwar years.[88] In the jazz of bop and cool, the bohemian night found its beat.[89]

17

A Walk on the Wild Side

Bohemia and the Beats

On the night of October 7, 1955, six unknown poets appeared at "a run down second-rate experimental art gallery in the Negro section of San Francisco," a "collection of angels" gathered to give a free reading of their verse. This "charming event" was conceived as a liberating moment of defiance, a conscious repudiation of "the system of academic poetry, official reviews, New York publishing machinery, national sobriety and generally accepted standards of good taste."[1] Publicized by a hundred postcards sent out by the poets and with posters hung in the Latin Quarter North Beach bars, the reading was hosted by master of ceremonies Kenneth Rexroth, American poetry's bohemian father figure. This personage of the eccentric Greenwich Village rebelliousness of the 1920s was now an aged advocate of "disengagement." The evening lived up to its billing. The bizarre collection of performers wove a tapestry of rhythmic radical eccentricities that were part surrealism, part anarchism, part Zen Buddhism, partly inspired by drugs and cheap wine. Everyone in the room was drunk or high on something. An ecstatic peak of intensity was reached when Allen Ginsberg built a rhapsodic outline of the United States as a civilization encased in its own nightmare, constrained and distorted by a coercive and ultimately destructive materialism and its many mechanizations which had overtaken whatever remained of American individualism:

> I saw the best minds of my generation destroyed by madness, starving
> hysterical naked, dragging themselves through the negro streets at dawn
> looking for an angry fix, angelheaded hipsters burning for the ancient
> heavenly connection to the starry dynamo in the machinery of the night
> ... who wandered around and around at midnight in the railroad yard

wondering where to go, and went, leaving no broken hearts, who lit cigarettes in boxcars racketing through snow toward lonesome farms in grandfather night.[2]

Hearing Ginsberg's "Howl" was a strangely sobering experience. It was unmistakably dark and focused emphatically on the night, which was obviously where the angry young men of the 1950s felt they had some room to roam, space to create, and possibility to live: "Though the dream is fast/ in a night of rain,/ dreams can be amassed/ where the night has lain."[3]

Published in 1956, "Howl" was the product of a tortured family history, a communist upbringing, and an acknowledged homosexuality, as well as an obvious challenge to the political economy and cultural philistinism of mainstream America.[4] It would soon be the center of an obscenity trial that helped to thrust Ginsberg and a circle of similarly disaffected literary figures increasingly into the public eye.[5] But it was only the most obviously notorious of a series of publications that came to be associated with the "beat generation," a name coined by a friend of Ginsberg and Jack Kerouac, John Clellon Holmes, who would later write the archetypal jazz novel, The Horn (1958). His Go (1952) was the first self-consciously beat novel of the 1950s.[6] Though it was singularly unsuccessful both financially and aesthetically, in it Holmes codified the character of the beats:

> They never read the papers, they did not follow with diligent and self conscious attention the happenings in the political and cultural arena; they seemed to have almost calculated contempt for logical argument. They operated on feelings, sudden reactions, expanding these far out of perspective to see in them profundities ... they could not define if put to it.... He came to know their world ... of dingy backstairs "pads," Times Square cafeterias, bebop joints, night-long wanderings, meetings on street corners, hitchhiking, a myriad of "hip " bars all over the city, and the streets themselves. It was inhabited by people "hungup" with drugs and other habits, searching out a new degree of craziness; and connected by the invisible threads of need, petty crimes of long ago, or a strange recognition of affinity. They kept going all the time, living by night, rushing around to "make contact," suddenly disappearing into jail or on the road only to turn up again and search one another out. They had a view of life that was underground, mysterious, and they seemed unaware of anything outside the realities of deals, a pad to stay in, "digging the frantic jazz," and keeping everything going.... Once [Kerouac] said to him ... "You know, everyone I know is kind of furtive, kind of beat. They all go along the street like they were guilty of something, but didn't believe in guilt. I can spot them immediately! And it's happening all over the country, to everyone; a sort of revolution of the soul."[7]

This down-and-out bohemianism was anticipated in the early 1950s by Chandler Brossard's depiction of New York's hipsters in *Who Walk in Darkness* (1952).[8] Holmes's *Go* (originally titled *The Daybreak Boys*, alluding to a New York river gang of the 1840s) was "a book about a new underground of young people pioneering the search for what lay 'at the end of the night' (A phrase of Kerouac's)."[9]

To be beat was, in the bebop language of the 1940s, to be down and out, to be physically debilitated for lack of a fix.[10] The beats extended this language of need to the realm of spirituality. "Angels of desolation," they wandered the night asking, "Why?" only to find that there wasn't "a decent answer."[11] By 1957, with the publication of Kerouac's *On The Road*, the beats were a phenomenon, the subject of sympathetic essays by Norman Mailer ("The White Negro") and Caroline Bird ("Born 1930: The Lost Generation") and hostile harangues by Norman Podhoretz ("The Know-Nothing Bohemians"), Diana Trilling ("The Other Night at Columbia"), Robert Brustein ("The Cult of Unthink"), and many others.[12] Beat communities such as San Francisco's North Beach began to experience the hostility of the authorities, who exerted their antagonistic pressure by curtailing liquor licensing and encouraging landlord discrimination. Police surveillance of the area was stepped up, and beats faced the usual harassments: bistro customers were rousted; interracial couples were subjected to threats and insults; apartments were raided, books seized and burned, and property trashed and destroyed. The beat night was demonized in the yellow journalism of the Hearst press: "Far out in the faceless jungle of nothingness ... their capital (North Beach) ... is dangerous to outsiders who roam its cobbled streets at night.... They play leap frog down Grant Avenue at 4 A.M."[13] The more mainstream magazine *Life* was little better, bemoaning the dreary disaffection of the beats, and regarding their sneering repudiation of American society—"Mom, Dad, Politics, Marriage, the Savings Bank, Organized Religion"—as a shadow on the bright light of postwar American civilization.[14]

Holmes saw things differently. More than any other figure who lived alongside and as part of the beat generation, he had a dispassionate analytic sense that allowed him to see what was unique in the beats, what separated them from experiences of the past and what distinguished them from the conformities of the present.[15] They were rebels but not without a cause, dissidents whose program was consciously that of the self, *enfants terribles* "turned inside out," nonconformists whose underground appeal lay in the *appearance* of a structureless aesthetics of disengagement with the established values of form. Kerouac's quintessentially beat prose was a case in point; his style assumed its power only when it shed its traditionalist skin to incorporate "burbling neologisms," "imitations of Jazz scat singing." This "spontaneous bop prosody," consciously patterned on the jazz riff, conceived of sentences as "breath separations of the mind," not unlike a horn player's physically overdetermined chording. It was not so much that Kerouac renounced form itself as that he searched for its control in jazz motifs rather than in standardized literary convention. The controlled cadence of his sentences thus moved to the rhythmic raciness and freedom of jazz, rather than any preordained logic of grammar, in a literary-musical idiom that would easily find new levels in the heady atmosphere of the 1960s.[16] As John Clellon Holmes suggested insightfully in diary fragments from 1948 to 1950, the late-night freneticism of bop was the entryway into "an authentic response" to the postwar world.[17] It was but a short step to the rock revolutions of the East and West Coasts: Kerouac, Ginsberg, and others inspired the rebellious antics of Tuli Kupferberg and the Fugs in Greenwich Village and the psychedelic bands of Haight–Ashbury, especially Jefferson Airplane and Jerry Garcia's Grateful Dead.[18]

The 1950s, in retrospect, seem an odd moment for the discovery of the rebel in the American soul.[19] It was a decade of expansive economic growth (now, admittedly, known to have been marked by profound imbalances and unsettling inequalities), something of a high-water mark in the burgeoning military–industrial complex, which drove prosperity forward on the greased wheels of job creation. Labor, that perennial dissident, appeared to have been domesticated: trade unions were recognized; wages improved; and the consuming capacity of the stable working-class household expanded considerably. If the happy worker was indeed a myth, it had much of the nation fooled. Women had supposedly not yet broken out of the "feminine mystique" that insulated them from past waves of feminist discontent and ostensibly blocked their consciousness from reaching the "second-wave" plateau of liberation that lay around the rocky corner of the 1960s. Blacks were in motion, and the segregationist Solid South was cracking. Rosa Parks notwithstanding, however, the national civil rights movement had yet to find the voice of Martin Luther King, let alone Malcolm X. Politics, from anything approaching a left-wing perspective, was a nightmare in which McCarthyism was only the most visible threat. Before the senator from Wisconsin really got rolling, Mickey Spillane had tapped into the deep, dark reservoir of popular anticommunism, riding the revelations of Soviet espionage surrounding the trial of the Rosenbergs to the gruesome logic of truly pulp fiction. Spillane's Mike Hammer potboiler One Lonely Night (1951) sold three million copies, its language one of vile retribution: "I killed more people tonight than I have fingers on my hands. I shot them in cold blood and enjoyed every minute of it.... They were Commies, ... red sons-of-bitches who should have died long ago." This was Captain America with an attitude.[20]

There was plenty of attitude in other areas as well. Rock and roll presented a terrifying spectacle for the stolid ruling order of complacent Middle America, and youth gangs and an emerging racial combativeness evident among black adolescents were troubling signs of authority's fragile hegemony. Increasing teenage access to the automobile—which in the 1950s was a vehicle of both unchecked mobility and sexual opportunity (as well as eroticized aesthetics, with its sleek, fin-enhanced design)—created a sense that youth were speeding out of control, drawn to the fast track of indulgence. Cheap paperbacks and comics were the corruption of impressionable minds, a sinister creation of "wicked men." One parental duo wrote to a psychiatrist complaining that such influences were eroding their sons' connection to civilization. "They behave as if drugged," moaned the mother. "We consider the situation to be as serious as an invasion of the enemy in war time, with as far reaching consequences as the atom bomb."[21] A moral panic over a supposed national epidemic of juvenile delinquency swept across America in the mid-1950s; criminalized youth were everywhere, according to inflammatory books such as 1,000,000 Delinquents (1955); and in California it was estimated that one in every four seventeen-year-olds had gone to proverbial, and criminalized, seed. Like all such scourges, juvenile delinquency threatened to "demoralize, disrupt, confuse, and destroy" the foundations of citizenship and to erode fundamental values, thus furthering the subversions of "the Communist conspiracy."[22] Small wonder that this dark conception of the young and their culture of differentiating themselves from their elders evoked Norman Mailer's rage. "A stench of fear has come out of every pore of American life," he railed, "and we suffer from a collective failure of nerve." In this context, Mailer explained, "the only courage ... has been the isolated courage of isolated people."[23] But if Mailer saw the hipster existentialist beat as a savior of the American self, others looked with revulsion on this youthful "nihilism," with its dogged rebelliousness pitted unambiguously against "the whole body of laws, customs, fears, habits of thought, and literary standards that had been accepted." Malcolm Cowley's literary survey of the mid-1950s found a direct parallel between the juvenile delinquency that agitated America and the beat generation, whose aesthetics of underground cool threatened the sacred, and pleasantly accommodating, idioms of conventional style.[24]

This bohemianism of the 1950s—with its supposedly dark designs on the literary canon and its anarchic challenge to the social fabric of hierarchy, authority, and a sense of place governed by age and its privileges— was connected to but different from a historical past. Urban Bohemias have been intimately associated with the street life, cafés and leisurely intellectual possibilities of the city night in which days of hard labor are displaced by evenings of discussion and twilight promenades. In Paris, Vienna, London, and Berlin this culture of the café had nurtured marginalized intellectuals, revolutionaries, and rebels for a century by the time the beats appeared on the American scene.[25] In New York's Greenwich Village a casually literary culture of genteel alienation had moved through varying stages.[26] It had embraced artists and homosexuals, radicals and writers, early feminism and late cold-water flats.[27] American bohemias have also lived and died in various other locales: Chicago's North Side; numerous West Coast enclaves, from the nineteenth-century Spanish- and French-influenced quarters of San Francisco to the artist colonies of the 1920s such as Carmel or, in the sunlit shadows of Los Angeles, Venice Beach in the late 1940s and 1950s; the graceful decay and unbridled hedonism of the French Quarter in New Orleans. Impossible to date exactly, American bohemias thrived most obviously in the interwar period.[28]

These walking communities—with their cheap rents, loft spaces, bookstores, climate of political and lifestyle tolerance (accentuating the rebellious and radical but retaining some space for a truly imaginative conservatism), sidewalk sociability, and neighborhood restaurant/bar/saloon night life—have succumbed to various pressures. At the core of their disintegration lies the accelerating tempo of urban life. Inner-city decay and all its attendant social dysfunctionalities, speculative frenzies in the real estate market, soaring costs of everyday life, and the consequent dispersal of the artists, writers, and dissidents who formed the truly human substance of bohemia spelled the death of a way of life in the last half of the twentieth century. It is not simply that in retreating to the small towns and countrysides of America the bohemians have spread themselves thinner and made their presence as a collective less visible; equally important is that the tempo of bohemian formation, which has always been a process of migration and transformation, has so quickened as to make the possibility of sustaining a bohemian locale increasingly remote. "Bohemian communities may germinate," notes Russell Jacoby, "but cannot take root before the boutiques and condominiums crowd them out. The hysteria of development poisons the conviviality of artists and perhaps the creativity as well." Walter Benjamin recalled his youthful attraction to the West End Café of bohemian Berlin: "I see myself," he noted in his memoirs, "waiting one night amid tobacco smoke on the sofa that encircled one of the central columns," admitting that he "did not yet possess that passion for waiting without which one cannot thoroughly appreciate the charm of a cafe."[29]

Who now can fathom a "passion for waiting"? In the 1990s such a notion seemed bizarre, Greenwich Village cafés charge sitting fees; elbowing tourists and New Jersey and Long Island commuters crowd the entryways to clubs; washrooms are reserved for the use of paying patrons only; where a band is playing, two-drink minimums and steep cover charges are the norm. Indeed, Greenwich Village as a bohemian space had largely died by the 1960s, when Kerouac bemoaned the passing of the brief-lived jazz culture of the 1940s and 1950s: "You've got to have mucho money.... the sad commercial atmosphere is killing jazz [which] ... belongs to open joyful ten-cent beer joints, as in the beginning."[30] In the 1960s the East Village emerged as the new locale of bohemian aspiration; as Eli Waldron reported in the *Saturday Evening Post* (1964), "Only the well-heeled, the very well-heeled, can afford the rates prevailing in Greenwich Village. The ill-heeled and struggling are fleeing to a new Bohemia ... the former ghetto of the Lower East Side." Yet in less than a decade the East Village was invaded by contractors intent on gentrification (many of them servicing children of the suburbs who were fleeing the antiseptic spaces of their birth); entire streets were overtaken by specialty restaurants frequented not by the poor of the neighborhood but by cash-dispensing or plastic-toting suburbanites; and Tompkins Square Park, padlocked at night, restricted access during the day to bona fide "residents." Greenwich Village's bohemia had lasted seventy-five years; that of the East Village could not survive ten.[31]

If the highway and its culture of travel did not directly invade the old, declining bohemias, it restructured metropolitan centers and surrounded long-established enclaves of living and socializing space in a death grid of speeding vehicles, polluting fumes, concrete and pavement, and engine-driven isolation—all of which led to the suburbs. Critics such as Jane Jacobs, Lewis Mumford, and William H. Whyte were quick to defend the embattled city as it was fractured by highways and twisted and tangled into a dull inertia of parking lots, underground concourses, and interchanges, all seemingly feeding the "vapid suburbanization of America" and the endless commercialization of the urban core. If inner-city decay threatened metropolitan centers of "high" culture or business tourism, these market attractions were walled in, becoming bastions of a "beseiged" white privilege, accessible only by automobile, limousine, or taxicab. Turn-of-the-century understandings that street life defined urban existence ("Standing on the street corner waiting for no one is power," beat poet Gregory Corso declared[32]) thus sank in a sea of development. To take New York City as perhaps the exemplary instance of this process is to grasp—as is evident in the results of Robert Moses's relentless dedication to choking the city with expressways servicing the suburbs—the extent to which by 1955 the automobile and its arteries had restructured the meaning of urban life in America. Surveying the wreckage in 1958, Whyte declared, "Even a Bohemia of sorts can be of help." By this date, however, whatever magnetic hangovers of its long past remained, bohemia had lost a good deal of its drawing power.[33]

This is the context in which the beat generation coalesced in the late 1940s and the 1950s. As the cities turned against the possibility of bohemias, the new bohemians, in Jacoby's words, "abandoned them for the highways, campuses, and countryside.... the beats became bohemian messengers in the age of the highway and the declining city.... In the period of urban sprawl, the beats were the last bohemians."[34] The argument can be extended. Beat sensibilities were bohemian, to be sure, but as the beats were déclassé, so too were they stripped of a sense of place. Utterly incapable of sustaining an environment of roots and stabilities, as a generation they addressed universals, not particulars, and their idiom was movement rather than stability. "In three hundred pages," complained Paul Goodman's review of Kerouac's On the Road in disbelief, "these fellows cross America eight times, usually camping on friends or relatives," displaying "the woeful emptiness of running away from even loneliness and vague discontent."[35] The beats were the last bohemians because, if they inherited the legacy of bohemia as estrangement, they were incapable of maintaining bohemia as a physical place, a living spatial organism somehow beyond the individual self. The beat generation passed through everywhere; it could settle nowhere. At the end of Holmes's Go the novel's protagonist, Paul, asks furtively, "Where is our home?" The anxiety of this lack of resolution gripped would-be beats, but the Kerouac-like figure seems to understand the dilemma and revel in it "as if what he pursued in that night lay still a little further on."[36] Like the so-called new bohemians of New York's East Village, the beats were "night people, and they move[d] in groups," given to the age-old pleasures of the avant-garde urban evening: "dancing, cool talk, and a 'connection,' be it in the form of dope or sex."[37] Kerouac's Lonesome Traveller (1960), which begins with a chapter titled "Piers of the Homeless Night," fuses images of night's bounties and homeless movement in homage to vanishing hoboes, skid row hotels, twenty-four-hour cafeterias, Negro whores, dimly lit clubs and dance bars—people and places "born of pride having nothing to do with a community," everything to do with the fraternities of the dark.[38] As Holmes would write in "Midnight Oil" (1965): "At least the deadened hours/ promise dawn and irony."[39]

The beats, however overripe the 1950s seemed for their particular angst, had hardly emerged untouched by the past. Lawrence Lipton, who sustained the beat milieu in southern California from his Venice Beach base, claimed in The Holy Barbarians (1959) to have been "as beat as any of today's beat generation" in the 1920s; he saw in that original postwar "spirit of revolt" the initial expropriation of the upper-class privilege of "defying convention," a process he dubbed the "democratization of amorality."[40] Literary outlaws such as William S. Burroughs and Nelson Algren also preceded the beats, willing them a legacy of creative nihilism and a dark negotiation with the machineries of power that would be reborn in the lives and lines of the beat generation.

Of the two, Burroughs, lionized by the beats as their patron saint, a sort of Prince of Darkness for the 1950s (and later godfather to hippies and punks and, according to Patti Smith, the inspiration for "heavy metal" music), had a longer history and a more anarchic influence on innovations of style.[41] Born to a socially registered St. Louis family, he was the proverbial exile, a déclassé rebel and antihero whose history from the 1920s to the late twentieth century encompassed a Harvard degree and wanderings throughout the United States, European capitals, and the Third World in an endless search for sex and drugs, "the uncut kick." At age forty, settled in Tangier, Burroughs managed to shed his class background and respectable family status. He had published his scandalous account of the drug life, Junkie, in 1953, but his major work, Naked Lunch (1959)—a further descent into the "perversions" of addiction and homosexuality— was five years away and would immerse him in a classic obscenity trial.[42] His life was a series of "busts": syphilis, forged prescriptions, drunk driving, narcotics possession, criminal imprudence, the haunting memory of a wife shot dead as the intoxicated Burroughs—blaming a faulty pistol— missed the target in a "William Tell" episode in Mexico. Never working in the occupational mainstream, he earned his keep as a detective, a cotton picker, an exterminator, a reporter, and a pickpocket, but obviously preferred his stints as a morphine addict and resident in a Moroccan male brothel. Incarcerated in dark depression—"A nightmare feeling of foreboding and desolation comes over me as a great mushroom-shaped cloud darkens the earth"[43]—Burroughs connected with Ginsberg and Kerouac precisely because his prose was unadorned with the usual clutter of literary pretension:

> A naked lunch is natural to us,
> we eat reality sandwiches.
> But allegories are so much lettuce.
> Don't hide the madness.[44]

To the extent that he believed in art, it was what could be lived beyond the range of conformity, what could be pushed in the face of convention. Burroughs ended *Junkie* with a beat manifesto, short and to the experiential point: "Kick is seeing things from a special angle. Kick is momentary freedom from the claims of the aging, cautious, nagging, frightened flesh, ... the final fix."[45]

Algren was more connected to the proletarian school of writing, for which the beats had little patience, but he too touched a dark nerve in the exposed sensibility of interwar alienation. Formed by the Great Depression, Algren wrote *Somebody in Boots* (1935), a hungry 1930s version of *On the Road* where kicks were replaced by raw realities. Riding the rails, hoboing it across America, landing in jail, busting heads with cops and Klansmen, frequenting tattoo parlors or dime-a-dance halls, experiencing the dark, deadly consequences of homelessness—all these experiences colored Algren's prose, producing a novel that, however superficially Kerouac-like, carried a tone of desperation rather than of frenzied odyssey. That Algren actually *did* these things, crossing paths with the bohemian, literary milieu of Chicago's North Side, placed him firmly in the ranks of beat predecessors, but his subject matter and style diverged significantly from the angst-driven productions of the late 1940s and 1950s. To be sure, *Somebody in Boots*, in the words of usually negative reviewers, haunted "the memory like music," carrying with it the "bitterness not of revolutionary fervor, but of disillusioned youth." But three of its four parts were prefaced by quotations from the *Communist Manifesto*. This was not a beat book; its transgressive tone owed too much to the orthodox left.[46]

Neverthless, Algren's inspirations were certainly beat, in the original underground meanings of the term: his subject matter of the dispossessed was contextualized in the dark recesses of the night, where Algren repeatedly sought food for his troubled thought. Suicidal, frustrated in love and literary accomplishment, temporarily institutionalized, he worked his way through the Communist Party milieu of fellow travelers and their Popular Front organizations via the endless stories the urban night could provide. Along with his friend and supporter, the similarly situated writer Jack

Conroy, Algren frequented Chicago's boxing rings, gambling dens, and gang hangouts, rubbing shoulders with con men and prostitutes, drinking heavily, and adopting the stance of the pugilistic loser. Introduced to East St. Louis's underground and vice district, he prowled it incessantly. Algren was now an accomplished author of the urban night. In March 1940 he received from his friend Richard Wright a copy of the African-American author's new novel, *Native Son*. The title had been Algren's original choice for *Somebody in Boots* but had been discarded by the publisher; Nelson freely offered it to Wright, who replied in an affectionate inscription, referring to Algren as "the best writer of good prose in the U.S.A."

Buoyed by Wright's praise, and acclimated to the dark subjects of his imaginative literary choice, Algren's 1940s productions included *Never Come Morning* (1942), an exploration of the making of a first-generation American ethnic hoodlum which earned him the condemnation of the Polish community, the surveillance of the FBI, and calls to ban the book from libraries; *The Neon Wilderness* (1947), a collection of short stories drawn from the urban night; and the justifiably celebrated *The Man with the Golden Arm* (1949). This account of urban criminality, including addiction, and its repression by a moralizing authority sustained by the capacity to oppress, was a deeper and more artistic treatment than the "how to do it" mechanics of Burroughs's later *Junkie*. Algren seemed to have gotten past the marginalization of the struggling author, but dead-end relationships and blow-ups with literary colleagues were common. Still, he had the oddly dualistic securities of long-standing friendships in the underworld and a growing presence in the international literary community, where he was able to consolidate an intense love affair with the French sensation and companion of Jean-Paul Sartre, Simone de Beauvoir. His writing having achieved a certain celebratory status and critical acclaim, with theatrical and film presentations placing it before a wider public, the stage was in some ways set for Algren's mid-1950s blowout, the powerful depiction of the New Orleans dispossessed, *A Walk on the Wild Side* (1956). It proved disappointingly unsuccessful, drawing spiteful reviews from the usual cast of characters associated with the literary establishment, Norman Podhoretz and Alfred Kazin leading the charge. Moreover, injury had been added to insult: convinced that he was on the verge of his deserved "score," Algren the gambler turned down $32,500 for the book, thinking there was more to be had from it. He was driven virtually to despair by his untimely tossing of the literary dice, his broken connection to de Beauvoir, and the savage response to *Wild Side*. He still had his ageing underworld connections, his "devotion to the outcasts," but he had squandered his chance. "The gates of his soul," Jack Conroy liked to say, "opened on the hell side." After 1956, Algren never got them closed.[47]

Deeply wounded by a climate of critical hostility, he was but one of many victims of a tightening literary canon that would soon exile the very idea of the writer as a compassionate social conscience of the dark dimensions of urban America. An obviously embittered Algren lashed out at the Cold War aesthetics of the "New Criticism." He aimed his satirical sights at the increasingly formalist fortress of a "loose federation" of scholastics who situated themselves "between the literary quarterlies, publishers' offices and book review columns," arriving "directly from their respective campuses armed with blueprints to which the novel and the short story would have to conform, ... presenting a view of American letters untouched by American life." Such bitterness, no matter how justified, has a way of overstepping its proper limits, spilling over into spheres where, in healthier contexts of artistic recognition, it would have no need to flow. If Algren could see some redeeming value in Kerouac's On the Road, his view of the other beats was less charitable. He had little time for the self-indulgence of Ginsberg and his ever present entourage, whom Algren regarded as "people who take it for granted that the proper function of the artist is to amuse." The beats were not much more than "aid and comfort to complacency," reminding Algren of a Greenwich Village announcement: "Classes in Non-Conformity Wednesday at 9. Please be on time."[48] Similarly dismissive readings of the beats would appear in other obscure corners of the literary left, where the cavalierly bohemian inattention to class exploitations drew the ire of those whose creative and political time in the trenches had turned them away from the long night wait "for the heavenly fix."[49]

Ironically, it was Kerouac, most in touch with an admittedly problematized working-class identity, who would come to be the core of the beat aesthetic. Moving Ginsberg in the direction of his style, inspiring Burroughs, canonizing Neal Cassady, Kerouac served as a prototypical beat in Holmes's analytic categorizations. And, of course, with the publication of On the Road he captivated a media hyped on the "wild youth" of the 1950s and their "frenetic search for Experience and Sensation."[50] Kerouac has been studied intensely, his work judged correctly to be an evolving autobiography of a life consumed by the search for an authentic American expression of the soul of freedom, translated into a voice uninhibited by convention. The ways in which Kerouac's writing found this voice in a prose of radicalized narrative spontaneity—with its fixation on the mythic constructions and elaborated historicizations of movement as freedom, the frontier as quest, and male friendship as the gendered boundary within which all life evolved—has been explored in useful studies, both critical and biographical.[51] There was a striking parallel between Kerouac's themes and those of a more overtly politicized set of "vag" writings from a generation before—Tom Kromer's *Waiting for Nothing* (1935) or Edward Dahlberg's *Bottom Dogs* (1930)—but those proletarian road narratives seemed incarcerated in the almost stereotypical fruits of wrath associated with the radicalism of fellow travelers who actually believed in the possibility of social transformation.[52] In finding his literary voice over the course of the 1950s, Kerouac seemed liberated from such a past, pouring out his words on the legendary 120-foot roll manuscript, writing a largely unpunctuated stream-of-consciousnes draft of *On the Road* in a matter of weeks, working endlessly at night. All his later prose would be an engagement with this original articulation of beat sensibilities which, when the instinctual mobility, allure of sex,[53] and masculine consensus are stripped away, reveal a profoundly despairing antimaterialist skepticism. Crossing the Sierra Madre Oriental at the end of the novel, Sal (Kerouac) and Dean (Neal Cassady) roll toward Mexico City, their pursuit of the end of their journey interrupted by the impoverished mountainous towns of native peoples: "Life was dense, dark, ancient.... All had their hands outstretched. They had come down from the back mountains and higher places to hold forth their hands for something they thought civilization could offer, and they never dreamed the sadness and the poor broken delusion of it. They didn't know that a bomb had come that could crack all our bridges and roads and reduce them to jumbles, and we would be as poor as they someday, and stretching out our hands in the same, same way."[54]

On the Road is permeated with this darkness. The irony of the quest for light and kicks is that it passes through, almost always, the night. As Gerald Nicosia has pointed out, the most frequently used words in the novel, repeated with the frequency of a litany, are *beat, star, vision, dream, lost, gone, sad, ghost*—and *night*.[55] Whatever the discoveries and revels of the night, moreover, "horrible nauseas possessed us in the morning."[56] In the night poems and dark dreams of *Dr. Sax* (1959), Kerouac's account of growing up as an immigrant French Canadian in the tenemented milltown of Lowell, Massachusetts, the horrors of the night are presented as fantasies of the apocalyptic shadowy world of an American "puberty myth." In these beginnings, Kerouac deliberately distinguishes *and* blurs lightness and darkness, as he did in *On the Road*: "The rain is really milk/ The night is really white/ The shroud is really seen/ By the white eyes of the light."[57] It was almost as though Kerouac thought of himself as born in the dark fears of the night, which it was then his literary responsibility to exorcise for all America:

> I was scared. The dark
>   was full of phantoms
> Come from the other side of death
>   to claim the hearts
> Of Sacrificial little children
>   laying up in the winter night[58]

"There is no end to the night," Kerouac proclaimed at the end of his short story "Jazz of the Beat Generation."[59] Henry Miller made much the same point in introducing *The Subterraneans* (1958), a book in which Kerouac exposed the sexual self-destructiveness of the beats in an anguished, autobiographical account of the failure of interracial love. Readers might wonder where Kerouac found the inspiration for such material, Miller noted, answering bluntly: "Man, he lay awake all night listening with eyes and ears. A night of a thousand years. Heard it in the womb, heard it in the cradle, heard it in school, heard it on the floor of life's stock exchange where dreams are traded for gold." Progress seemed derailed at the end of the beat road in this bleak exposition, but Miller saw Kerouac and other beats as prophets: "They're not riding the atom-powered Juggernaut," he insisted, adding for good measure his defense of raw factualism: "Believe me, there's nothing clean, nothing healthy, nothing promising about this age of wonders—except the telling."[60] For Kerouac the telling was a night tale, ultimately a book of dreams: "long outlines of personal experience and vision, night-long confessions full of hope that had become illicit and repressed by War, stirrings, rumblings of a new soul."[61] But there was little space for grappling with this "method," given its rejection by a complacent literati or its appropriation and stereotypical stylization in the media-pushed construction of the "beatnik," a designation Kerouac loathed by the late 1950s.[62]

John Clellon Holmes opens his affectionate and insightful essay on Kerouac with these words: "'A great rememberer redeeming life from darkness': thus Kerouac, self-described." This was a heavy burden to carry. It was all too easy to get lost in the darkness, especially when the backbiting uproar of the New Critics drowned one's perspective in an invective that could never effectively be answered. By 1962 the idealistic Kerouac wanderings, in which he had discovered the night's sensualities and sociabilities, the bonds of the road and the riff, and the meaning of these for a restless generation, had come to an end. He returned to his nightmares and a fruitless search for home and familialism that would end in Florida. There, tied to his mother, Kerouac was pressured toward a belligerent conservatism and a troubled self-destructiveness, both of which he had always harbored but seldom acknowledged publicly. For the next few years, his thought swirled in alcoholic genius, losing itself in macho acts of senseless bravado and the occasional "furies over Jews, negroes, intellectuals, & most of the other racial & class shibboleths which these years in the South, & off the road, have made seem like menaces to him." Holmes, one of his few remaining friends, commented in his journal: "No real place for him." In 1969, at the age of forty-seven, Kerouac died an alcoholic death. The night had caught up with the man who defined beat but who could not live it; it overtook him, but not before he had rewritten something of its histories.[63]

No doubt the inadequacy underlying all of this is perfectly evident in hindsight, especially the beat capacity to draw on black America in order to privilege "white" estrangements. In African-American circles the "white Negro" hardly meant what it did to hipster-sympathetic writers such as Norman Mailer; rather, it designated something that threatened to dilute and popularize in ways that would draw the public eye. Black beats were never quite "beat" enough to find their way to the limelight that Kerouac, Ginsberg, Cassady, Burroughs, Gregory Corso, and even the legendary Times Square hustler, Herbert Huncke, seemed to occupy with ease.[64] And yet the black–white connection attempted among the beats was both somewhat novel and, in its time, undoubtedly genuine. Rexroth, reviewing The Subterraneans in the San Francisco Chronicle, knew how to situate his blows below Kerouac's belt: "The story is all about jazz and Negroes. Now there are two things Jack knows nothing about—jazz and Negroes."[65]

The reduction of women to cardboard cutouts, pasted into the pages of beat prose and displaced with a cavalier misogyny, was evident to the women of the beat generation and is still painfully obvious almost forty years later. Yet, as in the case of African Americans, women's involvement in the beat night, if anything but a relationship of equality, did point in new directions.[66] For her part, Joyce Johnson would not have traded her moment with Kerouac and the beats, however subordinate, for a later liberation. She passed through the 1960s as years "never quite my time. They seemed anticlimactic, for all their fireworks.... The old intensities were blanding out into 'Do your own thing' ... Ecstasy had become chemical, forgetfulness could be had by prescription. Revolution was in the wind, but it never came." Looking backward, Johnson could see herself as a figure in the beat night of 1958; it was an experience she never "outgrew."[67]

The "Beat Brotherhood," for all its nonconformity, *was* undeniably sexist, even misogynist; women were sexualized and then silenced.[68] Curiously, the beats grappled, incompletely and inadequately no doubt, with the presence of homosexuality in ways that seemed far more explicit and sensitive than their lack of engagement with male–female relations.[69] This was because, as an expression of hypermasculinity, poised in combative opposition, the beat generation was always something of a beleaguered artistic maleness in which transgressive eroticism was negotiated within a clash of aesthetics governed, on all sides, by males. "Straight" in this sense, if gendered as exclusively male, connoted not so much conformist sexuality as a broader aesthetic of conventionality coded in respectability. Sexual hipsters had wider horizons: "*Never knock the way the other cat swings.*"[70] Yet the swinging was naturalized as an unquestioned "cat" prerogative. In their ritualized bonding on the mythical road, then, beat males constructed women in ways perfectly congruent with aspects of the mainstream culture's gendered deformities. It was not for nothing that Carolyn Cassady titled her account of years with Cassady, Kerouac, and Ginsberg *Off the Road* (1990).[71] Yet the small spaces afforded women in this beat milieu were, in their breaking of the staid rules of the petty-bourgeois mainstream, sufficient to draw and hold some women to the countercultural possibilities.[72] They longed for something different from the stifling life mapped out by an ossified parental generation and willed to them as their unalterable lot. "I think we were trying to shake the time," recalls Hettie Jones, "shake it off, shake it up, shake it down. A shakedown."[73]

In Alix Kates Shulman's novel *Burning Questions* (1978) a young women, Zane, flees the Midwest in search of such a "shakedown." She settles in Greenwich Village, where she delights in the bohemian rapport of the 1950s. Her first beat meal is an excursion into chaotic sociability: the kitchen table is cluttered with loaves of garlic bread, pots of spaghetti sauce, wine, and salad—a feast of communalism. Sandwiched between artists, Zane is enraptured by "the unending stream of words," incredulous at the range of conversation. She has found new possibilities, a place and a generational culture where expression—verbal, artistic, and sexual— is not only allowed but encouraged, almost demanded. Responding to the range of subjects discussed in the tiny Village flat, she notes, "It's a lot better than what they talk about in Indiana." "What do they talk about there?" she is asked. "Cars and clothes. And communists in the government," is her reply. In two short sentence fragments, Zane identified what to many was a peculiarly American "darkness at noon": the suburban materialism and political conformism that many beats rejected, that in their linked meaning located the beat generation within the social relations of the Cold War, and that pushed them toward what was left of the twentieth-century bohemian night.[74]

18

Noir

The Cultural Politics of Darkness

The Cold War reaches across the international history of the twentieth century, a disfigurement that leaves a frozen burn scorching the politics and culture of diverse moments, scarring East and West in ways different but reciprocal. More than a brief interlude associated with the post–Second World War campaigns of Senator Joseph McCarthy, the anticommunism central to the century's politics was a practice of containment that began with the making of the first revolutionary workers' state in the Soviet Union in 1917 and continued well after the implosion of actually existing socialism at the end of the 1980s.[1] The ugliness of this two-sided Cold War conditioned and pressured Stalinist atrocity as well as the evils of disingenuous democratic display: the Russian show trials and purges of the late 1930s[2] had their seemingly less bloody but hardly benign counterpart in the House Un-American Activities Committee (HUAC) hearings where the dubious practice of naming names turned the United States into an informer society in which people traded the honor of political conviction for the material securities of status and position.[3]

Bodies thus litter the political landscape. The extermination of the entire human apparatus of original Bolshevism in the degeneration of Stalinized Soviet life, not to mention the vast death march of induced famine in the countryside or the gulag of political and cultural repression, wrote finis to the liberatory hopes that many had associated with workers' revolution and the accomplishments of 1917. What followed in the United States was of course less chillingly terroristic, but the visible tip of an iceberg of denunciation with deadly consequences reaches from the Rosenbergs to lesser-known figures. The sensitive Canadian career diplomat and scholar of Japanese feudalism, E. H. Norman, finally committed suicide in Cairo after being hounded by McCarthyism's watchdogs for almost a decade.[4] Few areas of cultural life remained untouched by this ugliness, and as thousands were blacklisted from government circles, teaching jobs, journalist posts, Hollywood, and the arts community,[5] the Cold War at midcentury exercised a pernicious impact on avant-garde movements from abstract expressionism to modern jazz.[6]

Noir, both fiction and film, is one of those quintessentially modernist American cultural developments whose essence has, for generations of critics, proved notoriously difficult to locate with definitional precision.[7] As Raymond Borde and Étienne Chaumeton suggested in their *Panorama du film noir americain* (1955), it was the darkness at the heart of this new genre that lent it a certain coherence. This content coincided, interestingly, with a set of techniques—from off-centered shots and eerie lighting to night locations—many of which can be located in a materialized stylistics of wartime production overdetermined by budget constraints that affected the large studios as well as limiting the small producers. Noir is thus defined—first in substance but also in a congruent aesthetics—as disorientation. In its fundamental break with literary and cinematic convention, in which well-understood moral reference points had long been universally presented as statements of inherently timeless social values such as good, beauty, and honor, noir's core was its refusal to reproduce the parables of propriety. Instead, it introduced the destabilization of ambivalence and the challenging referent of reversal: good and evil were conjoined to the point of becoming indistinguishable; classical heroes and heroines were displaced by protagonists mired in the depths of depravity; motivations presented in their most base and disturbing light in animated narratives of chaos and confusion. Stylistically juxtaposing the bizzare and fantastic with a relentless sequence of realist snapshots, moreover, noir created an atmosphere of the ultranormal periodically ruptured by the weird, the violent, and the disturbing. All of this was often shot in closeup or tightly framed, lending it an offputting imbalance, claustrophobic in its containments. Audiences thus experienced noir, especially in its cinematic variants, as anguish and insecurity, a genre of apprehension.[8]

The background to this complex emergence of noir's forms, its prose as well as Hollywood variants, is thus multifaceted. Recent feminist commentary has often addressed noir as something of a male gaze, a fantasy of repression in which the desires and determinations of independent women are subordinated and brought back into the familialist fold of nurturing conventions. Such an interpretation certainly resonates with historical circumstances, especially in the United States, where the fluidity of gender relations was quite pronounced in the decades preceding noir's evolving place in popular culture. From the postwar 1920s to the economically pressured malaise of the Great Depression into the maelstrom of the 1940s, sexuality and male–female relations shifted gears dramatically. The resulting volatility in gender relations no doubt fed into the possibility that one dimension of anxiety addressed by noir would involve the subtle sustaining of male authority. There is no doubt much to recommend this reading, although some within critical feminist circles contend that the noir genre often provided an erosion of patriarchy's codes and conformities.[9]

If gender scripted noir's moment of emergence, so too did class. A part of the genre's origins lay in the depressingly stark 1930s realization that even the seemingly protected middle classes were facing economic insecurity, downward mobility, and consequent psychological turmoil. The translation of this socioeconomic unease into the dark artistic conventions of the 1940s allowed for noir's aesthetic purchase on a generation that had witnessed the capacity of boom to reverse to bust, sounding the death knell of complacent security and proclaiming an age of alienation. In Edward Hopper's oils, this representational engagement with estrangement found a uniquely American expression. The shadowed virtual photorealism of his archetypally noirish *Nighthawks* (1942) drew on themes the artist had explored earlier, pushing his 1920s articulations of anomie in more unambiguously alienated directions. Images of automats, drugstores, and burlesque houses, all crafted by Hopper in the late 1920s, gave way to post-1940 productions of office scenes, often shadowed in the night.[10] In these paintings, Hopper cast the commerce of the day in noirish juxtaposition to work time's supposed end, achieving an effect not unlike that of the David Mamet play and James Foley–directed 1992 film, *Glengarry Glen Ross*, in which darkness provides a context for capitalism's seamiest competitive manipulations and psychological damage to expose themselves. Hopper's *Summer Evening* (1947) typifies noir's rough-edged destiny of despair, the lighted porch framed by the night providing a venue pregnant with sensuality, conspiracy, and a hard-boiled cynicism drifting inevitably toward no good end.[11]

This hybrid representational evolution can be located in the lead-ups to and subsequent shadows of the Cold War.[12] Noir as a genre was born in the subterfuges of the Popular Front, where the programmatic suppression of revolutionary intention through integration into the mainstream of bourgeois order orchestrated a politics of accommodation always ostensibly turning on clandestine articulations of oppositional theory and practice.[13] Left-leaning Hollywood auteurs noirs made the most of this "cultural front" and gravitated to the ambivalences of noir instinctually, seeing in it "a shrewdly oblique strategy for an otherwise subversive realism."[14] A case in point was the quintessential Popular Front writer Vera Caspary, whose route from Jewish middle-class Chicago to Hollywood took her through two and a half years in the Communist Party in New York and Connecticut and involvement in the whirlwind activism of the cultural front of the 1940s. In her autobiography, The Secrets of Grown-Ups (1979), Caspary recalled engaging with the politics of the Anti-Nazi League, the League against War and Fascism, and the League of American Writers. She taught writing classes in order to earn money to bring refugee authors to America. "For the Left," she remembered, "these were fruitful years.... Almost every night there were fund-raising parties, benefits and concerts. There was a steady infux of new people coming to work in the studios—actors, writers, directors from New York, refugees from Europe." Caspary's thriller Laura (1942) became a film noir classic, although under Otto Preminger's 1944 direction it exemplified the subordination of the femme fatale to the male voice-over and, unlike Caspary's text, reduced women's experience to a superficial surface resistant to analysis.[15]

In the period of the Popular Front, then, noir attracted dissident authors and filmmakers, and was even to a certain extent crafted by them; in its capacity to build a critique of capitalism on the disintegrating rungs of conventional moral authority, noir was a voice raised against the sanctimoniousness of the socioeconomic context from within its particular confinements. This was not Marxist, pace Michael Denning's appreciation of the cultural front, as much as it was comfortably in alignment with the ambivalences of the Communist Party's relationship with capitalism and the American state.

The political certainties of the 1940s, during which the nation's moral core was a unified opposition to fascism, found themselves disintegrating and cut adrift in the realignments of post–Second World War anti-communism. With the Popular Front dismantled and the posture of reaction hardening dangerously day by day, it was impossible to make cinema Marxist at midcentury. But noir's formalistic darkness continued to allow the depiction of capitalism's unsavory undercurrents, to spin out the moral tales of an underground city where the productions of honest toil always lose out to the quick fixes of corruption and speculative vice, where the déclassé rich and the gangster predator rule an economy of easy money and its purchase on the good life.[16] In noir the attractions of the night always supersede those of the day, and, when given the choice, noir antiheroes inevitably choose betrayals and thefts, even murder, over honest toil and hard labor. That they could not win at capitalism's game is what no doubt made noir an attractive vehicle for Hollywood's progressives, among them the writers John Huston and Malvin Wald and the directors George E. Diskant and Jules Dassin.[17] But this message of doom and defeat also had its attractions in the Cold War climate of the reactionary 1950s, where the compensations of the hard-boiled style re-negotiated masculinity in an epoch of proletarian defeat and domestica-tion, both at the point of production and in the ideological arena.[18]

Noir's most successful cinematic expressions negotiated these shifting political contours in a unique fusion of heavy-handed German expres-sionism—orchestrated by expatriate directors such as Fritz Lang,[19] Otto Preminger,[20] Billy Wilder, Anatole Litvak, and Max Steiner—and the hard-boiled American prose style of Dashiell Hammett.[21] The Humphrey Bogart–Mary Astor 1941 production of Hammett's *The Maltese Falcon* (first published in 1930) marks the generally accepted debut of film noir.[22] On Califor-nia's Sunshine Coast—where heavy industry was weaker than in other geographic sectors, where old money was judged in decades rather than centuries, where rural America was physically quite close but socially so distant, and where the hustling boosterism of Hollywood lent the economic climate a fantasy-like hyperreality that seemed not all that far removed from the actualities of a political economy always on the verge of running away from itself—the potential for cultural and political fermentation was, as Mike Davis has suggested, truly bizarre.[23] "It is traumatic for an individual to lose a set of beliefs," writes the film noir critic Carl Richardson, whose exploration of the impact of the 1930s suggests that "for a world-wide coterie of intellectuals and artists, it is a dark, frustrating process. It is a film noir on a large scale."[24] Noir's aesthetics were tarnished from the genre's inception.

Out of the depths of the Great Depression came a series of real-life blows, their artistic renditions beginning with James M. Cain's novel *The Postman Always Rings Twice* (1934),[25] Horace McCoy's *They Shoot Horses Don't They?* (1935),[26] and Nathanael West's *The Day of the Locust* (1939). Stories of descent, debilitation, debauchery, and despair, these dark fictions seemed to replicate a part of the argument of Lewis Corey's [Louis Fraina's] unsettling analysis, *Crisis of the Middle Class* (1935). Captured artistically in Philip Evergood's painting *Dance Marathon* (1934), this "proletarian grotesque," in the words of Michael Denning, pushed images of play into the representational realm of its opposite: "The dance marathon" became "an allegory of an American capitalism in which endless, repetitive amusement and entertainment is oppressive, consuming the dreams of its youth," whose lives are squandered in economic depression, turning the pleasures of pastimes such as dance into the most routinized "wage labor."[27] In conjunction with Raymond Chandler's reconstruction of the world of the Los Angeles rich, as eyeballed by the tough-guy private dick Phillip Marlowe and always tarnished by a moral darkness that could be opened up to the light only by the vernacular of the people, such texts turned the page toward noir's urban futilities.[28] Two years before he died, Chandler wrote to his London solicitor, "I have lived my life on the edge of nothing."[29]

If the origins of this accommodation lay in the economic malaise of the 1930s, the final reconciliation was one of a seemingly psychological realpolitik, in which recognition of what was possible in the give-and-take of capitalism's ensembles of power was adapted to rather than challenged—with particular psychic costs.[30] The astute Afro-Caribbean Marxist C. L. R. James grasped the dualism of this cultural negotiation, appreciating its subtle subversions as well as its incarcerating incorporations. Noir institutionalized traditionalist values of individualism, and James located the attraction of the genre in the rugged American need to stand alone. The heroic fatalism of noir's protagonists was an almost universal self-reliance, apart from all structures of constituted authority and most emphatically distanced from law and propriety: "He had to be an ordinary guy—*one who went out and did the job himself.*" In the context of closed frontiers and obvious barriers to the mythic dreams of American acquisitive individualism, undeniable in the post-Depression epoch of capitalism's powerful monopolistic grasp on material power, noir sustained "a sense of active living, and in the bloodshed, the violence, the freedom from restraint to allow pent-up feelings free play," James discerned a possible release of "the bitterness, hate, fear, and sadism" that he saw simmering below the discontented surface of social relations.[31] If James saw in this narrative of cultural appropriation and understanding the potential of resistance, there was much to overcome to mobilize its possibilities. Not the least of noir's cultivations was the construction of a dark imagery whose predictable postures erased the living realities of day-to-day oppression in the distorted shadows of night's always unfulfilled dreams, sliding inevitably into the sinister hole of nightmarish fears from which the only exit appears a fantasy of forgetfulness.[32]

Noir's exploration of such themes often took on purely economic dimensions, albeit in ways that could blur into sexual pathologies, where the spent currency of erotic fulfillment generally had a crassly materialistic character. To be sure, there was the possibility of diversity always present in noir's unfolding dramas. In Chester Himes's novel *If He Hollers Let Him Go* (1945), for instance, racism found a bitter chronicler. Something of this would be born again in the soft-pedaling 1980s and 1990s with film adaptions of Walter Mosley's Easy Rawlins mysteries, *Devil in a Blue Dress*, *A Red Death*, and *White Butterfly*, but racial commentary was a rare intervention in the white plots of noir's acquisitive individualism.[33] Nevertheless, regardless of the route to noir's endnote, its cul-de-sac conclusion was universally marked by its darkened realism.

Chandler noted in 1950, the Cold War breaking all around him, "We still have dreams, but we know that most of them will come to nothing. And we also most fortunately know that it really doesn't matter." With the Hollywood Ten battling the blacklist, Chandler could declare, "This is not an age of reason or tolerance, but in Hollywood you don't learn to be a hero. You learn to be expedient—or you get to hell out."[34] There wasn't much, after all, beyond the big sleep: "What did it matter where you lay once you were dead? In a dirty sump or in a marble tower on top of a high hill? You were dead, you were sleeping the big sleep, you were not bothered by things like that."[35] The message would reappear in the twisted reversals of the staccato prose and spare aesthetics of the Los Angeles novels of James Ellroy: his nightmare-induced noir quartet—*The Black Dahlia* (1987), *The Big Nowhere* (1988), *L.A. Confidential* (1990), and *White Jazz* (1993)—had its origins in the author's mother's unresolved murder.[36] Noir proved a reservoir for the avant-garde aspirations of the 1940s and 1950s precisely because it seemed the perfect accommodation: it embraced alienation, tried to overcome it, reproduced the evil it aimed to transcend, and returned to the ever-troubling heart of darkness at the core of human existence. The contradictory impulse of the genre nurtured a profound moral ambivalence, a conspiracy of silencing anguish conscious in its intention to produce emotional insecurity: noir was nothing less, in the words of its original interpreters, than "*that state of tension instilled in the spectator when the pyschological reference points are removed. The aim of film noir was to create a specific alienation.*"[37] As one of its great character actors, Elisha Cook, Jr.—whose credits included thirteen major motion pictures, from *The Maltese Falcon* through *Phantom Lady* (1944), *The Big Sleep* (1946), *Born to Kill* (1947), *The Killing* (1956), and *Baby Face Nelson* (1957)—described his roles: "I played rats, pimps, informers, hopheads, and communists," a veritable catalogue of undesirables.[38] Noir typecast not the admirable hero but the fall-guy antihero.

This dark moral reversal was as much an articulation of form as of substance. Moods, rather than plots, dominate noir; as a cinematic genre it was built around frustrations and fears, claustrophobias and psychic chaos, an anxiety-ridden context of paranoia all too often embedded in a troubling experience of defeat. Film noir's human centerpieces were constructions of lonely obsessions, narrowed to the point that they suffocate those who could not effectively wrestle their own demons into the background where they belong, allowing "healthy" perspectives of human relationships and purposes to come into the foreground. Against idealized conceptions of families, communities, and commitments, noir presented a dark, foreboding culture of shocking individualism. In it, an endlessly alienated pursuit of illusive material gratifications short-circuited the American Dream, pushing it in the direction of an eminent imploding nightmare. In the plot lines of noir everything good was permeated with the polluting evils of greed and lust, excesses of the estranged self that manage to corrupt human vulnerability and force it toward its ugliest poles of (dis)attraction. Stylistic devices, from closeups of anguished faces to distorted lighting, mirror reflections, silhouetted figures, haunting flashbacks, outlandish camera angles, shadowed walls, and twisted profiles, contributed to the making of skewed perspectives. This formal presentation that there was something seriously awry in the human condition[39] had its material origins in both the scarcities (which constricted the possibilities of shooting, lighting, and editing) and the social perspectives of the Second World War.[40]

Above all else, noir elevated the night to a dark moment of human estrangement, a time and place of instability in which strivings for the unattainable produced the undoing of men and women. Their every act was shot in orchestrated night-on-night scenes that broke with cinematic tradition to present the oppositional possibilities of day and night. In The Night Has a Thousand Eyes (1947) Edward G. Robinson, playing a tormented psychic with the power to predict death, lives beneath the oppression of the stars, which fatally oversee his adventures: "I had become a reverse zombie, the world was dead and I was living."[41] Visual motifs thus translated into existential comment as the dark boundaries of existence constricted inward in a tightening knot of noir's capacity to effect a material transfiguration. The physicality of a scene became the tortured content of a soul.[42] "The Streets were dark with something more than night," declares Edward G. Robinson in The Woman in the Window (1945); Mark Stevens proclaims in The Dark Corner (1946), "I'm backed up in a dark corner and I don't know who's hitting me." In both scenes the spatial and shadowed context of enclosure, in conjunction with dialogue and the cinematic process of framing, moves from one of place to one of psyche—not unlike the HUAC settings in which the bright light of anticommunism shone illuminatingly through speeches of pathetic recantation.

After resisting the McCarthyite witch-hunt for two years, for instance, Lee J. Cobb found himself penniless and workless, his wife institutionalized as an alcoholic. He finally broke, naming twenty individuals as "known" Communists and identifying others within Actors' Equity as left-wingers. Finally able to secure employment, he suffered a massive coronary (his hospital bills were covered by Frank Sinatra) before landing the entirely appropriate role of the compliant Johnny Friendly in On the Waterfront (1954). Cobb's final statement to HUAC was a pusillanimous justification of his sad denouement: he thanked the modern-day inquisition for allowing him "the privilege of setting the record straight, ... further strengthening ... our Government and its efforts at home and abroad."[43] Film noir at least spared its audience such pathetic blandishments. All that the noir antihero could generally accomplish was a temporary stay of personal solitude, a quiet, desperate retreat from the confusion that relentlessly sinks optimism in the rough waves of impending darkness, a final futile statement or gesture.[44] Cobb might better have settled for as much.

To isolate a classic film noir presentation analytically is perhaps an impossibility, so diverse were the Hollywood offerings in this genre. Between The Maltese Falcon (1941) and Orson Welles's Touch of Evil (1958) the literally hundreds of films made encompassed a range of formalized types, from the socially critical commentary of The Naked City (1948) and Nightmare Alley (1947) through gangster films such as The Racket (1951) and The Asphalt Jungle (1950) to the generalized noir theme of fatalism and demoralization attendant on greed and the adventure of quests for pathological acquisitions, material, psychological, or sexual. In the last category can be placed many of the adaptations of classic Hammett and Chandler private-eye fiction, as well as Humphrey Bogart films such as High Sierra (1941), Key Largo (1948), Dead Reckoning (1947), and In a Lonely Place (1950). Ironically enough, the least successful variants of noir were consciously right-wing statements, such as the dour melodrama Ride the Pink Horse (1947), and explicit Cold War productions that attempted actually to address anti-communism frontally. I Was a Communist for the FBI (1951) pales in comparision, aesthetically and intellectually, with the materialized eroticization of estrangement evident in Double Indemnity (1944), The Postman Always Rings Twice (1946), or Clash by Night (1952). Yet, as revealed by one classic noir statement, the blacklisted director-in-exile Jules Dassin's Night and the City (1950), the imagery and representational force of noir was never all that far removed from the Cold War's stifling presence.[45]

Dassin was one of the premier Hollywood noir directors. Between 1941 and 1946 he directed eight shorts and features, including *Nazi Agent* (1942) and the light comedy *The Affairs of Martha* (1942), in which a servant writes a scandalous book about her employers. Dassin's true creative genius burst forth with the three critically acclaimed films, *Brute Force* (1947), *Thieves' Highway* (1949), and *The Naked City* (1948), some of which drew the ire of the FBI. The last had the stark presentation of a docudrama, but the other two marked Dassin as one of Hollywood's more socially conscious artists. Dassin was a champion of the mythic, proletarian conflict ubiquitous in the maelstrom of bourgeois order and his work was unrelenting in its condemnation of the meaninglessness and everyday violence of routinized life.

When his noir counterpart, imprisoned Ukrainian-Canadian Edward Dmytryk of the infamous Hollywood Ten, sought the favor of HUAC and purged himself by identifying Dassin as a supposed Communist, the latter—against whom there was little tangible evidence beyond Dmytryk's self-interested testimony—found himself persecuted and blacklisted. Dmytryk, the only member of the Hollywood Ten to recant in this way, went on to direct *The Sniper* (1952), a thinly veiled defense of political repression which elided deviance and dissidence in justifying the incarceration of sex offenders in mental hospitals (it was the time of Francis Farmer, after all).[46] In 1954 he directed the highly acclaimed *The Caine Mutiny* (1954), which carried the authoritarian message that even incompetent leaders deserve the regard of those serving under them, whose allegiance must be total and unwavering.[47] Meanwhile, rather than dignify HUAC and its project, Dassin had left the United States for England. His first film in exile was *Night and the City* (1950), a cinematic tour through the themes of noir shot against a background of darkest London: a Dickensian underworld of con men, hustlers, petty thieves, street urchins, dance hall girls, beggars, and bookies; a labyrinth of stairwells, bridges, construction sites, hideaways, constricted spaces, and parodied dangers.[48]

Inhabiting this terrain of the street and its foggy and smoky alleyways, through which he is almost always on the run, is an American expatriate on the proverbial make, Harry Fabian, played by the noir icon Richard Widmark. Fabian is forever in search of his rightful score, a man on the perpetual edge, for whom his long-suffering, golden-hearted girlfriend Mary Bristol provides a ready source of petty cash. But as Harry works himself toward the limelight of "being somebody," of actually "having it all," the stakes are raised to the point where nobody, and certainly not Mary, can pull him out of his fated demise. Harry, described by a romantic rival (whose genuine decency and somewhat homosexualized persona eliminates him from Mary's slightest consideration) as "an artist without an art," succumbs in the end to a betrayal of art and pays the ultimate price. Cynically befriending Gregorius, the innocent if patriarchal figure-head of European Greco-Roman wrestling and the disenchanted father of the unsavory, immigrant Kristol, the ruthlessly powerful criminal boss of London's emerging postwar commercialized wrestling scene, Harry Fabian uses his capacities as a con man to hustle his way into a potential rivalry with the underworld emperor. For a while, his capacity to con virtually everyone around him appears to be paying dividends. With Gregorius in his corner, his ventures bankrolled by his nightclub-owner employer, Nosseross, and his ploys playing out, Fabian's name is about to head the marquee of London wrestling's biggest coup: an epic, theatrical battle between classical, artistic Greco-Roman wrestling and the psychopathology of "the fight game" as epitomized in the person of Kristo's star performer, the subhuman "Strangler."

Yet Harry's apparently unfolding bonanza unravels as his con predictably oversteps itself and his markers are called in by those, such as Nosseross and Kristo, who hold the decisively powerful cards. In the end Harry is reduced to what he has always been, a man on the run (he complains in his last hour that he has forever been running, from welfare agents, his father, the police). An exile in his own adopted city (not unlike Dassin himself), a figure with a price on his head that few of his fellow hustlers can resist (again, not unlike Dassin in the world of Hollywood's HUAC), Harry is a doomed man scrambling through the night over war-bombed rubble, seeking futile refuge against the damp-darkened walls of the Thames or in the refuse of London's wharf rats. As the bridge swarms with Kristo's ready soldiers, he faces a dark dawn as a man whose time has finally run out. Without a word of politics, Dassin thus creates a commentary on the world of the Cold War, in which powerful forces of evil bring exile, frustration, and defeat to those "who just want to be somebody"—a line of pathos uttered by Fabian which predated Marlon Brando's famous On the Waterfront (1954) statement by four years.

Visually, the film is a condemnation of the cynical and desperate cor-ruptions of the postwar capitalist marketplace. In Beggar's Lane, one of Harry's cronies outfits professional panhandlers with false limbs and other props that make them a more viable conduit for cash. The metaphorical imagery is anything but light. A pit-like darkness symbolizes capitalism's incarceration of the working class, and the seediness of exchange relations offers a stark representation of the crass hucksterism of metropolitan capital. In the subterranean nightclub lair of the Silver Fox, an aptly named den of wily duplicity, a grotesque Nosseross strokes his cash like a caricature of the grasping, bloated exploiter, his life confined to the office from which he looks appropriately down upon the nocturnal theater in which a male clientele makes itself a ready sucker for every costly pseudo-sexual come-on. The underground emperor, Kristo, flanked by his lawyer and bodyguard, is the only figure who looms over London's skyline. Biding his time and eventually exacting his revenge, Kristo is the living embodiment of the fact not only that crime does pay but that it ultimately calls all the shots. In the background, smaller predators circle the ever-present human prey.

Money rules this universe of greed and corruption, emerging from transactions behind the scenes, manufactured from the wheelings and dealings of false bargains. Cash changes hands in thick, elastic-wrapped packages; bills are stroked sensually by those devoid of human eroticism; wealth talks the language of empty promise but can never actually secure anything of worth. Harry's obsessional pursuit of money and the fame he thinks it will secure him is the tragic flaw in a life of anguished movement that takes him only in the spiral of inevitable free fall into a final, friendless hell.

Mary tells Fabian in the end that he could have done anything: with brains, ambition, and hard work, he could have been a heroic figure, but his lack of art ensured that he would always pursue "the wrong things." In the London night Harry Fabian is eventually reduced to just such a "wrong thing": everything is for sale as a car speeds through Harry's increasingly claustrophobic world, announcing to all and sundry the thousand-pound price on his head. The man who had managed to "get it all" has signed his own death warrant by pushing the game of self-realization too far. The rules of class place and social station, bent to the point of snapping by those at the top of the small, social pyramid of London's subculture of the night street, are only so flexible. For the Harry Fabians they provide just enough give to rebound in death. Harry at least goes to his end with some grace, doing what he can to secure Kristo's blood money for Mary; she alone, in the London of the night, stands by the man who has offered her only the cold comfort of his own insatiable ambitions, and a willingness to do virtually anything to realize them.[49]

Night and the City is thus an ongoing social commentary on the labyrinth of postwar capitalism and its Cold War politics of repressive containment, a challenging exploration all the more effective precisely because it seems far removed from the subject of its caustic critique. Symbolized in Dassin's film as commercially promoted wrestling, capitalism is insightfully constructed as a staged event. This is a noir preface to postmodern theory's grasp of the critical importance of spectacle in a decaying order in which the marketing of images outpaces the production of goods—of which there is no sign whatever in the rotting darkness of Night and the City, where everything for sale is a recycled subterfuge, a crafted fraud. Roland Barthes's understanding of Parisian wrestling in roughly the same period suggests the significance of this spectacle and its relationship to noir as a genre. "The virtue of all-in wrestling is that it is the spectacle of excess," states Barthes in his opening analytic line, and noir and its Cold War subjects are also about excess. Wrestling, like noir, "abandons itself to the primary virtue of the spectacle, which is to abolish all motives and all consequences," a process the Cold War codified. Noir antiheroes are not unlike Barthes's wrestlers, nor are they all that different from those who purged themselves before HUAC: "The function of the wrestler is not to win; it is to go exactly through the motions which are expected of him.... a man who is down is exaggeratedly so, and completely fills the eyes of the spectators with the intolerable spectacle of his own powerlessness." Such a scene can be marketed and sold as spectacle because the genuineness of its content is beside the point: "What the public wants is the image of passion, not passion itself." The axiom is applicable to Night and the City's central locale, the Silver Fox nightclub, where a staged sensuality, in its darkly designed disingenuousness, poisons the capacity for passion between Nosseross (No Eros) and his calculatingly cold wife, Helen. Noir and wrestling elevate the "bastard" to the standard of humanity, as perhaps does capitalism. And to visualize such a bastard aesthetically is noir's contribution, a culture of darkness entirely congruent with postwar capitalism's politics of Cold War night. "Some fights," comments Barthes, "among the most successful kind, are crowned by a final charivari, a sort of unrestrained fantasia where the rules, the laws of the genre, the referee's censuring and the limits of the ring are abolished, swept away by a triumphant disorder ... [a] return to the orgy of evil which alone makes good wrestling." Noir's final frames could hardly be better described, nor capitalism's trajectory more aptly characterized.[50]

What Mike Davis calls the "transformational grammar" of noir was thus capable of sustaining an acute artistic paradox.[51] In the constricting sociopolitical climate of the Cold War, it played within conventional boundaries but caricatured those boundaries mercilessly. As Davis suggests, not only did noir shift the language of charming boosterism and optimistic ambition away from its veneer of social niceties and into the dark recesses of its sinister counterparts of greed and the materially induced manipulations (and worse) of hucksterism; it managed to represent themes literally outlawed in the moment of the Cold War freeze on social commentary.[52] Anticommunism had so suppressed the possibility of cinematic depictions of working-class life that noir's unsubtle exploitation of this equally unsubtle exercise of censorship merely followed the trajectory of exclusion by exaggerating the inversion of powerlessness. Noir thus created a dark reservoir of humanity whose marginality pushed past that of an organized proletariat into the shadowy isolations of rootlessness, where cab drivers, dance hall girls, war veterans, boxers, private detectives, and criminals symbolize the have-nots stripped even of the collectivity of wage-earning jobs and the associational authorities of unions, communities, and political activities. While capitalism was being reified in the post–Second World War years as a savior of humankind, the acquisitive individualism of the marketplace was darkened in noir's depiction of "bosses" as emperors of the underworld, tsars of the disreputable enterprises of the night: the clubs, bars, rings, and cul-de-sacs where cash always changes hands in the most sordid of ways. If race, a pivotal social divide, was also exorcised by the Cold War demons as too contentiously hot a political issue to handle without yet again introducing the potential of dissidence, noir's pressured whiteness managed to racialize otherness in the contorted savagery of dangerously powerful freaks and geeks.[53] These were usually used crassly by powerfully evil figures, who could nevertheless be undone by the simple humanity of their cretinous but ultimately innocent dupes. Even in noir's unashamedly misogynistic presentation of the inner tensions of gendered greed, the mere presence of the femme fatale had a powerful potential to subvert sexual stereotyping. Presented as a persistent frustration of male desire, the femme fatale defied a patriarchal culture's limiting subordinations of female place and tightening definitions of womanly need.[54] As Janey Place has suggested, noir women often disrupted the conventional narrative: their disorienting presentation of an unrepressed female sexuality combined with a rapacious materialism provided a rare cinematic articulation of women's strengths in the realms of Eros and accumulation.[55] The only winner in Night and the City is the old hag of the Silver Fox nightclub, shunned by beauty but rewarded by the beast of an owner, who wills her his property in a final act of revenge against his unfaithful and contemptuously repulsed wife.

Noir thus rewrote the script of Cold War culture. Even if its darkness submerged themes of social protest in the long night of alienation, noir refused to collapse the entirety of critical representation's repertoire into the soft, fleshy monotones of prettified propagandizing for an American Way of Life. Films such as Nicholas Ray's *They Live By Night* (1947) battled the censors' demands to curb social criticism, eliminate reference to war profiteering, and downplay depictions of postwar affluence as propelled by the consumer hucksters—such as used car dealers—who were the thieves of a new and crudely acquisitive social order.[56] Noir's elevation of the night and the searches for self-realization that unfolded within its darkness offered coded counterpoints to the jaded and jaundiced conventionalities of idealized families and communities. Noir presented an introspective, always fatally flawed, flight from such conformist confinement. It was an escape pushed by scarred backgrounds and unwholesome needs but one at least cognizant of human suffering and abuse, incapable of papering over the larger social ills that the Cold War attempted to deny and obfuscate.

This transgressively open-ended set of noir possibilities has proved particularly durable. Despite a middle-to-late 1950s Hollywood demand for a more prettified pontification of the bourgeoisie's many virtues, noir has managed to keep alive both a proletarian kernel and the political background of its formative moment. In Gordon Demarco's 1980s Trotskyist detective, Riley Kovachs, the "hard-boiled" takes a left turn, battling Stalinist union corruption, racism, and McCarthyism.[57] The neo-noir productions *Chinatown* (1974), *Taxi Driver* (1976), and *Blue Velvet* (1987) were but a cinematic preface to an onslaught of resurgent noir in the 1990s.[58] This extended from the big screen to the popularity of televised noirish series such as *Miami Vice* and *Homicide*, which had been preceded by such late 1950s productions as *Peter Gunn*, perhaps the most mass-directed introduction of the subtle subversions of jazz to a white mainstream audience.[59] Ideally suited to the rebirth was the "savage art" of the anarcho-communist-populist Jim Thompson, whose dark explorations of the underworld of the 1930s and 1940s had produced some of the most volatile fiction of the noir genre, moving well past Chandler and Hammett. The cinematic reconfiguration of noir under late capitalism commenced with two 1990 film versions of Thompson novels, *The Grifters* and *After Dark, My Sweet*.[60] Soon followed by the innovations of Quentin Tarantino and others, most of 1990s neo-noir had a decidedly destructive conception of the "family values" that had been pressured into the politics of mainstream culture at the time: *Reservoir Dogs* (1992), *Red Rock West* (1992), *Pulp Fiction* (1994), *The Last Seduction* (1994).[61] Throughout this explosion of dark cinema the gendered nature of greed—always present in traditional noir's inability to transcend a bifurcation of woman: evil and predatory temptress or saintly and victimized adornment—flows easily into late-twentieth-century constructions of masculine womanhood, every bit as capable as debased manhood of seizing whatever main chance presents itself.[62]

With noir's rebirth in the late twentieth century, it was less pressured by political containments than the productions of the 1940s and 1950s, and its sexualized possibility expanded considerably, freed from the earlier censorship of Will Hays, the Production Code, and the Catholic Legion of Decency.[63] Transgressive sexuality, from the subthemes of incest that figure forcefully in Chinatown and The Grifters to the bending content of homosexuality in The Last Seduction, fuses with the overarching theme of noir, money, and its disfiguring capacities. In the 1980s and 1990s, however, the proliferation of assembly-line mystery writers such as James Lee Burke, Lawrence Block, and their female counterpart, Sue Grafton, bleached noir of much of its darkness, smoothing its rough edges and filing down its open antagonisms. If there is a hard-boiled successor to Chandler and Hammett, it is Andrew Vachss. His private detective, Burke, is a product of child abuse and the ugliness of the state reformatory system, an eroticized avenger. A crusader untroubled by the moralities of Marlowe or Sam Spade, Burke is a mercenary of the night, a depoliticized defender of innocent children, the strong silent type gone outlaw. His turf is the city of darkness, the night markets where predators prowl for victims and where the rough justice of noir can still be found, although crafted somewhat differently from traditional noir's recognizable politics of representation.[64]

This fin-de-siècle rescripting of noir's nature, in which the Cold War is displaced, has left the contemporary genre twisting in the winds of a peculiar "end of history" culturalist climate. Nihilism, chaos, and sensationalism still blow with gusto.[65] But the subtle craft of noir's original imagery has been jettisoned, yet another casualty of the truly "big sleep" of capitalism's current ascendancy.

PART VIII

Race and Capitalist Crisis

18. Joe Hendricks, Untitled depiction of urban youth,
Rochester, New York (1970s).

19

Nights of Accumulation

Banditry, Mafias, and the
Contemporary Spirit of Capitalism

Capitalism's long history has intruded upon and contextualized the histories of transgression and the night for centuries. Defined by its dependence on the extraction of surplus from a propertyless wage-laboring population, and moved by a relentless logic of accumulation, capitalism's slow beginnings in the seventeenth century literally gathered steam in the eighteenth and nineteenth centuries. They adapted technological innovations to the cause of emerging social differentiation and an expanding division of labor; the consequences of the Industrial Revolution transformed first locales then countries, finally the globe itself. The interests of capital, quickly transcending national boundaries and necessitating a worldwide competitive scramble for markets, stimulated imperialism's expansion of empires. As new innovations in the structure and management of enterprise moved capital off the pedestal of the regionally based family firm and onto the wider stage of the multinational corporation, capitalism's twentieth-century history did not so much shift gears as create a set of new teeth with which accumulation could take bigger and bigger bites. Capitalism's history has been one of endlessly new imaginings, all premised on the acquisition and accumulation central to its drive. Of vital importance in this expansionary logic is capital's capacity to subordinate the dispossessed, whose production of surplus has, for hundreds of years, provided the material appropriations energizing capital's movements and productive expansions.[1]

Commentators on capitalism, especially those whose ideas are situated within a Marxist framework, have always differentiated the *productive* essence of truly capitalist exploitive relations from the predatory, often speculative, early mercantile exchange endeavors whose high-stakes gambles served to fuel the fires of the first Industrial Revolution.[2] To be sure, the transition from the exchange-driven mercantilism of the Age of Absolutism to the factory productions of the Age of Industry, with its attendant shift in social structure, the rise of the city, and the subordination of the country-side, entailed a range of cultural consequences—the time discipline explored by E. P. Thompson and others to the spiritual accommodations and adaptations studied by R. H. Tawney and Max Weber in their influential books on puritanism, Protestantism, and the rise of capitalism.[3] Not only did this constellation of change, paced by production, initiate swing shifts in class and state formations. It also altered the materially embedded appreciation and understanding of "need" itself, stimulating consumer appetite and creating a human nature of want that would have been unfathomable in earlier ages.[4] From the physiologically induced desire for the stimulant sugar (associated with the newly created proletariat of England in the late eighteenth and nineteenth centuries) to the psychic need for acquisition that sociologists associate with the *embourgeoisement* of affluent labor in "classless" America in the "end of ideology" 1950s, capitalism's history has been one of creating "need" in ways that change both the mind and the body as they are situated in social relations of power.[5]

Indeed, Tawney started and ended his study of religion and capitalism's rise with a set of aphorisms that highlighted how change can overwhelm those who would deny its inexorable march:

> The certainties of one age are the problems of the next. Few will
> refuse their admiration to the magnificent conception of a community
> penetrated from apex to foundation by the moral law, which was the
> inspiration of the great reformers, not less than of the better minds of
> the Middle Ages. But, in order to subdue the tough world of material
> interests, it is necessary to have at least so much sympathy with its
> tortuous ways as is needed to understand them. The Prince of Darkness
> has a right to a courteous hearing and a fair trial, and those who will
> not give him his due are wont to find that, in the long run, he turns
> the tables by taking his due and something over.

By the 1930s Keynes could write, "Modern capitalism is absolutely ir-religious, without internal union, without much public spirit, often, though not always, a mere congeries of possessors and pursuers." At that early date, admittedly one of crisis, capitalism was conceived as moving toward its night. As Tawney suggested, moreover, it did so by receding into its past, abandoning the *productive* revolutionism of its dynamic, centuries-long middle period and settling into a dark, predatory labyrinth of exchange where life itself becomes a market, and all markets are meant to be advantageously manipulated.[6]

Such warnings and denunciations were distant indeed by the closing decades of the twentieth century, when the spirit of capitalism seemed far removed from the revolutionary origins that had translated the transforming power of production into a material force capable of reversing spiritual authority. Some insist that late-twentieth-century capitalism has moved into a decidedly new mode of production, a postmodern economics governed not by the old standards of production, profit, and the conventional powers and properties associated with them but by new and rapidly evolving technologies of information. Markets are no longer held to be critically concerned with things and properties as commodities; instead, circulating knowledges constitute the fundamental power zones of the postmodern world. As the critically important writings of Fredric Jameson and David Harvey suggest, however, it is possible to situate such developments—which are not perhaps as ultimately transformative as their interpretive advocates suggest—within the long swings of capitalist change and reconstitution, materializing cultural movements in late capitalism's postmodern genres.[7]

Here, my purposes are more modest. Capitalism remains a system governed by the metaphorical laws and motivating logics of its past. Yet if one considers the contemporary spirit of capitalism, it is difficult not to see it entering a particularly dark period of brutalizing economic, cultural, social, and psychic barbarism, whatever its capacities to soften the blows of indifferent accumulation with consumer accoutrements and highly selective (on a global scale) material palliatives. Early revolutionary capitalism, with its powerful productive impulses, expanded the material possibilities for humankind immeasurably. It also conditioned intellectual breakthroughs of monumental benefit, shattering the fetters of ignorance and tradition and dismantling (albeit often without conscious intent) the most crudely incapacitating subordinations: serfdom, slavery, and superstition. This capitalism was, in fact, a progressive historical force, and one that at least offered a negotiation, as Tawney and Weber have shown, of the ethical complexities of individualism and social responsibility—however much that negotiation may have seemed to some an ideological facade.[8] Late capitalism, in decided contrast, has ossified into a night creature of predatory rapaciousness, a truly amoral marketplace beast with a single motivation: accumulation at any cost. It is a nightmarish reproduction of Marx's metaphors of the profit-driven order as a vampirish, werewolfish monster.[9] It is surely no accident, the ideas of any given epoch having an unmistakable relationship to the material context in which they are spawned, that at precisely the historical moment of this new world order's birth, sociobiology and neo-Darwinian thought experienced a reactionary revival. Human nature was increasingly constructed as a reified, gene-driven survivalism in which crass self-interest was elevated to the status of a motivating force in history; Andrew Ross has appropriately dubbed this result "the gangster theory of life."[10]

In the climate of late capitalism, business and crime have become increasingly congruent. Savings and loan scandals, bank bilkings, tax and trust-law evasions, junk-bond marketeering, offshore shelters, and conflicts of interest extend throughout the society to the pillars of political power. With the maze of interpenetrations that link legitimate and illicit capital, late capitalism truly does appear to operate on a gangster theory in which greed is the sole governance of acquisitive individualism's endless pursuits.[11] Capitalist crisis, linked less to production's shutdowns than to the effervescent destabilizations of mirage-like money, is now often seen as a potential catastrophic collapse. Commerce's launderings, sordid manufacture, and theft transactions threaten to topple a precarious social order in proverbial dominos fashion.[12]

Little can now be said or done to shore up this shaky material edifice. It is no longer possible, or necessary, to suggest some kind of association of capitalist accumulation and spiritual values, as it was in capitalism's revolutionary phase. Now, acquisition is the end that justifies any and all means. Not the puritan committed to production and profit, as in the seventeenth century, but the bandit and mafia community become the representational figures of capitalism in the last decades of the twentieth century. Rather than textiles or sugar or automobiles or electronics products, the commodities of late capitalism's booming dawn are often the purchases of the night, sold in the seedy markets of side streets and the boulevards of all-too-often tarnished dreams, where substances of mind and body alteration are the palliatives of choice. The contemporary spirit of capitalism is thus a nonspirit, a dark denial of any and all values save those that will secure the quickest possible return. This has always been the gangster creed, but whereas capitalism once hypocritically outlawed criminality, criminality has now reconfigured capitalism in its outlaw mold. In the words of Vincenzo Ruggiero, "From clean money to criminal money and vice versa, the direction seems to be reversible: while the Mafia does business, business *mafiosizes* itself."[13] To understand the ethical void of late capitalism, in which one production of the night is the escalating violence of accumulation on a world scale, one can perhaps follow no better historical route than that of the bandits and mafias who have come to occupy such a central place in the imagery of accumulation.[14]

Bandits—especially the social bandit whose acts of robbery and plunder pose a direct challenge to unjust, accumulative authority, redistributing wealth and income to those from whom it has been extracted, avenging the wrongs of the weak—predate capitalism by centuries. Antiquity's marauders, the ballad and literary evolution of Robin Hood and his outlaw band (which reached from the thirteenth through the nineteenth centuries), and the brigandage of the Mediterranean world all carried the lore and the lusts of the bandit through various historical periods. A 1585 report read matter-of-factly, "This year in Rome, we have seen more heads [of bandits] on the Ponte Sant'Angelo than melons on the marketplace," a disturbing analogy that linked expropriation and exchange, production and punishment.[15]

Yet the heroic age of the social bandit coincided, interestingly, with the progressive epoch of capitalism's sustained inroads on feudal structures, during which the disruptions and dispossessions associated with breaking the back of landed power and colonial structures of rule produced a traumatic and materially debilitating chaos for peasant producers. The time was thus ripe for a fusion of popular protest and social banditry, and in a wide array of dispersed geographical locales—from eastern and southern Europe to Africa, Latin America, and China—the late eighteenth, nineteenth, and early twentieth centuries saw the rise of the plebeian-sanctioned outlaw: the social bandit criminalized by the state and powerful interests but championed and protected by the *menu peuple* and revered for his refusal to succumb to authority.[16] Bred of deteriorating material conditions, banditry was the peasant proprietor's last stand. Increasingly translated to the urban barrio, it was an extreme recourse to extreme measures that galvanized the very few at the same time as its attractions were quite widespread. As Hobsbawm concludes:

> The bandit is brave, both in action and as victim. He dies defiantly and well, and unnumbered boys from slums and suburbs, who possess nothing but the common but nevertheless precious gift of strength and courage, can identify themselves with him. In a society in which men live by subservience, as ancillaries to machines of metal or moving parts of human machinery, the bandit lives and dies with a straight back.[17]

If the bandit was formed within this largely backward-looking, eminently masculinized defiance, he was nevertheless symbolic of something more than the selfish "gangster theory of life." Primitive notions of justice, of the good leader or avenger or figure of stature who will return prosperity and proper social relations to the people, animate the heroic mythology of the social bandit, including frontier outlaws of the Australian outback or the Turnerian American West. Just as the spirit of early capitalism was one of ethical renegotiation, so too the spirit of social banditry, arising out of progressive capital's admittedly harsh reconstructions of landed society, was a process of reconfiguring understandings of place and power, both of which were gripped tightly in the jaws of an obvious but poorly conceived dissolution. As the state, often under attack, followed particular tactics of repression and accommodation—at times warring against the guerrilla bandit, at times adapting social banditry to its hegemonic legitimation—the oppositional meaning of the bandit's primitive appropriation blurred in a confused clash of seemingly incompatible forces. That the bandit rarely reconstructed his relation to such processes of change in ways that could transform the social order was the tragedy of this limited form of resistance. But the bandit's refusal simply to adapt stoically to immiseration, unjust repression, and criminalization left a legacy of transgressive resistance, a saga of moral ambivalence that cut into the underside of capitalism's and colonialism's many undeniable conquests.

A particular variant of this preservationist bandit was the mafioso of the southern Italian olive-producing region of the Plain of Gioia Tauro. In Pino Arlacchi's words, this Calabrian subregion experienced a state of "permanent transition" from 1860 to 1950 as a monoculture fixated on olive production came increasingly "to resemble a game of chance." Class formation was characterized by rapid change: bonanza years facilitated the purchase of houses, livestock, and small farms so that landless laborers became small tenants, sharecroppers, or smallholders. But depressed periods always followed, forcing many to sell and readjust to the vicissitudes of propertyless laboring status. Even the ruling layers of society were never secure, and Arlacchi suggests that Calabria experienced a "circulation of elites," a process of power's constant reconstitution that encouraged conspicuous display of the acquisitions of prestige. Between 1860 and the Second World War, sectors of Calabrian society had been formed and reformed with such rapidity and lack of continuity that the entire social formation was governed only by an "extra-familial web of social relations both extremely thin and very limited." Institutions of authority were virtually absent, and interactions among families and individuals were those "of sovereign powers in conflict." The political economy of this society of "permanent transition" thus took on the trappings of an almost antiquated mercantile exchange network. Individual prestige came to be measured by the number of "adherences" a person was able to acquire, the number of "accounts" sealed in instrumental "friendships." The irony of mafia formation, then, was that for all its popularly misconceived familialist content, it originated in a counterfamilial network of power rooted in the materially induced decay of generations of instability.[18]

In the destabilized context of post-1840 Sicily, too, after feudalism was officially abolished and northern capitalist forces had moved into the region in what amounted to an attempted market coup, traditional feudal owners, arriviste entrepreneurs, and brigand-like enforcers sealed a hybrid class pact in the interests of coercing a stability that an incompletely formed and quite unpopular state proved unable to secure. This pact oppressed the small peasant proprietors and landless laborers (and thwarted and militarily suppressed their periodic uprisings), but also secured them some guarantee of the support system of obligations they needed to survive in the harsh new world of the capitalist marketplace.[19] State formation in southern Italy, particularly on the island of Sicily, never quite garnered the support of the indigenous population, which experienced the unification of Italy as a process of regional domination. A kind of combined and uneven development of inequality in governance was evident in the history of thwarted efforts at social change. Land reform failed, and in its wake came the suppression of rural unrest and the repression of the Palermo revolt of 1866; the parliamentary rebellion of 1873–1874, when only three of forty-eight deputies returned in Sicily were pro-government; and, in the growing school of Italian criminology, the increasing association of the "southern question" with that of "racial" inferiority.[20]

What was a mafia? In its Italian origins it was less something to which one belonged, than a set of behavioral practices. As Christopher Duggan has indicated, the notion that the mafia evolved historically as a clandestine, ceremonially initiated, strictly hierarchical, sinister body of criminals who allocated unto themselves specified spheres of control (like the camorra of Naples), has become embedded in its mythology.[21] In Italy, where the mafia was judged by the 1880s to be centered in prison society, that view of it was intimately connected to the primitive empiricism of early sociology and criminology. Its most irrational, xenophobic expression appeared in the United States, where a series of turn-of-the-century incidents of violence and intimidation undertaken under the supposed auspices of something called the Black Hand conditioned belief in a centralized body of extortion and crime associated with "dangerous foreigners." This perception hardened in the 1950s and 1960s with state-directed inquiries into the status of organized cartels of illicit activity. The notoriety associated with the so-called Appalachian convention of what was proclaimed a "Mafia Grand Council" in 1957, and testimonies of figures such as Joseph Valachi, who in 1963 revealed the existence of what he called Cosa Nostra, fed the panic over ethnic criminality. But all of this rather overblown argumentation has failed to establish the central role of a coherent criminal organization, and most reasoned discussion of the mafia stresses the significance not of criminal conspiracies but of a style of behavior.[22]

To behave like a mafioso was to be "a man of honor," a figure of respect in a society of intensely gendered understandings of esteem. Aggressive toughness and unscrupulous settling of scores were judged touchstones of valor and bravery, all cast within a dichotomized conception of life that elevated the masculine and the public and idealized the feminine and the private. Honor in its masculine variant was a virility that proved itself in deeds and postures, which at their extreme were capable of violence; it proclaimed manly worth in a voice of outward articulation, conditioning others to respect, fear, and submit. Feminine honor was largely sexual and kinship-composed, a chaste virginity or wifely subordination that sealed the bonds of patriarchal familialism in an inward-leaning repose of service and isolation. This gendered double standard was extended into class and status realms as well and stood beyond the strictures of law and state coercions. Within the overlapping circles of mafioso honor, or omertà, where the ability to be a man of stature encompassed the possibility of violence, it was more important that social relations were meant to be governed by tact, manners, courtesies, and kindnesses. All of this was used to solidify friendships and secure agreement without overt violence. But outside the circles of honor, in dealings with class "inferiors" or family and business enemies, such norms of behavior were to be scorned: false façades erected to facilitate the security of power, enforced by cunning and courage, fraud and ferocity, were legitimized as necessary maneuvers in the ultimately violent resolution of specific dealings. Thus the "honorable" man might, in deeds of demonstration, violate women for whom he felt no responsibility of omertà, defining his respect and virility in terms of his capacity to protect the honor of his own circle's women from such shame—which would reflect back on him—while ravaging the women of irretrievably dishonored layers of society. If those violated did not respond with appropriate acts of vendetta-like retribution (killing anyone who had shamed the circle of honor was the definitive response), they were forever relegated to a sub-

ordinate "caste" marked even in the territoriality of their living spaces—
likely the dirtiest and most depressing—in the village.

This gendered code of honor and its double standard was carried into
the male realms of business and sociopolitical authority. The mafioso
manner ensured that all transactions, from economic undertakings to
public festive life, were sites of endless challenge, combat, and competition.
Precisely because areas of mafioso strength emerged out of the weak-
nesses of a social formation lacking deeply rooted class structures, strong
institutional networks, and advancing state formation, the "war of each
against all" that governed relations among and within families in parts of
southern Italy made honor, rather than justice, an endless and infinitely
varied pursuit. Honor, as Arlacchi concludes, "was connected less with
justice than with domination and physical strength." As the history of the
Corleone family in Mario Puzi's novel and the trilogy of the *Godfather* films
(1972, 1974, 1990) indicates, "In the carrying out of his day-to-day 'duties,'
the *mafioso* did not follow any abstract ideal of morality and justice. He
sought honour and power, and in pursuit of his goals he was quite ready
to flout *any* established rule of conduct.... What determined the power of
the *mafioso* was victory in the struggle for supremacy—victory by whatever
means necessary."[23]

The mafioso's "family" was thus something of a primitive state, func-
tioning parallel to and serving as a surrogate for structures of governing
authority that could not, in specific Italian regions, command the allegiance of masses of people or secure their welfare. Mafia protections
safeguarded dominant material interests and sustained order, the tribute
exacted amounting to a tax; mafia mediations in contentious realms of
business and social life assumed a judicial function. As a proxy for the
incomplete state, the mafioso stood as a pragmatic, personal articulation
of dual power, albeit one that consolidated authority individually and in
ways that offered no *revolutionary* challenge to the ruling order. Rather,
depending on the circumstances, the mafia could be regarded by the
national state as potentially positive or threateningly disruptive. As class
intermediaries who eschewed both peasant/proletarian trials and deprivations *and* the encumbrances of large-scale ownership and ongoing accumulation, the traditional "men of honor" sided with money but were
not governed entirely by it. The mafiosi straddled the politics of state
formation but were never integrated into its finally decisive structures.
Their *omertà* encompassed limited wealth as well as many other factors,
political, material, and cultural, and beyond the maintenance of *omertà*
their commitments were always provisional and flexible.[24]

Post–Second World War developments, however, dramatically altered the terrain of *omertà* and the meaning of mafia.[25] The cumulative effect of a widening series of social, economic, political, and cultural change was that by the late 1960s and 1970s the traditional mafioso code of honor had been displaced by a relentless accumulative drive for wealth. Essentially urban, this development shattered *omertà* in a crisis of legitimation that left the mafiosi denigrated as deviant and marginalized as criminal rather than revered and respected. What remained of mafia authority was the gangster predation that infiltrated construction circles, exploited accumulative strategies (extortion, kickbacks, protection) that were blatantly illegal, and then fused with large business interests in pursuing legitimate entrepreneurial activity, often supplementing the power of money with the imposing provincialism of rugged mafioso intimidation. Thus mafia capitalism, as it emerged in the 1970s, combined the investment portfolio of contemporary business with the primitive enforcement mechanisms of traditional mafioso power. It did not so much exist alongside more pristine forms of capital as interpenetrate and reconfigure the social relations of production and exchange. The mafia spirit, no longer one of honor, entered wider and wider spheres of economic interaction. It promoted a rapacious accumulation and conspicuous consumption. No longer inhibited by the necessity of negotiating directly with the state and the judiciary, mafia capitalism evolved into a parallel power, sustained over time by a relentless war of position to secure to itself profit and power. As its economy and culture broke free of local and regional constraint, the new mafia internationalism of the 1970s keyed in on the trade in base morphine, which, once processed, offered market returns upward of 2,000 percent. Such material inducements linked Milan's mafias with like-minded elements in Asia, Afghanistan, Latin America, and urban America. For all of their notoriety, however, these were rather small fish in the expanding pond of the global drug trade, and their meager resources actually kept the American mafia in check. Their initiatives were usually subordinate to powerful U.S. military and financial groupings.[26]

Much of this history of change and transformation could be associated with the so-called crime families and developing gangsterism of America, where Italians followed on the heels of Jewish and Irish predecessors.[27] As these Italian "entrepreneurs" infiltrated the unions, the banks, the trucking industry, and the docks, it became harder and harder to distinguish the corporate from the criminal in their racketeering activities.[28] By the 1980s and 1990s, however, this predatory entrepreneurial gangsterism was shifting racial/ethnic place: new gang formations—African-American,

Chicano, Latino—assumed prominence in the world of organized criminal activity, which had become indistinguishable from the internationalized connections of drug peddling and, as a contemporary spirit of capitalism, had infused entire sectors of a growing underground economy.[29] Mafia families, the most successful of which had already integrated into mainstream business, could not adapt to the new drug economy, controlled on a world scale by entrepreneurial Latin American and Asian criminal cartels.

Some of the latter, especially those with Central and South American connections, were linked loosely via U.S. countersubversive and counterinsurgency forces to networks of reaction that crossed paths in the anti-Sandinista campaigns of the early 1980s. The American conditions that spawned this subterranean spirit of late capitalism were, ironically, precisely those that had bred the original connections of honor and wealth associated with old-style mafiosi in the destabilized political economies of southern Italy. American inner-city neighborhoods, from ghetto and barrio enclaves in Brooklyn, the South Bronx, and Manhattan to southside Chicago, South Central Los Angeles, and Miami, became, like the Sicilian and Calabrian countryside, regions of particular *social* underdevelopment in which institutions of protection and provisioning—from the schools and hospitals to employment bureaus, fire departments, mass transit, and welfare outlets—experienced years of neglect and abandonment.[30]

The material core of this violently restructured social disorder was the loss of employment: 450,000 low-skill industrial jobs employing inner-city workers disappeared in New York City between 1970 and 1984, and a further 300,000 waged positions were lost in Philadelphia, Boston, and Baltimore, pushing unemployment rates to an astounding 68 percent for black males in the Northeast.[31] In New York City, where manufacturing jobs dwindled from 1.1 million in 1950 to 300,000 in 1995, the mid-1970s saw a "planned shrinkage" aimed at "redundant" blacks and Puerto Ricans. Targeted to suffer losses in essential services in their ghetto neighborhoods in retribution for a wilting tax base—caused by landlords in flight, businesses in collapse, and the arrears characteristic of a political economy peopled by the unemployed and marginalized—the new victims of structural racism confronted the harsh conditions of late capitalism. Roger Starr, chief of New York's Housing and Development Administration, explained cynically, seemingly unconcerned about the racist implications of his blatant class agenda: "We should not encourage people to stay where their job possibilities are daily becoming more remote. Stop the Puerto Ricans and the rural blacks from living in the city ... it can no longer be the place of opportunity.... Our urban system is based on the theory of taking the peasant and turning him into an industrial worker. Now there are no industrial jobs. Why not keep him a peasant?"[32] Starr, noting that the city had violated the elementary teachings of Economics 101 by lending long and borrowing short in the development and mortgage markets of urban housing, appeared before legislative hearings with a wad of "bad paper" debt and called on a "fairy godmother" to come in and take it off his hands: nobody danced into the disaster with high-priced glass slippers.[33] The result was a context crying out for a parallel authority, a stateless state constructed from below. By the time of Ronald Reagan's second presidential term, more than one-third of black families in America lived at or below the official poverty line.[34] This is what contemporary gang culture, where the rough machismo and predatory acquisitive individualism of the street marketplace thrive, is all about. Few moments in the history of capitalism, outside of the rise of fascism, have been animated by a spirit as dark as this.[35]

The middle period of the twentieth century was thus marked by a fundamental dualism in the American inner city, where people of color—largely African-American and Latino (Puerto Rican and Chicano in their east and west localizations)—lived in a state of repressed destitution and coerced subordination, not to mention an environment of decay and danger.[36] On the one hand, periodic uprisings and rebellious implosions shattered social calm: zoot-suit riots and black mobilizations in the 1940s; the beginnings of civil rights agitation in the 1950s and early 1960s; the explosive rage that saw the ghettos torched and white power—economic and military—vanquished for brief moments in the 1960s of Watts, Harlem, and Detroit; the symbolically and politically potent eruption of inner-city youth and black factory workers in the organized revolutionism of the Young Lords, the Black Panthers, and the League of Revolutionary Black Workers in the late 1960s. On the other hand, the liberal order offered the proverbial carrot—Democratic Party patronage, programs of poverty and illiteracy alleviation and voter registration, phony youth employment initiatives, and a reformist ideology of integration—which, in the relatively flush times of this period, skimmed the surface of institutionalized racism.

At the level of state coercion, the countersubversive apparatus of localized police forces and covert, often murderous, FBI and CIA operations laid siege to the emerging leadership of revolt. Through campaigns of innuendo and intimidation, as well as overt terroristic assaults, these left the nascent cadre of resistance incapacitated, incarcerated, demoralized, destroyed, or dead. This clandestine war on domestic subversion, interestingly enough, paralleled the evolution of equally covert, technically illegal, police forces orchestrated by the nightriders of the Nixon administration such as G. Gordon Liddy. Their White House mandate was to administer a crackdown on drugs that would serve the useful ideological purpose of blaming foreign powers for the crisis of American cities and pragmatically justify the expansion of executive power that was the hallmark of presidential purpose in the early 1970s.[37] Within a decade this infrastructure would easily adapt to a seemingly inevitable fusion of interests: the valiant but cash-starved forces of international counter-subversion and the easy money of reaction's drug connection, personalized in the staff of a market-military complex of dispossessed businessmen and generals driven from their respective citadels of power by the likes of Nicaragua's "socialist" Sandinistas. All of this helped set the stage for the increasingly austere pressures of the last thirty years of the twentieth century. As funds for placation, however modest, dried up in a generalized post-1973 state fiscal crisis, the ghettos and, most particularly, their youth and newly arrived immigrants (often "illegals"), were written off as zones and personnel of primitive disaccumulation. Capital and the state expected no return from such quarters save that of self-destructive, chaotic violence. As schools and hospitals deteriorated and workplaces closed, the social costs of this process were increasingly obvious. By the 1980s the percentage of black and brown youth without work or living below the poverty line in urban America had climbed significantly, some estimates of the crisis indicating a 70 percent rate of joblessness among young people of color.[38] Unemployment among black youth in Los Angeles County soared to 45 percent, and 40 percent of families were living below or virtually on the poverty line. Ghetto high schools had a dropout rate approaching 50 percent, and 250,000 to 350,000 "latchkey children" aged five to fourteen were left without adult care from the end of the school day until the termination of their parents' work time.[39] Communities governed by such markers of basic material want were quickly scorned and typecast as the reconstituted environs of the "dangerous classes"—reconfigured in twentieth-century parlance as the "underclass"—requiring the governance of the heavy hand. Urban landscapes were thus turned into war zones featuring police helicopters, tanks outfitted with battering rams, new technologies of surveillance, fenced housing projects, and "pass" systems reminiscent of apartheid South Africa.[40] Black and Latino incarceration rates soared; American prisons became racial gulags; and the United States earned the dubious distinction of imprisoning its people at a rate—344 per 100,000—that outstripped all global competitors, including notoriously repressive regimes such as South Africa. On death row in the mid-1990s roughly 40 percent of inmates were African Americans, even though blacks constituted less than 15 percent of the country's population.[41] Male mortality rates in black America exceeded those of impoverished developing nations such as the Gambia, India, or El Salvador. Almost one in five black male deaths in the early 1990s were the result of homicide.[42]

In the face of this devastation, with programs of amelioration cut to the bare bone, inner-city neighborhoods were abandoned, judged redundant and expendable, an urban jungle to be policed with the menacingly hard hand of racist ugliness. One such body of regulation was the Los Angeles Police Department (LAPD), notorious for its brutalizing presence as an occupying army of vengeance and violence, architect of the late 1980s program of repression known as the Hammer. As Mike Davis and others have concluded, the outcome of this spiraling descent was something of a foregone conclusion: youth gangs whose origins perhaps lay in a fading memory of resurrecting the promise of black and Latino revolt associated with the Panthers and the Young Lords "evolved through the 1970s into a hybrid of teen cult and proto-Mafia." Ironically enough, these victims of a scorched-earth capitalist program of destruction and demoralization followed a Milton Friedmanesque neoclassical policy of maximizing their economic utility by exploiting the single marketplace that survived the devastation of the 1970s and 1980s: the dark spirit of predatory mercantile capitalism found a fitting resting place in the political economy of crack cocaine, a cheap, immediate "high" that could be sold on the street corner for the price of sex or a boosted VCR. The attributes of the mafiosi extended into a generalized ethos proved to have particular resonance in the rough enterprise of youth gangs. They conditioned a climate of escalating violence and an often cavalier disregard for life that the media have hyped with the customary journalistic fix of sensationalism.[43]

The evolution of African-American, Asian, and Latino gangs in the 1970s and 1980s took a particularly ruthless mafia form. Networks of unemployed youth plug into the exchange relations of the world market at its darkest, if perhaps not its weakest, link: crack provides a career path, however truncated and unpredictably volatile, for the young in need of dollars. Organized hierarchically, if loosely, the gangs have reintroduced a racialized omertà, becoming, in effect, the mercenary foot soldiers of the narco-imperialism orchestrated by powerful oligopolies such as the Hong Kong Tongs or the Columbian Medellín cartel.[44] Visible in their ostentatious display of jewelry and juice (the ghetto equivalent of influence and honor, reinforced by the advanced firepower of handguns and more exotic weapons), decked out in outlandishly expensive running shoes and designer T-shirts,[45] the drug-pushing gang members of the marketplaces of the night have inspired a cultural revolution of machismo street "attitude."[46] They push the parameters of black and Latino masculinity in explosively violent directions. Gang tactics of intimidation reinvent practices from the mob wars of the 1920s, now designated gangbangs and drive-bys. A mythologizing imagery is lyricized in gangsta rap's chronicles of misogynist exploits and violent coming-to-terms with racist America, symbolized by battles with the police. Ice Cube's "Endangered Species (Tales from the Darkside)" captures something of the genre's orientation:

> Every cop killer goes ignored,
> They just send another nigger to the morgue.
> A point scored. They could give a fuck about us.
> They'd rather catch us with guns and white powder...
> They'll kill ten of me to get the job correct
> To serve, protect, and break a nigga's neck.[47]

As Robin Kelley suggests, it would be erroneous to homogenize the culture of inner-city youth of color. The interesting exchange of aesthetics that connects gang experience, aerosol and graffiti artists, the highly differentiated regional and stylistic layers of hip-hop, and other forms of self-presentation common in the ghetto is decidedly two-sided, cutting into the racist structures of containment in a generalized stand of defiance but slicing out of repression in creatively different, often diametrically opposed, ways. Presented eloquently in John Singleton's film Boyz N the Hood (1991), this dualistic dynamism drives a diversified black urban culture in ways that white sociologies and contemporary theories have difficulty deciphering. They fail to come to grips with the fusion of racism's pervasively coercive containments, the pleasures of artistic and bodily transgressions and subtle arts of resistance, and, finally, the brutalizing conformity to realms of capitalism's project that phenomena such as the gangs illuminate.[48] However much gangs are not what ghetto and barrio youth are actually about, racism's ugliness—the brutalizing terror of police armies of occupation, and the dead ends of a political economy of exclusion, always beckoning with an illusory abundance—connects the separate spheres of street "color" in America in a chain that links strength and weakness. Thus, the cult stock of the gangs has, ironically, been bolstered by the cops and the state, whose incompetence and inability to derail the megabusiness of international cartel drug importing, processing, and large-scale distribution has to be papered over with the scapegoating of the small dealers of the street. The latter's symbolism, swagger, and intuitive clash with white authority offer a ready-made portrait of the enemy (young, black/brown, male, and thus indistinguishable from the homogenized depersonalized population of the inner city) which official-dom faces in its war on the lower ends of the drug trade. It is an odd war, however; one that repressive forces of the state love to lose. Out of day-to-day defeats are fashioned justifications for police brutality and a deflecting ideology that attributes the collapse of urban civil society to the irredeemable, drug-induced savagery of the American poor—many of whom are conveniently visible minorities.[49]

Meanwhile, as the price of pure cocaine dropped from $45,000 a kilo in 1984 to $11,000 in 1989, and street vials of crack, once marketed at $20 to $25, crashed through the price barrier of almost any consumer to bottom out at $5 or less, all evidence pointed to the futility of mass arrests of street-level dealers and SWAT-team raids on storefront distribution centers and houses of assignation. It was clear that more and more cocaine was flowing into the inner city, glutting the market, and equally apparent that the large distributors and processing importers, many of them linked to the politics of reaction in Central and South America (and thus connected clandestinely to U.S. international "countersubversion"), were hardly touched by the hostilities.[50] The return of heroin in the mid-1990s as a drug of choice among the ghetto poor—its price structure tailored to its targeted market's capability to pay—was yet another indication that the by then thirty-year-old declared war on drugs in America was more posture and pronouncement than serious strategic undertaking. Some of the most powerful international drug traffickers are able to parlay the intense poverty of their local settings into a social banditry mystique. They dispense largesse on an immense scale and, through bribes and patronage, insulate themselves from arrest and prosecution. As the U.S. Drug Enforcement Administration (DEA) sputters its rage, this contingent of modern-day Robin Hoods hoard bullion and build mansions, openly display their money, goods, and influence, and live the new spirit of capitalism's nights of accumulation.

The public relations show that sustains the sham war is truly diverse and includes international and domestic theaters of display. Invasions of weakened Central American states and the deposing of leaders who have outlived their usefulness (such as Panama's Noriega), the burning of peasant crops in Bolivia, plans to unleash coca-eating butterflies in Peru, the kidnappings of Mexican citizens, and the hoisting of a fleet of radar blimps over the Caribbean, are but some of the internationally staged acts.[51] The domestic scene reaches a certain curtain-lowering bravado in repressive sweeps of urban gangland. One such orchestration of the power of the modern-day gendarmes, mounted by then LAPD Chief Daryl Gates in April 1988, was a search-and-seize operation that witnessed 1,453 arrests—almost one "gangbanger" for every cop involved in the invasion. A year later the guest of honor at the LAPD's antidrug showtime was none other than Nancy Reagan. Sporting a police windbreaker, the fetching former first lady nibbled fruit salad in a luxury mobile home while Gates and his men busted the fourteen narco-terrorists of an alleged crack house. Then, touring the aftermath, her sense of taste offended by the tawdry wallpaper and drug-bust debris, Nancy snorted, "These people in here are beyond teaching and rehabilitation."[52] Did she mean the residents of the crack house, or South Central Los Angeles in general?

To be sure, the gangs are not exemplars of a Walt Disney variety of overachievement. No other grouping has so dramatically altered the statistical profile of violent crime in America: youth killings soared 371 percent between 1980 and 1992, and the dramatically increased number of those under the age of eighteen charged with murder (up 165 percent from 1985 to 1993) was unmistakably associated with the gang culture of retribution.[53] Gangs are of course heavily involved in the marketing of a host of illicit products, from guns and prostituted sex to a wide range of drugs, but members enter the trade as individuals, the lumpen capitalists of the underside of the drug business, not its powerful corporate linchpin. In the process, a mafioso style of contemporary capitalism has emerged, embracing a predator ideology and an acquisitive individualism reinforced by gang recourse to violence that has become commonplace.[54] But the gangs do not, for the most part, run and process drugs as a large-scale, corporate business venture. At the level of the urban street, for instance, each metropolitan center has hundreds of rock cocaine franchises and thousands of petty suppliers. Both layers sustain significant numbers of rogue entrepreneurs, whose coherent alignment with either "corporate headquarters" or the competing retail outlets is weak if not nonexistent. Like the world of capitalism which it emulates in its structures of distribution, the drug trade is highly concentrated in its upper echelons and a literal labyrinth of exchange possibilities at its base, many of them quite unconnected to one another and random in their techniques. The closer one gets to the consumer, especially those whose poverty ensures that their purchases are small and frequent, the more evident is this dispersed network of sales.[55] There are also some large dealers in the ghetto, of course. The Arkansas-born Chambers brothers managed to establish a cocaine empire in Detroit that grossed a tax-free $55 million annually before they were arrested, convicted, and jailed for their entrepreneurial successes.[56]

Yet even if gangs thus represent a truly primitive practice of accumulation with a correspondingly predatory emphasis, this rebirth of the original mafioso style has not secured to the young of the inner city the bulk of the superprofits of capital's most lucrative commodity. Gangs may well be "all about money now," as one San Diego member stated, but the dollars to be had are not the phenomenal sums often cited in the press, and the hours are long and wearing, from mid-afternoon to well into the darkest early-morning hours. Only a fraction of the drug trade's estimated $500 billion annual take ends up in the lumpenized entrepreneurial pockets of black and brown youth; they probably collect between $500 and $900 a week—much better than a job at McDonald's, of course, but hardly the road to riches, especially when the dangers and downside of the work are taken into consideration. Despite the caricatured overconsumption that figures in the outlaw spending of easily earned money, the accumulations are simultaneously primitive and paltry.[57] As Max Weber long ago grasped, if extraordinary capital accumulation "calls into play certain traditional, archaic cultural and personal qualities—predatory instincts, the use of violence, small group loyalties, boldness, and so on—ordinary capital accumulation depends on 'formally peaceful probabilities of gain'."[58] According to articles in sources as varied as the New Left Review and Fortune, the global trade in cocaine and other illicit substances is extraordinary only at the level of the street. As Hobsbawm commented in an assessment of the Colombian Medellín cartel: "Left to themselves and the principles of Adam Smith, the consortia of Medellín investors would no more see themselves as criminals than did the Dutch or English venturers into the Indies trade (including opium), who organized their speculative cargoes in much the same way.... It is basically an ordinary business that has been criminalized—as Colombians see it—by a U.S. which cannot manage its own affairs."[59]

But this ordinary business, driven by a logic of accumulation at any cost, is quite extraordinary in its violent, destructive consequences. Prior capitalisms have of course exploited the possibilities of drugs, especially opium, but the role of coca and cocaine production in Columbia, Peru, and Bolivia has, in the post-1975 years, disfigured indigenous politics and production in Latin America. It contributes to the weakening of class-based institutions such as trade unions and left-wing parties, funds repressive death squads, undermines diversified employment, and further marginalizes indigenous peoples, accentuating violence and distorting the political economy of everyday life. The drug trade mires these countries in a monoculture of criminality that masks their fundamental social ills and sinks them deeper and deeper into the dependencies of international debt.

In the consumer environs of the American inner city, the picture is equally dark. A minority made up of gang members, dealers, and users have appropriated the public space of barrio and ghetto neighborhoods, defining the material relations of urban life in terms of relentless and predatory acquisition. They seize what is left after inner-city parks have been gutted and abandoned by municipal authorities or sold, privatized, or concessioned as locked spaces for the "legitimate" (read "affluent") residents.[60] And they follow—on their own terms—the bitter logic of this profit-maximizing, commodity-conceptualized ethos.

Few texts convey the brutalizing banality of this contemporary spirit of capitalism more poignantly than Philippe Bourgois's anthropological study, In Search of Respect: Selling Crack in El Barrio (1995), which chronicles the broken bodies and barricaded buildings that symbolize the debilitation of an urban environment written off by large capital and its coercive and conciliatory arms of state power. Bourgois presents a unique view of the squalor and struggle for honor that mark the lives of barrio residents, many of whom came out of the gangs of the 1970s and 1980s. Cocaine, crack, and heroin were "the fastest growing—if not the only— equal opportunity employers of men in Harlem," unrivaled in their capacities as income-generating opportunities. Those who opted into this political economy of processing and selling were not capitalism's antagonists but its last fervent believers, passionate defenders of "Horatio Alger's version of the American Dream."[61] They embraced a barrio variant of mafioso omertà, fusing it with an acquisitive individualism that, in its late capitalist context, turned ultimately to violence to resolve its cycle of contradiction.[62]

That this entire edifice was night driven is evident in Bourgois's book. His method was to spend "hundreds of nights on the street and in crackhouses observing dealers and addicts." His fieldwork consisted of midnight lounging at "La Farmacia," a barrio street corner known for its "unique diversity of psychoactive substances." Often seduced by "the night's friendly aura," Bourgois came to depend on the night authority of those whose 3:00 A.M. "hoodlum-like demeanor" protected him. Their "shifts" ended between midnight and 4:00 A.M., and working on Thursdays and Fridays rather than Mondays and Tuesdays might spell the difference between economic survival and either descent into abusive use of crack, or internecine violence.[63]

The contemporary spirit of capitalism is thus a profound tragedy, a marketplace of omertà's dreams that slides irretrievably into "the brutal rhythms of ... the night."

> Especially after midnight, Beckman Avenue, along with other open-air drug markets of the South Bronx and Manhattan, had a Middle-Eastern-bazaar, street-theatre air. Crack users formed long queues to buy vials from pitchers hawking their wares, watched closely by managers, in turn supervised by enforcers standing near sleek, polished cars with dark windows, guns bulging under leather jackets. Young children played in the streets, stopping to watch the procession of cocaine whores strutting the street hoping to turn a quick trick in exchange for crack, or staring at sudden face-slappings of willful women or the shuckin' and jivin' of homeboys.[64]

Nelson George ruminates on this dark process, which "in this age of nine-millimeter justice" so often ends in a "thirst for immediate vengeance." He sees the rage and desperation bred of years of urban apartheid turned against the very victims of oppression: "Racism and incompetence have conspired with the terror of crackology ... to fill the overnight news with the dying gasp of neighborhood babies. Four died within an eight-day period in July and more have been shot since.... These murders were the stuff of nightmares."[65] Is it any wonder, asks Mike Davis, that "poor youths are hallucinating on their own desperado 'power trips'" when the obviousness of "the mean ethos of the age" is everywhere evident in mushrooming signs "of approaching helter-skelter" in which "a whole generation is being shunted toward some impossible Armageddon?"[66] In its dark dialogues and desperations, capitalism's late-twentieth-century spirit is an accumulative chaos running amok in barbarisms and brutalities. It has brought urban life to the end of an anguished cry, one that has been heard too faintly but grows louder with the passage of each disintegrative decade.

20

The Implosion of the City

Nights of Race Rage and Riot

The predatory primitive accumulations characteristic of late capitalism's barbaric acquisitive individualism have moved from the country to the city, their mafia-like organization as well as their illicit product filtered through particular class channels and spatial locales. From the rural "under-developed" context of peasant cultivation, bandit appropriation, and feudal-istic lordship, the circuits of contemporary accumulation lead logically to "overdeveloped" corporate organizations, bourgeois appetites, ostentatious styles, and urban markets where the commodity—processed and refined—reaps its profitable rewards and sows its bitter fruit.

Cities, sites of the development of civilization, as a host of urbane urbanist texts of the pre–New Left 1960s reveal—among them, Percival and Paul Goodman's *Communitas* (1960), Lewis Mumford's *The City in History* (1961), Jane Jacobs's *The Death and Life of Great American Cities* (1961)[1]—are only as resilient, however, as their hegemonic class vanguard. In the late twentieth century this political-economic contingent has served the city poorly. The future of urban life has been bartered for the speculative, megaproject quick fixes of a boosterist construction mania, often fueled by transitory spectacle and pie-in-the-sky promotionalism, a hucksterism adept at creating the illusion of urban place. "Nonplace" urban spaces such as Los Angeles and Atlanta are the archetypal locales of a new urban form.[2] Here the fantasy of a sanitized land/skyscape, backdropped by security-laden, commercialized, and privatized core constructions of so-called public space, plus the sprawl of slums and suburbs punctuated by islands of parking lots, finds its heartbeat in the shopping mall and its connective arteries in the expressway. In this imaginary urbanism, mythologized as the megacity, production and jobs are displaced by gentrification, architectural excess, and social neglect. Job loss is countered by expanding numbers of insatiable and aggressively self-serving nouveau riche professionals, and the proliferation of rent-accelerating offices. Metropolitan life contrasts excessive display and ever more vicious cycles of poverty and displacement.

The city trenches of confrontational class and race interest that were dug through the battles of urban life in the 1960s were, by the 1990s, largely evacuated in a retreat that recognizes, with an anguished sense of loss, the campaign of terror and assassination that has taken the pulse of the city and cashed in on its immediate possibilities. Detroit's Renaissance Complex and Atlanta's Omni Center are maze-like fortresses of brick, glass, and steel, monuments to money, while those racially dispossessed by the new urban revivalism are reduced to catering to transient professionals. The battle of urban culture, waged too often in the name of an illusory classless community, has been turned from one of an optimistic offense to a mere defensive, bureaucratized, minimalist preservationism.

If Atlanta is the ostensible success story in this narrative of displacement, Detroit, once affectionately known as Motown, is its sad and fearfully scarred failure. Murder City, as it came to be designated (its annual homicide statistic peaked at 686 in 1987, a rate of 63 per 100,000 population, which topped the national figures until nudged out of its pacesetting place by Washington, D.C.), "stands for an America that is over." Only the dreadful nostalgia of what once was is juxtaposed to what remains. The metaphor associated with the Motor City is that of war, and Detroit has been defeated. People, mostly white, have fled. Property has been simply left to rot—or burn, torched by arsonists who have managed to institutionalize their activity in the night-before-Halloween's Devil's Night; upward of four hundred fires illuminate the dark end-of-October decay in what has become a harvest season tourist event, drawing spectacle seekers from as far away as Japan. Meanwhile, jobs and services melt into the disaster pool, never to reappear. Two out of three Detroit-area residents, according to newspaper polls, are afraid to go downtown, a place of "the most awesome concentration of emerging ruins in the nation," both physical and human. Beneath the abandoned, prematurely decrepit skyscrapers— stripped of their fixtures and ostentatious façades by white capital in flight, or languidly blurring into the garbage-strewn lots and the boarded-up disheveled residences that are now the dwelling place of addicts and alcoholics or homeless squatters—is an ecology of rust and refuse in which the abandonment of things mirrors the seeming valuelessness of life. "A war was fought here," concludes Detroit poet Philip Levine. "American capitalism, armed with greed, racism, and the design for the world's gaudiest fish-tailed Cadillac took on the land, the air, and the people, and we all lost."[3] Small wonder that many have come to see cities as an obsolete way of organizing human activity. The political fashion of multiculturalism aside, the understanding that, outside of the protected towers of inner-city finance, exchange, and instantaneous communication, the urban centers of advanced capitalism have become capitals of the third world, is something of a two-edged sword that few want cutting the wrong (i.e. against their material interests) way.

As the nomenclature of the third world suggests, "race"—an ambiguous but nevertheless centrally important location in the demographics and development of the modern city—occupies a pivotal place in the degeneration and increasingly volatile climate of urban living.[4] Scapegoated by the complacent as the cause of metropolitan decay, people of color are in historical fact the victims of the destruction of the city.[5] Brought to urban centers by the lure of freedom and progress, the economics of secure waged employment and the networks of familialist and cultural survival the city has nurtured in the wake of the global dispersion of landed peasant societies, they have paid for their adaptations to the city with a persistent marginalization.[6]

Allowed to enliven the cultural shadows of the marketplace, such urban migrants have nevertheless always been categorized within a dark aesthetics of danger and exoticism. As racial animosities hardened in particular historical moments, the seemingly benign "attraction" at the cultural margins, consciously constructed out of the magnetic pull of the "perverse" other, could easily slip into brutally unmediated assault on the supposed pathologies of racial difference.[7] This was evident in such ugly nights of physical attack as the zoot-suit riots in Los Angeles in June 1943, when Anglo-American servicemen and civilians symbolically annihilated (through ritualized castration and shaming shaving, as well as physical beating) the pachuco Mexican Americans whose flamboyant dress and sexualized style had actually set a fashion tone and image of bravado appropriated by many urban youth, black, brown, and white.[8]

Beyond the presentation and improvisation of styles and genres associated with people of color, evident in dress, music, and sport, the material contribution of these increasingly urban populations has been and remains prodigious. They provide varied ruling classes with reserve armies of labor that have the dual advantage of depressing all wages and miring a substantial sector of laboring humanity in the substandard remunerations and insecurities of racially hierarchialized exploitation. Historically this has always left the pay envelopes of black, brown, and yellow workers thinner than those of whites. However much was accomplished in the civil rights struggles of the 1940s through the 1960s, they did little to lessen the obvious persistence of racism and its disfiguring and multi-faceted impact on urban life. Not surprisingly, then, the struggle for racial equality proves an uphill fight to address all aspects of prejudice and difference. Whatever their particularities, these usually find a common level in the economics of exploitation. As Dona Cooper Hamilton and Charles V. Hamilton have recently argued, in the United States the African-American civil rights movement was a social policy campaign aimed at ameliorating all special oppressions, whether rooted in race or in gender, through common struggles to achieve economic and class equality.[9]

Out of this crucible of contentious politics emerged an anguished articulation of "black power," an outpouring of demanding analysis that has survived in a shelf of 1960s texts.[10] It was but the tip of a burning iceberg of rage. James Baldwin's evocative and prophetic *The Fire Next Time* (1963) warned all Americans of what lay before them if the racist carnage, centuries old, was not brought to a halt:

> I could ... see that the intransigence and ignorance of the white world might make ... vengeance inevitable—a vengeance that does not really depend on, and cannot really be executed by, any person or organization, and that cannot be prevented by any police force or army: historical vengeance.... Everything now, we must assume, is in our hands; we have no right to assume otherwise. If we—and now I mean the relatively conscious whites and the relatively conscious blacks, who must, like lovers, insist on, or create, the consciousness of the others—do not falter in our duty now, we may be able, handful that we are, to end the racial nighmare, and achieve our country, and change the history of the world. If we do not now dare everything, the fulfillment of that prophecy, recreated from the Bible in song by a slave, is upon us: *God gave Noah, the rainbow sign, No more water, the fire next time.* [11]

Two years later, as the Watts rebellion in Los Angeles confirmed Baldwin's apocalyptic prognosis, the "low riders" of the Los Angeles ghetto saun-tered across the Folsom Prison yard and assembled on the basketball court. Amid smiles of jubilation and triumphant slapping of palms, one of their number stepped forward and swaggered into inner-city rhyme:

> They walking in fours and kicking in doors;
> dropping Reds and busting heads;
> drinking wine and committing crime, shooting and looting;
> high-sliding and low-riding, setting fires and slashing tires;

turning over cars and burning down bars;
making Parker mad and me glad;
putting an end to that "go slow" crap and putting sweet Watts on
    the map—
my black ass is in Folsom this morning but my black heart is in
    Watts!

Watts, once a place of subordination and shame, the physical space of black destitution and desperation, was now a rallying cry of prideful, cleansing rebellion.[12]

The riots led by blacks throughout the 1960s, of which Watts was but one of many, were happenings of resistance, spontaneous political explosions of a preprogrammatic sort. They were comparable, given the highly different experiences of black and white youth, to the more culturally ordered Woodstock phenomenon of the same period. Where white youth dropped out and tuned in, so to speak, black youth dropped in and turned out; if whites had the economic capacity to consume their youthful revolt in music and drugs, blacks spent their rebelliousness in a rage against the boundaries that had constricted their horizons and material possibilities. Watts and other ghetto rebellions, moreover, stood as a significant departure from the pattern of compromised "evolutionism" of racialized urban politics in the postwar period, as well as differing dramatically from a long history of race confrontation in the city.[13] The riots of the 1960s turned the race tables of rage, as nights of explosive violence moved toward the retribution and vengeance Baldwin had warned of. One hundred years and more of intimidating coercions, in which black Americans had ample reason to fear white violence and irrationality, was reversed in the middle years of the 1960s as black anger found its release in nights of cultivated revenge.

Historically, the race riot had undoubtedly been more rural than urban, an unleashed viciousness of New World plantation slavery which periodically subjected displaced Africans, incarcerated in systems of brutal bondage, to their white masters' coercive might and propensity to slaughter. It might well erupt as a consequence of slave flight or more collective forms of resistance, or it could be ignited by the panic-induced dark fantasies of fearful populations whose dominance was rooted in insecurity and profound material and psychic imbalances.[14] In the United States, the post-Emancipation period of the late 1860s and early 1870s can be interpreted as a momentous struggle for African-American liberation. In those years acts of imagination and creativity on the part of blacks and some supporting whites were resisted by rearguard terror, a persistently violent containment of people and passions in which bodies and aspirations were assaulted. With slavery abolished, the kind of race riot that had characterized black–white relations undoubtedly continued to have a rural presence but achieved a more concentrated expression in episodic urban explosions that sustained African-American subordination in recurring eruptions of white rage.[15]

Racist suppression of free blacks in urban America has a long history, reaching back to the early eighteenth century but flaring to prominence in the generalized nativist upsurge of the 1830s. Philadelphia was a center of this racist violence: at least seven major mob attacks against black people took place there in the years 1834–1838. From the populist pen of America's best-selling novelist of the time, George Lippard, came this passage from The Quaker City (1844):

> Why you see, a party of us one Sunday arternoon, had nothin' to do, so we got up a nigger riot. We have them things in Phil'delphy, once or twice a year, you know? I helped burn a nigger church, two orphans' asylums and a school-house. And happenin' to have a pump-handle in my hand, I aksedentally hit an old nigger on the head. Konsekance wos he died. That's why they call me Pump-Handle.[16]

The City of Brotherly Love was not alone in such actions. As David Roediger has suggested, rampaging white racists in the early republic were driven by a complex fusion of "rationalizing logic." Added to the economics of the seemingly threatened wage, and the sexual phobias concerning "amalgamation," was elite willingness to channel lower-class discontent away from its generalized hostility to privilege, property, and power by tacitly licensing attacks on the most dispossessed. Consequently, nights of swaggering resentment turned into race wars in which defenseless blacks were routinely scapegoated, often with chilling ugliness.[17]

If racist mobs were hardly exceptional in antebellum America, the most acute expressions of the modern race riot nevertheless date from the 1860s, obviously a crucible of change in the history of race relations in the United States. In New York the anti–Civil War draft riots of July 1863 left northern Republicans aghast at the immense property damage. The necessity of recalling five Union Army regiments to suppress the rampaging mobs and the death toll of more than a hundred persons (at least 10 percent of whom were blacks lynched by white rioters) brought the racial crisis to a public head. Many of the rioters were workers outraged not only that the military service legislated for all citizens could be avoided by whites with sufficient resources to muster the $300 commutation fee but that both black freemen and slaves were exempt. Terrorized by racist attack, blacks fled New York, the African-American population of the city plummeting by 20 percent between 1860 and 1865.[18] In 1866, Reconstruction riots in New Orleans and Memphis left scores dead and hundreds injured as white, police-led, officially sanctioned mobs attacked recently emancipated African Americans and their white allies: they marched on institutions of black political power; burned down schools, churches, and homes; raped, sexually assaulted, and shamed black women.[19] Between 1882 and 1927, of the more than five thousand lynchings in the United States, 70 percent of the victims were black. Atrocious attacks terrorized all African Americans and those whites who would consider supporting them. Any person who violated the codes of color or crossed boundaries of racial place could be subjected to a death penalty passed in the volatile court of racist vigilante justice.

During the early decades of the twentieth century, in urban race riots, north and south, paramilitary assaults on black communities and mob violence left no ambiguity about the continuing virulence of race hatred infecting much of white America. Among the many metropolitan centers where rioting whites attacked black people and their homes and institutions were Wilmington, North Carolina (1898); New York (1900); New Orleans (1900); Evansville and Greensburg, Indiana (1903 and 1906); Springfield, Ohio, and Springfield, Illinois (1904, 1906, 1908); East St. Louis (1917); Houston (1917); Chicago (1919); Washington, D.C. (1919); and Tulsa, Oklahoma (1921). As the titles of some historical treatments indicate, these "carnivals of fury" took place during "nights of violence." Inflamed by the construction of a moral panic, driven by unsubstantiated newspaper reports of black males harassing white women, Washington's race riot was but one of many in which police were ordered to arrest all young men found in "suspicious" neighborhoods after nightfall. Chicago's racial explosion, precipitated by a beach incident in which a black youth supposedly violated the informal segregation of Lake Michigan's shoreline, but complicated by legacies of long-standing class tensions among black and white workers, left thirty-five dead, some five hundred injured, and more than a thousand homeless. In Tulsa, an army of whites led by American Legionnaires, infuriated that African Americans had armed to protect an accused rapist from the lynch mob, invaded the black district of the town known as Little Africa and torched a square mile of territory. As fires burned through the night of May 31–June 1, 1921, black Tulsa was reduced to ashes.[20]

Such wanton violence stimulated varied defensive mobilizations on the part of American blacks, including the formation of the National

Association for the Advancement of Colored People (NAACP) as well as countless local contingents of "armed guards."[21] Liberal periodicals opened their pages to harsh condemnations of lynching and racist mob rule. But established authorities at federal, state, and local levels more often than not turned a blind eye to the ugly nights of riotous terror.[22]

This situation did not change markedly over the next decades, but with the increasing demands of African Americans for an end to racist exclusions and constraints during the Second World War years, a white backlash fired the engines of the race riot in the early 1940s. Black migration from the South to the North continued, and communism and anticommunism offered contending claims about the politics of race. A revived labor movement in which African Americans figured forcefully, demands for desegregation in the armed forces, and a world war fought against a Nazi state that proclaimed racial superiority a part of its raison d'être all contributed to an appreciation of the centrality of race in these years. Figures such as the African-American leader A. Philip Randolph expanded the agenda of an emerging civil rights movement and offered white racist reaction an increasingly visible target.

As tensions between blacks and whites heightened in the armed forces, various military camps were sites of pitched battles, some of which left soldiers dead. Off their bases, black soldiers faced brutal beatings and murderous assault by Jim Crow thugs, racist state troopers, and local police; within army jurisdictions, the African Americans who resisted the taunts and literal ambushes of racist elements often found themselves court-martialed for their trouble. The usual array of insults and humiliations stigmatized servicemen and servicewomen of color, just as the historically rooted phobias of threatened white power were quick to find their way to increasingly public platforms. In a Pennsylvania camp one white officer flew the tattered flag of sexual panic, long linked to race hatred: "Any cases between white and colored males and females," his posted notice read, "whether voluntary or not, is considered rape and during time of war the penalty is death."[23]

Small wonder that significant numbers of blacks refused to comply with the Selective Service Act: by 1943, African Americans totaled 35 percent of delinquent registrants; between 1941 and 1946, two thousand black males were sent to prison for dodging the draft. "Whitey's war" found little favor in the zoot-suiter, bebopping milieu of young urban blacks, which nurtured future revolutionaries such as Malcolm X and cultural rebels such as the trumpeter Dizzy Gillespie. Gillespie secured a failed draft status designation when he sidled up to his recruitment officer and offered a far from patriotic confession:

> Well, look, at this time, at this stage in my life here in the United States whose foot has been in my ass. The white man's foot has been in my ass.... At this point, I can never even remember having met a German. So if you put me out there with a gun in my hand and tell me to shoot at the enemy, I'm liable to create a case of "mistaken identity," of who I might shoot.

Malcolm appeared at his draft interview "costumed like an actor," from his yellow knob-toed shoes to his red, frizzed "bush conk." Leaning low toward the army psychiatrist, the eighteen-year-old adopted the centuries-old ploy of "puttin' on ole massa." But his stage-whispered words of hoarse conspiracy conveyed more than a mere theater of resentment: "I want to get sent down South. Organize them nigger soldiers, you dig? Steal us some guns and kill some crackers!"[24]

Wartime volatilities thus set the stage for a new round of urban conflagration: no fewer than 242 racial battles took place in forty-seven cities between March 1 and December 31, 1943. The issues were varied and complex, but at their base was the ever present racism of white America, its influence felt in labor markets, schools, scholarship, newspaper reports, cultural segregation, and the mass media. A country at war for democracy had demonstrably not shaken off the many shackles of enslavement. Langston Hughes spoke for many black war resisters:

> Looky here, America
> What you done done—
> Let things drift
> Until the riots come
> ...
> Now your policemen
> Let the mobs run free.
> I reckon you don't care
> Nothing about me.
> ...
> You tell me that hitler
> Is a mighty bad man
> I guess he took lessons
> From the ku klux klan.[25]

Among the violent urban implosions of 1943, two of the most significant were in the major metropolitan centers of Detroit and New York. In Motor City's enclave of factories essential to wartime production, the volatile mix of a black and white workforce recently recruited from the

Deep South and Appalachia, plus established institutions of governance and regulation built on white power (of Detroit's 3,600 police officers, perhaps forty were black), created an atmosphere of acute tension. Over the course of 1942 and into the first months of 1943 blacks and whites clashed in a series of skirmishes that affected schools, housing projects, workplaces, and national defense plants. Wildcat strikes and small-scale riots were commonplace. Even the FBI acknowledged that "white hoodlums" had "allegedly instituted a reign of terror among Negro residents of the Eight-Mile Road Community," and that "Klan-inspired" white mobs up to a hundred strong were reported to have "terrorized the Central Avenue section of Detroit's West Side," smashing windows of Negro residents. The *Wage Earner*, the voice of Detroit's Catholic trade unions, referred in early June 1943 to "a growing subterranean race war ... which can have no other ultimate result than an explosion of violence." A few weeks later what had rumbled underground raged openly in the streets.[26] Not unexpectedly, this racist violence—an unambiguous outcome of the white hatred, fear, and prejudice sustained in daylight's many marketplace exclusions, inequalities, and Jim Crow separations—found its forums of expression in the night.

Detroit's 1943 race riot was introduced in a secret FBI report with the following sentence: "Sunday night, June 20, 1943, was an exceptionally hot and sultry night and the amusement parks and recreational facilities in the Detroit area were jammed." One resort area was Belle Isle, a haven from the heat located in the Detroit River, accessible by a single bridge or one of several small ferries. Once the preserve of whites, Belle Isle had by 1943 become a playground increasingly frequented by blacks, and on the night of June 20 up to 90 percent of perhaps 100,000 people on the island were African Americans. As traffic jammed on the solitary bridge and tempers flared, racial taunts were hurled into the night air; fights broke out over trivial confrontations involving space, place, and petty proprieties; and by 11:30 P.M. the bridge was engulfed in a full-scale brawl. Sailors rushed from a nearby armory to support the outnumbered whites. Police were soon on the scene, making arrests, hustling off crowds of "goddam niggers," and emboldening the mob of five thousand angry whites who eventually traversed the bridge looking for isolated blacks to pummel. As dawn broke and the workday commenced, hostile white crowds milled about downtown, their resentments fueled by rumors of "atrocities." By nightfall on June 21 their numbers had swelled to some 100,000; it was worth a black person's life to be caught on the streets. The routines of production stopped, for workplaces were empty.

To quell the riot, white police ironically moved into black districts, killing a number of African Americans, beating others, incarcerating some, hospitalizing many. Pistol whipping, clubbing, and arrest were the order of the night for blacks who resisted in any way, who numbered in the *hundreds*. But although some arrests were made among the *thousands* of white rioters, dispersal, warning, and physical shoving were the norm. One black youth, Julian Witherspoon, greeted the police with the taunt "Heil Hitler"; he was shot in the back. When his peers responded to being lined up against a wall with the remark, "Shame we law-abiding citizens have to be treated like Fascists," a police officer was said to reply, "shoot any of them that moves, because we have plenty of bullets left, and you'll get the same as your buddy." Detroit seemed a war zone in which an occupying army of armed white officialdom, buttressed by marauding bands of white reserves of reaction, had displaced any semblance of due process and established "law and order".

Inflammatory news broadcasts warned that carloads of armed Negroes were reported to be on their way from Chicago to liberate Detroit. Gerald L. K. Smith used his fascist publication, the *Cross and Flag*, to incite race hatred by constantly alluding to the intimacies of black–white "mixing"; he sexualized the integrated housing projects, schools, restaurants, hotels, and streetcars or trains of Detroit as an "unnatural" threat of miscegenation, an abhorrent "promiscuousness." A lynch mob bent on "putting the niggers in their place" bathed the city in blood lust. Only after repeated proddings of African-American and trade-union leaders did city officials call on federal troops to restore order. By then, of course, the police and white racist mobs had sated their appetites for revenge with countless beatings and a number of killings; the message of the terror unleashed by affirmations of black identity had been branded into African-American bodies.

It took the declaration of martial law, with federal troops monitoring police brutality, to restrain whites seriously and bring the Detroit riot under control. White youth gangs jeered the troops as "nigger lovers," but within hours of their arrival some measure of at least superficial calm had been restored. When the smoke cleared and the final brutal statistics were compiled, the balance sheet told an unmistakable tale of inequality. Despite the significantly smaller numbers of blacks among the rioters, twenty five of the thirty-four dead were African/Americans, and seventeen of these had been shot to death by the police. Likewise, the 700 injured reported by hospitals and the almost 1,900 persons arrested indicated that whites, who outnumbered blacks in riot participation, had been less likely to be hurt or face a jail sentence. Even though white officials castigated black preachers, African-American community leaders, communists, and NAACP members as responsible for fomenting violence, a liberal coalition of religious and reform-minded organizations concluded that the Detroit riots of 1943 were, on the whole, a deplorable racist attack on the black community: "Negroes have been victimized by police in the name of law and order as well as by lawless mobs." The wounds of racism were now "open and raw."[27]

Some of the same configuration of forces led to violence in New York's Harlem in August 1943. When a white policeman shot a black army private at a hotel under surveillance as a "raided premise" on the evening of August 1, the pent-up anger of one of the largest and most culturally visible and vibrant urban African-American locales in the United States exploded. Frustrations were driven by a decade and more of economic malaise, the nationwide knowledge of the ill treatment of black servicemen, and the often brutalizing white face of police authority. Following small demonstrations at the local precinct station, Harlem—which had experienced a similar riot eight years earlier, in 1935—erupted in an attack on the symbolism and substance of racism in America. Targeting white-owned businesses, blacks smashed windows, looted stores, and torched buildings.[28] New York's municipal authorities, however, though they too blamed black leaders and communists, adopted a more liberal public profile than their Detroit counterparts and thereby successfully defused black resentment relatively quickly, restricting the riotous disorder to a single evening of chaotic property destruction. Nevertheless, six persons were killed and some 550 arrested; 1,450 stores were damaged or destroyed, with property loss said to exceed $5 million.[29]

The Harlem and Detroit riots of 1935 and 1943 thus stand as something of a transitional moment in the history of the race riot: for the first time, in any serious way, white terror began to be displaced by black agency. African Americans responded to the racist structures of life in the city with the antagonism of a race consciousness of civil rights, focused by wartime's ideological contradictions. That this awareness of rights and of a capacity to twist the arm of white authority forcefully were developed most acutely in black Harlem is no surprise. For decades New York's African-American community had harbored an indigenous intelligentsia, sustained significant connections among radicals both black and white, and stood proudly as the centerpiece of black urban culture in the United States. Detroit's black community was more precarious and more plebeian, and when it rose in angry resistance in 1943, the ranks of reaction were more threateningly hostile—a reminder that in much of white America, black demand for equality and fairness would continue to be met by the terror and threat of the lynch mob.[30]

Over the course of the 1950s the night remained for many African Americans a time of troubled anxiety and threatening terror. Particularly in the rural South the racist spirit of lynch law was alive and well, often buttressed and sustained by established courts and the authorities of order. The decade opened with the 1951 legal lynching of the Martinsville Seven (black men executed for allegedly having raped a white woman) in Virginia, and Willie McGee (also falsely accused and convicted of rape) in Mississippi. On Christmas Eve of that same year, NAACP activists Harriet and Harry T. Moore, engaged in a black voter registration drive in Florida, died at the hands of killers who placed a bomb beneath their home. The Communist journal *Masses and Mainstream* published Lorraine Hansberry's "Lynchsong," commemorating the nights of racist horror that still gripped much of America:

> My mother told me about
> The dark nights
> And dirt roads
> And torch lights
> And lynch robes
> . . .
>   sorrow night
>   and a sorrow night
> . . .
> The
> Faces of men
> Laughing white
> Faces of men
> Dead in the night

Out of such nights grew the groundswell of civil rights agitation associated with the left-orchestrated appeal to the United Nations, *We Charge Genocide* (1951); Martin Luther King, Jr.'s non-violent campaign to achieve civil rights and the year-long Montgomery, Alabama, bus boycott; the more aggressively radical early 1960s mobilizations of the Congress of Racial Equality (CORE) and the Student Non-Violent Co-ordinating Committee (SNCC); and the nationalist separatism of Elijah Muhammed's Black Muslims. These developments recast white–black relations in urban America, setting the stage for the confrontations of the 1960s.

The years 1963 and 1964 marked the continuity of violent racism in the American South. Four black girls were killed in the bombing of a Birmingham, Alabama, church; the black civil rights activist Medgar Evers was assassinated; and three "freedom riders," one black and two white, were murdered by racist vigilantes in Mississippi. Northern cities were thought to be places in which legal segregation and lynch law did not prevail, yet little headway had been made in establishing even a rudimentary equality: blacks and whites occupied highly different worlds with respect to housing, jobs, education, health, and welfare; their relationships to the institutions of governance and regulation, from the pinnacles of municipal power to the cop on the street, were as separate and unequal as in the virtual apartheid of the South. In spite of Lyndon Johnson's much-vaunted War on Poverty, statistics from the 1960s were unambiguous in their message. Ten million blacks were officially classified as impoverished by the Social Security Administration. A Department of Labor survey of a dozen black ghettos estimated conservatively that 10 percent of blacks were unemployed—three times the national average—and one in every five of those who did have jobs earned less than $60 weekly. Often excluded from the best-paying skilled and unionized work, African Americans were also confined to segregated housing in neighborhoods where schooling was poor, crime rates high, and policing rigorous and rough: estimates were that 50 to 90 percent of black males had, at some point in their lives, experienced arrest. Merchants gouged the ghetto resident, offering inferior goods at inflated prices and exploiting the poverty of the neighborhood to extract rates of credit return unimaginable in more affluent white sectors.[31]

All this, along with the nation's willingness to fight a war halfway around the world in Vietnam, an outpost of empire of questionable concern to most poor blacks, was the context in which Martin Luther King's "I Have a Dream" speech at the Lincoln Memorial (attended by 200,000 and viewed by millions on television) and Malcolm X's more inflammatory comment on the killing of President John F. Kennedy that the "chickens were coming home to roost" fell on receptive African-American ears. Malcolm would be cut down by the assassin's bullet in 1965, King in 1968, their deaths contributing significantly to the black rage that, fed by discrimination and destitution, engulfed urban America in the 1964–1968 years.[32] As James Baldwin knew in 1963, black people had run out of patience with white America; it was time for the truly transgressive fire. And it would burn brightest at night. Urban blacks turned darkness from a time and place of fear to a space in which the demand for a new day could be voiced.

The long, hot summers of the mid-1960s and the April 1968 days of fury precipitated by police shootings and arrests in the black community and the assassinations of beloved black leaders were among the most serious threats to public order in the long and checkered history of the United States.[33] Commencing in mid-July 1964, rioting in the urban ghetto began, understandably, in Harlem, the epicenter of the black metropolis, then spread to outlying New York districts such as Brooklyn's Bedford-Stuyvesant, and then on to Rochester, various New Jersey cities, Philadephia and Dixmoor, Illinois. The August 1965 Watts riots in Los Angeles rekindled the flames of black rage in the worst urban conflagration since the East St. Louis race riot and massacre of 1917. The death toll and the arrest count broke into newly dangerous dimensions. The Watts riots, front-page news across the nation for more than a week, left thirty-four dead, more than a thousand injured, nearly four thousand facing criminal charges, and property damage that soared into the tens of millions of dollars.[34] Smaller explosions occurred in Chicago and San Diego, but it was the massive looting, arson, and tumultuous disorder of Watts that captured public attention, its rallying cry "Burn, baby, burn" searing the divided consciences of black and white America.

The next summer witnessed seemingly unending urban rioting in black America. Affecting more than two dozen cities, the 1966 riots never reached the heights of the Watts rebellion, but collectively they marked a rising pattern of African-American revolt, establishing the year as the most violent in a decade that seemed perched on the edge of animosity's abyss. By June 1967, with an increasingly fractious black leadership predicting the most turbulent summer ever and white authority trembling in the face of an obviously incendiary danger, cities prepared for the worst. They got even more than they bargained for. Riots broke out across the nation, from Nashville, Cleveland, and Boston in June to Cincinnati, Buffalo, Newark, and Milwaukee later in the summer. Detroit's uprising, that year, like all such ghetto rebellions a product of decades of inner-city malaise and black discontent that was no longer containable, outstripped in its death and devastation anything seen in America since the New York City draft riots of 1863.[35] Less than a year later, with the assassination of Martin Luther King, major riots erupted in Washington (where an unprecedented eight thousand were arrested), Baltimore, and Chicago, and lesser disturbances in more than a hundred cities.[36] From 1963 to 1968, 341 riots had shattered the illusory calm of 265 cities, leaving 221 dead and tens of thousands facing criminal charges.[37] A century after the Emancipation Proclamation had abolished slavery in the United States, black America served notice that its subordination was no longer acceptable. If whites were to rule with racist brutality and African Americans were to remain little more than the dispossessed of the world's most affluent nation—the daylight hours being a constant reminder of the oppressions and exploitations of inequality's persistence—the nights would burn, illuminating black resistance and refusal.

Detroit well illustrates the race-driven urban explosions of the 1960s.[38] During the 1950s and early 1960s the city had won awards for its adept handling of the problems of racial discrimination, and its mayor, Jerome P. Cavanagh, was hailed nationally as a far-sighted urban leader in the vanguard of progressive political change. Nevertheless, by 1967 the so-called model city was a seething cauldron of discontent, with African Americans underrepresented in skilled and professional jobs, adequate housing, and the amenities—spatial as well as cultural—of city life. Increasingly concentrated in an emerging ghetto, Detroit's black population was likelier to be young, poor, sick, educationally deprived, and out of work than its white residents. Understandably, then, blacks gravitated to various institutional expressions of resistance. Detroit boasted the largest branch of the NAACP in the nation, but a host of more radical, often locally based, bodies developed over the course of the 1960s to champion the cause of black nationalism, among them the Group of Advanced Leadership (GOAL); the Revolutionary Action Movement (RAM) and its defense order, the Black Guard; Wayne State University's black student group UHURU (Swahili for Freedom Now); and the nationally connected chapter of CORE. Other black mobilizations were in the making, including the Republic of New Africa, which campaigned for an independent black nation, and the League of Revolutionary Black Workers, a militant organization based in the auto plants and premised on a Marxist appreciation of the need to address the related experiences of race and class. A particular target of all such expressions of increasing black consciousness was the infamously racist Detroit police force. As the city commemorated the twentieth anniversary of the 1943 riot with a 200,000-strong walk for freedom, backed by the major institutional expressions of the labor, civil rights, and black nationalist movements and supported by the liberal Cavanagh administration, Detroit was a mix of contradictory sensibilities. Most whites, privileged in terms of their work and welfare, infused their view of the future with optimism and hope; blacks, far less well off, were moving resolutely toward a confrontation with their own frustrations and resentments.[39]

This mix, having brewed for years, reached its boiling point on Sunday July 23, 1967. Characteristically, the beginnings of the eruption were an event of the night. Following a Saturday that had been hot and muggy, the after-hours clubs of Detroit's black ghetto, whose "blind pig" origins lay in the post–Second World War refusal of middle-class downtown bars and restaurants to serve black patrons, were packed. One such Twelfth Street establishment was hosting a party for two Vietnam servicemen, its dingy second-floor apartment packed to the rafters with upward of a hundred African Americans, roughly half men and half women. Around 4:00 A.M. the place was raided, doors broken down with sledgehammers, owners and patrons placed under arrest. A crowd gathered on Twelfth Street, a twenty-four-hour summer venue. Jocular at first, the assembly turned combative when those in police custody were, according to eye-witnesses, kicked and pushed down the stairs while handcuffed, beaten with nightsticks and gun butts, and mishandled, especially the black women, in ways that offended the street onlookers. Taunts and jeers escalated to calls for retribution and attacks on "Whitey," as much a pejorative directed at the authority status of the police as a racial epithet; the crowd two-thousand-strong now grew increasingly hostile and moved menacingly toward the police, who were being bombarded with bottles, beer cans, and rocks. Beating a hasty retreat, the cops left the crowd in control of the scene, emboldened with the sense that it had secured a victory over oppression and struck a blow for freedom. Less than fifteen minutes later, as an officer in charge of the precinct returned to Twelfth Street to deal with what he thought was "a little trouble," he could do nothing but fend off projectiles and withdraw. With windows being broken and stores looted, the riot was underway.[40]

For the first four hours of the street battles, a holiday, carnivalesque atmosphere prevailed in the largely young crowd caught up in an "epidemic of excitement." Having backed the police into retreat, roving crowds achieved a sense of invincibility that soared as further police actions proved incapable of defusing the volatile situation. Between 8:00 A.M. and noon on Sunday the ranks of rioters swelled to almost ten thousand, and window breaking and looting escalated to arson. Rumors of blacks being bayoneted by white police spread through the crowd, and moderate black leaders—brought to the scene to quiet and disperse the rioters—were jeered, their proposals rejected with a hostility that left them scared and scarred. The city's liberal white power centers, reluctant to sanction force and perhaps recognizing that they could not sustain it when outnumbered so dramatically, ordered the police not to use firearms. The riotous crowd made the most of this moment of license. Only in retrospect did some looters come to the deeply dark conclusion that white police "Seemed to be enjoying seeing 12th Street tore down."

At 4:00 P.M., after twelve hours of chaos, Mayor Cavanagh finally appealed to Michigan's governor to authorize the use of the National Guard. By this time, however, fires were burning out of control in a hundred-block area west of Twelfth Street, and Detroit, according to syndicated columnist Jimmy Breslin, was "bitter with smoke," the sky "a red glow." Over the course of that day and the next some 825 fire alarms signaled "probably the worst fire emergency ever faced by an American city in modern times." Meanwhile, the mounting death toll included black looters trapped in store basements and white store owners beaten as they attempted to protect their property.

On Sunday the National Guard, state troopers, and Detroit police stepped up the attempt to control the riot with physical intimidation. The result was a night of escalating violence. Police were now ordered to use fire-arms to apprehend looters, and to shoot to kill if they themselves were fired upon. More than a thousand persons were arrested. In the excessively humid, 90-degree night of July 23 and the early morning hours of July 24, the nature of the confrontation shifted. Amid the rubble of destruction, the sooty air, and heat of the arsonists' flames, rioters and looters continued to run amok, but adding to the inflamed disorder was the night's project of police revenge. The riot had turned from a revolt of blacks against police and property, the symbol of economic power, to a quest for vengeful control. "They are savages," said one policeman of black rioters, while cries rang out in dark alleyways, "Control those coons. Shoot 'em in the nuts!" Thereafter the streets were a scene of carnage, the nights punctuated with gunfire. In the notorious Algiers Motel incident on the night of July 25, three young blacks were shot to death and a number of others, as well as some whites, were beaten and terrorized by Detroit police—who managed, in the aftermath of the riot, to avoid conviction. Supposedly precipitated by sniper fire, the Algiers massacre almost certainly had more to do with violent racism, exacerbated by the obvious sexual alliances of white women and black men at the hotel.[41] The riot had become a rationalizing cover for racist murder.

It was days before anything resembling calm was restored in the ravaged inner city; not until late in the first week of August were all troops withdrawn. No mere tally of losses, in human and property terms, can summarize the destruction of the Motor City's 1967 riot, but the figures do convey some of the dimensions of the carnage: 43 riot-related deaths; well over a thousand injured and 7,231 arrested; 2,509 stores looted, burned, or destroyed, property loss well in excess of $50 million.[42] Mayor Cavanagh surveyed post-riot Detroit and commented, "We stand amidst

the ashes of our hopes." The raw racism underlying American social relations had been exposed, and blacks had refused to remain complacent
victims.[43] There was no more waiting for next time; the fire had come
to urban America. It had come with darkness, a blaze of the night. The
response from white America was predictable: Detroit's officials, bolstered
by thousands of National Guardsmen, state troopers, and the federally
deployed armed forces of the United States, slapped a curfew on the city,
restricting activity and movement from 9:00 P.M. to 5:00 A.M.

In the ranks of the academically fearful, events such as Detroit's 1967
riot precipitated a rush to conservative, often racist, judgment, E. C.
Banfield's The Unheavenly City (1968) providing one of the most bluntly
sociological formulations. Riots were written off as "outbreaks of the
animal spirits," a pastime of the youthful "underclass" who could be
counted on to loot and burn "mainly for fun and profit."[44] It was as
though the carnivalesque atmosphere of certain aspects and times of urban,
racially prompted riots necessarily typecast them as thoroughly frivolous
events, unconnected to any wider relations of deprivation and dissent.
This crudely functionalist reductionism also colored many liberal analyses
which, however much they might recognize the roots of black rioting in
the legitimate grievances of African Americans, cornered the history of
urban racial disorder in a pseudohistorical oppositional evolutionism. In
such readings the riotous racist attacks on precarious African-American
populations which had predominated in the pre–Second World War years
were somehow invested with "communal" content, whereas the black
riots of the 1960s, portents of which occurred as early as 1943, were
"outbursts" against property, dominated by looting, and thus driven by
the acquisitive individualism of the "commodity."[45] But no such natural
history of communal/commodity opposition exists in the shifting pattern
of race rage in the United States, for commodities and communal concerns are neither the preserve of race categories nor capable of being
disentangled. Black rioters attacked property and appropriated commodities
not out of some instinctual accumulative drive but as an expression, albeit
often inarticulate, of pent-up frustrations and animosities rooted in a
generations-old, racially defined experience of dispossession. In the inner-
city neighborhoods of black America this state of insecurity and need, in
its underlying structures of racial inequality, was always about communal
and commodity necessities and desires. The fires that torched the U.S.
cities in the 1960s illuminated such reciprocities.

In doing so, they moved the history of urban conflagration closer to
yet another decisive reckoning, one that would develop in circumstances

of accelerated change. By the 1980s such disturbances had extended to Britain, where a volatile climate of urban dispossession, Caribbean immigration, and heightened racial tensions exploded in the London districts of Brixton, Finsbury Park, Peckham, Southall, and Lewisham, as well as in similar neighborhoods of Birmingham, Liverpool, Bristol, and elsewhere. Indeed, as a consequence of the social deformations of capitalism's increasing internationalism and global reach, the modern city in general was often perceived as a powder keg, its dangerous, exposed fuse that of "race." The expanding parameters of urban conflagration reconfigured the character of the race riot in the late capitalism of the United States, where significant ethnoracial destabilizations unfolded in tandem with the long continuities of racism's presence, both structural and subjective.

Indicative of the altered state of urban racial dynamics and tensions in the United States of the 1980s was the central place of Miami, where the race wars of 1980 and 1989 opened and closed with nights of looting, shooting, beating, and burning and days that were not much better. The toll for these two major events included more than twenty dead, roughly fifteen hundred arrested, and property damage into the hundreds of millions of dollars. In many ways the stories were old ones: police brutality culminating in the deaths of African Americans enraged a black community, whose riotous rampage left the neighboring African-American districts of Liberty City and Overtown devastated. In the 1980 event, the final straw in a riot waiting to happen was the acquittal by an all-white jury of four white police officers charged with beating a black insurance salesman to death. The context was complicated well beyond the usual black/white opposition by the presence in Miami of a large Hispanic population, a recent addition to the race equation which leavened the load of tension and antagonism. The 1989 riot, initiated when a Latino cop fired on and killed a black motorcyclist (whose passenger died in the ensuing collision), was also followed by the officer's eventual acquittal, even though an original jury (supposedly influenced by fears of African-American rioting) returned a guilty verdict at the first trial. In both legal proceedings, however, there was considerable difficulty in securing what was considered an impartial judicial venue: the 1980 case was tried in Tampa; the 1989 case's final appeal, having been moved five times, eventually reached a verdict in Orlando. At the root of everything was the widening range of animosity in which a culture clash traditionally associated with long-standing black/white antagonism was complicated by African-American resentment of Mexican and Cuban immigrants, by white politicians' scapegoating of these same Hispanic people, and by shrinking funds available for inner-city programs. Miami, a late capitalist melting pot that simply refused to liquefy race difference, was one of several metropolitan centers where old and new racisms, born of new internationalist demographics, collided in a generalized disorder of power, subordination, and vengeful reaction.[46]

This was the background, as well, to the 1992 Rodney King riots, which have taken on the trappings of a literary text in postmodernism's free-floating book on race and riot.[47] Los Angeles is indeed grist for this particular mill,[48] and its 1992 riots have been interpreted in various ways. One reading presents the uprising as a Banfield-like loot fest precipitated by "an abundance of young men with time on their hands." Another interpretation stresses black protest against discrimination and brutality. Others suggest a late capitalist "bread riot" driven by a broad spectrum of the multiracial dispossessed, a *Blade Runner*-esque illumination of the city's descent into street anarchy in which white migrations and municipal authority's willingness to write off the urban core economically and socially resulted in a "survival of the unfittest" that left a racialized underclass in control of urban space. Emphasis has been placed on the race riot as a multiethnic battle that prefigures twenty-first-century forms of street protest in which, it is predicted, "territorially based ethnic tensions" will erupt in chaotic clashes of cultures and colors.[49] What emerges from an interrogation of the Rodney King riots is the extent to which it signals, in its dispersals and complexities, a new fusion of forces in the race-related upheavals of the capitalist city.

The basic facts of the Los Angeles riot are well known. In the early morning hours of March 3, 1991, a speeding car occupied by three black males ran a red light on a California highway. Eventually, after a chase in which the fleet Hyundai outraced the freeway cops, the vehicle pulled over, a large black man jumped out and, clutching his behind, laughed crazily and danced for the unamused husband-and-wife Highway Patrol team. By this time, twenty-one LAPD officers were on the scene; the black man was soon beaten senseless, at least four cops kicking him and raining baton blows on his crawling, then prostrate, body; several stun-gun blasts punctuated the personal touch; orders were given to strike the victim again. A brutal beating, to be sure, but nothing really new to the racial terrorism of the urban night, where white cops and Americans of color routinely confront one another in an unequal exchange of violence and abuse that helps seal the subordination of race, whatever the rhetorics of liberation and equality. So commonplace was the "incident" that officers' radio messages from the scene were transmitted to department headquarters in a language of cavalier, bantering banality: "I've got a victim with ... ha ha ... head injuries." Yet the subdued and beaten traffic offender, a man later identified as Rodney G. King, has been written into the history of the fin-de-siècle American city, a chapter in the race rage that runs like a dark thread through the economic, social, political, and cultural relations of the twentieth century.

Although similar treatment has been an every-night occurrence faced by countless black Americans, the vicious police beating of Rodney King attained an unprecedented visibility, and was transformed into a major historical event, because it was captured on a gritty, shadowed home video recording, shot under the cover of night's darkness by an onlooking white. In eighty-one seconds of suffering, Rodney King exposed hundreds of thousands of hours of brutality. Night's terrors for African Americans were, finally, brought into the public light of day. For once, the evidence seemed unassailable, and in the court of the people the armed police officers stood convicted of an ugly, almost murderous, assault. The proof was visible, not only in video footage but in Rodney King's silent body, on which was stamped the record of the night's violence: a split inner lip, partial paralysis of the face, a dislodged eye socket, nine skull fractures, a shattered cheekbone, the bruises of fifty-six blows, and a broken leg.

Yet a little over one year later, all four officers—three via acquittals and one on the declaration of a mistrial—escaped conviction. The trial, subject to a number of change-of-venue appeals by defense lawyers, was eventually held in lily-white Simi Valley (home to 2,000 of the LAPD's total force of 8,300), where the defendants, if not the victim, did indeed get a jury of their peers: eleven whites and one Hispanic decided the fate of the charged officers. Rodney King, who on the advice of his counsel never testified during the trial, was portrayed as a hulking animal, ostensibly high on some inner-city drug, and whose refusal to acknowledge verbally his submission to the police established his dangerous defiance and proved that he was in "control" of his own beating. A traffic violation, committed by a black who responded to police intimidation with a carnivalesque but nonviolent parody, threatening only in its display of disdain, had somehow earned the vicious beating administered by the chain of command of the LAPD.[50]

Within hours of the verdict, sections of Los Angeles erupted in understandable rage. For five nights the fires burned again: buildings were torched, stores looted, passing motorists pelted with debris or, in extreme cases, hauled from their vehicles and brutally assaulted. The National Guard was quick to appear on the scene, followed by U.S. Army and Marine troops, FBI agents, and border patrol guards; a dusk-to-dawn curfew tried to curtail the night's capacity to exact its particular toll of vengeance. When the smoke had cleared, fifty-eight were dead, 2,300 injured, 1,150 buildings destroyed and possibly as many as ten thousand damaged. Whole blocks had been leveled, the estimates of property damage ranging from $785 million to $1 billion. Almost 9,500 were arrested, although not all ended up facing charges. Moreover, the shock waves of the acquittal of the police officers responsible for Rodney King's beating reverberated throughout the continent, and sympathetic uprisings rocked Seattle, San Francisco, Long Beach, Madison, Atlanta, Newark, Detroit, New York, Washington, Chicago, Philadelphia, and Toronto. A case of police brutality more than a year old, and one that originally caused protest but not riotous confrontation, had galvanized the urban underprivileged into acts of resistance and revenge that rekindled the fires of the ever-changing history of race riot.[51]

The 1992 Los Angeles riots differed, in many respects, from earlier race-ignited urban implosions. First, the uprising was not spontaneously generated out of the moment of an "incident" of brutality, as African-American protests had been from the 1940s to the 1960s. Rather, in its overexposure, the hyperbrutality of the night of March 3, 1991, seared the consciousness of a nation and blurred into a public memory that could never quite shake its grittily gruesome images, however much they seemed, after a time, almost unreal, the product of presentation rather than a terrifying history that had actually happened. The longevity of this process, in which the videotaped beating was televised repeatedly over the course of a year and more, numbed people's recognition of the deeply racist structures of insulation that stood between the obviously guilty officers and an actual conviction, lulling the public—black, brown, yellow, and white—into the security that a wrong would be righted. When that satisfaction was legally denied, the packaged memory of Rodney King beaten senseless was impossible either to lose or to accept. As one woman proclaimed in the midst of the resulting wreckage, "We've been trusting too long. We trusted the jury to do right. I'm so mad at us for trusting."[52]

Second, although all such disturbances are the products of decades of discontent, the Rodney King riots were driven by the pervasive economic malaise that has ensnared the generation postdating the affluence, black nationalist mobilizations, and civil rights liberalism of the 1960s. Impaled on the economic horns of a dilemma that proclaimed a new national prosperity while it left black and brown youth of the inner city to the far from tender mercies of a two-tiered wage system, a dismantled social services sector (education, health, welfare), the flight of manufacturing capital, and the obliteration of unionized jobs, people of color in Los Angeles were the abandoned victims of an orchestrated recession vicious in its ravages. "Pay close attention to what these people were stealing," commented the poet Meri Nana-Anna Danquah, "food, diapers, toys. No one mentioned economics." The enervating economic slide that had taken so many youth of color into the depths of material despair was perhaps the fundamental backdrop of these riots, unlike the climate of the 1960s ghetto revolts. Whereas possibility burned in the Black Power looting and burning of that decade, the difference in 1992 was precisely the lack of optimism and hope. In Lynell George's words, the L.A. rebellion became "unfocused, its battle cry cacophonous." African-American commentators rightly asked, "What does this signify? What kind of phoenix's gonna rise out of these particular ashes?" Rioters responded to those who threatened them, "Go ahead and kill us. We're already dead." All that could be said, apparently, was that "maybe it had to burn ... like how sometimes you have to burn a field. To make something new." But nothing much was new; despite L.A.'s rosy post-riot promises for the future, there were still no jobs, no resources. To many an African American, L.A. merely meant Lower Alabama.[53]

Third, a central reason why the promise of nights of rage was so subdued as to be almost invisible in the original erasures of the 1992 conflagration was that the power of opposition, like the experiences of dispossession, had become complicated to the point not of focused clarity but of dispersed plurality. The rioters—ironically enough, given the black–white antagonism evident in the Rodney King beating—were a rainbow coalition of the urban poor, drawn from the eclectic colors of America's immigrant-infused inner-city demographic mosaic. Of the almost 9,500 arrested, only 30 percent were black, fully 37 percent Latino, and a surprising 7 percent white; most significantly, the remaining 26 percent of those caught in the dragnet of repression were classified as "other/unknown." Blacks constituted the bulk of those rioting and arrested on the first night of the uprising, but subsequent evenings saw increasing Latino involvement as Mexican and Central American jobless youth took to the streets. Complicating matters further, this second wave of the discontented and dispossessed struck purposively at the Korean petty-bourgeois elements of South Central Los Angeles, their small family shops the targets of preference for arsonists and looters. If the acquittal of four white officers guilty of the brutalizing of a black male precipitated the riots of 1992, it also unleashed the pent-up frustrations and dark underside of multiethnic tension and antagonism. In the aftermath, hundreds of so-called illegal aliens were rounded up as the LAPD linked arms with federal forces such as the Immigration and Naturalization Service and the Border Patrol to conduct a campaign of terror and deportation aimed at disrupting an increasingly politicized Central American community. Similarly, in a massive nocturnal invasion of African-American and Latino neighborhoods, the city police and National Guard conducted postmidnight street and house sweeps, aided by their proliferating data banks on supposed gang members (in which the figures on "classified" youth soared from 14,000 to over 150,000 in the late 1980s and early 1990s); almost 50 percent of young male blacks in Los Angeles County were reviled in the rhetoric of regulatory "data" collection as dangerous gang members. Ostensibly searching for items looted in the riots, local police, immigration officials, and FBI agents created a state of martial law that constructed Los Angeles at night as a marketplace of ill-gotten gain which it was "legitimate" for authority to ransack. Ideologically, this repression reached its political apogee in violent police attacks on Crips and Blood "truce" meetings, which sometimes temporarily forged a politics of liberation solidarity in night gatherings of five to seven hundred gang youth. The L.A. night thus bred low-intensity warfare, a counterinsurgency aimed at disrupting and destabilizing the transgressive ferment that late capitalism's first multiethnic urban riot had uncapped.[54]

The nights of Rodney King rioting, then, in their multidimensionality, marked a significant realignment of the race riot as urban rebellion. Described by Mike Davis as a hybrid social revolt encompassing not only black protest, but a modern "bread" riot by the multiracial urban poor and an interethnic conflict in which elements of the "colored" lower orders launched an anti-Asiatic pogrom, the uprising produced a first impression of inchoate militancy.[55] Subsequent events, in which state repression in the service of "colorless" capitalist (read "real white power") interests melded segments of this dispersed plurality of the urban poor together, conditioned the formation and political evolution of a nascent rainbow coalition. Composed as it was of the highly volatile human material ground down in South Central L.A. and other districts of the urban poor, the emerging politics of the 1990s oppositional night was inflammatory indeed. The burning embers illuminated both the possibility of new opportunities (gang truces and politicization as well as awareness of the importance of solidarities among the exploited and oppressed) and the problematic depths of racism's ugly backlashes, which could cut through inner-city neighborhoods in revengeful rages directed at the Other

(Koreans) beyond the *original* Other.[56] The Los Angeles riots, in which African Americans, Hispanics, Asians, and whites found themselves caught in a rebellious motion both liberating and threatening, exposed the dark and the light at the end of a long historical tunnel of urban race riots. The fire next time, as prophesied in 1963 and confirmed by the Rodney King riots in their decisive difference, may leave so little standing that it will be impossible to see light and dark again. But after 1992 it was no longer possible to deny the insight animating Baldwin's plea for change:

> America, of all the Western nations, has been best placed to prove the uselessness and obsolescence of the concept of color. But it has not dared to accept this opportunity, or even to conceive of it as an opportunity.... White Americans find it as difficult as white people elsewhere do to divest themselves of the notion that they are in possession of some intrinsic value that black people need, or want ... Alas, this value can scarcely be corroborated.... The white man's unadmitted — and apparently, to him, unspeakable—private fears and longings are projected on to the Negro. The only way he can be released from the Negro's tyrannical power over him is to consent, in effect, to become black himself, to become a part of that suffering and dancing country that he now watches wistfully from the heights of his lonely power and, armed with spiritual traveller's checks, visits surreptitiously after dark.[57]

PART IX
Conclusion

19. Bertall, *La Barricade* from *The Communists of Paris* (1871).

21

Dark Cultures and the Politics of Transgression/ Transformation

I like the night and many of its transgressive people. These are the hours in which I, and so many others with whom I share a tenuous and usually unspoken bond, *live*. Writing these many chapters, I have found it easy to see the attractions of a postmodernist sensibility in which identities of transgression (often sustained in the dark hours of the evening and early morning) and the struggles of marginalized Others (pushed to the peripheries of power's bright day) come to the forefront, where they are presented as reversals of the degradations and distortions necessary to authority's continuity. For those drawn to the prospects of social transformation, the night seemingly offers a view from below, a set of understandings of difference and an empathetic engagement with the many deviances constructed over the ages to sustain subordination. An almost libidinal charge comes with involvement in topics of transgression and the night, where sensualities and sociabilities, aesthetics and the arts of resistance, are an unmistakable presence, a pleasurable reminder that life is not only about the travails and timidities of a tortured accommodation. To look into the night, to grope one's way through its thick darkness and past its opaque inhibited visions, is to see with varying degrees of clarity the sights and sites of intriguingly challenging and endlessly diverse resiliencies, moments in the making of a truly new world.

And this is the potential and promise of a postmodernist perspective and the politics, however unstated, of transgression. In forcing one to look at the precarious edges of experience, where oppression's meanings are negotiated and sometimes reconstructed, the postmodernist politics

of identity necessarily opens one's eyes to perspectives and places that
have too routinely been out of sight and out of mind, often for centuries.
For some, no doubt, this is, in the parlance of our times, an empowering
process of shifting the terms whereby entrenched authority universally
naturalizes historical narratives of inequality glorified: the cleansing of
churchly crusades of conquest; the mythologizing of monarchies and their
right to rule; the romance of entrepreneurship and the individual initiative
that condemns collectivities apparently capable of only lesser destinies of
toil; the mapping of contributions that conceptualize vast reaches of human
contribution, from motherhood to the musics of marked peoples, as
somehow cartographically missing. The night is where counters to that
conventional wisdom often find a space to grow and growl, a place
welcoming in its shadowed obscurities, where the voice of subjectivity,
long suppressed, finds a rare articulation. "In Night," declares Elie Wiesel,
concisely characterizing the three parts of his autobiographical Holocaust
meditation on human evil and self-destruction, "it is the 'I' who speaks;
in the [narratives of Dawn and The Accident] it is the 'I' who listens and
questions."[1]

Historians, political theorists, sociologists, and others who comment
on power's reign have been slow to grasp this significance, although
contemporary literature, attentive to what Jim Carroll has called "the
obscure members of the cosmopolitan night," has been relentless in its
use of metaphorical darkness.[2] As a parallel to the histories of the night
presented throughout this book, the fiction of late capitalism—especially
at its geographical and social margins—repeatedly conjoins the socioeconomic othering of imperialism's global subordinations with the inversions of a transgressive sexuality, fusing the oppression and liberation
of alternative in narratives of the night.[3] Where, as in the case of Cuba,
such themes can be explored against the backdrop of revolution, the
tapestry of emancipation's ironies is rich indeed.[4] The point is underlined
in Marge Piercy's fictionalization of gender relations in the Paris of the
turbulent late eighteenth century.[5] Drawn to the night, the novelist sees
what the archives of day's power often deny and destroy. A zone of de-
construction (I use the word descriptively rather than theoretically), the
night can be grasped historically as both a figment of power's imaginative
fears, a dark designation illuminating the historicized traumas of hegemonic regimes,[6] and as an actual place and space in which the ubiquitous
contestations of everyday life were fought out on a terrain that afforded
slightly more opportunity for engagement by the oppressed and the
exploited. If this engagement was not always of the sort sanctified by

traditionalist prejudice of what constitutes event and actuality, it can nevertheless be explored and read within the relations of power and subordination.[7] One needs to understand this and seek out the remnants of experiences cherished for what they were, for what they promised, and for what they could become.

It is that becoming, the movement from dark transgressive cultures to social transformation, that concerns me most and that leaves me, for all my predilections, ultimately skeptical of a postmodernist politics of the reification of identity and Otherness. It is of course appropriate to savor the particularities of the range of subjective experience traversed in a centuries-long walk through the aesthetics and activities of the night. Pornographers and pirates, bandits and beats, communards and crack dealers were undeniably agents whose understandings of their historical selves seldom met on anything approximating common ground. Readers might rightly conclude that I have produced a text in which the parts loom larger than the whole. This would be congruent with a postmodern appreciation, which would accentuate the night's fragmentations and pluralities, a swirl of differentiation in which no connections and commonalities manage to surface in the sea of darkness. For the playfully postmodern, it is possible to revel in such discursiveness, but there is a dark side to this theoretical moment as well, espoused in the pessimism of Georges Bataille. "We lack daylight to the extent that we lack the night that we are," he has written, adding a comment that could well be applied to the range of dark cultures I have sampled in these histories of the night: "What happens to us when, disintoxicated, we learn what we are? Lost among babblers in a night in which we can only hate the appearance of light which comes from babbling."[8] This is the inner subjectivity of the dangers that power has always, in various guises, used the night to deploy.

Am I drunk with the illusion of night's possibilities? In claiming sobriety, I refuse, in some senses, both of these ultimatist postmodern responses, although I draw in some ways on the sentiments of each. On the one hand, to embrace the particularities of night's many chapters, celebrating them on their own terms as a way of retreating into the parochialities, however pleasurable, of each, is to limit the meaning of dark cultures to that of self-definition and subjective sensuality, to condemn them to a permanent state of marginality, and to refuse to look night's restraints in their evil eye. On the other hand, to find in the transgressions of the night only an incoherent babble that proves to outsiders a lack of self-identity, or to see the night as something only to be taken back from some dangerous, all-powerful force, is to impose a closure that seems unduly harsh and insensitive to what has, over time, been a persistent process of creation, adaptation, and renewal. That this process is a product of desire, often constrained by danger, is all too evident in the histories of the night, which show repression and resistance engaged in a constant tug-of-war whose stakes—as moments of revolutionary potential (the 1790s) or reactionary backlash (Nazism in the 1930s) indicate—are high indeed. "We built the night out of the materials of despair and dreams," writes the novelist of the Bahian waterfront, Jorge Amado.[9]

That despair and those dreams (postmodernism's repudiation of all metanarratives of interpretation and all master categories of analytic thought aside)[10] are situated within the rise and transformation of global capitalism, the determining and foundational feature of human experience in the modern world. This is where we still live and struggle. In metaphorical terms, capitalism's daylight powers are ever the prelude to night's cultures of transgression, marginality, and alternative. There is no possibility of adequately seeing power and its consequences only from below, just as the night cannot really be understood apart from the day.

If Foucault accentuates night's opportunities and forces us to look to their possibilities, Marx reminds us—never more decisively than now, when he is most resolutely rebuked—that we cannot do so without a sober appreciation of the day's determinations. To be sure, Marx's political economy, poised to challenge the dismal science of bourgeois thought on its own terms, understated the vehicles and vehemence of popular opposition to and distance from the debasements of capitalist institutions and authority. This structured power invested age-old hierarchies of gender and racial difference with newly potent meanings as the modern world emerged from the layered shell of older social formations. One purpose of this book is to emphasize the long resilience of everynight resistance and refusal, which remains underappreciated in a world capable of canonizing ideas of the great tradition but blind to the dark doings of the marginal and the transgressive. Darkness, contra Hannah Arendt, was never only a time of evil, even in the most unfortunate historical periods of reaction and retribution.[11]

Marxist critique has nevertheless looked inadequately into the night and paid insufficient attention to dimensions of subordination, marginalization, and transgression not directly and unambiguously connected, via the wage and struggles over its contents, to the labor–capital relation. But that relation was central to the evolution of other arenas of social contestation. Running through the dense darkness of histories of the night, then, lie undeniable connective tissues, materialist links in the chains that men and women must shed if their days, as well as their nights, are to be truly free.

That such struggles bridge night and day is as evident as their embeddedness in a history that has, for centuries, been truly global in its reach and calamitous consequences. The highest stage of the capitalist day reached into the dark continents and reconfigured the meaning of the night for the entirety of the world's peoples. Postmodernism's capacity to clone analytic modes supposedly attentive to a differentiated postcoloniality, however attractive as a recognition of difference on a world scale, may actually paper over the many imperialist interconnections that link first and third worlds. Postmodernism's purchase on the experience of the disintegration of "actually existing socialism" seems weak at best in contemporary Russia or the beleaguered planned economies of Cuba or China.[12]

This book, then, is no postmodern celebration of fragmentation, ephemerality, and social indetermination. It does not so much champion marginalization and transgression as acknowledge their *coerced* being, explore their cultural resiliencies, and suggest that their historicized presence, constrained limitations, and capacities to articulate a challenge to ensconced power are never islands unto themselves. They are always reciprocally related to the material world of production and exchange, where oppression and exploitation are universal attributes of night's freedoms and fears as well as day's more transparent politics of inequality. To break out of these cultures of darkness, to take what is imaginative and sustaining in them and move such forces decisively in the direction of social transformation, demands not the isolations of subjectivity, self, and limited satisfactions but the cultivation of ever widening sociabilities. Difference, however much it is to be defended, is never in and of itself an antidote to oppression and exploitation, which override the particularisms of specific identities, but rather an invaluable and thoroughly understandable palliative in periods terrorized by the continuities of power's constraints. Social transformation, initiated in part in the dark cultures of the night, can proceed to its logical conclusion only through the movements and mobilizations that, building on difference, actually break it down and bring together the forced fragmentations of capitalism's tyrannical, eminently pluralistic, order.

Like Marx's words, the metaphorical bats with which this book opened, the project of social transformation, subdued and seemingly still in the caves and crevices of capitalism's powerful days of oppression and exploitation, historically emerged in nights, representational and real, of strange flights that have taken men and women of diverse background and sociocultural place into varied activities. In their nocturnal lives these disparate people have accommodated and resisted, transgressed and tithed, challenged and sustained the varied but reinforcing powers of a capitalism that has the ultimate project of subordinating the vast majority of humankind. Its dependence on accumulation is a relentlessly unending quest to keep the foundational difference of the modern world, material inequality, forever secure. From this essential practice of exploitation, which separates countries into classes and the world into spheres of capitalist, imperialist interest, flow the many estrangements and permanently disfiguring oppressions of times past and present, where class, race, and gender have come to be lived as codified difference across centuries of accumulation and avarice. In the night this difference has sometimes found a space and a time to present its own face, but seldom has the countenance been unmarked by power's ravages, and at times the disfigured visage of challenge has been pushed violently into uncomfortable spaces of confinement. If the bat of night's transformative potential is to fly free, it must shed its singular identity as a bat, join with other species of the day and night, learn to do more than retreat in the face of daylight's challenges, and colonize all places and times. It must build a society that walks and flies, that inhabits the boulevards of light as well as the skies of dusk. This is humanity's project as well, a part of which will be shaped by the dark transgressive cultures made in the long night of capitalist containment.

Notes

Introduction

1. Karl Marx and Friedrich Engels, *Manifesto of the Communist Party*, original 1848 (New York: Arrow Editions, 1933), p. 7.
2. For an introduction only consider the statements in Rodney Hilton, ed., *The Transition from Feudalism to Capitalism* (London: New Left Books, 1976); Ellen Meiksins Wood, *The Pristine Culture of Capitalism: An Historical Essay on Old Regimes and Modern States* (London: Verso, 1991).
3. See, for instance, Harvey J. Kaye, *The Powers of the Past: Reflections on the Crisis and Promise of History* (Minneapolis: University of Minnesota Press, 1991).
4. For the original Fukuyama statement, see Francis Fukuyama, "The End of History," *The National Interest* 16 (Summer 1989): 3–18, and the more complex elaborations in *The End of History and the Last Man* (New York: Macmillan, 1992).
5. Consider for the 1840s and the 1920s the following accounts: Marx and Engels, *The German Ideology* (New York: International Publishers, 1939), esp. pp. 79–194; Perry Anderson, *Considerations on Western Marxism* (London: New Left Books, 1976).
6. See Ellen Meiksins Wood, *The Retreat from Class: A New "True" Socialism* (London: Verso, 1986).
7. For left responses to the constellation of forces addressed by Fukuyama see Lutz Niethammer, *Posthistoire: Has History Come to an End?* (London: Verso, 1992); Joseph McCarney, "Shaping Ends: Reflections on Fukuyama," *New Left Review*, 202 (November–December 1992), pp. 37–54; Perry Anderson, "The Ends of History," in Anderson, *A Zone of Engagement* (London: Verso, 1992), pp. 279–375.
8. I have surveyed the problematic character of this work, as it applies to historical analysis, in Bryan D. Palmer, *Descent into Discourse: The Reification of Language and the Writing of Social History* (Philadelphia: Temple University Press, 1992). See, as well, Ellen Meiksins Wood and John Bellamy Foster, eds., *In Defense of History: Marxism and the Postmodern Agenda* (New York: Monthly Review Press, 1997). For a useful collection of material, pro and con, relating to

postmodern history, see Keith Jenkins, ed., *The Postmodern History Reader* (London and New York: Routledge, 1997).

9. Ellen Wood, "Identity Crisis," *In These Times*, 13 June 1994, pp. 28–29; Wood, *The Pristine Culture of Capitalism*.

10. Recent attempts to provide histories and geographies of the night thus converge with my purpose. Note Joachim Schlor, *Nights in the Big City: Paris, Berlin, London, 1840–1930* (London: Reaktion Books, 1998); Luc Bureau, *Geographie de la nuit* (Montreal: L'Hexagone, 1997).

11. See especially the comments on night/darkness in Michel Foucault, *Madness and Civilization: A History of Insanity in the Age of Reason* (New York: Vintage, 1965), pp. 85–116.

12. David Macey, *The Lives of Foucault: A Biography* (New York: Pantheon, 1993), p. 389.

13. John Rajchman, "Foucault's Art of Seeing," *October*, 44 (Spring 1988): 89–117.

14. "Intellectuals and Power: Michel Foucault and Gilles Deleuze," in Russell Ferguson et al., eds., *Discourses: Conversations in Postmodern Art and Culture* (Cambridge, Mass.: MIT Press, 1990), pp. 14–16.

15. J. G. Merquoir, *Foucault* (Berkeley: University of California Press, 1985), p. 155.

16. Karl Marx, "The Holy Family," in Marx and Engels, *Collected Works, Volume 4, 1844–1845* (New York: International Press, 1976), p. 36.

17. See Karl Marx, "Proceedings of the Sixth Rhine Province Assembly. Third Article. Debates on the Law of the Thefts of Wood," and "Justification of the Correspondent from the Mosel," in Marx and Engels, *Collected Works, Volume 1, 1835–1843* (New York: International Press, 1976), pp. 224–63, 355; Erica Sherover-Marcuse, *Emancipation and Consciousness: Dogmatic and Dialectical Perspectives in the Early Marx* (Oxford: Blackwell, 1986), pp. 17–44.

18. This was a part of what Gramsci was grappling with in his discussion of hegemony, which involved not only the coercive power of capital and the state but also the capacity of such forces to create consensual, but disturbingly collective, accommodation among the subaltern groups. See Antonio Gramsci, *Selections from the Prison Notebooks* (New York: International Press, 1971).

19. Fredric Jameson, *Postmodernism, or, The Cultural Logic of Late Capitalism* (Durham, N.C.: Duke University Press, 1991), pp. 11–12.

20. The bat metaphor was first used in Vilfred Pareto, *Les Systèmes Socialistes*, Vol. II (Paris, 1902), and is elaborated on in Bertell Ollman, *Alienation: Marx's Concept of Man in Capitalist Society* (Cambridge: Cambridge University Press, 1971), pp. 3–11.

Chapter 1

1. See Patricia Hills, "John Sloan's Images of Working-Class Women," *Prospects* 5 (1980): 157–96; Joshua Brown, "A Spectator of Life—A Reverential, Enthusiastic, Emotional Spectator," *American Quarterly* 49 (June 1997): 356–84; Marianne Doezema, *George Bellows and Urban America* (New Haven: Yale University Press, 1992); Milton Brown, *American Painting from the Armory Show to the Depression* (Princeton: Princeton University Press, 1955), pp. 9–38.

2. See Theodore Dreiser, "The City Awakes," in *The Color of a Great City* (New York: Boni & Liveright, 1923), esp. pp. 5–7; and, on O'Keeffe, Abraham A.

Davidson, *Early American Modernist Painting, 1910–1925* (New York: Harper & Row, 1981), p. 206.

3. Henrik de Leeuw, *Sinful Cities of the Western World* (New York: Citadel Press, 1934), pp. 251–52.

4. Benton's recollections of New York in this period, overlapping with those of the Ashcan School, focus on the bohemianism of artistic circles. See Thomas Hart Benton, *An Artist in America* (Columbia: University of Missouri Press, 1968), esp. pp. 37–64; Michael Denning, *The Cultural Front: The Laboring of American Culture in the Twentieth Century* (London: Verso, 1995), pp. 65, 74, 133.

5. See Henry Adams, *Thomas Hart Benton: Drawing from Life* (New York: Abbeville Press, 1990), p. 137; Adams, *Thomas Hart Benton: An American Original* (New York: Knopf, 1989), pp. 165–67; Mathew Baigell, *Thomas Hart Benton* (New York: Harry N. Abrams, n.d.), pp. 111–13. Highly suggestive is Erika Doss, *Benton, Pollock, and the Politics of Modernism: From Regionalism to Abstract Expressionism* (Chicago: University of Chicago Press, 1991). On comparisons of the night and the western frontier, see Murray Melbin, "Night as Frontier," *American Sociological Review* 43 (February 1978): 3–22.

6. See Joseph Burke and Colin Caldwell, *Hogarth: The Complete Engravings* (London: Alpine, n.d.), esp. pp. 177–80; Ronald Paulson, *Hogarth: His Life, Art, and Times* (New Haven: Yale University Press, 1974), esp. pp. 175–81, 219.

7. T. S. Eliot, "The Love Song of J. Alfred Prufrock," in *Selected Poems* (London: Faber & Faber, 1952), p. 13.

8. On the notorious Black Act enacted in England in 1723, see E. P. Thompson, *Whigs and Hunters: The Origin of the Black Act* (New York: Pantheon, 1975). An intriguing discussion is found in Wolfgang Schivelbusch, *Disenchanted Night: The Industrialization of Light in the Nineteenth Century* (Berkeley: University of California Press, 1988).

9. Jean Baudrillard, *The Transparency of Evil: Essays on Extreme Phenomena* (London: Verso, 1993), pp. 44–45.

10. Loren Eiseley, *The Night Country: Reflections of a Bone Hunting Man* (New York: Scribner, 1971), pp. 3–4.

11. Note the discussion in Maurice Agulhon, *Marianne into Battle: Republican Imagery and Symbolism in France, 1789–1880* (Cambridge: Cambridge University Press, 1981); Eric Hobsbawm, "Man and Woman in Socialist Iconography," *History Workshop Journal* 6 (Autumn 1978): 121–38; Agulhon, "On Political Allegory: A Reply to Eric Hobsbawm," *History Workshop Journal* 8 (Autumn 1979): 167–73; Sally Alexander, Anna Davin, and Eve Hostettler, "Labouring Women: A Reply to Eric Hobsbawm," *History Workshop Journal* 8 (Autumn 1979): 174–82.

12. See *Roy DeCarava: A Retrospective* (New York: Museum of Modern Art, 1996); Roy DeCarava and Langston Hughes, *The Sweet Flypaper of Life* (New York: Simon & Schuster, 1955); Sherry Turner DeCarava, "Celebration," in James Alinder, ed., *Roy DeCarava: Photographs* (Carmel, Calif.: Friends of Photography, 1981), pp. 7–20; A. D. Coleman, "Roy DeCarava: Thru Black Eyes," *Popular Photography* (April 1970): 68–71, 113–15, 118–19, 168; Elton C. Fax, *Seventeen Black Artists* (New York: Dodd, Mead, 1971), pp. 167–87; Ruth Wallen, "Reading the Shadows—the Photography of Roy DeCarava," *Exposure* 27 (Fall 1990): 13–26.

13. George Rawick, *From Sundown to Sunup: The Making of the Black Community* (Westport, Conn.: Greenwood, 1972), p. 12. Note, as well, Charles Joyner, *Down by the Riverside: A South Carolina Slave Community* (Urbana: University of Illinois Press,

1984), p. 127: "It was not the days of drudgery in the rice fields but the hours of off time that most shaped the contours of slave culture."

14. For the classic statement on the self-emancipation of slaves see W. E. B. DuBois, *Black Reconstruction in America, 1860–1880* (Cleveland: World, 1964). See also DuBois, *The Souls of Black Folk* (New York: Fawcett, 1964); Charles S. Johnson, *Shadow of the Plantation* (Chicago: University of Chicago Press, 1934); Ralph Ellison, *Invisible Man* (New York: Random House, 1952); David Bradley, *The Chaneysville Incident* (New York: Harper & Row, 1981); and the disturbingly insightful commentary on Chester Himes—author of *If He Hollers Let Him Go* (1945) and a series of successful black detective novels—in Fred Pfeil, "Policiers Noirs," in Pfeil, *Another Tale to Tell: Politics and Narrative in Postmodern Culture* (London: Verso, 1990), pp. 64–68.

15. *Roy DeCarava: A Retrospective*, p. 25.

Chapter 2

1. Karl Marx, "The So-Called Primitive Accumulation," in Marx, *Capital: A Critical Analysis of Capitalist Production*, Volume I (New York: International, 1967), p. 715. For an account emphasizing the longevity of the English peasantry, see J. M. Neeson, "An Eighteenth-Century Peasantry," in John Rule and Robert Malcolmson, eds., *Protest and Survival: Essays for E. P. Thompson* (London: Merlin Press, 1993), pp. 24–59.

2. See, among other sources, Teodor Shanin, ed., *Peasants and Peasant Society* (Harmondsworth: Penguin, 1971).

3. On the history of climate, see the special issue, *Journal of Interdisciplinary History* 10 (Spring 1980).

4. Johan Huizinga, *The Waning of the Middle Ages* (Harmondsworth: Penguin, 1979), pp. 28–29.

5. Emile Guillaumin, *The Life of a Simple Man*, ed. and intro. Eugene Weber (Hanover, N.H.: University Press of New England, 1983), pp. 148, 150–51, 158, 195. John Berger, *Pig Earth* (London: Writers & Readers, 1979), p. 201, states that the peasant's determination is "to hand on the means of survival (if possible made more secure, compared to what he inherited) to his children."

6. Robert Darnton, "Peasants Tell Tales: The Meaning of Mother Goose," in Darnton, *The Great Cat Massacre and Other Episodes in French Cultural History* (New York: Basic Books, 1984), p. 34.

7. Antonio Gramsci, *Selections from the Prison Notebooks* (New York: International Press, 1971), p. 358.

8. See esp. Berger, *Pig Earth*, pp. 195–213, but note the more sobering assessment of the peasantry in Marcus Hindus, *Red Bread: Collectivization in a Russian Village* (Bloomington: Indiana University Press, 1988). For indications of the destabilizing changes within the peasantry that contributed to economic differentiation, demographic revolution, and socioeconomic transformation, see T. H. Ashton and C. H. E. Philpin, eds., *The Brenner Debate: Agrarian Class Structure and Economic Development in Pre-Industrial Europe* (Cambridge: Cambridge University Press, 1985); Teodor Shanin, ed., *Late Marx and the Russian Road: Marx and "The Peripheries of Capitalism"* (New York: Monthly Review Press, 1983); V. I. Lenin, *The Development of Capitalism in Russia* (Moscow: Progress, 1964); Wally

Seccombe, *A Millennium of Family Change: Feudalism to Capitalism in Northwestern Europe* (London: Verso, 1992).

9. Berger, *Pig Earth*, p. 197. Note the development of a theory of peasant resistance in James C. Scott, *Weapons of the Weak: Everyday Forms of Peasant Resistance* (New Haven: Yale University Press, 1985); Scott, *Domination and the Arts of Resistance: Hidden Transcripts* (New Haven: Yale University Press, 1990). Peasant proverbs and conventional wisdom are discussed in Natalie Zemon Davis, "Proverbial Wisdom and Popular Errors," in Davis, *Society and Culture in Early Modern France* (Stanford, Calif.: Stanford University Press, 1975), pp. 227–70.

10. Eric Hobsbawm, *Age of Extremes: The Short History of the Twentieth Century, 1914–1991* (London: Michael Joseph, 1994), pp. 289–93, 352–57, 379–83. Peasant displacement in the post–World War II period is an important theme in Philip McMichael, *Development and Social Change: A Global Perspective* (Thousand Oaks, Calif.: Pine Forge Press, 1996).

11. Joseph Roux, *Pensées* (1885), quoted in Theodore Zeldin, *France, 1848–1945: Ambition and Love* (Oxford: Oxford University Press, 1979), p. 132.

12. Charles-Leonard Pfeiffer, *Taste and Smell in Balzac's Novels* (Tuscon: University of Arizona Press, 1949); Alain Corbin, "Les Paysans de Paris," *Ethnologie Française* 2 (1980): 169–76; Herbert J. Hunt, *Balzac's Comédie Humaine* (London: Athlone Press, 1959).

13. Karl Marx, "The Eighteenth Brumaire of Louis Bonaparte," in Karl Marx and Friedrich Engels, *Selected Works* (Moscow: Progress, 1968), p. 172. A similar perspective dominates discussion of the peasantry in Gramsci, *Selections from the Prison Notebooks*. For a diatribe against Marx on the peasantry, which descends into attack on the twentieth-century socialist (Stalinist) assault on the rural population, see David Mitrany, *Marx against the Peasant: A Study in Social Dogmatism* (Chapel Hill: University of North Carolina Press, 1951).

14. Friedrich Engels, "The Peasant Question in France and Germany," in Marx and Engels, *Selected Works*, p. 633. For an account that confirms Engels's assessment of the peasantry, see Guillaumin, *Life of a Simple Man*, pp. 186–90.

15. See Teodor Shanin, *The Awkward Class: Political Sociology of Peasantry in a Developing Society—Russia, 1910–1925* (Oxford: Oxford University Press, 1972); Lenin, *The Development of Capitalism in Russia*; Michael Löwy, *The Politics of Combined and Uneven Development: The Theory of Permanent Revolution* (London: Verso, 1981); E. J. Hobsbawm, "Peasant Land Occupations," *Past & Present* 62 (February 1974): 120–52.

16. See Eugen Weber, *Peasants into Frenchmen: The Modernization of Rural France* (Stanford, Calif.: Stanford University Press, 1976), pp. 3–22; Weber, *France: Fin de Siècle* (Cambridge, Mass.: Harvard University Press, 1986), pp. 52, 62; Zeldin, *France, 1848–1945*, pp. 131–34.

17. Weber, *Peasants into Frenchmen*, p. 12.

18. *The Complete Letters of Vincent Van Gogh*, Volume II (London, 1958), p. 370, quoted in G. E. M. de Ste. Croix, *The Class Struggle in the Ancient Greek World: From the Archaic Age to the Arab Conquest* (London: Duckworth, 1981), pp. 209–10. The quotation on the physical peasant is from an 1822 source cited in Weber, *Peasants into Frenchmen*, p. 6. Note that Ste. Croix, who reads the Van Gogh painting in an unambiguously positive way, still manages to fall into ambivalence. He concludes simultaneously that "the 'Potato Eaters' are poor, but they are not evidently miserable" (p. 210) and that "the miserably poor

'Potato Eaters'" were depicted by Van Gogh with "heartrending sympathy" (p. 278).

19. Consider, as well, the imaginative reading of Van Gogh's *A Pair of Boots* (1887), a painting of peasant shoes, in Fredric Jameson, *Postmodernism, or, The Cultural Logic of Late Capitalism* (Durham, N.C.: Duke University Press, 1991), p. 7. On the conditions of the peasantry see, as well, Marx, "The Eighteenth Brumaire of Louis Bonaparte," pp. 172–74.

20. Brillat-Savarin, quoted in Fernand Braudel, *Capitalism and Material Life, 1400–1800* (New York: Harper & Row, 1973), p. 66.

21. Quoted in Piero Camporesi, *The Anatomy of the Senses: Natural Symbols in Medieval and Early Modern Italy* (Cambridge: Polity Press, 1994), p. 196.

22. Guillaumin, *Life of a Simple Man*, p. 102

23. Emmanuel Le Roy Ladurie, *Montaillou: The Promised Land of Error* (New York: Vintage, 1979), pp. 277–78.

24. Darnton, "Peasants Tell Tales," pp. 13, 31–32. On storytelling and the legalities of pardon tales, see Natalie Zemon Davis, *Fiction in the Archives: Pardon Tales and Their Tellers in Sixteenth-Century France* (Stanford, Calif.: Stanford University Press, 1987).

25. This highly complex issue is addressed adroitly in Seccombe, *A Millennium of Family Change*, most pointedly on pp. 38–40, 78–82, 121–24. For contrasting statements on peasant families in England and France, see Peter Laslett, *The World We Have Lost* (London: Methuen, 1971); Alan Macfarlane, *The Origins of English Individualism* (Oxford: Basil Blackwell, 1978); Keith Wrightson and David Levine, *Poverty and Piety in an English Village: Terling, 1525–1700* (New York: Academic Press, 1979), esp. pp. 82–91; Richard M. Smith, "Kin and Neighbours in a Thirteenth-Century Suffolk Community," *Journal of Family History* 4 (1979): 219–56; J. L. Flandrin, *Families in Former Times: Kinship, Household, and Sexuality* (New York: Cambridge University Press, 1979); Emmanuel Le Roy Ladurie, *The Peasants of Languedoc* (Urbana: University of Illinois Press, 1980).

26. See Wally Seccombe, "Marxism and Demography," *New Left Review* 137 (January–February 1983): 39–41, and Michael Mitterauer and Richard Seider, *The European Family: Patriarchy to Partnership from the Middle Ages to the Present* (Oxford: Basil Blackwell, 1982).

27. Natalie Zemon Davis, *The Return of Martin Guerre* (Cambridge, Mass.: Harvard University Press, 1983), pp. 6–18.

28. Le Roy Ladurie, *Montaillou*, p. 24.

29. Berger, "A Question of Place," in *Pig Earth*, pp. 1–4; Alain Corbin, *The Foul and the Fragrant: Odor and the French Social Imagination* (Cambridge, Mass.: Harvard University Press, 1986), pp. 16–18, 36, 120, 187, 212; Piero Camporesi, *Bread of Dreams: Food and Fantasy in Early Modern Europe* (Chicago: University of Chicago Press, 1989), pp. 44–45; Captain John G. Bourke, *Scatological Rites of All Nations: A Dissertation upon the Employment of Excrementitious Remedial Agents in Religion* (New York: Anthropological Society, 1934), p. 240; Reay Tannahill, *Flesh and Blood: A History of the Cannibal Complex* (London: Hamish Hamilton, 1975); Camporesi, *Juice of Life: The Symbolic and Magic Significance of Blood* (New York: Continuum, 1995), esp. pp. 18, 29.

30. Richard Cobb titled an essay on the French peasant novel (*le roman regional*) "Blood and Soil." See his *Promenades: An Historian's Appreciation of Modern French Literature* (Oxford: Oxford University Press, 1980), pp. 45–51.

31. Michel Foucault, *I, Pierre Rivière, having slaughtered my mother, my sister, and my brother: A Case of Parricide in the 19th Century* (New York: Pantheon, 1973). On parricide, see also Davis, *Fiction in the Archives*, pp. 12, 60, 103 (and also 7 on wife killing); Manfredi Piccolomini, *The Brutus Revivial: Parricide and Tyrannicide during the Renaissance* (Carbondale: University of Southern Illinois Press, 1991).

32. Darnton, "Peasants Tell Tales," pp. 42, 53–55.

33. Claude-Henri Rocquet, *Bruegel: or The Workshop of Dreams* (Chicago: University of Chicago Press, 1991), pp. 139, 171.

34. Pierre Goubert, *The Ancien Régime: French Society, 1600–1750* (London: Weidenfeld & Nicolson, 1973), pp. 108–09.

35. Davis, *Fiction in the Archives*, p. 44; Richard Cobb, "L'Affaire Perken: A Double Murder on the Franco-Dutch Border, 1809," in Cobb, *A Sense of Place* (London: Duckworth, 1975), esp. p. 54; Goubert, *The Ancien Régime*, pp. 103–07; Olwen H. Hufton, *The Poor of Eighteenth Century France, 1750–1789* (Oxford: Clarendon Press, 1974); Barbara Hanawalt, *Crime and Conflict in English Communities, 1300–1348* (Cambridge, Mass.: Harvard University Press, 1979), pp. 76–83; Michel Mollat, *The Poor in the Middle Ages: An Essay in Social History* (New Haven: Yale University Press, 1986), esp. pp. 191–294; Alan Macfarlane, *Justice and the Mare's Ale: Law and Disorder in Seventeenth-Century England* (Oxford: Basil Blackwell, 1981), pp. 158, 180, 189, for specific comment on the night, but the book in general confirms the place of darkness in harboring criminals; Weber, *Peasants into Frenchmen*, p. 54; Richard Cobb, *The Police and the People: French Popular Protest, 1795–1820* (London: Oxford University Press, 1970), p. 305; Guillaumin, *The Life of a Simple Man*, p. 50; Alain Corbin, *The Village of Cannibals: Rage and Murder in France, 1870* (Cambridge, Mass.: Harvard University Press, 1992), pp. 53–55; E. P. Thompson, *Whigs and Hunters: The Origin of the Black Act* (New York: Pantheon, 1975); Camporesi, *Bread of Dreams*, pp. 92–102; Jean Verdon, *La Nuit au Moyen Age* (Paris: Perrin, 1994), esp. pp. 67–88; Robert Mandrou, *Introduction to Modern France, 1500–1640: An Essay in Historical Psychology* (New York: Harper Torchbooks, 1975), pp. 56, 236–37; Michael Kunze, *Highroad to the Stake: A Tale of Witchcraft* (Chicago: University of Chicago Press, 1987), p. 135.

36. Camporesi, *Bread of Dreams*, p. 96. Note, as well, Davis, "Proverbial Wisdom," pp. 255–57, 264.

37. William H. McNeill, *Keeping Together in Time: Dance and Drill in Human History* (Cambridge, Mass.: Harvard University Press, 1995), p. 41; John R. Gillis, "Peasant, Plebeian and Proletarian Marriage in Britain, 1600–1900," in David Levine, ed., *Proletarianization and Family History* (New York: Academic Press, 1984), pp. 129–62; Gillis, *For Better for Worse: British Marriages, 1600 to the Present* (Oxford: Oxford University Press, 1985), pp. 13, 15, 109–12.

38. Gillis, "Peasant, Plebeian and Proletarian Marriage," p. 137; G. M. Foster, "Anatomy of Envy: A Study of Symbolic Behaviour," *Current Anthropology* 13 (April 1972): 165–202; Foster, "Peasant Society and the Image of the Limited Good," *American Anthropologist* 67 (April 1965): 156–202; Gustav Gluck, *Pieter Brueghel the Elder* (London: Hyperion, n.d.), p. 34; Zeldin, *France, 1848–1945*, p. 132.

39. Braudel, *Capitalism and Material Life*, p. 92.

40. Ibid, pp. 90–91, and for the chapter on "Daily Bread," pp. 66–120; Mandrou, *Introduction to Modern France, 1500–1640*, pp. 13–22. See, as well, the wide-ranging discussion in Victor V. Magagna, *Communities of Grain: Rural Rebellion in*

Comparative Perspective (Ithaca: Cornell University Press, 1991). The counter-posing of a bread-nexus to a cash-nexus is central to E. P. Thompson, "The Moral Economy of the English Crowd," in *Customs in Common* (London: Merlin Press, 1991), p. 189.

41. Davis, *The Return of Martin Guerre*, p. 24, for the quite limited historical evidence, and for the artistic license of the film, *Le Retour de Martin Guerre* (1982), directed by Daniel Vigne.

42. Robert Brenner, "The Origins of Capitalist Development: A Critique of Neo-Smithian Marxism," *New Left Review* 104 (July–August 1977): 25–92; various essays, two by Brenner, in Ashton and Philpin, *The Brenner Debate*; Ian Kershaw, "The Great Famine and Agrarian Crisis in England, 1315–1322," in Rodney H. Hilton, ed., *Peasants, Knights, and Heretics: Studies in Medieval English Social History* (Cambridge: Cambridge University Press, 1976), pp. 85–132; Jean Chesneaux, "Pre-Capitalist Societies: Have They a Common Past?" and "Capitalism: the Great Unifier of History," in Chesneaux, *Pasts and Futures; or What Is History For?* (London: Thames & Hudson, 1978), pp. 73–82; Mark Bloch, *French Rural History: An Essay on Its Basic Characteristics* (Berkeley and Los Angeles: University of California Press, 1973), p. 26; R. H. Tawney, *The Agrarian Problem in the Sixteenth Century* (New York: Harper & Row, 1967), p. 112; Fernand Braudel, *The Mediterranean and the Mediterranean World in the Age of Philip II*, Volume I (New York: Harper & Row, 1972), pp. 602–06, on grain crises in Sicily; C. Lis and H. Soly, *Poverty and Capitalism in Pre-Industrial Europe* (Atlantic Highlands, N.J.: Humanities Press, 1979), pp. 75, 78, 84, 102, 107–08, 135, 173–74; William H. McNeill, *Plagues and Peoples* (Garden City, N.Y.: Doubleday, 1976); Michael W. Flinn, *The European Demographic System, 1500–1820* (Baltimore: Johns Hopkins University Press, 1981), esp. pp. 47–64; Andrew B. Appleby, "Epidemics and Famine in the Little Ice Age," *The Journal of Interdisciplinary History* 10 (Spring 1980): 643–64; Le Roy Ladurie, *The Peasants of Languedoc*, pp. 133–42, 198–99, 244; Emmanuel Le Roy Ladurie, *The French Peasantry, 1450–1660* (Berkeley: University of California Press, 1987), pp. 271–76; Trevor Aston, ed., *Crisis in Europe, 1560–1660* (Garden City: Doubleday, 1967), esp. E. J. Hobsbawm, "The Crisis of the Seventeenth Century," pp. 5–62; John Illife, *The African Poor: A History* (Cambridge: Cambridge University Press, 1987), p. 6; James Hunter, *The Making of the Crofting Community* (Edinburgh: John Donald, 1976); T. M. Devine, *The Great Highland Famine: Hunger, Emigration, and the Scottish Highlands in the 19th Century* (Edinburgh: John Donald, 1988); Daniel J. Casey and Robert E. Rhodes, eds., *Views of the Irish Peasantry, 1800–1916* (Hamden, Conn.: Archon Books, 1977); Samuel Clark and James Donnelly, eds., *Irish Peasants: Violence and Political Unrest, 1780–1914* (Madison: University of Wisconsin Press, 1983).

43. This paragraph draws mainly on Camporesi, *Bread of Dreams*, with quotations taken from pp. 56, 58, 61, 74–75, 85. But see, as well, J. Delumeau, *La Peur en Occident (XIVe–XVIIIe siècles): Une cité assiégée* (Paris: Fayard, 1978), esp. pp. 162–64; Le Roy Ladurie, *The Peasants of Languedoc*, p. 135; Robert Jutte, *Poverty and Deviance in Early Modern Europe* (Cambridge: Cambridge University Press, 1994); A. L. Beier, "Vagrants and the Social Order in Elizabethan England," *Past & Present* 64 (August 1974): 3–29; and for a challenging argument that dearth could contribute to social stability, John Walter and Keith Wrightson, "Dearth and the Social Order in Early Modern England," *Past & Present* 71 (May 1976): 2–42. A cautious statement is Peter Laslett, "Did the Peasants

Really Starve? Famine and Pestilence in Pre-Industrial Society," in Laslett, *The World We Have Lost*, pp. 113–34.

44. Goubert, *The Ancien Régime*, pp. 118–19; Braudel, *Capitalism and Material Life*, pp. 92–95; Georges Duby, *The Early Growth of the European Economy: Warriors and Peasants from the Seventh to the Twelfth Century* (London: Weidenfeld & Nicolson, 1973), p. 29.

45. Camporesi, *Bread of Dreams*, esp. pp. 18, 24–25, 125–29, 137–50; Bourke, *Scatalogical Rites*, pp. 89–91.

46. Camporesi, *Bread of Dreams*, pp. 17–18.

47. The Bruegel material that follows builds on Robert L. Delevoy, *Bruegel: Historical and Critical Study* (Paris: Skira, 1959); the imaginatively suggestive Rocquet, *Bruegel*; Arturo Bov, *Bruegel: The Life and Work of the Artist* (London: Thames & Hudson, 1971); John E. T. C. White, *Pieter Bruegel and the Fall of the Art Historian* (Newcastle upon Tyne: University of Newcastle upon Tyne, 1978).

48. Quotations are from Delevoy, *Bruegel*, pp. 11, 16, 24–25, 34, 43, 117.

49. Camporesi, *Bread of Dreams*, pp. 80–81. See also Delevoy, *Bruegel*, pp. 61–62; Bovi, *Bruegel*, p. 35; Michael A. Mullett, *Popular Culture and Popular Protest in Late Midieval and Early Modern Europe* (London: Croom Helm, 1987), pp. 97, 99; T. J. Clark, *Images of the People: Gustav Coubert and the 1848 Revolution* (London: Thames & Hudson, 1973), p. 93; Georges Duby, *The Three Orders: Feudal Society Imagined* (Chicago: University of Chicago Press, 1980).

50. Rocquet, *Bruegel*, pp. 103–04, 115.

51. For an account of Carnival, see Emmanuel Le Roy Ladurie's *Carnival in Romans: A People's Uprising at Romans, 1579–1580* (Harmondsworth: Penguin, 1981).

52. Note the discussions in Emmanuel Le Roy Ladurie, *Love, Death, and Money in the Pays d'Oc* (Harmondsworth: Penguin, 1984); Jacques Le Goff, *Your Money or Your Life: Economy and Religion in the Middle Ages* (New York: Zone Books, 1988), esp. pp. 40–41.

53. See esp. Delevoy, *Bruegel*, pp. 68–95.

54. Duby, *The Three Orders*, quotation from p. 1; Huizinga, *The Waning of the Middle Ages*, pp. 54–64; Roland Mousnier, "The Social Structures of the Kingdom of France," in Mousnier, *Peasant Uprisings in Seventeenth-Century France, Russia, and China* (New York: Harper & Row, 1970), pp. 3–31. For a critique of Mousnier, see Armand Arriaza, "Mousnier and Barber: The Theoretical Underpinning of the 'Society of Orders' in Early Modern Europe," *Past & Present* 89 (November 1980): 39–57.

55. Bloch, *French Rural History*, p. 170; Rodney Hilton, *Bond Men Made Free: Medieval Peasant Movements and the English Rising of 1381* (London: Temple Smith, 1973), esp. pp. 63–135; George A. Collier with Elizabeth Lowery Quaratiello, *Basta! Land and the Zapatista Rebellion in Chiapas* (Oakland, Calif.: Institute for Food and Development Policy, 1994). Henry Heller's *Iron and Blood: Civil Wars in Sixteenth Century France* (Kingston: McGill–Queen's University Press, 1991), is an attempt to critique the prevailing view of stability associated with a conception of medieval society as one of "orders."

56. Le Roy Ladurie, *The French Peasantry*, p. 65.

57. Hilton, *Bond Men Made Free*; R. B. Dobson, *The Peasants' Revolt of 1381* (London: Macmillan, 1970); Friedrich Engels quoted in James M. Stayer, *The German Peasants' War and Anabaptist Community of Goods* (Montreal: McGill–Queen's University Press, 1991), p. 19. See, as well, Engels, "The Peasant War In Germany,"

in Karl Marx and Friedrich Engels, *Collected Works,Volume* 10 (New York: International Press, 1978), pp. 397–482; Peter Blickle, *The Revolution of 1525: The German Peasants' War from a New Perspective* (Baltimore: Johns Hopkins University Press, 1981). I am drawing loosely on Benedict Anderson, *Imagined Communities: Reflections on the Origins and Spread of Nationalism* (London: Verso, 1991). But note also Christopher Hill, "The Norman Yoke," in John Saville, ed., *Democracy and the Labor Movement: Essays in Honour of Dona Torr* (London: Lawrence & Wishart, 1954), pp. 11–66; and Hill, "Pottage for Freeborn Englishmen: Attitudes to Wage-Labor," in Hill, *Change and Continuity in 17th Century England* (London: Weidenfeld & Nicolson, 1974), pp. 219–38. For the use of the term "worldly ban," see Stayer, *The German Peasants' War,* p. 71.

58. E. J. Hobsbawn, *Primitive Rebels: Studies in Archaic Forms of Social Movement in the 19th and 20th Centuries* (Manchester: Manchester University Press, 1959); Hobsbawm, *Bandits* (New York: Dell, 1969); Peter Stallybrass, "'Drunk with the Cup of Liberty': Robin Hood, the Carnivalesque, and the Rhetoric of Violence in Early Modern England," in Nancy Armstrong and Leonard Tennenhouse, eds., *The Violence of Representation: Literature and the History of Violence* (London: Routledge, 1989), pp. 45–76; Louis A. Perez, Jr., *Social Banditry and Peasant Protest in Cuba, 1878–1918* (Pittsburgh: University of Pittsburgh Press, 1989); Linda Lewin, "The Oligarchical Limitations of Social Banditry in Brazil: The Case of the 'Good' Thief Antonio Sylvino," *Past & Present* 82 (February 1979): 116–146; Brent D. Shaw, "Bandits in the Roman Empire," *Past & Present* 105 (November 1984): 3–52; Jean Chesneaux, *Peasant Revolts in China, 1840–1949* (London: Thames & Hudson, 1973). On Robin Hood, see the many essays in Hilton, *Peasants, Knights, and Heretics,* pp. 221–318.

59. Eric Wolf, *Peasant Wars of the Twentieth Century* (New York: Harper & Row, 1969); Joseph Tharamangalam, "Indian Peasant Uprisings: Myth and Reality," *Journal of Peasant Studies* 13 (April 1986): 116–34; Gerard Chaliand, *The Peasants of North Vietnam* (Harmondsworth: Penguin, 1968); A. Neuberg (pseud.), *Armed Insurrection* (1928; New York: St. Martin's Press, 1970); E. J. Hobsbawm, "Vietnam and the Dynamics of Guerrilla War," in Hobsbawm, *Revolutionaries: Contemporary Essays* (New York: Pantheon, 1973), pp. 163–76; "Report on an Investigation of the Peasant Movement In Hunan" (1927), in *Selected Works of Mao Tse-tung* (Peking: Foreign Languages Press, 1967), p. 33. Mao's theory of peasant leadership was developed as the Stalinist Comintern abandoned the advanced workers of the Chinese cities, who were exterminated by the forces of reaction in the late 1920s. See Jean Chesneaux, *The Chinese Labor Movement, 1919–1927* (Stanford, Calif.: Stanford University Press, 1968); Harold R. Isaacs, *The Tragedy of the Chinese Revolution* (Stanford, Calif.: Stanford University Press, 1961).

60. Friedrich Engels, *The German Revolutions: The Peasant War in Germany* and *Germany—Revolution and Counter-Revolution,* ed. Leonard Krieger (Chicago: University of Chicago Press, 1967), p. 35.

61. Camporesi, *Bread of Dreams;* Bloch, *French Rural History,* p. 169.

62. See Jacques Le Goff, *The Birth of Purgatory* (Chicago: University of Chicago Press, 1984).

63. Norman Cohn, *The Pursuit of the Millennium: Revolutionary Messianism in Medieval and Reformation Europe and its Bearing on Modern Totalitarian Movements* (New York: Harper & Row, 1961), pp. 213, 226–36; Hilton, *Bond Men Made Free,* pp. 159–60, 178,

211, 215, 221–22; Stayer, *The German Peasants' War*, pp. 42, 60–62, 73, 95–96; Lee Palmer Wandel, *Voracious Idols and Violent Hands: Iconoclasm in Reformation Zurich, Strasbourg, and Basel* (Cambridge: Cambridge University Press, 1995); E. Belfort Bax, *The Peasants War in Germany, 1525–1526* (1899; New York: August M. Kelley, 1968); Bax, *The Rise and the Fall of the Anabaptists* (1903; New York: American Scholar, 1966).

64. See, for England and the aftermath of 1381, Margaret Aston, "Lollardy and Sedition, 1381–1431," in Hilton, *Peasants, Knights, and Heretics*, pp. 273–318; and for Anabaptism, Werner O. Packull, *Mysticism and the Early South German–Austrian Anabaptist Movement, 1525–1531* (Kitchener, Ont.: Herald Press, 1977); James M. Stayer, *Anabaptists and the Sword* (Lawrence, Kan.: Coronado Press, 1972); and the documentary collection, Michael G. Baylor, ed., *The Radical Reformation* (Cambridge: Cambridge University Press, 1991).

65. Stayer, *The Peasants' War*, p. 42; Le Roy Ladurie, *The French Peasantry*, pp. 275–386; Mousnier, *Peasant Uprisings*; David Sabean, "The Communal Basis of Pre-1800 Peasant Uprisings in Western Europe," *Comparative Politics* 8 (April 1976): 355–64; Sabean, *Power in the blood: Popular Culture and Village Discourse in Early Modern Germany* (Cambridge: Cambridge University Press, 1984); Yves-Marie Berce, *History of Peasant Revolts: The Social Origins of Rebellion in Early Modern France* (Cambridge: Polity Press, 1990); Maureen Perrie, *Pretenders And Popular Monarchism in Early Modern Russia* (Cambridge: Cambridge University Press, 1995); Philip Longworth, "The Pretender Phenomenon in Eighteenth-Century Russia," *Past & Present* 66 (February 1975): 29–60; Jean Chesneaux, *Peasant Revolts in China, 1840–1949* (London: Thames & Hudson, 1973); Susan Naquin, *Millenarian Rebellion in China: The Eight Trigrams Uprising of 1813* (New Haven: Yale University Press, 1976); James Bunyan Parsons, *Peasant Rebellions of the Late Ming Dynasty* (Tuscon: University of Arizona Press, 1970); Magagna, *Communities of Grain*, pp. 244–48; George Wilson, "Pursuing Millennium in the Meji Restoration," in Tetsuo Najita and J. Victor Koschmann, eds., *Conflict in Modern Japanese History: The Neglected Tradition* (Princeton: Princeton University Press, 1982), pp. 176–94; Herbert B. Bix, *Peasant Protest in Japan, 1590–1884* (Cambridge, Mass.: Harvard University Press, 1986); Louis A. Perez, *Lords of the Mountain: Social Banditry and Peasant Protest in Cuba, 1878–1918* (Pittsburgh: University of Pittsburgh Press, 1989), p. 43. The notion of the good king/emperor, most explicit in the seventeenth-century Russian peasant search for "the good tsar," is generalized in Mullett, "Language and Action in Peasant Revolts," in *Popular Culture and Popular Protest*, pp. 71–109.

66. Le Roy Ladurie, *Montaillou*, pp. viii, 13, 23, 87, 100, 143, 151–55, 247–49, 327, 341, 346–47. On Cathars in other contexts, see John N. Stephens, "Heresy in Medieval and Renaissance Florence," *Past & Present* 54 (February 1972): 25–60; Lutz Kaelber, "Weavers into Heretics? The Social Organization of Early-Thirteenth-Century Catharism in Comparative Perspective," *Social Science History* 21 (Spring 1997): 111–37. For the Established Church's evolving prohibition of incest—a matter largely of noble, princely, and monarchial property rights in kinship—see Georges Duby, *The Knight, the Lady, and the Priest: The Making of Modern Marriage in Medieval France* (New York: Pantheon, 1983). On blasphemy's physicality, see Lyndal Roper, *Oedipus and the Devil: Witchcraft, Sexuality and Religion in Early Modern Europe* (London: Routledge, 1994), p. 34.

67. Carlo Ginzburg, *The Cheese and the Worms: The Cosmos of a Sixteenth-Century Miller*

(Harmondsworth: Penguin, 1982), and also Ginzburg, "High and Low: The Theme of Forbidden Knowledge in the Sixteenth and Seventeenth Centuries," *Past & Present* 73 (November 1976): 28–41. For other accounts of peasant reading and religion, see Natalie Zemon Davis, "Printing and the People," in *Society and Culture*, esp. pp. 194–209; Foucault, I, *Pierre Rivière*, pp. 101–02. For a stimulating discussion of cheese and its meanings in this context, see Piero Camporesi, "The Cursed Cheese," in Camporesi, *The Anatomy of the Senses: Natural Symbols in Medieval and Early Modern Italy* (Cambridge: Polity Press, 1994), pp. 37–63.

68. Urban settings were also the site of many nocturnal discussions, e.g. Mark Phillips, *The Memoir of Marco Parenti: A Life in Medici Florence* (Princeton: Princeton University Press, 1987).

69. For magic in earlier periods, see Valerie I. J. Flint, *The Rise of Magic in Early Medieval Europe* (Princeton: Princeton University Press, 1991); Richard Kieck-hefer, *Magic in the Middle Ages* (Cambridge: Cambridge University Press, 1989). This paragraph draws in particular on Keith Thomas, *Religion and the Decline of Magic* (New York: Scribner, 1971); Christopher Hill, "Science and Magic," in Hill, *The Collected Essays of Christopher Hill: Vol. Three, People and Ideas in 17th Century England* (Amherst: University of Massachusetts Press, 1986), pp. 274–96; Camporesi, *Bread of Dreams*, pp. 91–98; Carlo Ginzburg, *Night Battles: Witchcraft and Agrarian Cults in the Sixteenth and Seventeenth Centuries* (New York: Viking Penguin, 1985). Magic also figures prominently in Davis, *The Return of Martin Guerre*.

Chapter 3

1. Friedrich Sorge, *The Labor Movement in the United States: A History from Colonial Times to 1890* (Westport, Conn: Greenwood, 1977), p. 123.

2. Keith Thomas, *Religion and the Decline of Magic* (New York: Scribner, 1971), p. 46. For an introduction to this text, see Jonathan Barry, "Introduction: Keith Thomas and the Problem of Witchcraft," in Jonathan Barry et al., eds., *Witchcraft in Early Modern Europe: Studies in Culture and Belief* (Cambridge: Cambridge University Press, 1996), pp. 1–45. For critiques of Thomas, see Christina Larner, *Enemies of God: The Witch-Hunt in Scotland* (London: Chatto & Windus, 1981); S. Clark, "Inversion, Mis-rule, and the Meaning of Witchcraft," *Past & Present* 87 (1980): 98–127; R. Walinski-Kiehl, "'Godly State': Confessional Conflict and Witchhunting in Early Modern Germany," *Mentalities* 5 (1988): 13–24; and E. P. Thompson, "Anthropology and the Discipline of Historical Context," *Midland History* 1 (1972): 51–55. Note as well Robin Briggs, *Witches and Neighbors: The Social and Cultural Context of European Witchcraft* (New York: Viking, 1996).

3. Jeffrey B. Russell, *A History of Witchcraft: Sorcerers, Heretics, and Pagans* (London: Thames & Hudson, 1980), p. 8.

4. Mary Russo, *The Female Grotesque: Risk, Excess, Modernity* (London: Routledge, 1994).

5. Piero Camporesi, *Juice of Life: The Symbolic and Magic Significance of Blood* (New York: Continuum, 1995), esp. p. 19.

6. See Carolyn Merchant, "Nature as Disorder: Women and Witches," in *The Death of Nature: Women, Ecology, and the Scientific Revolution* (San Francisco: Harper

& Row, 1983), pp. 127–48.

7. See Georges Bataille, "The Christian Era: From Christian Condemnation to Morbid Exaltation (Or from Christianity to Satanism)," in The Tears of Eros (San Francisco: City Lights, 1989), pp. 79–80. Edward J. Teijirian, Sexuality and the Devil: Symbols of Love, Power and Fear in Male Psychology (New York: Routledge, 1990) is a contemporary psychotherapist's exploration of the symbolism of sexuality as it relates to images and consciousness of the devil.

8. For an introduction to "white magic," see Charles Grant Loomis, White Magic: An Introduction to the Folklore of Christian Legend (Cambridge, Mass.: Mediaeval Academy of America, 1948).

9. An excellent social history of political factionalism and social tension in the Friuli is Edward Muir, Mad Blood Stirring: Vendetta and Factions in Friuli during the Renaissance (Baltimore: Johns Hopkins University Press, 1993).

10. This paragraph draws on the stimulating study of Carlo Ginzburg, Night Battles: Witchcraft and Agrarian Cults in the Sixteenth and Seventeenth Centuries (New York: Viking Penguin, 1985)

11. For a committed statement of a folklorist drawn to the subjectivism of witchcraft, see Jeanne Favret-Saada, Deadly Words: Witchcraft in the Bocage (Cambridge: Cambridge University Press, 1980). Another sympathetic contemporary account is T. M. Luhrmann, Persuasions of the Witch's Craft: Ritual Magic and Witchcraft in Present-day England (Oxford: Blackwell, 1989). See, as well, Diane Purkiss, The Witch in History: Modern and Twentieth Century Representations (New York: Routledge, 1996).

12. John Demos, "Underlying Themes in the Witchcraft of Seventeenth-Century New England," in Stanley Katz, ed., Essays in Politics and Social Development in Colonial America (Boston: Little, Brown, 1971), p. 117. For a slightly different framing of this interpretive dualism, see M. J. Kephart, "Rationalists vs. Romantics among Scholars of Witchcraft," in Max Marwick, Witchcraft and Sorcery: Selected Readings (Harmondsworth: Penguin, 1990), pp. 326–42. Kephart claims the status of a "cultural materialist," following the interpretive direction of Marvin Harris, Cows, Pigs, Wars, and Witches (New York: Random House, 1974), distancing himself from the views of Margaret Murray, The Witch Cult in Western Europe (1921), Europe's Inner Demons (1975), and Norman Cohn, The Pursuit of the Millennium (1961). Such texts either acknowledge the existence of covens and cults or insist that the ideas of the witch be treated seriously. See, as well, William Monter, "The Historiography of European Witchcraft: Progress and Prospects," Journal of Interdisciplinary History 2 (1972): 435–53.

13. H. R. Trevor-Roper, "The European Witch Craze of the Sixteenth and Seventeenth Centuries," in Trevor-Roper, The Crisis of the Seventeenth Century: Religion, the Reformation, and Social Change (London: Oxford University Press, 1972), pp. 90–192.

14. Thomas, Religion and the Decline of Magic, pp. 435–585.

15. Carlo Ginzburg, "The Inquisitor as Anthropologist," and "Clues," in Ginzburg, Myths, Emblems, Clues (London: Melbourne & Henley, 1990), pp. 96–125, 156–64; Ginzburg, Ecstasies: Deciphering the Witches' Sabbath (New York: Pantheon, 1991). For a critique of Ginzburg, see Perry Anderson, "Nocturnal Enquiry: Carlo Ginzburg," in Anderson, A Zone of Engagement (London: Verso, 1992), pp. 207–29. On microhistory and Ginzburg's place within it, see Edward Muir, "Introduction: Observing Trifles," in Muir and Guido Ruggiero, eds.,

Microhistory and the Lost Peoples of Europe (Baltimore: Johns Hopkins University Press, 1991), pp. vii–xxviii.

16. These paragraphs draw on Ginzburg, *Ecstasies*, and Anderson, "Nocturnal Enquiry."

17. Reginald Scott, *The Discoverie of Witchcraft* (London, 1584), and Thomas Middleton, *A Tragi-Coomedie Called The Witch* (London, 1778), both quoted in K. M. Briggs, *Pale Hectate's Team: An Examination of the Beliefs on Witchcraft and Magic among Shakespeare's Contemporaries and His Immediate Successors* (London: Routledge & Kegan Paul, 1962), p. 81.

18. John Ashton, *The Devil in Britain and America* (London: Ward & Downey, 1896), pp. 165–66.

19. Piero Camporesi, *Bread of Dreams: Food and Fantasy in Early Modern Europe* (Chicago: University of Chicago Press, 1989), pp. 161–62; E. William Monter, *Witchcraft in France and Switzerland: The Borderlands during the Reformation* (Ithaca: Cornell University Press, 1976), p. 200; G. R. Quaife, *Godly Zeal and Furious Rage: The Witch in Early Modern Europe* (London: Croom Helm, 1987), pp. 199–209; Sandra Shulman, *Nightmare: The World of Terrifying Dreams* (New York: Macmillan, 1979); Michael J. Harner, "The Role of Hallucinogenic Plants in European Witchcraft," in Harner, ed., *Hallucinogens and Shamanism* (New York: Oxford University Press, 1973); Bernard Barnett, "Drugs of the Devil," *New Scientist* 27 (July 1965): 222–25; Barnett, "Witchcraft, Psychopathology, and Hallucinations," *British Journal of Psychiatry* 111 (1965): 439–45; A. Allen, "Toads: The Biochemistry of the Witches' Cauldron," *History Today* 29 (April 1979): 265–68. On ergotism and the Salem Witch Trials of 1692, see Linda R. Caporael, "Ergotism: The Satan Loosed in Salem?" *Science* 192 (1976): 21–26; N. P. Spanos and Jack Gottlieb, "Ergotism and the Salem Village Witch Trials," *Science* 194 (24 December 1976): 1390–94; M. K. Matossian, "Ergot and the Salem Witchcraft Affair," *American Scientist* 70 (1982): 355–57. On ergot, see Camporesi, *Bread of Dreams*, p. 127. More skeptical is Robert Mandrou, *Introduction to Modern France, 1500–1640* (New York: Harper, 1977), pp. 219–20.

20. See Fernando Cervantes, "The Devil's Encounter With America," in Jonathan Barry et al., eds., *Witchcraft in Early Modern Europe: Studies in Culture and Belief* (Cambridge: Cambridge University Press, 1996), pp. 119–44; Elsie Clews Parsons, "Witchcraft among the Pueblos: Indian or Spanish?" and Clyde Kluckholm, "Navaho Witchcraft," in Max Marwick, ed., *Witchcraft and Sorcery: Selected Readings* (Harmondsworth: Penguin, 1990), pp. 235–39, 246–62; Natalie Zemon Davis, *Women on the Margins: Three Seventeenth-Century Lives* (Cambridge, Mass.: Harvard University Press, 1995), pp. 123, 126; Sayed Idries Shah, *Oriental Magic* (London: Rider and Company, 1956), pp. 149–72; Philip A. Kuhn, *Soulstealers: The Chinese Sorcery Scare of 1768* (Cambridge, Mass.: Harvard University Press, 1990).

21. See Anderson, "Nocturnal Enquiry," pp. 228–29. Ginzburg's studies of the *benandanti* and of Menocchio's heresies lack the close reconstruction of villages in Emmanuel Le Roy Ladurie's *Montaillou: The Promised Land of Error* (New York: Vintage, 1979). Anderson notes that Ginzburg's *Ecstasies* rests on a "declaration of faith in the perennity of the nocturnal region of twisted gait and swaying trance," which is, "of its nature, unadorned with evidence." (p. 226) See, as well, Robin Briggs, ""Many Reasons Why: Witchcraft and the Problem of Multiple Explanation," in Barry et al., eds., *Witchcraft in Early Modern Europe*, p. 59.

22. Fernand Braudel, *The Mediterranean and the Mediterranean World in the Age of Philip II*, Volume I (New York: Harper & Row, 1972) pp. 37–38.

23. Piero Camporesi, *The Fear of Hell: Images of Damnation and Salvation in Early Modern Europe* (Cambridge: Polity Press, 1990), p. 4. On Manichaeanism, see Jeffrey Richards, *Sex, Dissidence, and Damnation: Minority Groups in the Middle Ages* (London: Routledge, 1994), pp. 42–73.

24. Norman Cohn, *Europe's Inner Demons: An Enquiry Inspired by the Great Witch-Hunt* (New York: Basic Books, 1975), p. 209.

25. Camporesi, *Bread of Dreams*, pp. 95–96; Cohn, *Europe's Inner Demons*, pp. 206–24; Gustav Henningsen, "The Ladies from Outside: An Archaic Pattern of the Witches' Sabbath," in Bengt Ankarloo and Gustav Henningsen, eds., *Early Modern European Witchcraft: Centres and Peripheries* (Oxford: Clarendon Press, 1990), pp. 191–215.

26. See Richards, *Sex, Dissidence and Damnation*, pp. 74–87; G. R. Quaife, *Godly Zeal and Furious Rage: The Witch in Modern Europe* (London: Croom Helm, 1987), pp. 79–112.

27. Lyndal Roper, *Oedipus and the Devil: Witchcraft, Sexuality, and Religion in Early Modern Europe* (London: Routledge, 1994), p. 240, see also pp. 199–248; also Roper, "Witchcraft and Fantasy in early modern Germany," in Barry et al., eds., *Witchcraft in Early Modern Europe*, pp. 207–36. On women as witnesses before inquisitions, see Clive Holmes, "Women: Witnesses and Witches," *Past & Present* 140 (August 1993): 45–78. For another account, less sexually and psychically developed, linking inquisitor and witch in embedded mythology, see Maruizio Bertolotti, "The Ox's Bones and the Ox's Hide: A Popular Myth, Part Hagiography and Part Witchcraft," in Muir and Ruggerio, eds., *Microhistory*, pp. 42–70.

28. Quotations from Quaife, *Godly Zeal and Furious Rage*, pp. 98–99; Camporesi, *Bread of Dreams*, p. 98; Richards, *Sex, Dissidence, and Damnation*, p. 75; C. L'Estrange Ewen, *Witchcraft and Demonianism: A Consise Account Derived from Sworn Depositions and Confessions Obtained in the Courts of England and Wales* (London: Heath Cranton, 1933), pp. 88–89; John Ashton, *The Devil in Britain and America* (London: Ward & Downey, 1896), p. 168; Middleton, *The Witch*, quoted in Briggs, *Pale Hecate's Team*, p. 81; and on the eating of incestuous and other infants, Norman Cohn, "The Myth of Satan and his Human Servants," in M. Douglas, ed., *Witchcraft, Confessions and Accusations* (London: Tavistock, 1970). For a discussion on patriarchy, see Marianne Hester, "Patriarchal Reconstruction and Witch Hunting," in Barry et al., eds., *Witchcraft in Early Modern Europe*, pp. 288–30. For a detailed account of one witch-hunter's fascination with and repulsion by Sabbat sexual practices, see Gerhild Scholz Williams, *Defining Dominion: The Discourses of Magic and Witchcraft in Early Modern France and Germany* (Ann Arbor: University of Michigan, 1995), esp. pp. 111–15. For a broad statement, see James A. Brundage, *Law, Sex, and Christian Society in Medieval Europe* (Chicago: University of Chicago Press, 1987).

29. Williams, *Defining Dominion*, p. 87. See, as well, Marianne Hester, *Lewd Women and Wicked Witches: A Study of the Dynamics of Male Domination* (London: Routledge, 1992).

30. For discussions of antiquity, cults, early demonization of heretics, and the coming of hegemonic Christianity, see Pennethorne Hughes, *Witchcraft* (Harmondsworth: Penguin, 1969), pp. 21–68, and Ruth Martin, *Witchcraft and the*

Inquisition in Venice, 1550–1650 (Oxford: Basil Blackwell, 1989), pp. 9–79. Martin has useful accounts of the inquisitorial catalogues. See also Cohn, Europe's Inner Demons, pp. 1–78, which has especially strong sections on Waldensians and changing views of the devil. On the devil specifically, see Jeffrey Burton Russell's The Devil: Perceptions of Evil from Antiquity to Primitive Christianity (Ithaca: Cornell University Press, 1977) and The Prince of Darkness: Radical Evil and the Power of Good in History (Ithaca: Cornell University Press, 1988). Inquisitorial texts are explored in the fascinating examination in Williams, Defining Dominion.

31. Alan Macfarlane, Witchcraft in Tudor and Stuart England (London: Routledge & Kegan Paul, 1970), p. 151.

32. Harris, Cows, Pigs, Wars, Witches, pp. 225, 236–40; Emmanuel Le Roy Ladurie, Les Paysans de Languedoc (Paris: 1966), pp. 407–13, cited in Larner, Enemies of God, pp. 27–28.

33. Malcolm Gaskill, "Witchcraft in Early Modern Kent: Stereotypes and the Background to Accusations," in Barry et al., eds., Witchcraft in Early Modern Europe, pp. 257–87.

34. Thomas, Religion and the Decline of Magic, p. 520. See also the discussion of fraud and malice in Christina Hole, Witchcraft in England (London: Batsford, 1945), pp. 72–84.

35. Richards, Sex, Dissidence, and Damnation, p. 87, offers a succinct summary of the standard conclusions.

36. See Eric J. Hobsbawm and Terence Ranger, eds., The Invention of Tradition (Cambridge: Cambridge University Press, 1983); Benedict Anderson, Imagined Communities: Reflections on the Origins and Spread of Nationalism (London: Verso, 1991).

37. For more on nineteenth-century France, see Emmanuel Le Roy Ladurie, La Sorcieré de Jasmin (Paris: Editions du Seuil, 1983) For the twentieth-century folkloric study of bewitching, see Favret-Saada, Deadly Words.

38. Thus, "the notion of a polarity between a 'learned,' 'continental,' and 'demonological' set of beliefs held by the elite and a popular concern with witchcraft which centred on maleficium is a gross oversimplification. A much more common impression is that of a jumble of popular and 'educated' beliefs which were mobilised into an agitated interaction by the conditions of a mass witch hunt." From Jim Sharpe, "The Devil in East Anglia: The Mathew Hopkins Trials Reconsidered," in Barry et al., eds., Witchcraft in Early Modern Europe, p. 252. See also Clive Holmes, "Popular Culture? Witches, Magistrates and Divines in Early Modern England," in Steven Kaplan, ed., Understanding Popular Culture: Europe from the Middle Ages to the Nineteenth Century (New York: Mouton, 1984), pp. 85–110.

39. Philip Mayer, "Witches," in Marwick, ed., Witchcraft and Sorcery, p. 54; Thomas, Religion and the Decline of Magic, pp. 570–83. On the continuity of witchcraft and the important issues it raises, see Ian Bostridge, "Witchcraft Repealed," and William de Blecourt, "On the Continuation of Witchcraft," both in Barry et al., eds., Witchcraft in Early Modern Europe, pp. 309–52.

40. There is a large literature on Puritanism in the Old and New Worlds. For background on England, see Christopher Hill, Society and Puritanism in Pre-Revolutionary England (London: Panther, 1969). For New England intellectual history, see Perry Miller, The New England Mind: The Seventeenth Century (New York: Macmillan, 1939), which understates the significance of witchcraft. For the Antichrist, see Christopher Hill, Antichrist in Seventeenth-Century England (London:

Verso, 1990). For a broad interpretation of the wilderness and Puritanism, see Alan Heimert, "Puritanism, the Wilderness, and the Frontier," *New England Quarterly* 26 (1953): 361–82, and Kai T. Erickson, *Wayward Puritans: A Study in the Sociology of Deviance* (New York: Wiley & Sons, 1966). The quotations from Cotton Mather, which Erickson draws upon, are from Cotton Mather, *Wonders of the Invisible World* (Boston, 1693), in Samuel G. Drake, ed., *The Witchcraft Delusion in New England* (Roxbury, Mass.: Elliot Woodward, 1866), pp. 16–17, 80–81, 94–95.

41. See Richard Godbeer, *The Devil's Dominion: Magic and Religion in Early New England* (Cambridge: Cambridge University Press, 1992), pp. 24–152.

42. David D. Hall, *Worlds of Wonder, Days of Judgment: Popular Religious Belief in Early New England* (New York: Oxford University Press, 1989).

43. On the powerful historical role of the idea of the convenant, see Donald Harman Akenson, *God's Peoples: Covenant and Land in South Africa, Israel, and Ulster* (Kingston: McGill–Queens University Press, 1991).

44. Godbeer, *The Devil's Dominion*, pp. 4–5; Erikson, *Wayward Puritans*, pp. 67–141.

45. Quoted in John Putnam Demos, *Entertaining Satan: Witchcraft and the Culture of Early New England* (New York: Oxford University Press, 1982), pp. 3–17.

46. Godbeer, *The Devil's Dominion*, pp. 162–63.

47. This paragraph draws on Demos, *Entertaining Satan*, although I do not wholeheartedly accept his arguments about the psychic imbalances at work among "possessed" adolescent women. For Connecticut, see the older work by John M. Taylor, *The Witchcraft Delusion in Colonial Connecticut, 1647–1697* (1908; New York: Burt Franklin, 1971).

48. See the excellent material and argument gathered in Paul Boyer and Stephen Nissenbaum, eds., *Salem Village Witchcraft: A Documentary Record of Local Conflict in Colonial New England* (Belmont, Calif.: Wadsworth Publishing, 1972); Boyer and Nissenbaum, *Salem Possessed: The Social Origins of Witchcraft* (Cambridge, Mass.: Harvard University Press, 1974).

49. See Winthrop Jordan, *White Over Black: American Attitudes Toward the Negro, 1550–1812* (Baltimore: Penguin, 1969), esp. 199–205.

50. Marion L. Starkey, *The Devil in Massachusetts: A Modern Inquiry into the Salem Witch Trials* (New York: Knopf, 1949), pp. 9–11.

51. See Osborne and Good testimony in Charles W. Upham, *Salem Witchcraft: With an Account of Salem Village and a History of Opinions on Witchcraft and Kindred Subjects*, Volume I (New York: Ungar Publishing, 1966), pp. 12–22. On Sarah Good, see Erikson, *Wayward Puritans*, p. 143; and the sparse but background documentation in Boyer and Nissenbaum, eds., *Salem Village Witchcraft*, pp. 139–47.

52. Upham, *Salem Witchcraft*, Volume II, pp. 23–29.

53. Ibid., pp. 26–27; Gilbert Osofsky, ed., *Puttin' On Ole Massa: The Slave Narratives of Henry Bibb, William Wells Brown, and Solomon Northup* (New York: Harper Torchbooks, 1969), Bibb quotation is from p. 9. Note also the account of voodoo, witches, and African and Creole folklore in Charles Joyner, *Down by the Riverside: A South Carolina Slave Community* (Urbana: University of Illinois Press, 1984); Eugene D. Genovese, *Roll, Jordan, Roll: The World the Slaves Made* (New York: Pantheon, 1974), pp. 209–32.

54. Upham, *Salem Witchcraft*, Volume II, p. 32; Boyer and Nissenbaum, *Salem Possessed*, p. 2.

55. Boyer and Nissenbaum, *Salem Possessed*, p. 220.

56. See the brief but fascinating discussion of the link between witchcraft and peasant attempts to preserve and revive the Saturday half-holiday in Henry Heller, *Labour, Science and Technology in France, 1500–1620* (Cambridge: Cambridge University Press, 1996), pp. 143–47.

57. Karl Marx, "Speech at the Anniversary of *The People's Paper*," in Karl Marx and Friedrich Engels, *Collected Works, Volume XIV, 1855–1856* (New York: International, 1980), pp. 655–56.

58. See, for example, Robert Darnton, *The Literary Underground of the Old Regime* (Cambridge, Mass: Harvard University Press, 1983).

Chapter 4

1. Lawrence Stone, "Magic, Religion, and Reason," in Stone, *The Past and the Present Revisited* (London: Routledge, 1987), p. 189.

2. Peter Nagy, *Libertinage et Revolution* (Paris: Gallimard, 1975). On class, see the comments on Sade in Roland Barthes, *Sade, Fourier, Loyola* (New York: Hill & Wang, 1976), p. 130.

3. David Foxton, *Libertine Literature in England, 1660–1745* (Hyde Park, N.Y.: University Books, 1965), p. 52; G. S. Rousseau and Roy Porter, eds., preface to *Sexual Underworlds of the Enlightenment* (Manchester: Manchester University Press, 1987), p. 9. Rousseau and Porter are not making strict separations between aristocratic and bourgeois, but use the latter term to designate a position of status.

4. V. S. Pritchett, "The Harlot's Progress," *New York Review of Books*, October 31 1963, p. 1; J. H. Plumb, introduction to *Memoirs of Fanny Hill* (New York: Putnam, 1965), p. xiii; Nancy Miller, "'I's' in Drag: The Sex of Recollection," *Eighteenth Century* 22 (1981): 54; Anne Taylor, *Male Novelists and Their Female Voices: Literary Masquerades* (Troy, N.Y., 1981), p. 93, quoted in Peter Sabor's introduction to John Cleland, *Memoirs of a Woman of Pleasure* (New York: Oxford University Press, 1985), pp. xvi–xvii.

5. On *Fanny Hill's* legal status, see John Sutherland, *Offensive Literature: Decensorship in Britain, 1960–1982* (London: Junction Books, 1982), pp. 32–40, as well as scattered references throughout Edward de Grazia, *Girls Lean Back Everywhere: The Law of Obscenity and the Assault on Genius* (New York: Random House, 1992).

6. John Cleland, *Memoirs of a Woman of Pleasure*, ed. Peter Sabor (New York: Oxford University Press, 1985), p. 1. Another edition, introduced by George Woodcock, is Cleland, *Fanny Hill: Memoirs of a Woman of Pleasure* (Markham, Ont.: Fitzhenry & Whiteside, 1989), p. 3.

7. Randolph Trumbach, "Erotic Fantasy and Male Libertinism in Enlightenment England," in Lynn Hunt, ed., *The Invention of Pornography: Obscenity and the Origins of Modernity* (New York: Zone, 1993), pp. 259–71. See, as well, Trumbach, "London's Sodomites: Homosexual Behaviour and Western Culture in the Eighteenth Century," *Journal of Social History* 11 (1977): 1–33, and a number of other Trumbach writings, including comment on sapphists in "London's Sapphists: From Three Sexes to Four Genders in the Making of Modern Culture," in Julia Epstein and Kristina Straub, eds., *Body Guards: The Cultural Origins of Gender Ambiguity* (New York: Routledge, 1991), pp. 112–41.

8. Leo Braudy, "Fanny Hill and Materialism," *Eighteenth-Century Studies* 4 (1970–1971): 21–40; also Susan Sontag, "The Pornographic Imagination," *Partisan*

Review 2 (1967):195–96; Raymond K. Whitely, "Rationalizing a Rogue: Themes and Techniques in the Novels of John Cleland" (PhD thesis, Dalhousie University, 1978), pp. 430–43. On Cleland, see also William H. Epstein, *John Cleland: Images of a Life* (New York: Columbia University Press, 1974).

9. This suggestion of Lord Shaftesbury's significance is found in Randolph Trumbach, "Erotic Fantasy and Male Libertinism," pp. 270–71. See also Lawrence Klein, "The Third Earl of Shaftesbury and the Progress of Politeness," *Eighteenth-Century Studies* 18 (1984–1985): 186–214; Klein, "Liberty, Manners, and Politeness in Early Eighteenth-Century England," *Historical Journal* 32 (1989): 583–605.

10. Note Randolph Trumbach, "Modern Prostitution and Gender in *Fanny Hill*: Libertine and Domesticated Fantasy," in Rousseau and Porter, eds., *Sexual Underworlds of the Enlightenment*, pp. 69–85.

11. Quoted in Foxon, *Libertine Literature*, p. 56.

12. Leo Braudy, *The Frenzy of Renown: Fame and Its History* (New York: Oxford University Press, 1986), p. 386.

13. See the discussion in Walter Kendrick, *The Secret Museum: Pornography in Modern Culture* (New York: Viking, 1987), pp. 1–66.

14. Lawrence Stone, *The Family, Sex, and Marriage in England, 1500–1800* (New York: Harper & Row, 1977), p. 539.

15. Steven Marcus, *The Other Victorians: A Study of Sexuality and Pornography in Mid-Nineteenth-Century England* (New York: Basic Books, 1966); Kendrick, *Secret Museum*, pp. 1–2.

16. Lynn Hunt, "Introduction: Obscenity and the Origins of Modernity, 1500–1800," in Hunt, ed., *The Invention of Pornography*, pp. 13–15.

17. E. P. Thompson, "Glandular Aggression," *New Society* 19 (January 1967): 100.

18. G. Steiner, "Night Words: High Pornography and Human Privacy," in D. Holbrook, ed., *The Case Against Pornography* (La Salle, Ill.: Open Court, 1973); L. Lederer, ed., *Take Back the Night: Women on Pornography* (New York: William Morrow, 1980).

19. Marcus, *The Other Victorians*, p. 272, and Thompson, "Glandular Aggression," p. 100.

20. Note the discussion in Jean Gagnon, *Pornography in the Urban World* (Montreal: Art Metropole, 1986), pp. 38–39. This discussion draws on Anne Cauquelin, *La Ville la Nuit* (Paris: Coll. Politique eclatee, 1977), pp. 142–45. Of course some on the fundamentalist right, as well as some radical feminists, attempt to reduce much contemporary art to the status of pornography. See Wendy Steiner's account of the Robert Mapplethorpe exhibition scandal and other such developments in *The Scandal of Pleasure: Art in an Age of Fundamentalism* (Chicago: University of Chicago Press, 1996).

21. Richard S. Randall, *Freedom and Taboo: Pornography and the Politics of a Self Divided* (Berkeley: University of California Press, 1989), p. 261: "In the pornographic within, transgressive wishes are mediated by our capacity for thought and imagination and by our ability to create and use representation. Transgressive images, words, and ideas give symbolic form to these forbidden impulses and desires and serve as external attachments for them. Disturbing as they may sometimes be, neither the fantasies nor their external manifestation in pornographic expression can be considered alien."

22. Quoted in Foxon, *Libertine Literature*, pp. 56–57.

23. On Restif, the most developed brief study is David Coward, "The Sublimations of a Fetishist: Restif de la Bretonne (1734–1806)," in Robert P. Maccubbin, ed., 'Tis Nature's Fault: Unauthorized Sexuality During the Enlightenment (Cambridge: Cambridge Universty Press, 1987), pp. 98–108. See also Patrick J. Kearney, A History of Erotic Literature (London: Macmillan, 1982), pp. 86–93; Kendrick, The Secret Museum, pp. 17–21; Lucienne Frappier-Mazur, "Truth and the Obscene Word in Eighteenth-Century Pornography," and Kathryn Norberg, "The Libertine Whore: Prostitution in French Pornography from Margot to Juliette," in Hunt, ed., The Invention of Pornography, pp. 203–52. On Restif and nineteenth-century prostitution, see Charles Bernheimer, Figures of Ill Repute: Representing Prostitution in Nineteenth-Century France (Cambridge, Mass.: Harvard University Press, 1989), pp. 17–26.

24. See Rodney A. Smolla, Jerry Falwell v. Larry Flynt: The First Amendment on Trial (New York: St. Martin's Press, 1988).

25. The general quotations concerning the historical origins and context of pornography in the above paragraphs are drawn from Lynn Hunt, "Introduction," The Invention of Pornography, pp. 11, 13, 15.

26. See Peter Fryer, ed., Forbidden Books of the Victorians: Henry Spenser Ashbee's Bibliographies of Erotica (London: Odyssey, 1970); Steven Marcus, The Other Victorians, pp. 34–76, contains a chapter on Ashbee that attempts a psychoanalytic reading of his erotic obsessions. It has been suggested that Ashbee either authored or was involved in the publication, sometime between 1885 and 1895, of the classic English statement My Secret Life (New York: Grove Press, 1966), a text commented on in detail by Marcus, pp. 77–196. See also Kearney, A History of Erotic Literature, pp. 126–28.

27. See Christopher Hill, The World Turned Upside Down: Radical Ideas during the English Revolution (New York: Viking Press, 1972), pp. 247–60, from which quotations are drawn; Tim Harris, "'Lives, Libertines, and Estates': Rhetorics of Liberty in the Reign of Charles II," in Harris et al., eds., The Politics of Religion in Restoration England (Oxford: Basil Blackwell, 1990), pp. 217–42; E. P. Thompson, Witness Against the Beast: William Blake and the Moral Law (New York: New Press, 1993), esp. pp. 22–32; Lawrence Stone, "Libertine Sexuality in Post-Restoration England: Group Sex and Flagellation among the Middling Sort in Norwich in 1706–07," Journal of the History of Sexuality 2 (1992): 511–25; Stone, The Family, Sex, and Marriage, pp. 483–602. It is an interesting question as to whether Fanny Hill drew on the existence of such aristocratic brothels or stimulated their development. See Trumbach, "Erotic Fantasy and Male Libertinism," p. 271, and Nancy Armstrong's suggestions about the relationship of literature and marriage in Desire and Domestic Fiction (New York: Oxford University Press, 1987).

28. Quoted in Stone, The Family, Sex, and Marriage, p. 538.

29. G. S. Rousseau, "The Sorrows of Priapus: Anticlericalism, Homosocial Desire, and Richard Payne Knight," in Rousseau and Porter, eds., Sexual Underworlds, pp. 101–53; James G. Turner, "The Properties of Libertinism," in Maccubbin, ed., 'Tis Nature's Fault, esp. p. 81; Marcus, The Other Victorians, p. 286; Margaret C. Jacob, "The Materialist World of Pornography," in Hunt, ed., The Invention of Pornography, pp. 157–202. Contrasts in seventeenth- and eighteenth-century libertinism are sketched in Roy Porter, "Mixed Feelings: The Enlightenment and Sexuality in Eighteenth-Century Britain," in Paul-Gabriel Bouce, ed.,

Sexuality in Eighteenth Century Britain (Manchester: Manchester University Press, 1982), pp. 3–4, but they may be overdrawn.

30. On the Dilettanti, see Trumbach, "Erotic Fantasy and Male Liberation," in Hunt, ed., *The Invention of Pornography*, pp. 271–74, 279–81; Cecil Harcourt-Smith, *The Society of the Dilettanti, Its Regalia and Pictures* (London: Macmillan, 1932); Lionel Crust, *History of the Society of Dilettanti* (London: Macmillan, 1914); Reverend John Selby Watson, *Biographies of John Wilkes and William Cobbett* (London: William Blackwood, 1870), p. 8; Oscar Sherwin, *A Gentleman of Wit and Fashion: The Extraordinary Life and Times of George Selwyn* (New York: Twayne, 1963), esp. pp. 45–46, 98. On Dashwood, see Louis Kronenberger, *The Extraordinary Mr. Wilkes: His Life and Times* (Garden City, N.Y.: Doubleday, 1974), pp. 11–14; John Brewer, *Party Ideology and Popular Politics at the Accession of George III* (Cambridge: Cambridge University Press, 1976), pp. 10, 43, 107; Betty Kemp, *Sir Francis Dashwood* (London: Macmillan, 1967).

31. See Horace Walpole, *Memoirs of the Reign of George III*, Volume I (London, 1894), pp. 136–38, 248; Trumbach, "Erotic Fantasy and Male Libertinism," in Hunt, ed., *The Invention of Pornography*, pp. 274–79; Watson, *Biographies of John Wilkes and William Cobbett*, p. 8; Raymond Postgate, *"That Devil Wilkes"* (London: Constable & Company, 1930), pp. 23–29; Horace Bleackley, *Life of John Wilkes* (London: John Lane, 1917), pp. 48–51; W. F. Rae, *Wilkes, Sheridan, Fox: The Opposition Under George the Third* (Toronto: Adam Stevenson, 1874), pp. 12–14; Audrey Williamson, *Wilkes: "A Friend to Liberty"* (London: George Allen & Unwin, 1974), esp. pp. 26–42; Sherwin, *Gentleman of Wit*, pp. 47–53.

32. Peter Quennell, *The Profane Virtues: Four Studies of the Eighteenth Century* (New York: Viking Press, 1945), pp. 178–79.

33. Wilkes is a much studied figure. There is an excellent, insightful discussion in John Brewer, *Party Ideology and Popular Politics*, pp. 163–200, and Wilkesite radicalism is often alluded to in a detailed study of a slightly earlier period in Nicholas Rogers, *Whigs and Cities: Popular Politics in the Age of Walpole and Pitt* (Oxford: Oxford University Press, 1989), esp. pp. 385–86. In addition to treatments cited in note 31, see William Purdie Treloar, *Wilkes and the City* (London: John Murray, 1917); George Rudé, *Wilkes and Liberty: A Social Study of 1763 to 1774* (London: Oxford University Press, 1962); and Peter D. G. Thomas, *John Wilkes: A Friend to Liberty* (Oxford: Clarendon Press, 1996), quotation from p. 220. The Thomas biography follows the chronology of O. A. Sherrard's *A Life of John Wilkes* (New York: Dodd, Mead, 1930). Additional quotations in this paragraph are from Postgate, *That Devil Wilkes*, p. 32; Bleackley, *Life of Wilkes*, pp. 66–70.

34. This paragraph draws on the standard sources on Wilkes, but for particulars see the narrative in Thomas, *John Wilkes*; Postgate, *"That Devil Wilkes"*, esp. pp. 30–31 on Churchill, and p. 26 on libertine alteration of texts; Williamson, *Wilkes*, pp. 83–86; and George Nobbe, *The North Briton: A Study in Political Propaganda* (New York: AMS Press, 1966); Rudé, *Wilkes and Liberty*. The historical significance of Wilkes and freedom of the press is addressed in Donald Thomas, *A Long Time Burning: The History of Literary Censorship in England* (London: Routledge & Kegan Paul, 1969), pp. 92–112. More generally, see Fredrick S. Siebert, *Freedom of the Press in England, 1476–1776: The Rise and Decline of Government Controls* (Urbana: University of Illinois Press, 1952).

35. Quoted in Thomas, *John Wilkes*, p. 66.

36. Quoted in Williamson, *Wilkes*, pp. 84–85.

37. Quoted in Kearney, *A History of Erotic Literture*, p. 72.

38. Bleackley, *Life of John Wilkes*, p. 134.

39. Rudé, *Wilkes and Liberty*.

40. This argument draws on the excellent interpretation in Brewer, *Party Ideology and Popular Politics*, pp. 163–200. See, as well, Stone, *The Family, Sex, and Marriage*, pp. 621–22; Mary Thale, ed., *The Autobiography of Francis Place* (Cambridge: Cambridge University Press, 1972), pp. 45, 51, 58; and, for contextual background, Nicholas Rogers, "Aristocratic Clientage, Trade and Independency: Popular Politics in PreRadical Westminster," *Past & Present* 61 (November 1973): 70–106. Note the argument on patriotism and Englishness in Linda Colley, *Britons: Forging the Nation, 1707–1837* (New Haven: Yale University Press, 1992), pp. 105–17.

41. See Williamson, *Wilkes*, pp. 207–35; Quennell, *The Profane Virtues*, pp. 208–18.

42. Lynn Hunt, "Pornography and the French Revolution," in Hunt, ed., *The Invention of Pornography*, pp. 301–31; Peter Wagner, *Eros Revived: Erotica of the Enlightenment in Europe and America* (London: Secker & Warburg, 1988), p. 6. See, as well, Edward A. Tiryakian, "From Underground to Convention: Sexual Anomie as an Antecedent to the French Revolution," *Social Theory* 5 (1984): 289–307. For background, note the essays in Lynn Hunt, ed., *Eroticism and the Body Politic* (Baltimore: Johns Hopkins University Press, 1990); Dorinda Outram, *The Body and the French Revolution: Sex, Class, and Political Culture* (New Haven: Yale University Press, 1989).

43. Stone, *The Family, Sex, and Marriage*, p. 535.

44. See Timo Airaksinen, *The Philosophy of the Marquis de Sade* (London and New York: Routledge, 1995).

45. See Roland Barthes, "Sade II: Bringing Order," in Barthes, *Sade, Fourier, Loyola*, pp. 160–61; Roberta J. Hackel, *De Sade's Quantitative Moral Universe: Of Irony, Rhetoric, and Boredom* (Paris: Mouton, 1976).

46. The above paragraphs draw on and quote from Simone de Beauvoir, "Must We Burn Sade?" in De Beauvoir, *The Marquis de Sade: An Essay* (New York: Grove Press, 1953), pp. 11, 29; Ronald Hayman, *De Sade: A Critical Biography* (New York: Thomas Crowell, 1978), pp. xxv–xxvi, 229, quoting Michel Foucault, *Madness and Civilization: A History of Insanity in the Age of Reason* (New York: Vintage, 1973); Georges Bataille, *Literature and Evil* (London: Calder & Boyars, 1973), p. 86; Pierre Klossowski, *Sade My Neighbor* (Evanston, Ill.: Northwestern University Press, 1992), p. 121.

47. There are some useful comments on sadism in Kaja Silverman, *Male Subjectivity at the Margins* (New York and Routledge: London, 1992). For sadism's relationship to confinement and its relationship to "the natural habitat of unreason," state repression's fortresses, and punishing edifices of constraint, see Foucault, *Madness and Civilization*, pp. 208–10.

48. These two paragraphs draw on interpretive statements in De Beauvoir, *The Marquis de Sade*, p. 82; Angela Carter, *The Sadeian Woman: An Exercise in Cultural History* (London: Virago, 1979), pp. 24–25; Jane Gallop, *Intersections: A Reading of Sade with Bataille, Blanchot, and Klossowski* (Lincoln: University of Nebraska Press, 1981), pp. 5–16. On biographical detail the older Gilbert Lely, *The Marquis de Sade: A Biography* (London: Elek Books, 1961) and Norman Gear, *The Divine Demon: A Portrait of the Marquis de Sade* (London: Fredrick Muller, 1963)

have been surpassed by the detailed Maurice Lever, *Sade: A Biography* (New York: Farrar, Straus & Giroux, 1993). For a briefer, more accessible work that contains a useful annotation on Sade's major publications, see Donald Thomas, *The Marquis de Sade* (London: Weidenfeld & Nicolson, 1976).

49. Sontag, "On Pornography," p. 194. For a hostile reading of attempts to "rehabilitate" Sade, see Roger Shattuck, *Forbidden Knowledge: From Prometheus to Pornography* (New York: St. Martin's Press, 1996), esp. pp. 229–99, which concludes: "The divine marquis represents forbidden knowledge that we may not forbid. Consequently, we should label his writings carefully: potential poison, polluting to our moral and intellectual environment."

50. For a recent important study that places Sade at the center of a historicized discussion of censorship, see Nicholas Harrison, *Circles of Censorship: Censorship and its Metaphors in French History, Literature, and Theory* (Oxford: Clarendon Press, 1995).

51. Bataille, *Literature and Evil*, p. 94. See, as well, De Beauvoir, *Marquis de Sade*, pp. 25–26; Roger Shattuck, *Forbidden Knowledge: From Prometheus to Pornography* (New York: Harcourt Brace, 1996), pp. 229–300.

52. This draws on, but develops differently, arguments in Frances Ferguson, "Sade and the Pornographic Legacy," *Representations* 36 (Fall 1991): 1–21. It also parallels arguments about Samuel Richardson, the seventeenth-century English author and commentator on libertinism, put forward in Terry Eagleton, *The Rape of Clarissa: Writing, Sexuality and Class Struggle in Samuel Richardson* (Oxford: Basil Blackwell, 1982), esp. pp. 14–16. Note, as well, R. F. Brissenden, *Virtue in Distress: Studies in the Novel of Sentiment from Richardson to Sade* (London: Macmillan, 1974), esp. p. 35, which Eagleton interprets as Brissenden claiming Richardson's *Clarissa* (1747–48) is "a drastic demystification of sentimentalist ideology, a violent defacing of the myths of 'natural goodness' with which a benevolently weeping bourgeoisie concealed from itself its own exploitative practice." For interpretations emphasizing anomie and alienation in Richardson, again paralleling my argument about Sade, see Edward Copeland, "Remapping London: *Clarissa* and the Woman in the Window," and James Grantham Turner, "Lovelace and the Paradoxes of Libertinism," both in Margaret Anne Doody and Peter Sabor, eds., *Samuel Richardson: Tercentenary Essays* (Cambridge: Cambridge University Press, 1989), pp. 51–88.

53. Quoted in Thomas, *Marquis de Sade*, p. 184, although I am in disagreement with Thomas's literalist argument about Blake's ignorance of Sade and thus have a diametrically opposed reading of the passage. On the wider symbolism of the Bastille, and with particular reference to Sade, see Hans-Jurgen Lusebrink and Rolf Reichardt, *The Bastille: A History of a Symbol of Despotism and Freedom* (Durham, N.C.: Duke University Press, 1997), esp. pp. 31–33, 43, 66.

54. Simon Schama, *Citizens: A Chronicle of the French Revolution* (New York: Knopf, 1989), pp. 391–93, 399, 407, 455. Schama presents comments on Sade's period as "revolutionary" citizen that are highly and ideologically simplified. Not much better is Emmet Kennedy, *A Cultural History of the French Revolution* (New Haven and London: Yale University Press, 1989), p. 106, which suggests a relationship between Sade's erotic terror and the Terror. The standard biographies of Sade, cited above, are a more reliable entrée into this period: details are available in Lever, *Sade*.

55. See Michel Foucault, *The History of Sexuality, Volume I: An Introduction* (New York:

Vintage, 1980), pp. 148–49. For details on Sade and freedom and imprisonment, see Lever, *Sade*, pp. 345–52, 452–57.

56. Marquis de Sade, *The 120 Days of Sodom and Other Writings* (New York: Grove Press, 1966), pp. 599–672; Carter, *The Sadeian Woman*, pp. 148–50; and the broader discussion in Joel Whitebook, *Perversion and Utopia: A Study in Psychoanalysis and Critical Theory* (Cambridge, Mass.: MIT Press, 1995).

57. Iain McCalman, *Radical Underworld: Prophets, Revolutionaries, and Pornographers in London, 1795–1840* (Cambridge, Mass: Cambridge University Press, 1988). Consider, as well, the fascinating arguments in two articles by Nicholas Rogers, "Pigott's Private Eye: Radicalism and Sexual Scandal in Eighteenth-Century Britain," *Journal of the Canadian Historical Association* (1993): 247–64 and "Royal Soap? Class and Gender in the Queen Caroline Affair," *Left History* 2 (Spring 1994): 5–26.

58. Marcus, *The Other Victorians*, pp. 266–87; Kendrick, *The Secret Museum*, pp. 125–57; Thompson, "Glandular Aggression."

Chapter 5

1. Quoted in Robert Birley, *The English Jacobins From 1789 to 1802: The Gladstone Memorial Prize Essay, 1924* (London: Oxford University Press, 1924), p. 7.

2. Quoted in E. P. Thompson, *The Making of the English Working Class* (New York: Vintage, 1963), p. 83.

3. For an introduction, see E. J. Hobsbawm, *The Age of Revolution: Europe, 1789–1848* (London: Weidenfeld and Nicolson, 1962).

4. The contested historiography of the French Revolution is now immense. For a sobering Marxist critique of both revisionist and orthodox materialist accounts, see George C. Comninel, *Rethinking the French Revolution: Marxism and the Revisionist Challenge* (London: Verso, 1987). For an indication of new, culturalist approaches, see the massive four-volume edited history by Keith Michael Baker et al., eds., *The French Revolution and the Creation of Modern Political Culture* (Oxford: Pergamon Press, 1987). On Saint-Just, see Annie Besant, *History of the Great French Revolution: A Course of Six Lectures* (London: Freethought, 1885), pp. 26, 282–84.

5. Hobsbawm, *Age of Revolution*, pp. 42–72.

6. These paragraphs draw on Thompson, *The Making of the English Working Class*, esp. pp. 36, 87, 90, 94, 763; Birley, *The English Jacobins*, p. 6; Walter Phelps Hall, *British Radicalism, 1791–1797* (London: P. S. King & Son, 1912), pp. 57–73. See also Albert Goodwin, *The Friends of Liberty: The English Democratic Movement in the Age of the French Revolution* (Cambridge, Mass.: Harvard University Press, 1979), pp. 99–135 and 171–207; and John Dinwiddy, "Interpretations of Anti-Jacobinism," in Mark Philp, ed., *The French Revolution and British Popular Politics* (Cambridge: Cambridge University Press, 1991), pp. 38–49. An excellent documentary collection, covering most of the important pamphet ground, is Marilyn Butler, ed., *Burke, Paine, Godwin and the Revolution Controversy* (Cambridge: Cambridge University Press, 1984).

7. Not to be confused with "Jacobitism," an earlier political phenomenon that sought to reverse the settlement of 1688, which secured a Stuart restoration and overturned the Whig politics of the Hanoverian accession. See Eveline Cruickshanks, ed., *Ideology and Conspiracy: Aspects of Jacobitism, 1689–1759* (Edin-

burgh: John Donald, 1982). For an introduction to eighteenth-century Jacobinism, see Gwyn A. Williams, *Artisans and Sans-Culottes: Popular Movements In France and Britain during the French Revolution* (London: Edward Arnold, 1968).

8. François Furet, "Revolution français et tradition jacobine," in Colin Lucas, ed., *The Political Culture of the French Revolution*, Volume 3 of Baker et al., eds., *The French Revolution and the Creation of Modern Political Culture*, pp. 329–38. On the ideological assimilation of Jacobinism and Bolshevism see, as well, Ferene Feher, *The Frozen Revolution: An Essay on Jacobinism* (New York: Cambridge University Press, 1987). Essential reading is Trotsky's discussion of "Jacobinism and Social Democracy," the final chapter of *Our Political Tasks* (1904). Trotsky's essay was written as a Menshevik polemic against Lenin, but is not to be confused with the conservative menshevism, a pragmatic hostility to all bolshevik practice as "*intelligenskii*, narrowly factional, jacobin." For an exciting attempt to address popular memory, historiographic revisionism, and the challenge to the ideals and popular initiatives of 1789, see Steven Laurence Kaplan, *Farewell, Revolution: Disputed Legacies: France, 1789/1989* (Ithaca: Cornell University Press, 1995).

9. Albert Goodwin, *The Friends of Liberty: The English Democratic Movement in the Age of the French Revolution* (Cambridge, Mass: Harvard University Press, 1979), pp. 19–31.

10. Edward Smith, *The Story of the English Jacobins: Being An Account of the Persons Implicated in the Charges of High Treason, 1794* (London: Cassell, Petter & Galpin, 1881), pp. v–vi. Note also Malcolm I. Thomis and Peter Holt, *Threats of Revolution in Britain, 1789–1848* (Hamden, Conn.: Archon Press, 1977), p. 5.

11. Birley, *The English Jacobins*, p. 6.

12. Mary Thale, ed., *Selections from the Papers of the London Corresponding Society, 1792–1799* (Cambridge: Cambridge University Press, 1983), esp. pp. 5–8; Thompson, *The Making of the English Working Class*, pp. 17–18. For a brief introduction to the LCS and the British Jacobins of the 1790s, see H. T. Dickinson, *British Radicalism and the French Revolution* (Oxford: Blackwell, 1985), pp. 1–24.

13. The above paragraphs draw on and quote from Thompson, *The Making of the English Working Class*, pp. 123, 141; Edward Smith, *The Story of the English Jacobins: Being An Account of the Persons Implicated in the Charges of High Treason, 1794* (London: Cassell, Petter, & Galpin, 1881), p. 137; Thale, ed., *Selections from the Papers of the LCS*, p. 140.

14. See Thompson, *The Making of the English Working Class*, pp. 122–23, 156–60, 182–85. On Thelwall in general, many sources might be cited, among them: Geoffrey Gallop, "Ideology and the English Jacobins: The Case of John Thelwall," *Enlightenment and Dissent* 5 (1986): 3–20; Iain Hampsher-Monk, "John Thelwall and the Eighteenth-Century Radical Response to Political Economy," *Historical Journal* 34 (1991): 1–20; Charles Cestre, *John Thelwall: A Pioneer of Democracy and Social Reform in England During the French Revolution* (London: Swan Sonnenschein, 1906). The most useful single source is Gregory Claeys, ed., *The Politics of English Jacobinism: Writings of John Thelwall* (University Park: Pennsylvania State University Press, 1995), which contains a significant introduction (pp. xiii–lvi) as well as Thelwall's major writings. The Claeys quotation is from p. xiv, also p. xxiii. Two Thelwall tracts, as well as other radical writings of the period, are collected in Claeys, ed., *Political Writings of the 1790s: Volume 4, Radicalism and Reform, 1793–1800* (London: William Pickering, 1995).

15. Quoted in Philip Anthony Brown, *The French Revolution in English History* (London: George Allen & Unwin, 1918), p. 112.
16. Thale, ed., *Selections from the Papers of the London Corresponding Society*, pp. 135–40; Smith, *The Story of the English Jacobins*, pp. 109–10. On Citizen Groves, see Thompson, *Making of the English Working Class*. On Lovett, see William Lovett, *My Life and Struggles in Pursuit of Bread, Truth and Knowledge Etc.* (1867: London: MacGibbon and Kee, 1967).
17. These paragraphs draw on Thompson, *The Making of the English Working Class*, pp. 17–20; "Hardy's Account of His Arrest," in Thale, ed., *Selections from the Papers of the London Corresponding Society*, pp. 157–58; Claeys, ed., *The Politics of English Jacobinism: The Writings of John Thelwall*, pp. xxiii–xxvii; G. D. H. Cole and Raymond Postgate, *The British Common People, 1746–1946* (London: Methuen, 1961), pp. 160–61. Francis Place recalled the 28th Anniversary of Hardy's acquittal in 1822 at the Crown and Anchor Tavern in the Strand. See the full account in Smith, *The Story of the English Jacobins*, pp. 177–78. On the tradition of metropolitan dining in remembrance of the acquitals, see James A. Epstein, *Radical Expression: Political Language, Ritual, and Symbol in England, 1790–1850* (New York: Oxford University Press, 1994), p. 151. For Burke, see R. B. McDowell, ed., *The Correspondence of Edmund Burke (September 1794–April 1796)*, Volume 7 (Chicago: University of Chicago Press, 1969), p. 282.
18. Thompson, *The Making of the English Working Class*, pp. 189, 103–06, 140–41; Ian Sellers, "William Roscoe, the Roscoe Circle, and Radical Politics in Liverpool, 1787–1807," *Transactions of the Historical Society of Lancashire and Cheshire* 120 (1968), pp. 45–62; R. B. Rose, "The 'Jacobins' of Liverpool, 1789–1793," *Liverpool Bulletin* 9 (1960–1961); Tom Garvin, "Defenders, Ribbonmen and Others: Underground Political Networks in Pre-Famine Ireland," *Past & Present* 96 (August 1982): 142–45; Terry Eagleton, *Heathcliff and the Great Hunger: Studies in Irish Culture* (London: Verso, 1995), p. 85; Gwyn A. Williams, *When Was Wales? A History of the Welsh* (London: Black Raven Press, 1985), esp. pp. 167–72.
19. Claeys, ed., *The Politics of English Jacobinism: The Writings of John Thelwall*, p. xxvii.
20. An exceptionally rich account of the persecution of Thelwall is E. P. Thompson, "Hunting the Jacobin Fox," *Past & Present* 142 (February 1994): 94–139.
21. On this process, see E. P. Thompson, "Disenchantment or Default? A Lay Sermon," in Conor Cruise O'Brien and William Dean Vanech, eds., *Power & Consciousness* (New York: New York University Press, 1969), pp. 149–82. On the circle of Romantic Jacobins, see Nicholas Roe, *Wordsworth and Coleridge: The Radical Years* (Oxford: Clarendon Press, 1988); William Haller, *The Early Life of Robert Southey, 1774–1803* (New York: Columbia University Press, 1917), pp. 51, 134, 158–59, 231, 268–69, 274; Marilyn Butler, *Romantics, Rebels and Reactionaries: English Literature and Its Background, 1760–1830* (Oxford: Oxford University Press, 1981); Michael Henry Schrivener, *Radical Shelley: The Philosophical Anarchism and Utopian Thought of Percy Bysshe Shelley* (Princeton: Princeton University Press, 1982), pp. 3–34; David Duff, *Romance and Revolution: Shelley and the Politics of a Genre* (Cambridge: Cambridge University Press, 1994).
22. Thompson, "Disenchantment or Default?" p. 179; Thomas Love Peacock, *Nightmare Abbey by the Author of Headlong Hall* (1818; Oxford and New York: Woodstock Books, 1992), Introduction, and pp. 15–16, 72, 76–77; Roe, *Wordsworth and Coleridge: The Radical Years*, pp. 1, 20. On Coleridge, see the

conservative account in Molly Lefebvre, *Samuel Taylor Coleridge: A Bondage of Opium* (London: Quartet, 1977). For an earlier defeat, see Christopher Hill, *The Experience of Defeat: Milton and Some Contemporaries* (London: Faber & Faber, 1984).

23. Thale, ed., *Selections from the Papers of the LCS*, pp. 447–50.

24. All quotations from Thompson, "The Jacobin Fox."

25. On the naval mutinies, see Thompson, *The Making of the English Working Class*, pp. 148, 167–68, 185, 482; Marianne Elliott, *Partners in Revolution: The United Irishmen and France* (New Haven: Yale University Press, 1982), pp. 134–44; and the fuller treatment in Roger Wells, *Insurrection: The British Experience, 1795–1803* (Gloucester: Alan Sutton, 1983), pp. 79–109, 265.

26. For the fall of Irish Jacobinism, see Dorothy Thompson, "Seceding from the Seceders: The Decline of the Jacobin Tradition in Ireland, 1790–1850," in Thompson, *Outsiders: Class, Gender and Nation* (London: Verso, 1993), pp. 134–63.

27. On the United Irishmen, see Elliott, *Partners in Revolution*; Elliott, "Ireland," in Otto Dann and John Dinwiddy, eds., *Nationalism in the Age of the French Revolution* (London and Ronceverte: Hambledon Press, 1988), pp. 71–86; R. R. Madden, *The United Irishmen: Their Lives and Times* (Dublin: James Duffy, 1846); and for the Irish links to the French Revolution, see Liam Swords, *The Green Cockade: The Irish in the French Revolution, 1789–1815* (Sandycove: Glendale, 1989). For the United States, Richard J. Twomey, *Jacobins and Jeffersonians: Anglo-American Radicalism in the United States, 1790–1820* (New York: Garland, 1989). Thelwall thought that, in 1794 alone, eighty thousand radical sympathizers emigrated to America. See Claeys, ed., *The Politics of English Jacobinism: The Writings of John Thelwall*, p. xxv. The quotations on Canada are from Bryan D. Palmer, *Working-Class Experience: The Rise and Reconstitution of Canadian Labor, 1800–1980* (Toronto: Butterworth's, 1983), p. 46. For two detailed accounts of the United Irishmen and the United Englishmen, see Wells, *Insurrection*, esp. pp. 131–77, and Goodwin, *Friends of Liberty*, pp. 416–50.

28. Thompson, *The Making of the English Working Class*, pp. 472–78.

29. On Despard, see Thompson, *The Making of the English Working Class*, pp. 472–84; Goodwin, *Friends of Liberty*, pp. 464–70; Wells, *Insurrection*; Elliott, *Partners in Revolution*; Iain McCalman, *Radical Underworld: Prophets, Revolutionaries, and Pornographers in London, 1795–1840* (Cambridge: Cambridge University Press, 1988), pp. 11–15; Peter Linebaugh, *A Dish with One Spoon: The American Experience of Slavery and the Commons in the Transformation of Three Officers of the English Crown into Freedom Fighters for the United Irish* (Toledo, Ohio: University of Toledo, 1999), pp. 12–16.

Chapter 6

1. Edmund Burke, *Reflections on the Revolution in France*, ed. Conor Cruise O'Brien (Harmondsworth: Penguin, 1969), pp. 173, 279–80, 313, 161, 275, 372, 92–93. Also note the discussion in "Frankenstein's French Revolutions," in Fred Botting, *Making Monstrous: Frankenstein, Criticism, Theory* (Manchester and New York: Manchester University Press, 1991), pp. 139–63.

2. On the symbolic importance of the monster in the Middle Ages, see David Williams, *The Function of the Monster in Mediaeval Thought and Literature* (Montreal: McGill–Queen's University Press, 1996).

3. Background on monsters can be found in Chris Baldick, "The Politics of

Monstrosity," in In Frankenstein's Shadow: Myth, Monstrosity, and Nineteenth-Century Writing (Oxford: Clarendon Press, 1987), pp. 10–29; Christopher Hill, "The Many-Headed Monster in Late Tudor and Early Stuart Political Thinking," in Charles H. Carter, ed., From the Renaissance to the Counter-Reformation (New York: Random House, 1965), pp. 296–324.

4. Michel Foucault, Madness and Civilization: A History of Insanity in the Age of Reason (New York: Vintage, 1973), p. 209.

5. Margaret L. Carter, Specter or Delusion? The Supernatural in Gothic Fiction (Ann Arbor: UMI Research, 1987); Tzvetan Todorov, The Fantastic: A Structural Approach to a Literary Genre (Ithaca: Cornell University Press, 1975); David Punter, The Literature of Terror: A History of Gothic Fictions from 1765 to the Present Day (London: Longman, 1980); Devendra P. Varma, The Gothic Flame (New York: Russell & Russell, 1966); and for a brief overview, Lowry Nelson, Jr., "Night Thoughts on the Gothic Novel," Yale Review 52 (December 1962): 236–57.

6. Noel Carroll, The Philosophy of Horror: or Paradoxes of the Heart (New York: Routledge, 1990), pp. 4–5. See, as well, Arthur Clayborough, The Grotesque in Art and Literature (Oxford: Clarendon Press, 1965).

7. Foucault, Madness and Civilization, p. 209. For an insightfully suggestive reading of the literary history of this period, see David Punter, The Romantic Unconscious: A Study in Narcissism and Patriarchy (New York: New York University Press, 1990).

8. See Brian J. Frost, "Blood, Diablerie, and Undeath," in Frost, The Monster with a Thousand Faces: Guises of the Vampire in Myth and Literature (Bowling Green, Ohio: Bowling Green State University Popular Press, 1989), pp. 6–9.

9. Foucault, Madness and Civilization, pp. 209–10.

10. See, for instance, Steven Earl Forry, Hideous Progenies: Dramatizations of "Frankenstein" from Mary Shelley to the Present (Philadelphia: University of Pennsylvania Press, 1990); Roxana Stuart, Stage Blood: Vampires of the Nineteenth-Century Stage (Bowling Green, Ohio: Bowling Green State University Popular Press, 1994).

11. Donna Haraway, Primate Visions: Gender, Race, and Nature in the World of Modern Science (New York: Routledge, 1989), p. 378: "Monsters share more than the word's root with the verb 'to demonstrate': monsters signify."

12. Gilles Deleuze and Félix Guattari, Anti-Oedipus: Capitalism and Schizophrenia (New York: Viking, 1990), p. 112.

13. Botting, Making Monstrous, p. 161. See, as well, Roger Shattuck, Forbidden Knowledge: From Prometheus to Pornography (New York: Harcourt Brace, 1996), esp. pp. 77–108.

14. Franco Moretti, Signs Taken for Wonders: Essays in the Sociology of Literary Forms (London: Verso, 1988), p. 83.

15. J. M. Hill, "Frankenstein and the Physiognomy of Desire," American Imago 32 (1975): 358. For a useful discussion of "The Politics of Monstrosity," see Baldick, In Frankenstein's Shadow, pp. 10–30. Note Foucault, Madness and Civilization, p. 210: "Was this conversion not authorized by the survival and the re-awakening of the fantastic in places where unreason had been reduced to silence?" See, as well, Jutta Held, "Between Bourgeois Enlightenment and Popular Culture: Goya's Festivals, Old Women, Monsters, and Blind Men," History Workshop Journal 23 (Spring 1987): 49–50.

16. R. E. Foust, "Monstrous Image: Theory of Fantasy Antagonists," Genre 13 (Winter 1980): esp. 442, 452–53; Sigmund Freud, "The Uncanny," in The

Standard Edition of the Complete Psychological Works of Sigmund Freud, ed. James Strachey, Volume 17 (London: Hogarth Press, 1955), pp. 234–35.

17. Nina Auerbach, *Our Vampires, Ourselves* (Chicago: University of Chicago Press, 1995), esp. p. 41; Richard Dellamora, *Masculine Desire: The Sexual Politics of Victorian Aestheticism* (Chapel Hill: University of North Carolina Press, 1990), pp. 69–85; Norine Dresser, *American Vampires: Fans, Victims & Practitioners* (New York: W. W. Norton, 1989), p. 109. Note, as well, Auerbach's comments on contemporary women's vampire films such as *Near Dark* (pp. 186–92). For other statements on female vampires and *Carmilla*, see James B. Twitchell, *The Living Dead: A Study of the Vampire in Romantic Literature* (Durham, N.C.: Duke University Press, 1981), pp. 39–73; Alok Bhalla, *Politics of Atrocity and Lust: The Vampire Tale as a Nightmare History of England in the Nineteenth Century* (New Delhi: Sterling, 1990).

18. Bonnie Zimmerman, "Lesbian Vampires," *Jump Cut* 24/25 (March 1981): 23–24. While addressing a slightly different subject, the comments in Valerie Traub, "The Ambiguities of 'Lesbian' Viewing Pleasure: The (Dis)Articulations of *Black Widow*," in Julia Epstein and Kristina Staub, eds., *Body Guards: The Cultural Politics of Gender Ambiguity* (New York: Routledge, 1991), pp. 305–28, are relevant.

19. Richard Dyer, "Children of the Night: Vampirism as Homosexuality, Homosexuality as Vampirism," in Susannah Radstone, ed., *Sweet Dreams: Sexuality, Gender, and Popular Fiction* (London: Lawrence & Wishart, 1988), pp. 47–72; Christopher Craft, "'Kiss Me with those Red Lips': Gender and Inversion in Bram Stoker's Dracula," *Representations* 8 (Fall 1984): 107–33; and some of the suggestions in Jacqueline LeBlanc, "'It is not good to note this down': *Dracula* and the Erotic Technologies of Censorship," in Carol Margaret Davison, *Bram Stoker's Dracula: Sucking Through the Century, 1897–1997* (Toronto: Dundurn, 1997), pp. 249–68.

20. Punter, *The Literature of Terror*, pp. 411–12.

21. Judith Halberstam, *Skin Shows: Gothic Horror and the Technology of Monsters* (Durham, N.C.: Duke University Press, 1995), pp. 136, 27. Note, as well, the discussions in Eric Naiman, "When a Communist Writes Gothic: Aleksandra Kollontai and the Politics of Disgust," *Signs* 22 (August 1996): 1–29; Veronica Hollinger, "The Vampire and the Alien: Gothic Horror and Science Fiction," in Davison, *Bram Stoker's Dracula*, pp. 213–30; Carroll, *Philosophy of Horror*, p. 201. For a banal statement by Stephen King, see *Danse Macabre* (New York: Berkley Books, 1987), p. 39.

22. On Stoker, see Daniel Farson, *The Man Who Wrote Dracula: The Biography of Bram Stoker* (London: Michael Joseph, 1973). This text introduces the highly sexualized content of vampirism, while claiming Stoker had no inkling of any erotic aspects in the mythology. See, as well, Ernest Jones, *On the Nightmare* (New York: Grove Press, 1951), pp. 98–130; Jan B. Gordon, "The 'Transparency' of Dracula," in Davison, ed., *Bram Stoker's Dracula*, pp. 95–121. On historical vampire and werewolf mythologies see, among other sources, Montague Summers, *The Vampire: His Kith and Kin* (New Hyde Park: University Books, 1960); Clive Leatherdale, *The Origins of Dracula: The Background to Bram Stoker's Gothic Masterpiece* (London: William Kimbler, 1987); Paul Barber, *Vampires, Burial and Death* (New Haven: Yale University Press, 1988); Jan E. Perkowski, *Vampires of the Slavs* (Cambridge, Mass.: Slavica Publishers, 1976); Brian J. Frost,

The Monster with a Thousand Faces: Guises of the Vampire in Myth and Literature (Bowling Green, Ohio: Bowling Green State University Popular Press, 1989). For werewolves, see Charlotte F. Otten, ed., *A Lycanthropy Reader: Werewolves in Western Culture* (Syracuse: Syracuse University Press, 1986); Jones, *On the Nightmare*, pp. 131–53.

23. See Havelock Ellis, *The Psychology of Sex: A Manual for Students* (New York: Emerson, 1964), p. 209. For a suggestion of the congruence of Stoker's *Dracula* and Freudian perspectives, see Stephanie Moss, "The Psychiatrist's Couch: Hypnosis, Hysteria, and Proto-Freudian Performance in *Dracula*," in Davison, *Bram Stoker's Dracula*, pp. 123–46.

24. On place and the imagined community of Transylvania, note Gerald Walker and Lorraine Wright, "Locating *Dracula*: Contextualising the Geography of Transylvania," in Davison, *Bram Stoker's Dracula*, pp. 49–74.

25. This paragraph draws on Moretti, *Signs Taken for Wonders*, pp. 90–98; Ken Gelder, *Reading the Vampire* (London: Routledge, 1994), pp. 17–22. See, as well, the complementary argument in Alok Bhalla, "'Seeking Whom He May Devour': Dracula, Lucy, and Mina as Predators and Victims in an Hobbesian Jungle," in *The Politics of Atrocity and Lust*, pp. 35–56, 68–69, and the suggestive statement in Stephen D. Arata, "The Occidental Tourist: *Dracula* and the Anxiety of Reverse Colonisation," *Victorian Studies* 33 (1990): 621–45. For an alternative assessment of Dracula as "feudalism's death warmed up," see Baldick, *In Frankenstein's Shadow*, esp. p. 148. An interesting reading appears in Halberstam, *Skin Shows*, pp. 86–106. Halberstam opens by suggesting a link between Dracula and anti-Semitism, by which the stereotypical representation of the Jew's avaricious relation to money is related to the Count's acquisitive needs. A broader historical account with a useful discussion of the dimension of imperialism appears in Patrick Brantlinger, "Imperial Gothic: Atavism and the Occult in the British Adventure Novel, 1880–1914," in Brantlinger, *Rule of Darkness: British Literature and Imperialism, 1830–1914* (Ithaca: Cornell University Press, 1988). For other important contextualizations of Bram Stoker's *Dracula*, see Carol Margaret Davison, "Bram Stoker's *Dracula*: Sucking Through the Century, 1897–1997," and Richard Anderson, "Dracula, Monsters, and the Apprehension of Modernity," in Davison, *Bram Stoker's Dracula*, pp. 19–40, 321–30.

26. See the quotations from Marx in Gelder, *Reading the Vampire*, pp. 20–22, and Alok Bhalla, "The Age of Empire: The Victorian Horror Tale and *Varney the Vampire*," in Bhalla, ed., *Politics of Atrocity and Lust*, pp. 20–25. See also Robert Paul Wolff, *Moneybags Must Be So Lucky: On the Literary Structure of Capital* (Amherst: University of Massachusetts Press, 1988). The most useful single introduction to the vampire imagery in Marx and Engels is the excellent discussion in Chris Baldick, "Karl Marx's Vampires and Grave-diggers," in Baldick, *In Frankenstein's Shadow*, pp. 121–40. See also Friedrich Engels, *The Condition of the Working-Class in England in 1844* (London: Allen & Unwin, 1968), p. 278; Karl Marx, *Grundrisse: Introduction to a Critique of Political Economy* (Penguin: Harmondsworth, 1973), pp. 461, 646, 660; Karl Marx, *Capital*, Volume I (New York: International, 1967), pp. 394–427; Friedrich Engels, "The English Ten Hours' Bill," in Karl Marx and Friedrich Engels, *Collected Works, Volume 10* (New York: International, 1978) p. 288.

27. Moretti, *Signs Taken for Wonders*, pp. 107–08; Auerbach, *Our Vampires, Ourselves*, pp. 192, 220.

28. On another level see Alex Potts, "Beautiful Bodies and Dying Heroes: Images of Ideal Manhood in the French Revolution," *History Workshop Journal* 30 (Autumn 1990): 1–21

29. On Wollstonecraft, Godwin, and their relationship, see Mike Game, *Harmless Lovers? Gender, Theory, and Personal Relationships* (London: Routledge, 1993), pp. 59–81, 107–13.

30. Godwin's diary records simply, "Born of Mary, 20 minutes after 11, at night." Note the catalogue for *Mary Wollstonecraft & Mary Shelley: Visionary Daughters of Albion—A Bicentenary Celebration, May 3–September 13* (New York: New York Public Library, Center for the Humanities, Edna Barnes Salomon Room, 1997), p. 1.

31. On Godwin there are many writings. See, for instance, Ford K. Brown, *The Life of William Godwin* (London and Toronto: J. M. Dent, 1926); R. G. Grylls, *William Godwin and His World* (London: Odhams Press, 1953); Don Locke, *A Fantasy of Reason: The Life and Thought of William Godwin* (London: Routledge & Kegan Paul, 1980); George Woodcock, *William Godwin: A Biographical Study* (Montreal: Black Rose, 1989); Mark Philp, *Godwin's Political Justice* (Ithaca: Cornell University Press, 1986); and Mark Philp, ed., *Collected Novels and Memoirs of William Godwin*, Volume I (London: William Pickering, 1992), esp. pp. 13–17, 85–146. On Wollstonecraft, see Claire Tomalin, *The Life and Death of Mary Wollstonecraft* (New York: Harcourt, Brace, 1974); and Janet Todd and Marilyn Butler, eds., *The Works of Mary Wollstonecraft: Volume 5—A Vindication of the Rights of Men, A Vindication of the Rights of Woman, Hints* (London: William Pickering, 1989). On the relationship of Godwin and Wollstonecraft, see especially Ralph M. Wardle, ed., *Godwin & Mary: Letters of William Godwin and Mary Wollstonecraft* (Lawrence: University of Kansas Press, 1966). The *Anti-Jacobin Review* poem is from Woodcock, *William Godwin*, p. 162. Hostility to Mary Wolstonecraft remains. See Richard Cobb, "Mary Wollstonecraft," in Cobb, *Tour de France* (London: Duckworth, 1976), pp. 72–85.

32. On Mary Shelley there is much scholarship; I have drawn upon Betty T. Bennett, ed., *The Letters of Mary Wollstonecraft Shelley: Volume I—"A Part of the Elect"* (Baltimore and London: Johns Hopkins University Press, 1980); Julian Marshall, *The Life and Letters of Mary Wollstonecraft Shelley* (London: Richard Bentley, 1889); Richard Church, *Mary Shelley* (London: Gerald Howe, 1928); R. Glynn Grylls, *Mary Shelley: A Biography* (London: Oxford University Press, 1938); Elizabeth Nitchie, *Mary Shelley: Author of "Frankenstein"* (New Brunswick: Rutgers University Press, 1953); Jane Dunn, *Moon in Eclipse: A Life of Mary Shelley* (New York: St. Martin's Press, 1978); Anne K. Mellor, *Mary Shelley: Her Life, Her Fiction, Her Monsters* (New York: Routledge, 1988); Jane Blumberg, *Mary Shelley's Early Novels: "This Child of Imagination and Misery"* (London: Macmillan, 1993); Muriel Spark, *Mary Shelley* (London: Constable, 1988). Most intriguing on the father–daughter relation are Katherine C. Hill-Miller, *"My Hideous Progeny": Mary Shelley, William Godwin, and the Father–Daughter Relationship* (Newark, N.J.: University of Delaware Press, 1995), which contains an insightful analysis of *Mathilda*, pp. 101–27; and U. C. Knoepflmacher, "Thoughts on the Aggression of Daughters," in George Levine and U. C. Knoepflmacher, eds., *The Endurance of Frankenstein: Essays on Mary Shelley's Novel* (Berkeley: University of California Press, 1979), pp. 88–119.

33. See the suggestively speculative comments in Christopher Small, "Shelley and Frankenstein," in *Ariel Like a Harpy: Shelley, Mary and Frankenstein* (London: Victor Gollancz, 1972), pp. 100–21.

34. For the sake of convenience, I utilize the 1831 edition as presented in Mary Shelley, *Frankenstein*, ed. Johanna M. Smith (New York: St. Martin's Press, 1992), quotations from pp. 51, 56–59, 71, 98–99, 102, 121, 185. On historical context, see Tim Marshall, *Murdering to Dissect: Grave-robbing, Frankenstein and the Anatomy Literature* (Manchester: Manchester University Press, 1995). Baldick, "The Monster Speaks: Mary Shelley's Novel," in *In the Shadow of Frankenstein*, pp. 30–62, is a valuable brief introduction to the novel. For a gendered reading of the compulsive quest for knowledge and its mysteries, see Eugenia C. DeLamotte, *Perils of the Night: A Feminist Study of Nineteenth-Century Gothic* (New York: Oxford University Press, 1990), pp. 43–92.

35. Quoted in Dunn, *Moon in Eclipse*, p. 95.

36. William Patrick Day, *In the Circles of Fear and Desire: A Study of Gothic Fantasy* (Chicago: University of Chicago Press, 1985), p. 139.

37. Note the pertinent general discussion of parental anxiety and its relation to the creation of monsters in Haraway, *Primate Visions*, p. 378.

38. Consider the stimulating discussion in Barbara Creed, *The Monstrous-Feminine: Film, Feminism, Psychoanalysis* (New York: Routledge, 1993). Creed uses the horror film to challenge the conventional wisdom that monsters and monstrosity conceptualize women only as victim; she argues that the prototypical origin of monstrosity is the female reproductive body.

39. See the forceful statement in Ellen Moers, "Female Gothic," in Levine and Knoepflmacher, eds., *The Endurance of Frankenstein*, pp. 77–87; Robert Kiely, *The Romantic Novel in England* (Cambridge, Mass.: Harvard University Press, 1972), p. 161; and the imaginative discussion in Halberstam, *Skin Shows*, pp. 28–52. See, as well, Naiman, "When a Communist Writes Gothic," pp. 1–29; and Roger Shattuck, *Forbidden Knowledge: From Prometheus to Pornography* (New York: St. Martin's Press, 1996), pp. 93–95.

40. Smith, ed., *Frankenstein*, p. 58. The gender ambiguity of this first description of the monster might lend credence to the argument about the centrality of androgyny in William Veeder, *Mary Shelley and Frankenstein: The Fate of Androgyny* (Chicago: University of Chicago Press, 1986), but I remain unconvinced by that interpretation.

41. See Kate Ellis, "Monsters in the Garden: Mary Shelley and the Bourgeois Family," in Levine and Knoepflmacher, eds., *The Endurance of Frankenstein*, pp. 123–42.

42. Mellor, *Shelley: Her Life, Her Fictions, Her Monsters*, p. 40.

43. The absent mother is a strong motif in much criticism on *Frankenstein*. See the varied commentaries in Hill-Miller, *"My Hideous Progeny"*, pp. 59–100; Marc Rubenstein, "My Accursed Origin: The Search for the Mother in *Frankenstein*," *Studies in Romanticism* 15 (Spring 1976): 165–94. Note the interesting argument in Gordon Hirsch, "The Monster was a Lady: On the Psychology of Mary Shelley's *Frankenstein*," *Hartford Studies in Literature* 7 (1975): 116–53.

44. Johanna M. Smith, "'Cooped Up': Feminine Domesticity in *Frankenstein*," in Smith, ed., *Frankenstein*, pp. 270–85; Mary Poovey, *The Proper Lady and the Woman Writer: Ideology as Style in the Works of Mary Wollstonecraft, Mary Shelley, and Jane Austen* (Chicago: University of Chicago Press, 1984), pp. 114–42; Ellis, "Monsters

in the Garden," in Levine and Knoepflmacher, eds., *Endurance of Frankenstein*, pp. 123–42; Anca Vlasopolos, "*Frankenstein's* Hidden Skeleton: The Psycho-Politics of Oppression," *Science-Fiction Studies* 10 (1983): 125–36; Mary Lowe-Evans, *Frankenstein: Mary Shelley's Wedding Guest* (New York: Twayne Publishers, 1993).

45. Mellor, *Shelley: Her Life, Her Fiction, Her Monsters*, quotation from p. 115; see also pp. 89–126.

46. Smith, ed., *Frankenstein*, pp. 40, 44, 45, 56.

47. For more on nature, see Peter Brooks, "'Godlike Science/Unhallowed Arts': Language, Nature, and Monstrosity," in Levine and Knoepflmacher, eds., *The Endurance of Frankenstein*, pp. 88–122, and for a positive reading of the potential of science, not often broached in the feminist criticism, see Samuel Holmes Vasbinder, *Scientific Attitudes in Mary Shelley's Frankenstein* (Ann Arbor: UMI Research Press, 1984). A broad assessment of the relationship of nature and woman is Carolyn Merchant, *The Death of Nature: Women, Ecology, and the Scientific Revolution* (San Francisco: Harper & Row, 1983).

48. Joseph Conrad, *Heart of Darkness* (Harmondsworth: Penguin, 1983), contains "a number of uncanny resemblances to the design of *Frankenstein*," as noted by Baldick, *In the Shadow of Frankenstein*, p. 165.

49. Smith, ed., *Frankenstein*, pp. 124–28, 140–43; Barbara Johnson, "My Monster/My Self," *Diacritics* 12 (1982): 2–10; Gayatri Chakravorty Spivak, "Three Women's Texts and a Critique of Imperialism," *Critical Inquiry* 12 (Autumn 1985): 256.

50. Paul O'Flinn, "Production and Reproduction: The Case of Frankenstein," *Literature & History* 9 (Autumn 1983): 194, 201. Rosemary Jolly informed me of the banning of *The Rocky Horror Picture Show*, which had taken on in South Africa a certain cult status, much as it did in North America in the 1970s.

51. H. L. Malchow, "Frankenstein's Monster and Images of Race in Nineteenth-Century Britain," *Past & Present* 139 (May 1993): 90–130; Milton A. Mays, "*Frankenstein*, Mary Shelley's Black Theodicy," *Southern Humanities Review* 3 (Winter 1969): 146–53; Milton Millhauser, "The Noble Savage in Mary Shelley's *Frankenstein*," *Notes and Queries* 190 (June 1946): 248–50. For context on women and abolitionism, see Clare Midgley, *Women Against Slavery: The British Campaign, 1780–1870* (London: Routledge, 1992); Vron Ware, "An Abhorrence of Slavery: Subjection and Subjectivity in Abolitionist Politics," in Ware, *Beyond the Pale: White Women, Racism, and History* (London: Verso, 1992), pp. 47–116.

52. Spivak, "Three Women's Texts," pp. 255–56.

53. Carlyle quoted in Baldick, *In Frankenstein's Shadow*, pp. 90–102, which also contains a wider discussion of the Irish and the image of Frankenstein.

54. See Harold Bloom, "Frankenstein, or the New Prometheus," *Partisan Review* 32 (1965): 618.

55. Smith, ed., *Frankenstein*, p. 106. But see, as well, Warren Montag, "The Workshop of Filthy Creation: A Marxist Reading of *Frankenstein*," in Smith, ed., *Frankenstein*, esp. pp. 106–07.

56. *Letters of Mary Wollstonecraft Shelley*, Volume I, p. 49, quoted in O'Flinn, "Production and Reproduction," p. 195.

57. Mellor, *Mary Shelley: Her Life, Her Fiction, Her Monsters*, p. 70; Smith, ed., *Frankenstein*, p. 142.

58. Karl Marx, *The Revolutions of 1848: Political Writings, Volume 1*, ed David Fernbach (Harmondsworth: Penguin, 1973), pp. 73, 79, quoted in Baldick, *In Frankenstein's Shadow*, p. 127.

59. Moretti, *Signs Taken for Wonders*, pp. 85–90.

60. Note the comments in Klaus Theweleit, *Male Fantasies: Volume 1: Women Floods Bodies History* (Minneapolis: University of Minnesota Press, 1987), pp. 264–65, 360.

61. Marx, *Grundrisse*, p. 458; Marx, "Speech at the Anniversary of *The People's Paper*," in Karl Marx and Friedrich Engels, *Collected Works, Volume 14* (New York: International, 1980) pp. 655–56; Martin Tropp, *Mary Shelley's Monster* (Boston: Houghton Mifflin, 1976), p. 81; James P. Cannon, "The Frankenstein of Rationalized Production in the 1920s," from a New York lecture, "Revolutionary Perspective in America," 20 December 1930, in James P. Cannon Papers, State Historical Society of Wisconsin, Madison, Microfilm Reel 32.

62. Karl Marx and Friedrich Engels, "Manifesto of the Communist Party," in *Selected Works* (Moscow: Progress, 1968), p. 38.

Chapter 7

1. These paragraphs quote from and draw on Karl Marx, "The Working Day," in *Capital*, Volume 1 (New York: International, 1967), pp. 231–302. On time, see as well E. P. Thompson, "Time, Work-Discipline and Industrial Capitalism," *Past & Present* 38 (December 1967): 56–97.

2. See Jacques Rancière, *The Nights of Labor: The Workers' Dream in Nineteenth-Century France* (Philadelphia: Temple University Press, 1981), which contains a useful introduction to Rancière by Donald Reid, pp. xv–xxxvii.

3. For a depiction of such conditions late into the Victorian period, see Raphael Samuel, "The Workshop of the World: Steam Power and Hand Technology in mid-Victorian Britain," *History Workshop Journal* 3 (Spring 1977): 6–72.

4. On bakers, parades, and public image, see the discussions in Alfred F. Young, "Plebeian Culture and Eighteenth-Century American Radicalism," in Margaret Jacob and James Jacob, eds., *The Origins of Anglo-American Radicalism* (London: George Allen & Unwin, 1984), pp. 200–04; Susan G. Davis, *Parades and Power: Street Theatre in Nineteenth-Century Philadelphia* (Philadelphia: Temple University Press, 1986), p. 128; Sean Wilentz, "Artisan Republican Festivals and the Rise of Class Conflict in New York City, 1788–1837," in Michael H. Frisch and Daniel J. Walkowitz, eds., *Working-Class America: Labor, Community, and American Society* (Urbana: University of Illinois Press, 1983), p. 47; Charles G. Steffen, *The Mechanics of Baltimore: Workers and Politics in the Age of Revolution, 1763–1812* (Urbana: University of Illinois Press, 1984), p. 93; David Montgomery, "The Working Classes of the American Preindustrial City, 1780–1830," *Labor History* 9 (Winter 1968): 13–14; "Account of the Grand Federal Procession in Philadelphia, 4 July 1788," *American Museum* 4 (July 1788): 68. For general background on bakers and other crafts in early America, see Richard B. Morris, *Government and Labor in Early America* (New York: Octagon, 1965).

5. These paragraphs draw on many sources, but see in particular Steven Laurence Kaplan, *The Bakers of Paris and the Bread Question, 1700–1775* (Durham, N.C.: Duke

University Press, 1996), esp. pp. 227–31, 265, 425; Ian McKay, "Capital and Labor in the Halifax Baking and Confectionary Industry during the Last Half of the Nineteenth Century," *Labour/Le Travailleur* 3 (1978): 88–91; McKay, "Bondage in the Bakehouse? The Strange Case of the Journeyman Bakers, 1840–1880," in Royden Harrison and Jonathan Zeitlin, eds., *Divisions of Labor: Skilled Workers and Technological Change in Nineteenth-Century England* (Brighton: Harvester, 1985), pp. 47–86.

6. For the image of the prostitute prodigal daughter, see Felix Labisse's 1943 painting, depicted in Georges Bataille, *The Tears of Eros* (San Francisco: City Lights, 1989), p. 188.

7. Sara C. Maza, *Servants and Masters in Eighteenth-Century France: The Uses of Loyalty* (Princeton: Princeton University Press, 1983), pp. 124–25; Leonore Davidoff and Catherine Hall, *Family Fortunes: Men and Women of the English Middle Class, 1780–1850* (Chicago: University of Chicago Press, 1987), pp. 388–96; "The Servant Problem: A Sketch from Fanny Hurst's Novel *Lummox*," *The Worker* (Toronto) March 26, 1926, quoted in Genevieve Leslie, "Domestic Service in Canada, 1880–1920," in *Women at Work: Ontario, 1850–1930* (Toronto: Canadian Women's Educational Press, 1974), p. 85; and Magdalena Fahrni, "The Rhetoric of Order: Respectability, Deviance, and the Criminalizing of Class in Ontario, 1880–1914" (MA thesis, Queen's University, Kingston, Canada, 1993). Fahrni contains an excellent and extensive citation of the voluminous literature on servants.

8. For varied readings of the Munby–Cullwick narrative, see Anne McClintock, *Imperial Leather: Race, Gender, and Sexuality in the Colonial Contest* (New York: Routledge, 1995), pp. 132–80; Derek Hudson, *Munby, Man of Two Worlds: The Life and Diaries of Arthur J. Munby, 1812–1910* (Cambridge: Gambit, 1974); Liz Stanley, *The Diaries of Hannah Cullwick: Victorian Maidservant* (New Brunswick: Rutgers University Press, 1984); Leonore Davidoff, "Class and Gender in Victorian England," in Judith L. Newton, Mary P. Ryan, and Judith Walkowitz, eds., *Sex and Class in Women's History* (London: Routledge & Kegan Paul, 1983), pp. 16–71; Carol Mavor, *Pleasures Taken: Performances of Sexuality and Loss in Victorian Photographs* (Durham, N.C.: Duke University Press, 1995), pp. 71–116; Peter Stallybrass and Allon White, "Below Stairs: The Maid and the Family Romance," in Stallybrass, *The Politics and Poetics of Transgression* (Ithaca: Cornell University Press, 1986), pp. 149–70; Liz Stanley, "Biography as Microscope or Kaleidoscope?: The Case of 'Power' in Hannah Cullwick's Relationship with Arthur Munby," *Women's Studies International Forum* 10 (1987): 19–31; Julia Swindell, "Liberating the Subject? Autobiography and 'Women's History': A Reading of *The Diaries of Hannah Cullwick*," in Personal Narrative Group, ed., *Interpreting Women's Lives: Feminist Theory and Personal Narratives* (Bloomington: Indiana University Press, 1989), pp. 24–38; Heather Dawkins, "The Diaries and Photographs of Hannah Cullwick," *Art History* 10 (June 1987): 154–87; Griselda Pollack, "The Dangers of Proximity: The Spaces of Sexuality and Surveillance in Word and Image," *Discourse* 16 (Winter 1993).

9. Robert Gordon and Andrew Forge, *Degas* (London: Thames & Hudson, 1988), p. 66; Christopher Benfey, *Degas in New Orleans: Encounters in the Creole World of Kate Chopin and George Washington Cable* (New York: Knopf, 1997).

10. This paragraph draws most directly on the readings of Mavor, *Pleasures Taken*, and McClintock, *Imperial Leather*, although I do not necessarily accept all of

the arguments in these texts. I follow convention in referring to Hannah by her first name and Munby by his surname, but this implies no hierarchy of authority, as Mavor's discussion makes clear.

11. See, for instance, McClintock, *Imperial Leather*, p. 143; Michel Foucault, *Madness and Civilization: A History of Insanity in the Age of Reason* (New York: Vintage, 1973), pp. 207–10.

12. Michel Foucault, "The Eye of Power," in Colin Gordon et al., eds., *Power/Knowledge: Selected Interviews and Other Writings, 1972–1977* (New York: Pantheon, 1980), pp. 153–54. For discussions of vision and its significance, which some have argued has been denigrated by new regulatory modes and new postmodernist conceptions, see Martin Jay, *Downcast Eyes: The Denigration of Vision in Twentieth-Century French Thought* (Berkeley: University of California Press, 1993); and the essays in David Michael Levin, ed., *Modernity and the Hegemony of Vision* (Berkeley: University of California Press, 1993).

13. E. P. Thompson, *The Making of the English Working Class* (Harmondsworth: Penguin, 1970), pp. 292–93; Henry Mayhew, *London Labour and the London Poor* (New York: Dover Publications, 1968); Charles Booth, *Life and Labour of the People of London* (London, 1902); Gareth Stedman Jones, *Outcast London: A Study in the Relationship between Classes in Victorian Society* (London: Penguin, 1971); Mariana Valverde, *The Age of Light, Soap, and Water: Moral Reform in English Canada, 1885–1925* (Toronto: McClelland & Stewart, 1991). A richly detailed treatment is Alain Faure, "Sordid Class, Dangerous Class? Observations on Parisian Ragpickers and Their Cites During the Nineteenth Century," *International Review of Social History* 41 (1996): 157–76.

14. Thomas Boyle, *Black Swine in the Sewers of Hampstead: Beneath the Surface of Victorian Sensationalism* (New York: Viking, 1989); James Greenwood, *The Seven Curses of London* (Oxford: Basil Blackwell, 1981); P. J. Keating, ed., *Into Unknown England, 1866–1913: Selections from the Social Explorers* (Manchester: Manchester University Press, 1976); Kellow Chesney, *The Victorian Underworld* (New York: Schocken, 1972); Deborah Gorham, "'The Maiden Tribute of Modern Babylon' Revisited," *Victorian Studies* 21 (Spring 1978): 353–79. For a colonial account, see General Sir George MacMunn, *The Underworld of India* (London: Jarrolds, 1933).

15. Rosalind Williams, *Notes on the Underground: An Essay on Technology, Society, and the Imagination* (Cambridge, Mass.: MIT Press, 1990). See, as well, Wendy Lesser, *The Life below the Ground: A Study of the Subterranean in Literature* (Boston: Faber & Faber, 1987); Christopher Prendergast, *Paris and the Nineteenth Century: Writing the City* (Cambridge, Mass.: Blackwell, 1992), esp. pp. 74–101.

16. On Sue, see Charles Arol Isetts, "Eugène Sue: A Writer for the People" (PhD dissertation, Miami University, Ohio, 1974). On Hugo, note Suzanne Guerlac, *The Impersonal Sublime: Hugo, Baudelaire, Lautréamont* (Stanford: Stanford University Press, 1990), pp. 13–67; Priscilla Parkhurst Ferguson, *Paris as Revolution: Writing the Nineteenth Century City* (Berkeley: University of California Press, 1994), esp. pp. 154–62.

17. Louis Chevalier, *Laboring Classes and Dangerous Classes in Paris during the First Half of the Nineteenth Century* (New York: Howard Fertig, 1973), esp. pp. 107–10. For a critique of Chevalier, see Barrie M. Ratcliffe, "Classes laborieuses et classes dangereuses à Paris pendant la premiere moitie du XIXe siècle?: The Chevalier Thesis Reexamined," *French Historical Studies* 17 (Fall 1991): 542–74.

18. Irving Howe, "Céline: The Sod beneath the Skin," in Howe, *Decline of the New*

(New York: Harcourt, Brace, & World, 1970), p. 54. For a late-twentieth-century excursion into a similiar world, see Jennifer Toth, *The Mole People: Life in the Tunnels beneath New York City* (Chicago: Chicago Review Press, 1993).

19. Wolfgang Schivelbusch, *Disenchanted Night: The Industrialization of Light in the Nineteenth Century* (Berkeley: University of California Press, 1988).

20. Donald Reid, *Paris Sewers and Sewermen: Realities and Representations* (Cambridge, Mass: Harvard University Press, 1991), pp. 20–21.

21. Ibid., pp. 25–52.

22. Chevalier, *Laboring Classes and Dangerous Classes*, p. 109. Of generalized relevance is Nicholas Green, *The Spectacle of Nature: Landscape and Bourgeois Culture in Nineteenth-Century France* (Manchester: Manchester University Press, 1990).

23. For figures, see Theodore Zeldin, *France, 1848–1945: Ambition and Love* (Oxford: Oxford University Press, 1979), pp. 305–14; Greenwood, *The Seven Curses of London*, pp. 179–180; Fraser Harrison, *The Dark Angel: Aspects of Victorian Sexuality* (Glasgow: Fonana/Collins, 1979), pp. 216–56. For a "classic" encyclopedic mid-nineteenth-century reform tract presenting a history of prostitution, see William W. Sanger, *The History of Prostitution: Its Extent, Causes and Effects Throughout the World* (New York: Eugenics Publications, 1937). Note the discussion of the Parisian "spermal economy" in Rupert Christiansen, *Paris Babylon: The Story of the Paris Commune* (New York: Viking, 1994), pp. 80–92.

24. Reid, *Paris Sewers and Sewermen*, esp. p. 23, but see also, on Parent-Duchâtelet, Chevalier, *Laboring Classes and Dangerous Classes*; Charles Bernheimer, *Figures of Ill Repute: Representing Prostitution in Nineteenth-Century France* (Cambridge, Mass.: Harvard University Press, 1989); Jann Matlock, *Scenes of Seduction: Prostitution, Hysteria, and Reading Difference in Nineteenth-Century France* (New York: Columbia University Press, 1994), pp. 23–48; Alain Corbin, "Commercial Sexuality in Nineteenth-Century France: A System of Images and Regulation," in Catherine Gallagher and Thomas Laqueur, eds., *The Making of the Modern Body: Sexuality and Society in the Nineteenth Century* (Berkeley: University of California Press, 1987), pp. 209–18.

25. Note the discussion in Alain Corbin, *Women for Hire: Prostitution and Sexuality in France after 1850* (Cambridge, Mass: Harvard University Press, 1990). Among the most stimulating and rich studies of prostitution is an account of twentieth-century Chinese experience: Gail Hershatter, *Dangerous Pleasures: Prostitution and Modernity in Twentieth-Century Shanghai* (Berkeley: University of California Press, 1997).

26. Chevalier, *Laboring Classes and Dangerous Classes*, pp. 303–04. For photographic representation of locations around Les Halles and Rue Saint-Denis, see *Atget Paris* (Paris: Hazan, 1992), pp. 65–93, 142–54.

27. Jann Matlock, *Scenes of Seduction*, quotations from pp. 81, 106, but see pp. 60–121 in general.

28. On republican imagery, see Maurice Agulhon, *Marianne into Battle: Republican Imagery and Symbolism in France, 1789–1880* (Cambridge: Cambridge University Press, 1981), and for historical context Philip Nord, *The Republican Moment: Struggles for Democracy in Nineteenth-Century France* (Cambridge, Mass.: Harvard University Press, 1995).

29. This paragraph draws primarily on the stimulating and richly complex account in Bernheimer, *Figures of Ill Repute*, although my orientation is not necessarily the same on every interpretive point. Note the short account in Bataille, *The Tears of Eros*, pp. 142–61.

30. See Arnold Hauser, *The Social History of Art: Naturalism, Impressionism, The Film Age* (New York: Vintage, 1951), pp. 4, 63–64, 111–13; Bernheimer, *Figures of Ill Repute*, pp. 104–07; Patricia Mainardi, *Art and Politics of the Second Empire: The Universal Expositions of 1855 and 1867* (New Haven: Yale University Press, 1987).

31. See T. J. Clark, "Olympia's Choice," in *The Painting of Modern Life: Paris in the Art of Manet and His Followers* (New York: Knopf, 1985), pp. 79–146; and the useful counter-reading in Bernheimer, "Manet's Olympia: The Figuration of Scandal," in *Figures of Ill Repute*, pp. 89–128. For background, Otto Friedrich, *Olympia's Paris in the Age of Manet* (New York: Simon & Schuster, 1992). Note as well Valverde, *Age of Light, Soap, and Water*, pp. 78–79.

32. Greenwood, *Seven Curses of London*, pp. 173–74. For a discussion of the literary representation of prostitution in this period, see Amanda Anderson, *Tainted Souls and Painted Faces: The Rhetoric of Fallenness in Victorian Culture* (Ithaca: Cornell University Press, 1993).

33. Judith R. Walkowitz, *Prostitution and Victorian Society: Women, Class, and the State* (Cambridge: Cambridge University Press, 1980); Shannon Bell, *Reading, Writing & Rewriting the Prostitute Body* (Bloomington: University of Indiana Press, 1994), pp. 55–64.

34. Charles van Onselen, "Prostitutes and Proletarians, 1886–1914," in *Studies in the Social and Economic History of the Witwatersrand, 1886–1914, Volume I: New Babylon* (New York: Longman, 1982), pp. 103–62. For balanced accounts of "white slavery," see Ruth Rosen, *The Lost Sisterhood: Prostitution in America, 1900–1918* (Baltimore: Johns Hopkins University Press, 1982), pp. 112–36; Timothy J. Gilfoyle, *City of Eros: New York City, Prostitution, and the Commercialization of Sex, 1790–1920* (New York: W. W. Norton, 1992), pp. 251–97.

35. Quotations from Tristan in Matlock, *Scenes of Seduction*, pp. 58–59.

36. Judith R. Walkowitz, *City of Dreadful Delight: Narratives of Sexual Danger in Late Victorian London* (Chicago: University of Chicago Press, 1992), pp. 191–228; Elaine Showalter, *Sexual Anarchy: Gender and Culture at the Fin de Siècle* (New York: Viking, 1990), p. 127; Wendy Mitchinson, *The Nature of Their Bodies: Women and Their Doctors in Victorian Canada* (Toronto: University of Toronto Press, 1991); Angus McLaren, *A Prescription for Murder: The Victorian Serial Killings of Dr. Thomas Neill Cream* (Chicago: University of Chicago Press, 1993). For one attempt to identify Jack the Ripper, see Donald McCormick, *The Identity of Jack the Ripper* (London: Jarrolds, 1959).

37. Amy Gilman Srebnick, *The Mysterious Death of Mary Rogers: Sex and Culture in Nineteenth-Century New York* (Oxford: Oxford University Press, 1995). Note Gramsci's comment: "The detective novel was born in the margins of literature dealing with 'causes célèbres'." See Antonio Gramsci, *Selections from Cultural Writings*, ed. David Forgacs and Geoffrey Nowell-Smith (Cambridge, Mass.: Harvard University Press, 1985), p. 369. For another account, in a different regional context, see John Burke, *The Legend of Baby Doe: The Life and Times of the Silver Queen of the West* (Lincoln: University of Nebraska Press, 1974).

38. Kathy Peiss, *Cheap Amusements: Working Women and Leisure in Turn-of-the-Century New York* (Philadelphia: Temple University Press, 1986); Carolyn Strange, *Toronto's Girl Problem: The Perils and Pleasures of the City, 1880–1930* (Toronto: University of Toronto Press, 1995); Wayne Roberts, *Honest Womanhood: Feminism, Feminity, and Class Consciousness Among Toronto Working Women, 1896–1914* (Toronto: New Hogtown Press, 1976); Lori Rotenberg, "The Wayward Worker: Toronto's Prostitute at

the Turn of the Century," in Janice Acton et al., eds., *Women at Work: Ontario, 1850–1930* (Toronto: Women's Press, 1974), pp. 33–70; Peter Ward, ed., *The Mysteries of Montreal: Memoirs of a Midwife by Charlotte Fuhrer* (Vancouver: University of British Columbia Press, 1984); Judith Fingard, *The Dark Side of Life in Victorian Halifax* (Halifax: Pottersfield Press, 1989), pp. 95–113.

39. Christine Stansell, *City of Women: Sex and Class in New York, 1789–1860* (New York: Knopf, 1986), pp. 63–75; William Sanger, *History of Prostitution*, pp. 29, 450–699; Luc Sante, *Low Life: Lures and Snares of Old New York* (New York: Vintage, 1992), pp. 177–95. An exquisitely crafted study of New York prostitution is Gilfoyle, *City of Eros.*

40. C. S. Clark, *Of Toronto the Good, A Social Study: The Queen City of Canada as It Is* (Toronto: Coles Reprint, 1970), p. 106.

41. John D'Emilio and Estelle B. Freedman, *Intimate Matters: A History of Sexuality in America* (New York: Harper & Row, 1988), pp. 130–38; Anne M. Butler, *Daughters of Joy, Sisters of Misery: Prostitutes in the American West, 1865–90* (Urbana: University of Illinois Press, 1987); Robert R. Dykstra, *The Cattle Towns: A Social History of the Kansas Cattle Trading Centers Abilene, Ellsworth, Wichita, Dodge City, and Caldwell, 1867 to 1885* (New York: Atheneum, 1974); James H. Gray, *Red Lights on the Prairies* (New York: Signet, 1971); Rosen, *Lost Sisterhood*, pp. 71–92; Al Rose, *Storyville, New Orleans: Being an Authentic, Illustrated Account of the Notorious Red Light District* (Mobile: University of Alabama Press, 1974); Herbert Asbury, *The French Quarter: An Informal History of the New Orleans Underworld* (New York: Knopf, 1936); Asbury, *The Barbary Coast: An Informal History of the San Francisco Underworld* (Garden City: Knopf, 1933); Jacqueline Baker Barnhart, "Working Women: Prostitution in San Francisco from the Gold Rush to 1900" (PhD dissertation, University of California, Santa Barbara, 1976); Lucie Cheng Hirata, "Free, Indentured, Enslaved: Chinese Prostitutes in Nineteenth-Century America," *Signs* 5 (Autumn 1979): 3–29.

42. Walt Whitman, *New York Dissected*, ed. Emory Holloway and Ralph Adimari (New York, 1936), p. 6, cited in D'Emilio and Freedman, *Intimate Matters*, p. 49. Of the Bowery, an area rife with nineteenth-century prostitution, Luc Sante, *Low Life*, p. 361, states: "The Bowery is the capital of night. On its sidewalks, people are crashing through saloon doors, shouldering through crowds looking for a fight, looking for lost fathers or husbands, hooking out-of-towners to try to sell them worthless junk at wild prices, raising money for a bed, picking cigar butts out of the gutter, flashing rolls of bills to impress newly met acquaintances, preaching the gospel to nobody at all, selling stolen watches from under their coats, selling newspapers, selling favors, selling *themselves*" (emphasis added).

43. See Ray Allen Billington, *The Protestant Crusade, 1800–1860: A Study of the Origins of American Nativism* (New York: Rinehart, 1952), pp. 98–108; D'Emilio and Freedman, *Intimate Matters*, p. 131.

44. Fingard, *The Dark Side of Life in Victorian Halifax*, pp. 104–13.

45. Butler, *Daughters of Joy, Sisters of Mercy*; Sylvia Van Kirk, *"Many Tender Ties": Women in Fur Trade Society, 1670–1870* (Winnipeg: Watson & Dwyer, 1980).

46. Gilfoyle, *City of Eros*, pp. 36–43; Iver Bernstein, *The New York City Draft Riots: Their Significance for American Society and Politics in the Age of the Civil War* (New York: Oxford University Press, 1990), pp. 32, 34; Samuel Prime, *Life in New York* (New York, 1847), pp. 175–76; Richard Symanski, *The Immoral Landscape: Female*

Prostitution in Western Societies (Toronto: Butterworths, 1981), pp. 138–42; Noel Ignatiev, How the Irish Became White (New York: Routledge, 1995), pp. 40–42. See, as well, B. O. Flower, Civilization's Inferno; or, Studies in the Social Cellar (Boston: Arena, 1893), p. 103.

47. Consider the varied and often contending positions in Bernheimer, Figures of Ill Repute, pp. 266–74; Wendy Steiner, The Scandal of Pleasure: Art in an Age of Fundamentalism (Chicago: University of Chicago Press, 1995), p. 83; Leo Steinberg, "The Philosophical Brothel," October 44 (Spring 1988): 17–74; Charles Harrison, Francis Franscina, and Gill Perry, Primitivism, Cubism, Abstraction: The Early Twentieth Century (New Haven: Yale University Press, 1993), esp. pp. 107–13; Fredric Jameson, "Modernism and Imperialism," in Seamus Deane, ed., Nationalism, Colonialism and Literature (Minneapolis: University of Minnesota Press, 1990), pp. 50–51.

48. Note the useful first-hand account for the early twentieth century in Hendrik De Leeuw, Sinful Cities of the Western World (New York: Citadel Press, 1934).

Chapter 8

1. See Mariana Valverde, "The Dialectic of the Familiar and the Unfamiliar: 'The Jungle' in Early Slum Travel Writing," Sociology 30 (August 1996): 493–509; Anne McClintock, Imperial Leather: Race, Gender, and Sexuality in the Colonial Contest (New York: Routledge, 1995), pp. 118–22; Douglas A. Lorimer, Colour, Class, and the Victorians: English Attitudes to the Negro in the Mid-nineteenth Century (New York: Holmes & Meier, 1978); Thomas Richards, The Imperial Archive: Knowledge and the Fantasy of Empire (London: Verso, 1993). Consider, as well, the two chapters, "Cities of Darkness and Light," and "Cities and Countries," in Raymond Williams, The Country and the City (Frogmore: Paladin, 1975), pp. 259–79, 347–68. For slightly different contextualizations, Alex Potts, "Picturing the Modern Metropolis: Images of London in the Nineteenth Century," History Workshop Journal 26 (Autumn 1988): 28–56; Peter Bailey, "'In Darkest England and the Way Out': The Salvation Army, Social Reform, and the Labor Movement, 1885–1910," International Review of Social History 29 (1984): 133–71; John McBratney, "Imperial Subjects, Imperial Space in Kipling's Jungle Book," Victorian Studies 35 (Spring 1992): 277–93.

2. E. A. Blair [George Orwell], "L'Empire Britannique en Birmanie," Le Progrès Civique, May 4, 1929, pp. 22–24, translated and quoted in Bernard Crick, George Orwell: A Life (London: Secker & Warburg, 1980), pp. 101–02.

3. George Orwell, The Road to Wigan Pier (Harmondsworth: Penguin, 1977), p. 127.

4. See Crick, Orwell, pp. 76–103, quotation from p. 100; Peter Stansky and William Abrahams, The Unknown Orwell (London: Constable, 1972), pp. 121–76; Michael Shelden, Orwell: The Authorised Biography (London: Heinemann, 1991), esp. pp. 85–123. Aside from Burmese Days, Orwell's most acute writings relating to his service in imperialism are: "A Hanging" (1931) and "Shooting an Elephant" (1936), in The Collected Essays, Journalism and Letters of George Orwell: Volume 1: An Age Like This, 1920–1940, ed. Sonia Orwell and Ian Angus (New York: Harcourt Brace Jovanovich, 1968), pp. 44–48, 235–42. For an account of another troubled Englishman, whose negotiations with imperialism and Indian culture resulted in "authentic encounter," one in which the colonizing

missionary became "a marginal man, a courier between cultures who wore the authorized livery of neither," see E. P. Thompson, *Alien Homage: Edward Thompson and Rabindranath Tagore* (Delhi: Oxford University Press, 1993).

5. Shelden, *Orwell: The Authorised Biography*, p. 103.

6. H. Feis, *Europe: The World's Banker, 1870–1914* (New Haven: Yale University Press, 1930), p. 467.

7. For a succinct statement, see the sections on imperialism and militarism in E. H. Carr, ed., *Bukharin and Preobrazhensky: The ABC of Communism* (Harmondsworth: Penguin, 1969), pp. 146–62.

8. A stimulating, wide-ranging sociological account is Michael Mann, *The Sources of Social Power: Volume 1—A History of Power from the Beginning to AD. 1760* (Cambridge: Cambridge University Press, 1986).

9. For accounts of theories of imperialism that address the early-twentieth-century literature, see Anthony Brewer, *Marxist Theories of Imperialism: A Critical Survey* (London: Routledge, 1989); Victor G. Kiernan, *Marxism and Imperialism* (London: Edward Arnold, 1974); and the contentious but stimulating and challenging Bill Warren, *Imperialism: Pioneer of Capitalism* (London: Verso, 1980). Ernest Mandel, *Marxist Economic Theory*, Volume II (New York: Monthly Review Press, 1968), esp. pp. 441–84, presents a brief, coherent statement on the economic dimensions of modern imperialism.

10. Orwell, "Why I Joined the Independent Labor Party" (1938) in *Collected Essays*, Volume I, p. 337. For a brief, accessible account of imperialism in Burma, see V. G. Kiernan, *The Lords of Humankind: European Attitudes to the Outside World in the Imperial Age* (Harmondsworth: Penguin, 1972), pp. 81–85.

11. I draw on and quote from Orwell, *The Road to Wigan Pier*, pp. 123–27; George Orwell, *Burmese Days* (New York: Popular Library, 1958), p. 61; Crick, *Orwell*, pp. 76–93; Shelden, *Orwell*, pp. 108–09; Raymond Williams, *Orwell* (London: Flamingo, 1984), esp. pp. 7–9; Williams, *The Country and the City*, pp. 337–42. For general statements on homosexuality, see Orwell, *Collected Essays*, Volume I, pp. 56–57, 71. For an account of Orwell's anti-feminism and capacity to ignore women that largely bypasses his colonial period and avoids race, see Deirdre Beddoe, "Hindrances and Help–Meets: Women in the Writings of George Orwell," in Christoper Norris, ed., *Inside the Myth: Orwell—Views from the Left* (London: Lawrence & Wishart, 1984), pp. 139–54.

12. The illustration is reproduced in Patrick J. Kearney, *A History of Erotic Literature* (London: Macmillan, 1982), pp. 104–05.

13. For a discussion of race and the "class body," see Michel Foucault, *The History of Sexuality, Volume I: Introduction* (New York: Vintage, 1980), esp. pp. 120–27. On homoeroticism, see the intriguing analysis in Kaja Silverman, "White Skin, Brown Masks: The Double Mimesis, or With Lawrence in Arabia," *Differences* 1 (1989): 3–54; and for later periods Ted Morgan, *Literary Outlaw: The Life and Times of William S. Burroughs* (New York: Avon, 1988), pp. 234–71; Michelle Green, *The Dream at the End of the World: Paul Bowles and the Literary Renegades in Tangiers* (New York: Harper, 1992).

14. Among many sources, see: Mary Louise Pratt, *Imperial Eyes: Travel Writing and Transculturation* (London: Routledge, 1992), esp. pp. 86–101; McClintock, *Imperial Leather*, pp. 41–42; Sander Gilman, *Difference and Pathology: Stereotypes of Sexuality, Race, and Madness* (Ithaca: Cornell University Press, 1985), pp. 45, 76–128;

Lorimer, Color, Class and the Victorians, p. 132; Ann Laura Stoler, Race and the Education of Desire: Foucault's History of Sexuality and the Colonial Order of Things (Durham, N.C.: Duke University Press, 1995), esp. pp. 39–54; Stoler, "Carnal Knowledge and Imperial Power: Gender, Race, and Morality in Colonial Asia," in Micaela di Leonardo, ed., Gender at the Crossroads of Knowledge: Feminist Anthropology in a Postmodern Era (Berkeley: University of California Press, 1991), pp. 55–101; David Brion Davis, The Problem of Slavery in Western Culture (Harmondsworth: Penguin, 1970), p. 505; John Butcher, The British in Malaya, 1880–1914 (Kuala Lumpur: Oxford University Press, 1979); Joanna de Groot, " 'Sex' and 'Race': The Construction of Language and Image in the Nineteenth Century," in Susan Mendus and Jane Rendall, eds., Sexuality and Subordination: Interdisciplinary Studies of Gender in the Nineteenth Century (London: Routledge, 1989), pp. 89–128.

15. Ian Buruma, "Revenge in the Indies," New York Review of Books, August 11, 1994, pp. 30–32; Philip Mason, Birth of a Dilemma: The Conquest and Settlement of Rhodesia (London: Oxford University Press, 1958), p. 244.

16. Kiernan, The Lords of Humankind, pp. 135–43. On Western feminists and women of color, see Antoinette Burton, "The Feminist Quest for Identity: British Imperial Suffragism and 'Global Sisterhood,' 1900–1915," Journal of Women's History 3 (Fall 1991): 46–81; Vron Ware, Beyond the Pale: White Women, Racism, and History (London: Verso, 1992), pp. 117–66.

17. See Ronald Hyam, Empire and Sexuality: The British Experience (Manchester: Manchester University Press, 1990), and the critique in Stoler, Race and the Education of Desire, pp. 174–176. An excellent and wide-ranging collection, diverse in its appreciation of gender and the significance of sexuality, is Andrew Parker et al., eds., Nationalisms and Sexualities (New York: Routledge, 1992).

18. Jeff Nunokawa, "For Your Eyes Only: Private Property and the Oriental Body in Dombey and Son," in Jonathan Arac and Harriet Ritvo, eds., Macropolitics of Nineteenth Century Literature (Philadelphia: University of Pennsylvania Press, 1991), pp. 138–58.

19. See V. I. Lenin, "Preface to the French and German Editions," in Imperialism, The Highest Stage of Capitalism (Peking: Foreign Languages Press, 1965), p. 9.

20. Edward W. Said, Orientalism (New York: Vintage, 1979), esp. pp. 6, 207; Ann Laura Stoler, "Making Empire Respectable: The Politics of Race and Sexual Morality in 20th Century Colonial Cultures," American Ethnologist 16 (1989): esp. 635. For critiques of Said's masculinization of orientalism, see Sara Mill, Discourses of Difference: An Analysis of Women's Travel Writing and Colonialism (London: Routledge, 1991); Billie Mellman, Women's Orients: English Women and the Middle East, 1718–1918—Sexuality, Religion, and Work (Ann Arbor: University of Michigan Press, 1992); Reina Lewis, Gendering Orientalism: Race, Femininity and Representation (London: Routledge, 1996); Jane Miller, Seductions: Studies in Reading and Culture (London: Virago, 1996), pp. 118–22; and the later comments of Stoler, Race and the Education of Desire, pp. 174–75. Note, finally, the broad, general discussion in Gyan Prakash, "Postcolonial Criticism and Indian Historiography," in Linda Nicholson and Steven Seidman, eds., Social Postmodernism Beyond Identity Politics (Cambridge: Cambridge University Press, 1995), pp. 87–100; Dipesh Chakrabarty, "Postcoloniality and the Artifice of History: Who Speaks for 'Indian' Pasts?" Representations 37 (Winter 1992):1–26.

21. See, for instance, the writings of Frantz Fanon, especially *Black Skin, White Masks* (New York: Grove Press, 1967), esp. pp. 41–62. For historical background, see Jose Piedra, "In Search of the Black Stud," and Maria Carrion, "The Queen's Two Bawdies: *El Burlador de Sevilla* and the Teasing of Historicity," in Louise Fradenburg and Carla Freccero, eds., *Premodern Sexualities* (London: Routledge, 1996), pp. 23–70. Note, as well, Irene L. Gendzier, *Frantz Fanon: A Critical Study* (London: Wildwood House, 1973), esp. pp. 50–56; Robert Young, *White Mythologies: Writing History and the West* (London: Routledge, 1990), pp. 153–56; Stoler, *Race and the Education of Desire*, pp. 169–71; Homi Bhabha, "Remembering Fanon: Self, Psyche, and the Colonial Condition," in Patrick Williams and Laura Chrisman, eds., *Colonial Discourse and Post-Colonial Theory* (New York: Columbia University Press, 1994), pp. 112–23; Diana Fuss, "Interior Colonies: Frantz Fanon and the Politics of Identification," *Diacritics* 24 (Spring/Fall 1994): 20–42; Jock McCulloch, *Colonial Psychiatry and "The African Mind"* (Cambridge: Cambridge University Press, 1995). For other marginalized women, see Sharon Tifany and Kathleen Adams, *The Myth of the Wild Woman* (Cambridge: Schenkman, 1985); L. Hyun-Yi Kang, "The Desiring of Asian Female Bodies: Interracial Romance and Cinematic Subjection," *Visual Anthropology Review* 9 (Spring 1993): 5–21.

22. See Fernando Cervantes, *The Devil in the New World: The Impact of Diabolism in New Spain* (New Haven: Yale University Press, 1994), esp. pp. 75–97.

23. See Stoler, *Race and the Education of Desire*, pp. 177–83. Consider, as well, the fictional exploration of related themes in Linda Spalding, *Daughters of Captain Cook* (Toronto: Lester & Orpen Dennys, 1988), and, in another context, Catherine Hall, "Imperial Man: Edward Eyre in Australasia and the West Indies, 1833–1866," in Bill Schwarz, ed., *The Expansion of England: Race, Ethnicity and Cultural History* (London: Routledge, 1996), pp. 130–70.

24. In this regard, though dealing with an earlier period, Christopher Hill's chapter "'Going Native': 'The Noble Savage'" is instructive. See Hill, *Liberty Against the Law: Some Seventeenth-Century Controversies* (London: Allen Lane, 1996), pp. 145–61.

25. Cervantes, *The Devil in the New World*, esp. p. 78.

26. G. E. M. de Ste. Croix, *The Class Struggle in the Ancient Greek World* (London: Duckworth, 1981), pp. 453–503. See, as well, Michael W. Doyle, *Empires* (Ithaca: Cornell University Press, 1986), esp. pp. 11–103; Loveday Alexander, ed., *Images of Empire* (Sheffield: Sheffield Academic Press, 1991); P. D. A. Garnsey and C. R. Whittaker, eds., *Imperialism in the Ancient World* (Cambridge: Cambridge University Press, 1978). Slavery in Ancient Greece is discussed insightfully in M. I. Finley, *Ancient Slavery and Modern Ideology* (Harmondsworth: Penguin, 1980) and Finley, *Economy and Society in Ancient Greece* (Harmondsworth: Penguin, 1983).

27. See Mary Campbell, *The Witness and the Other World: Exotic European Travel Writing, 400–1600* (Ithaca: Cornell University Press), esp. pp. 87–121, quoting Columbus on p. 111; Said, *Orientalism*, esp. pp. 49–92; Kiernan, *The Lords of Humankind*, pp. 112–50; Eric R. Wolf, *Europe And the People Without a History* (Berkeley: University of California Press, 1982), pp. 24–72; Eduardo Galeano, *Open Veins of Latin America: Five Centuries of the Pillage of a Continent* (New York: Monthly Review Press, 1973), pp. 21–22; Eric Williams, *From Columbus to Castro: The History of the Caribbean, 1492–1969* (London: Andre Deutsch, 1970), p. 20.

28. Cannibalism is treated broadly in Hans Askenasy, *Cannibalism: from Sacrifice to Survival* (New York: Prometheus, 1994); Reay Tannahill, *Flesh and Blood: A History of the Cannibal Complex* (London: Abbacus, 1996). Its relation to the conquest of America is discussed in Tzvetan Todorov, *The Conquest of America: The Question of the Other* (New York: Harper Perennial, 1992), pp. 154–57, 179–80, 188.

29. For an analytically rich interpretation, see Inga Clendinne, "The Cost of Courage in Aztec Society," *Past & Present* 107 (May 1985): 44–89. Todorov's *Conquest of America* contains much on the Aztecs.

30. Williams, *From Columbus to Castro*, pp. 18–45; C. L. R. James, *The Black Jacobins: Toussaint L'Ouverture and the San Domingo Revolution* (New York: Vintage, 1963), pp. 3–5; Philip P. Boucher, *Cannibal Encounters: Europeans and Island Caribs, 1492–1763* (Baltimore: Johns Hopkins University Press, 1992); L. F. S. Upton, "The Extermination of the Beothuks of Newfoundland," *Canadian Historical Review* 48 (June 1977): 133–53; A. G. Bailey, *The Conflict of European and Eastern Algonkian Cultures, 1504–1700* (Toronto: University of Toronto Press, 1969); Cornelius Jaenen, *Friend and Foe: Aspects of French–Amerindian Cultural Contact in the Sixteenth and Seventeenth Centuries* (Toronto: McClelland & Stewart, 1976); Bruce Trigger, *The Children of the Aataentsic: A History of the Huron People to 1660* (Montreal: McGill–Queen's University Press, 1976); Calvin Martin, "The European Impact on the Culture of a Northeastern Algonquian Tribe: An Ecological Interpretation," *William & Mary Quarterly* 31 (1974): 3–26; Karl H. Schlesier, "Epidemics and Indian Middlemen: Rethinking the Wars of the Iroquois, 1609–1653," *Ethnohistory* 23 (1976): 129–45; William M. Denevan, ed., *The Native Population of the Americas in 1492* (Madison: University of Wisconsin Press, 1992); Olive Patricia Dickason, *The Myth of the Savage: And the Beginnings of French Colonialism in the Americas* (Edmonton: University of Alberta Press, 1984); and the broad-ranging Ronald Wright, *Stolen Continents: The "New World" Through Indian Eyes* (Toronto: Penguin Books, 1992). For the ecological reading of empire, see Alfred W. Crosby, Jr., *The Columbian Exchange: Biological and Cultural Consequences of 1492* (Westport, Conn.: Greenwood, 1972); Crosby, Jr., *Ecological Imperialism: The Biological Expansion of Europe, 900–1900* (Cambridge: Cambridge University Press, 1986); William Cronon, *Changes in the Land: Indians, Colonists, and the Ecology of New England* (New York: Hill & Wang, 1983); Timothy Silver, *A New Face on the Countryside: Indians, Colonists, and Slaves in South Atlantic Forests, 1500–1800* (Cambridge: Cambridge University Press, 1990).

31. On Abbot, see Boucher, *Cannibal Encounters*, p. 27; Colin Steele, *English Interpreters of the Iberian New World from Purchas to Stevens, 1603–1726: A Bibliographical Study* (Oxford: Dolphin, 1975), p. 21; John Parker, *Books to Build an Empire* (Amsterdam: N. Israel, 1965), p. 259; Margaret Hogden, *Early Anthropology in the Sixteenth and Seventeenth Centuries* (Philadelphia: University of Pennsylvania Press, 1964), p. 200.

32. Consider the discussions in Christopher Hill, "Daniel Defoe (1660–1731) and Robinson Crusoe," in Hill, *The Collected Essays of Christopher Hill, Volume 1: Writing and Revolution in Seventeenth Century England* (Amherst: University of Amherst Press, 1985), pp. 105–30; Stephen Hymer, "Robinson Crusoe and the Secret of Primitive Accumulation," *Monthly Review* 23 (1971): 11–36; Ian Watt, *Myths of Modern Individualism: Faust, Don Quixote, Don Juan, Robinson Crusoe* (Cambridge: Cambridge University Press, 1996), esp. pp. 141–92; Warren Montag, *The Unthinkable Swift: The Spontaneous Philosophy of a Church of England Man* (London: Verso, 1994), pp.

131–38. More wide-ranging, but touching on similar issues, is Diana Loxley, *Problematic Shores: The Literature of Islands* (London: Macmillan, 1990).

33. Richard C. Trexler, *Sex and Conquest: Gendered Violence, Political Order, and the European Conquest of the Americas* (Ithaca: Cornell University Press, 1985). For other statements on the berdache, especially in northern woodlot tribes, see Gary Kinsman, *The Regulation of Desire: Homo and Hetero Sexualities* (Montreal: Black Rose Books, 1996), pp. 92–93; Jonathan Goldberg, "Sodomy in the New World: Anthropologies Old and New," in Michael Warner, ed., *Fear of a Queer Planet: Queer Politics and Social Theory* (Minneapolis: University of Minnesota Press, 1993), pp. 3–18; Evelyn Blackwood, "Sexuality and Gender in Certain Native American Tribes: The Case of Cross-Gender Females," *Signs* 10 (1984): 27–42. For a more sober view of the Caribs, see the moderate views of the pirates' priest, Father Labat, presented in Everild Young, FRGS, and Kjeld Helweg-Larsen, *The Pirates' Priest: The Life of Pere Labat in the West Indies, 1693–1705* (London: Jarrold's, 1965), pp. 48–77.

34. McClintock, *Imperial Leather*, pp. 24–28; Nancy L. Paxton, "Mobilizing Chivalry: Rape in British Novels about the Indian Uprising of 1857," *Victorian Studies* 35 (Fall 1992): 5–30; and for background, Kiernan, *Lords of Humankind*, pp. 33–78; Edward John Thompson, *The Other Side of the Medal* (New Delhi: Oxford University Press, 1989). On the Nat Turner rebellion, see William Styron, *The Confessions of Nat Turner* (Toronto: Signet, 1967), and the compilation, John B. Duff and Peter M. Mitchell, *The Nat Turner Rebellion: The Historical Event and the Modern Controversy* (New York: Harper & Row, 1971), as well as Eugene D. Genovese, "William Styron Before the People's Court," in Genovese, *In Red and Black: Marxian Explorations in Southern and Afro-American History* (New York: Vintage, 1971), pp. 200–17, a review of John Henrik Clarke et al., *William Styron's Nat Turner: Ten Black Writers Respond* (Boston: Beacon Press, 1968).

35. For a popular account of the Inca conquest, see Wright, *Stolen Continents*, pp. 64–83, quoted poem from p. 83.

36. See Eric Williams, *Capitalism & Slavery* (New York: Capricorn, 1966); Peter Wilson Coldham, *Emigrants in Chains: A Social History of Forced Emigration to the Americas, 1607–1776* (Baltimore: Johns Hopkins University Press, 1992); David Eltis, "Free and Coerced Transatlantic Migrations: Some Comparisons," *American Historical Review* 88 (1983): 251–80; Hilary McD. Beckles, *White Servitude and Black Slavery in Barbados, 1627–1715* (Knoxville: University of Tennessee Press, 1989); David W. Galenson, *White Servitude in Colonial America: An Economic Analysis* (Cambridge, Mass.: Harvard University Press, 1981); Russell R. Menard, "From Servants to Slaves: The Transformation of the Chesapeake Labor System," *Southern Studies* 16 (Winter 1977): 355–90; and the wide-ranging collection Paul E. Lovejoy and Nicholas Rogers, eds., *Unfree Labor in the Development of the Atlantic World* (London: Frank Cass, 1994). For a later period, see David Northrup, *Indentured Labor in the Age of Imperialism, 1834–1922* (Cambridge: Cambridge University Press, 1995); and of interest with respect to Asian indentured labor: Peter Richardson, *Chinese Mine Labor in the Transvaal* (London: Macmillan, 1982); Walton Look Lai, *Indentured Labor, Caribbean Sugar: Chinese and Indian Migrants to the British West Indies, 1838–1918* (Baltimore: Johns Hopkins University Press, 1993).

37. Farley Grubb, "The Long-Run Trend in the Value of European Immigrant Servants, 1654–1831: New Measurements and Intepretations," *Research in*

Economic History 14 (1992): 167–240; David Eltis, "Europeans and the Rise and Fall of African Slavery in the Americas: An Interpretation," *American Historical Review* 98 (December 1983): 1399–423; Winthrop D. Jordan, *White Over Black: American Attitudes Toward the Negroe, 1550–1812* (Baltimore: Penguin, 1968).

38. Williams, *Capitalism and Slavery*, and, for comment, Barbara L. Solow and Stanley L. Engerman, eds., *British Capitalism and Caribbean Slavery: The Legacy of Eric Williams* (Cambridge: Cambridge University Press, 1987); C. Duncan Rice, *The Rise and Fall of Black Slavery* (London: Macmillan, 1975); Seymour Drescher, *Capitalism and Antislavery: British Mobilization in Comparative Perspective* (New York: Oxford University Press, 1987); Robin Blackburn, *The Overthrow of Colonial Slavery, 1776–1848* (London: Verso, 1988); Stanley L. Engerman, "The Slave Trade and British Capital Formation in the Eighteenth Century: A Comment on the Williams Thesis," *Business History Review* 46 (Winter 1972): 430–43; Roger Anstey, "'Capitalism and Slavery': A Critique," *Economic History Review* 21 (1968), pp. 307–20.

39. See Blackburn, *The Overthrow of Colonial Slavery, 1776–1848*, pp. 1–32; Sidney W. Mintz, *Sweetness and Power: The Place of Sugar in Modern History* (New York: Viking, 1985), pp. 19–74; Richard S. Dunn, *Sugar and Slaves: The Rise of the Planter Class in the English West Indies, 1624–1713* (New York: W. W. Norton, 1972); Dale W. Tomich, *Slavery in the Circuit of Sugar: Martinique and the World Economy* (Baltimore: Johns Hopkins University Press, 1990); Robert W. Fogel, *Without Consent or Contract: The Rise and Fall of American Slavery* (New York: W. W. Norton, 1989), pp. 17–40; Paul E. Lovejoy, "The Volume of the Atlantic Slave Trade: A Synthesis," *Journal of African History* 23 (1983): 473–501; Peter Linebaugh, "All the Atlantic Mountains Shook," *Labor/Le Travailleur* 10 (Autumn 1982): 87–122. For the perspective from Africa, see Walter Rodney, *How Europe Underdeveloped Africa* (Washington: Howard University Press, 1981), pp. 73–146. On Brazil, note the important study: Gilberto Freyre, *The Masters and the Slaves: A Study in the Development of Brazilian Civilization* (New York: Knopf, 1956). For other monoculture economies, note the case of coffee, detailed in William Roseberry, Lowell Gudmundson, and Mario Samper Kutschbach, eds., *Coffee, Society, and Power in Latin America* (Baltimore: Johns Hopkins University Press, 1995); Charles Bergquist, *Coffee and Conflict in Columbia, 1886–1910* (Durham, N.C.: Duke University Press, 1988).

40. David Brion Davis, *The Problem of Slavery in the Age of Revolution, 1770–1823* (Ithaca: Cornell University Press, 1975), p. 41.

41. Mary Turner, *Slaves and Missionaries: The Disintegration of Jamaican Slave Society, 1787–1834* (Urbana: University of Illinois Press, 1982). Turner presents a useful case study of the slave–missionary relation.

42. Philip D. Curtin, *The Image of Africa: British Ideas and Action, 1780–1850* (Madison: University of Wisconsin Press, 1964), esp. p. 9; Lorimer, *Color, Class, and the Victorians*, quotation from p. 147; Patrick Brantlinger, *Rule of Darkness: British Literature and Imperialism, 1830–1914* (Ithaca: Cornell University Press, 1988), esp. the excellent chapter "The Genealogy of the Myth of the 'Dark Continent'," pp. 173–98; Dorothy Hammond and Alta Jablow, *The Africa that Never Was: Four Centuries of British Writing about Africa* (New York: Twayne, 1970), pp. 49–113, quotation from p. 94; Jordan, *White Over Black*, pp. 269–311, develops a contextual background; and a study of American views is presented in Michael McCarthy, *Dark Continent: Africa as Seen by Americans* (Westport, Conn.: Greenwood Press, 1983).

43. McClintock, *Imperial Leather*, pp. 207–31. For other brief readings of such advertisements, see Lorimer, *Color, Class, and the Victorians*, pp. 89–90; Carol Mavor, *Pleasures Taken: Performances of Sexuality and Loss in Victorian Photographs* (Durham, N.C.: Duke University Press, 1995), pp. 94–100. Also suggestive, in another national context, is Mariana Valverde, *The Age of Light, Soap, and Water: Moral Reform in English Canada, 1885–1925* (Toronto: McClelland & Stewart, 1991).

44. For Britain, see Lorimer, *Color, Class, and the Victorians*, pp. 95–89; Henry Mayhew, *London Labor and the London Poor*, Volume III (London: Griffin, Bohn & Company, 1861), pp. 190–95. The United States minstrels are discussed in Alexander Saxton, *The Rise and Fall of the White Republic: Class Politics and Mass Culture in Nineteenth-Century America* (London: Verso, 1990), pp. 165–82; David R. Roediger, *The Wages of Whiteness: Race and the Making of the American Working Class* (London: Verso, 1991), pp. 115–32; Eric Lott, *Love and Theft: Blackface Minstrelsy and the American Working Class* (New York: Oxford University Press, 1993). Note, as well, George H. Rehin, "Harlequin Jim Crow: Continuity and Covergence in Blackface Clowning," *Journal of Popular Culture* 9 (1975–1976): 682–701.

45. Brantlinger, *Rule of Darkness*, p. 184, alluding to the stamp design depicted in Roland Oliver, *Sir Harry Johnston and the Scramble for Africa* (London: Chatto & Windus, 1957).

46. Kathryn Castle, *Britannia's Children: Reading Colonialism Through Children's Books and Magazines* (Manchester: Manchester University Press, 1996); Anne Bloomfield, "Drill and Dance as Symbols of Imperialism," in J. A. Mangan, ed., *Making Imperial Mentalities: Socialisation and British Imperialism* (Manchester: Manchester University Press, 1990), pp. 74–95.

47. See Michel Foucault, "Appendix: The Discourse on Language," in *The Archaelogy of Language & The Discourse of Language* (New York: Pantheon, 1972), p. 229. Consider, as well, the imaginative arguments from later periods in C. L. R. James, *Beyond a Boundary* (New York: Pantheon, 1983); Ariel Dorfman, *The Empire's Old Clothes: What the Lone Ranger, Babar, and Other Innocent Heroes Do to Our Minds* (New York: Pantheon, 1983).

48. For an account of mid-twentieth-century sociology's grappling with this matter, see Rene Maunier, *The Sociology of Colonies: An Introduction to the Study of Race Contact* (London: Routledge & Kegan Paul, 1949).

49. Clarke quoted in Brantlinger, *Rule of Darkness*, pp. 126–27.

50. On the Saint Dominigue masters' profligacy, see C. L. R. James, *The Black Jacobins: Toussaint L'Ouverture and the San Domingo Revolution* (New York: Vintage, 1963), esp. pp. 27–61. Robert William Fogel and Stanley L. Engerman attempt to dismiss "breeding" as mere myth in *Time on the Cross: The Economics of American Negro Slavery* (Boston: Little, Brown, 1974), pp. 78–86, but note the evidence in Richard Sutch, "The Breeding of Slaves for Sale and the Westward Expansion of Slavery, 1850–1860," in Stanley L. Engerman and Eugene D. Genovese, eds., *Race and Slavery in the Western Hemisphere: Quantitative Studies* (Princeton: Princeton University Press, 1975), pp. 173–210; Herbert G. Gutman and Richard Sutch, "Victorians All? The Sexual Mores and Conduct of Slaves and Their Masters," in Paul A. David et al., *Reckoning With Slavery: A Critical Study in the Quantitative History of American Negro Slavery* (New York: Oxford University Press, 1976), p. 155.

51. The downplaying of slavery's horror was an understandable component of the slaveholders' ideology, as is suggested in Eugene D. Genovese, *The World*

The Slaveholders Made: Two Essays in Interpretation (New York: Vintage, 1971). I find contemporary historiography's efforts in this direction less appealing: Fogel and Engerman, Time on the Cross, replied to at length in Herbert G. Gutman, Slavery and the Numbers Game: A Critique of Time on the Cross (Urbana: University of Illinois Press, 1975); Paul A. David et al., Reckoning with Slavery: A Critical Study in the Quantitative Study of American Negro Slavery (New York: Oxford University Press, 1976). On slavery diversity and the comparative differences for slaves in various locales, see the essays in Laura Foner and Eugene D. Genovese, eds., Slavery in the New World: A Reader in Comparative History (Englewood Cliffs: Prentice-Hall, 1969). For the range of responses developed by American slaves to deal with their oppression and exploitation, see Stanley Elkins, Slavery: A Problem in American Institutional and Intellectual Life (Chicago: University of Chicago Press, 1959); Eugene D. Genovese, Roll, Jordan, Roll: The World the Slaves Made (New York: Pantheon, 1974); Herbert G. Gutman, The Black Family in Slavery and Freedom, 1750–1925 (New York: Pantheon, 1976). A consise statement on slave resistance is James Oakes, "The Political Significance of Slave Resistance," History Workshop Journal 22 (Autumn 1986): 89–107.

52. Quotations from Eugene D. Genovese, From Rebellion to Revolution: Afro-American Slave Revolts in the Making of the Modern World (Baton Rouge: Louisiana State University Press, 1979), pp. 2, 96; Herbert Aptheker, American Negro Slave Revolts (New York: International, 1943), p. 15. On Haiti and Toussaint L'Ouverture, see James, The Black Jacobins; Carolyn E. Fick, The Making of Haiti: The Saint Domingue Revolution from Below (Knoxville: University of Tennessee Press, 1990); Madison Smartt Bell, All Souls' Rising (New York: Pantheon, 1995); Wenda Parkinson, "This Gilded African": Toussaint L'Ouverture (London: Quartet, 1980); Blackburn, The Overthrow of Colonial Slavery, 1776–1848, pp. 213–64.

53. This paragraph draws on the excellent introduction in Genovese, From Rebellion to Revolution, pp. 1–50, as well as the rich detail in Aptheker, American Negro Slave Revolts. See, as well, Genovese, Roll, Jordan, Roll, pp. 587–660; Gerald W. Mullin, Slave Resistance in Eighteenth-Century Virgina (New York: Oxford University Press, 1972); Jack D. L. Holmes, "The Abortive Slave Revolt at Pointe Coupee, Louisiana, 1795," Louisiana History 11 (Fall 1970): 341–62; Tommy R. Young II, "The United States Army and the Institution of Slavery in Louisiana, 1803–1815," Louisiana Studies 13 (Fall 1974): 201–22. Abigail B. Bakan, Ideology and Class Conflict in Jamaica: The Politics of Rebellion (Montreal: McGill–Queen's University Press, 1990), pp. 50–67; Mary Reckford Turner, "The Jamaican Slave Rebellion of 1831," Past & Present 40 (July 1968):108–25; and for a dissenting view on Brazil, Carl N. Degler, Neither Black nor White: Slavery and Race Relations in Brazil and the United States (New York: Macmillan, 1971). John W. Cromwell, "The Aftermath of Nat Turner's Insurrection," Journal of Negro History 5 (April 1920): 208–34, is still worth reading.

54. George P. Rawick, From Sundown to Sunup: The Making of the Black Community (Westport, Conn.: Greenwood, 1972), p. 112; Frederick Law Olmsted, A Journey in the Back Country, 1853–1854 (New York: Schocken, 1970), p. 444; Aptheker, American Negro Slave Revolts, pp. 69, 103, 245; Mullen, Flight and Rebellion, esp. p. 142; Genovese, Roll, Jordan, Roll, pp. 617–20 (on patrols), and pp. 648–57 (on runaways).

55. Genovese, Roll, Jordan, Roll, p. 588; Genovese, From Rebellion to Revolution.

56. Genovese, From Rebellion to Revolution, esp. pp. 43, 90, 96–97; Peter Linebaugh,

"All The Atlantic Mountains Shook," pp. 87–122; Jesse Lemish, "Jack Tar in the Streets: Merchant Seamen in the Politics of Revolutionary America," *William & Mary Quarterly* 25 (1968), 371–407. On Christophe, see James, *The Black Jacobins*; Fick, *The Making of Haiti*; and Hubert Cole, *Christophe: King of Haiti* (London: Eyre & Spottiswoode, 1967).

57. Peter Linebaugh, "What If C. L. R. James Had Met E. P. Thompson in 1792?" *Urgent Tasks: Journal of the Revolutionary Left* 12 (Summer 1981): 108–10; Linebaugh, *The London Hanged: Crime and Civil Society in the Eighteenth Century* (London: Allen Lane, 1991), pp. 136, 169–70, 348–51, 415; Peter Linebaugh and Marcus Rediker, "The Many-Headed Hydra: Sailors, Slaves and the Atlantic Working Class in the Eighteenth Century," and Julius S. Scott, "Afro-American Sailors and the International Communication Network: The Case of Newport Bowers," both in Colin Howell and Richard Twomey, eds., *Jack Tar in History: Essays in the History of Maritime Life and Labor* (Fredericton, N.B.: Acadiensis Press, 1991), pp. 11–52; Edward Scobie, *Black Britannia: A History of Blacks in Britain* (Chicago: Johnson, 1972), pp. 66–84. Consider, as well, the account of a much later period: Laura Tabili, *"We Ask for British Justice": Workers and Racial Difference in Late Imperial Britain* (Ithaca: Cornell University Press, 1994).

Chapter 9

1. Michel Foucault, *Discipline and Punish: The Birth of the Prison* (New York: Pantheon, 1977), quotation from pp. 227–28, 256, but note the general discussion of "panopticism" and "complete and austere institutions", pp. 195–256, which can be read alongside Stanley Elkins's discussion of slavery's "closed" nature, and its relation to a "concentration camp" in *Slavery: A Problem in American Institutional and Intellectual Life* (Chicago: University of Chicago Press, 1968). Of direct relevance is the discussion in Peter Linebaugh and Marcus Rediker, "The Many Headed Hydra: Sailors, Slaves and the Atlantic Working Class in the Eighteenth Century," in Colin Howell and Richard J. Twomey, eds., *Jack Tar in History: Essays in the History of Maritime Life and Labor* (Fredricton, N.B.: Acadiensis Press, 1991), esp. p. 35 with reference to eighteenth-century class opposition that moved *eastward* from plantations and vessels to the streets of metropolitan London: "A central theme in this cycle was the many-sided resistance to confinement—on ships, in workshops, in prisons, or even in empires—and the simultaneous search for autonomy."

2. Johnson quoted in Peter Linebaugh, "'All the Atlantic Mountains Shook'," *Labour/Le Travail* 10 (1982): 101. See, as well, Christopher Hill, *The World Turned Upside Down: Radical Ideas During the English Revolution* (New York: Viking, 1972), pp. 32–45; Immanuel Wallerstein, *The Modern World-System: Capitalist Agriculture and the Origins of the World Economy in the Sixteenth Century* (New York: Academic Press, 1974).

3. Benedict Anderson, *Imagined Communities: Reflections on the Origin and Spread of Nationalism* (London: Verso, 1983); Richard Thomas, *Imperial Archive: Knowledge and the Fantasy of Empire* (London: Verso, 1993). Given the focus of this chapter, consider as well the material gathered in David F. Marley, *Pirates and Engineers: Dutch and Flemish Adventurers in New Spain (1607–1697)* (Windsor: Netherlandic Press, 1992).

4. Foucault, *Discipline and Punish*, pp. 293–94.

5. On a modernist chapter in this narrative, focusing on the mercenary Bob Denard and the "Perfume Islands," the Comoros, see Samantha Weinberg, *Last of the Pirates: The Search for Bob Denard* (New York: Pantheon, 1994). For an account of recent pirate historiography, emphasizing the "romantic" vs. the "realist" assessment of maritime banditry, see Lawrence Osborne, "A Pirate's Progress," *Lingua Franca* 8 (March 1988): 34–42.

6. For a broad discussion of states, sovereignty and global violence, see the intriguing Janice E. Thomson, *Mercenaries, Pirates, and Sovereigns: State-Building and Extraterritorial Violence in Early Modern Europe* (Princeton: Princeton University Press, 1994).

7. For brief accounts of this ancient piracy, see Edward Lucie-Smith, *Outcasts of the Sea: Pirates and Piracy* (New York: Paddington Press, 1978), pp. 28–35; Robert C. Ritchie, *Captain Kidd and the War Against the Pirates* (Cambridge, Mass.: Harvard University Press, 1986), pp. 2–6; Nancy K. Sandars, *The Sea Peoples: Warriors of the Ancient Mediterranean, 1250–1150 B.C.* (London: Thames & Hudson, 1978), pp. 116–202; F. J. Tritsch, "The 'Sackers' of Cities and the Movement of Population," in P. A. Crossland and Ann Birchall, eds., *Bronze Age Migrations in the Aegean* (London: Duckworth, 1973), pp. 233–38; Henry A. Ormerod, *Piracy in the Ancient World: An Essay in Mediterranean History* (Chicago: Argonaut, 1967), pp. 102–03.

8. See especially Fernand Braudel, *The Mediterranean and the Mediterranean World in the Age of Philip II*, Volume I (New York: Harper & Row, 1972), pp. 130–31; Dian H. Murray, *Pirates of the South China Coast, 1790–1810* (Stanford: Stanford University Press, 1987); Ritchie, *Captain Kidd*, pp. 5–9.

9. On Drake see, among many possible sources, Derek Wilson, *The World Encompassed: Francis Drake and His Great Voyage* (New York: Harper & Row, 1977); and the popular account in Robert Carse, *The Age of Piracy: A History* (New York: Rinehart, 1957), pp. 62–94.

10. Fernand Braudel, *The Mediterranean and the Mediterranean World in the Age of Philip II*, Volume II (New York: W. W. Norton, 1973), pp. 865–91.

11. Wesley F Craven, "The Earl of Warwick, a Speculator in Piracy," *Hispanic American Historical Review* 10 (1930): 457–79; Kenneth R. Andrews, "Sir Robert Cecil and Mediterranean Plunder," *English Historical Review* 87 (1972): 513–32; Kenneth R. Andrews, *Elizabethan Privateering: English Privateering During the Spanish War, 1585–1603* (Cambridge: Cambridge University Press, 1964), esp. pp. 104–05; Gordon Connell-Smith, *Forerunners of Drake: A Study of English Trade with Spain in the Early Tudor Period* (London: Green, 1954), pp. 136–51.

12. Ritchie, *Captain Kidd*, pp. 11–26.

13. Marcus Rediker, *Between the Devil and the Deep Blue Sea: Merchant Seamen, Pirates, and the Anglo-American Maritime World, 1700–1750* (Cambridge: Cambridge University Press, 1987), pp. 260–61; Christopher Hill, "Radical Pirates?" in Margaret Jacob and James Jacob, eds., *The Origins of Anglo-American Radicalism* (London: George Allen & Unwin, 1984), p. 22; C. and R. Bridenbaugh, *No Peace Beyond the Line: The English in the Caribbean, 1624–1690* (New York: Oxford University Press, 1972), p. 394.

14. The allusions to night raids are meant only to indicate the general issue, which is easily documented by endless detailed reference. See Captain Charles Johnson [Daniel Defoe], *A General History of the Pyrates*, ed. Manuel Schonhorn (1724; Columbia: University of South Carolina Press, 1972), p. 50; [Le Golif,]

The Memoirs of a Buccaneer: Being a Wondrous and Unrepentant Account of the Prodigious Adventures and Amours of King Louis XIV's Loyal Servant Louis Adhemar Timothee Le Golif, ed. G. Alaux and A. t'Serstevens (London: George Allen & Unwin, 1954), p. 30; and on Morgan, David Cordingly, Under the Black Flag: The Romance and Reality of Life Among the Pirates (New York: Random House, 1995), pp. 43–48; John Esquemeling, The Buccaneers of America: A True Account of the Most Remarkable Assaults Committed of Late Years Upon the Coasts of the West Indies by the Buccaneers of Jamaica and Tortuga (Both English and French) (London: Swann Sonnenschein, 1893), p. 346 and, for an account of Portobello, pp. 140–49. A general popular overview is David Cordingly, ed., Pirates: Terror on the High Seas from the Caribbean to the South China Sea (Atlanta: Turner, 1996).

15. There are various editions of the Esquemeling volume. For the fullest text available to me I have consulted John Esquemeling, The Buccaneers of America: A True Account of the Most Remarkable Assaults Committed of Late Years Upon the Coasts of The West Indies by the Buccaneers of Jamaica and Tortuga (Both English and French) (London: Swan Sonnenschein, 1893). An abridged, accessible modern version is Alexander Olivier Esquemelin, The Buccaneers of America (Baltimore: Penguin, 1969). The different names Esquemelin/Esquemeling are a consequence of Anglicized publication, and I follow Esquemeling in future reference. On the authorship of the 1724 history of the pirates, see, for the original argument that Johnson was Defoe, the writings of John Robert Moore, Defoe in the Pillory and Other Studies (Bloomington: University of Indiana Press, 1939); and Moore, Daniel Defoe: Citizen of the Modern World (Chicago: University of Chicago Press, 1958). Revisionist skepticism is presented by P. N. Furbank and W. R. Owens in The Canonisation of Daniel Defoe (New Haven: Yale University Press, 1988), esp. pp. 100–14. Their position is accepted in the history by David Cordingly, Under the Black Flag: The Romance and the Reality of Life among the Pirates (New York: Random House, 1995), p. xx. I have employed the Daniel Defoe–attributed authorship edition, edited by Manuel Schonhorn, A General History of the Pyrates (1724; Columbia: University of South Carolina Press, 1972), which contains an introduction, "The Life of Defoe," pp. xi–xlii. For an account of Defoe and criminality, see Lincoln B. Faller, Crime and Defoe: A New Kind of Writing (Cambridge: Cambridge University Press, 1993).

16. The most accessible summary of this literature is Cordingly, Under the Black Flag, but see as well Edward Lucie-Smith, Outcasts of the Sea: Pirates and Piracy (New York: Paddington Press, 1978), p. 238. For a typical example of the genre of pirate literature that proliferated in the early twentieth century, see Arthur D. Howden Smith, Porto Bello Gold (New York: Brentano's, 1924).

17. Quoted in Warren Montag, The Unthinkable Swift: The Spontaneous Philosophy of a Church of England Man (London: Verso, 1994), p. 131.

18. [Le Golif] Memoirs of a Buccaneer, p. 53.

19. Gay's opera Polly, Act II, Scene 9, suggests that some pirates borrowed extensively from indigenous people: "You talk downright Indian," says one figure to a pirate, expressing criticism of his understanding of honor. See Christopher Hill, Liberty Against the Law: Some Seventeenth-Century Controversies (London: Allen Lane, 1996), p. 160. On the Caribs, see Everild Young, FRGS, and Kjeld Helweg-Larsen, The Pirates' Priest: The Life of Pere Labat in the West Indies, 1693–1705 (London: Jarrold's, 1965), pp. 48–77.

20. C. H. Haring, *The Buccaneers in the West Indies in the XVII Century* (London: Methuen, 1910), p. 66–70; Immanuel Wallerstein, *The Modern World System II: Mercantilism and the Consolidation of the European World Economy, 1600–1750* (New York: Academic Press, 1980), pp. 157–61.

21. Esquemeling (1893), *The Buccaneers of America*, pp. 58–61; Robert F. Marx, *Pirate Port: The Story of the Sunken City of Port Royal* (London: Pelham Books, 1968), pp. 11–12, 66–70; Clinton V. Black, *The Pirates of the West Indies* (Cambridge: Cambridge University Press, 1989), p. 18.

22. These paragraphs draw on B. R. Burg, *Sodomy and the Pirate Tradition: English Sea-Rovers in the Seventeenth-Century Caribbean* (New York: New York University Press, 1984), pp. 128–31; Haring, *Buccaneers in the West Indies*, p. 69; Marcus Rediker, *Between the Devil and the Deep Blue Sea: Merchant Seamen, Pirates, and the Anglo-American World, 1700–1750*, pp. 255, 274–75; Cordingly, *Under the Black Flag*, p. 105; P. K. Kemp and C. Lloyd, *The Brethren of the Coast* (London: Heinemann, 1960); C. M. Senior, *A Nation of Pirates: English Piracy in its Heyday* (New York: Crane, Russak, 1976), p. 48; Arthur L. Hayward, ed., *Lives of the Most Remarkable Criminals* (New York, 1927 reprint), p. 37; S. Charles Hill, "Episodes of Piracy in Eastern Waters," *Indian Antiquary* 49 (1920): 37. Le Golif's account is *Memoirs of a Buccaneer*, pp. 87–110, while the quotation on pirate courts and law comes from Johnson, *History of the Pyrates*, p. 222. For accounts of prison sexuality, see the survey on research in William Simon and John Gagnon, *Sexual Conduct* (Chicago: Aldine, 1973), pp. 235–49, as well as the older study, J. F. Fishman, *Sex in Prison* (London: John Lane, 1935).

23. [Le Golif] *Memoirs of a Buccaneer*, pp. 37–53.

24. Rediker, *Between the Devil and the Deep Blue Sea*, pp. 254–87, with quotation from Barnaby Slush on p. 287. For the egalitarian order of buccaneers see, as well, Johnson, *History of the Pyrates*, pp. 88–89, 117, 139, 145, 195, 214, 222, 352, 423; Esquemeling, *Buccaneers of America*, p. 58; Haring, *Buccaneers of the West Indies*, p. 73.

25. Paul Avrich, *The Haymarket Tragedy* (Princeton: Princeton University Press, 1984), p. 56. Note, as well, the essay "Life under the Death's Head: Anarchism and Piracy," by Gabriel Kuhn in Ulrike Klausmann, Marion Meinzerin, and Gabriel Kuhn, *Women Pirates and the Politics of the Jolly Roger* (Montreal: Black Rose, 1997), pp. 255–79.

26. On social banditry, see Eric J. Hobsbawm, *Primitive Rebels: Studies in Archaic Forms of Social Movements in the 19th and 20th Centuries* (Manchester: Manchester University Press, 1959), esp. pp. 5–28; Hobsbawm, *Bandits* (Harmondsworth: Penguin, 1969), pp. 13–31. Note, as well, the discussion in Christopher Hill, *Liberty Against the Law: Some Seventeenth-Century Controversies* (London: Allen Lane, 1996).

27. See C. M. Senior, *A Nation of Pirates: English Piracy in its Heyday* (New York: Crane, Russak, 1976), p. 29. One unwilling crew member described the pirate lifestyle: "Prodigious drinking, monstrous cursing, hideous blasphemies and open defiance of Heaven and contempt of Hell itself was the constant employment, unless when sleep sometimes abated the noise and revelings" (quoted in Lucie-Smith, *Outcasts of the Sea*, p. 199).

28. These three paragraphs draw on evidence in the following, although the admittedly contentious interpretation around the pirate "nation" is my own: Haring, *Buccaneers in the West Indies*, p. 274; Senior, *A Nation of Pirates*, pp. 30–31,

48–77; Eric Williams, *From Columbus to Castro: The History of the Caribbean, 1492–1969* (London: Andre Deutsch, 1970), p. 83; Ritchie, *Captain Kidd*, p. 232; Rediker, *Between the Devil and the Deep Blue Sea*, pp. 254–57. On the pirate flag, note the brief discussion in Cordingly, *Under the Black Flag*, pp. 114–19, and in Rediker, *Between the Devil and Deep Blue Sea*, pp. 279–281, who concludes, "the consciousness of kind never took national shape." I am using "nation" more metaphorically and less precisely.

29. On these ideas, note Christopher Hill, *The World Turned Upside Down: Radical Ideas During the English Revolution* (New York: Viking Press, 1972); and the essay on pirates in Hill, *Liberty Against the Law*, pp. 110–22.

30. Hill, "Radical Pirates?" pp. 17–32; Rediker, *Between the Devil and the Deep Blue Sea*, pp. 267–69.

31. Hill, "Radical Pirates?" esp. pp. 18–19, 27–28; Johnson, *History of the Pyrates*, pp. 383–439, with quotations from pp. 417, 426–27, 435, 437; Eric R. Wolf, *Europe and the People Without History* (Berkeley: University of California Press, 1982), p. 155; Auguste Toussaint, *History of the Indian Ocean* (Chicago: University of Chicago Press, 1966), p. 146.

32. Burg, *Sodomy and the Pirate Tradition*. For an introductory overview on women and pirates, see Jo Stanley, *Bold in Her Breeches: Women Pirates across the Ages* (San Francisco: Harper, 1995).

33. See Burg, *Sodomy and the Pirate Tradition*, pp. 80–84, 112–21; Senior, *A Nation of Pirates*, pp. 38–39, 57; [Le Golif] *Memoirs of a Buccaneer*; Lucie-Smith, *Outcasts of the Sea*, 197–200; Johnson, *History of the Pyrates*, pp. 156–65, 428, 623–26; Cordingly, *Under the Black Flag*, pp. 56–78; Hill, "Radical Pirates?" pp. 19, 27. On divorce among the pirates, see also J. H. Lefroy, *Memorials of the Discovery and Early Settlement of the Bermudas or Somers Islands, 1515–1685* (London: Longmans Green, 1877), pp. 2, 46, 100, 197–98, 224–25. For radical endorsement of polygamy and embrace of its freedoms, see Christopher Hill, *Milton and the English Revolution* (London: Faber & Faber, 1977), pp. 136–39.

34. On Read and Bonny, as well as other women, see Klausmann, Meinzerin and Kuhn, *Women Pirates and the Politics of the Jolly Roger*, pp. 163–223. For an overstated argument on lesbianism, see Susan Baker, "Ann Bonny and Mary Read," in Nancy Myron and Charlotte Bauch, eds., *Women Remembered: A Collection of Biographies* (Berlin: Erinnerungen an Frauen, 1977).

35. This paragraph draws on material in Cordingly, *Under the Black Flag*, pp. 194–240; and Rediker, *Between the Devil and the Deep Blue Sea*, pp. 281–87.

36. For pirate marooning, see Black, *Pirates of the West Indies*, pp. 15–16; George Woodbury, *The Great Days of Piracy in the West Indies* (New York: W. W. Norton, 1951), p. 130; Cordingly, *Under the Black Flag*, pp. 100, 135–40. On the linguistic origins of the terminology of slave runaways as maroons, see Richard Price, *The Guiana Maroons: A Historical and Bibliographical Introduction* (Baltimore: Johns Hopkins University Press, 1976), pp. 2–3; E. Kofi Agorsah, ed., *Maroon Heritage: Archaelogical, Ethnographic, and Historical Perspectives* (Kingston, Jamaica: Canoe Press, 1994), pp. 2, 89. For pirate–maroon connections, see Richard Price, ed., *Maroon Societies: Rebel Slave Communities in the Americas* (Garden City: Anchor, 1973), pp. 14, 55–57; Peter H. Wood, *Black Majority: Negroes in Colonial South Carolina from 1670 through the Stono Rebellion* (New York: W. W. Norton, 1974), p. 52; Violet Barbour, "Privateers and Pirates of the West Indies," *American Historical Review* 16 (1911): 564; Michael Craton, *Testing the*

Chains: Resistance to Slavery in the British West Indies (Ithaca: Cornell University Press, 1982), p. 64.

37. See Gwendolyn Midlo Hall, *Social Control in Slave Plantation Societies: A Comparison of St Domingue and Cuba* (Baltimore: Johns Hopkins University Press, 1971), p. 62.

38. As an introduction to maroon societies, see Eugene D. Genovese, *From Rebellion to Revolution: Afro-American Slave Revolts in the Making of the Modern World* (Baton Rouge: Louisiana State University Press, 1979), pp. 51–81; and the excellent collection, Price, ed., *Maroon Societies*. See also Herbert Aptheker, "Maroons within the Present Limits of the United States," *Journal of Negro History* 24 (1939): 167–84. Slave flight is treated in Gerald W. Mullin, *Flight and Rebellion: Slave Resistance in Eighteenth-Century Virginia* (New York: Oxford University Press, 1972); John Hope Franklin and Loren Schweninger, *Runaway Slaves: Rebels on the Plantation* (New York: Oxford University Press, 1999).

39. On the Seminole maroons and their wars, see Kenneth W. Porter, "Florida Slaves and Free Negroes in the Seminole War, 1835–1842," *Journal of Southern History* 30 (1964): 427–50; Porter, "Relations Between Negroes and Indians Within the Present Limits of the United States," *Journal of Negro History* 17 (July 1932): 287–367; and Porter, *The Black Seminoles: History of a Freedom-Seeking People* (Gainesville: University Press of Florida, 1996), revised and edited by Alcione M. Amos and Thomas P. Senter; John W. Blassingame, *The Slave Community: Plantation Life in the Ante-Bellum South* (New York: Oxford University Press, 1972), pp. 121–24; Michael Paul Rogin, *Fathers and Children: Andrew Jackson and the Subjugation of the American Indian* (New Brunswick, N.J.: Transaction, 1991). There is an oddly climactic deterministic suggestion about the Seminole maroons in Carl N. Degler, *Neither Black nor White: Slavery and Race Relations in Brazil and the United States* (New York: Macmillan, 1971), pp. 51–52. For a general account of Indian–slave relations, see William S. Willis, "Divide and Rule: Red, White, and Black in the Southeast," *Journal of Negro History* 48 (July 1963): 157–76.

40. The literature on the Jamaican maroons is extensive; see Mavis C. Campbell, *The Maroons of Jamaica: A History of Resistance, Collaboration, and Betrayal* (Granby, Mass.: Bergin & Garvey, 1988).

41. Vic Reid, *Nanny Town* (Kingston: Jamaica Publishing House, 1983), p. 38, quoted in Carolyn Cooper, "'Resistance Science': Afrocentric Ideology in Vic Reid's *Nanny Town*," in Agorsah, ed., *Maroon Heritage*, p. 110. This edited collection contains the best ethnographic and anthropological introduction to aspects of surviving maroon culture in Jamaica, including the historical background of maroons, their distinct cultures, and their heritages of music and warfare. See, as well, the anthropological account of a surviving maroon community in Katherine Dunham, *Journey to Accompong* (New York: Henry Holt, 1946).

42. On polygamy and European distaste, see Price, ed., *Maroon Societies*, pp. 19, 241, 346–47, 354, which quotes at one point a disdainful depiction published in Bryan Edwards, *Observations on the Disposition, Character, Manners, and Habits of Life of the Maroon Negroes of the Island of Jamaica...* (1807).

43. I have drawn liberally on the exciting arguments in Cooper, "'Resistance Science': Afrocentric Ideology in Vic Reid's *Nanny Town*," and Kamu Brathwaite, "Nanny, Palmares, and the Caribbean Maroon Connexion," both in Agorsah,

ed., *Maroon Heritage*, pp. 109–39. The Brathwaite essay presents a strong statement on mythologizing Nanny, especially with respect to the buttocks and
bullets story (pp. 120–22). For an example of historical reproduction of this
lore, see Michael Craton, *Testing the Chains: Resistance to Slavery in the British West
Indies*, p. 81. I have drawn the quoted poetry from the Cooper essay, pp. 113–
14, which draws on Louise Bennett, "Jamaica Oman," in *Selected Poems*, ed.
Mervyn Morris (Kingston: Sangster's 1982), pp. 21–22; Laura Goodison,
"Nanny," in *I Am Becoming My Mother* (London: New Beacon Books, 1986), pp.
44–45. For other brief statements on maroon women, see Lucille Mathurin
Mair, *The Rebel Woman in the British West Indies under Slavery* (Kingston: Institute of
Jamaica, 1975), and Alan Tuelon, "Maroon Chieftainess," *Caribbean Quarterly* 19
(December 1973): 20–27.

44. Genovese, *From Rebellion to Revolution*, p. 63; Craton, *Testing the Chains*, p. 65; and
on Saint Domingue: Caroyn E. Frick, *The Making of Haiti: The Saint Domingue
Revolution from Below* (Knoxville: University of Tennessee Press, 1990); C. L. R.
James, *The Black Jacobins: Toussaint L'Ouvertre and the San Domingo Revolution* (New
York: Vintage, 1963). On Surinam, Captain John Gabriel Stedman, *Narrative of
a Five Years Expedition Against the Revolted Negroes of Surinam* (Amherst: University of
Massachusetts Press, 1971), has a highly useful abridgement; Richard Price
and Sally Price, eds., *Stedman's Surinam: Life in an Eighteenth-Century Slave Society*
(Baltimore: Johns Hopkins University Press, 1992); and for an invaluable
guide to the published material, with a strong introduction, see Richard
Price, ed., *The Guiana Maroons: A Historical and Biographical Introduction* (Baltimore:
Johns Hopkins University Press, 1976). Genovese, *From Rebellion to Revolution*,
pp. 139–66, contains a useful bibliographic essay, while other contexts are
covered in Price, ed., *Maroon Societies*, and Bernard A. Marshall, "Maroonage
in Slave Plantation Societies: A Case Study of Dominica, 1785–1815," *Caribbean
Quarterly* 22 (June–September 1976): 26–32.

45. Kamau Brathwaite, "9 Veridian—for GrandeeNanny," in "Nanny, Palmares
and the Caribbean Maroon Connexion," in Agorsah, ed., *Maroon Heritage*,
p. 134.

46. See the discussion in Ariel Dorfman, *The Empire's Old Clothes: What the Lone Ranger,
Babar, and Other Innocent Heroes Do to Our Minds* (New York: Pantheon, 1983).

47. For a treatment of this complicated process as it relates to West Indian
cricket, see the imaginatively engaging account in C. L. R. James, *Beyond a
Boundary* (New York: Pantheon, 1983).

Chapter 10

1. E. P. Thompson, *The Making of the English Working Class* (Harmondsworth: Penguin,
1980), p. 458.

2. See Marcel van der Linden, ed., *Social Security Mutualism: The Comparative History
of Mutual Benefit Societies* (Bern: Peter Lang, 1996), a huge volume that contains
twenty-eight essays organized into an introduction, a concluding account of
international dimensions, and treatment of the following regions: Anglo-
Saxon world; southern Europe; central and eastern Europe; western and
northern Europe; Asia and Latin America.

3. On the Masonic stress on antiquity (in which the Order was traced to Adam

and Eve, dated with the building of King Solomon's Temple), see Lynn Dumenil, *Freemasonry and American Culture, 1880–1930* (Princeton: Princeton University Press, 1984), p. 33.

4. For a statement on Ireland, see John Campbell, "Friendly Societies in Ireland, 1800–1980," in van der Linden, ed., *Social Security Mutualism*, pp. 65–82.

5. Freemasonry is perhaps an exception to this generalization, having deeper and more oppositional political roots in the upheavals predating the Age of Revolution, particularly those of seventeenth-century England. See the excellent study by Margaret C. Jacob, *Living the Enlightenment: Freemasonry and Politics in Eighteenth-Century Europe* (New York: Oxford University Press, 1991).

6. Rowland Berthoff, *An Unsettled People: Social Order and Disorder in American History* (New York: Harper & Row, 1971), pp. 444–56. For discussion of the mutual benefit society and fraternalism in the "white settler" dominions and the United States, see the accounts on the United States, Canada, Australia, and New Zealand in van der Linden, ed., *Social Security Mutualism*, pp. 83–206.

7. *Rules of the Independent Order of Oddfellows, Manchester Unity Friendly Society* (Chorlton-upon-Medlock: Odd Fellows, 1879), p. 3.

8. Jacob, *Living the Enlightenment*, pp. 13–14.

9. James L. Ridgely, *The Odd-Fellows Pocket Companion: A Correct Guide to All Matters Relating to Odd-Fellowship* (Cincinnati: Odd Fellows, 1867), pp. 44–45; Rev. A. B. Gosh, *The Odd Fellows Improved Pocket Manual* (Cincinnati: Odd Fellows, 1867), pp. 44–45; Ancient Order of United Workmen, *Ritual* (n.p., n.d.), p. 29.

10. John R. Gillis, *Youth and History: Tradition and Change in European Age Relations, 1770–the Present* (New York: Academic Press, 1981), p. 80; Margaret C. Jacob, *Living the Enlightenment*, p. 8.

11. These paragraphs draw on many sources. At the broadest and most general level, Wilson Carey McWilliams's *The Idea of Fraternity in America* (Berkeley: University of California Press, 1973) introduces issues that are now being dealt with in more detail by social historians. Ritual's importance is addressed in E. J. Hobsbawm, *Primitive Rebels: Studies in Archaic Forms of Social Movement in the 19th and 20th Centuries* (Manchester: Manchester University Press, 1959), pp. 150–74, the quotation on initiation is from p. 158. The most detailed account of masonic rituals in the late nineteenth century appears in Dumenil, *Freemasonry and American Culture*, pp. 32–73, from which I have drawn liberally. Note, as well, Darryl Jean-Guy Newbury, "'No Atheist, Eunuch or Woman': Male Associational Culture and Working-Class Identity in Industrializing Ontario, 1840–1880" (MA thesis, Queen's University, 1992), pp. 51–101, esp. pp. 76–79; Mary Ann Clawson, "Nineteenth-Century Women's Auxiliaries and Fraternal Orders," *Signs* 12 (Autumn 1986): 53.

12. For a more sustained argument relating to Canada, see Bryan D. Palmer, "Mutuality and the Masking/Making of Difference: Mutual Benefit Societies in Canada, 1850–1950," in van der Linden, ed., *Social Security Mutualism*, pp. 111–46.

13. Jno Ervin, Jr., *The Manchester Unity of Oddfellows Friendly Benefit Society* (Halifax, N.S.: Oddfellows, 1870), p. 35.

14. On the process of family formation alluded to here, see Wally Seccombe's discussion of the mature proletarian household in Seccombe, "Marxism and Demography," *New Left Review* 137 (January–February 1983), pp. 44–47.

15. Obviously the fraternal order crossed class lines, and nothing in this chapter

is meant to suggest that the friendly society was a uniquely working-class institution. Studies that lay stress on the middle-class character of the lodge include D. H. Doyle, "The Functions of Voluntary Associations in a Nineteenth-Century American Town," *Social Science History* 1 (September 1977): 333–58; Roy Rosenzweig, "Boston Masons, 1900–1935: The Lower Middle-Class in a Divided Society," *Journal of Voluntary Action Research* 6 (July 1977): 119–24; Mary Ann Clawson, *Constructing Brotherhood: Class, Gender and Fraternalism* (Princeton, N.J.: Princeton University Press, 1989), pp. 176–77. No study has been able to get around the extent to which workers were a presence in virtually all fraternal orders, and in some cases their numbers were an absolute, even overwhelming, majority. See also Lynne Marks, *Revivals and Roller Rinks: Religion, Leisure, and Identity in Late Nineteenth-Century Small-Town Ontario* (Toronto: University of Toronto Press, 1996), pp. 108–16; Christopher J. Anstead, "Fraternalism in Victorian Ontario: Secret Societies and Cultural Hegemony" (PhD diss., University of Western Ontario, 1992), pp. 184–88, 376.

16. P. H. and J. H. Gosden, *The Friendly Societies in England, 1815–1875* (Manchester: Manchester University Press, 1961), p. 2.

17. David Neave, "Friendly Societies in Great Britain," in van der Linden, ed., *Social Security Mutualism*, p. 48; Hobsbawm, *Primitive Rebels*, pp. 157–60; Edith G. Firth, ed., *The Town of York, 1815–1834* (Toronto: Champlain Society, 1966), pp. 77–78; Michael S. Cross, ed., *The Workingman in the Nineteenth Century* (Toronto: Oxford University Press, 1974), p. 240; J. I. Cooper, "The Quebec Ship Labourers' Benevolent Society," *Canadian Historical Review* 30 (December 1949): 339–40; John Iliffe, "The Creation of Group Consciousness Among the Dockworkers of Dar es Salaam, 1929–1950," in Richard Sandbrook and Robin Cohen, eds., *The Development of an African Working Class: Studies in Class Formation and Action* (Toronto: University of Toronto Press, 1975), p. 55.

18. Ervin, *Manchester Unity of Oddfellows*, p. 36.

19. On Morgan, Freemasonry, and anti-Masonic fears, see Ronald Formisano and Kathleen Smith Kutolowski, "Antimasonry and Masonry: The Genesis of Protest, 1826–1827," *American Quarterly* 29 (Summer 1977): 139–65; David Brion Davis, "Some Themes of Counter–Subversion: An Analysis of Anti-Masonic, Anti-Catholic, and Anti-Mormonism Literature," *Mississippi Valley Historical Review* 47 (September 1960): 205–44; Clawson, *Constructing Brotherhood*, pp. 115–17; and for Masonry in the United States, Dumenil, *Freemasonry and American Culture*, and for an examination of the early period, Steven C. Bullock, *Revolutionary Brotherhood: Freemasonry and the Transformation of the American Social Order, 1730–1840* (Chapel Hill, University of North Carolina Press, 1996). Also note Captain William Morgan, *The Mysteries of Freemasonry* (New York: Wilson, n.d.), pp. 1–9. A series of useful documents are presented in David Brion Davis, ed., *The Fear of Conspiracy: Images of Un-American Subversion from the Revolution to the Present* (Ithaca and London: Cornell University Press, 1971), pp. 66–94, Armstrong quotation from pp. 82–83.

20. Cited in Thompson, *The Making of the English Working Class*, p. 461.

21. Bryan D. Palmer, *Working-Class Experience: Rethinking the History of Canadian Labour, 1800–1981* (Toronto: McClelland & Stewart, 1991), p. 59; *Report of the Royal Commission on the Relations of Labor and Capital in Canada*, "Ontario Evidence, Volume II" (Ottawa: Queen's Printer, 1889), p. 813.

22. *Rules of the Independent Order of Oddfellows*, p. 3.

23. David Montgomery, "Labor in the Industrial Era," in Richard B. Morris, ed., *The United States Department of Labor History of the American Worker* (Washington, D.C.: Government Printing, 1976), p. 121.

24. C. S. Davies, *History of Macclesfield* (Manchester, 1961), p. 180, quoted in Thompson, *The Making of the English Working Class*, p. 461.

25. Quoted in Bryan D. Palmer, *A Culture in Conflict: Skilled Workers and Industrial Capitalism in Hamilton, Ontario, 1860–1914* (Kingston: McGill–Queen's University Press, 1979), p. 43. See, as well, James P. Cannon, "A Fraternal Order for the U.S. Workers," MS. [1927?] in Cannon Files, Prometheus Research Library, New York.

26. Henry Leonard Stillson, *The History and Literature of Oddfellowship: The Three-Link Fraternity* (Boston, 1897), p. 49; W. J. Morris, *Pocket Lexicon of Canadian Freemasonry* (Perth: Courrier, 1889), p. 36; W. W. Dodge, *The Fraternal and Modern Banquet Orator* (Chicago, 1903); *Constitution for the Government of the Grand Legion of Ontario Select Knights of the A.O.U.W. and Subordinate Legions Under its Jurisdiction* (London, 1886), quoted in Newbury, "'No Atheist, Eunuch or Woman'," p. 69; Cecil J. Houston and William J. Smyth, *The Sash Canada Wore: A Historical Geography of the Orange Order in Canada* (Toronto: University of Toronto Press, 1980), p. 151; Carl Berger, *The Sense of Power: Studies in the Ideas of Canadian Imperialism, 1867–1914* (Toronto: University of Toronto Press, 1970), pp. 134–35.

27. Alvin J. Schmidt and Nicholas Babchuk, "The Unbrotherly Brotherhood: Discrimination in Fraternal Orders," *Phylon* 34 (Fall 1973): 276; Edward Nelson Palmer, "Negro Secret Societies," *Social Forces* 23 (December 1944): 208–10; Simon Cordery, "Fraternal Orders in the United States: A Quest for Protection and Identity," in van der Linden, ed., *Social Security Mutualism*, pp. 87–90; Chuen-Yan Lai, "The Chinese Consolidated Benevolent Association in Victoria," *BC Studies* 15 (1972): 53–67.

28. On women's auxiliaries, see the account in Clawson, *Constructing Brotherhood*, pp. 178–210.

29. See the early comment on the gendered nature of fraternalism in Noel Gist, "Secret Societies: A Cultural Study of Fraternalism in the United States," *University of Missouri Studies* 15 (October 1940): esp. p. 40. Note Michael Carnes, *Secret Ritual and Manhood in Victorian America* (New Haven: Yale University Press, 1989); Clawson, *Constructing Brotherhood*; and the brief statement in Marks, *Revivals and Roller Rinks*, pp. 108–16, which is perhaps overly blunt. On the antiquated masculinism of the Masons, see Henry Robertson, *A Digest of Masonic Jurisprudence, Especially Applicable to Canadian Lodges* (Toronto: Hunter Rose, 1889), p. 57, and William Nicholls, *Jachin and Boaz; or, An Authentic Key to the Door of Freemasonry, both Ancient and Modern* (London, 1797), p. 9, both quoted in Newbury, "'No Atheist, Eunuch, or Woman'," pp. 83, 85. The quoted lines of verse are from The English Workingman's Benefit Society, *Presentations on May 21 (Whitsun Monday)* (Montreal, 1866), p. 7.

30. Clawson, *Constructing Brotherhood*, pp. 211–42; David M. Smith, "'The Best Game on Earth': The Transformation of the Independent Order of Foresters, 1874–1905" (MA thesis, Queen's University, 1996).

31. See Palmer, "Mutuality and the Masking/Making of Difference," in van der Linden, ed., *Social Security Mutualism*, pp. 138–46; Lizabeth Cohen, *Making a New*

16. Catherine LeGrand, "Living in Macondo: Economy and Culture in a United Fruit Company Banana Enclave (Santa Marta, Colombia, 1890–1930)," MS., 1995; Lauren Derby, "Haitians, Magic, and Money: Raza and Society in the Haitian–Dominican Borderlands, 1900 to 1937," Comparative Studies in Society and History 36 (1994): 520; Nancie L. Gonzalez, "The Christian Palestinians of Honduras: An Uneasy Accommodation," in Nancie L. Gonzalez and Carolyn S. McCommon, eds., Conflict, Migration, and the Expression of Ethnicity (Boulder: Westview Press, 1989), p. 79.

17. For critiques of Michael T. Taussig's The Devil and Commodity Fetishism in South America, see the summary of sources cited in Edelman, "Landlords and the Devil." See, as well, William Rowe and Vivian Schelling, Memory and Modernity: Popular Culture in Latin America (London: Verso, 1991), esp. pp. 63, 72–73.

18. Quote from Taussig, Devil and Commodity Fetishism, p. 18. Taussig has recently presented a revised interpretation, drawing less on Marx and more on Bataille and Nietzsche. See Michael Taussig, "The Sun Gives Without Receiving: An Old Story," Comparative Studies in Society and History 37 (1995): 368–98.

19. As background, see Catherine LeGrand, Frontier Expansion and Peasant Protest in Colombia, 1830–1938 (Albuquerque: University of New Mexico Press, 1986).

20. Eric J. Hobsbawm, "Peasant Movements in Colombia," International Journal of Economic and Social History 8 (1976): 166–86; Hobsbawm, Age of Extremes: The Short Twentieth Century, 1914–1991 (London: Michael Joseph, 1994), p. 290; Hobsbawm, Bandits (New York: Dell, 1969), p. 59; Taussig, Devil and Commodity Fetishism, p. 86.

21. Taussig, Devil and Commodity Fetishism, pp. 96–97, 109–11.

22. This is not unrelated to the Colombian peasantry's adaptation to the international cocaine trade. See Hobsbawm, Age of Extremes, p. 366; Charles Bergquist, Labor in Latin America: Comparative Essays on Chile, Argentina, Venezuela, and Colombia (Stanford: Stanford University Press, 1986), pp. 369–70. Note the cryptic entry under the title "Cocaine" in Taussig, "The Sun Gives Without Receiving," pp. 385–86, where a gruesome story of cocaine transport is told by a peasant proprietor. On the notion of "hidden transcripts," see James C. Scott, Domination and the Arts of Resistance: Hidden Transcripts (New Haven: Yale University Press, 1990), and, for an earlier statement, Scott, Weapons of the Weak: Everyday Forms of Peasant Resistance (New Haven: Yale University Press, 1985).

23. Consider, for instance, the discussion of another Bolivian context in Olivia Harris, "The Dead and the Devils among the Bolivian Laymi," in Maurice Bloch and Jonathan Parry, eds., Death and the Regeneration of Life (Cambridge: Cambridge University Press, 1982), pp. 45–73.

24. On the miners' history and traditions see, among other sources, June Nash, "The Devil in Bolivia's Nationalized Tin Mines," Science and Society 36 (1972): esp. 221–24; Nash, We Eat the Mines and the Mines Eat Us: Dependency and Exploitation in Bolivian Tin Mines (New York: Columbia University Press, 1979), esp. pp. 1–56; Herbert Klein, Parties and Political Change in Bolivia, 1880–1952 (Cambridge: Cambridge University Press, 1969).

25. Taussig has recently suggested, drawing on Friedrich Nietzsche's Twilight of the Idols (or How to Philosophize with a Hammer) (Harmondsworth: Penguin, 1990), that the devil as a Great Imitator does not "give without receiving." See Taussig, "The Sun Gives Without Receiving," p. 397.

26. The preceding paragraphs draw on the rich accounts in Nash, "The Devil in Bolivia's Tin Mines," pp. 221–33; Nash, We Eat the Mines; Nash, ed., I Spent My Life in the Mines: The Story of Juan Rojas, Bolivian Tin Miner (New York: Columbia University Press, 1992), esp. pp. 236–40; Taussig, Devil and Commodity Fetishism, pp. 168, 181.

27. This reading is different from but draws on Nash, We Eat the Mines, pp. 155–69; Taussig, The Devil and Commodity Fetishism, esp. pp. 211–13.

28. Americo Parades, Folktales of Mexico (Chicago: University of Chicago Press, 1970); Edelman, "Landlords and the Devil," p. 58.

29. See the thorough discussion in Nash, We Eat the Mines, pp. 125–46.

30. Dale Tomich, "Liberté ou Mort: Republicanism and Slave Revolt in Martinique, February 1831," History Workshop Journal 29 (Spring 1990): 89–91.

31. Note the rich treatment in John Cowley, Carnival, Canboulay, and Calypso Traditions in the Making (Cambridge: Cambridge University Press, 1996).

32. On the violent potential of carnival, note the discussion in Daniel Touro Linger, Dangerous Encounters: Meanings of Violence in a Brazilian City (Stanford: Stanford University Press, 1992). A recent ethnography of Latino machismo presents a more benign reading. See Matthew C. Gutmann, The Meanings of Macho: Being a Man in Mexico City (Berkeley: University of California Press, 1996).

33. The above quotes and perspective are drawn from Susan Campbell, "Carnival, Calypso, and Class Struggle: Nineteenth Century Trinidad," History Workshop Journal 26 (Autumn 1988): 1–27.

34. Linger, Dangerous Encounters, p. 81.

35. Nancy Scheper-Hughes, Death without Weeping: The Violence of Everyday Life in Brazil (Berkeley: University of California Press, 1992), p. 504; Linger, Dangerous Encounters, p. 98.

36. Note, as well, the discussion of the carnivalesque and of New Orleans Mardi Gras in the 1870s in Christopher Benfey, Degas in New Orleans: Encounters in the Creole World of Kate Chopin and George Washington Cable (New York: Knopf, 1997), pp. 171–93.

37. Lee Palmer Wandel, Voracious Idols and Violent Hands: Iconoclasm in Reformation Zurich, Strasbourg, and Basel (Cambridge: Cambridge University Press, 1995), pp. 176–81.

38. Emmanuel Le Roy Ladurie, Carnival in Romans: A People's Uprising at Romans, 1579–1580 (New York: Penguin, 1979).

39. J. Paul Getty Museum, Handbook of the Collections (Malibu: Getty Museum, 1991), p. 128.

40. Rowe and Schelling, Memory and Modernity, esp. pp. 131–37. The most obvious inversion, that of transvestism, is central to Brazilian carnival. See Linger, Dangerous Encounters, and Scheper-Hughes, Death Without Weeping, pp. 480–504.

41. Roberto DeMatta, "Carnival in Multiple Planes," in John J. MacAloon, ed., Rite, Drama, Festival, Spectacle: Rehearsals Toward a Theory of Cultural Performance (Philadelphia: Institute for the Study of Human Issues, 1984), pp. 208–40; Victor Turner, "Carnival in Rio: Dionysian Drama in an Industrializing Society," in Turner, The Anthropology of Performance (New York: Cambridge University Press, 1986), pp. 123–38.

42. For a description of a carnivalesque religious festival among Australian aboriginal peoples that stresses the significance of night, torchlit processions and dance, see Émile Durkheim's 1912 text The Elementary Forms of the Religious

Life (New York: Free Press, 1965), p. 249, quoted in Linger, *Dangerous Encounters*, p. 51.

43. George Lipsitz, "Mardi Gras Indians: Carnival and Counter-Narrative in Black New Orleans," in *Time Passages: Collective Memory and American Popular Culture* (Minneapolis: University of Minnesota Press, 1990), p. 242.

44. Samuel Charters, *The Roots of Blues: An African Search* (London: Macmillan, 1981), pp. 68–69; Jason Berry, Jonathan Foose, and Tad Jones, *Up From the Cradle of Jazz: New Orleans Music Since World War II* (Athens: University of Georgia Press, 1986), pp. 203–39.

45. Rowe and Schelling, *Memory and Modernity*, pp. 66, 89–91.

46. This is not, of course, the only way to interpret the developing relations of locale and capitalism's global reach. For an assessment that stresses the capacity of indigenous peasant cultures to resist wage labor and shift the relational boundaries of political economy, see Carol A. Smith, "Local History in Global Context: Social and Economic Transitions in Western Guatemala," *Comparative Studies in Society and History* 26 (1984):193–228.

47. Derby, "Haitians, Magic, and Money," esp. pp. 516–26. For more on the 1937 *El Masacre*, see Thomas Fiehrer, "Political Violence in the Periphery: The Haitian Massacre of 1937," *Race and Class* 32 (October–December 1990): 1–20; Michael Malek, "The Dominican Republic's General Rafael L. M. Trujillo and the Haitian Massacre of 1937: A Case of Subversion in Inter-Caribbean Relations," *Secolas Annals* 11 (March 1980): 137–55. Arcahaie and zombies are discussed in Zora Neale Hurston, *Tell My Horse: Voodoo and Life in Haiti and Jamaica* (New York: Harper & Row, 1990), pp. 139–78; Wade Davis, *Passage of Darkness: The Ethnobiology of the Haitian Zombie* (Chapel Hill: University of North Carolina Press, 1988). For a novel set in New York that draws on this Haitian experience, see Andrew Vachss, *Sacrifice* (New York: Knopf, 1991). Excellent histories and anthropologies of Haiti, offering much useful comment on voodoo, include Carolyn E. Fick, *The Making of Haiti: The Saint Domingue Revolution from Below* (Knoxville: University of Tennessee Press, 1992); Joan Dayan, *Haiti, History, and the Gods* (Berkeley: University of California Press, 1998).

48. See Peter Worsley, *The Trumpet Shall Sound: A Study of "Cargo" Cults in Melanesia* (London: Paladin, 1970); Charles Van Onselen, *Chibaro: African Mine Labour in Southern Rhodesia, 1900–1933* (London: Pluto Press, 1980), pp. 177–78, 197–98. Note, as well, the discussion of witchcraft in June Nash, *In the Eyes of the Ancestors: Belief and Behavior in a Maya Community* (New Haven: Yale University Press, 1970).

49. Jacques Chevalier, *Civilization and the Stolen Gift: Capital, Kin, and Cult in Eastern Peru* (Toronto: University of Toronto Press, 1982), esp. pp. 377–430, quotations from pp. 411, 423; J. Siskind, *To Hunt in the Morning* (London: Oxford University Press, 1973), p. 147.

50. Karl Marx, "The Future Results of the British Rule in India" [1853], in Marx and Engels, *Collected Works, Volume 12: 1853–1854* (New York: International, 1979), quoted in the concluding sentence of Chevalier, *Civilization and the Stolen Gift*, p. 430; Aijaz Ahmad, *In Theory: Classes, Nations, Literatures* (London: Verso, 1992), pp. 221–42. For an overly critical engagement with Ahmad, see the review by Benita Perry in *History Workshop Journal* 36 (Autumn 1993): 232–42. Consider, as well, many of the essays in Jean Chesneaux, *Pasts and Futures or What is*

History For? (London: Thames & Hudson, 1976), esp. "Pre-Capitalist Societies: Have They a Common Past?" and "Capitalism: the Great Unifier of History," pp. 73–82.

51. Maurice Godelier, *The Mental and the Material: Thought Economy and Society* (London: Verso, 1986), p. 168.

Chapter 13

1. George Lestey [Lesly], "Lament of the Sodomites" (1675), in Paul Hallam, *The Book of Sodom* (London: Verso, 1993), p. 142.

2. Lauren Derby, "Haitians, Magic, and Money: *Raza* and Society in the Haitian–Dominican Borderlands, 1900 to 1937," *Comparative Studies in Society and History* 36 (1994): 519.

3. June Nash, *We Eat the Mines and the Mines Eat Us: Dependency and Exploitation in Bolivian Tin Mines* (New York: Columbia University Press, 1979), p. 141.

4. On the "mine marriage," see T. Dunbar Moodie with Vivienne Ndatshe, *Going for Gold: Men, Mines, and Migration* (Witwatersrand: Witwatersrand University Press, 1994), pp. 121–58; Moodie (with Vivienne Ndatshe and British Sibuyi), "Migrancy and Male Sexuality on the South African Gold Mines," in Martin Bauml Duberman, Martha Vicinus, and George Chauncey, Jr., eds., *Hidden from History: Reclaiming the Gay & Lesbian Past* (New York: New American Library, 1989), pp. 411–25; Patrick Harries, "Symbols and Sexuality: Culture and Identity on the Early Witwatersrand Gold Mines," *Gender and History* 2 (1990): 329.

5. Michel Foucault, *The History of Sexuality, Volume I: Introduction* (New York: Vintage, 1980), p. 49; Leo Bersani, "The Gay Daddy," *Homos* (Cambridge, Mass.: Harvard University Press, 1995), p. 81.

6. See the discussions in David M. Halperin, *Saint Foucault: Towards a Gay Hagiography* (New York: Oxford University Press, 1995), pp. 67–68; Eve Kosofsky Sedgwick, *Tendencies* (Durham, N.C.: Duke University Press, 1993), pp. xii–xiii; Martha Vicinus, "'They Wonder to Which Sex I Belong': The Historical Roots of the Modern Lesbian Identity," in Henry Abelove, Michele Aina Barale, and David M. Halperin, eds., *The Lesbian and Gay Studies Reader* (New York: Routledge, 1993), pp. 432–52. Note, as well, two theoretical statements on representation: Annamarie Jagose, *Lesbian Utopics* (New York: Routledge, 1994), and Earl Jackson, Jr., *Strategies of Deviance: Studies in Gay Male Representation* (Bloomington: Indiana University Press, 1995). For useful comment on queer theory, see the overview by Annamarie Jagose, *Queer Theory: An Introduction* (New York: New York University Press, 1996), and Linda Nicholson and Steve Seidman, eds., *Social Postmodernism: Beyond Identity Politics* (Cambridge: Cambridge University Press, 1995), esp. Steven Seidman, "Deconstructing Queer Theory or the Under-theorization of the social and the ethical," pp. 116–41. For a review of the links of queer theory and AIDS activism, and the important statement on queer theory and its dominant paradigms of severing queer identity from specific race, class, and gender experiences, see Rosemary Hennessy, "Queer visibility in commodity culture," ibid., pp. 142–83.

7. Note the argument in Sally O'Driscoll, "Outlaw Readings: Beyond Queer Theory," *Signs* 22 (Autumn 1996): 30–51.

8. Reina Lewis, *Gendering Orientalism: Race, Femininity, and Representation* (London: Routledge, 1996), pp. 180–81; Robert Surieu, *Sarve e Naz: An Essay on Love and the Representation of Erotic Themes in Ancient Iran* (Geneva: Nagel, 1967), pp. 135–45; Arlo Karlen, *Sexuality and Homosexuality* (New York: W. W. Norton, 1971), pp. 232–33; David F. Greenberg, *The Construction of Homosexuality* (Chicago: University of Chicago Press, 1988), p. 117; citations on the *Kama Sutra* and harem lesbianism are referenced in Devagana Desai, *Erotic Sculpture of India: A Socio-Cultural Study* (New Delhi: Tala McGraw Hill, 1975), p. 172.

9. Guy Poirier, "Masculinities and Homosexualities in French Renaissance Accounts of Travel to the Middle East and North Africa," in Jacqueline Murray and Konrad Eisenbichler, eds., *Desire and Discipline: Sex and Sexuality in the Premodern West* (Toronto: University of Toronto Press, 1996), p. 157.

10. Bret Hinsch, *Passions of the Cut Sleeve: The Male Homosexual Tradition in China* (Berkeley: University of California Press, 1990), p. 2.

11. See the excellent essay "Double Consciousness in Sappho's Lyrics," in John J. Winkler, *The Constraints of Desire: The Anthropology of Sex and Gender in Ancient Greece* (New York: Routledge, 1990), pp. 162–87.

12. Winkler, *The Constraints of Desire*; Greenberg, *The Construction of Homosexuality*, pp. 184–241; Kenneth J. Dover, *Greek Homosexuality* (Cambridge, Mass.: Harvard University Press, 1978); David M. Halperin, "Sex Before Sexuality: Pederasty, Politics, and Power in Classical Athens," in Duberman et al., eds., *Hidden from History*, pp. 37–53; David M. Halperin, *One Hundred Years of Homosexuality: And Other Essays on Greek Love* (New York: Routledge, 1990); William Armstrong Percy III, *Pederasty and Pedagogy in Archaic Greece* (Urbana: University of Illinois Press, 1996); Michel Foucault, *The Use of Pleasure: The History of Sexuality, Volume II* (New York: Vintage, 1986); Richard A. Posner, *Sex and Reason* (Cambridge, Mass.: Harvard University Press, 1992), pp. 146–51.

13. See Hans Mayer, *Outsiders: A Study in Life and Letters* (Cambridge, Mass: MIT Press, 1984), pp. 143–46. He presents evidence critical of pederasty from a range of commentators beyond the usual citations from Plato, who wrote that same-sex activity "willfully contributes to the withering away of the human race, and sows the seed on rock and stone where it cannot take root and come to its natural fruition."

14. John Boswell, *Same-Sex Unions in Premodern Europe* (New York: Villard, 1994), pp. 53–107.

15. Foucault, *The Use of Pleasure*, pp. 97, 253–54; Halperin, *One Hundred Years of Homosexuality*, pp. 68–69.

16. Foucault, *The History of Sexuality, Volume I*, p. 101. For a selection from the Talmud, see Hallam, *The Book of Sodom*, pp. 105–08, which also contains the relevant biblical passages, pp. 5–12. On this biblical context, see Jonathan Goldberg, ed., *Reclaiming Sodom* (London: Routledge, 1994), particularly "Genesis: 19," pp. 25–27, and Robert Alter, "Sodom as Nexus: The Web of Design in Biblical Narrative," pp. 28–42. As Eve Kosofsky Sedgwick notes in *Epistemology of the Closet* (Berkeley: University of California Press, 1990), p. 35, the increasingly strong glare of heterosexist AIDS-phobia has focused attention on anal pleasure and its medical and metaphorical meanings. For powerful political and theoretical statements, see many of the essays in Douglas Crimp, ed., *AIDS: Cultural Analysis and Cultural Activism* (Cambridge, Mass.: MIT Press, 1989), esp. Leo Bersani, "Is the Rectum a Grave?," pp. 197–222, also

reprinted in Goldberg, *Reclaiming Sodom*, pp. 249–64; Goldberg, *Sodometries: Renaissance Texts, Modern Sexualities* (Stanford: Stanford University Press, 1992), pp. 1–26.

17. Alter, "Sodom as Nexus," p. 33.

18. John Boswell, *Christianity, Social Tolerance, and Homosexuality: Gay People in Western Europe from the Beginning of the Christian Era to the Fourteenth Century* (Chicago: University of Chicago Press, 1980), esp. pp. 269–332; R. I. Moore, *The Formation of a Persecuting Society* (Oxford: Basil Blackwell, 1987), esp. pp. 92–93; Hallam, *The Book of Sodom*, p. 109; Poirier, "Masculinities and Homosexualities in French Renaissance Accounts," pp. 123–54.

19. Gregory W. Bredbeck, *Sodomy and Interpretation: Marlowe to Milton* (Ithaca: Cornell University Press, 1991), p. 5.

20. Boswell, *Christianity, Social Tolerance, and Homosexuality*, pp. 261–64; Louise Fradenburg and Carla Freccero, eds., *Premodern Sexualities* (New York: Routledge, 1996), pp. 99–116, 153–74.

21. Steve Brown, "The Boyhood of Shakespeare's Heroines: Notes on Gender Ambiguity in the Sixteenth Century," *Studies in English Literature* 30 (1990): 243–63; Bruce R. Smith, *Homosexual Desire in Shakespeare's England* (Chicago: University of Chicago Press, 1991).

22. Alan Bray, "Homosexuality and the Signs of Male Friendship in Elizabethan England," *History Workshop Journal* 29 (Spring 1990), pp. 1–19; two useful edited collections are Kent Gerard and Gert Hekma, eds., *The Pursuit of Sodomy: Male Homosexuality in Renaissance and Enlightenment Europe* (New York: Harrington Park Press, 1988), and Jonathan Goldberg, ed., *Queering the Renaissance* (Durham, N.C.: Duke University Press, 1994). Note, as well, Greenberg, *The Construction of Homosexuality*, pp. 301–46; Joseph Cady, "'Masculine Love', Renaissance Writing and the 'New Invention' of Homosexuality," in Claude Summers, ed., *Homosexuality in Renaissance and Enlightenment England: Literary Representations in Historical Context* (New York: Haworth Press, 1992), pp. 9–40; Cady, "The 'Masculine Love' of 'The Princes of Sodom'—'Practicing the Art of Ganymede' at Henri III's Court: The Homosexuality of Henri III and his Mignons in Pierre de L'Estoile's *Memoires-Journaux*," in Murray and Eisenbichler, eds., *Desire and Discipline*, pp. 123–54; James M. Saslow, *Ganymede in the Renaissance: Homosexuality in Art and Society* (New Haven: Yale University Press, 1986); A. L. Rowse, *Homosexuals in History: A Study of Ambivalence in Society, Literature and the Arts* (New York: Macmillan, 1977), pp. 6–90; Jonathan Goldberg, "The History that Will Be," in Fradenburg and Freccero, eds., *Premodern Sexualities*, pp. 1–22.

23. B. R. Burg, *Sodomy and the Pirate Tradition: English Sea Rovers in the Seventeenth-Century Caribbean* (New York: New York University Press, 1984); Hallam, *Book of Sodom*, p. 37.

24. Greenberg, *The Construction of Homosexuality*, pp. 342–45; Joao Tevisan, *Perverts in Paradise* (London: G.M.P. 1986), pp. 47–54, 97 (other sections appear in Hallam, *The Book of Sodom*, pp. 202–03); Gary Kinsman, *The Regulation of Desire: Homo and Hetero Sexualities* (Montreal: Black Rose Books, 1996), p. 98.

25. For an introduction through a brief collection of original documents, see Mark Blasius and Shane Phelan, eds., *We Are Everywhere: A Historical Sourcebook of Gay and Lesbian Politics* (New York: Routledge, 1997), pp. 1–33.

26. Lillian Faderman, *Surpassing the Love of Men: Romantic Friendship and Love Between*

Women from the Renaissance to the Present (New York: William Morrow, 1981), esp. pp. 23–102; Valerie Traub, "The (In)Significance of 'Lesbian' Desire in Early Modern England," in Goldberg, ed., *Queering the Renaissance*, pp. 62–83; Judith C. Brown, "Lesbian Sexuality in Medieval and Early Modern Europe," in Duberman et al., eds., *Hidden from History*, pp. 67–75; Kathy Lavezzo, "Sobs and Sighs Between Women: the Homoerotics of Compassion in *The Book of Margery Kempe*," in Fradenburg and Freccero, eds., *Premodern Sexualities*, pp. 175–98.

27. James Holstun, "'Will You Rent Our Ancient Love Asunder?': Lesbian Elegy in Donne, Marvell, and Milton," *English Literary History* 54 (1987): 835–67; Harriette Andreadis, "The Sapphic Platonics of Katherine Philips, 1632–1664," *Signs* 15 (1989): 34–60; Elizabeth Harvey, "Ventiloquizing Sappho: Ovid, Donne, And the Erotics of the Feminine Voice," *Criticism* 31 (1989): 115–38; Judith Brown, *Immodest Acts: The Life of a Lesbian Nun in Renaissance Italy* (New York: Oxford University Press, 1986).

28. Stephen Greenblatt, "Fiction and Friction," in Greenblatt, *Shakespearian Negotiations: The Circulation of Social Energy in Renaissance England* (Oxford: Clarendon Press, 1988), p. 67; Ann Rosalind Jones and Peter Stallybrass, "Fetishizing Gender: Constructing the Hermaphrodite in Renaissance Europe," in Julia Epstein and Kristina Straub, eds., *Body Guards: The Cultural Politics of Gender Ambiguity* (New York: Routledge, 1991), pp. 80–111; Lorraine Daston and Katherine Park, "Hermaphrodites in Renaissance France," *Critical Matrix* 1 (1985): 1–19; Daston and Park, "The Hermaphrodite and the Orders of Nature: Sexual Ambiguity in Early Modern France," in Fradenburg and Freccero, eds., *Premodern Sexualities*, pp. 117–36; Donald Stone, Jr., "The Sexual Outlaw in France, 1605," *Journal of the History of Sexuality* 2 (1992): 597–608; Michael de Cossart, *Antonio Beccadelli and the Hermaphrodite* (Liverpool: Janus Press, 1984); on transvestism in general, Marjorie Garber, *Vested Interests: Cross-Dressing and Cultural Anxiety* (New York: Routledge, 1992), as well as the briefer statement in Garber, "The Chic of Araby: Transvestism, Transsexualism and the Erotics of Cultural Appropriation," in Epstein and Straub, eds., *Body Guards*, pp. 223–47; and on the hermaphrodite, see Thomas Laqueur, *Making Sex: Body and Gender from the Greeks to Freud* (Cambridge, Mass.: Harvard University Press, 1990), pp. 135–42.

29. Milton and Lesly quoted in Bredbeck, *Sodomy and Interpretation*, pp. 214, 218, and another passage from Lesly's *Fire and Brimstone*, "Lament of the Sodomites," appears in Hallam, *The Book of Sodom*, pp. 141–42. Note, as well, Bruce W. Holsinger, "Sodomy and Resurrection: The Homoerotic Subject of the *Divine Comedy*," in Fradenburg and Freccero, eds., *Premodern Sexualities*, pp. 243–74; and Roger Shattuck, *Forbidden Knowledge: From Prometheus to Pornography* (New York: St. Martin's Press, 1996), pp. 49–75.

30. Hallam, *The Book of Sodom*, pp. 229–32. On Marlow, see Jonathan Goldberg, "Sodomy and Society: The Case of Christopher Marlowe," *Southwest Review* 69 (1984): 371–78; Hans Mayer, "Christopher Marlow and King Edward II of England," in *Outsiders*, pp. 155–66; and Bredbeck, *Sodomy and Interpretation*.

31. Note the arguments in Jeffrey Weeks, "Sins and Disease," *History Workshop Journal* 1 (1976): 211–19; Weeks, *Coming Out: Homosexual Politics in Britain from the Nineteenth Century to the Present* (Totowa: Barnes & Noble 1977); Weeks, "Discourse, Desire, and Sexual Deviance: Some Problems in the History of Homosexuality," in Ken Plummer, ed., *The Making of the Modern Homosexual*

(London: Hutchinson, 1981); David M. Halperin, "'Homosexuality': A Cultural Construct (An Exchange with Richard Schneider)," in *One Hundred Years of Homosexuality*, pp. 41–53; Halperin, *Saint Foucault*; Robert Padgug, "Sexual Matters: Rethinking Sexuality in History," in Duberman et al., eds., *Hidden from History*, pp. 54–66; and for a parallel argument on heterosexuality, see Jonathan Ned Katz, *The Invention of Heterosexuality* (New York: Dutton, 1995).

32. For the range of sodomitical possibilities in the premodern period, see Richard Davenport-Hines, *Sex, Death, and Punishment: Attitudes to Sex and Sexuality in Britain Since the Renaissance* (London: Collins, 1990), pp. 56–104. The most accessible statements of the supposedly realist/essentialist school are John Boswell, "Revolutions, Universals, and Sexual Categories," in Duberman et al., eds., *Hidden from History*, pp. 17–36; and Cady, "The Masculine Love of the Princes of Sodom," in Murray and Eisenbichler, eds., *Desire and Discipline*, pp. 123–54. A useful compilation of texts relating to this set of interpretive positions is Edward Stein, ed., *Forms of Desire: Sexual Orientation and the Social Constructionist Controversy* (New York: Routledge, 1990).

33. Karl Marx, "The Eighteenth Brumaire of Louis Bonaparte," in Karl Marx and Friedrich Engels, *Selected Works* (Moscow: Progress, 1963), p. 97. Note Eve Kosofsky Sedgwick, *Epistemology of the Closet* (Berkeley: University of California Press, 1990), esp. pp. 44–48, and Weeks, *Invented Moralities*, p. 6.

34. See the short statement by Mary McIntosh, "The Homosexual Role," *Social Problems* 16 (1968): 182–92. Also consider the discussion of the hierarchialization of reproductive/nonreproductive sexualities in Henry Abelove, "Some Speculations on the History of 'Sexual Intercourse' during the 'Long Eighteenth Century' in England," *Genders* 6 (1989): 125–30. Blasius and Phelan, eds., *We Are Everywhere*, pp. 37–57, presents documents on this period that link sexual liberation, political speech, and the French Revolution, a set of conjunctures discussed in an earlier chapter.

35. Faderman, *Surpassing the Love of Men*, pp. 23–30, 40; Greenberg, *The Construction of Homosexuality*, pp. 320, 332; Karlen, *Sexuality and Homosexuality*, p. 142; Kristina Straub, "The Guilty Pleasures of Female Theatrical Cross Dressing and the Autobiography of Charlotte Clarke," in Epstein and Straub, eds., *Body Guards*, pp. 142–66; Theo van der Meer, "Tribades Tried: Female Same-Sex Offenders in Late Eighteenth-Century Amsterdam," *Journal of the History of Sexuality* 1 (1991): 424–45; Joan DeJean, *Fictions of Sappho, 1546–1937* (Chicago: University of Chicago Press, 1989); and aspects of the argument in Martha Vicinus, "'They Wonder to which Sex I Belong': The Historical Roots of the Modern Lesbian Identity," in Dennis Altman et al., eds., *Which Homosexuality?* (London: G.M.P., 1989), pp. 171–98. Faderman's stress on romantic friendship, while certainly valid in terms of recovering a past of woman–woman relations, needs to be supplemented with a more extensive exploration of early same-sex eroticism among women.

36. The literature on this is vast. For a bibliographic overview, see the note on sources on sodomy in Randolph Trumbach, "Erotic Fantasy and Male Libertinism in Enlightenment England," in Lynn Hunt, ed., *The Invention of Pornography: Obscenity and the Origins of Modernity, 1500–1800* (New York: Zone, 1993), pp. 253–382, with sources cited on pp. 388–90. Greenberg, *The Construction of Homosexuality*, pp. 301–46, is another overview. There is a series of important articles in Robert Purks Maccubbin, ed., *'Tis Nature's Fault: Unauthorized Sexuality*

during the Enlightenment (Cambridge: Cambridge University Press, 1995), pp. 109–91. Trumbach's work also appears in "Sodomitical Assaults, Gender Roles, and Sexual Development in Eighteenth-Century London," in Gerard and Hekma, eds., *Male Homosexuality in Renaissance and Enlightenment Europe*, pp. 407–32; "The Birth of the Queen: Sodomy and the Emergence of Gender Equality in Modern Culture, 1600–1750," in Duberman et al., eds., *Hidden from History*, pp. 129–40; "Gender and the Homosexual Role in Modern Western Culture: The Eighteenth and Nineteenth Centuries Compared," in Altman et al., eds., *Which Homosexuality?*, pp. 149–69; "Sodomy Transformed: Aristocratic Libertinage, Public Reputation, and the Gender Revolution of the Eighteenth Century," *Journal of Homosexuality* 19 (1990): 105–24.

37. Greenberg, *The Construction of Homosexuality*, p. 311, citing Luiz Mott's work on Lisbon.

38. Randolph Trumbach, "London's Sapphists: From Three Sexes to Four Genders in the Making of Modern Culture," in Epstein and Straub, eds., *Body Guards*, pp. 112–41. On theatricality and this process, see Laura Levine, *Men in Women's Clothing: Anti-theatricality and Effeminization, 1579–1642* (Cambridge: Cambridge University Press, 1994).

39. Greenberg, *The Construction of Homosexuality*, pp. 332–33; Gerald Howson, *Thief-Taker General: Jonathan Wild and the Emergence of Crime and Corruption as a Way of Life in Eighteenth-Century England* (New Brunswick: Rutgers University Press, 1970), p. 49; and Hallam, "Ned Ward: The Mollies," in *The Book of Sodom* pp. 111–14. See, as well, Michel Rey, "Police and Sodomy in Eighteenth-Century Paris: From Sin to Disorder," in Gerard and Hekma, eds., *The Pursuit of Sodomy*, pp. 129–46.

40. Lee Edelman, "The Sodomite's Tongue and the Bourgeois Body in Eighteenth-Century England," in Edelman, *Homographesis: Essays in Gay Literary and Cultural Theory* (New York: Routledge, 1994), pp. 121–28. For more discussion of the late-nineteenth-century significance of race, see Siobban Somerville, "Scientific Racism and the Emergence of the Homosexual Body," *Journal of the History of Sexuality* 5 (October 1994): 243–66. Contrast Abdul R. JanMohamed, "Sexuality on/of the Racial Border: Foucault, Wright, and the Articulation of 'Racialized Sexuality'," in Donna C. Stanton, ed., *Discourses of Sexuality: From Aristotle to AIDS* (Ann Arbor: University of Michigan Press, 1992), pp. 94–116, with Ann Laura Stoler, *Race and the Education of Desire: Foucault's History of Sexuality and the Colonial Order of Things* (Durham, N.C.: Duke University Press, 1995).

41. Foucault, *The History of Sexuality, Volume I*, p. 43. Note, as well, Greenberg, *The Construction of Homosexuality*, pp. 397–433; Katz, *The Invention of Heterosexuality*, pp. 19–32. For women and lesbians, note Lillian Faderman, "The Morbidification of Love Between Women by Nineteenth-Century Sexologists," *Journal of Homosexuality* 4 (1978): 73–90. For a brief statement, see Neil Miller, "The 'Invention' of Homosexuality," in Miller, *Out of the Past: Gay and Lesbian History from 1869 to the Present* (New York: Vintage, 1995), pp. xvii–xxv. Miller also contains a useful introductory statement on early sexology, pp. 13–28. This is a subject introduced with original documents, counter-proposals from the late-nineteenth-century world of Whitman and Carpenter, and the British medicalization of "inversion" in Blasius and Phelan, eds., *We Are Everywhere*, pp. 63–131, 179–93.

42. Note the arguments in two essays by George Chauncey, "From Sexual

Inversion to Homosexuality: Medicine and the Changing Conceptualization of Female Deviance," *Salmagundi* 58–59 (Fall–Winter 1982–1983): 114–46, and "Christian Brotherhood or Sexual Perversion? Homosexual Identities and the Construction of Sexual Boundaries in the World War I Era," *Journal of Social History* 19 (1985): 189–211.

43. For women, see Faderman, *Surpassing the Love of Men*, pp. 103–89; Carroll Smith-Rosenberg, "The Female World of Love and Ritual: Relations between Women in Nineteenth-Century America," *Signs* 1 (1975): 1–29; and for men, aspects of the aestheticism delineated in Robert K. Martin, "Knights-Errant and Gothic Seducers: The Representation of Male Friendship in Mid-Nineteenth-Century America," and Martha Vicinus, "Distance and Desire: English Boarding School Friendships, 1870–1920," in Duberman et al., eds., *Hidden From History*, pp. 169–82, 212–31. On Whitman, see Miller, *Out of the Past*, pp. 3–12; Jonathan Katz, *Gay American History* (New York: Crowell, 1976); Justin Kaplan, *Walt Whitman: A Life* (New York: Bantam, 1982); and Gay Wilson Allen, *The New Walt Whitman Handbook* (New York: New York University Press, 1986).

44. Whitman, *Leaves of Grass* (1860), quoted in Kaplan, *Walt Whitman*, p. 237.

45. Adrienne Rich, "Compulsory Heterosexuality and Lesbian Experience," *Signs* 5 (1980): 631–60; and Richard Dellamora, "Homosexual Scandal and Compulsory Heterosexuality in the 1890s," in Dellamora, *Masculine Desire: The Sexual Politics of Victorian Aestheticism* (Chapel Hill: University of North Carolina Press, 1990), pp. 193–217.

46. E. P. Thompson, *The Making of the English Working Class* (New York: Vintage, 1963), pp. 9–11; Miller, *Out of the Past*, p. 49, for Wilde's famous statement.

47. Mayer, *Outsiders*, pp. 167–221; Robert Aldrich, *The Seduction of the Mediterranean: Writing, Art and Homosexual Fantasy* (London: Routledge, 1993); Dellamora, *Masculine Desire*. For another perspective, see the intriguing suggestions in Wayne Koestenbaum, *Double Talk: The Erotics of Male Literary Collaboration* (London: Routledge, 1989). In another milieu, note the account of Douglas Shand-Tucei, *Boston Bohemia, 1881–1900—Ralph Adams Cram: Life and Architecture* (Amherst: University of Massachusetts Press, 1995).

48. Sheila Rowbotham and Jeffrey Weeks, *Socialism and the New Life: The Personal and Sexual Politics of Edward Carpenter and Havelock Ellis* (London: Pluto Press, 1977), and, for the milieu in general, Judith R. Walkowitz, *City of Dreadful Delight: Narratives of Sexual Danger in Late-Victorian London* (Chicago: University of Chicago Press, 1992), pp. 135–70; Phyllis Grosskurth, *Havelock Ellis* (New York: Knopf, 1980), pp. 93–106; Blasius and Phelan, eds., *We Are Everywhere*, pp. 79–131; Vern L. Bullough, *Science in the Bedroom: The History of Sex Research* (New York: Basic Books, 1994), pp. 34–91.

49. See Mayer, *Outsiders*, pp. 223–29; Miller, *Out of the Past*, pp. 44–54; Dellamora, *Masculine Desire*, pp. 193–212; Ed Cohen, *Talk on the Wilde Side* (New York: Routledge, 1993); Lewis Chester, David Leitch, and Colin Simpson, *The Cleveland Street Affair* (London: Weidenfeld & Nicolson, 1976); Theo Aronson, *Prince Eddy and the Homosexual Underworld* (New York: Barnes & Noble, 1994); James R. Kincaid, *Child-Loving: The Erotic Child and Victorian Culture* (London: Routledge, 1992), pp. 232–34.

50. An extract appears in Blasius and Phelan, eds., *We Are Everywhere*, pp. 199–213.

51. Hallam, "The Phoenix of Sodom," in *The Book of Sodom*, pp. 115–22; Lee Edelman, "Seeing Things: Representation, the Scene of Surveillance and the

Spectacle of Gay Male Sex," in Goldberg, ed., *Reclaiming Sodom*, pp. 265–68; Jeffrey Weeks, "Inverts, Perverts, and Mary-Annes: Male Prostitution and the Regulation of Homosexuality in Nineteenth and Early Twentieth Century England," in Duberman et al., eds., *Hidden from History*, pp. 202–10. On transvestism in the late nineteenth and early twentieth centuries, see Angus McLaren, *The Trials of Masculinity: Policing Sexual Boundaries, 1870–1930* (Chicago: University of Chicago Press, 1997), pp. 207–32.

52. See the extraordinarily rich accounts in Steven Maynard, "Through a Hole in the Lavatory Wall: Homosexual Subcultures, Police Surveillance, and the Dialectics of Discovery, Toronto, 1890–1930," *Journal of the History of Sexuality* 5 (October 1994): 207–42; Maynard, "'Horrible Temptations': Sex, Men, and Working-Class Male Youth in Urban Ontario, 1890–1935," *Canadian Historical Review* 78 (June 1997): 191–235.

53. Consider, for example, the overview of nineteenth-century Canadian experience presented in Steven Maynard, "In Search of 'Sodom North': The Writing of Lesbian and Gay History in English Canada, 1970–1990," *Canadian Review of Comparative Literature* 21 (March–June 1994): 117–32; Kinsman, *The Regulation of Desire*, pp. 98–147. For Canada see, as well, Lorna Hutchinson, "Buggery Trials in Saint John, 1806: The Case of John M. Smith," *University of New Brunswick Law Journal* 40 (1991): 130–48; Steven Maynard, "Rough Work and Rugged Men: The Social Construction of Masculinity in Working-Class History," *Labour/Le Travail* 23 (Spring 1989): 159–68; Terry Chapman, "'An Oscar Wilde Type': 'The Abominable Crime of Buggery' in Western Canada, 1890–1920," *Criminal Justice History* 4 (1983): 97–118; Chapman, "Male Homosexuality: Legal Restraints and Social Attitudes in Western Canada, 1890–1920," in Louis Knafla, ed., *Law and Justice in a New Land: Essays in Western Canadian Legal History* (Toronto: Carswell, 1986). See the more generalized statement in Richard Davenport-Hines, "Dance as They Desire: The Construction and Criminalization of Homosexuality," in Davenport-Hines, *Sex, Death, and Punishment: Attitudes to Sex and Sexuality in Britain since the Renaissance* (London: Collins, 1990), pp. 105–56.

54. See Burton, "The Terminal Essay," from *The Book of the Thousand Nights and a Night* (1886), in Blasius and Phelan, eds., *We Are Everywhere*, pp. 85–91.

55. Katz, *Gay American History*, p. 574; George Chauncey, *Gay New York: Gender, Urban Culture, and the Making of the Gay Male World, 1890–1940* (New York: Basic, 1994), p. 37; Herbert Asbury, *The Gangs of New York: An Informal History of the Underworld* (New York: Capricorn Books, 1970), pp. 187–90. For comment on same-sex activity in pre-1870 New York, see Greenberg, *The Construction of Homosexuality*, pp. 355–56; Michael Lynch, "'Here is Adhesiveness': From Friendship to Homosexuality," *Victorian Studies* 29 (1985): 67–96.

56. This paragraph draws on original documentation presented in Katz, *Gay American History*, pp. 39–53; and on the depiction of the Bowery of the 1890s as gay haven and spectacle in Chauncey, *Gay New York*, pp. 33–45.

57. Havelock Ellis, *Studies in the Psychology of Sex: Sexual Inversion, Volume II* (New York: Random House, 1936), pp. 350–51. Ellis's remarks address the homosexual subculture of any large American city. My remarks, for reasons of clarity and space only, focus on New York. See the broader discussions in Jonathan Katz's documentary collection, *Gay American History*, which details the "scandals" of miscegenous same-sex eroticism (p. 49) in places such as St. Louis, New

Orleans or Washington. See also John D'Emilio and Estelle B. Freedman, *Intimate Matters: A History of Sexuality in America* (New York: Harper & Row, 1988), pp. 227–29; James Burnham, "Early References to Homosexual Communities in American Medical Writings," *Medical Aspects of Human Sexuality* 7 (1973): 40–49.

58. Chauncey, *Gay New York*, p. 3. The following paragraphs draw on and quote from Chauncey's text.

59. Chauncey, *Gay New York*, pp. 6, 42–44, citing Ralph Werther [a.k.a. Earl Lind, Jennie June], *Autobiography of an Androgyne* (1918) and *The Female Impersonators* (1922), both texts edited and published by Alfred W. Herzog of the New York–based *Medico-Legal Journal*.

60. These paragraphs draw primarily on Chauncey, *Gay New York*. Note, as well, Kevin J. Mumford, *Interzones: Black/White Sex Districts in Chicago and New York in the Early Twentieth Century* (New York: Columbia University Press, 1997), pp. 73–92. On public washrooms and the tearoom, see the historically and empirically sensitive treatment in Maynard, "Through a Hole in the Lavatory Wall," and Edelman, "Tearooms and Sympathy; or the Epistemology of the Water Closet," in *Homographesis*, pp. 148–71. On jazz age Harlem, see the pioneering statement by Eric Garber, "A Spectacle in Color: The Lesbian and Gay Subculture of Jazz Age Harlem," in Duberman et al., eds., *Hidden from History*, pp. 318–31. Note, as well, Hendrik de Leeuw, *Sinful Cities of the Western World* (New York: Citadel Press, 1934), pp. 260–67, which discusses the commercialized eroticism of Harlem and the homosexual subcultures of Times Square and Greenwich Village.

61. Compare Chauncey's social history in *Gay New York* and Sedgwick's *Epistemology of the Closet* for sophisticated commentary on the meaning of "the closet." See, as well, David Van Leer, "The Beast of the Closet: Sedgwick and the Knowledge of Homosexuality," in *The Queening of America: Gay Culture in Straight Society* (New York: Routledge, 1995).

62. Chauncey, *Gay New York*, pp. 331–54. He presents copious evidence on the rise of repression, but see as well the more general statements in Greenberg, *The Construction of Homosexuality*, pp. 434–54, and Kinsman, *The Regulation of Desire*, pp. 107–212.

63. Katz, *Gay American History*, pp. 82–90; Chauncey, *Gay New York*, p. 332; *James P. Cannon as We Knew Him: By Thirty-Three Comrades, Friends, and Relatives* (New York: Pathfinder, 1976), p. 66.

64. Note David Van Leer, *The Queening of America*, for an intriguing reading of the effect on homosexuality and its representation. For the stage, see Nicholas de Jongh, *Not in Front of the Audience: Homosexuality on Stage* (London: Routledge, 1992), esp. pp. 49–85. On film, see Vito Russo, *The Celluloid Closet: Homosexuality in the Movies* (New York: Harper & Row, 1981); Richard Dyer, *Now You See It: Studies in Lesbian and Gay Film* (New York: Routledge, 1990).

65. See Gordon Heath, *Deep are the Roots: Memoirs of a Black Expatriate* (Amherst: University of Massachusetts Press, 1992); David Leeming, *James Baldwin: A Biography* (New York: Henry Holt, 1994), esp. pp. 21–73; and Lee Edelman, "The Part for the (W)hole: Baldwin, Homophobia, and the Fantasmatics of 'Race'," in *Homographesis*, pp. 42–77.

66. Consider, for instance, comment on Jean Genet in Leo Bersani, "The Gay Outlaw," in *Homos*, pp. 113–84; Edmund White, *Genet: a Biography* (New York:

Knopf, 1993); or on Allen Ginsberg in Barry Miles, *Ginsberg: A Biography* (New York: Simon & Schuster, 1989); Michael Schumacher, *Dharma Lion: A Biography of Allen Ginsberg* (New York: St. Martin's Press, 1992).

67. Quoted in Richard Davenport-Hines, "Nights of Insult: Male Homosexuality since the 1940s," in *Sex, Death, and Punishment*, pp. 286–329.

68. Drucilla Cornell, *Transformations: Recollective Imagination and Sexual Difference* (New York: Routledge, 1993), p. 193. As some psychologists, psychoanalysts, and "expert" medical figures functioned as prominent agents of repression vis-à-vis the gay world, it is easy to condemn the loosely designated Freudian tradition. For a corrective to this reaction, see Henry Abelove, "Freud, Male Homosexuality, and the Americans," *Dissent* 34 (Winter 1987): 59–69.

69. On the personal traumas of adapting to gay identity in this period, see the moving account in Martin Duberman, *Cures: A Gay Man's Odyssey* (New York: Penguin, 1992). Another life history is presented in Alan Helms, *Young Man from the Provinces: A Gay Life Before Stonewall* (Boston: Faber & Faber, 1995). Political difficulties are chronicled in John D'Emilio, "Dreams Deferred: The Birth and Betrayal of America's First Gay Liberation Movement," in *Making Trouble*, pp. 17–56. Katz, *Gay American History*, pp. 174–95, presents documents detailing various "cures" for homosexuality, among them psychoanalysis, electroshock, abstinence, lobotomy, emetic aversion therapy, and castration. Lesbians faced the same onslaught; see Lillian Faderman, *Odd Girls and Twilight Lovers: A History of Lesbian Life in Twentieth-Century America* (New York: Columbia University Press, 1991), pp. 134–38. For the question of homosexual doubt and trauma in an earlier period, see Jeffrey Weeks, *Sex, Politics and Society: The Regulation of Sexuality since 1800* (London: Longman, 1989), p. 105.

70. John D'Emilio, *Sexual Politics, Sexual Communities: The Making of a Homosexual Minority in the U.S., 1940–1970* (Chicago: University of Chicago Press, 1983); D'Emilio, "Gay Politics, Gay Community: San Francisco's Experience," in *Making Trouble: Essays on Gay History, Politics, and the University* (New York: Routledge, 1992), pp. 74–95; Esther Newton, *Cherry Grove, Fire Island: Sixty Years in America's First Gay and Lesbian Town* (New York: Beacon, 1993); Frances Fitzgerald, *Cities on a Hill: A Journey Through Contemporary American Cultures* (New York: Simon & Schuster, 1986), pp. 25–120; Peter M. Nardi, David Sanders, and Judd Marmor, eds., *Growing up Before Stonewall: Life Stories of Some Gay Men* (London: Routledge, 1994); Eric Marcus, *Making History: The Struggle for Gay and Lesbian Equal Rights, 1945–1990* (New York: HarperCollins, 1992); Mark Abrahamson, *Urban Enclaves: Identity and Place in America* (New York: St. Martin's Press, 1996), pp. 103–20; Blasius and Phelan, eds., *We Are Everywhere*, pp. 241–842, presents a useful and extensive compilation of documents on the post-1950 development of a gay and lesbian politics of emancipation. For the episodic confrontations and their background, see Martin Duberman, *Stonewall* (New York: Penguin, 1994); Randy Shilts, *The Mayor of Castro Street* (New York: St. Martin's Press, 1982); Miller, *Out of the Past*, pp. 363–421. Arthur Bell provides a recollection of a year in the emerging gay liberation movement in *Dancing the Gay Lib Blues: A Year in the Homosexual Liberation Movement* (New York: Simon & Schuster, 1971). For British struggles for law reform, see Stephen Jeffery Poulter, *Peers, Queers, & Commons: The Struggle for Gay Law Reform from 1950 to the Present* (London: Routledge, 1991).

71. Note Stan Persky, *Buddy's: Meditations on Desire* (Vancouver: New Star, 1989); Ed Jackson and Stan Persky, eds., *Flaunting It! A Decade of Gay Journalism from the Body*

Politic (Vancouver: New Star, 1982); Kinsman, *The Regulation of Desire*, pp. 288–329; D'Emilio, "Saturday Night," in *Making Trouble*, pp. 196–201.

72. For Georges Bataille, see *Eroticism: Death and Sensuality* (San Francisco: City Lights, 1986); *The Tears of Eros* (San Francisco: City Lights, 1989); and *The Transparency of Evil: Essays on Extreme Phenomena* (London: Verso, 1993). For discussions of S/M, see the contrasting perspectives on Foucault in Halperin, *Saint Foucault* and James Miller, *The Passion of Michel Foucault* (New York: Doubleday, 1993). The quotation is from a text of dubious value, Frank Browning, *The Culture of Desire: Paradox and Perversity in Gay Lives Today* (New York: Crown, 1993), pp. 82–83. See, as well, the useful discussions of S/M and public sex in Bersani, "Is the Rectum a Grave?" pp. 197–222; Tim Edwards, *Erotics and Politics: Gay Male Sexuality, Masculinity and Feminism* (London: Routledge, 1994), esp. pp. 74–109; Wouter Geurtsen, "Sex in the Margins," and Jon Binnie, "The Twilight World of the Sadomasochist," in Stephen Whittle, ed., *The Margins of the City: Gay Men's Urban Lives* (Aldershot: Arena, 1994), pp. 143–69. Note, as well, the wide-ranging discussion in Mark Simpson, *Male Impersonators: Men Performing Masculinity* (London: Routledge, 1994).

73. For one overview, drawing on oral history, see Marcus, *Making History*. Depictions of the gay milieu appear in Simon LeVay and Elisabeth Nonas, *City of Friends: A Portrait of the Gay and Lesbian Community in America* (Cambridge, Mass.: MIT Press, 1995); Gilbert Herdt, ed., *Gay Culture in America: Essays from the Field* (Boston: Beacon Press, 1992). Note, as well, Tim McCaskell, "The Bath Raids and Gay Politics," in Frank Cunningham et al., eds., *Social Movements/Social Change: The Politics and Practice of Organizing* (Toronto: Garamond, 1988), pp. 169–88; Michael Denneny et al., eds., *The Christopher Street Reader* (New York: Coward–McCann, 1983).

74. Bersani, *Homos*, p. 19.

75. Narayan, quoted in Bersani, "Is the Rectum a Grave?" p. 197.

76. Mark Abrahamson, *Urban Enclaves: Identity and Place in America* (New York: St. Martin's Press, 1996), p. 120, citing *New York Times*, 16 February 1994, p. A10.

77. See Andre Picard, *The Gift of Death: Confronting Canada's Tainted Blood Tragedy* (Toronto: HarperCollins, 1995).

78. The literature on HIV and AIDs is now immense and ranges from journalistic accounts of the spread of the devastatation through more scientific treatises to some amazingly rich cultural commentary. Among the legion of texts, see Randy Shilts, *And the Band Played On: Politics, People, and the AIDS Epidemic* (New York: St. Martin's Press, 1987); Larry Kramer, *Reports from the Holocaust: The Making of an AIDS Activist* (New York: St. Martin's Press, 1989); Fenton Johnson, *Geography of the Heart: A Memoir* (New York: Charles Scribner, 1996); Padraig O'Malley, ed., *The AIDS Epidemic: Private Rights and Public Interest* (Boston: Beacon Press, 1989). On the issue of backlash, see Simon Watney, *Policing Desire: Pornography, AIDS, and the Media* (Minneapolis: University of Minnesota Press, 1987); Cindy Patton, *Inventing AIDS* (New York: Routledge, 1990); Richard Davenport-Hines, "Hating Others: AIDS," in *Sex, Death, and Punishment*, pp. 330–84; Michael Warner, "Media Gays: A New Stone Wall," *Nation* 265 (14 July 1997): 15–19. Note, as well, Susan Palmer, *AIDS as an Apocalyptic Metaphor in North America* (Toronto: University of Toronto Press, 1997).

79. On this process, see Bersani, "Is the Rectum a Grave?" and note, as well,

Cindy Patton, "Refiguring Social Space," in Linda Nicholson and Steven Seidman, eds., *Social Postmodernism: Beyond Identity Politics* (Cambridge: Cambridge University Press, 1995), pp. 216–49. By the late 1990s there were those who were returning to the dark landscapes of homoerotic desire, refusing the limitations of gay respectability by living sexual lives of responsible choice, demanding the right to their unleashed sexual passions in the context of practices that are HIV/AIDS aware and safe but deviantly nonconventional. See Mitchell Raphael, "Sex Rebel is Anti-Gay, in his Way," *Toronto Star*, August 23, 1997. There were also more mainstream voices of respectability who, from various quarters, claimed that the assimilation of gays and the quieting and suppression of their sexuality had killed much of the artistic creativity of transgressive homoeroticism. Clearly, this was related to the process of various submissions associated with the terror of AIDS and HIV. Note Daniel Harris, *The Rise and Fall of Gay Culture* (New York: Hyperion, 1997).

80. Consider the statement, pitched toward theoretical issues, in Steven Seidman, "Deconstructing Queer Theory or the Under-theorization of the Social and the Ethical," in Nicholson and Seidman, eds., *Social Postmodernism*, pp. 116–41.

81. Faderman, *Surpassing the Love of Men*, esp. pp. 145–230, quotation from pp. 199–200; Faderman, *Odd Girls and Twilight Lovers*, pp. 11–36. See also Carroll Smith-Rosenberg, "The Female World of Love and Ritual: Relations Between Women in Nineteenth Century America," in *Disorderly Conduct: Visions of Gender in Victorian America* (New York: Oxford University Press, 1985), pp. 53–76; Lesbian History Group, *Not a Passing Phase: Reclaiming Lesbians in History, 1840–1985* (London: Women's Press, 1985), esp. essays by Sheila Jeffreys (pp. 19–28), Elaine Miller (pp. 29–54), and Pam Johnson (pp. 55–76). For a slightly later period, see Elizabeth Lapovsky Kennedy, "'But we would never talk about it': the Structures of Lesbian Discretion in South Dakota, 1928–1933," in Ellen Lewin, *Inventing Lesbian Cultures in America* (Boston: Beacon, 1996), pp. 15–39.

82. On passing women, lesbianism, prisons, and gender ambiguity, see Katz, *Gay American History*, pp. 65–73, 225–45; Garber, *Vested Interests*, pp. 67–92; Caroll Smith-Rosenberg, "Hearing Women's Worlds: A Feminist Reconstruction of History," and "The New Woman as Androgyne: Social Disorder and Gender Crisis, 1870–1936," in *Disorderly Conduct*, pp. 39–40, 270–90; Faderman, *Surpassing the Love of Men*, pp. 254–94; Julie Wheelwright, *Amazons and Military Maids: Women Who Dressed as Men in the Pursuit of Life, Liberty and Happiness* (London: Pandora, 1989). See, as well, fiction posing as history in Don Akenson's mischievous *At Face Value: The Life and Times of Eliza McCormack/John White* (Montreal: McGill–Queen's University Press, 1990). Besides Garber's *Vested Interests*, see the essays on cross-dressing in Richard Ekins and Dave King, eds., *Blending Genders: Social Aspects of Cross-Dressing and Sex Changing* (London: Routledge, 1996).

83. Faderman, *Surpassing the Love of Woman*, pp. 239–53, contains an accessible introduction to the sexologists, with the quotation on pp. 252–53. See, as well, Faderman, *Odd Girls and Twilight Lovers*, pp. 37–61, and for another account, see Noreen O'Connor and Joanna Ryan, *Wild Desires and Mistaken Identities* (New York: Columbia University Press, 1993).

84. Miller, *Out of the Past*, pp. 75–91, 137–47, 183–96; Sonja Ruehl, "Inverts and

Experts: Radclyffe Hall and the Lesbian Identity," in Rosalind Brunt and Caroline Rowan, eds., *Feminism, Culture & Politics* (London: Lawrence & Wishart, 1986), pp. 15–36; Lucie Delarue-Mardrus, *The Angel and the Perverts* (New York: New York University Press, 1995); Shari Benstock, "Paris Lesbianism and the Politics of Reaction, 1900–1940," in Duberman et al., eds., *Hidden from History*, 332–46; Chauncey, *Gay New York*, pp. 227–44; Caroline Ware, *Greenwich Village, 1920–1930: A Comment on American Civilization in the Post-War Years* (New York: Houghton Mifflin, 1935), pp. 55, 96, 237, 253; Faderman, *Odd Girls and Twilight Lovers*, pp. 62–92.

85. On Smith, blueswomen, and sexual transgression, see Katz, *Gay American History*, pp. 76–82; Chris Albertson, *Bessie* (New York: Stein & Day, 1974), pp. 13, 116–26, 140; William Barlow, *"Looking Up at Down": The Emergence of Blues Culture* (Philadelphia: Temple University Press, 1989), pp. 199–200; Garber, "A Spectacle in Color: The Lesbian and Gay Subculture of Jazz Age Harlem," in Duberman et al., eds., *Hidden from History*, pp. 318–32. See, as well, Mumford, *Interzones*, pp. 79–84. For a recently published discussion of "crossover" traditions in African-American music, including that of trans-vestism, see Marybeth Hamilton, "Sexual Politics and African-American Music; or, Placing Little Richard in History," *History Workshop Journal* 46 (Autumn 1998): 161–76.

86. Consider the accounts of bars in Elizabeth Lapovsky Kennedy and Madeline D. Davis, *Boots of Leather, Slippers of Gold: The History of a Lesbian Community* (New York: Penguin, 1993); Rochella Thorpe, "A House Where Queers Go: African-American Lesbian Night Life in Detroit, 1940–1975," in Lewin, ed., *Inventing Lesbian Cultures*, pp. 40–62.

87. Joan Nestle, "The Bathroom Line," in Nestle, *A Restricted Country* (Ithaca: Fire-brand Books, 1987), pp. 37–39.

88. Leslie Feinberg, *Stone Butch Blues* (Ithaca, N.Y.: Firebrand Books, 1993), p. 4.

89. The centrality of night and darkness to gay lives and aesthetics is nicely illuminated in Maurice van Lieshout, "Leather Nights in the Woods: Locating Male Homosexuality and Sadomasochism in a Dutch Highway Rest Area," in Gordon Brent Ingram, Anne-Marie Bouthillette, and Yolande Retter, eds., *Queers in Space: Communities/Public Places/Sites of Resistance* (Seattle: Bay Press, 1997), pp. 339–56; The Hall Carpenter Archives Gay Men's Oral History Group, *Walking After Midnight* (London: Routledge, 1989); and Derek McCormack's novel of gay teenage life *Dark Rides* (Toronto: Gutter Press, 1996). On the coercive side of the dark, see the early fictional statement of Daniel Curzon, *Something You Do in the Dark* (New York: G. P. Putnam, 1971).

90. John Rechy, *City of Night* (New York: Grove Press, 1963), p. 11. Rechy is currently completing a novel exploring themes of sexual outlawry and exile on the eve of the 'discovery' of AIDS. It is tentatively titled *The Coming of the Night*. See Mitchell Raphael, "Sex Rebel is Anti-Gay, in His Way." Note as well the significance of night entries in Rechy's diary-like docudrama of L.A.'s sexual underground in the 1970s: *The Sexual Outlaw: A Documentary* (New York: Grove Press, 1977).

91. Karl Marx, "The Working Day," from *Capital*, Volume 1, quoted in Saul K. Padover, ed., *Karl Marx on America and the Civil War* (New York: McGraw-Hill, 1972), p. 20.

Chapter 14

1. Priscilla Parkhurst Ferguson, *Paris as Revolution: Writing the 19th-Century City* (Berkeley: University of California Press, 1994). She presents her textualization of Paris as revolution based on Walter Benjamin's conceptualization of the metropolitan capital's time–space as "a dream time," while the novelist Marge Piercy fictionalizes gender relations in the Paris of the French Revolution, acutely aware of the contrasts of day and night in her novel *City of Darkness, City of Light* (New York: Ballantine, 1996).

2. On Everett, see Melvyn Dubofsky, *We Shall Be All: A History of the Industrial Workers of the World* (Chicago: Quadrangle, 1969), pp. 339–43; Norman H. Clark, "Everett, 1916 and After," *Pacific Northwest Quarterly* 57 (April 1966): 57–64; and, for the quoted verse, Walker C. Smith, *The Everett Massacre: A History of the Class Struggle in the Lumber Industry* (Chicago: I.W.W. Publishing Bureau, 1918).

3. Mary V. Dearborn, *Queen of Bohemia: The Life of Louise Bryant* (Boston: Houghton Mifflin, 1996), p. 146. For accounts of the Red Scare of these years, see William Preston, Jr., *Aliens and Dissenters: Federal Suppression of Radicals, 1903–1933* (Urbana: University of Illinois Press, 1994); Robert K. Murray, *Red Scare: A Study in National Hysteria* (Minneapolis: University of Minnesota Press, 1955).

4. Jan Valtin, *Out of the Night* (New York: Alliance Book Corporation, 1941). Valtin receives brief mention in Harvey Klehr and Ronald Radosh, *The Amerasia Spy Case: Prelude to McCarthyism* (Chapel Hill: University of North Carolina Press, 1996), p. 150.

5. The literature on 1968 is immense. Quotations and content drawn from David Caute, *The Year of the Barricades: A Journey Through 1968* (New York: Harper & Row, 1988); Herve Bourges, ed., *The French Student Revolt: The Leaders Speak* (New York: Hill & Wang, 1968); Gabriel Cohn-Bendit and Daniel Cohn-Bendit, *Obsolete Communism: The Left-Wing Alternative* (London: Penguin, 1969); Bernard E. Brown, *The French Revolt: May 1968* (New York: McCaleb-Seiler, 1970); Norman Mailer, *The Armies of the Night: History as a Novel; the Novel as History* (New York: Signet, 1968); David Farber, *Chicago '68* (Chicago: University of Chicago Press, 1988).

6. Mona Ozouf, *Festivals and the French Revolution* (Cambridge, Mass: Harvard University Press, 1988), pp. 1–3.

7. Ozouf, *Festivals and the French Revolution*; Daniel Guerin, *Class Struggle in the First French Republic: Bourgeois and Bras Nus, 1793–1795* (London: Pluto, 1973). See as well, Lionel Gossman, "Michelet and the French Revolution," in François Furet and Mona Ozouf, eds., *The French Revolution and the Creation of Modern Political Culture: Volume 3—The Transformation of Political Culture, 1789–1848* (New York: Pergamon Press, 1989), pp. 639–64; Lynn Hunt, *Politics, Culture, and Class in the French Revolution* (London: Methuen, 1986).

8. James A. Leith, *Space and Revolution: Projects for Monuments, Squares, and Public Buildings in France, 1789–1799* (Montreal: McGill–Queen's University Press, 1991). See also James A. Leith, *The Idea of Art as Propaganda in France, 1750–1799* (Toronto: University of Toronto Press, 1965); Leith, "Symbols in the French Revolution: The Strange Metamorphoses of the Triangle," in Leith, ed., *Symbols in Life and Art* (Kingston: McGill–Queen's University Press, 1987). For a general theoretical statement, see Nancy Fraser, "Politics, Culture, and the Public Sphere: Toward a Postmodern Conception," in Linda Nicholson and Steven

Seidman, eds., *Social Postmodernism: Beyond Identity Politics* (Cambridge: Cambridge University Press, 1995), pp. 287–314.

9. This paragraph draws on Ozouf, *Festivals and the French Revolution*, pp. 33–60; P. A. Kropotkin, *The Great French Revolution, 1789–1793* (New York: G. P. Putnam, 1909), pp. 177–79.

10. Dearborn, *Queen of Bohemia*, p. 86.

11. On Tatlin and the monument, see Rene Fulop-Miller, *The Mind and Face of Bolshevism* (New York: Knopf, 1928), pp. 144–46; Mildred Constantine and Alan Fern, *Revolutionary Soviet Film Posters* (Baltimore: Johns Hopkins University Press, 1974), pp. 5–7; James von Geldern, *Bolshevik Festivals, 1917–1920* (Berkeley: University of California Press, 1993), pp. 86, 196–97.

12. These paragraphs draw on the rich account in von Geldern, *Bolshevik Festivals*.

13. See Lynn Mally, *Culture of the Future: The Proletkult Movement in Revolutionary Russia* (Berkeley: University of California Press, 1990); Nina Tumarkin, *Lenin Lives! The Lenin Cult in Soviet Russia* (Cambridge, Mass: Harvard University Press, 1997).

14. Consider the varied accounts in Richard Stites, *Revolutionary Dreams: Utopian Vision and Experimental Life in the Russian Revolution* (New York: Oxford University Press, 1989); Irene Masing-Delich, *Abolishing Death: A Salvation Myth of Russian Twentieth-Century Literature* (Stanford: Stanford University Press, 1992); Eric Naiman, *Sex in Public: The Incarnation of Early Soviet Ideology* (Princeton: Princeton University Press, 1997).

15. See, among other sources, Louis Chevalier, *Laboring Classes and Dangerous Classes In Paris During the First Half of the Nineteenth Century* (New York: Howard Fertig, 1973); Charles Prendergast, *Paris and the Nineteenth Century: Writing the City* (Cambridge, Mass: Blackwell, 1992); Priscilla Parkhurst Ferguson, *Paris as Revolution: Writing the Nineteenth-Century City* (Berkeley: University of California Press, 1994).

16. The literature on the Commune is extensive. Standard accounts include Frank Jellinek, *The Paris Commune of 1871* (London: Victor Gollancz, 1937); Stewart Edwards, *The Paris Commune of 1871* (London: Eyre & Spottiswoode, 1971); Louis M. Greenberg, *Sisters of Liberty: Marseille, Lyon, Paris and the Reaction to a Centralized State, 1868–1871* (Cambridge, Mass.: Harvard University Press, 1971). A useful and wide-ranging collection is James A. Leith, ed., *Images of the Commune* (Montreal: McGill–Queen's University Press, 1978).

17. Among the many accounts of the Commune, I have quoted from Thomas March, *The History of the Paris Commune of 1871* (London: Swan, Sonnenschein & Company, 1896), esp. pp. 15, 84, 100–15. Perhaps the best "eye-witness" nineteenth-century account is Prospe Olivier Lissagaray, *History of the Commune of 1871*, trans. Eleanor Marx Aveling (London: Reeves & Turner, 1886). Other first-person accounts include Rev. W. Gibson, *Paris During the Commune* (London: Methodist Book Room, 1895); Ernest Alfred Vizetelly, *My Adventures in the Commune, Paris, 1871* (London: Chatto & Windus, 1914); and the pre-Commune account of a climate of fear attendant on Prussian invasion in Nathan Sheppard, *Shut up in Paris* (London: Richard Bentley & Son, 1871).

18. See Edwards, *The Paris Commune of 1871*, pp. 277–312; Gibson, *Paris during the Commune*, p. 239; James A. Leith, "The War of Images Surrounding the Commune," in Leith, ed., *Images of the Commune*, pp. 101–50.

19. See the exciting treatment by Gay L. Gullickson, *Unruly Women of Paris: Images of the Commune* (Ithaca: Cornell University Press, 1996).

20. This paragraph draws on original documentary material in Stewart Edwards,

ed., *The Communards of Paris, 1871* (London: Thames & Hudson, 1973), pp. 140–57.

21. Karl Marx, "The Civil War in France," in Karl Marx and Friedrich Engels, *Selected Works* (Moscow: Progress, 1968), p. 311.

22. R. W. Postgate, ed., *Out of the Past: Some Revolutionary Sketches* (London: Labor Publishing, 1922), p. 116; Vizetelly, *My Adventures in the Commune*, pp. 292–347.

23. Quoted in Rupert Christiansen, *Paris Babylon: The Story of the Paris Commune* (New York: Viking, 1995), p. 367.

24. On Parisian prostitutes and the Commune, see Neil Stewart, *Blanqui* (London: Victor Gollancz, 1939), p. 298; Frank Jellinek, *The Paris Commune of 1871*, pp. 277–78; Christiansen, *Paris Babylon*, pp. 83–92, 346. The quotation is from Roger L. Williams, *The French Revolution, 1870–1871* (London: Weidenfeld & Nicolson, 1969), p. 151.

25. See, for instance, F. B. Smith, "Some British Reactions to the Commune," in Eugene Kamenka, ed., *Paradigm for Revolution? The Paris Commune 1871–1971* (Canberra: Australian National University Press, 1972), p. 87; E. P. Thompson, *William Morris: Romantic to Revolutionary* (New York: Pantheon, 1977).

26. See Paul Avrich, *The Haymarket Tragedy* (Princeton: Princeton University Press, 1984).

27. Michelle Perrot, "The First of May 1890 in France: the Birth of a Working-class Ritual," in Pat Thane and Geoffrey Crossick, eds., *The Power of the Past: Essays for Eric Hobsbawm* (Cambridge: Cambridge University Press, 1984), pp. 143–72; Perrot, *Workers on Strike: France, 1871–1890* (New Haven: Yale University Press, 1987); Leopold H. Haimson and Charles Tilly, eds., *Strikes, Wars, and Revolutions in an International Perspective: Strike Waves in the Late Nineteenth and Twentieth Centuries* (Cambridge: Cambridge University Press, 1989); Philip S. Foner, *May Day: A Short History of the International Workers' Holiday, 1886–1986* (New York: International, 1986).

28. John Sommerfield, *May Day* (London: Lawrence & Wishart, 1936), p. 192. For comments on May Day in New York in this period that also reflect a sense of loss, see Mary McCarthy, *Intellectual Memoirs: New York, 1936–1938* (San Diego: Harcourt Brace, 1992), pp. 1–3; Richard Wright, *American Hunger* (New York: Perennial, 1979), pp. 130–35. A more positive assessment of May Day and the United States' "cultural front" appears in Michael Denning, *The Cultural Front: The Laboring of American Culture in the Twentieth Century* (London: Verso, 1996), pp. 53–114.

29. This account relies on the most thorough and sensitive discussion of both the strike and the Pageant: Steve Golin, *The Fragile Bridge: Paterson Silk Strike 1913* (Philadelphia: Temple University Press, 1988). For other accounts, see Martin Green, *New York, 1913: The Armory Show and the Paterson Strike Pageant* (New York: Collier, 1988); Linda Nochlin, "The Paterson Strike Pageant of 1913," *Art in America* 52 (May–June 1974): 67–68; Joyce L. Kornbluth, ed., *Rebel Voices: An I.W.W. Anthology* (Ann Arbor: University of Michigan Press, 1968), pp. 197–226; Steven Watson, *Strange Bedfellows: The First Avant-Garde* (New York: Abbeville Press, 1991), esp. pp. 166–187, 401–02, 410.

30. See Dubofsky, *We Shall Be All*, pp. 263–90.

31. Quoted in Dubofsky, *We Shall Be All*, p. 279; William D. Haywood, *Bill Haywood's Book: The Autobiography of William Dudley Haywood* (New York: International, 1929), pp. 261–77, esp. p. 262.

32. See the account in Golin, *The Fragile Bridge*, pp. 157–78, with the long quotation on p. 166.
33. For the traditional pessimistic postmortems on the pageant, see Dubofsky, *We Shall Be All*, pp. 280–85; Golin's summary of Flynn's negative assessment in *The Fragile Bridge*, pp. 170–78; and Kornbuth, ed., *Rebel Voices*, pp. 215–25.
34. Helmut Gruber, *Red Vienna: Experiment in Working-Class Culture, 1919–1934* (New York: Oxford University Press, 1991), pp. 109–11. See, as well, Anson Rabinbach, *The Crisis of Austrian Socialism: From Red Vienna to Civil War, 1927–1934* (Chicago: University of Chicago Press, 1983).
35. This discussion draws on the suggestive work of Temma Kaplan, "Civic Rituals and Patterns of Resistance in Barcelona, 1890–1930," in Thane and Crossick, eds., *Power of the Past*, pp. 173–94; Kaplan, *Red City, Blue Period: Social Movements in Picasso's Barcelona* (Berkeley: University of California Press, 1992).
36. On Barcelona and the Blue and Rose periods, see Pierre Daix and Georges Boudaille, *Picasso: The Blue and Rose Periods* (Greenwich: New York Graphic Society, 1967); Arianna Stassinopoulos Huffington, *Picasso: Creator and Destroyer* (New York: Simon & Schuster, 1988), pp. 32–48; and the impressively detailed and judicious John Richardson, *A Life of Picasso, Volume I: 1881–1906* (New York: Random House, 1991). Kaplan, *Red City, Blue Period*, pp. 37–57, summarizes much for the early years and offers suggestions on the cultural significance of Picasso's return to Barcelona in 1913 and 1916–1917. See, as well, Paul Morand, "Catalan Nights," in *Fancy Goods: Open All Night* (New York: New Directions, 1984), pp. 65–95.
37. Huffington, *Picasso*, pp. 231–33; Kaplan, *Red City, Blue Period*, pp. 179–87. *Guernica* is the subject of a number of sophisticated studies. See Herschel B. Chipp, *Picasso's "Guernica": History, Transformations, Meanings* (Berkeley: University of California Press, 1989); Sir Anthony Blunt, *Picasso's "Guernica"* (Oxford: Oxford University Press, 1969); Rudolf Arnheim, *The Genesis of a Painting: Picasso's "Guernica"* (Berkeley: University of California Press, 1980).
38. Stephen Spender, "Guernica," in Murray A. Sperber, ed., *And I Remember Spain: A Spanish Civil War Anthology* (New York: Macmillan, 1974), pp. 151–52.
39. Kaplan, *Red City, Blue Period*, esp. pp. 165–88. For general accounts of the Spanish Civil War and this context, see Burnett Bolloten, *The Spanish Civil War: Revolution and Counterrevolution* (Chapel Hill: University of North Carolina Press, 1991); Ronald Fraser, *Blood of Spain: An Oral History of the Spanish Civil War* (New York: Pantheon, 1979); Hugh Thomas, *The Spanish Civil War* (New York: Harper, 1961); and Felix Morrow, *Revolution and Counter-Revolution in Spain* (New York: Pathfinder, 1974).

Chapter 15

1. *S. M. Eisenstein: Selected Works*, Volume 1 (1988), pp. 281, 283, quoted in Malcolm Quinn, *The Swastika: Constructing the Symbol* (London: Routledge, 1994), p. 3.
2. For a discussion of film, see Susan Sontag, "Fascinating Fascism," in Sontag, *Under the Sign of Saturn* (New York: Noonday Press, 1980), pp. 73–108.
3. As an introduction, see Herman Klauss, "On Festivities in the Schools," in George L. Mosse, ed., *Nazi Culture: Intellectual, Cultural and Social Life in the Third*

Reich (London: W. H. Allen, 1966), pp. 127–32; Jost Dulffer, *Nazi Germany, 1933–1945: Faith and Annihilation* (London: Arnold, 1992), pp. 111–116; Detlev J. K. Peukert, *The Weimar Republic: The Crisis of Classical Modernity* (London: Allen Lane, 1991), pp. 104–06; Karin Hausen, "Mother's Day in the Weimar Republic," in Renate Bridenthal, Atina Grossmann, and Marion Kaplan, eds., *When Biology Became Destiny: Women in Weimar and Nazi Germany* (New York: Monthly Review Press, 1984), pp. 131–52.

4. Leon Trotsky, "What Is National Socialism?" (November 2, 1933), reprinted in Trotsky, *The Struggle Against Fascism in Germany* (New York: Pathfinder, 1971), p. 406. Note the recent academic studies in David F. Crew, ed., *Nazism and German Society, 1933–1945* (London: Routledge, 1994): Alf Ludtke, "The 'Honor of Labor': Industrial Workers and the Power of Symbols Under National Socialism" (pp. 67–109), and Ian Kershaw, "The 'Hitler Myth': Image and Reality in the Third Reich" (pp. 197–217).

5. On the broad appeal of the Nazi program, which encompassed the cultural and the political, the social and the economic, packaged in a national program of advance, see William Burstein, *The Logic of Evil: The Social Origins of the Nazi Party, 1925–1933* (New Haven: Yale University Press, 1996).

6. On clashes between Communists and Nazis, see Eve Rosenhaft, *Beating the Fascists? The German Communists and Political Violence, 1929–1933* (Cambridge: Cambridge University Press, 1983).

7. Among many commentaries, note Eric Hobsbawm, *The Age of Extremes: The Short Twentieth Century* (London: Michael Joseph, 1994), pp. 116–18; Fritz Stern, *Dreams and Delusions: National Socialism in the Drama of the German Past* (New York: Vintage, 1989), esp. pp. 166–68; Richard Bessel, "Political Violence and the Nazi Seizure of Power," in Bessel, ed., *Life in the Third Reich* (Oxford: Oxford University Press, 1987), pp. 1–16.

8. Herman Rauschning, *The Beast from the Abyss* (London: William Heinemann, 1941), pp. 68–69, 149–151. See also Rauschning, *The Revolution of Nihilism: Warning to the West* (New York: Longmans, Green & Company, 1939); Rauschning, *Makes of Destruction: Meetings and Talks in Revolutionary Germany* (London: Eyre & Spottiswoode, 1942).

9. Quoted in Klaus Theweleit, *Male Fantasies: Volume 1—Women, Floods, Bodies, History* (Minneapolis: University of Minnesota Press, 1987), p. 127. For later soldiers, see Omer Bartov, "The Conduct of War: Soldiers and the Barbarization of Warfare," in Michael Geyer and John W. Boyer, eds., *Resistance Against the Third Reich, 1933–1990* (Chicago: University of Chicago Press, 1994), pp. 39–52.

10. Egon Haas, "Foreword by the Translator," in Margarete von Falkensee, *Blue Angel Nights: Erotic Escapades in Germany of the 1920s* (New York: Carol & Graf, 1986), p. 6. The novel originally appeared in 1931 under the title *The Pleasure Garden*. On metaphors of darkness see, as well, Norman Geras, "Marxists Before the Holocaust," *New Left Review* 224 (July–August 1997), pp. 19–38, and the representational imagery developed in Yehuda Bauer, *The Holocaust in Historical Perspective* (Seattle: University of Washington Press, 1978), esp. pp. 37–38.

11. Maria Tatar, *Lustmord: Sexual Murder in Weimar Germany* (Princeton: Princeton University Press, 1995).

12. For the Weimar Republic, see Peukert, *The Weimar Republic*; Warren B. Morris, Jr., *The Weimar Republic and Nazi Germany* (Chicago: Nelson-Hall, 1982); David

Abraham, *The Collapse of the Weimar Republic* (Princeton: Princeton University Press, 1981). A local study is William Sheridan Allen, *The Nazi Seizure of Power: The Experience of a Single German Town* (Chicago: Quadrangle, 1965). On the repression of the "impure," whatever their outcast status, see, among other sources, Jeremy Noakes, "Social Outcasts in the Third Reich," in Richard Bessel, ed., *Life in the Third Reich* (Oxford: Oxford University Press, 1987), pp. 83–96; Michael Burleigh and Wolfgang Wippermann, *The Racial State: Germany, 1933–1945* (Cambridge: Cambridge University Press, 1991), pp. 113–97; Detlev J. K. Peukert, "The Genesis of the 'Final Solution' from the Spirit of Science," in David F. Crew, ed., *Nazism and German Society, 1933–1945* (London: Routledge, 1994), pp. 274–99. Obviously the literature on eugenics, race, and "national socialism" is relevant. See Paul Weindling, *Health, Race and German Politics Between National Unification and Nazism, 1870–1945* (Cambridge: Cambridge University Press, 1989); Henry Friedlander, *The Origins of Nazi Genocide: From Euthanasia to the Final Solution* (Chapel Hill: University of North Carolina Press, 1995); Gisela Bock, "Sterilization and Medical Massacres in National Socialist Germany: Ethics, Politics, and the Law," in Manfred Berg and Geoffrey Cocks, eds., *Medicine and Modernity: Public Health and Medical Care in 19th and 20th Century Germany* (Cambridge: Cambridge University Press, 1997).

13. On aspects of ideology, see George L. Mosse, *The Crisis of German Ideology: Intellectual Origins of the Third Reich* (New York: Grosset & Dunlap, 1964); Shulamit Volkov, "The Written Matter and the Spoken Word: On The Gap Between Pre-1914 and Nazi Anti-Semitism," in François Furet, ed., *Unanswered Questions: Nazi Germany and the Genocide of the Jews* (New York: Schocken, 1989), pp. 33–53.

14. Leon Trotsky, "The Tragedy of the German Proletariat: The German Workers Will Rise Again!—Stalinism Never," in Trotsky, *The Struggle Against Fascism in Germany*, p. 375. See the concise statement in Gunter W. Remmling, "The Destruction of the Workers' Mass Movement in Nazi Germany," in Michael N. Dobkowski and Isidor Wallimann, eds., *Radical Perspectives on the Rise of Fascism in Germany, 1919–1945* (New York: Monthly Review Press, 1989), pp. 215–30.

15. This is not to deny the complexity of class relations: certainly some workers did support Hitler and the Nazis; equally undeniable is the weakened state of political opposition resulting from the post-1928 clashes of Communist (KPD) and Social Democratic (SPD) Parties.

16. Note David Abraham, "State and Classes in Weimar Germany," *Politics & Society* 7 (1977): 229–66. A range of theoretical views on fascism are presented in Dobkowski and Wallimann, eds., *Radical Perspectives*, pp. 21–215, a section introduced with a revised variant of the Abraham essay. For a summary of East German scholarship, see Andreas Dorpalen, *German History in Marxist Perspective: The East German Approach* (Detroit: Wayne State University Press, 1985), pp. 308–463.

17. Detlev J. K. Peukert, *Inside Nazi Germany: Conformity, Opposition, and Racism in Everyday Life* (London: B. T. Batsford, 1987), pp. 42–44. On the Nazis and social democracy, see Donna Harsch, *German Social Democracy and the Rise of Nazism* (Chapel Hill: University of North Carolina Press, 1993); Richard Breitman, *German Social Democracy and the Weimar Republic* (Chapel Hill: University of North Carolina Press, 1981); Robert A. Gates, "German Socialism and the Crisis of 1929–1933," *Central European History* 7 (1974): 332–59; Adolf Sturmthal, *The*

Tragedy of European Labor, 1918–1939 (New York: Columbia University Press, 1943);
Ben Fowkes, "Defense of Democracy or Advance to Socialism? Arguments
within German Social Democracy in the Mid-1920s," in Dobkowski and
Wallimann, eds., *Radical Perspectives*, pp. 247–66.

18. Kurt Patzold, "Terror and Demagoguery in the Consolidation of the Fascist
Dictatorship in Germany, 1933–1934," in Dobkowski and Wallimann, eds.,
Radical Perspectives, pp. 231–46; Richard Bessel, "Political Violence and the Nazi
Seizure of Power," in Bessel, ed., *Life in the Third Reich*, pp. 1–16.

19. Quoted in Richard Plant, *The Pink Triangle: The Nazi War Against Homosexuals* (Edinburgh: Mainstream, 1987), p. 106.

20. See Allan Merson, *Communist Resistance in Nazi Germany* (London: Lawrence &
Wishart, 1985); Tim Mason, "Labor in the Third Reich, 1933–1939," *Past &
Present* 33 (April 1966): 112–41; Ben Fowkes, *Communism in Germany under the
Weimar Republic* (London: Macmillan, 1984); Eric D. Weitz, *Creating German
Communism, 1890–1990: From Popular Protests to Socialist State* (Princeton: Princeton
University Press, 1997), pp. 233–310.

21. See, among other studies that relate this to homosexuality, Harry Oosterhuis,
"Medicine, Male Bonding, and Homosexuality in Nazi Germany," *Journal of
Contemporary History* 32 (April 1997): 187–206.

22. This paragraph draws on material in James D. Steakley, *The Homosexual Emancipation Movement in Germany* (New York: Arno, 1975); Vern L. Bullough, *Science in
the Bedroom: The History of Sex Research* (New York: Basic Books, 1994), pp. 57–
92; Plant, *The Pink Triangle*; Claudia Schoppmann, *Days of Masquerade: Life Stories of
Lesbians During the Third Reich* (New York: Columbia University Press, 1996);
Erwin J. Haeberle, "Swastika, Pink Triangle, and Yellow Star: The Destruction
of Sexology and the Persecution of Homosexuals in Nazi Germany," in Martin
Duberman, Martha Vicinus, and George Chauncey, Jr., eds., *Hidden from History:
Reclaiming the Gay and Lesbian Past* (New York: New American Library, 1989), pp.
365–79; Michael Burleigh and Wolfgang Wippermann, *The Racial State: Germany,
1933–1945* (Cambridge: Cambridge University Press, 1991), pp. 184–86;
Christopher Isherwood, *Christopher Isherwood and His Kind, 1929–1939* (New York:
Farrar, Straus & Giroux, 1976), esp. pp. 13–29; Isherwood, *The Berlin Stories:
The Last of Mr. Norris and Goodbye to Berlin* (New York: New Directions, 1945);
Jonathan Fryer, *Isherwood: A Biography of Christopher Isherwood* (London: New English
Library, 1977), esp. pp. 112–24; Stan Persky, "Berlin/Boyopolis," in Persky,
Then We Take Berlin: Stories from the Other Side of Europe (Toronto: Knopf, 1995), pp.
129–220. Persky's account seems to want to reproduce Isherwood's erotic
encounters fifty years later. For an intriguing contemporary attempt to relate
the "perversions" of fascism and the "perversions" of sexual transgression,
including commercialized homosexuality, see Hendrik De Leeuw, *Sinful Cities
of the Western World* (New York: Citadel, 1934), pp. 223–46. Note, finally, the
documentary collection Mark Blasius and Shane Phelan, eds., *We Are Everywhere: A Historical Sourcebook of Gay and Lesbian Politics* (New York: Routledge, 1997),
pp. 63–178.

23. Harry Ooserhuis, "The 'Jews' of the Antifascist Left: Homosexuality and
Socialist Resistance to Nazism," in G. Hekma, H. Ooserhuis, and J. Steakley,
eds., *Gay Men and the Sexual History of the Political Left* (London: Routledge, 1995),
pp. 227–57. A recent treatment of Roehm is Eleanor Hancock, "'Only the
Real, the True, the Masculine Held its Value': Ernst Rohm, Masculinity, and

Male Homosexuality," *Journal of the History of Sexuality* 8 (April 1998): 616–41.

24. Ian Kershaw, *The "Hitler Myth": Image and Reality in the Third Reich* (Oxford: Clarendon Press, 1987). Kershaw stresses that the "Roehm Putsch" was motivated by fear of Roehm's ambitions to take over the army, which is undoubtedly true, but in displacing Roehm, Hitler and others rationalized their coup with the violence and rhetoric of homophobia.

25. See Oosterhuis, "Medicine, Male Bonding, and Homosexuality in Nazi Germany," pp. 187–206.

26. R. Lautman, "Categorisation in Concentration Camps as a Collective Fate: A Comparision of Homosexuals and Jehovah's Witnesses," *Journal of Homosexuality* 19 (1990): 67–88.

27. The number of castrations was not large, but the coercive message of even a few cases was powerful enough. See G. J. Giles, "'The Most Unkindest Cut of All': Castration, Homosexuality, and Nazi Justice," *Journal of Contemporary History* 27 (January 1992): 41–61.

28. The above paragraphs draw on Plant, *The Pink Triangle*; Eugen Kogan, *The Theory and Practice of Hell* (New York: Berkeley, 1968). See, as well, Heinz Herger, *The Men with the Pink Triangle* (Boston: Alyson, 1980); Max Gallo, *The Knight of the Long Knives* (New York: Harper & Row, 1972); Saul Friedlander, *Nazi Germany and the Jews—Volume 1: The Years of Persecution, 1933–1939* (New York: HarperCollins, 1997), pp. 113–14, 203, 205–07, 236, 247, 302. An excellent brief account of homosexual repression is in Burleigh and Wippermann, *The Racial State*, pp. 182–97. For an account of homosexuals and concentration camps, see Ruediger Lautmann, "Gay Prisoners in Concentration Camps," in Michael Berebaum, ed., *A Mosaic of Victims: Non-Jews Persecuted and Murdered by the Nazis* (London: Macmillan, 1990), pp. 200–21. For a dramatization of homosexuality and the concentration camps, see Martin Sherman, *Bent* (New York: Avon, 1979).

29. For a broad historical discussion of German Jewry, see Fritz Stern, "The Burden of Success: Reflections on German Jewry," in *Dreams and Delusions*, pp. 97–14.

30. An overview of modern anti-Semitism with interesting analytic implications is found in Peter Loewenberg, *Fantasy and Reality in History* (New York: Oxford University Press, 1995), pp. 172–91. The most strident and exaggerated interpretive case, emphasizing the inevitability of the "Final Solution" given the German people's virulent anti-Semitism, is perhaps Daniel Jonah Goldhagen's popularly acclaimed *Hitler's Willing Executioners: Ordinary Germans and the Holocaust* (New York: Knopf, 1996). For a critique of Goldhagen, see Norman G. Finkelstein, "Daniel Jonah Goldhagen's 'Crazy' Thesis: A Critique of Hitler's Willing Executioners," *New Left Review* 224 (July–August 1997): 39–87.

31. See Lisa Fittko, *Solidarity and Treason: Resistance and Exile, 1933–1940* (Evanston: Northwestern University Press, 1993), p. 43. "A census had been announced. Suddenly, all residents were ordered to be at the address where they were legally registered on the appointed night. Every home would be checked, everyone would be counted. The census was aimed at us illegals! And this meant that we, the illegals, would have to spend the night in parks, on benches, in dark streets, backyards, and alleys.... We were wild game in season." For an account of early atrocities, including much anti-Semitic

terror, see Alexandra Richie, *Faust's Metropolis: A History of Berlin* (New York: Carrol & Graf, 1998), pp. 407–74.

32. Among the excellent studies of this assault on the status and rights of German Jews, providing detail and dimensions impossible to treat adequately here, see Karl A. Schleunes, *The Twisted Road to Auschwitz: Nazi Policy Toward German Jews, 1933–1939* (Urbana: University of Illinois Press, 1990); Saul Friedlander, *Nazi Germany and the Jews*; Karl A. Schleunes, "Retracing the Twisted Road: Nazi Policies Toward German Jews, 1933–1939," and Saul Friedlander, "From Anti-Semitism to Extermination: A Historiographical Study of Nazi Policies Toward the Jews and an Essay in Interpretation," in François Furet, *Unanswered Questions: Nazi Germany and the Genocide of the Jews* (New York: Schocken, 1989), pp. 3–32, 54–70. A brief statement appears in William Carr, "Nazi Policy Against the Jews," in Bessel, ed., *Life in the Third Reich*, pp. 69–82.

33. For a recent survey of the happenings of *Kristallnacht*, see Friedlander, *Nazi Germany and the Jews*, pp. 269–76.

34. A useful collection of essays, establishing the stages in the making of the Final Solution, is Christopher R. Browning, *Fateful Months: Essays on the Emergence of the Final Solution* (London: Holmes & Meier, 1985). The Holocaust is now the subject of an immense literature. See the brief summary and citation of major sources in Stanely G. Payne, *A History of Fascism, 1914–1945* (Madison: University of Wisconsin Press, 1995), pp. 380–81; Michael R. Marrus, "History of the Holocaust: A Survey of Recent Literature," *Journal of Modern History* 59 (March 1987): 114–60.

35. The classic account of German resistance is Peter Hoffmann, *The History of German Resistance* (Cambridge, Mass.: MIT Press, 1977) supplemented by much subsequent literature, including Theodore Hamerow, *On the Road to Wolf's Lair: German Resistance to Hitler* (Cambridge, Mass.: Harvard University Press, 1997). Hamerow stresses official military challenges and clandestine plots. A wide-ranging recent account is Anton Gill, *An Honorable Defeat: A History of German Resistance to Hitler, 1933–1945* (New York: Henry Holt, 1994). On memory of this darkness and its relationship to resistance to fascism, see a number of essays in Michael Geyer and John W. Boyer, eds., *Resistance Against the Third Reich, 1933–1990* (Chicago: University of Chicago Press, 1994), esp. Geoffrey Cocks, "Repressing, Remembering, Working Through: German Psychiatry, Psycho-therapy, Psychoanalysis, and the 'Missed Resistance' in the Third Reich," and Michael Geyer, "Resistance as Ongoing Project: Visions of Order, Obligations to Strangers, and Struggles for Civil Society, 1933–1990," pp. 312–50, as well as the useful collection, Luisa Passerini, ed., *Memory and Totalitarianism: Volume 1 of the International Yearbook of Oral History and Life Stories* (Oxford: Oxford University Press, 1992). Note, finally, the treatment of memory in Jane Kramer, *The Politics of Memory: Looking for Germany in the New Germany* (New York: Random House, 1996). Kramer deals with journalism in the 1988–1995 years.

36. See many of the essays in the excellent collection, David F. Crew, ed., *Nazism and German Society, 1933–1945* (London: Routledge, 1994).

37. On resistance and containment, see Tim Mason, "The Containment of the Working Class in Nazi Germany," in Jane Caplan, ed., *Nazism, Fascism, and the Working Class* (Cambridge: Cambridge University Press, 1995), pp. 231–73; Mason, "Labor in the Third Reich, 1933–1939," *Past & Present* 33 (April 1936): 112–41; Daniel Guerin, *The Brown Plague: Travels in Late Weimar and Early Nazi Germany*

(Durham, N.C.: Duke University Press, 1994), esp. pp. 123–52; Klaus-Michael Mallmann and Gerhard Paul, "Omniscient, Omnipotent, Omnipresent? Gestapo, Society, and Resistance," in Crew, ed., Nazism and German Society, pp. 166–96; Peukert, Inside Nazi Germany, pp. 118–34; Herbert Steiner, "The Role of Resistance in Austria, with Special Reference to the Labor Movement," and Alf Ludtke, "The Appeal of Exterminating 'Others': German Workers and the Limits of Resistance," in Geyer and Boyer, eds., Resistance Against the Third Reich, pp. 167–72, 53–74; Terence Prittie, Germans Against Hitler (London: Hutchinson, 1964); Max Horbach, Out of the Night (1967; New York: F. Fell, 1969).

38. On White Rose, see Christiane Moll, "Acts of Resistance: The White Rose in the Light of New Archival Evidence," in Geyer and Boyer, eds., Resistance Against the Third Reich, pp. 173–200; Annette E. Dumbach and Jud Newborn, Shattering the German Night: The Story of the White Rose (Boston: Beacon Press, 1986); Terence Prittie, Germans against Hitler (London: Hutchinson, 1964), pp. 153–78; and for the leaflet documentation quoted, Inge Scholl, The White Rose: Munich, 1942–1943 (Middletown, Conn.: Wesleyan University Press, 1973).

39. The White Rose were not Marxists, and certainly not Gramscians, but note the discussion of passive revolution in Antonio Gramsci, Selections from the Prison Notebooks (New York: International, 1971), pp. 106–20. An extraordinary account of the Italian fascist experience and the working class is Luisa Passerini, Fascism in Popular Memory: The Cultural Experience of the Turin Working Class (Cambridge: Cambridge University Press, 1987).

40. The following discussion focuses on Berlin, but other locales could be addressed. Consider for context the discussion in Robin Lenman, "Politics and Culture: The State and the Avant-Garde in Munich, 1886–1914," in Richard J. Evans, ed., Society and Politics in Wilhelmine Germany (London: Croom Helm, 1978), pp. 90–111.

41. For an example of the satirical, see a compilation of the leftist cabaret performer Kurt Tucholsky, Deutschland, Deutschland uber alles: Photographs assembled by John Heartfield (Amherst: University of Amherst Press, 1972). On American cabaret in the Popular Front period, see Michael Denning, The Cultural Front: The Laboring of American Culture in the Twentieth Century (London: Verso, 1996), pp. 325–28.

42. On "degenerate" art, see the excellent commentary and catalogue of an exhibit in Stephanie Barron et al., "Degenerate Art": The Fate of the Avant-Garde in Nazi Germany (Los Angeles: LACMA, 1991).

43. Among many studies, see George Grosz, A Little Yes and a Big No: the Autobiography of George Grosz (New York: Dial Press, 1946); Irwin Beith Lewis, George Grosz: Art and Politics in the Weimar Republic (Madison: University of Wisconsin Press, 1971); Barbara McCloskey, George Grosz and the Communist Party: Art and Radicalism in Crisis, 1918–1936 (Princeton: Princeton University Press, 1997).

44. On cabaret, see the rich study of Peter Jelavich, Berlin Cabaret (Cambridge, Mass.: Harvard University Press, 1993); and the useful collection, Laurence Senelick, ed., Cabaret Performance: Volume II: Europe, 1920–1940—Sketches, Songs, Monologues, Memoirs (Baltimore: Johns Hopkins University Press, 1993).

45. On Dietrich, the archetype of Weimar sexuality, see Donald Spoto, Blue Angel: the Life of Marlene Dietrich (New York: Doubleday, 1992).

46. Note the stimulating discussion in Linda Mizejewski, *Divine Decadence: Fascism, Female Spectacle, and the Makings of Sally Bowles* (Princeton: Princeton University Press, 1992), which I draw on but do not totally agree with. Mizejewski ends her book with the quotation from Ross, which appeared in Sarah Caudwell, "Reply to Berlin," *New Statesman*, October 3, 1986, pp. 28–29. See, as well, Isherwood, "Sally Bowles," in *The Berlin Stories*, section titled "Goodbye to Berlin," pp. 21–76; Margarete von Falkensee, *Blue Angel Nights [The Pleasure Garden]* (New York: Carroll & Graf, 1986). Films such as *Cabaret* displeased Isherwood because they tended to portray the night scene washed of grittiness, which Isherwood, and apparently Bowles as well, thought both important and attractive. Cabaret women and their sexuality should be contextualized in terms of Nazi constructions of womanhood. See Claudia Koonz, *Mothers in the Fatherland: Women, the Family, and Nazi Politics* (New York: St. Martin's Press, 1987); Bridenthal et al., eds., *When Biology Became Destiny*, and two essays, Gisela Bock, "Antinatalism, Maternity, and Paternity in National Socialist Racism," and Adelheid von Saldern, "Victims or Perpetrators? Controversies about the Role of Women in the Nazi State," in Crew, ed., *Nazism and German Society*, pp. 110–40 and pp. 141–65, respectively.

47. These two paragraphs draw on material in Guerin, *The Brown Plague*, pp. 65–68 and pp. 165–72; Christine Fournier, "'Ring' Youth Gangs," *Die neue Weltbuhne*, January 20, 1931; Eve Rosenhaft, "Organising the 'Lumpenproletariat': Cliques and Communists in Berlin during the Weimar Republic," in Richard J. Evans, ed., *The German Working Class, 1888–1933: The Politics of Everyday Life* (London: Macmillan, 1982), pp. 174–219; Peukert, *The Weimar Republic*, pp. 93, 254. I have not been able to read the major German collection on the subject: Helmut Lessing and Manfred Liebel, eds., *Wilde Cliquen* (Bensheim, 1981). For early Socialist Youth groups, see Alex Hall, "Youth in Rebellion: The Beginnings of the Socialist Youth Movement, 1904–1914," in Richard J. Evans, ed., *Society and Politics in Wilhelmine Germany* (London: Croom Helm, 1978), pp. 241–66.

48. The best source in English on the Edelweiss Pirates is Peukert, *Inside Nazi Germany*, esp. pp. 134, 154–72. An accessible, short account is Peukert, "Youth in the Third Reich," in Bessel, ed., *Life in the Third Reich*, pp. 25–40, and the brief comment in Gill, *An Honourable Defeat*, pp. 196–200. See, as well, Tim Mason, "The Containment of the Working Class in Nazi Germany," in Mason, *Nazism, Fascism and the Working Class*, p. 237; Daniel Horn, "Youth Resistance in the Third Reich," *Journal of Social History* 7 (1973): 26–50. There are references to the Pirates in the excellent general discussion of youth in Burleigh and Wippermann, *The Racial State*, pp. 201–41. A brief passage in Terence Prittie, *Germans Against Hitler* (London: Hutchinson, 1964), p. 159, suggests that Edelweiss groups were linked to banned Catholic associations and were often a clandestine, oppositional contingent within the Hitler Youth, but this seems a rather narrow understanding.

49. On the "swing kids," aside from the 1993 Hollywood movie of the same name, see Michael H. Kater, *Different Drummer: Jazz in the Culture of Nazi Germany* (Oxford: Oxford University Press, 1992), esp. pp. 102–10, 148–62, 193–94; Kater, "Forbidden Fruit? Jazz in the Third Reich," *American Historical Review* 94 (February 1994): 11–43; "Hans Massaquoi," in Studs Terkel, ed., *The Good*

War: An Oral History of World War Two (New York: Pantheon, 1984), pp. 500–01; Earl R. Beck, "The Anti-Nazi 'Swing Youth,' 1942–1945," *Journal of Popular Culture* 19 (Winter 1985): 45–53; Peukert, *Inside Nazi Germany*, pp. 166–69; scattered comment in Burleigh and Wippermann's discussion of youth and the Third Reich in *The Racial State*, pp. 201–41; and the brief aside in Eric Hobsbawm, *The Jazz Scene* (New York: Pantheon, 1989), p. 229.

Chapter 16

1. Eric Hobsbawm, *The Jazz Scene* (New York: Pantheon, 1993), pp. xii–xvi. For jazz influences in this period, see Michael H. Kater, *Different Drummer: Jazz in the Culture of Nazi Germany* (Oxford: Oxford University Press, 1992), pp. 10, 48, 71, 76, 78, 82; James Lincoln Collier, *The Making of Jazz: A Comprehensive History* (Boston: Houghton Mifflin, 1978), pp. 320, 335; Leonard Feather, *The Encyclopedia of Jazz* (New York: Horizon, 1955), p. 21. A treatment of Louis Armstrong is Laurence Bergreen, *Louis Armstrong: An Extravagant Life* (New York: Broadway Books, 1997).

2. For a discussion of creolization, see Marshall Stearns, *The Story of Jazz* (New York: New American Library, 1958), pp. 11–45. Note the essay by Luc Sante, "Really the Blues," *New York Review of Books*, August 11, 1994, pp. 46–52. For the argument that this process was not entirely benign, see Peter Fryer, "The 'Discovery' and Appropriation of African Music and Dance," *Race & Class* 39 (January–March 1998): 1–20.

3. Prison work chants are studied in Bruce Jackson, *Wake Up Dead Man* (Cambridge, Mass.: Harvard University Press, 1972); John Lomax, *Adventures of a Ballad Hunter* (New York: Macmillan, 1947); Alan Lomax, *The Land Where the Blues Began* (New York: Pantheon, 1993), pp. 256–313.

4. Virtually all commentary on jazz and blues uses the night as a backdrop out of which the history of these genres, the practice of performance, and the aesthetics of the music develop. For jazz, note the centrality of night in Geoff Dyer, *But Beautiful: A Book About Jazz* (New York: North Point Press, 1996). For blues, one of the rare critics and commentators to accord the night its obvious place of conceptual importance is Paul Garon, *Blues and the Poetic Spirit* (San Francisco: City Lights, 1975), pp. 115–19. Note, as well, the discussion of blues and jazz aesthetics and the night, developed out of an appreciation of Harlem poetry, in James De Jongh, *Vicious Modernism: Black Harlem and the Literary Imagination* (Cambridge: Cambridge University Press, 1990), pp. 21–26.

5. LeRoi Jones, *Blues People: Negro Music in White America* (New York: Apollo, 1963), pp. 17–18, 41, 61, 67. For a critique of Jones, see Ralph Ellison, "Blues People," in Ellison, *Shadow and Act* (New York: Signet, 1966), pp. 241–50. On slavery and the work song, see Eugene D. Genovese, *Roll, Jordan, Roll: The World the Slaves Made* (New York: Pantheon, 1974), pp. 318–74; Charles Joyner, *Down by the Riverside: A South Carolina Slave Community* (Urbana: University of Illinois Press, 1984), pp. 1, 59; William Barlow, *"Looking Up at Down": The Emergence of Blues Culture* (Philadelphia: Temple University Press, 1989), pp. 13–17; Dena J. Epstein, *Sinful Times and Spirituals: Black Folk Music to the Civil War* (Urbana: University of Illinois Press, 1974).

6. For an excellent analytically poised discussion, see James H. Cone, *The Spirituals and the Blues: An Interpretation* (Maryknoll, N.Y.: Orbis Books, 1991).

7. On the Mississippi River Delta background, see Robert Palmer, *Deep Blues* (New York: Penguin, 1982); William Ferris, *Blues from the Delta* (Garden City, N.Y.: Doubleday, 1978). One of the more detailed discussions of the process of transplantation is found in James Lincoln Collier, *The Making of Jazz: A Comprehensive History* (Boston: Houghton Mifflin, 1978). See, as well, Houston A. Baker, Jr., *Blues, Ideology, and Afro-American Literature: A Vernacular Theory* (Chicago: University of Chicago Press, 1984), pp. 1–14. On Congo Square, see Jerah Johnson, "New Orleans's Congo Square: An Urban Setting for Early Afro-American Cultural Formation," *Louisiana History* 32 (Spring 1991): 117–57.

8. For a collection of essays relevant to these processes, see James H. Dormon, ed., *Creoles of Color of the Gulf South* (Knoxville: University of Tennessee Press, 1996). Note, as well, Christopher Benfey, *Degas in New Orleans: Encounters in the Creole World of Kate Chopin and George Washington Cable* (New York: Knopf, 1997); George Washington Cable, *Creoles and Cajuns: Stories of Old Louisiana* (Garden City, N.Y.: Doubleday, 1959).

9. Cone, *The Spirituals and the Blues*, pp. 1, 7. For a congruent argument, in which interpretation of the blues as irreligious is challenged, see Jon Michael Spenser, *Blues and Evil* (Knoxville: University of Tennessee Press, 1993).

10. See the highly suggestive argument in Hobsbawm, *The Jazz Scene*, pp. 3–8; Collier, *The Making of Jazz*, pp. 30–34; and to some extent Sidney Finkelstein, *Jazz: A People's Music* (New York: Citadel Press, 1948), pp. 9–30; Lawrence Levine, *Black Culture and Black Consciousness: Afro-American Folk Thought from Slavery to Freedom* (New York: Oxford University Press, 1977), p. 296; Paul Oliver, *The Story of the Blues* (Philadelphia: Chilton Book Company, 1969).

11. Quoted in Cone, *The Spirituals and the Blues*, p. 109.

12. Iain Lang, *Jazz in Perspective: The Background of the Blues* (London: Hutchinson, 1948), pp. 30–31.

13. In what follows I draw eclectically on lyrics and artists. For a more thorough canvassing of the recordings and men and women associated with the blues, see Paul Oliver, ed., *The Blackwell Guide to Blues Records* (Oxford: Blackwell Reference, 1989), which contains particularly useful essays and discographies on subjects and chronological periods such as "classic blues" and women singers, the 1930s, and Chicago and the post–Second World War North. For other argument along these lines, see Cone, *The Spirituals and the Blues*, and the suggestions in Albert Murray, *The Hero and the Blues* (New York: Viking, 1995); Murray, *The Blue Devils of Nada: A Contemporary American Approach to Aesthetic Statement* (New York: Vintage, 1997); Houston A. Baker, Jr., *Afro-American Poetics: Revisions of Harlem and the Black Aesthetic* (Madison: University of Wisconsin Press, 1988), pp. 147, 150, 156–59. Note, as well, the general arguments about popular music, with specific reference to jazz and blues, in George Lipsitz, *Dangerous Crossroads: Popular Music, Postmodernism and the Poetics of Place* (London: Verso, 1994), 4, 13–14, 27, and especially the essay "Albert King, Where Y'at?" pp. 171–82; Lipsitz, *Time Passages: Collective Memory and American Popular Culture* (Minneapolis: University of Minnesota Press, 1990), pp. 3–4.

14. On the origins of the designation "blues," see Barlow, *"Looking Up at Down"*, pp. 8–9; Paul Oliver, *The Meaning of the Blues* (New York: Collier, 1963), p. 333;

Collier, *The Making of Jazz*, p. 37; John J. Niles, "Shout Coon Shout," *Musical Quarterly* 16 (October 1930): 519–21.

15. Quoted in Litwack, *Been in the Storm So Long: The Aftermath of Slavery* (New York: Vintage, 1980), pp. 387, 292.

16. Lyrics quoted in Hobsbawm, *The Jazz Scene*, pp. xlv–xlvii, which also contains a short, useful statement on railroads.

17. Lyrics quoted in Alan Lomax, *The Land Where the Blues Began* (New York: Pantheon, 1993), p. 171, and see, for other comment and lyrics related to railroads, and to work gangs associated with them, pp. 142–44, 167–85.

18. On Thomas and the railroad song and Blind Lemon Jefferson see Barlow, "Looking Up at Down", pp. 60–72; Samuel Charters, *The Bluesmen* (New York: Oak, 1967), pp. 175–89. The lyric quoted comes from Eric Sackheim, compiler, *The Blues Line: A Collection of Blues Lyrics from Leadbelly to Muddy Waters* (Hopewell, N.J.: Ecco Press, 1993), "Easy Rider Blues," p. 91.

19. Lyrics quoted in Paul Oliver, *Blues Fell This Morning: Meaning in the Blues* (Cambridge: Cambridge University Press, 1993), p. 59.

20. Quoted in Cone, *The Spirituals and the Blues*, pp. 122–23.

21. See Ralph Ellison, "Blues People," p. 250.

22. Quoted in Barlow, "Looking Up at Down", p. 3.

23. On the nature and dimensions of pre–First World War black migrations and laboring lives, see John Hope Franklin, *From Slavery to Freedom: A History of Negro Americans* (New York: Knopf, 1947), pp. 397–402; Florette Henri, *Black Migration: Movement North, 1900–1920* (Garden City, N.Y.: Doubleday, 1976), pp. 26–34; Philip S. Foner, *Organized Labor and the Black Worker, 1619–1981* (New York: International, 1982), pp. 64–136; Hobsbawm, *The Jazz Scene*, p. 14; William M. Tuttle, Jr., "Labor Conflict and Racial Violence: The Black Worker in Chicago, 1894–1919," *Labor History* 10 (1969): 86–111; and the insightful passage in Toni Morrison, *Jazz* (New York: Penguin, 1992), pp. 33–35.

24. *Jazz Monthly*, December 1963, p. 28, quoted in Barlow, "Looking Up at Down", p. 262.

25. Lyrics quoted in Ann Douglas, *Terrible Honesty: Mongrel Manhattan in the 1920s* (New York: Noonday, 1995), p. 398.

26. Note the detailed account of Cincinnati in Steven C. Tracey, *Going to Cincinnati: A History of Blues in the Queen City* (Urbana and Chicago: University of Illinois Press, 1993).

27. On the making of the urban blues milieu in this period, see the most recent study of rural to urban black migration, Carole Marks, *Farewell—We're Good and Gone: The Great Black Migration* (Bloomington: Indiana University Press, 1989); and the older study, Elliott Rudwick, *From Plantation to Ghetto* (New York: Hill & Wang, 1976).

28. Eugene Victor Wolfenstein, *The Victims of Democracy: Malcolm X and the Black Revolution* (Berkeley: University of California Press, 1981), pp. 42–86.

29. On the underworld, see the study Ronald L. Morris, *Wait Until Dark: Jazz and the Underworld, 1880–1940* (Bowling Green: Bowling Green University Popular Press, 1980); and for the 1940s, Wolfenstein, *Victims of Democracy*, pp. 153–207.

30. The Memphis scene is discussed admirably and fully in James Dickerson, *Goin' Back to Memphis: A Century of Blues, Rock'n'Roll, and Glorious Soul* (New York: Schirmer Books, 1996); Barlow, "Looking Up at Down", pp. 202–29, from which I draw the quoted lyrics. Paul Oliver's *The Story of the Blues* presents a dis-

cussion of Beale Street, pp. 47–57. For Bessie Smith, I draw on the brief discussion in Collier, *The Making of Jazz*, p. 118. For blues recollections see, as well, Samuel Charters, *Sweet as the Showers of Rain* (New York: Oak Publications, 1977), p. 50; Mike Rowe, *Chicago Blues: The City and the Music* (New York: Da Capo, 1975), p. 96; B. B. King, *Blues All Around Me: The Autobiography of B. B. King* (New York: Avon, 1996), p. 117.

31. On the history of "race" records and the exploitation of black artists, see Barlow, *"Looking Up at Down"*, pp. 128–35, 328–34; Francis Davis, *The History of the Blues: The Roots, the Music, the People, from Charley Patton to Robert Cray* (New York: Hyperion, 1995), pp. 202–05; George Lipsitz, *Rainbow at Midnight: Labor and Culture in the 1940s* (Urbana: University of Illinois Press, 1994), pp. 303–34; and, specifically on the Chess brothers, Rowe, *Chicago Blues*.

32. This draws on arguments and lyrics in Paul Garon, *Blues and the Poetic Spirit* (San Francisco: City Lights, 1996), pp. 115–19; Sterling A. Brown, *Southern Roads* (New York: Harcourt Brace, 1932), pp. 52–64; Sackheim, compiler, *The Blues Line*, p. 192. On Robert Johnson, see Barlow, *"Looking Up at Down"*, pp. 45–50; Palmer, *Deep Blues*; Samuel Charters, *Robert Johnson* (New York: Oak Publications, 1973); Alan Greenberg, *Love in Vain: The Life and Legend of Robert Johnson* (Garden City, N.Y.: Doubleday, 1983); Peter Guralnick, *Searching for Robert Johnson* (New York: Dutton, 1989). On Charley Patton, note the analytic statement in Cone, *The Spirituals and the Blues*, p. 112.

33. For a general statement that coincides with this particular analysis, see Robin D. G. Kelley, *Race Rebels: Culture, Politics, and the Black Working Class* (New York: Free Press, 1994), pp. 17–54.

34. An intriguing recent account of blues, left politics, and the "cultural front" of the 1930s and 1940s is Michael Denning, *The Cultural Front: The Laboring of American Culture in the Twentieth Century* (London: Verso, 1996), esp. pp. 348–60.

35. Charley Patton, "Mean Black Moan" (on Chicago strike), quoted in Barlow, *"Looking Up at Down"*, p. 38; L. C. Williams, "Strike Blues," quoted in Garon, *Blues and the Poetic Spirit*, p. 134; Mississippi John Hurt, "Spike Driver Blues," in Sackheim, compiler, *The Blues Line*, p. 226; Leadbelly, "Bourgeois Blues," in Oliver, *Blues Fell This Morning*, pp. 168–69.

36. Red Nelson, "Cryin' Mother Blues," quoted in John Postgate, *A Plain Man's Guide to Jazz* (New York: Oak Publications, 1973), p. 8.

37. On Patton, see Barlow, *"Looking Up at Down"*, pp. 33–40; David Evans, "Charley Patton: Conscience of the Delta," in Robert Sacre, ed., *The Voice of the Delta: Charley Patton* (Liege: Presses Universitaires, 1987), pp. 111–220; Palmer, *Deep Blues*, pp. 48–89; Samuel Charters, *The Bluesmen* (New York: Oak Publications, 1967), pp. 34–56.

38. Barlow, *"Looking Up at Down"*, pp. 263–66; Garon, *Blues and the Poetic Spirit*, pp. 103–08; Jon Michael Spencer, *Blues and Evil* (Knoxville: University of Tennessee Press, 1993), p. 75; Ralph Ellison, *Invisible Man* (New York: Signet, 1952), pp. 131–34; Paul Garon, *The Devil's Son-in-Law: The Story of Peetie Whiteshaw and His Songs* (London: Studio Vista, 1971).

39. Garon, *Blues and the Poetic Spirit* presents a series of small discussions of many of these themes, including specific attention to aggressive behavior and alcohol and drugs, pp. 65–71, 91–102. This is not unrelated to the important complications Ann DuCille has attempted to develop with respect to our appreciation of blues as a "signifying" statement of African-American

experience. See Ann DuCille, "Blues Notes on Black Sexuality: Sex and the Texts of Jessie Fauset and Nella Larsen," *Journal of the History of Sexuality* 3 (January 1993): 418–44.

40. Eddie Boyd, "Five Long Years," and Big Joe Williams, "Overhauling Blues," quoted in Garon, *Blues and the Poetic Spirit*, pp. 131, 138; Robert Johnson, "Terraplane Blues," in Sackheim, compiler, *The Blues Line*, p. 218.

41. Quoted in Garon, *Blues and the Poetic Spirit*, p. 140.

42. For a contemporary treatment of blues women, see Angela Y. Davis, *Blues Legacies and Black Feminism: "Ma" Rainey, Bessie Smith, and Billie Holiday* (New York: Pantheon, 1998). The lines from Ma Rainey's "Prove It on Me" are quoted in Barlow, *"Looking Up at Down"*, p. 160.

43. Quoted in Garon, *Blues and the Poetic Spirit*, p. 139.

44. Quoted in Barlow, *"Looking Up at Down"*, pp. 148–49.

45. See Garon, *Blues and the Poetic Spirit*, p. 71; Lynne Segal, *Is The Future Female? Troubled Thoughts on Contemporary Feminism* (London: Virago, 1987), p. 151. For context, see Kevin J. Mumford, *Interzones: Black/White Sex Districts in Chicago and New York in the Early Twentieth Century* (New York: Columbia University Press, 1997).

46. This draws on arguments and lyrics in Barlow, *"Looking Up at Down"*, pp. 135–74; Garon, *Blues and the Poetic Spirit*, pp. 57–65; Hazel V. Carby, "It Jus Be's Dat Way Sometime: The Sexual Politics of Women's Blues," in Ellen Carol DuBois and Vicki L. Ruiz, eds., *Unequal Sisters: A Multicultural Reader in U.S. Women's History* (New York: Routledge, 1990), pp. 246–48; Lang, *Jazz in Perspective*, p. 65; and Nellie Florence, "Jacksonville Blues," in Sackheim, compiler, *The Blues Line*, p. 40.

47. For other comment on transgressive sexuality and African-American music, see Marybeth Hamilton, "Sexual Politics and African-American Music; or, Placing Little Richard in History," *History Workshop Journal* 46 (Autumn 1998): 161–76; Ann DuCille, "Blues Notes on Black Sexuality."

48. This discussion draws explicitly on Douglas, *Terrible Honesty*, pp. 409–14; Barlow, *"Looking Up at Down"*, pp. 164–79; Collier, *The Making of Jazz*, pp. 108–22; Bud Freeman, *Crazeology: The Autobiography of a Chicago Jazzman* (Urbana: University of Illinois Press, 1989), p. 14; and for Smith's sexuality, Chris Albertson, *Bessie* (New York: Stein & Day, 1974), pp. 116–22. See, as well, Ralph J. Gleason, *Celebrating the Duke: And Louis, Bessie, Billie …* (New York: Da Capo, 1995), pp. 27–32.

49. For an introduction to Muddy Waters as pacesetter, see James Rooney, *Bossmen: Bill Munroe and Muddy Waters* (New York: Da Capo, 1971).

50. See the overview presented in Arnold Shaw, *Honkers and Shouters: The Golden Years of Rhythm and Blues* (New York: Macmillan, 1978). For a powerful statement of the period, penned by a white Jewish bluesman, see Mezz Mezzrow, *Really the Blues* (London: Flamingo, 1993).

51. Among many sources that could be cited on the Chicago Blues, see Barlow, *"Looking Up at Down"*, pp. 287–324; some of the depictions in Samuel Charters, *The Legacy of the Blues: Art and Lives of Twelve Great Bluesmen* (New York: DeCapo, 1977); Rowe, *Chicago Blues*, from which I draw the lyric of Sonny Boy Williamson II's "Unseeing Eye," p. 170; Oliver, *The Story of the Blues*, pp. 105–15; Davis, *The History of the Blues*, pp. 134–38, 180–88. On white rock adaptations, note the often dismissive commentary in Oliver, *The Story of the Blues*, pp. 157–

68; Garon, *Blues and the Poetic Spirit*, pp. 21–50; and the overview in Charlie Gillett, *The Sound of the City: The Rise of Rock and Roll* (New York: Pantheon, 1983).

52. My reading of jazz follows the largely positive literature. For a strong negative critique of jazz as mass-produced, formulaic repetition, see Theodor W. Adorno, "Perennial Fashion—Jazz," in Adorno, *Prisms* (Cambridge, Mass.: MIT Press, 1982), pp. 119–32. Introductions to the complex totality of jazz, largely bypassed in this essay, are Robert Gottlieb, ed., *Reading Jazz: A Gathering of Autobiography, Reportage, and Criticism from 1919 to Now* (New York: Pantheon, 1996); Barry Kernfeld, ed., *The New Grove Dictionary of Jazz* (New York: St. Martin's Press, 1994). On the centrality of early rhythmic improvisation, see Ingrid Monson, *Saying Something: Jazz Improvisation and Interaction* (Chicago: University of Chicago Press, 1996). Two histories include the richly detailed Ted Gioia, *The History of Jazz* (New York: Oxford University Press, 1997) and the more popularly accessible Burton Peretti, *Jazz in American Culture* (Chicago: Ivan Dee, 1997).

53. On the opaque beginnings of jazz—where much that needs to be known will likely remain buried in obscurity—see Stearns, *The Story of Jazz*, pp. 33–110; Jack Vincent Buerkle and Danny Barker, *Bourbon Street Black: The New Orleans Black Jazzman* (New York: Oxford University Press, 1973), esp. pp. 3–21; Leroy Ostransky, *The Anatomy of Jazz* (Seattle: University of Washington Press, 1960), pp. 148–84; Kathy J. Ogren, *The Jazz Revolution: Twenties America & the Meaning of Jazz* (Oxford: Oxford University Press, 1989), pp. 11–56; Samuel Barclay Charters, *Jazz: New Orleans, 1885–1963* (New York: Oak Publications, 1963). Quotes are from Alan Lomax, *Mister Jelly Roll* (Berkeley: University of California Press, 1950), p. 86; and Hobsbawm, *The Jazz Scene*, p. 16.

54. For this history, see Al Rose, *Storyville, New Orleans: Being an Authentic Illustrated Account of the Notorious Red Light District* (Tuscaloosa: University of Alabama Press, 1974); Ruth Rosen, *The Lost Sisterhood: Prostitution in America, 1900–1918* (Baltimore: Johns Hopkins University Press, 1982).

55. On the Original Dixieland Jazz Band see H. O. Brunn, *The Original Dixieland Jazz Band* (Baton Rouge: Louisiana University Press, 1960); Lewis A. Erenberg, *Steppin' Out: New York Nightlife and the Transformation of American Culture, 1890–1930* (Chicago: University of Chicago Press, 1981), pp. 251–53.

56. Freeman, *Crazeology*, pp. 17, 7, 36. On African-American dance and jookin', see Katrina Hazzard-Gordon, *Jookin': The Rise of Social Dance Formations in African-American Culture* (Philadelphia: Temple University Press, 1990); Robin D. G. Kelley, *Race Rebels: Culture, Politics and the Black Working Class* (New York: Free Press, 1994), pp. 46–47; Zora Neale Hurston, "Characteristics of Negro Expression," in Nancy Cunard, ed., *Negro Anthology* (New York: Negro Universities Press, 1969). On Bix Beiderbecke, see Richard M. Sudhalter and Philip R. Evans with William Dean-Myatt, *Bix: Man and Legend* (New Rochelle, N.Y.: Arlington House, 1974).

57. For an interpretation of jazz stressing the significance of racism, see Gene Lees, *Cats of Any Color: Jazz, Black and White* (New York: Oxford University Press, 1994).

58. On the Jazz Age, popularization, and swing, see the full account in Gunther Schuller, *The Swing Era: The Development of Jazz, 1930–1945* (New York: Oxford University Press, 1989); and for Kansas City, see the excellent study, Nathan W. Pearson, Jr., *Goin' to Kansas City* (Urbana: University of Illinois Press, 1987); Martin Williams, "What Happened in Kansas City?" in *Jazz Heritage* (New

York: Oxford University Press, 1985), pp. 17–28; Ross Russell, *Jazz Style in Kansas City and the Southwest* (Berkeley: University of California Press, 1971). On the New York nightclub scene, where jazz was popular, see Erenberg, *Steppin' Out*, and Douglas, *Terrible Honesty*—white jazzmen, Beiderbecke, and Tucker are discussed on pp. 358–71, 414–43.

59. Neil Leonard, *Jazz: Myth and Religion* (New York: Oxford University Press, 1987), p. 28. On Goodman, see Ross Firestone, *Swing, Swing, Swing: The Life and Times of Benny Goodman* (New York: W. W. Norton, 1993), and for Goodman's roots in the white jazz of ethnic Chicago, William Howland Kenney, *Chicago Jazz: A Cultural History, 1904–1930* (New York: Oxford University Press, 1993).

60. For a wonderful compilation of black jazz recollections, see Dempsey J. Travis, ed., *An Autobiography of Black Jazz* (Chicago: Urban Research Institute, 1983), which contains a Cab Calloway recollection of the mob's Cotton Club influence, pp. 227–28. See, as well, Lang, *Jazz in Perspective*, pp. 91–92.

61. See, for instance, Tyler Stovall, *Paris Noir: African Americans in the City of Light* (Boston: Houghton Mifflin, 1996); Bill Moody, *The Jazz Exiles: American Musicians Abroad* (Reno: University of Nevada Press, 1990); Fryer, "The 'Discovery' and Appropriation of African Music and Dance," p. 13. For the origins of this movement, note the case of Josephine Baker, detailed in Josephine Baker and Jo Bouillon, *Josephine* (New York: Marlowe and Company, 1988); Lynn Haney, *Naked at the Feast: The Biography of Josephine Baker* (London: Robson Books, 1995); Phyllis Rose, *Jazz Cleopatra: Josephine Baker in Her Time* (New York: Vintage, 1991).

62. Note Denning's placement of Holiday and others at the conjuncture of Popular Front politics and cultural innovation in Denning, *The Cultural Front*, pp. 338–48.

63. Collier, *The Making of Jazz*, pp. 292–312; Neil Leonard, *Jazz and the White Americans: The Acceptance of a New Art Form* (Chicago: University of Chicago Press, 1962), pp. 111–18, 167–72; Eric Hobsbawm, "Billie Holiday," in Hobsbawm, *Uncommon People: Resistance, Rebellion, and Jazz* (London: Weidenfeld & Nicolson, 1998), pp. 293–94. For biographies of Billie Holiday, see Stuart Nicholson, *Billie Holiday* (London: Gollancz, 1995); John Chilton, *Billie's Blues: The Billie Holiday Story, 1933–1959* (New York: Stein & Day, 1975).

64. How all of this worked itself out was often a local matter, as detailed in the insightful account of George Lipsitz, *A Life in the Struggle: Ivory Perry and the Culture of Opposition* (Philadelphia: Temple University Press, 1988). Note the excellent discussion in Robin D. G. Kelley, "The Riddle of the Zoot: Malcolm Little and Black Cultural Politics During World War II," in *Race Rebels*, pp. 161–81, which quotes Ellison, p. 161, and the complementary wide-ranging account in Denning, *The Cultural Front*. See also Jon Parrish, *The Color of Jazz: Race and Representation in Postwar American Culture* (Jackson: University of Mississippi Press, 1997), pp. 3–22.

65. See Denning, *The Cultural Front*, pp. 309–19; Hobsbawm, "The People's Swing," in *Uncommon People*, pp. 274–80. On Ellington note, as well, Edward Hasse, *Beyond Category: The Life and Genius of Duke Ellington* (New York: Simon & Schuster, 1993); Mark Tucker, ed., *The Duke Ellington Reader* (New York: Oxford University Press, 1993); [Duke] Edward Kennedy Ellington, *Music is My Mistress* (Garden City, N.Y.: Doubleday, 1973); Ken Rattenbury, *Duke Ellington: Jazz Composer* (London: Yale University Press, 1990); Gleason, *Celebrating the Duke*, pp. 153–271.

66. For an introduction, see Frank Kofsky, *Black Nationalism and the Revolution in Music* (New York: Pathfinder, 1970), pp. 125–38; Eric Lott, "Double V, Double-Time: The Bebop's Politics of Style," *Callallo* 11 (1988): 597–605; Jones, *Blues People*, pp. 187–211. Denning links jazz and the generalized cultural ferment of what he calls the CIO years in *The Cultural Front*, pp. 328–38.

67. Accounts of some of these founders include Mike Hennessey, *Klook: The Story of Kenny Clarke* (London: Quartet Books, 1990); Laurent de Wilde, *Monk* (New York: Marlowe, 1997); Thomas Fitterling, *Thelonious Monk: His Life and Work* (Berkeley: Berkeley Hills Books, 1997). Note the wide-ranging discussion of bebop and its practitioners in Scott de Veaux, *The Birth of Bebop: A Social and Musical History* (Berkeley: University of California Press, 1997), esp. pp. 167–270.

68. For introductions to bop, see the analytically rich de Veaux, *Birth of Bebop*; Francis Davis, *Bebop and Nothingness: Jazz and Pop at the End of the Century* (New York: Schirmer Books, 1996), esp. pp. 11–35; Thomas Owens, *Bebop and Its Players* (New York: Oxford University Press, 1995); Collier, *The Making of Jazz*, pp. 341–62; Stearns, *The Story of Jazz*, pp. 155–72; Hobsbawm, *The Jazz Scene*, pp. 82–90. On Parker, blues, and bop, see Pearson, *Goin' to Kansas City*, pp. 204–13; Sidney Finkelstein, *Jazz: A People's Music* (New York: Citadel Press, 1948), pp. 227–38; Whitney Balliett, "The Measure of 'Bird,'" *Saturday Review* 39 (March 17, 1956): 34, quoted in Ostransky, *The Anatomy of Jazz*, p. 270; and for some snapshots of the personnel, Max Harrison, *A Jazz Retrospect* (London: Quartet, 1991), pp. 15–22, 28–31; 88–93; Gary Giddins, *Riding on a Blue Note: Jazz and American Pop* (New York: Oxford University Press, 1981), pp. 213–251; Whitney Balliett, *Goodbyes and Other Messages: A Journal of Jazz, 1981–1990* (New York: Oxford University Press, 1991), pp. 18–22, 37–39, 42–45.

69. Gene Santoro, "The Prince of Darkness," in Santoro, *Dancing in Your Head: Jazz, Blues, Rock, and Beyond* (New York: Oxford University Press, 1994), p. 166; Roy Porter with David Keller, *There and Back: The Roy Porter Story* (Baton Rouge: Louisiana State University Press, 1991), pp. 21, 52–66; A. B. Spellman, *Black Music: Four Lives* (New York: Schocken Books, 1970), quoted in Collier, *The Making of Jazz*, p. 360; Ostransky, *The Anatomy of Jazz*, pp. 254–79, which draws on a range of late 1940s and 1950s jazz criticism. Langston Hughes, *The Best of Simple* (New York: Hill & Wang, 1961), pp. 117–18, quoted in Kofsky, *Black Nationalism and the Revolution in Music*, pp. 270–71. Note, as well, James Lester, *Too Marvelous for Words: The Life and Genius of Art Tatum* (New York: Oxford University Press, 1994). For a counter-view, stressing bebop's continuities with earlier jazz, see Mark C. Gridley, *Jazz Styles: History and Analysis* (Englewood Cliffs, N.J.: Prentice-Hall, 1988), pp. 143–76. On the Gillespie–Parker productions of this period, see Max Harrison, *A Jazz Retrospect* (London: Quartet, 1991), pp. 88–93. Martin Williams, *Jazz in Its Time* (New York: Oxford University Press, 1989), pp. 184–206.

70. John Clellon Holmes, *The Horn* (New York: Random House, 1958).

71. Paul F. Berliner, *Thinking in Jazz: The Infinite Art of Improvisation* (Chicago: University of Chicago Press, 1994), p. 88.

72. The citations for hangin' out and jammin' could be endless, but note Berliner, *Thinking in Jazz*, pp. 36–59; Art Farmer, *The Art of Art Farmer* (New York: Charles Colin, 1984). On Central Avenue, see Art and Laurie Pepper, *Straight Life: The Story of Art Pepper* (New York: Schirmer Books, 1979), p. 41; Johnny Otis,

Upside Your Head! Rhythm and Blues on Central Avenue (Hanover: Wesleyan University Press, 1993), p. 4; Johnny Otis, *Listen to the Lambs* (New York: W. W. Norton, 1968), pp. 107–20, 171–75; Roy Porter with David Keller, *There and Back: The Roy Porter Story* (Baton Rouge: Louisiana State University Press, 1991), pp. 52–66. On Montreal, see John Gilmore, *Swinging in Paradise: The Story of Jazz in Montreal* (Montreal: Vehicule Press, 1988), pp. 115–40. Canadian jazz is explored in Mark Miller, *Melodious Racket: The Lost History of Jazz in Canada, 1914–1949* (Toronto: Mercury Press, 1997). An exceptional local history is Paul de Barros, *Jackson Street After Hours: The Roots of Jazz in Seattle* (Seattle: Sasquatch Books, 1994). For the important California scene in general, see Ted Gioia, *West Coast Jazz: Modern Jazz in California, 1945–1960* (New York: Oxford University Press, 1992).

73. Dicky Wells, as told to Stanley Dance, *The Night People: Reminiscences of a Jazzman* (Boston: Crescendo, 1971); Whitney Balliett, *Night Creature: A Journal of Jazz, 1975–1980* (New York: Oxford University Press, 1981).

74. Holmes, *The Horn*, p. 50.

75. More traditional formalists, such as the supremely elegant vision-impaired jazz pianist Art Tatum, managed to survive bebop's challenges and, in the process, adapt to the limitations imposed on black artists with a kind of Olympian satisfaction in their prestige and accomplishments. See James Lester, *Too Marvelous for Words: The Life and Genius of Art Tatum* (New York: Oxford University Press, 1994).

76. See Ostransky, *The Anatomy of Jazz*, pp. 272–73; and the commentary on early Charlie Parker and Dizzy Gillespie recordings in Martin Williams, *Jazz in Its Time* (New York: Oxford University Press, 1989), pp. 184–97, 201–06. There is a useful collection of commentary on bebop drawn from a wide range of texts in Meltzer, ed., *Reading Jazz*, pp. 175–207.

77. On Parker, commentary is now extensive and almost any account of modern jazz relates the history of the 1940s and Bird. See Carl Woideck, *Charlie Parker: His Music and Life* (Ann Arbor: University of Michigan Press, 1996). For a sampling of other discussion, see Collier, *The Making of Jazz*, pp. 362–76; Robert George Reisner, *Bird: The Legend of Charlie Parker* (New York: Da Capo, 1973); Ross Russell, *Bird Lives!* (New York: Charterhouse, 1973); Leonard, *Jazz and the White Americans*, p. 158; Stearns, *The Story of Jazz*, pp. 160–67. Quotations from and about Parker are from Brian Priestley, *Charlie Parker* (New York: Hippocrane, 1984), pp. 11, 24; Nat Shapiro and Nat Hentoff, eds., *Hear Me Talkin' to Ya* (New York: Rinehart, 1955), p. 405. For a withering assault on Bird, still capable of recognizing his genius, see Dave Dexter, Jr., *The Jazz Story: From the 90s to the 60s* (Englewood Cliffs, N.J.: Prentice-Hall, 1964), pp. 145–56. An insightful interpretation is found in Parrish, *The Color of Jazz*, pp. 42–78.

78. For Holiday, see Collier, *The Making of Jazz*, pp. 303–12; Billie Holiday with William Dufty, *Lady Sings the Blues* (New York: Lancer, 1965); John Chilton, *Billie's Blues* (New York: Stein & Day, 1975); and the verse from Stuart Z. Perkhoff, *Visions from the Tribe* (Denver: Black Ace, 1976), quoted in Meltzer, ed., *Reading Jazz*, pp. 211–12. See also the discussion of Holiday in Davis, *Blues Legacies and Black Feminism*.

79. Priestley, *Charlie Parker*, pp. 11, 24.

80. Among other accounts, see Art and Laurie Pepper, *Straight Life*; Chet Baker, *As Though I Had Wings: The Lost Memoir* (New York: St. Martin's Press, 1997); Janet Coleman and Al Young, *Mingus/Mingus: Two Memories* (New York: Limelight,

1991); Charles Mingus, *Beneath the Underdog: His World as Composed by Mingus* (New York: Random House, 1991); Porter with Keller, *There and Back*; Norwood "Pony" Poindexter, *The Pony Express: Memoirs of a Jazz Musician* (Frankfurt: J.A.S. Publikationen, 1985). Critical commentary, not always favorable, can be found in Williams, *Jazz in Its Time*, pp. 236–39. For a discussion that is hostile to Mingus's *Beneath the Underdog*, but not to his abilities as a bassist, see Whitney Balliett, *Goodbye and Other Messages: A Journal of Jazz, 1981–1990* (New York: Oxford University Press, 1991), pp. 149–55, 247–51; for more on Mingus, and on Pepper as a legend, see Balliett, *Night Creature*, p. 115; Leonard, *Jazz: Myth and Religion*, pp. 79–92, 110–11; Gary Giddins, "The Whiteness of the Wail," in Giddins, *Riding on a Blue Note: Jazz and American Pop* (New York: Oxford University Press, 1981), pp. 252–57.

81. Drew Page, *Drew's Blues: A Sideman's Life with the Big Bands* (Baton Rouge: Louisiana State University Press, 1980), p. i.

82. Collier, *The Making of Jazz*, p. 407; Berliner, *Thinking in Jazz*, p. 822–23; Shapiro and Hentoff, eds., *Hear Me Talkin' to Ya*, pp. 371–82; Nat Hentoff, *The Jazz Life* (New York: Da Capo, 1978), pp. 75–97; Poindexter, *Pony Express*; Art and Laurie Pepper, *Straight Life*; T. Fetterling, *Thelonious Monk* (Berlin: Orcos, 1987), p. 62; and, for a thorough account of the cabaret laws, Paul Chevigny, *Gigs: Jazz and the Cabaret Laws in New York City* (New York: Routledge, 1991). On jazz as protest, the standard account is Finkelstein, *Jazz: A People's Music*, which stresses the accomplishment of jazz as a protest against racist oppression (esp. pp. 27–30). See, as well, Hobsbawm, *The Jazz Scene*, pp. 229–47.

83. Miller, *Such Melodious Racket*, p. 230.

84. See the comments in Finkelstein, *Jazz: A People's Music*, pp. 235–38.

85. For a survey of jazz experience prior to the shifts of the mid-1950s, see Leonard Feather, *The Encyclopedia of Jazz* (New York: Horizon Press, 1955). Subsequent developments are related in the analytically acute Frank Kofsky, *Black Nationalism and the Revolution in Music*, which places Coltrane in a central place, as do most serious scrutinies, among them: Gridley, *Jazz Styles*, pp. 279–300; Collier, *The Making of Jazz*, pp. 478–493.

86. For New Orleans, see Jason Berry, Jonathan Foose, and Tad Jones, *Up From the Cradle of Jazz: New Orleans Music Since World War I* (Athens and London: University of Georgia Press, 1986); and the photo essay on New Orleans jazz families, Lee Friedlander, *The Jazz People of New Orleans* (London: Jonathan Cape, 1992). For the first Chicago school, largely white, see Kenney, *Chicago Jazz*; Postgate, *A Plain Man's Guide to Jazz*, pp. 48–53; on the second, African-American, Chicago school, see Gridley, *Jazz Styles*, pp. 268–78; Ekkehard Jost, *Free Jazz* (New York: Da Capo, 1994). Ornette Coleman is the subject of a useful essay in Charles O. Hartman, *Jazz Text: Voice and Improvisation in Poetry, Jazz, and Song* (Princeton: Princeton University Press, 1991), pp. 57–75, and the biography John Litweiler, *Ornette Coleman: A Harmolodic Life* (New York: Da Capo, 1994).

87. Jim Godbolt, *A History of Jazz in Britain, 1919–1950* (London: Quartet Books, 1984); S. Frederick Starr, *Red and Hot: The Fate of Jazz in the Soviet Union, 1917–1980* (New York: Oxford University Press, 1983); Leo Feigin, ed., *Russian Jazz: New Identity* (London: Quartet Books, 1985).

88. On the birth of cool jazz and the place of Miles Davis, see Francis Davis, *Bebop and Nothingness*, pp. 40–47; Bill Cole, *Miles Davis: A Musical Biography* (New York: Morrow, 1974); Miles Davis with Quincy Troupe, *Miles: The Autobiography*

(New York: Simon & Schuster, 1989); Jack Chambers, *Milestones*, 1: *The Music and Times of Miles Davis to 1960* (Toronto: University of Toronto Press, 1983); Gary Carner, *The Miles Davis Companion: Four Decades of Commentary* (New York: Schirmer Books, 1996); Gleason, *Celebrating the Duke*, pp. 131–47; Gridley, *Jazz Styles*, pp. 177–225; Collier, *The Making of Jazz*, pp. 408–36; Jones, *Blues People*, pp. 211–20. See, finally, the overview of this period and the immediately preceding years in Denning, *The Cultural Front*. A lament for the late-twentieth-century demise of jazz is Eric Nisenson, *Blue: The Murder of Jazz* (New York: St. Martin's Press, 1997).

89. See the suggestive treatment of jazz and New York's Village in Parrish, *The Color of Jazz*, pp. 23–41. For later developments, note Hobsbawm, "Jazz since 1960," in *Uncommon People*, pp. 281–92.

Chapter 17

1. Allen Ginsberg, *Howl: Original Draft Facsimile*, ed. Barry Miles (New York: Harper & Row, 1986), p. 3.

2. For descriptions of the night of "Howl's" delivery, see "First Reading at the Six Gallery" and other documents in *Howl: Original Draft Facsimile*, pp. 165–68. An example of critical commentary on Ginsberg's "Howl" is Gregory Stephenson, *The Daybreak Boys: Essays on the Literature of the Beat Generation* (Carbondale: Southern Illinois University Press, 1990), pp. 50–58, while a wide array of contemporary discussion appears in Lewis Hyde, ed., *On the Poetry of Allen Ginsberg* (Ann Arbor: University of Michigan Press, 1984), pp. 23–84.

3. John Clellon Holmes, "Night Music" [1950], in Holmes, *Night Music: Selected Poems* (Fayetteville: University of Arkansas Press, 1989), p. 12.

4. For the poem's biographical context see, among many sources, James E. Breslin, "Allen Ginsberg's 'Howl'," in Breslin, *From Modern to Contemporary* (Chicago: University of Chicago Press, 1984), pp. 77–109.

5. On the legal history of "Howl" and other commentary, see *Howl: Original Draft Facsimile*, pp. 169–74; Barry Miles, *Ginsberg: A Biography* (New York: Simon & Schuster, 1989), pp. 188–247; Michael Schumacher, *Dharma Lion: A Biography of Allen Ginsberg* (New York: St. Martin's Press, 1992), pp. 188–264; "Big Bad Day for Bards at Bay: Trial Over Howl and Other Poems," *Life* 43 (September 9, 1957): 105–08. The first biography of Ginsberg was Jane Kramer, *Allen Ginsberg in America* (New York: Random House, 1969).

6. Jack Kerouac's *The Town and the City* (New York: Harcourt Brace, 1950) had appeared two years earlier, but it can be argued that there was nothing particularly "beat" about Kerouac's first novel. Ginsberg describes the prose of the book as "regular ... writing in the forms of Thomas Wolfe ... lengthily constructed sentences ... musical, rhythmical constructions." See Allen Ginsberg, *Allen Verbatim: Lectures on Poetry, Politics, Consciousness* (New York: McGraw-Hill, 1974), pp. 151–52. In many ways it was a preface, in form and content, to *On the Road*, but had not yet broken out of its literary culture's boundaries. See, as well, John Tytell, *Naked Angels: Kerouac, Ginsberg, Burroughs* (New York: Grove Weidenfeld, 1991), pp. 149–56.

7. John Clellon Holmes, *Go* (1952; Mamaroneck, N.Y.: Paul P. Appel, 1977), pp. 35–36, portions of which are quoted in Russell Jacoby, *The Last Intellectuals:*

American Culture in the Age of Academe (New York: Basic Books, 1987), p. 66. On Holmes, see Cynthia S. Hamilton, "The Prisoner of Self: The Work of John Clellon Holmes," in A. Robert Lee, ed., *The Beat Generation Writers* (London: Pluto, 1996), pp. 114–27; Stephenson, *The Daybreak Boys*, pp. 90–104.

8. Chandler Brossard, *Who Walk in Darkness* (New York: New Directions, 1952); and Brossard, "Redemption," in Gene Feldman and Max Gartenberg, eds., *The Beat Generation and the Angry Young Men* (New York: Dell, 1958), pp. 134–55.

9. Holmes, *Go*, p. xiii.

10. David W. Maurer, *Language of the Underworld* (Lexington: University Press of Kentucky, 1981), p. 281. For a brief discussion of the emergence of the term, see Edward Halsey Foster, *Understanding the Beats* (Columbia: University of South Carolina Press, 1992), pp. 6–7.

11. Jack Kerouac, *Desolation Angels* (London: Andre Deutsch, 1966), p. 35.

12. Norman Mailer, "The White Negro: Superficial Reflections on the Hipster" [originally published in *Dissent*, 1957], in Mailer, *Advertisements for Myself* (New York: G. P. Putnam's Sons, 1959), pp. 331–75; Caroline Bird, "Born 1930: The Unlost Generation," *Harper's Bazaar*, February 1957, pp. 104–05; Norman Podhoretz, "The Know Nothing Bohemians," *Partisan Review* 25 (Spring 1958): 305–18, reprinted in Podhoretz, *Doings and Undoings: The Fifties and After in American Writing* (New York: Farrar Straus, 1964); Diana Trilling, "The Other Night at Columbia: A Report from the Academy," *Partisan Review* 26 (Spring 1959): 214–30; Robert Brustein, "The Cult of Unthink," *Horizon* 1 (September 1958): 38–44, 134–35. An excellent bibliographic compilation of original commentary on the beats is found in Lee Bartlett, *The Beats: Essays in Criticism* (Jefferson, N.C.: McFarland, 1981), pp. 198–202.

13. See Francis J. Rigney and L. Douglas Smith, *The Real Bohemia: A Sociologial and Psychological Study of the "Beats"* (New York: Basic Books, 1961), pp. 151–76.

14. Paul O'Neil, "The Only Rebellion Around," *Life* 47 (November 30, 1959): 115–30, quoted in Jacoby, *The Last Intellectuals*, p. 66.

15. Holmes, "This is the Beat Generation," in Holmes, *Passionate Opinions: The Cultural Essays* (Fayetteville: University of Arkansas Press, 1988), pp. 58–63. For other Holmes commentary, see Holmes, "Unscrewing the Locks: The Beat Poets," in Bartlett, ed., *The Beats*, pp. 5–14; and the early Holmes collection, *Nothing More to Declare* (New York: Dutton, 1967), which contains not only "This is the Beat Generation" [1952] but also "The Philosophy of the Beat Generation" [1958].

16. Robert M. Lindner, *Rebel without a Cause: The Story of a Criminal Psychopath* (New York: Grove Press, 1944), and the 1955 Nicholas Ray directed film, *Rebel without a Cause*, which pushed James Dean to stardom as a prototype 1950s rebel. Mailer's "The White Negro," pp. 344–46, called for an essential sympathy with the psychopathology explored by Lindner, arguing that "not every psychopath is an extreme case," and that individual growth could benefit from the creative repudiations of the psychopath. Note Bird, "The Unlost Generation," pp. 104–05. On Kerouac's style, see John Montgomery, *Kerouac West Coast: A Bohemian Pilot—Detailed Navigational Instructions* (Palo Alto: Fels and Firn Press, 1976); Ginsberg, *Allen Verbatim*, pp. 151–60; John Tytell, *Naked Angels: Kerouac, Ginsberg, Burroughs* (New York: Grove Weidenfeld, 1991), pp. 143–44; Regina Weinreich, *The Spontaneous Poetics of Jack Kerouac: A Study of the Fiction* (New York: Marlowe, 1995), pp. 8–10; Warren Tallman, "Kerouac's

Sound," *Tamarack Review* 11 (Spring 1959): 58–74. Kerouac is the centerpiece of a sourcebook by Arthur and Kit Knight, *Kerouac and the Beats: A Primary Sourcebook* (New York: Paragon House, 1988). These authors have produced another useful volume: *The Beat Vision: A Primary Sourcebook* (New York: Paragon, 1987).

17. John Clellon Holmes, "Crazy Days, Numinous Nights: 1948–1950," in Arthur and Kit Knight, eds., *The Beat Vision*, p. 79.

18. David Szatmary, *A Time to Rock: A Social History of Rock 'N Roll* (New York: Schirmer Books, 1996), pp. 159–82.

19. For links of the beats and the New Left of the 1960s, see Jack Newfield, *A Prophetic Minority: The American New Left* (London: Anthony Blond, 1967), pp. 35–48.

20. Extensive citation could be provided. See, for a mere glimpse of the issues, Stephen Brier, ed., *Who Built America? Working People and the Nation's Economy, Politics, Culture, and Society—Volume II: From the Gilded Age to the Present* (New York: Pantheon, 1992), pp. 479–542; quotation from Mickey Spillane, *One Lonely Night* (New York: Signet, 1951).

21. William Graebner, *Coming of Age in Buffalo: Youth and Authority in the Postwar Era* (Philadelphia: Temple University Press, 1990); Brier, ed., *Who Built America?*, pp. 530–35; H. F. Moorhouse, "The 'Work Ethic' and 'Leisure' Activity: the Hot Rod in Postwar America," in Patrick Joyce, ed., *The Historical Meanings of Work* (Cambridge: Cambridge University Press, 1987), pp. 237–57; J. Bernard, "Teenage Culture: An Overview," *The Annals of the American Academy of Political and Social Science* 338 (November 1961): 4; David Gartman, *Auto Opium: A Social History of American Automobile Design* (London: Verso, 1994), pp. 136–81.

22. Jacoby, *The Last Intellectuals*, pp. 63–65; James Gilbert, *A Cycle of Outrage: America's Reaction to the Juvenile Delinquent in the 1950s* (New York: Oxford University Press, 1986); Daniel Bell, "The Myth of the Crime Waves," in Bell, *The End of Ideology* (New York: Free Press, 1962), esp. pp. 157–58; David Matza and Gresham Sykes, "Juvenile Delinquency and Subterranean Values," *American Sociological Review* 26 (October 1961): 712–19. For Kerouac's repudiation of a connection between his writing, the beats, and juvenile delinquency, see Helen McNeil, "The Archaeology of Gender in the Beat Movement," in Lee, ed., *The Beat Generation Writers* (London: Pluto, 1996), pp. 187–88.

23. Mailer, "The White Negro," pp. 338–39.

24. Malcolm Cowley, *The Literary Situation* (New York: Viking, 1954), p. 241, quoted in Jacoby, *The Last Intellectuals*, pp. 64–65; Adam Gussow, "Bohemia Revisited: Malcolm Cowley, Jack Kerouac, and On the Road," *Georgia Review* 38 (1984): 291–311.

25. See, for instance, Jerrold Seigel, *Bohemian Paris* (New York: Viking, 1986); Cesar Grana, *Bohemian Versus Bourgeois: French Society and the French Man of Letters in the Nineteenth Century* (New York: Basic Books, 1964); W. Scott Haine, *The World of the Paris Café: Sociability among the French Working Class, 1789–1914* (Baltimore: Johns Hopkins University Press, 1996).

26. See June Sochen, *The New Woman: Feminism in Greenwich Village, 1910–1920* (New York: Quadrangle, 1972); Judith Schwarz, *Radical Feminists of Heterodoxy: Greenwich Village, 1912–1940* (Norwich: New Victoria, 1986); Edward Shils, *Portraits: A Gallery of Intellectuals* (Chicago: University of Chicago Press, 1997), pp. 111–12.

27. For Greenwich Village, the original important statement was Caroline F. Ware, *Greenwich Village, 1920–1930* (Boston: Houghton Mifflin, 1935). Also useful, especially for the earlier pre–First World War and War context is Allen Churchill, *The Improper Bohemians* (New York: E. P. Dutton, 1959); Steven Watson, *Strange Bedfellows: The First American Avant-Garde* (New York: Abbeville Press, 1991). Essential reading is the richly illustrated collection of essays, Rick Beard and Leslie Cohen Berlowitz, eds., *Greenwich Village: Culture and Counterculture* (New Brunswick: Rutgers University Press, 1993).

28. Attempts to survey American bohemianism start with the useful Albert Parry, *Garrets and Pretenders: A History of Bohemianism in America* (New York: Covici Friede, 1933), and move to the more flippant Emily Hahn, *Romantic Rebels: An Informal History of Bohemianism in America* (Boston: Houghton Mifflin, 1967). On early radical bohemians, see Mary V. Dearborn, *Queen of Bohemia: The Life of Louise Bryant* (New York: Houghton Mifflin, 1996); and for a later particular setting, see John Arthur Maynard, *Venice West: The Beat Generation in Southern California* (New Brunswick: Rutgers University Press, 1991); Lawrence Lipton, *The Holy Barbarians* (New York: Julian Messner, 1959).

29. Jacoby, *The Last Intellectuals*, pp. 27–53; Walter Benjamin, "A Berlin Chronicle," in Benjamin, *One Way Street and Other Writings* (London: New Left Books, 1979), pp. 310–11.

30. Jack Kerouac, *Lonesome Traveller* (New York: McGraw-Hill, 1960), p. 114.

31. Hahn, *Romantic Rebels*, pp. 385–91, while Jacoby, *The Last Intellectuals*, pp. 40–53, presents a general overview. For an updated note, see Robert Fitch, *The Assassination of New York* (London: Verso, 1993). On the East Village and bohemia, see John Gruen, *The New Bohemia: Art, Music, Drama, Sex, Film, Dance in New York's East Village* (Chicago: A Cappella Books, 1990).

32. Kerouac, *Lonesome Traveller*, p. 108.

33. For defenders of the city, see Lewis F. Fried, *Makers of the City* (Amherst: University of Massachusetts Press, 1990). This paragraph also draws on Jacoby, *The Last Intellectuals*, pp. 40–44, 60; Robert Caro, *The Power Broker: Robert Moses and the Fall of New York* (New York: Vintage, 1975); Marshall Berman, *All That Is Solid Melts Into Air: The Experience of Modernity* (New York: Simon & Schuster, 1982), pp. 290–348. For a celebration of the car and the highway, see John B. Rae, *The Road and the Car in American Life* (Cambridge, Mass.: MIT Press, 1971).

34. Jacoby, *The Last Intellectuals*, pp. 53, 71. See, as well, the discussion of rootlessness and alienation in Rigney and Smith, *The Real Bohemia*, pp. 16–24, 66–81.

35. Paul Goodman, *Growing Up Absurd* (London: Sphere, 1970), p. 224.

36. Holmes, *Go*, p. 311.

37. Hahn, *Romantic Rebels*, pp. 289–90.

38. Kerouac, *Lonesome Traveller*.

39. Holmes, "Midnight Oil," in *Night Music*, p. 40.

40. Lipton, *The Holy Barbarians*, pp. 7, 272–83; Maynard, *Venice West*, is, among other things, an account of Lipton that offers much commentary on his book.

41. On Burroughs, see Ted Morgan, *Literary Outlaw: The Life and Times of William S. Burroughs* (New York: Avon, 1988); Eric Mottram, *William Burroughs: The Algebra of Need* (London: Boyars, 1977); Jennie Skerl, *William S. Burroughs* (Boston: Twayne, 1985); and the brief statement in Stephen Godfrey, "From Naked Lunch to Shotgun Painting," *Globe and Mail* (Toronto, July 13, 1988).

42. William S. Burroughs, *Naked Lunch* (New York: Grove Press, 1966), and for

the obscenity trial, see Edward de Grazia, *Girls Lean Back Everywhere: The Law of Obscenity and the Assault on Genius* (New York: Random House, 1992), pp. 480–95; Michael B. Goodman, *Contemporary Literary Censorship: The Case History of Burroughs' Naked Lunch* (London: Scarecrow, 1981).

43. William S. Burroughs, *Cities of the Red Night* (New York: Holt, Rinehart, & Winston, 1981), p. 332.

44. Allen Ginsberg, "On Burroughs' Work," in Ginsberg, *Reality Sandwiches, 1953–1960* (San Francisco: City Lights Books, 1963), quoted in Robin Lydenberg, *Word Cultures: Radical Theory and Practice in William S. Burroughs' Fiction* (Chicago: University of Illinois Press, 1987), p. 9.

45. William S. Burroughs, *Junkie* (New York: Ace, 1953), and note, as well, Frank D. McConnell, "William Burroughs and the Literature of Addiction," *Massachusetts Review* 8 (1967): 665–80. For the critical reception of Burroughs over the course of three decades, see Jennie Skerl and Robin Lydenberg, eds., *William S. Burroughs at the Front: Critical Reception, 1959–1989* (Carbondale: Southern Illinois University Press, 1991); Bartlett, *The Beats*, pp. 14–40, 202–08, the latter pages providing a useful bibliography; and Tytell, *Naked Angels*, pp. 36–51, 111–40. On the centrality of "kicks" to the beat experience, see Rigney and Smith, *The Real Bohemia*, pp. 43–65.

46. Nelson Algren, *Somebody in Boots* (New York: Vanguard Press, 1935); and for comment, see Morris Dickstein, "Depression Culture: The Dream of Mobility," in Bill Mullen and Sherry Linkon, eds., *Radical Revisions: Rereading 1930s Culture* (Urbana: University of Illinois Press, 1996), pp. 231–32; and the standard source on Algren, Bettina Drew, *Nelson Algren: A Life on the Wild Side* (Austin: University of Texas Press, 1989), pp. 75–97.

47. See Algren's books, *Never Come Morning* (New York: Harper & Brothers, 1942); *The Neon Wilderness* (Garden City, N.Y.: Doubleday, 1947); *The Man with the Golden Arm* (Garden City, N.Y.: Doubleday, 1949); *A Walk on the Wild Side* (Greenwich, Conn.: Fawcett, 1956). For commentary on this period, see Drew, *Nelson Algren*; Douglas Wixson, *Worker–Writer in America: Jack Conroy and the Tradition of Midwestern Literary Radicalism, 1898–1990* (Urbana: University of Illinois Press, 1994), pp. 450–72; Michael Denning, *The Cultural Front: The Laboring of American Culture in the Twentieth Century* (London: Verso, 1996), which contains discussion of Algren (pp. 70, 78, 209, 215, 224, 227–28, 234, 237, 251–54, 465).

48. Drew, *Nelson Algren*, esp. pp. 293–95. See the insightful essay John Clellon Holmes, "Arm: A Memoir," in Holmes, *Representative Men: The Biographical Essays* (Fayetteville: University of Arkansas Press, 1988), pp. 241–62.

49. For standard left critiques of the beats, see Guy Daniels, "Post-Mortem on San Francisco," *The Nation* 187 (August 2, 1958): 53–55; John G. Roberts, "The Frisco Beat," *Mainstream* 11 (July 1958): 11–26. On the communist poet Thomas McGrath and the beats, see the entire issue of *TriQuarterly* 70 (Fall 1987), but especially the essay by E. P. Thompson, "Homage to Thomas McGrath," esp. pp. 125–26. Note the full version of McGrath, "After the Beat Generation," in McGrath, *The Movie at the End of the World: Collected Poems* (Chicago: Swallow Press, 1980), pp. 162–63.

50. For a more overtly political Latin American equivalent to *On the Road*, see Ernesto Che Guevara, *The Motorcycle Diaries: A Journey Around South America* (London: Verso, 1995).

51. Beginning with the biographical, see Dennis McNally, *Desolate Angel: Jack Kerouac,*

the Beat Generation, and America (New York: Random House, 1979); Barry Gifford and Lawrence Lee, Jack's Book: An Oral Biography of Jack Kerouac (New York: St. Martin's Press, 1978); Gerald Nicosia, Memory Babe: A Critical Biography of Jack Kerouac (New York: Viking, 1983); Ann Charters, Kerouac: A Biography (New York: Warner Paperback, 1973). Critical commentary on the Kerouac body of writing, conveniently gathered in Ann Charters, ed., The Portable Jack Kerouac (New York: Viking, 1995), includes: Warren French, Jack Kerouac (Boston: Twayne, 1986); Tytell, Naked Angels; Regina Weinreich, The Spontaneous Poetics of Jack Kerouac: A Study of the Fiction (New York: Marlowe, 1995); R. J. Ellis, "'I Am Only a Jolly Storyteller': Jack Kerouac's On the Road and Visions of Cody," in Lee, The Beat Generation Writers, pp. 37–60; Tim Hunt, Kerouac's Crooked Road (Handen, Conn.: Archon Books, 1981). Note, as well, Chris Challis, Quest for Kerouac (London: Faber & Faber, 1984).

52. Denning, The Cultural Front, pp. 186–91.
53. Sex was fundamental. See Lawrence Lipton, The Erotic Revolution: An Affirmative View of the New Morality (Los Angeles: Sherbourne Press, 1965), pp. 124, 278.
54. Kerouac, On the Road (New York: Signet, 1958), p. 246.
55. Nicosia, Memory Babe, p. 348.
56. Kerouac, On the Road, p. 184.
57. Jack Kerouac, Dr. Sax (New York: Grove Press, 1959), p. 161. For comment on Dr. Sax, see Nicosia, Memory Babe, pp. 391–410.
58. Jack Kerouac, Mexico City Blues (New York: Grove Press, 1959), p. 89.
59. Kerouac, "Jazz of the Beat Generation," in Charters, ed., The Portable Jack Kerouac, p. 232. See, as well, Kerouac, "New York Scenes," in Kerouac, Lonesome Traveler, pp. 104–17, first published under the title, "Beat Night Life of New York."
60. Henry Miller, "Preface," in Kerouac, The Subterraneans (New York: Avon, 1958), pp. 6–7.
61. See Jack Kerouac, Book of Dreams (San Francisco: City Lights, 1961); quotation from Kerouac, "On the Origins of a Generation," in Kerouac, Good Blonde and Others (San Francisco: Grey Fox Press, 1993), p. 60.
62. For a glimpse of the conventional construction of the beatnik, see Brier, Who Built America?, p. 531.
63. Holmes, "The Great Pretender," and "Perpetual Visitor," both in Representative Men, pp. 113, 151, 149. For Kerouac's last years, see the standard accounts in his biographies by Charters, McNally, and Nicosia. See also the lavishly illustrated book by Steve Turner, Jack Kerouac: Angel-headed Hipster (New York: Viking, 1996).
64. See, for instance, Johnny Otis, "White Negroes," in Upside Your Head! Rhythm and Blues on Central Avenue (Hanover: Wesleyan University Press, 1993), pp. 162–64, and the discussion in A. Robert Lee, "Black Beats: The Signifying Poetry of LeRoi Jones/Amiri Baraka, Ted Joans and Bob Kaufman," in Lee, ed., The Beat Generation Writers, pp. 158–77; Imamu Amiri Baraka, The Autobiography of LeRoi Jones/Amiri Baraka (New York: Freundlich Books, 1984).
65. Quoted in Nicosia, Memory Babe, p. 568.
66. See Brenda Knight, Women of the Beat Generation: The Writers, Artists, and Muses at the Heart of a Revolution (Berkeley: Conari Press, 1996).
67. Joyce Johnson, Minor Characters: Life with Kerouac and the Beat Generation (London: Virago, 1994), pp. 261–62. See, as well, Johnson's novel In the Night Café (New York: Washington Square Press, 1989).

68. Eliot D. Allen, "That Was No Lady—That Was Jack Kerouac's Girl," in Richard E. Langford, ed., *Essays in Modern American Literature* (Deland, Flor.: Stetson University Press, 1963), pp. 97–102. Note the sociological discussion of beat women in Rigney and Smith, *The Real Bohemia*, pp. 82–97.

69. Note Catharine R. Stimpson, "The Beat Generation and the Trials of Homosexual Liberation," *Salmagundi* 58/59 (Fall/Winter 1982–1983): 373–92.

70. Holmes, "Neal Cassady: The Gandy Dancer," in *Representative Men*, p. 206. Consider the argument about "the flight from responsibility" in Barbara Ehrenreich, *The Hearts of Men: American Dreams and the Flight from Commitment* (New York: Anchor, 1983).

71. Carolyn Cassady, *Off the Road: My Years with Cassady, Kerouac, and Ginsberg* (New York: Penguin, 1990).

72. See, as well, Wini Breines, "The 'Other' Fifties: Beats and Bad Girls," in Joanne Meyerowitz, ed., *Not June Cleaver: Women and Gender in Postwar America, 1945–1960* (Philadelphia: Temple University Press, 1994), pp. 382–408; Helen McNeil, "The Archaelogy of Gender in the Beat Movement," and Amy L. Friedman, "'I Say My New Name': Women Writers of the Beat Generation," in Lee, ed., *The Beat Generation Writers*, pp. 178–215; Hettie Jones, *How I Became Hettie Jones* (New York: Dutton, 1990); Diane Di Prima, *Memoires of a Beatnik* (San Francisco: Last Gasp, 1988), p. 392.

73. Jones, *How I Became Hettie Jones*, p. 34.

74. Alix Kates Shulman, *Burning Questions* (New York: Knopf, 1978), p. 64, quoted in Breines, "The 'Other' Fifties," pp. 392–93. On the beats and anti-communism, see Rigney and Smith, *The Real Bohemia*, pp. 164–65. On the beats and cultural developments with the Soviet Union, see Inger Thorup Lauridsen and Per Dalgard, eds., *The Beat Generation and the Russian New Wave* (Ann Arbor: Ardis, 1990). For the climate of this period, see Doug Dowd, "Cry 'Havoc!' and Let Slip the Dogs of War: McCarthyism, Korea, and other Nightmares," *Monthly Review* 48 (April 1997): 32–42; this essay is a chapter in Dowd's more extensive discussion of much of the twentieth century in Dowd, *Blues for America: A Critique, a Lament, and Some Memories* (New York: Monthly Review Press, 1997). On the suffocating climate of the family, see Elaine Tyler May, *Homeward Bound: American Families in the Cold War Era* (New York: Basic Books, 1988); Wini Breines, *Young, White, and Miserable: Growing up Female in the Fifties* (Boston: Beacon, 1992); Brett Harvey, *The Fifties: A Women's Oral History* (New York: HarperCollins, 1993); and sections of Wendy Kozol, *Life's America: Family and Nation in Postwar Photojournalism* (Philadelphia: Temple University Press, 1994).

Chapter 18

1. This position, in which the Cold War is extended back in time, as well as perhaps forward into the future, seems to me congruent with positions adopted by William Appleman Williams. See, for example, *The Tragedy of American Diplomacy* (New York: Delta, 1962); Paul M. Buhle and Edward Rice-Maximin, *William Appleman Williams: The Tragedy of Empire* (New York and London: Routledge, 1995). On McCarthy, see David M. Oshinsky, *A Conspiracy So Immense: The World of Joe McCarthy* (New York: Free Press, 1983); Richard M. Fried, *Nightmare in Red: The McCarthy Era in Perspective* (New York: Oxford University Press, 1990).

2. See, for instance, *The Case of Leon Trotsky: Report of Hearings on the Charges Made against*

Him in the Moscow Trials by the Preliminary Commission of Inquiry (New York: Harper & Brothers, 1937).

3. The Hollywood blacklist is explored in Victor S. Navasky, *Naming Names* (New York: Viking, 1980); Patrick McGilligan and Paul Buhle, eds., *Tender Comrades: A Backstory of the Hollywood Blacklist* (New York: St. Martin's Press, 1997), as well as in the more wide-ranging statement, Larry Ceplair and Steven Englund, *The Inquisition in Hollywood: Politics in the Film Community, 1930–1960* (Berkeley: University of California Press, 1983); and for a particular figure, see Lester Cole, *Hollywood Red: The Autobiography of Lester Cole* (Palo Alto, Calif.: Ramparts Press, 1981). Note, as well, Sally Belfrage, *Un-American Activities: A Memoir of the Fifties* (New York: Harper, 1994).

4. On the Rosenbergs, see the older statement in John Wexley, *The Judgement of Julius and Ethel Rosenberg* (New York: Cameron & Kahn, 1955), and the more acclaimed Ronald Radosh and Joyce Milton, *The Rosenberg File: A Search for Truth* (New York: Vintage, 1984). E. H. Norman's case remains controversial. See Peyton V. Lyon, "The Loyalties of E. Herbert Norman," *Labour/Le Travail* 28 (Fall 1991): 219–59; James Barros, *No Sense of Evil: Espionage, the Case of Herbert Norman* (Toronto: Deneau, 1986); Roger W. Bowen, *Innocence is Not Enough: The Life and Death of Herbert Norman* (Vancouver: Douglas & McIntyre, 1986).

5. Note David Caute, *The Great Fear: The Anti-Communist Purge Under Truman and Eisenhower* (New York: Simon & Schuster, 1979); Len Scher, *The Un-Canadians: True Stories of the Blacklist Era* (Toronto: Lester, 1992).

6. Consider Frank Kofsky, "Black Music: Cold War 'Secret Weapon'," in Kofsky, *Black Nationalism and the Revolution in Music* (New York: Pathfinder, 1970), pp. 109–22; Serge Guilbault, *How New York Stole the Idea of Modern Art: Abstract Expressionism, Freedom, and the Cold War* (Chicago: University of Chicago Press, 1983). For a general cultural history of the Cold War, see Tom Engelhardt, *The End of Victory Culture: Cold War America and the Disillusioning of a Generation* (New York: Basic, 1995). For the context of the cultural front, see Michael Denning in *The Cultural Front: the Laboring of American Culture in the Twentieth Century* (London: Verso, 1996). Denning provides a sense of the progressive opposition's immediate historical background.

7. On problems of definition and the range of writings, related especially to film noir, see Alain Silver, "Introduction," in Alain Silver and James Ursini, eds., *Film Noir Reader* (New York: Limelight, 1996), pp. 3–15.

8. I have drawn on the useful abbreviated statement in Raymond Borde and Etienne Chaumeton, "Towards a Definition of Film Noir," in Silver and Ursini, eds., *Film Noir Reader*, pp. 17–25.

9. On female repression and male power, and the extended engagement with this position, see Janey Place, "Women in Film Noir," in E. Ann Kaplan, ed., *Women and Film Noir* (London: British Film Institute, 1978), p. 50; Elizabeth Cowie, "Film Noir and Women," in Joan Copjec, ed., *Shades of Noir: A Reader* (London: Verso, 1993), pp. 121–66. Note, as well, Woody Haut, *Pulp Culture: Hardboiled Fiction and the Cold War* (London: Serpent's Tail, 1995), pp. 106–31.

10. For other comment on noir and the office, see Fredric Jameson, "The Synoptic Chandler," in Copjec, ed., *Shades of Noir*, pp. 33–56.

11. Hopper's works, and biographical and analytic perspectives, are found in Gail Levin, *Edward Hopper: An Intimate Biography* (New York: Knopf, 1995); Deborah Lyons and Adam D. Weinberg, *Edward Hopper and the American Imagination* (New

York: Whitney Museum/W. W. Norton, 1995); Wieland Schmied, *Edward Hopper: Portraits of America* (New York: Prestel-Verlag, 1995); Gail Levin, *Edward Hopper: The Art and the Artist* (New York: Whitney Museum/W. W. Norton, 1980); Gail Levin, "Edward Hopper: The Influence of Theatre and Film," *Arts Magazine* 55 (October 1980): 123–27; Erika Doss, "Edward Hopper, Nighthawks, and Film Noir," *Postcript: Essays in Film and the Humanities* 2 (Winter 1983): 14–36.

12. On contextualization, see Charles Higham and Joel Greenberg, *Hollywood in the Forties* (New York: A. S. Barnes, 1968), and Dana Polan, *Power and Paranoia: History, Narrative and the American Cinema, 1940–1950* (New York: Columbia University Press, 1986).

13. I reject the uncritical readings of the Popular Front that have captivated much of the political and cultural historiography of this period, as evident in Denning, *The Cultural Front,* and Maurice Isserman, *Which Side Were You On? The American Communist Party during the Second World War* (Middletown, Conn: Wesleyan University Press, 1982). For an alternative reading more in line with my views, see Michael Goldfield, "Recent Historiography of the Communist Party USA," in Mike Davis et al., eds., *The Year Left: An American Socialist Yearbook* (London: Verso, 1985), pp. 315–58.

14. Mike Davis, *City of Quartz: Excavating the Future in Los Angeles* (New York: Vintage, 1992), p. 41.

15. On Caspary, see Denning, *The Cultural Front,* pp. 144–45, 228; Vera Caspary, *The Secrets of Grown-Ups* (New York: McGraw-Hill, 1979). For a feminist critique of *Laura,* see Karen Hollinger, "Film Noir, Voice-over, and the Femme Fatale," in Silver and Ursini, *Film Noir Reader,* pp. 247–50.

16. For background, see the discussions in David E. Ruth, *Inventing the Public Enemy: The Gangster in American Culture, 1918–1934* (Chicago: University of Chicago Press, 1996); Robert Warshow, "The Gangster as Tragic Hero," in Warshow, *The Immediate Experience: Movies, Comics, Theatre and Other Aspects of Popular Culture* (New York: Anchor Books, 1962), pp. 83–88; George Grella, "The Gangster Novel: The Urban Pastoral," in David Madden, ed., *Tough Guy Writers of the Thirties* (Carbondale: University of Southern Illinois Press, 1968), pp. 186–98.

17. Peter Biskind, "'They Live by Night' by Daylight," *Sight and Sound* 45 (Autumn 1976): 218–22.

18. See the readings provided by Ken Worpole, *Dockers and Detectives: Popular Reading/Popular Writing* (London: Verso, 1983); Ernest Mandel, *Delightful Murder: A Social History of the Crime Story* (London: Pluto, 1984); Madden, *Tough Guy Writers of the Thirties*; and, albeit in less overt political terms, Frank Krutnik, *In a Lonely Street: Film Noir, Genre, Masculinity* (New York: Routledge, 1991). For a recent gay reading of film noir, see the fascinating set of arguments in Robert J. Corber, *Homosexuality in Cold War America: Resistance and the Crisis of Masculinity* (Durham, N.C.: Duke University Press, 1997), pp. 23–104.

19. See Alfred Appel, Jr., "The Director: Fritz Lang's American Nightmare," *Film Comment* 10 (November–December 1974): 12–17.

20. Richard Lippe, "At the Margins of Film Noir: Preminger's Angel Face," in Silver and Ursini, eds., *Film Noir Reader,* pp. 161–76.

21. See William F. Nolan, *Hammett: A Life at the Edge* (New York: Congdon & Weed, 1983); Diane Johnson, *Dashiell Hammett: A Life* (New York: Random House,

1983); Robert I. Edenbaum, "The Poetics of the Private-Eye: The Novels of Dashiell Hammett," in Madden, *Tough Guy Writers of the Thirties*, pp. 80–103.

22. For commentary on the German contribution and the hard-boiled style to noir, see Paul Schrader, "Notes on Film Noir," in Silver and Ursini, eds., *Film Noir Reader*, pp. 55–56. On *The Maltese Falcon*, see Irving Malin, "Focus on 'The Maltese Falcon': The Metaphysical Falcon," in Madden, *Tough Guy Writers of the Thirties*, pp. 104–09. An introduction to crime fiction, which structured some of the aesthetics of noir, is found in Jerry Palmer, *Thrillers: Genesis and Structure of a Popular Genre* (London: Edward Arnold, 1978); Palmer, *Potboilers: Methods, Concepts, and Case Studies in Popular Fiction* (New York: Routledge, 1991).

23. As an introduction to noir and Los Angeles, see the breathtaking argument in Mike Davis's *City of Quartz*, pp. 36–46.

24. Carl Richardson, *Autopsy: An Element of Realism in Film Noir* (Metuchen, N.J.: Scarecrow, 1992), p. 183.

25. On the importance of Cain, see Joyce Carol Oates, "Man Under Sentence of Death: The Novels of James M. Cain," in Madden, *Tough Guy Writers of the Thirties*, pp. 110–28.

26. See Thomas Sturak, "Horace McCoy's Objective Lyricism," in Madden, *Tough Guy Writers of the Thirties*, pp. 137–62.

27. Michael Denning, *The Cultural Front: The Laboring of American Culture in the Twentieth Century* (London: Verso, 1996), p. 183.

28. On Chandler, see Fredric Jameson, "The Synoptic Chandler," in Copjec, ed., *Shades of Noir*, pp. 33–56; Herbert Ruhm, "Raymond Chandler: From Bloomsbury to the Jungle—and Beyond," in Madden, *Tough Guy Writers of the Thirties*, pp. 171–85; and Fred Pfeil, *White Guys: Studies in Postmodern Domination and Difference* (London: Verso, 1995), pp. 105–66. For statements on noir and urbanism, see David Reid and Jayne L. Walker, "Strange Pursuit: Cornell Woolrich and the Abandoned City of the Forties," in Copjec, ed., *Shades of Noir*, pp. 57–96; Nicholas Christopher, *Somewhere in the Night: Film Noir and the American City* (New York: Free Press, 1997).

29. Quoted in Frank McShane, *The Life of Raymond Chandler* (London: Jonathan Cape, 1976), p. 1.

30. For a rather benign view, see Deborah Thomas, "Psychoanalysis and Film Noir," in Ian Cameron, ed., *The Movie Book of Film Noir* (London: Studio Vista, 1992), pp. 71–87.

31. C. L. R. James, *American Civilization*, ed. Anna Grimshaw and Keith Hart (Oxford: Blackwell, 1993), pp. 121, 127, quoted in Robert J. Corber, *Homosexuality in Cold War America: Resistance and the Crisis of Maculinity* (Durham, N.C.: Duke University Press, 1997), pp. 27–28.

32. See the discussion of LA noir in Norman M. Klein, *The History of Forgetting: Los Angeles and the Erasure of Memory* (London: Verso, 1997), pp. 73–93.

33. Comment on Himes, whose other work focused on Harlem, can be found in Manthia Diawara, "Noir by Noirs: Towards a New Realism in Black Cinema," in Copjec, ed., *Shades of Noir*, pp. 261–78; Fred Pfeil, "Policiers Noirs," in Pfeil, *Another Tale to Tell: Politics and Narrative in Postmodern Culture* (London: Verso, 1990), pp. 64–68; Denning, *The Cultural Front*, pp. 221, 227–28, 252, 257, 447–49. See, as well, Chester Himes, *My Life of Absurdity: The Later Years* (New York: Paragon House, 1976). Note the argument in Eric Lott, "The Whiteness of Film Noir," in Mike Hill, *Whiteness: A Critical Reader* (New York:

New York University Press, 1996), pp. 81–101.

34. Quoted in Philip Durham, *Down These Mean Streets a Man Must Go: Raymond Chandler's Knight* (Chapel Hill: University of North Carolina Press, 1963), pp. 76–77.

35. Raymond Chandler, *The Big Sleep* (1939; New York: Vintage, 1976), pp. 215–16.

36. See James Ellroy, *My Dark Places* (New York: Vintage, 1997).

37. Borde and Chaumeton, "Towards a Definition of Film Noir," in Silver and Ursini, eds., *Film Noir Reader*, p. 25.

38. Cook quoted in Nicholas Christopher, *Somewhere in the Night: Film Noir and the American City* (New York: Free Press, 1997), pp. 49–50.

39. See the discussion in George Lipsitz, *Rainbow at Midnight: Labor and Culture in the 1940s* (Urbana: University of Illinois Press, 1994), pp. 279–302; and the introduction J. P. Telotte, "Noir Narration," in Telotte, *Voices in the Dark: The Narrative Patterns of Film Noir* (Urbana: University of Illinois Press, 1989), pp. 1–39.

40. See Krutnik, *In a Lonely Street*, p. 21.

41. Quoted in Alain Silver and Elizabeth Ward, eds., *Film Noir: An Encyclopedic Reference to the American Style* (Woodstock: Overlook Press, 1979), p. 204.

42. For another reading of space, see Joan Copjec, "The Phenomenal Non-phenomenal: Private Space in Film Noir," in *Shades of Noir*, pp. 167–98.

43. For Cobb, see Navasky, *Naming Names*, pp. 268–73.

44. Consider the statements on styles and motifs in film noir in Janey Place and Lowell Peterson, "Some Visual Motifs of Film Noir," and Robert Porfirio, "No Way Out: Existential Motifs in the Film Noir," both in Silver and Ursini, eds., *Film Noir Reader*, pp. 65–94.

45. For guides to film noir, see the abbreviated and much criticized statement by Raymond Durgnat, "Paint it Black: The Family Tree of Film Noir," in Silver and Ursini, eds., *Film Noir Reader*, pp. 37–52, and the more extensive compendium presented in Silver and Ward, *Film Noir: An Encyclopedic Reference to the American Style*. Snapshot depictions of particular films appear in Barry Gifford, *Devil Thumbs a Ride & Other Unforgettable Films* (New York: Grove Press, 1988).

46. Frances Farmer was a left actress who worked with the Group Theatre in the 1930s and had modest success in Hollywood before being incarcerated in a mental asylum in the 1940s. Her life is memorialized in the 1982 film *Frances*, starring Jessica Lange; for a fictional account, see Gordon DeMarco, *The Canvas Prison* (San Francisco: Germinal Press, 1982).

47. See Lipsitz, *Rainbow at Midnight*, p. 291.

48. Dassin was indeed a Communist, although only loosely affiliated with the Party. On Dassin, see McGilligan and Buhle, eds., *Tender Comrades*, esp. pp. 199–224, a collection of interviews with blacklisted Hollywood figures. It also contains extensive reference to the despised Dmytryk.

49. Commentary on *Night and the City* appears in Glenn Erickson, "Expressionist Doom in Night in the City," in Silver and Ursini, eds., *Film Noir Reader*, pp. 203–07; Nicholas Christopher, *Somewhere in the Night: Film Noir and the American City* (New York: Free Press, 1997), pp. 75–84.

50. Wrestling as spectacle and its relationship to noir is touched on briefly in Christopher, *Somewhere in the Night*, pp. 81–83; I have drawn on the particular analysis in Roland Barthes, "The World of Wrestling," in Barthes, *Mythologies* (London: Granada, 1983), pp. 15–25. For a more general statement on

spectacle, see Guy Debord, *Comments on the Society of the Spectacle* (London: Verso, 1990).

51. Davis, *City of Quartz*, p. 38.
52. See, as well, Haut, *Pulp Culture*.
53. Note the discussion in Charles Shapiro, "'Nightmare Alley': Geeks, Cons, Tips, and Marks," in Madden, *Tough Guy Writers of the Thirties*, pp. 218–23.
54. See, for instance, Palmer, *Hollywood's Dark Cinema*, pp. 139–66; Hollinger, "Film Noir, Voice-Over, and the Femme Fatale," in Silver and Ursini, eds., *Film Noir Reader*, pp. 243–58.
55. Janey Place, "Women in Film Noir," in Kaplan, *Women in Film Noir*, pp. 35–54.
56. Lipsitz, *Rainbow at Midnight*, pp. 296–97.
57. See the DeMarco trilogy: *October Heat* (1979); *The Canvas Prision* (1982); and *Frisco Blues* (1985).
58. Among many possible commentaries, note Fred Pfeil, "Home Fires Burning: Family Noir in Blue Velvet and Terminator 2," in Copjec, ed., *Shades of Noir*, pp. 227–60; Fredric Jameson, *Postmodernism, or, The Cultural Logic of Late Capitalism* (Durham, N.C.: Duke University Press, 1991), pp. 19–20, 279–96; Edward Gallafent, "Echo Park: Film Noir in the 'Seventies'," and Leighton Grist, "Moving Targets and Black Widows: Film Noir in Modern Hollywood," both in Cameron, ed., *The Movie Book of Film Noir*, pp. 254–85.
59. See, for instance, Jeremy G. Butler, "Miami Vice, the Legacy of Film Noir," and James Ursini, "Angst at Sixty Fields per Second," both in Silver and Ursini, eds., *Film Noir Reader*, pp. 289–306, 275–87.
60. See Robert Polito, *Savage Art: A Biography of Jim Thompson* (New York: Knopf, 1995).
61. Note Robert G. Porfirio, "The Dark Age of American Film: A Study of the American Film Noir" (PhD diss., Princeton University, 1979); Todd Erickson, "Movement Becomes Genre," in Silver and Ursini, eds., *Film Noir Reader*, pp. 307–30.
62. Among the important, and differing, statements on women and noir, see Hollinger, "Film Noir, Voice-over, and the Femme Fatale," pp. 243–360; Cowie, "Film Noir and Women," pp. 121–66; R. Barton Palmer, *Hollywood's Dark Cinema: The American Film Noir* (New York: Twayne, 1994), pp. 139–68; and the essays in E. Ann Kaplan, *Women and Film Noir*.
63. On this background, see Gregory D. Black, *Hollywood Censored: Morality Codes, Catholics, and the Movies* (Cambridge: Cambridge University Press, 1994).
64. Andrew Vachss's writings include *Flood* (1985); *Strega* (1987); *Blue Belle* (1988); *Hard Candy* (1989); *Blossom* (1990); *Sacrifice* (1991); *Shella* (1993); *Born Bad* (1994); *Down in the Zero* (1994); *Batman: The Ultimate Evil* (1995); *Footsteps of the Hawk* (1995); *False Allegations* (1996); and *Another Chance to Get it Right: A Children's Book for Adults* (1995). For commentary, see Gary Dretzka, "Disturbed Avenger: Seeking Evil with Andrew Vachss' Urban Vigilante," *Chicago Tribune* (June 11, 1989;) Paul Mann, "A Heart and a Fist," *Saturday Review* in *Vancouver Sun*, June 1, 1991.
65. Obviously I do not agree with the ultimatist ideological posturing of Francis Fukuyama's understanding that the implosion of the Soviet Union in 1989 resolved the global confrontation of communism and capitalism in the latter's rightful and unambiguous favor, thus homogenizing the future of politics. The crisis of capitalist restoration in the former Soviet Union, which unfolded

with terrifying rapidity over the course of the 1990s, confirms the banality of any "end of history" posturing. Nevertheless, the cultural impact of this process is singularly important, especially in the capitalist West, as the evolution of noir suggests. See Francis Fukuyama, "The End of History," *The National Interest* 16 (Summer 1989): 3–18, and the more complex elaborations in Fukuyama, *The End of History and the Last Man* (1992). Significant readings of the problems posed in Fukuyama include Joseph McCarney, "Shaping Ends: Reflections on Fukuyama," *New Left Review* 202 (November–December 1992): 37–54; Perry Anderson, "The Ends of History," in Anderson, *A Zone of Engagement* (London: Verso, 1992), pp. 279–375.

Chapter 19

1. Comment on capitalism's centuries-long history is endless. See, among many other discussions, Rodney Hilton, "Capitalism—What's in a Name?" in Rodney Hilton, ed., *The Transition from Feudalism to Capitalism* (London: New Left Books, 1976), pp. 145–58.
2. Consider, for instance, the essays in Elizabeth Fox Genovese and Eugene D. Genovese, *Fruits of Merchant Capital: Slavery and Bourgeois Property in the Rise and Expansion of Capitalism* (Oxford: Oxford University Press, 1983); C. H. George, "The Origins of Capitalism: A Marxist Epitome and a Critique of Wallerstein's *Modern World-System*," *Marxist Perspectives* 3 (1980): 70–100; and the debates over the transition from feudalism to capitalism in two pivotal collections of essays, Hilton, ed., *The Transition from Feudalism to Capitalism*, and T. H. Ashton and C. H. E. Philpin, eds., *The Brenner Debate: Agrarian Class Structure and Economic Development in Pre-Industrial Europe* (Cambridge: Cambridge University Press, 1987).
3. See E. P. Thompson, "Time, Work-Discipline, and Industrial Capitalism," in Thompson, *Customs in Common* (London: Merlin, 1991), pp. 352–403; R. H. Tawney, *Religion and the Rise of Capitalism* (1926; Harmondsworth: Penguin, 1967); Max Weber, *The Protestant Ethic and the Spirit of Capitalism* (1926; London: Allen & Unwin, 1974); Christopher Hill, "Protestantism and the Rise of Capitalism," in Hill, *Change and Continuity in 17th Century England* (London: Weidenfeld & Nicolson, 1974), pp. 81–102.
4. See Neil McKendrick, John Brewer, and J. H. Plumb, *The Birth of Consumer Society: The Commercialization of Eighteenth-Century England* (Bloomington: Indiana University Press, 1982).
5. Consider the wide-ranging discussion in Susan Willis, "Sweet Dreams: Profits and Payoffs in Commodity Capitalism," in Willis, *A Primer for Daily Life* (London: Routledge, 1991), pp. 133–57; and the specific statements in Sidney Mintz, *Sweetness and Power* (New York: Viking, 1985), pp. 45–46; W. Loyd Warner and Paul S. Lunt, *The Social Life of a Modern Community* (New Haven: Yale University Press, 1941); W. Lloyd Warner, *American Life: Dream and Reality* (Chicago: University of Chicago Press, 1953); Daniel Bell, *The End of Ideology* (Glencoe, Ill.: Free Press, 1960).
6. Keynes and Tawney quoted from Tawney, *Religion and the Rise of Capitalism*, pp. 275–76, 280.
7. Fredric Jameson, *Postmodernism, or, The Cultural Logic of Late Capitalism* (Durham,

N.C.: Duke University Press, 1991); David Harvey, *The Condition of Postmodernity: An Enquiry into the Origins of Cultural Change* (Oxford: Basil Blackwell, 1989).

8. The notion that capitalism and the bourgeoisie could, in specific periods, serve the interests of humanity and play a historically progressive, even revolutionary, role figures in the discussion by Terry Eagleton, *The Illusions of Postmodernism* (Oxford: Blackwell, 1996).

9. It is appropriate that the metaphor of the vampire was also extended to a commodity of significance in late capitalism's history, heroin. See the discussion of heroin addiction as a vampire-like phenonomenon that produces "the living dead" in Edward Jay Epstein, *Agency of Fear: Opiates and Political Power in America* (London: Verso, 1990), pp. 23–45.

10. Richard Dawkins, *The Selfish Gene* (London: Oxford University Press, 1976), which Andrew Ross draws from in *The Chicago Gangster Theory of Life: Nature's Debt to Society* (London: Verso, 1994).

11. For an engaging impressionistic statement, see Charles Derber, *The Wilding of America: How Greed and Violence are Eroding our Nation's Character* (New York: St. Martin's Press, 1996), esp. pp. 37–60.

12. Pino Arlacchi, *Mafia Business: The Mafia Ethic and the Spirit of Capitalism* (London: Verso, 1987), p. 232.

13. Vincenzo Ruggiero, "The Camorra: 'Clean' Capital and Organised Crime," in Frank Pearce and Michael Woodiwiss, eds., *Global Crime Connections: Dynamics and Control* (London: Macmillan, 1993), p. 157.

14. This script is easily read in the contemporary political economy of California. See Richard Walker, "California Rages against the Dying of the Light," *New Left Review* 209 (January–February 1995): 42–74, for detail and suggestive contextualization.

15. Quoted in Fernand Braudel, *The Mediterranean and the Mediterranean World in the Age of Philip II*, Volume II (New York: Harper & Row, 1973), pp. 734–54, quotation from pp. 737–38.

16. J. L. H. Keep, "Bandits and the Law in Muscovy," *Slavonic Review* 35 (December 1956): 201–23; E. J. Hobsbawm, *Primitive Rebels: Studies in Archaic Forms of Social Movement in the 19th and 20th Centuries* (Manchester: Manchester University Press, 1959), pp. 13–29; Hobsbawm, *Bandits* (New York: Dell, 1969); Linda Lewin, "The Oligarchical Limitations of Social Banditry in Brazil: The Case of the 'Good Thief' Antonio Sylvino," *Past & Present* 82 (February 1979): 116–46; Louis A. Perez, Jr., *Social Banditry and Peasant Protest in Cuba, 1878–1918* (Pittsburgh: University of Pittsburgh Press, 1989); and the essays in Richard W. Slatta, *Bandidos: The Varieties of Latin American Banditry* (Westport, Conn.: Greenwood Press, 1987); Donald Crummey, ed., *Banditry, Rebellion, and Social Protest in Africa* (London: James Currey, 1986), pp. 89–192, 373–96.

17. Hobsbawm, *Bandits*, pp. 114–15. For a critique of Hobsbawm's influential formulations, see Pat O'Malley, "Social Bandits, Modern Capitalism, and the Traditional Peasantry: a Critique of Hobsbawm," *Journal of Peasant Studies* 6 (1979): 489–501.

18. Pino Arlacchi, *Mafia, Peasants, and Great Estates: Society in Traditional Calabria* (Cambridge: Cambridge University Press, 1983), pp. 89–111.

19. Anton Blok, "The Peasant and the Brigand: Social Banditry Reconsidered," *Comparative Studies in Society and History* 14 (1972): 495–504; Blok, *The Mafia of a Sicilian Village, 1860–1960* (New York: Harper Torchbooks, 1974); Hobsbawm,

Primitive Rebels, pp. 30–56; Henner Hess, Mafia and Mafiosi: The Structure of Power (Farnborough: Saxon House, 1973).

20. For a brief survey of this Sicilian history and its links to mafia formation, see Christopher Duggan, Fascism and the Mafia (New Haven: Yale University Press, 1989), pp. 20–52. On Italian criminology, see Daniel Pick, "The Faces of Anarchy: Lombroso and the Politics of Criminal Science in Post-Unification Italy," History Workshop Journal 21 (Spring 1986): 60–86. The context of Sicilian poverty forms the basis of a later discussion in Danilo Dolci, Poverty in Sicily: A Study of the Province of Palermo (Harmondsworth: Penguin, 1966).

21. On Naples and the camorra, see Arthur Train, Courts, Criminals, and the Camorra (London: Chapman & Hall, 1912); Vincenzo Ruggiero, "The Camorra: 'Clean' Capital and Organized Crime," in Pearce and Woodiwiss, eds., Global Crime Connections, pp. 141–61.

22. Duggan, Fascism and the Mafia, esp. pp. 15–19, 2–6. For the United States, see Joseph L. Albini, The American Mafia: Genesis of a Legend (New York: Appleton-Crofts, 1971); Dwight C. Smith, The Mafia Mystique (New York: Basic Books, 1975); Frederic D. Homer, Guns and Garlic: Myths and Realities of Organized Crime (West Lafayette, Ind.: Purdue University Press, 1974); Peter Maas, The Valachi Papers (New York: Putnam, 1968); and for a later period, see Nicholas Pileggi, Wise Guy: Life in a Mafia Family (New York: Pocket Books, 1985). Note the early sociological statement Robert Anderson, "From Mafia to Cosa Nostra," American Journal of Sociology 71 (1965): 302–10. A summary of the early sociological and criminological issues is Mary McIntosh, The Organisation of Crime (London: Macmillan, 1975), esp. pp. 42–58.

23. This discussion draws upon Arlacchi, Mafia Business, pp. 3–20, quotations from pp. 14–15. See, as well, Arlacchi, Mafia, Peasants, and Great Estates, pp. 111–21.

24. For a detailed exploration of some of this history, see Duggan, Fascism and the Mafia, while the power and class location of the mafia is discussed in Arlacchi, Mafia Business, pp. 21–54. Hobsbawm, Primitive Rebels, pp. 30–56, offers useful commentary on the parallel state and some discussion of the class character of mafiosi, which he regards as tied more directly to wealth than does Arlacchi. Note, as well, Michele Pantaleone, The Mafia and Politics (London: Chatto & Windus, 1966); Alan Cassels, Fascist Italy (New York: Thomas Y. Crowell, 1968), p. 70. The historical processes relevant to mafia formation were obviously at the core of much of Gramsci's attempts to theorize Italian history. See Antonio Gramsci in Selections from the Prison Notebooks (New York: International, 1973).

25. A personalized account is Gavin Maxwell, The Ten Pains of Death (London: Longman's, 1959).

26. On the postwar transformation, see Pantaleone, The Mafia and Politics, which also contains a discussion of the beginnings of heroin's importance, pp. 180–94; Arlacchi, Mafia Business, pp. 57–186, with a discussion of heroin in the 1970s, pp. 187–211; Blok, The Mafia of a Sicilian Village, pp. 213–30; Frank Pearce, Crimes of the Powerful: Marxism, Crime and Deviance (London: Pluto Press, 1976).

27. See Daniel Bell, "Crime as an American Way of Life: A Queer Ladder of Social Mobility," in Bell, The End of Ideology, pp. 115–36; Humbert S. Nelli, The Business of Crime: Italians and Syndicate Crime in the United States (New York: Oxford

University Press, 1976). On Capone, see F. D. Pasley, *Al Capone: The Biography of a Self-Made Man* (London: Faber & Faber, 1931); John Kobler, *Capone: The Life and World of Al Capone* (Greenwich, Conn.: Fawcett, 1971); Laurence Bergreen, *Capone: The Man and the Era* (New York: Simon & Schuster, 1994).

28. Francis A. J. Ianni, *A Family Business: Kinship and Social Control in Organized Crime* (New York: Russell Sage–Basic Books, 1972); Jonathan Kwitny, *Vicious Circles: The Mafia in the Marketplace* (New York: W. W. Norton, 1979); Mary McIntosh, "The Growth of Racketeering," *Economy and Society* 2 (1973): 35–69; John Landesco, *Organized Crime in Chicago* (Chicago: University of Chicago Press, 1968). On the literary representation of the gangster, see Michael Denning, *The Cultural Front: The Laboring of American Culture in the Twentieth Century* (London: Verso, 1996), pp. 254–58.

29. Philippe Bourgois, *In Search of Respect: Selling Crack in El Barrio* (Cambridge: Cambridge University Press, 1995), p. 75.

30. The classic liberal statement is Kenneth B. Clark, *Dark Ghetto: Dilemmas of Social Power* (New York: Harper Torchbooks, 1965).

31. Charles Derber, *The Wilding of America: How Greed and Violence Are Eroding Our Nation's Character* (New York: St. Martin's Press, 1996), p. 127.

32. Robert Fitch, *The Assassination of New York* (London: Verso, 1993), pp. viii, 216. Roger Starr later offered a series of defensive explanations for his statement and for the nature of the crisis in New York, among them Starr, *The Rise and Fall of New York City* (New York: Basic Books, 1985). A more sophisticated, but no less transparent, liberal response appears in Mario Cuomo, *The New York Idea: An Experiment in Democracy* (New York: Crown, 1994).

33. Fitch, *The Assassination of New York*, pp. 208, 216. Note, as well, the general discussion in Walter Stafford, "Whither the Great Neo-Conservative Experiment in New York City," in James Jennings, ed., *Race, Politics, and Economic Development: Community Perspectives* (London: Verso, 1992), pp. 101–16; and the wide-ranging collection of writings in John Hull Mollenkopf and Manuel Castells, eds., *Dual City: Restructuring New York* (New York: Russell Sage, 1991). For a humorous journalistic account of the period, see William E. Geist, *City Slickers: The Espresso Emergency Squad, the Hanger King and Other Tales of New York in the 1980s* (New York: Penguin, 1987).

34. Robin D. G. Kelley, *Yo' Mama's DisFUNKtional! Fighting the Culture Wars in Urban America* (Boston: Beacon Press, 1997), p. 46.

35. Consider the discussion of corrupt police, escalating criminality, and violence relating to Miami's "Little Havana"—site of one of the first battles waged in the state-directed drug war—in Paul Eddy, Hugo Sabogal, and Sara Walden, *The Cocaine Wars* (New York: W. W. Norton, 1988), pp. 232–46. More on Little Havana is found in Mark Abrahamson, *Urban Enclaves: Identity and Place in America* (New York: St. Martin's Press, 1996), pp. 85–102.

36. Environmental historians have begun to address the high costs of this process, and how it is paid in particular race and class ways. See, for instance, Andrew Hurley, *Class, Race, and Industrial Pollution in Gary, Indiana, 1945–1980* (Chapel Hill: University of North Carolina Press, 1995); Mike Davis, "The Case for Letting Malibu Burn," *Environmental History Review* 19 (Summer 1995): 1–36.

37. See Edward Jay Epstein, *Agency of Fear: Opiates and Political Power in America* (London: Verso, 1990).

38. See Keith Jennings, "Understanding the Persisting Crisis of Black Youth

Unemployment," in Jennings, ed., *Race, Politics, and Economic Development*, pp. 151–64; Kelley, *Yo' Mama's DisFUNKtional!*, pp. 46–47; R. Daniels, "Confronting the 'State of Emergency'," *Z Magazine* 6 (June 1993): 16; and for a detailed Detroit case study, Thomas J. Sugrue, *The Origins of the Urban Crisis: Race and Inequality in Postwar Detroit* (Princeton: Princeton University Press, 1996).

39. For a discussion of inner-city education and the catastrophic impact of poverty, see Ann C. Diver-Stamnes, *Lives in the Balance: Youth, Poverty, and Education in Watts* (Albany: State University of New York Press, 1995).

40. Kelley, *Yo' Mama's DisFUNKtional*, pp. 47–48.

41. Peter Linebaugh, "Gruesome Gertie at the Buckle of the Bible Belt," *New Left Review* 209 (January–February 1995): esp. 16, 18. For a thorough accounting of the issues involved in the death penalty, including discussion of its racialized content, see Hugo Adam Bedau, *The Death Penalty in America: Current Controversies* (New York: Oxford University Press, 1997), where a table (pp. 65–66) detailing the racial composition of death row indicates that the combined percentage of blacks and latinos on death row (48.3%) surpasses that of whites (48%) even though these two groupings do not come close to approaching that of whites in terms of the percentage of the total population.

42. C. J. L. Murray, "Mortality among Black Men," *New England Journal of Medicine* 322 (January 18, 1991): 205–06.

43. As an introduction to the phenomena outlined in the preceding two paragraphs, there is no better starting place than Mike Davis, *City of Quartz: Excavating the Future in Los Angeles* (New York: Vintage, 1992), esp. pp. 265–322. See, as well, Edward W. Soja, *Postmodern Geographies: The Reassertion of Space in Critical Social Theory* (London: Verso, 1989); two articles by the journalist L. Bing, "Confessions from the Crossfire," *LA Weekly* 10 (6–12 May 1988): 22–24, 26, 140; "When You're a Crip (or Blood)," *Harper's Magazine* 278 (March 1989): 51–59; Jimmie L. Reeves and Richard Campbell, *Cracked Coverage: Television News, the Anti-Cocaine Crusade, and the Reagan Legacy* (Durham, N.C.: Duke University Press, 1994); Craig Reinarman and Harry G. Levine, "The Crack Attack: Politics and Media in America's Latest Drug Scare," in Joel Best, ed., *Images of Issues: Typifying Contemporary Social Problems* (New York: Aldine de Gruyter, 1989), pp. 115–35; Clarence Lusane, *Pipe Dream Blues: Racism and the War on Drugs* (Boston: South End Press, 1991).

44. See William B. Sanders, *Gangbangs and Drive-bys: Grounded Culture and Juvenile Gang Violence* (New York: Aldine de Gruyter, 1994); Diver-Stamnes, *Lives in the Balance*, pp. 71–88; Felix M. Padilla, *The Gang as an American Enterprise* (New Brunswick: Rutgers University Press, 1993); Anne Campbell, *The Girls in the Gang* (Oxford: Blackwell, 1991).

45. On Chicano gang style, see James Diego Vigil, *Barrio Gangs: Street Life and Identity in Southern California* (Austin: University of Texas Press, 1988).

46. For an important discussion of the gendered configuration of gang experience, see Anne Campbell's *The Girls in the Gang*. A rare attempt to address sensitively the gendered making of the inner city is Bourgois, *In Search of Respect*. Bourgois's explicit chapters discuss the gendered nature of the street, the particular oppressions faced by women, the crisis of families and children, and the vulnerabilities of fathers. Note, as well, the discussion of gender in H. Edward Ransford, *Race and Class in American Society: Black, Latino, Anglo* (Rochester, Vt.: Schenkman Books, 1994), pp. 133–66.

47. On gangsta rap, see Robin D. G. Kelley, *Race Rebels: Culture, Politics, and the Black Working Class* (New York: Free Press, 1994), pp. 183–228, with lyrics from Ice Cube quoted on p. 203. The many other sources on rap include Brian Cross, *It's Not About a Salary: Rap, Race and Resistance in Los Angeles* (London: Verso, 1993), Houston A. Baker, Jr., *Black Studies, Rap, and the Academy* (Chicago: University of Chicago Press, 1993).

48. See a similar argument in Kelley, *Yo' Mama's DisFUNKtional*. Note, as well, Michael Eric Dyson, *Between God and Gangsta Rap: Bearing Witness to Black Culture* (New York: Oxford University Press, 1996); Cross, *It's Not About a Salary*; Russell A. Potter, *Spectacular Vernaculars: Hop-Hop and the Politics of Postmodernism* (Albany: State University of New York Press, 1995).

49. Consider Bourgois, *In Search of Respect*, pp. 109–13; and note the general discussion of the street drug trade in Mercer Sullivan, "Crime and the Social Fabric," in Mollenkopf and Castells, eds., *Dual City*, pp. 236–40.

50. See Epstein, *Agency of Fear*, esp. pp. 7–16; Edward S. Herman, *The Real Terror Network: Terrorism in Fact and Propaganda* (Montreal: Black Rose, 1992), pp. 80, 90; and the articles in *San Jose Mercury News*, August 19, August 20, and September 20, 1996.

51. Epstein, *Agency of Fear*, p. 11.

52. Davis, *City of Quartz*, pp. 267–68.

53. Derber, *The Wilding of America*, p. 107.

54. Note the discussion of violence and a culture of terror in Bourgois, *In Search of Respect*, pp. 34–35, and the remarks on gangs and drugs in Diver-Stamnes, *Lives in the Balance*, 71–88.

55. Davis, *City of Quartz*, pp. 309–17. For an account of street-level dealing in a Chicago Puerto Rican gang, see Felix M. Padilla, *The Gang as an American Enterprise* (New Brunswick: Rutgers University Press, 1993). The East Harlem case is documented with intimate detail in Bourgois, *In Search of Respect*, pp. 77–113. See, as well, Robert Jackall, *Wild Cow-Boys: Urban Marauders & the Forces of Order* (Cambridge, Mass.: Harvard University Press, 1997).

56. William Adler, *Land of Opportunity: One Family's Quest for the American Dream in the Age of Crack* (Boston: Atlantic Monthly, 1995).

57. Contrast the sums made by upper-level dealers, detailed in Patricia A. Adler, *Wheeling and Dealing: An Ethnography of an Upper-Level Drug Dealing and Smuggling Community* (New York: Columbia University Press, 1993). Note the comments on minimum-wage crack dealers in Bourgois, *In Search of Respect*, pp. 91–93; Padilla, *The Gang as an American Enterprise*, pp. 152–82; and the first-hand account in Sanders, *Gangbangs and Drive-bys*, p. 141.

58. Quoted in Arlacchi, *Mafia Business*, p. 160.

59. Mike Davis, "Los Angeles: Civil Liberties between the Hammer and the Rock," *New Left Review* 170 (July–August 1988): 53; Louis Kraar, "The Drug Trade," *Fortune* 20 (1988): 29; Susan Willis, "Sweet Dreams: Profits and Payoffs in Commodity Capitalism," pp. 151–57; Davis, *City of Quartz*, p. 311; E. J. Hobsbawm, "Murderous Colombia," *New York Review of Books*, November 20, 1986, p. 35.

60. On parks and recreational space, see Kelley, *Yo' Mama's DisFUNKtional*, pp. 44–45, 50–53.

61. See, as well, Merton's reading of Chicago street criminals in Robert K. Merton, "Opportunity Structure: The Emergence, Diffusion, and Differentiation of a

Sociological Concept, 1930s–1950s," in Fred Adler and William S. Laufer, eds., *The Legacy of Anomie Theory: Advances in Criminological Theory* (New Brunswick: Transaction Books, 1994), pp. 6, 3–78; and Max Frankel, "Drug War, II," *New York Times Magazine*, January 26, 1995.

62. Bourgois, *In Search of Respect*, esp. pp. 3, 326. Note, as well, Martin Sanchez Jankowski, *Islands in the Street: Gangs and American Urban Society* (Berkeley: University of California Press, 1991).

63. Bourgois, *In Search of Respect*, pp. 13, 19, 20, 30, 103, 314. For comment on Bourgois, see Derber, *The Wilding of America*, pp. 96–98. A journalistic statement appeared in Bourgois, "Just Another Night on Crack Street," *New York Times Sunday Magazine*, November 12, 1989, p. 53.

64. Jackall, *Wild Cow-Boys*, p. 22.

65. Nelson George, *Buppies, B-Boys, Baps, & Bohos: Notes on Post-Soul Black Culture* (New York: Harper Perennial, 1992), pp. 299–301.

66. Davis, *City of Quartz*, p. 316.

Chapter 20

1. These works and other relevant texts are discussed in Russell Jacoby, *The Last Intellectuals: American Culture in the Age of Academe* (New York: Basic, 1987), pp. 54–71.

2. M. Webber, "The Urban Place and the Nonplace Urban Realm," in Webber et al., eds., *Explorations into Urban Structure* (Philadelphia: University of Pennsylvania Press, 1964), pp. 79–153.

3. Jerry Herron, *AfterCulture: Detroit and the Humiliation of History* (Detroit: Wayne State University Press, 1993); Ze'ev Chafets, *Devil's Night: And Other True Tales of Detroit* (New York: Random House, 1990); Dan Georgakas and Marvin Surkin, *Detroit: I Do Mind Dying: A Study in Urban Revolution* (New York: St. Martin's Press, 1975); John J. Bukowczyk and Douglas Aikenhead with Peter Slavcheff, eds., *Detroit Images: Photographs of the Renaissance City* (Detroit: Wayne State University Press, 1989), p. 257; Camilio Jose Vergara, "Postindustrial City: Detroit Waits for the Millennium," *Nation* (18 May 1992): 660–64.

4. I am in agreement with current biological thinking that has established the extent to which "race" is a social construction rather than a physiological separation. Nevertheless, it is apparent to all social historians that it is a critical category in historical analysis, an obvious divide that runs through the nineteenth- and twentieth-century North American experience. I will not therefore place it in quotation marks unless I wish to flag a particular, often ironic, meaning. For a pertinent discussion, see Barbara J. Fields, "Ideology and Race in American History," in J. Morgan Kousser and James M. McPherson, eds., *Region, Race, and Reconstruction: Essays in Honor of C. Vann Woodward* (New York: Oxford University Press, 1982), pp. 143–78. On the importance of race in the crisis of the American city, see Robert A. Beauregard, *Voices of Decline: The Postwar Fate of U.S. Cities* (Oxford: Blackwell, 1993).

5. The literature on this subject is vast, but consider the liberal articulation of the problem in terms of crime in Mercer Sullivan, "Crime and the Social Fabric," in John Hull Mollenkopf and Manuel Castells, eds., *Dual City: Restructuring New York* (New York: Russell Sage Foundation, 1991), pp. 225–44; and the radical attempt to address reciprocal developments in the collected essays

in James Jenning, ed., *Race, Politics, and Economic Development: Community Perspectives* (London: Verso, 1992).

6. Note the discussion of African Americans in Detroit in Mark Abrahamson, *Urban Enclaves: Identity and Place in America* (New York: St. Martin's Press, 1996), pp. 49–66; Thomas J. Sugrue, *The Origins of the Urban Crisis: Race and Inequality in Postwar Detroit* (Princeton: Princeton University Press, 1996). The classic sociological statement is St. Clair Drake and Horace R. Cayton, *Black Metropolis: A Study of Negro Life in a Northern City* (1945; New York: Harper & Row, 1962).

7. For an exciting historical statement, see Kevin J. Mumford, *Interzones: Black/ White Sex Districts in Chicago and New York in the Early Twentieth Century* (New York: Columbia University Press, 1997). Conceptually, note the statement in Stephen Nathan Haymes, *Race, Culture, and the City: A Pedagogy for Black Urban Struggle* (Albany: State University of New York, 1995).

8. See Mauricio Mazon, *The Zoot-Suit Riots: The Psychology of Symbolic Annihilation* (Austin: University of Texas Press, 1984); Robin D. G. Kelley, *Race Rebels: Culture, Politics, and the Black Working Class* (New York: Free Press, 1994), pp. 161–82.

9. Dona Cooper Hamilton and Charles V. Hamilton, *The Dual Agenda: The African-American Struggle for Civil and Economic Equality* (New York: Columbia University Press, 1997).

10. See, among many variegated examples, Robert L. Allen, *Black Awakening in Capitalist America* (Garden City, N.Y.: Doubleday, 1970); Stokely Carmichael and Charles V. Hamilton, *Black Power* (New York: Vintage, 1967); Eugene Victor Wolfenstein, *The Victims of Democracy: Malcolm X and the Black Revolution* (Berkeley: University of California Press, 1981). For a feminist critique, one that emerged in the late 1970s and 1980s, see Michele Wallace, *Black Macho and the Myth of the Superwoman* (London: Verso, 1990).

11. James Baldwin, *The Fire Next Time* (New York: Dell, 1964), pp. 140–41. On Baldwin, see James Leeming, *James Baldwin: A Biography* (New York: Henry Holt, 1994).

12. Reds were barbituates and Parker was a reference to the Los Angeles Chief of Police at the time. See Eldridge Cleaver, *Soul on Ice* (New York: Delta, 1968), pp. 26–27.

13. James O'Toole, *Watts and Woodstock: Identity and Culture in the United States and South Africa* (New York: Viking, 1973), pp. 87–91, notes that before Watts precipitated a cohort of rebellious youth from ghetto gangs into the politics of social transformation, there was a leadership vacuum in Watts, filled only partially by religious organizations and Democratic Party loyalists.

14. Consider the statement in Orlando Patterson, *Slavery and Social Death: A Comparative Study* (Cambridge, Mass.: Harvard University Press, 1982).

15. For an invaluable overview, see Herbert Shapiro, *White Violence and Black Response: From Reconstruction to Montgomery* (Amherst: University of Massachusetts Press, 1988).

16. Accounts of Philadelphia race riots and the wider context of American nativist and racial violence in the 1830s include: John M. Werner, *Reaping the Bloody Harvest: Race Riots in the United States During the Age of Jackson, 1824–1849* (New York: Oxford University Press, 1986); Michael Feldberg, *The Turbulent Era: Riot and Disorder in Jacksonian America* (New York: Oxford University Press, 1980); John M. Runcie, "'Hunting the Nigs' in Philadelphia, 1834," *Pennsylvania History* 39

(April 1972):187–218; Elizabeth M. Geffen, "Violence in Philadelphia in the 1840s and 1850s," in Roger Lane and John J. Turner, eds., *Riot, Rout and Tumult: Readings in American Social and Political Violence* (Westport, Conn.: Greenwood, 1978), pp. 112–32. The Lippard quotation and a summary of the Philadelphia race riot in this period appear in Noel Ignatiev, *How The Irish Became White* (New York: Routledge, 1995), pp. 124–46.

17. David R. Roediger, *The Wages of Whiteness: Race and the Making of the American Working Class* (London: Verso, 1991), pp. 108–10. See, as well, Alexander Saxton, *The Rise and Fall of the White Republic: Class Politics and Mass Culture in Nineteenth-Century America* (London: Verso, 1990).

18. See the excellent account in Iver Bernstein, *The New York City Draft Riots: Their Significance for American Society and Politics in the Age of the Civil War* (New York: Oxford University Press, 1990); as well as older treatments: Albon P. Man, Jr., "Labor Competition and the New York City Draft Riots of 1863," *Journal of Negro History* 36 (October 1951): 376–405; Michael Wallace, "The Uses of Violence in American History," in Lane and Turner, eds., *Riot, Rout, and Tumult*, p. 13.

19. See Wallace, "The Uses of Violence," p. 14; Shapiro, *White Violence and Black Response*, pp. 6–7; Gilles Vandal, "The Origins of the New Orleans Riot of 1866, Revisited," *Louisiana History* 22 (1981): 135–65; John Carver Edwards, "Radical Reconstruction and the New Orleans Riot of 1866," *International Review of History and Political Science* (August 1973): 48–64; Bobby L. Lovett, "Memphis Riots: White Reaction to Blacks in Memphis, May 1865–July 1866," *Tennessee Historical Quarterly* (Spring 1979): 9–33; James Gilbert Ryan, "The Memphis Riots of 1866: Terror in a Black Community During Reconstruction," *Journal of Negro History* (July 1977): 243–77.

20. Among the many studies, see William Ivy Hair, *Carnival of Fury: Robert Charles and the New Orleans Race Riot of 1921* (Baton Rouge: Louisiana State University Press, 1982); Roberta Senechal, *The Sociogenesis of a Race Riot: Springfield, Illinois in 1908* (Urbana: University of Illinois Press, 1990); Robert V. Hayes, *A Night of Violence: The Houston Riot of 1917* (Baton Rouge: Louisiana State University Press, 1976); Elliott M. Rudwick, *Race Riot at East St. Louis, July 2, 1917* (Carbondale: Southern Illinois University Press, 1964); William M. Tuttle, Jr., *Race Riot: Chicago in the Red Summer of 1919* (New York: Atheneum, 1970); Scott Ellsworth, *Death in a Promised Land: The Tulsa Race Riot of 1921* (Baton Rouge: Louisiana State University Press, 1982); Shapiro, *White Violence and Black Response*, pp. 93–118, 180–85; Arthur I. Waskow, *From Race Riot to Sit-in: 1919 and the 1960s* (Garden City, N.Y.: Anchor Books, 1967), pp. 1–218.

21. It is possible that in some cases the formation of black defense guard units owed something to the experience and quite recent legacy of the revolutionary Industrial Workers of the World, who also faced establishment vigilante violence in the First World War years. See Ellsworth, *Death in a Promised Land*, pp. 25–33.

22. See the overview of black responses, white authority's inaction, and the continuity of terror in the 1920s and 1930s in Shapiro, *White Violence and Black Response*, pp. 119–300.

23. See Richard Dalfiume, *Fighting on Two Fronts: Desegregation of the Armed Forces, 1939–1953* (Columbia: University of Missouri Press, 1969); Roi Ottley, *"New World A-Coming": Inside Black America* (New York: Arno Reprint, 1969), pp. 311–14;

Neil A. Wynn, *The Afro-American and the Second World War* (New York: Holmes & Meier, 1975).

24. Kelley, *Race Rebels*, pp. 171–72, drawing on Dizzy Gillespie with Al Fraser, *To Be or Not … to Bop: Memoirs* (Garden City, N.Y.: Doubleday, 1979), pp. 119–20; Malcolm X with Alex Haley, *The Autobiography of Malcolm X* (New York: Grove Press, 1964), pp. 104–07; George Q. Flynn, "Selective Service and American Blacks during the Second World War," *Journal of Negro History* 69 (Winter 1984): 14–25; Robert A. Hill, ed., *The FBI's RACON: Racial Conditions In the United States During World War II* (Boston: Northeastern University Press, 1995), esp. pp. 1–4.

25. Langston Hughes, "Beaumont to Detroit, 1943," *Common Ground* (Fall 1943), p. 104, quoted in Shapiro, *White Violence and Black Response*, p. 340.

26. Writing on the Detroit 1943 riot is extensive. See Dominic J. Capeci, Jr., *Race Relations in Wartime Detroit: The Sojourner Truth Controversy* (Philadelphia: Temple University Press, 1984); Robert Shogan and Tom Craig, *The Detroit Riot* (Philadelphia: Chilton Books, 1964); Alfred McClung Lee and Norman Raymond Humphrey, *Race Riot* (New York: Dryden Press, 1943); Alan Clive, *State of War: Michigan in World War II* (Ann Arbor: University of Michigan Press, 1979), pp. 136–62; Howard Sitkoff, "The Detroit Race Riot of 1943," *Michigan History* 53 (Fall 1969): 183–206; B. J. Widick, *Detroit: City of Race and Class Violence* (Chicago: Quadrangle, 1972), pp. 93–111; Shapiro, *White Violence and Black Response*, pp. 310–30; Hill, ed., *The FBI's RACON*, pp. 111–54.

27. Among other sources, see Widick, *Detroit: City of Race and Class Violence*, pp. 99–112; Shapiro, *White Violence and Black Response*, pp. 310–30; Sidney Fine, *Violence in the Model City: The Cavanagh Administration, Race Relations, and the Detroit Riot of 1967* (Ann Arbor: University of Michigan Press, 1989), p. 1.

28. Shapiro, *White Violence and Black Response*, pp. 261–72 (on the 1935 riot) and pp. 330–37 (on 1943); Claude Brown, *Manchild in the Promised Land* (New York: New American Library, 1965), pp. 12–15; Hill, ed., *The FBI's RACON*, pp. 209–11.

29. Shapiro, *White Violence and Black Response*, p. 332; Hill, ed., *The FBI's RACON*, p. 209; Dominic J. Capeci, Jr., *The Harlem Riot of 1943* (Philadelphia: Temple University Press, 1977). For the liberal containment of the riots of 1935, which no doubt served as something of a model, see Mark Naison, *Communists in Harlem during the Depression* (Urbana: University of Illinois Press, 1983), pp. 140–50.

30. For one comparison, see Alex L. Swan, "The Harlem and Detroit Riots of 1943: A Comparative Analysis," *Berkeley Journal of Sociology* 16 (1971–1972): 75–93.

31. For a summary of this context, see Robert M. Fogelson, *Violence as Protest: A Study of Riots and Ghettos* (Garden City, N.Y.: Doubleday, 1971), pp. 79–104, where the quotations and developments of the above paragraphs can be found.

32. On Malcolm X see, among other studies, Wolfenstein, *The Victims of Democracy*; Malcolm X with Haley, *The Autobiography of Malcolm X*. For King, David L. Lewis, *King: A Biography* (Urbana: University of Illinois, 1970). Although focused on Malcolm, Cornel West, "Malcolm X and Black Rage," in West, *Race Matters* (New York: Vintage, 1994), pp. 133–52, also contains comment on King.

33. For brief accessible liberal overviews, see Robert Fogelson, "Violence as Protest," in Lane and Turner, Jr., eds., *Riot, Rout, and Tumult*, pp. 327–48; Fogelson, *Violence as Protest*; Waskow, *From Race Riot to Sit-In*; Morris Janowitz,

"Collective Racial Violence," in Hugh Davis Graham and Ted Robert Gurr, eds., *Violence in America: Historical and Comparative Perspectives* (Beverly Hills: Sage Publications, 1979), pp. 261–86. See, as well, Milton Viorts, *Fire in the Streets: American in the 1960s* (New York: Simon & Schuster, 1979), pp. 307–420; and for the urban policy implications, see Dennis E. Gale, *Understanding Urban Unrest: From Reverend King to Rodney King* (London: Sage, 1996).

34. The Watts riots are much studied. See Nathan Cohen, ed., *The Los Angeles Riots: A Socio-Psychological Study* (New York: Praeger, 1970); Jerry Cohen and William S. Murphy, *Burn, Baby, Burn! The Watts Riot* (New York: Avon, 1966); Gerald Horne, *Fire This Time: The Watts Uprising and the 1960s* (Charlottesville: University Press of Virginia, 1995); Robert Conot, *Rivers of Blood, Years of Darkness* (New York: Bantam, 1967).

35. For an exhaustive study of all aspects of the 1967 riot, see Fine, *Violence in the Model City*. On the background to Detroit's explosive riot, see the detailed examination in Sugrue, *The Origins of the Urban Crisis*, as well as the lesser statements in Leonard Gordon, *A City in Racial Crisis: The Case of Detroit Pre- and Post- the 1967 Riot* (New York: William C. Brown, 1971); Mark Abrahamson, *Urban Enclaves: Identity and Place in America* (New York: St. Martin's Press, 1996), pp. 49–66.

36. H. Bruce Franklin, *Back Where You Came From: A Life in the Death of an Empire* (New York: Harper's Magazine Press, 1975), p. 23.

37. Fine, *Violence in the Model City*, p. 299; Bryan T. Downes, "A Critical Re-examination of the Social and Political Characteristics of Riot Cities," *Social Science Quarterly* 5 (September 1970): 351–52.

38. For early accounts, see Hubert G. Locke, *The Detroit Riot of 1967* (Detroit: Wayne State University Press, 1969); J. A. Lukacs, "Postscript on Detroit: 'Whitey Hasn't Got the Message'," *New York Times Magazine*, August 27, 1967; Gary Wills, *The Second Civil War* (New York: New American Library, 1968).

39. For introductions to this period and its developments, see Fine, *Violence in the Model City*, pp. 17–126; James A. Geschwender, *Class, Race, and Worker Insurgency: The League of Revolutionary Black Workers* (Cambridge: Cambridge University Press, 1977), pp. 17–82.

40. For a perspective on the riot penned by a ghetto resident and son of one of the owners of the "blind pig," see William Walter Scott III, *Hurt, Baby, Hurt* (Ann Arbor: New Ghetto Press, 1970). On Twelfth Street, see George Henderson, "Twelfth Street: An Analysis of a Changed Neighborhood," *Phylon* 25 (Spring 1964): 91–96; Harold Black and James Wiley, "Dissecting a Riot Neighborhood," *Nation's Cities* 6 (September 1968): 18–20.

41. Aside from Fine, *Violence in the Model City*, pp. 271–90, see John Hershey, *The Algiers Motel Incident* (New York: Knopf, 1968).

42. For a treatment of those who lost their lives during the riot, see Van Gordon Sauter and Burleigh Hines, *Nightmare in Detroit: A Rebellion and Its Victims* (Chicago: Henry Regnery, 1968).

43. These paragraphs draw on the standard source on the Detroit riot, encyclopedic in detail: Fine, *Violence in the Model City*.

44. Edward C. Banfield, *The Unheavenly City* (Boston: Little, Brown, 1968); Banfield, "Rioting Mainly for Fun and Profit," in James Q. Wilson, ed., *The Metropolitan Enigma* (Cambridge, Mass.: Harvard University Press, 1968), pp. 283–308. Something of this late-1960s approach survives in the 1990s with neo-

conservative writing such as that of Dinesh D'souza, *The End of Racism: Principles for a Multiracial Society* (New York: Free Press, 1995), which addresses African-American rioting in the 1990s with the statement, "Behavior that would be regarded as pathological anywhere else is considered routine, and sometimes glamorous, in the ghetto" (pp. 16–17). For a critique of this thinking, see Robin D. G. Kelley, *Yo' Mama's DisFUNKtional! Fighting the Culture Wars in Urban America* (Boston: Beacon Press, 1997).

45. Note, especially, Morris Janowitz, "Collective Racial Violence: A Contemporary History," in Graham and Gurr, eds., *Violence in America*, esp. pp. 263–69; Hans Mattick, "The Form and Content of Recent Riots," *Midway* (Summer 1968): 3–32; Anthony Oberschall, "The Los Angeles Riot of August 1965," *Social Problems* 15 (Winter 1968): 322–34.

46. A Neil, "America's Latin Beat: A Survey of South Florida," *The Economist*, October 16, 1982, supplement; Dennis E. Gale, *Understanding Urban Unrest: From Reverend King to Rodney King* (London: Sage, 1996), pp. 104–07; A. Portes and A. Stepick, eds., *City on the Edge: The Transformation of Miami* (Berkeley: University of California Press, 1993).

47. For an illuminating series of statements—of understandably uneven analytic and political significance—that place the Los Angeles riot of 1992 within a set of postmodernist sensibilities, see Robert Gooding-Williams, ed., *Reading Rodney King/Reading Urban Uprising* (New York: Routledge, 1993).

48. Background on late capitalist Los Angeles can be gleaned from a number of texts, some of quite populist construction, others cast in more purposively complex analytic formulations. See, for instance, Lynell George, *No Crystal Stair: African-Americans in the City of Angels* (London: Verso, 1992); David Rieff, *Los Angeles: Capital of the Third World* (New York: Simon & Schuster, 1991); Reyner Banham, *Los Angeles: The Architecture of Four Ecologies* (New York: Penguin, 1990); Norman M. Klein, *The History of Forgetting: Los Angeles and the Erasure of Memory* (London: Verso, 1997); Mike Davis, *City of Quartz: Excavating the Future in Los Angeles* (New York: Vintage, 1992); Edward W. Soja, *Postmodern Geographies: The Reassertion of Space in Critical Social Theory* (London: Verso, 1989); Richard Walker, "California Rages against the Dying of the Light," *New Left Review* 209 (January–February 1995): 42–74.

49. For the range of interpretations, consult the articles in Mark Baldassare, ed., *The Los Angeles Riots: Lessons for the Urban Future* (Boulder: Westview Press, 1994).

50. For various interpretations and pieces of evidence assembled in these paragraphs, see the essays in Gooding-Williams, ed., *Reading Rodney King*. For an NAACP-sponsored study of the issue of police/minority relations set against the Rodney King beating, see Charles J. Ogletree, Jr., et al., *Beyond the Rodney King Story: An Investigation of Police Conduct in Minority Communities* (Boston: Northeastern University Press, 1995).

51. See Dennis E. Gale, *Understanding Urban Unrest: From Reverend King to Rodney King* (London: Sage, 1996); Melvin L. Oliver, James H. Johnson, Jr., and Walter C. Farrell, Jr., "Anatomy of a Rebellion: A Political Economy Analysis," in Gooding-Williams, ed., *Reading Rodney King*, pp. 117–41.

52. Lynell George, "Waiting for the Rainbow Sign," *New Left Review* 193 (May–June 1992): 79.

53. George, *No Crystal Stair*, p. 5; George, "Waiting for the Rainbow Sign," pp. 75–79; D'souza, *The End of Racism*, p. 17, quoting a citation from Luis Rodriguez,

"Deciphering L.A. Smoke Signals," *National Catholic Reporter*, May 22, 1992, p. 20. Davis, "Uprising and Repression in L.A.," and Rhonda M. Williams, "Accumulation as Evisceration: Urban Rebellion and the New Growth Dynamics," in Gooding-Williams, ed., *Reading Rodney King*, pp. 82–96, 142–56, contain comments on the destructive economic climate and its impact on inner-city youth of color in L.A., as does Davis, *City of Quartz*.

54. See especially Oliver et al., "Anatomy of a Rebellion," and Davis, "Uprising and Repression in L.A."

55. Davis, "Uprising and Repression in L.A.," pp. 142–43.

56. For sensitive statements on the complex issue of Koreans and the Rodney King riots, see Sumi K. Cho, "Korean Americans vs. African Americans: Conflict and Construction," and Elaine H. Kim, "Home is Where the Han Is: A Korean-American Perspective on the Los Angeles Upheavals," in Gooding-Williams, ed., *Reading Rodney King*, pp. 196–235.

57. Baldwin, *The Fire Next Time*, pp. 124–29. Consider, as well, Richard Delgado, *The Coming Race War? And Other Apocalyptic Tales of America After Affirmative Action and Welfare* (New York: New York University Press, 1996).

Chapter 21

1. Elie Wiesel, *The Night Trilogy: Night, Dawn, The Accident* (New York: Hill & Wang, 1987), p. 3. For a rare historical exploration, see Robert C. Allen, *Horrible Prettiness: Burlesque and American Culture* (Chapel Hill: University of North Carolina Press, 1991).

2. Jim Carroll, *The Basketball Diaries* (New York: Penguin, 1995), p. 189.

3. Consider, for instance, two contemporary novels of homosexuality and Argentina: Hector Bianciotti, *What the Night Tells the Day* (New York: New Press, 1995); Colm Toibin, *The Story of the Night* (New York: Henry Holt, 1996).

4. Reinaldo Arenas, *Before Night Falls* (New York: Viking, 1993); Pico Iyer, *Cuba and the Night* (New York: Vintage, 1996); Paul Julian Smith, *Vision Machines: Cinema, Literature, and Sexuality in Spain and Cuba, 1983–1993* (London: Verso, 1996).

5. Marge Piercy, *City of Darkness, City of Light* (New York: Fawcette Columbine, 1996).

6. The late nineteenth century, with its scientist penchant for biological explanations and capacity to characterize all nontraditional behaviors as disease-driven, posited that, "man, in fact, is a less evolved being as regards his inhibitions at night than during the day, and his brain is far more liable to disturbance of the controlling functions in disease." See "Cocainism," from the *Quarterly Journal of Inebrity*, reproduced in *Canada Lancet* (July 1891): 340–41. My thanks to Dan Malleck for bringing this source to my attention.

7. Consider the imaginative discussions of night dance in Alma Guillermoprieto, *Samba* (New York: Vintage, 1990); Celeste Fraser Delgado and Jose Esteban Munoz, eds., *Everynight Life: Culture and Dance in Latin/o America* (Durham, N.C.: Duke University Press, 1997).

8. Georges Bataille, *Inner Experience* (Albany: State University of New York Press, 1988), esp. pp. xxxii; Phillipe Sollers, "The Novel and the Experience of Limits," in Sollers, *Writing and the Experience of Limits* (New York: Columbia University Press, 1983), p. 197; Danielle Marx-Scouras, *The Cultural Politics of Tel*

Quel: Literature and the Left in the Wake of Engagement (University Park: Pennsylvania State University Press, 1996), pp. 89–90.

9. Jorge Amado, *Shepherds of the Night* (New York: Avon, 1988), p. xi.

10. For a response to these rejections from those who continue to embrace the validity of Marxist, historical materialist readings of the past, see Ellen Meiksins Wood and John Bellamy Foster, eds., *In Defense of History: Marxism and the Postmodern Agenda* (New York: Monthly Review Press, 1997).

11. See, for example, Hannah Arendt, *Men in Dark Times* (New York: Harcourt Brace Jovanovich, 1955).

12. Note the brief commentary in David Harvey, *The Condition of Postmodernity: An Enquiry into the Origins of Cultural Change* (Oxford: Basil Blackwell, 1990), esp. pp. 116–17; Bryan Palmer, "Poststructuralism/Postmodernism, Internationalism, and Socialism," *Socialist Alternatives* 2 (Winter 1993): 48–62.

Index